VIDEO GAMES AND GAMING CULTURE

Critical Concepts in Media and Cultural Studies

Edited by
Mark J. P. Wolf

Volume II
Design and Theory

LONDON AND NEW YORK

First published 2016
by Routledge
2 Park Square, Milton Park, Abingdon, Oxon OX14 4RN

and by Routledge
711 Third Avenue, New York, NY 10017

Routledge is an imprint of the Taylor & Francis Group, an informa business

British Library Cataloguing in Publication Data
A catalogue record for this book is available from the British Library

Library of Congress Cataloging in Publication Data
A catalog record for this book has been requested

ISBN: 978-1-138-81125-6 (Set)
ISBN: 978-1-138-81129-4 (Volume II)

Typeset in Times New Roman
by Book Now Ltd, London

Publisher's Note
References within each chapter are as they appear in the original complete work

CONTENTS

CONTENTS

ACKNOWLEDGEMENTS

The Publishers would like to thank the following for permission to reprint their material:

Greg Costikyan, 'I Have No Words & I Must Design', *Interactive Fantasy: The Journal of Role-Playing and Story-Making Systems*, 2 (London: Hogshead Publishing, 1994), pp. 192–211.

Doug Church, 'Formal Abstract Design Tools', *Game Developer* magazine, August 1999, reprinted in Katie Salen and Eric Zimmerman (eds), *The Game Design Reader: A Rules of Play Anthology* (Cambridge, MA: The MIT Press, 2006), pp. 366–380.

Marc LeBlanc, 'Tools for Creating Dramatic Game Dynamics', Game Developer's Conference (GDC), 1999, reprinted in Katie Salen and Eric Zimmerman (eds), *The Game Design Reader: A Rules of Play Anthology* (Cambridge, MA: The MIT Press, 2006), pp. 438–459.

Robin Hunicke, Marc LeBlanc, and Robert Zubek, 'MDA: A Formal Approach to Game Design and Game Research', *19th National Conference of Artificial Intelligence*, San Jose, California, 2004.

Karen Collins, 'An Introduction to the Participatory and Non-Linear Aspects of Video Games Audio', in Stan Hawkins and John Richardson (eds), *Essays on Sound and Vision* (Helsinki, Finland: Helsinki University Press, 2007), pp. 263–298.

Karen Collins, 'In the Loop: Creativity and Constraint in 8-bit Video Game Audio', *Twentieth-Century Music*, 4/2, 2007.

Nick Monfort and Ian Bogost, 'Chapter 4: Pac-Man', *Racing the Beam: The Atari Video Computer System* (Cambridge, MA: The MIT Press, 2009), pp. 65–79.

Henry Jenkins, 'Game Design as Narrative Architecture', in Noah Wardrip-Fruin and Pat Harrigan (eds), *First Person: New Media as Story, Performance, and Game* (Cambridge, MA: The MIT Press, 2004), pp. 118–130.

Mark J. P. Wolf, 'Theorizing Navigable Space in Video Games', in Stephan Günzel, Michael Liebe, and Dieter Mersch (eds), *DIGAREC Keynote-Lectures 2009/10* (Potsdam, Germany: Potsdam University Press, 2011), pp. 18–48.

University of Minnesota Press for permission to reprint Alexander R. Galloway, 'Gamic Action, Four Moments', *Gaming: Essays on Algorithmic Culture* (Minneapolis, MN: University of Minnesota Press, 2006), pp. 1–38.

Rune Klevjer, 'In Defense of Cutscenes', in Frans Mäyrä (ed.), *Proceedings of Computer Games and Digital Cultures Conference* (Tampere, Finland: Tampere University Press, 2002), pp. 191–202.

Routledge for permission to reprint Jesper Juul, 'Fear of Failing? The Many Meanings of Difficulty in Video Games', in Bernard Perron and Mark J. P. Wolf (eds), *The Video Game Theory Reader 2* (New York, NY: Routledge, 2008), pp. 237–252.

Bernard DeKoven, 'Changing the Game', *The Well-Played Game* (New York, NY: Doubleday, 1978), pp. 39–59, reprinted in Katie Salen and Eric Zimmerman (eds), *The Game Design Reader: A Rules of Play Anthology* (Cambridge, MA: The MIT Press, 2006), pp. 518–537.

Human Kinetics for permission to reprint David Myers, 'Computer Game Semiotics', *Play & Culture*, 4(4), 1991, 334–345. © Human Kinetics Publishers, Inc.

Lars Konzack, 'Computer Game Criticism: A Method for Computer Game Analysis', in Frans Mäyrä (ed.), *Proceedings of Computer Games and Digital Cultures Conference* (Tampere, Finland: Tampere University Press, 2002), pp. 89–100.

The author for permission to reprint Espen Aarseth, 'Playing Research: Methodological Approaches to Game Analysis', Digital Art and Culture conference, Melbourne, Australia, May 19–23, 2003, and also published in *Fine Art Forum*, 17(8), August 2003, and available at hypertext.rmit.edu.au/dac/papers/Aarseth.pdf.

Roberto Dillon, 'Towards the Definition of a Framework and Grammar for Game Analysis and Design', *International Journal of Computer and Information Technology*, 3(2), March 2014, 188–193.

Edizioni Unicopli, Costa and Nolan for permission to reprint David Myers, 'Bombs, Barbarians, and Backstories: Meaning-making within *Sid Meier's Civilization*', in Matteo Bittanti (ed.), *Ludologica. Videogames d'Autore: Civilization and its Discontents. Virtual History. Real Fantasies* (Milan, Italy: Edizioni Unicopli, Costa and Nolan, 2005).

Sage for permission to reprint Thomas H. Apperley, 'Genre and Game Studies', *Simulation Gaming*, 37(1), 2006, 6–23.

Will Brooker, 'Camera-Eye, CG-Eye: Videogames and the "Cinematic"', *Cinema Journal*, 48(3), Spring 2009, 122–128.

Wayne State University Press for permission to reprint Brett Camper, 'Color-Cycled Space Fumes in the Pixel Particle Shockwave: The Technical Aesthetics of *Defender* and the Williams Arcade Platform, 1980–82', in Mark J. P. Wolf (ed.), *Before the Crash: Early Video Game History* (Detroit, MI: Wayne State University Press, 2012), pp. 168–188. © 2012 Wayne State University Press, with the permission of Wayne State University Press.

Ian Bogost, 'Procedural Rhetoric', *Persuasive Games: The Expressive Power of Video Games* (Cambridge, MA: The MIT Press, 2010), pp. 1–64.

Disclaimer

INTRODUCTION TO VOLUME II

Mark J. P. Wolf

Part 4: Video game design and formal aspects

Much of what is written about video games concerns their design and formal aspects, following academic approaches found in the study of art, literature, film, and television. Such discussions help in the understanding of games, the development of shared terminology, the formation of conventions and genres, and can even lead to new ideas for future directions for video games. Most of these issues arise in the first essay, game designer Greg Costikyan's "I Have No Words & I Must Design" (1994), written at a time when game design vocabulary was still very limited. It is an early attempt to formalize many of the elements found in games and tries defining them in general terms useful to the design industry. Striving in much the same direction five years later, game designer Doug Church's essay, "Formal Abstract Design Tools" (1999), argues that "a better understanding of design tools will lead to greater creativity and better design" and that a precise design vocabulary, along with the development of new game design tools that such a discussion will encourage, will speed up the evolution of game design, something which has certainly happened with the rise of video game studies.

Inspired by Church's essay, Marc LeBlanc's essay, "Tools for Creating Dramatic Game Dynamics" (1999), builds on his work, developing a more conceptual framework for the refinement of game design ideas. LeBlanc is also one of the authors, along with Robin Hunicke and Robert Zubek, of the essay "MDA: A Formal Approach to Game Design and Game Research" (2004), which presents the Mechanics, Dynamics, and Aesthetics (MDA) framework, a formal approach to the understanding of games that tries to bridge the gap between design, criticism, and research in an attempt to create better communication between these areas.

Sound design is often overlooked in favor of graphics, which are easier to reproduce and analyze as images, and which are even emphasized in the name "video games" (as opposed to "games with video and audio"). The next two essays, by video game sound theoretician Karen Collins, "An Introduction to the Participatory and Non-Linear Aspects of Video Games Audio" (2007) and "In the Loop: Creativity and Constraint in 8-bit Video Game Audio" (2008), introduce several of the basic concerns in the study of video game sound. The first essay examines how video game sound differs from other types of soundtracks, due to the addition of player interactivity, which forces a game's soundtrack to become

1

nonlinear, sometimes looped, and able to interactively readjust itself to changing game events while still maintaining some level of musical consistency. The second essay takes a historical look at game sound, in particular, the early days of 8-bit audio, which forced composers to work within very specific aesthetic and technical limitations. Both essays are fine examples of how the study of video game sound can enrich the gaming experience. Another overlooked topic is the translation process that occurs when games are ported from one platform to another. A detailed, comprehensive look at this process, using the adaptation of *Pac-Man* (1980) to the Atari VCS 2600, is the topic of the next essay, "Pac-Man" from the book *Racing the Beam: The Atari Video Computer System* (2009) by Nick Montfort and Ian Bogost.

With the rise of three-dimensional graphics and increasingly detailed and complex game worlds, analyses of video game space have grown more frequent. Henry Jenkins's essay, "Game Design as Narrative Architecture" (2004), goes beyond the ludology-narratology dichotomy to argue "for an understanding of game designers less as storytellers and more as narrative architects." Building on Don Carson's idea of environmental storytelling, Jenkins describes how spatial storytelling can evoke preexisting narrative associations, provide a place for enacted events, and produce embedded narratives and emergent narratives. Next, taking a more structural look at game world spaces, my own essay, "Theorizing Navigable Space in Video Games" (2009), attempts to find a way to discuss the wide range of video game spaces and the resulting structures that they form in a meaningful way and one which can also hopefully account for new forms of spaces which are yet to appear.

Alexander R. Galloway's "Gamic Action, Four Moments", the opening chapter in his book *Gaming: Essays on Algorithmic Culture* (2006), looks at video games as action and as "algorithmic cultural objects". Crossing the axis between diegetic and nondiegetic with the axis between operator (player) and the machine, Galloway creates four quadrants, the "four moments" through which he precedes to analyze formals aspects of the video game medium. Focusing specifically on one aspect of games, Rune Klevjer's essay, "In Defense of Cutscenes" (2002), argues for the value of the cut-scene, examining the relationship "between the ergodic and the representational, and between play and narration" and showing the way cut-scenes contribute meaning to gameplay sequences. The last essay of the section, Jesper Juul's "Fear of Failing? The Many Meanings of Difficulty in Video Games" (2008), looks at the role of failure in video games, whether or not players prefer games where they do not feel responsible for failing, and the flow channel between anxiety and boredom. All three of these essays demonstrate analyses of particular aspects of video games and show the rich theoretical complexities and possibilities that one can find in the medium.

Part 5: Video game theory, methodology, and analysis

The first essay in this section, Bernard DeKoven's "Changing the Game", a chapter from his book *The Well-Played Game* (1978), considers games more broadly and looks at how games can be changed; the bending of rules versus the breaking of them, the addition of rules, and the way play communities follow rules and allow them to be changed, according to the needs of the members of the community. The essay, then, is a kind of meditation on how rules function and their purpose, thus seeing the changing of rules as a kind of meta-game one level up from the game in question itself, with its own set of meta-rules. It is this kind of consciousness that encourages one to consider games on multiple levels and, likewise, the analysis of games themselves. The next essay, "Computer Game Semiotics" (1991), is the work of David Myers, one of the few game theorists writing in the 1980s and 1990s. He begins by justifying games as an object of study and then applies structuralist analyses, borrowing from Propp, Levi-Strauss, and Greimas, to find the underlying structures of video games and examines three games of the time.

Although conceptual tools from film theory and literary theory have been applied to video games, it was soon realized that new methodologies would be needed for the critical analysis of video games, due to their interactivity, nonlinearity, and other peculiarities of the medium. Some authors writing about video games turned their analytical queries to the methods themselves, seeking and suggesting new ways of analyzing games. Lars Konzack's essay, "Computer Game Criticism: A Method for Computer Game Analysis" (2002), develops a new method for analyzing games, based on Konzack's perception of seven different layers of the computer game: hardware, program code, functionality, game play, meaning, referentiality, and socio-culture. Building on Konzack's work, Espen Aarseth suggested further methodologies for studying games in his essay, "Playing Research: Methodological Approaches to Game Analysis" (2003), even giving a typology of game research and an account of his own playing research in *The Elder Scrolls III: Morrowind* (2002). In a more recent example of scholarship pertaining to game analysis, Roberto Dillon's essay, "Towards the Definition of a Framework and Grammar for Game Analysis and Design" (2014), details his proposed "A.G.E." method, which examines core player Actions, the resulting Gameplay that follows, and the emotional Experience of the players involved. Dillon's model is also formalized into a grammar that can be used by analyst and game designer alike, applied to game criticism as well as game design.

While the foregoing essays in this section were very broad in their application, applying to a wide range of games, the next four essays are examples of detailed analyses which go in-depth with a narrower focus. The first essay, David Myers's "Bombs, Barbarians, and Backstories: Meaning-making within *Sid Meier's Civilization*" (2005), concentrates on *Civilization* (1991), discussing its "spiral-like history", its use of recursive replay, and the socio-cultural values embedded in the game. Thomas H. Apperley's essay, "Genre and Game Studies" (2006), looks at how prior conceptions of genre from other media have been applied to video games, in the area of marketing and elsewhere, arguing that such generic categories and descriptions fail to provide an understanding of the medium, something which he attributes to the tension between the "narratological" and "ludological" divide. Will Brooker's essay, "Camera-Eye, CG-Eye: Videogames and the 'Cinematic'" (2009), argues that the dominant camera style in video games is more like avant-garde cinema than conventional Hollywood cinema, or even blockbuster special effects cinema. Brett Camper's essay, "Color-Cycled Space Fumes in the Pixel Particle Shockwave: The Technical Aesthetics of *Defender* and the Williams Arcade Platform, 1980–82" (2012), takes a thorough examination of how the aesthetics of Williams's *Defender* (1980) was influenced by the technology of the platform used by the game and the relationship between the arcade game and the larger company platform used for arcade games of the time.

The final essay in this section, Ian Bogost's "Procedural Rhetoric" from his book *Persuasive Games: The Expressive Power of Video Games* (2010), discusses how video games can convey messages through what he calls "procedural rhetoric". Just as in stories told in traditional media, where the way actions are connected to consequences makes an implicit claim as to how things work (for example, a criminal gets punished before the end of a film, to show that crime does not pay), video games cannot only convey ideas in a similar fashion, but do so directly through the player's ability to choose different courses of action and compare the consequences following each. All the essays in this section demonstrate the video game's uniqueness as a medium and how consideration of its own peculiarities can cause one to reconsider not only the methodologies applied to their analysis but perhaps view the analyses of other media in a new light as well.

Part 4

VIDEO GAME DESIGN AND FORMAL ASPECTS

23

I HAVE NO WORDS & I MUST DESIGN

Greg Costikyan

Source: *Interactive Fantasy: The Journal of Role-Playing and Story-Making Systems*, 2 (London: Hogshead Publishing, 1994), pp. 192–211.

Context

"I Have No Words" was written in the early 1990s, at a time when virtually nothing had been written on the subject of game design as a discipline, before game studies as a discipline or *Game Developer* magazine existed. Since Chris Crawford's *Journal of Computer Game Design* had recently stopped publishing, there seemed no obvious venue for its publication. In 1994, James Wallis, who ran a small tabletop RPG company called Hogshead, invited me to write for its magazine, *Interactive Fantasy*, a small journal that ran intelligent discussions about RPG design, and so I sent him this piece. In retrospect, the emphasis on "decision making" may betray my leanings as a strategy gamer, and be less applicable to games that depend on fast action, but on the whole, I think it holds up well.

There's a lotta different kinds of games out there. A helluva lot. Cart-based, computer, CD-ROM, network, arcade, PBM, PBEM, mass-market adult, wargames, card games, tabletop RPGs, LARPs, freeforms. And, hell, don't forget paintball, virtual reality, sports, and the horses. It's all gaming.

But do these things have anything at all in common? What is a game? And how can you tell a good one from a bad one?

Well, we can all do the latter: "Good game, Joe," you say, as you leap the net. Or put away the counters. Or reluctantly hand over your Earth Elemental card. Or divvy up the treasure. But that's no better than saying, "Good book," as you turn the last page. It may be true, but it doesn't help you write a better one.

As game designers, we need a way to analyze games, to try to understand them, and to understand what works and what makes them interesting.

We need a critical language. And since this is basically a new form, despite its tremendous growth and staggering diversity, we need to invent one.

7

What is a game, anyhow?

It's not a puzzle

In *The Art of Computer Game Design*, Chris Crawford contrasts what he calls "games" with "puzzles." Puzzles are static; they present the "player" with a logic structure to be solved with the assistance of clues. "Games," by contrast, are not static, but change with the player's actions.

Some puzzles are obviously so; no one would call a crossword a "game." But, according to Crawford, some "games" a really just puzzles—Lebling & Blank's Zork, for instance. The game's sole objective is the solution of puzzles: finding objects and using them in particular ways to cause desired changes in the game-state. There is no opposition, there is no roleplaying, and there are no resources to manage; victory is solely a consequence of puzzle solving.

To be sure, Zork is not entirely static; the character moves from setting to setting, allowable actions vary by setting, and inventory changes with action. We must think of a continuum, rather than a dichotomy; if a crossword is 100% puzzle, Zork is 90% puzzle and 10% game.

Almost every game has some degree of puzzle-solving; even a pure military strategy game requires players to, e.g., solve the puzzle of making an optimum attack at this point with these units. To eliminate puzzle-solving entirely, you need a game that's almost entirely exploration: Just Grandma and Me, a CD-ROM interactive storybook with game-like elements of decision-making and exploration, is a good example. Clicking on screen objects causes entertaining sounds and animations, but there's nothing to "solve," in fact, no strategy whatsoever.

A puzzle is static. A game is interactive.

It's not a toy

According to Will Wright, his Sim City is not a game at all, but a toy. Wright offers a ball as an illuminating comparison: It offers many interesting behaviors, which you may explore. You can bounce it, twirl it, throw it, dribble it. And, if you wish, you may use it in a game: soccer, or basketball, or whatever. But the game is not intrinsic in the toy; it is a set of player-defined objectives overlaid on the toy.

Just so Sim City. Like many computer games, it creates a world that the player may manipulate, but unlike a real game, it provides no objective. Oh, you may choose one: to see if you can build a city without slums, perhaps. But Sim City itself has no victory conditions, no goals; it is a software toy.

A toy is interactive. But a game has goals.

It's not a story

Again and again, we hear about story. Interactive literature. Creating a story through roleplay. The idea that games have something to do with stories has such a hold on designers' imagination that it probably can't be expunged. It deserves at least to be challenged.

Stories are inherently linear. However much characters may agonize over the decisions they make, they make them the same way every time we reread the story, and the outcome is always the same. Indeed, this is a strength; the author chose precisely those characters, those events, those decisions, and that outcome, because it made for the strongest story. If the characters did something else, the story wouldn't be as interesting.

Games are inherently non-linear. They depend on decision-making. Decisions have to pose real, plausible alternatives, or they aren't real decisions. It must be entirely reasonable for a player to make a decision one way in one game, and a different way in the next. To the degree that you make a game more like a story—more linear, fewer real options—you make it less like a game.

Consider: you buy a book, or see a movie, because it has a great story. But how would you react if your gamemaster were to tell you, "I don't want you players to do that, because it will ruin the story?" He may well be right, but that's beside the point. Gaming is NOT about telling stories.

That said, games often, and fruitfully, borrow elements of fiction. Roleplaying games depend on characters; computer adventures and LARPs are often driven by plots. The notion of increasing narrative tension is a useful one for any game that comes to a definite conclusion. But to try to hew too closely to a storyline is to limit players' freedom of action and their ability to make meaningful decisions.

The hypertext fiction movement is interesting, here. Hypertext is inherently non-linear, so that the traditional narrative is wholly inappropriate to hypertext work. Writers of hypertext fiction are trying to explore the nature of human existence, as does the traditional story, but in a way that permits multiple viewpoints, temporal leaps, and reader construction of the experience. Something—more than hypertext writers know—is shared with game design here, and something with traditional narrative; but if hypertext fiction ever becomes artistically successful (nothing I've read is), it will be through the creation of a new narrative form, something that we will be hard-pressed to call "story."

Stories are linear. Games are not.

It demands participation

In a traditional artform, the audience is passive. When you look at a painting, you may imagine things in it, you may see something other than what the artist intended, but your role in constructing the experience is slight: The artist painted. You see. You are passive.

When you go to the movies, or watch TV, or visit the theater, you sit and watch and listen. Again, you do interpret, to a degree; but you are the audience. You are passive. The art is created by others.

When you read a book, most of it goes on in your head, and not on the page; but still. You're receiving the author's words. You're passive.

9

It's all too, too autocratic: the mighty artist condescends to share his genius with lesser mortals. How can it be that, two hundred years after the Revolution, we still have such aristocratic forms? Surely, we need forms in spirit with the times; forms which permit the common man to create his own artistic experience.

Enter the game. Games provide a set of rules; but the players use them to create their own consequences. It's something like the music of John Cage: he wrote themes about which the musicians were expected to improvise. Games are like that; the designer provides the theme, the players the music.

A democratic artform for a democratic age.

Traditional artforms play to a passive audience. Games require active participation.

So what is a game?

A game is a form of art in which participants, termed players, make decisions in order to manage resources through game tokens in the pursuit of a goal.

Decision-making

I offer this term in an effort to destroy the inane, and overhyped, word "interactive." The future, we are told, will be interactive. You might as well say, "The future will be fnurglewitz." It would be about as enlightening.

A light switch is interactive. You flick it up, the light turns on. You flick it down, the light turns off. That's interaction. But it's not a lot of fun.

All games are interactive: The game state changes with the players' actions. If it didn't, it wouldn't be a game: It would be a puzzle.

But interaction has no value in itself. Interaction must have purpose.

Suppose we have a product that's interactive. At some point, you are faced with a choice: You may choose to do A, or to do B.

But what makes A better than B? Or is B better than A at some times but not at others? What factors go into the decision? What resources are to be managed? What's the eventual goal?

Aha! Now we're not talking about "interaction." Now we're talking about decision-making.

The thing that makes a game a game is the need to make decisions. Consider Chess: it has few of the aspects that make games appealing—no simulation elements, no roleplaying, and damn little color. What it's got is the need to make decisions. The rules are tightly constrained, the objectives clear, and victory requires you to think several moves ahead. Excellence in decision-making is what brings success.

What does a player do in any game? Some things depend on the medium. In some games, he rolls dice. In some games, he chats with his friends. In some games, he whacks at a keyboard. But in every game, he makes decisions.

10

At every point, he considers the game state. That might be what he sees on the screen. Or it might be what the gamemaster has just told him. Or it might be the arrangement on the pieces on the board. Then, he considers his objectives, and the game tokens and resources available to him. And he considers his opposition, the forces he must struggle against. He tries to decide on the best course of action.

And he makes a decision.

What's key here? Goals. Opposition. Resource management. Information. Well talk about them in half a mo.

What decisions do players make in this game?

Goals

Sim City has no goals. Is it not a game?

No, as its own designer willingly maintains. It is a toy.

And the only way to stay interested in it for very long is to turn it into a game—by setting goals, by defining objectives for yourself. Build the grandest possible megalopolis; maximize how much your people love you; build a city that relies solely on mass transit. Whatever goal you've chosen, you've turned it into a game.

Even so, the software doesn't support your goal. It wasn't designed with your goal in mind. And trying to do something with a piece of software that it wasn't intended to do can be awfully frustrating.

Since there's no goal, Sim City soon palls. By contrast, Sid Meier and Bruce Shelley's Civilization, an obviously derivative product, has explicit goals—and is far more involving and addictive.

"But what about roleplaying games?" you may say. "They have no victory conditions."

No victory conditions, true. But certainly, they have goals; lots of them, you get to pick. Rack up the old experience points. Or fulfill the quest your friendly GM has just inflicted on you. Or rebuild the Imperium and stave off civilization's final collapse. Or strive toward spiritual perfection. Whatever.

If, for some reason, your player characters don't have a goal, they'll find one right quick. Otherwise, they'll have nothing better to do but sit around the tavern and grouse about how boring the game is. Until you get pissed off and have a bunch of orcs show up and try to beat their heads in.

Hey, now they've got a goal. Personal survival is a good goal. One of the best.

If you have no goal, your decisions are meaningless. Choice A is as good as Choice B; pick a card, any card. Who cares? What does it matter?

For it to matter, for the game to be meaningful, you need something to strive toward. You need goals.

What are the players' goals? Can the game support a variety of different goals? What facilities exist to allow players to strive toward their various goals?

Opposition

Oh, say the politically correct. Those bad, icky games. They're so competitive. Why can't we have cooperative games?

"Cooperative games" generally seem to be variants of "let's all throw a ball around." Oh golly, how fascinating, I'll stop playing Mortal Kombat for that, you betcha.

But are we really talking about competition?

Yes and no; many players do get a kick out of beating others with their naked minds alone, which is at least better than naked fists. Chess players are particularly obnoxious in this regard. But the real interest is in struggling toward a goal.

The most important word in that sentence is: struggling.

Here's a game. It's called Plucky Little England, and it simulates the situation faced by the United Kingdom after the fall of France in World War II. Your goal: preserve liberty and democracy and defeat the forces of darkness and oppression. You have a choice: A. Surrender. B. Spit in Hitler's eye! Rule Britannia! England never never never shall be slaves!

You chose B? Congratulations! You won!

Now, wasn't that satisfying? Ah, the thrill of victory.

There is no thrill of victory, of course; it was all too easy, wasn't it? There wasn't any struggle.

In a two-player, head-to-head game, your opponent is the opposition, your struggle against him; the game is direct competition. And this is a first-rate way of providing opposition. Nothing is as sneaky and as hard to overcome as a determined human opponent is. But direct competition isn't the only way to do it.

Think of fiction. The ur-story, the Standard Model Narrative, works like this: character A has a goal. He faces obstacles B, C, D, and E. He struggles with each, in turn, growing as a person as he does. Ultimately, he overcomes the last and greatest obstacle.

Do these obstacles all need to be The Villain, The Bad Guy, The Opponent, The Foe? No, though a good villain makes for a first rate obstacle. The forces of nature, cantankerous mothers-in-law, crashing hard-drives, and the hero's own feelings of inadequacy can make for good obstacles, too.

Just so in games.

In most RPGs, the "opposition" consists of non-player characters, and you are expected to cooperate with your fellow players. In many computer games, the "opposition" consists of puzzles you must solve. In LARPs, the "opposition" is often the sheer difficulty of finding the player who has the clue or the widget or the special power you need. In most solitaire games, your "opposition" is really a random element, or a set of semi-random algorithms you are pitted against.

Whatever goals you set your players, you must make the players work to achieve their goals. Setting them against each other is one way to do that, but not the only one. And even when a player has an opponent, putting other obstacles in the game can increase its richness and emotional appeal.

The desire for "cooperative games" is the desire for an end to strife. But there can be none. Life is the struggle for survival and growth. There is no end to strife, not this side of the grave. A game without struggle is a game that's dead.

What provides opposition? What makes the game a struggle?

Managing resources

Trivial decisions aren't any fun. Remember Plucky Little England?

There wasn't any real decision, was there?

Or consider Robert Harris's Talisman. Each turn, you roll the die. The result is the number of spaces you can move. You may move to the left, or to the right, around the track.

Well, this is a little better than a traditional track game; I've got a choice. But 99 times out of a 100, either there's no difference between the two spaces, or one is obviously better than the other. The choice is bogus.

The way to make choices meaningful is to give players resources to manage. "Resources" can be anything: Panzer divisions. Supply points. Cards. Experience points. Knowledge of spells. Ownership of fiefs. The love of a good woman. Favors from the boss. The good will of an NPC. Money. Food. Sex. Fame. Information.

If the game has more than one "resource," decisions suddenly become more complex. If I do this, I get money and experience, but will Lisa still love me? If I steal the food, I get to eat, but I might be caught and have my hand cut off. If I declare against the Valois, Edward Plantagenet will grant me the Duchy of Gascony, but the Pope may excommunicate me, imperiling my immortal soul.

These are not just complex decisions; these are interesting ones. Interesting decisions make for interesting games.

The resources in question have to have a game role; if "your immortal soul" has no meaning, neither does excommunication. (Unless it reduces the loyalty of your peasants, or makes it difficult to recruit armies, or . . . but these are game roles, *n'est-ce pas?*) Ultimately, "managing resources" means managing game elements in pursuit of your goal. A "resource" that has no game role has nothing to contribute to success or failure, and is ultimately void.

What resources does the player manage? Is there enough diversity in them to require tradeoffs in making decisions? Do they make those decisions interesting?

Game tokens

You effect actions in the game through your game tokens. A game token is any entity you may manipulate directly.

In a boardgame, it is your pieces. In a cardgame, it is your cards. In a roleplaying game, it is your character. In a sports game, it is you yourself.

What is the difference between "resources" and "tokens?" Resources are things you must manage efficiently to achieve your goals; tokens are your means of managing them. In a board wargame, combat strength is a resource; your counters are tokens. In a roleplaying game, money is a resource; you use it through your character.

Why is this important? Because if you don't have game tokens, you wind up with a system that operates without much player input. Will Wright and Fred Haslam's Sim Earth is a good example. In Sim Earth, you set some parameters, and sit back to watch the game play out itself. You've got very little to do, no tokens to manipulate, no resources to manage. Just a few parameters to twiddle with. This is mildly interesting, but not very.

To give a player a sense that he controls his destiny, that he is playing a game, you need game tokens. The fewer the tokens, the more detailed they must be; it is no coincidence that roleplaying games, which give the player a single token, also have exceptionally detailed rules for what that token can do.

What are the players' tokens? What are these tokens' abilities? What resources do they use? What makes them interesting?

Information

I've had more than one conversation with a computer game designer in which he tells me about all the fascinating things his game simulates—while I sit there saying, "Really? What do you know. I didn't realize that."

Say you've got a computer wargame in which weather affects movement and defense. If you don't tell the player that weather has an effect, what good is it? It won't affect the player's behavior; it won't affect his decisions.

Or maybe you tell him weather has an effect, but the player has no way of telling whether it's raining or snowing or what at any given time. Again, what good is that?

Or maybe he can tell, and he does know, but he has no idea what effect weather has—maybe it cuts everyone's movement in half, or maybe it slows movement across fields to a crawl but does nothing to units moving along roads. This is better, but not a whole lot.

The interface must provide the player with relevant information. And he must have enough information to be able to make a sensible decision.

That isn't to say a player must know everything; hiding information can be very useful. It's quite reasonable to say, "you don't know just how strong your units are until they enter combat," but in this case, the player must have some idea of the range of possibilities. It's reasonable to say, "you don't know what card you'll get if you draw to an inside straight," but only if the player has some idea what the odds are. If I might draw the Queen of Hearts and might draw Death and might draw the Battleship Potemkin, I have absolutely no basis on which to make a decision.

More than that, the interface must not provide too much information, especially in a time-dependent game. If weather, supply state, the mood of my commanders, the fatigue of the troops, and what Tokyo Rose said on the radio last night can all

14

affect the outcome of my next decision, and I have to decide some time in the next five seconds, and it would take me five minutes to find all the relevant information by pulling down menus and looking at screens, the information is still irrelevant. I may have access to it, but I can't reasonably act on it.

Or let's talk about computer adventures; they often display information failure. "Oh, to get through the Gate of Thanatos, you need a hatpin to pick the lock. You can find the hatpin on the floor of the Library. It's about three pixels by two pixels, and you can see it, if your vision is good, between the twelfth and thirteenth floorboards, about three inches from the top of the screen. What, you missed it?"

Yeah, I missed it. In an adventure, it shouldn't be ridiculously difficult to find what you need, nor should victory be impossible just because you made a wrong decision three hours and thirty-eight decision points ago. Nor should the solutions to puzzles be arbitrary or absurd.

Or consider freeforms. In a freeform, a player is often given a goal, and achieving it requires him to find out several things—call them Facts A, B, and C. The freeform's designer had better make damn sure that A, B, and C are out there somewhere—known to other characters, or on a card that's circulating in the game—whatever, they have to be there. Otherwise, the player has no chance of achieving his goal, and that's no fun.

Given the decisions players are required to make, what information do they need? Does the game provide the information as and when needed? Will reasonable players be able to figure out what information they need, and how to find it?

Other things that strengthen games

Diplomacy

Achieving a goal is meaningless if it comes without work, if there is no opposition; but that doesn't mean all decisions must be zero-sum. Whenever multiple players are involved, games are strengthened if they permit, and encourage, diplomacy.

Games permit diplomacy if players can assist each other—perhaps directly, perhaps by combining against a mutual foe. Not all multiplayer games do this; in Charles B. Darrow's Monopoly, for instance, there's no effective way to either help or hinder anyone else. There's no point in saying, "Let's all get Joe," or "Here, you're a novice, I'll help you out, you can scratch my back later," because there's no way to do it.

Some games permit diplomacy, but not much. In Lawrence Harris's Axis & Allies, players can help each other to a limited degree, but everyone is permanently Axis or permanently Allied, so diplomacy is never a key element to the game.

One way to encourage diplomacy is by providing non-exclusive goals. If you're looking for the Ark of the Covenant, and I want to kill Nazis, and the Nazis have the Ark, we can work something out. Maybe our alliance will end when the French Resistance gets the Ark, and we wind up on opposite sides, but actually, such twists are what make games fun.

15

But games can encourage diplomacy even when players are directly opposed. The diplomatic game par excellence is, of course, Calhammer's Diplomacy, in which victory more often goes to the best diplomat than to the best strategist. The key to the game is the Support order, which allows one player's armies to assist another in an attack, encouraging alliance.

Alliances never last, to be sure; Russia and Austria may ally to wipe out Turkey, but only one of them can win. Eventually, one will stab the other in the back.

Fine. It's the need to find allies, retain them, and persuade your enemies to change their stripes that makes sure you'll keep on talking. If alliances get set in stone, diplomacy comes to an end.

Computer games are almost inherently solitaire, and to the degree they permit diplomacy with NPC computer opponents, they generally don't make it interesting. Network games are, or ought to be, inherently diplomatic; and as network games become more prevalent, we can expect most developers from the computer design community to miss this point entirely. As an example, when the planners of interactive TV networks talk about games, they almost exclusively talk about the possibility of downloading cart-based (Nintendo, Sega) games over cable. They're doing so for a business reason: billions are spent annually on cart-based games, and they'd like a piece of the action. They don't seem to realize that networks permit a wholly different kind of gaming, which has the potential to make billions in its own right—and that this is the real business opportunity.

How can players help or hinder each other? What incentives do they have to do so? What resources can they trade?

Color

Monopoly is a game about real estate development. Right?

Well, no, obviously not. A real estate developer would laugh at the notion. A game about real estate development needs rules for construction loans and real estate syndication and union work rules and the bribery of municipal inspectors. Monopoly has nothing to do with real estate development. You could take the same rules, change the board, pieces, and cards, and make it into a game about space exploration, say. Except that your game would have as much to do with space exploration as Monopoly has to do with real estate development.

Monopoly isn't really about anything. But it has the color of a real estate game: named properties, little plastic houses and hotels, play money. And that's a big part of its appeal.

Color counts for a lot: as a simulation of World War II, Lawrence Harris's Axis & Allies is a pathetic effort. Ah, but the color! Millions of little plastic airplanes and battleships and tanks! Thundering dice! The world at war! The game works almost solely because of its color.

Or consider Chadwick's Space 1899. The rules do nothing to evoke the Burroughsian wonders, the pulp action thrills, and the Kiplingesque Victorian charms to be gained from the game's setting. Despite a clean system and a detailed world, it is curiously colorless, and suffers for it.

Pageantry, detail, and sense of place can greatly add to a game's emotional appeal. This has almost nothing to do with the game qua game; the original Nova edition of Axis & Allies was virtually identical to the Milton Bradley edition. Except that it had a god-awful garish paper map, some of the ugliest counters I've ever seen, and a truly amateurish box. I looked at it once, put it away, and never looked at it again.

Yet the Milton Bradley edition, with all the little plastic pieces, still gets pulled out now and again . . . Same game. Far better color.

How does the game evoke the ethos and atmosphere and pageantry of its setting? What can you do to make it more colorful?

Simulation

Many games simulate nothing. The oriental folk-game Go, say; little stones on a grid. It's abstract to perfection. Or John Horton Conway's Life; despite the evocative name, it's merely an exploration of a mathematical space.

Nothing wrong with that. But.

But color adds to a game's appeal. And simulation is a way of providing color.

Suppose I think, for some reason, that a game on Waterloo would have great commercial appeal. I could, if I wanted, take Monopoly, change "Park Place" to "Quatre Bras" and the hotels to plastic soldiers, and call it Waterloo. It would work.

But wouldn't it be better to simulate the battle? To have little battalions maneuvering over the field? To hear the thunder of guns?

Or take Star Wars: The Roleplaying Game, which I designed. I could have taken Gygax & Arneson's Dungeons & Dragons and changed it around, calling swords blasters and the like. But instead, I set out to simulate the movies, to encourage the players to attempt far-fetched cinematic stunts, to use the system itself to reflect something about the atmosphere and ethos of the films.

Simulation has other value, too. For one, it improves character identification. A Waterloo based on Monopoly would do nothing to make players think like Wellington and Napoleon; Kevin Zucker's Napoleon's Last Battles does much better, forcing players to think about the strategic problems those men faced.

And it can allow insight into a situation that mere narrative cannot. It allows players to explore different outcomes—in the fashion of a software toy—and thereby come to a gut understanding of the simulation's subject. Having played at least a dozen different games on Waterloo, I understand the battle, and why things happened the way they did, and the nature of Napoleonic warfare, far better than if I had merely read a dozen books on the subject.

Simulating something almost always is more complicated than simply exploiting a theme for color. And it is not, therefore, for every game. But when the technique is used, it can be quite powerful.

How can elements of simulation strengthen the game?

Variety of encounter

"You just got lucky."

Words of contempt; you won through the vagaries of chance. A game that permits this is obviously inferior to ones where victory goes to the skilled, smart, and strong. Right? Not necessarily.

"Random elements" in a game are never wholly random. They are random within a range of possibilities. When, in a board wargame, I make an attack, I can look at the Combat Results Table. I know what outcomes are possible, and my chances of achieving what I want to achieve. I take a calculated risk. And over the whole game, I make dozens or hundreds of die-rolls; given so much reliance on randomness, the "random element" regresses to a mean. Except in rare cases, my victory or defeat will be based on my excellence as a strategist, not on my luck with the dice.

Randomness can be useful. It's one way of providing variety of encounter.

And what does that mean?

It means that the same old thing all over again is fucking boring. It means that players like to encounter the unexpected. It means that the game has to allow many different things to happen, so there's always something a little different for the players to encounter.

In a game like Chess, that "something different" is the ever-changing implications of the positions of the pieces. In a game like Richard Garfield's Magic: The Gathering, it's the sheer variety of cards, and the random order in which they appear, and the interesting ways in which they can be combined. In Arneson & Gygax's Dungeons & Dragons, it's the staggering variety of monsters, spells, etc., etc., coupled with the gamemaster's ingenuity in throwing new situations at his players.

If a game has inadequate variety, it rapidly palls. That's why no one plays graphic adventures more than once; there's enough variety for a single game, but it's the same thing all over again the next time you play. That's why Patience, the solitaire cardgame, becomes dull pretty fast; you're doing the same things over and over, and reshuffling the cards isn't enough to rekindle your interest, after a time.

What things do the players encounter in this game? Are there enough things for them to explore and discover? What provides variety? How can we increase the variety of encounter?

Position identification

"Character identification" is a common theme of fiction. Writers want readers to like their protagonists, to identify with them, to care what happens to them. Character identification lends emotional power to a story.

The same is true in games. To the degree you encourage players to care about "the side," to identify with their position in the game, you increase the game's emotional impact.

The extreme case is sports; in sports, your "position" is you. You're out there on the baseball diamond, and winning or losing matters, and you feel it deeply when you strike out, or smash the ball out of the park. It's important to you.

So important that fistfights and bitter words are not uncommon, in every sport. So important that we've invented a whole cultural tradition of "sportsmanship" to try to prevent these unpleasant feelings from coming to the fore.

Roleplaying games are one step abstracted; your character isn't you, but you invest a lot of time and energy in it. It's your sole token and the sum total of your position in the game. Bitter words, and even fistfights, are not unknown among roleplayers, though rather rarer than in sports.

Getting players to identify with their game position is straightforward when a player has a single token; it's harder when he controls many. Few people feel much sadness at the loss of a knight in Chess or an infantry division in a wargame. But even here, a game's emotional power is improved if the player can be made to feel identification with "the side."

One way to do that is to make clear the player's point of view. Point of view confusion is a common failing of boardgame designers. For instance, Richard Berg's Campaigns for North Africa claims to be an extraordinary realistic simulation of the Axis campaign in Africa. Yet you, as player, spend a great deal of time worrying about the locations of individual pilots and how much water is available to individual battalions. Rommel's staff might worry about such things, but Rommel assuredly did not. Who are you supposed to be? The accuracy of the simulation is, in a sense, undermined, not supported, by the level of detail.

What can you do to make the player care about his position? Is there a single game token that's more important than others to the player, and what can be done to strengthen identification with it? If not, what is the overall emotional appeal of the position, and what can be done to strengthen that appeal? Who "is" the player in the game? What is his point of view?

Roleplaying

HeroQuest has been termed a "roleplaying boardgame." And, as in a roleplaying game, each player controls a single character, which, in HeroQuest's case, is a single plastic figure on the board. If you are a single character, are you not "playing a role?" And is the characterization of this game as a "roleplaying" game therefore justified?

No, to both questions.

The questions belie confusion between "position identification" and "roleplaying." I may identify closely with a game token without feeling that I am playing a role.

Roleplaying occurs when, in some sense, you take on the persona of your position. Different players, and different games, may do this in different ways: perhaps you try to speak in the language and rhythm of your character. Perhaps you talk as if you are feeling the emotions your character feels. Perhaps you talk as you normally do, but you give serious consideration to "what my character would do in this case" as opposed to "what I want to do next."

Roleplaying is most common in, naturally, roleplaying games. But it can occur in other environments, as well; I, for one, can't get through a game of Vincent Tsao's Junta without talking in a phony Spanish accent somewhere along the line. The game makes me think enough like a big man in a corrupt banana republic that I start to play the role.

Roleplaying is a powerful technique for a whole slew of reasons. It improves position identification; if you think like your character, you're identifying with him closely. It improves the game's color, because the players become partly responsible for maintaining the willing suspense of disbelief, the feeling that the game world is alive and colorful and consistent. And it is an excellent method of socialization.

Indeed, the connection with socialization is key: roleplaying is a form of performance. In a roleplaying game, roleplayers perform for the amusement of their friends. If there aren't any friends, there's no point to it.

Which is why "computer roleplaying games", so-called, are nothing of the kind. They have no more connection with roleplaying than does HeroQuest. That is, they have the trappings of roleplaying: characters, equipment, stories. But there is no mechanism for players to ham it up, to characterize themselves by their actions, to roleplay in any meaningful sense.

This is intrinsic in the technology. Computer games are solitaire; solitaire gamers have, by definition, no audience. Therefore, computer games cannot involve roleplaying.

Add a network, and you can have a roleplaying game. Hence the popularity of MUDs.

How can players be induced to roleplay? What sorts of roles does the system permit or encourage?

Socializing

Historically, games have mainly been used as a way to socialize. For players of Bridge, Poker, and Charades, the game is secondary to the socialization that goes on over the table.

One oddity of the present is that the most commercially successful games are all solitary in nature: cart games, disk-based computer games, CD-ROM games. Once upon a time, our image of gamers was some people sitting around a table and playing cards; now, it's a solitary adolescent, twitching a joystick before a flickering screen.

Yet, at the same time, we see the development of roleplaying, in both tabletop and live-action form, which depends utterly on socialization. And we see that the most successful mass-market boardgames, like Trivial Pursuit and Pictionary, are played almost exclusively in social settings.

I have to believe that the solitary nature of most computer games is a temporary aberration, a consequence of the technology, and that as networks spread and their bandwidth increases, the historical norm will reassert itself.

When designing any game, it is worthwhile to think about the game's social uses, and how the system encourages or discourages socialization. For instance, almost every network has online versions of classic games like Poker and Bridge. And in almost every case, those games have failed to attract much usage.

The exception: America Online, which permits real-time chat between players. Their version of network bridge allows for table talk. And it has been quite popular.

Or as another example, many tabletop roleplaying games spend far too much effort worrying about "realism" and far too little about the game's use by players. Of what use is a combat system that is extraordinarily realistic, if playing out a single combat round takes fifteen minutes, and a whole battle takes four hours? They're not spending their time socializing, talking, and hamming it up; they're spending time rolling dice and looking things up on charts. What's the point in that?

How can the game better encourage socialization?

Narrative tension

Nebula-award winning author Pat Murphy says that the key element of plot is "rising tension." That is, a story should become more gripping as it proceeds, until its ultimate climactic resolution.

Suppose you are a Yankees fan. Of course, you want to see the Yankees win. But if you go to a game at the ballpark, do you really want to see them develop a 7 point lead in the first inning and wind up winning 21 to 2? Yes, you want them to win, but this doesn't make for a very interesting game. What would make you rise from your seat in excitement and joy is to see them pull out from behind in the last few seconds of the game with a smash homerun with bases loaded. Tension makes for fun games.

Ideally, a game should be tense all the way through, but especially so at the end. The toughest problems, the greatest obstacles, should be saved for last. You can't always ensure this, especially in directly competitive games: a Chess game between a grandmaster and a rank beginner is not going to involve much tension. But, especially in solitaire computer games, it should be possible to ensure that every stage of the game involves a set of challenges, and that the player's job is done only at the end.

In fact, one of the most common game failures is anticlimax. The period of maximum tension is not the resolution, but somewhere mid-way through the game. After a while, the opposition is on the run, or the player's position is unassailable. In most cases, this is because the designer never considered the need for narrative tension.

What can be done to make the game tense?

They're all alike under the dice. Or phosphors. Or what have you

We're now equipped to answer the questions I posed at the beginning of this article.

Do all the myriad forms of gaming have anything in common? Most assuredly. All involve decision-making, managing resources in pursuit of a goal; that's true whether we're talking about Chess or Seventh Guest, Mario Brothers or Vampire, Roulette or Magic: The Gathering. It's a universal; it's what defines a game.

How can you tell a good game from a bad one? The test is still in the playing; but we now have some terms to use to analyze a game's appeal. Chess involves complex and difficult decisions; Magic has enormous variety of encounter; Roulette has an extremely compelling goal (money—the real stuff). More detailed analysis is possible, to be sure, and is left as an exercise for the reader.

Is the analytical theory presented here hermetic and complete? Assuredly not; there are games that defy many, though not all, of its conclusions (e.g., Candyland, which involves no decision-making whatsoever). And no doubt there are aspects to the appeal of games it overlooks.

It is to be considered a work in progress: a first stab at codifying the intellectual analysis of the art of game design. Others are welcome, even encouraged, to build on its structure—or to propound alternative theories in its defiance.

If we are to produce works worthy to be termed "art," we must start to think about what it takes to do so, to set ourselves goals beyond the merely commercial. For we are embarked on a voyage of revolutionary import: the democrative transformation of the arts. Properly addressed, the voyage will lend grandeur to our civilization; improperly, it will create merely another mediocrity of the TV age, another form wholly devoid of intellectual merit.

Acknowledgement

The author wishes to acknowledge the contributions of Chris Crawford, Will Wright, Eric Goldberg, Ken Rolston, Doug Kaufman, Jim Dunnigan, Tappan King, Sandy Peterson, and Walt Freitag, whose ideas he has liberally stolen.

Orthographical note

In normal practice, the names of traditional games, e.g., chess, go, poker, are uncapitalized, as is usual with common nouns. The names of proprietary games are written with Initial Caps. This usage is inconsistent with the thesis that games are an artform, and that each game, regardless of its origins, must be viewed as an oeuvre. I capitalize all game names, throughout the article.

We capitalize *Beowulf*, though it is the product of folk tradition rather than a definite author, just as we capitalize *One Hundred Years of Solitude*. In the same fashion, I capitalize Chess, though it is the product of folk tradition rather than a definite designer, just as I capitalize Dungeons & Dragons. It may seem odd, at first, to see Chess treated as a title, but I have done so for particular reasons.

I have also, whenever possible, attempted to mention a game's designer upon its first mention. When I have omitted a name, it is because I do not know it.

24

FORMAL ABSTRACT DESIGN TOOLS

Doug Church

Source: *Game Developer*, August 1999, 44–50. Reprinted in Katie Salen and Eric Zimmerman (eds), *The Game Design Reader: A Rules of Play Anthology* (Cambridge, MA: The MIT Press, 2006), pp. 366–380.

Context

Written after we had finished three or four games at the game development company Looking Glass, "Formal Abstract Design Tools" was my attempt to share with the public some of the ways we discussed and thought about games. We were frustrated with the lack of any terminology that was more specific than "fun;" my essay's response was split evenly between "This is cool and useful, how can I help?" and "You can't mandate and legislate design—design comes from designers, not from executive boardrooms!" I still believe that a better understanding of design tools will lead to greater creativity and better design, and that we still have a lot of thinking and experimenting to do. This article originally appeared in the August 1999 issue of *Game Developer* magazine.

Introduction

What is a modern computer game made of? It fuses a technical base with a vision for the player's experience. All of the disciplines involved (design, art, audio, levels, code, and so on) work together to achieve this synthesis.

In most disciplines, industry evolution is obvious: The machines we play on are far more powerful, screens have better resolution and more colors, paint and modeling tools are more sophisticated, audio processing is faster, and sound cards are more capable. Technical issues not even in our vocabulary ten years ago are solved and research continues with essentially infinite headroom. The technical base on which games stand (game code and content creation tools) is evolving.

Across all genres and companies, we build on our own and others' past ideas to expand technical limits, learn new techniques and explore possibilities. Ignoring an anomaly or two, no single company or team would be where it is now had it been forced to work in a vacuum.

Design, on the other hand, is the least understood aspect of computer game creation. It actualizes the vision, putting art, code, levels, and sound together into what players experience, minute to minute. Clever code, beautiful art, and stunning levels don't help if they're never encountered. Design tasks determine player goals and pacing. The design is the game; without it, you would have a CD full of data, but no experience.

Sadly, design is also the aspect that has had the most trouble evolving. Not enough is done to build on past discoveries, share concepts behind successes, and apply lessons learned in one domain or genre to another. Within genres (and certainly within specific design teams), particular lines have evolved significantly. But design evolution still lags far behind the evolution of overall game technology.

How do we talk about games?

The primary inhibitor of design evolution is the lack of a common design vocabulary. Most professional disciplines have a fairly evolved language for discussion. Athletes know the language of their sport and of general physical conditioning, engineers know the technical jargon of their field, doctors know Latin names for body parts and how to scribble illegible prescriptions. In contrast, game designers can discuss "fun" or "not fun," but often the analysis stops there. Whether or not a game is fun is a good place to start understanding, but as designers, our job demands we go deeper.

We should be able to play a side-scrolling shooter on a Game Boy, figure out one cool aspect of it, and apply that idea to the 3D simulation we're building. Or take a game we'd love if it weren't for one annoying part, understand why that part is annoying, and make sure we don't make a similar mistake in our own games. If we reach this understanding, evolution of design across all genres will accelerate. But understanding requires that designers be able to communicate precisely and effectively with one another. In short, we need a shared language of game design.

A language without borders

Our industry produces a wide variety of titles across a range of platforms for equally varied audiences. Any language we develop has to acknowledge this breadth and get at the common elements beneath seemingly disparate genres and products. We need to be able to put our lessons, innovations, and mistakes into a form we can all look at, remember, and benefit from.

A design vocabulary would allow us to do just that, as we could talk about the underlying components of a game. Instead of just saying, "That was fun," or "I don't know, that wasn't much fun," we could dissect a game into its components, and attempt to understand how these parts balance and fit together. A precise vocabulary would improve our understanding of and facility with game creation.

This is something we already do naturally with many technical innovations, since they are often much easier to isolate within a product or transfer to another project. A texture mapper or motion capture system is easily encapsulated. When everyone at the office gathers around some newly released game, major technical "evaluation" is done in the first five minutes: "Wow, nice texture mapping," or "Those figures rock" or "Still don't have a sub-pixel accurate mapper? What is their problem?" or "Man, we have to steal that special effect." But when the crowd disperses, few observations have been made as to what sorts of design leaps were in evidence and, more importantly, what worked and what didn't.

Design is hard to point at directly on a screen. Because of this, its evolutionary path is often stagnant. Within a given genre, design evolution often occurs through refinement. This year's real-time strategy (RTS) games clearly built on last year's RTS games. And that will continue, because design vocabulary today is essentially specific to individual games or genres. You can talk about balancing each race's unit costs, or unit count versus power trade-offs. But we would be hard pressed to show many examples of how innovations in RTS games have helped role-playing games (RPGs) get better. In fact, we might have a hard time describing what could be shared.

These concerns lead to the conclusion that a shared design vocabulary could be very useful. The notion of "Formal Abstract Design Tools" (or FADT, as they'll be referred to from here on) is an attempt to create a framework for such a vocabulary and a way of going about the process of building it.

Examining the phrase, we have: "formal," implying precise definition and the ability to explain it to someone else; "abstract," to emphasize the focus on underlying ideas, not specific genre constructs; "design," as in, well, we're designers; and "tools," since they'll form the common vocabulary we want to create.

"Design" and "tools" are both largely self-explanatory. However, some examples may help clarify "formal" and "abstract." For instance, claiming that "cool stuff" qualifies as a FADT violates the need for formality, since "cool" is not a precise word one can explain concretely—various people are likely to interpret it very differently. On the other hand, "player reward" is well defined and explainable, and thus works. Similarly, a "+2 Giant Slaying Sword" in an RPG is not abstract, but rather an element of one particular game. It doesn't qualify as a FADT because it isn't abstract. The general notion that a magic sword is based on—a mechanic for delivering more powerful equipment to the player—is, however, a good example of a FADT, so the idea of a "player power-up curve" might meet the definition above.

Let's create a design vocabulary—what could possibly go wrong?

Before we start investigating tools in more detail and actually look at examples, some cautionary words. Abstract tools are not bricks to build a game out of. You don't build a house out of tools; you build it with tools. Games are the same way. Having a good "player power-up curve" won't make a game good. FADT are not magic ingredients you add and season to taste. You do not go into a product proposal meeting saying, "This game is all about player power-up curves." As a designer, you still have to figure out what is fun, what your game is about, and what vision and goals you bring to it.

But a design vocabulary is our tool kit to pick apart games and take the parts that resonate with us to realize our own game vision, or refine how our own games work. Once you have thought out your design, you can investigate whether a given tool is used by your game already. If it is, are you using it well, or is it extraneous? If it isn't used, should it be, or is the tool not relevant for your game? Not every construction project needs a circular power saw (sadly), and not every game needs every tool. Using the right tools will help get the shape you want, the strength you need, and the right style.

Similarly, tools don't always work well together—sometimes they conflict. The goal isn't to always use every tool in every game. You can use an individual tool in different ways, and a given tool might just sit in a toolbox waiting to see if it is needed. You, the designer, wield the tools to make what you want—don't let them run the show.

Tools would be useful—where do we find them?

Therefore, we need a design vocabulary, a set of tools underlying game design practice. There is no correct or official method to identify them. One easy way to start looking is to take a good game and describe concretely some of the things that work well. Then, from concrete examples of real game elements, we can attempt to abstract and formalize a few key aspects and maybe find ourselves a few tools.

There isn't enough space here to exhaustively analyze each tool or game—the goal here is to give an overview of the ideas behind and uses of FADT, not a complete view of everything. With that in mind, we'll start with a quick tour of some games, tools, and ideas. Since we are looking for examples of good game design, we'll start by examining *Mario 64*. Once we have explored some concrete aspects of the game itself, we'll step back and start looking for things to abstract and formalize that we can apply to other genres and titles.

Mario 64 game play

Mario 64 blends (apparent) open-ended exploration with continual and clear direction along most paths. Players always have lots to do but are given a lot of choice about which parts of the world they work on and which extra stars they go for. The game also avoids a lot of the super-linear, what's-on-the-next-screen feel of side-scrolling games and gives players a sense of control. In *Mario*, players spend most of their time deciding what they want to do next, not trying to get unstuck, or finding something to do.

A major decision in the design was to have multiple goals in each of the worlds. The first time players arrive in a world, they mostly explore the paths and directions available. Often the first star (typically the easiest to get in each world) has been set up to encourage players to see most of the area. So even while getting

that first star, players often see things they know they will need to use in a later trip. They notice inaccessible red coins, hatboxes, strange contraptions, and so on, while they work on the early goals in a world. When they return to that world for later goals, players already know their way around and have in their heads some idea about how their goals might be achieved, since they have already visited the world and seen many of its elements.

Mario's worlds are also fairly consistent and predictable (if at times a bit odd). Players are given a small, simple set of controls, which work at all times. Simple though the controls are, they are very expressive, allowing rich interaction through simple movement and a small selection of jumping moves. The controls always work (in that you can always perform each action) and players know what to expect from them (for example, a triple jump goes a certain distance; a hip drop may defeat opponents). Power-ups are introduced slowly, and are used consistently throughout (for example, metal Mario can always walk under water).

These simple, consistent controls, coupled with the very predictable physics (accurate for a *Mario* world), allow players to make good guesses about what will happen should they try something. Monsters and environments increase in complexity, but new and special elements are introduced slowly and usually build on an existing interaction principle. This makes game situations very discernable it's easy for the players to plan for action. If players see a high ledge, a monster across the way, or a chest under water, they can start thinking about how they want to approach it.

This allows players to engage in a pretty sophisticated planning process. They have been presented (usually implicitly) with knowledge of how the world works, how they can move and interact with it, and what obstacles they must overcome. Then, often subconsciously, they evolve a plan for getting to where they want to go. While playing, players make thousands of these little plans, some of which work and some of which don't. The key is that when the plan doesn't succeed, players understand why. The world is so consistent that it's immediately obvious why a plan didn't work. This chasm requires a triple jump, not a standing jump; maybe there was more ice than the player thought; maybe the monster moves just a bit too fast. But players get to make a plan, try it out, and see the results as the game reacts. And since that reaction made sense, they can, if needed, make another plan using the information learned during the first attempt.

This involves players in the game, since they have some control over what they want to do and how they want to do it. Players rarely feel cheated, or like they wanted to try something the game didn't support. By offering a very limited set of actions, but supporting them completely, the world is made real for players. No one who plays *Mario* complains that they want to hollow out a cave and make a fire and cook fish, but cannot. The world is very simple and consistent. If something exists in the world, you can use it.

Great! But I'm not writing *Mario 64*. I mean, it's already been written

So *Mario* has some cool game design decisions. In the context of *Mario* itself, we have examined briefly how they work together, what impact they have on the players' experience and how these design decisions, in general, push the player toward deeper involvement in the game world. But if you're developing a car-racing game, you can't just add a hip-drop and hope it will work as well as it does in *Mario*. So, it's time to start abstracting out some tools and defining them well enough to apply them to other games.

Looking back at the *Mario* example, what tools can we derive from these specific observations? First, we see there are many ways in which players are encouraged to form their own goals and act on them. The key is that players know what to expect from the world and thus are made to feel in control of the situation. Goals and control can be provided and created at multiple scales, from quick, low-level goals such as "get over the bridge in front of you" to long-term, higher-level goals such as "get all the red coins in the world." Often players work on several goals, at different levels, and on different time scales.

This process of accumulating goals, understanding the world, making a plan and then acting on it, is a powerful means to get the player invested and involved. We'll call this "intention," as it is, in essence, allowing and encouraging players to do things intentionally. Intention can operate at each level, from a quick plan to cross a river to a multi-step plan to solve a huge mystery. This is our first FADT.

> INTENTION: *Making an implementable plan of one's own creation in response to the current situation in the game world and one's understanding of the game play options.*

The simplicity and solidity of *Mario's* world makes players feel more connected to, or responsible for, their actions. In particular, when players attempt to do something and it goes wrong, they are likely to realize why it went wrong. This leads to another tool, "perceivable consequence." The key is that not only did the game react to the player; its reaction was also apparent. When I make the jump, either it works or it doesn't. *Mario* uses this tool extensively at a low level (crossing a river, avoiding a rolling boulder, and so on). Any action you undertake results in direct, visible feedback.

PERCEIVABLE CONSEQUENCE: *A clear reaction from the game world to the action of the player.*

We have examined the ideas behind some parts of *Mario* and abstracted out two potential design tools. Note also how *Mario* uses these tools in conjunction; as players create and undertake a plan, they then see the results of the plan, and know (or can intuit) why these results occurred. The elements discussed are certainly not the only cool parts of *Mario*, nor the only tools that Mario uses, but hopefully this discussion gives an idea of how the process works. Later, we'll return to examine how multiple tools work with each other. But first, let's see if intention and perceivable consequence can be applied to some other games.

Same tools, different games

Perceived consequence is a tool often used in RPGs, usually with plot or character development. A plot event will happen, in which the game (through characters or narration) essentially comes out and says, "Because of X, Y has happened." This is clearly a fairly pure form of perceived consequence.

Often, however, RPGs are less direct about consequence. For example, the player may decide to stay the night at an inn, and the next morning he may be ambushed. Now, it may be that the designers built this in the code or design of the game. ("We don't want people staying in town too much, so if they start staying at the inn too often, let's ambush them.") However, that causality is not perceivable by the player. While it may be an actual consequence, to the player it appears random.

There are also cases where the consequence is perceivable, but something still seems wrong. Perhaps there's a fork in the road, where players must choose a direction. As a player travels down the chosen path, an encounter with bandits occurs, and the bandit leader proclaims, "You have entered the valley of my people; face my wrath." This is clearly a consequence, but not of a decision players thought they were making. Players bemoan situations where they are forced into a consequence by the designers, where they are going along playing a game and suddenly are told, "You had no way of knowing, but doing thing X results in horrible thing Z."

The story unfolds in *Final Fantasy VIII*

Here we can look at how *Mario* uses the perceivable consequence tool in order to gain some insight into how to make it work for us without frustrating players. In *Mario*, consequences are usually the direct result of a player decision. Rarely do players following a path through the game suddenly find themselves in a situation where the game basically says, "Ha ha, you had no way of knowing, but you should have gone left," or "Dead end! Now you get crushed." Instead, they see they can try a dangerous jump, a long roundabout path, or maybe a fight. And if it goes wrong, they understand why.

The story unfolds in *Final Fantasy VIII.*

So it should come as no surprise that, in RPGs, often the best uses of consequence come when they are attached to intentional actions. Being given a real choice to do the evil wizard's bidding or resist and face the consequences has both intention and consequence. And when these tools work together, players are left feeling in control and responsible for whatever happens. However, being told, "Now you must do the evil wizard's bidding" by the designer, and then being told, "As you did the evil wizard's bidding, the following horrible consequences have occurred," is far less involving for the player. So while both examples literally have perceived consequence, they don't cause the same reactions in the player.

Same game, different tool

Of course, there are reasons why RPGs often force players into a given situation, even at the cost of removing some of the player's feeling of control. The usual reason is to give the designer greater control of the narrative flow of the game. It is clear that "story" is another abstract tool, used in various ways across all game styles in our industry. But it's important to remember that, although books tell stories, when we say "story" is an abstract tool in game design, we don't necessarily mean expository, pre-written text. In our field, "story" really refers to any narrative thread that is continued throughout the game.

The most obvious uses of story in computer and video games can be found in adventure-game plot lines. In this game category, designers have written the story in advance, and players have it revealed to them through interactions with characters, objects, and the world. While we often try to set up things to give players a sense of control, all players end up with the same plot.

But story comes into play in *NBA Live*, too. There, the story is what happens in the game. Maybe it ends up in overtime for a last-second three-pointer by a star player who hasn't been hitting his shots; maybe it is a total blowout from the beginning and at the end the user gets to put in the benchwarmers for their moment of glory. In either case, the player's actions during play created the story. Clearly, the story in basketball is less involved than that of most RPGs, but on the other hand it is a story that is the player's—not the designer's—to control. And as franchise and season modes are added to sports games and team rivalries and multi-game struggles begin, story takes on a larger role in such games.

STORY: *The narrative thread, whether designer-driven or player-driven, that binds events together and drives the player forward toward completion of the game.*

Using multiple tools: cooperation, conflict, confusion

Adventure games often have little intention or perceivable consequence. Players know they will have to go everywhere, pick up everything, talk to everyone, use each thing on each other thing and basically figure out what the designer intended. At the lowest level, there is intention along the lines of, "I bet this object is the one I need," and just enough consequence that players can say, "That worked—the plot is advancing." But there is little overall creation of goals and expression of desires by players. While the player is doing things, it's usually obvious that only a few possibilities (the ones the designers pre-built) work, and that all players must do one of these or fail.

But as we've also seen, this loss of some consequence and most intention comes with a major gain in story. By taking control away from the player in some spaces, the designer is much freer to craft a world full of tuned-up moments in which the designer scripts exactly what will happen. This allows moments that are very powerful for players (moments that often feel as involving as player-directed actions, if not more so). So here is a space where tools conflict, where intention and story are at odds—the more we as designers want to cause particular situations, the less control we can afford to give players.

Once again, tools must be chosen to fit the task. Being aware of what game you want to develop allows you to pick the tools you want and suggests how to use them. You cannot simply start adding more of each tool and expect the game to work.

Concrete cases of multiple tool use

An interesting variant of the intention versus story conflict is found in traditional SquareSoft console RPGs (for example, the *Final Fantasy* series and *ChronoTrigger*). These games essentially give each tool its own domain in the game. The plot is usually linear, with maybe a few inconsequential branches. However, character and combat statistics are free form, complex systems, which have a variety of items, statistics, and combo effects that are under player control. Players must learn about these systems and then manage the items and party members to create and evolve their party.

During exploration of the game world, the plot reveals itself to the player. The designer creates cool moments that are shown to players, in the game, but are not player-driven. Despite little intention in terms of the plot, players are given some control of the pacing as they explore. While exploring, however, players find objects and characters. These discoveries impact the combat aspects of the game. Combat in the game is entirely under the players' control, as they decide what each character does, which abilities and items to use, and handle other details. Thus, players explore the story while combat contains intention and consequence.

SquareSoft games are, essentially, storybooks. But to turn the page, you have to win in combat. And to win in combat, you have to use the characters and items that come up in the story. So the consequences of the story, while completely preset and identical for all players, are presented (usually) right after a very intentional combat sequence. The plot forces you to go and fight your former ally, but you are in complete control of the fight itself.

Rather than trying to use all three tools at once, the designers use intention and consequence in the combat system, and story and consequence in the actual unfolding of the story. So, the designers get to use all the tools they want and tie the usage together in the game. However, they make sure that tools can be strongly utilized when called on. They don't try to put them in places where it would be hard to make them work effectively.

With a bit of a stretch, one can say that sports and fighting games actually mix all three of the tools into one. The story in a game of *NHL 99* is the scoring, the missed checks or the penalty shot. While this story is somewhat basic, it's completely owned by the player. Each player makes his or her own decision to go for the win by pulling the goalie, or not. And, most importantly, the decision and resulting action either works or does not, driving the game to a player-driven conclusion. Unlike adventure games, there is no trying to guess what the designer had in mind, no saving and loading the game 20 times until you click on the right object. You go in, you play the game, and it ends.

Similarly, in a fighting game, every controller action is completely consistent and visually represented by the character on-screen. In *Tekken*, when Eddy Gordo does a cartwheel kick, you know what you're going to get. As the player learns moves, this consistency allows planning—intention—and the reliability of the world's reactions makes for perceived consequence. If I watch someone play, I can see how and why he or she is better than I am, but all players begin the game on equal footing. The learning curve is in figuring out the controls and actions (in that it's player-learning alone that determines skill and ability in the game). The fact that actions have complete intention and consequence allows this.

In sports games, you direct players, select an action, and watch something happen in response to that action, which gives you feedback about what you tried to do. The player does direct the action—a crosscheck missed, a slap shot deflected, a pass gone wrong—but one level removed. While watching the action on screen, one sees everything that happens, but can't be sure exactly why it happened. This is because the basis of most sports games is a statistical layer, and thus the same actions with the controller can lead to different results. When you combine the different player ratings with the die-rolling going on behind the

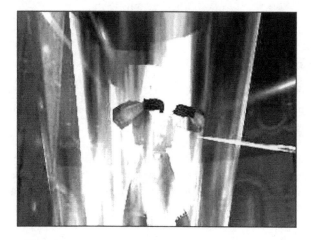

The outcome of consequences in *Final Fantasy VIII*.

scenes, the probabilities make sense, but may not be apparent to the player. The intention is still there, but the perceived consequence is much less immediate. This removal of direct control (and the entire issue of directing action) through a statistical layer, which the player can intuit but not directly see, is often present in RPG combat. Thus, in *Tekken*, I can't say, "Man, bad luck, if only I'd rolled better," or "Yeah, now that I'm a tenth-level ninja, I can do that move," but in *NBA Live* or an RPG, I often do.

Tool-based analysis

A fighter has a simple story ("I had just a sliver of health left, but I feinted a kick and then did my triple punch combo—barely finished him off"), but it's the player's story. There is no, "Man, I can't believe I missed that shot," or "Why did I go and do that?" or "How come my check didn't work?" A simple story, backed up by complete intention in a game that provides clear consequences, makes a very powerful experience for the player. So, both fighting games and, with some obfuscation of consequence, sports games, attempt to fuse intention and consequence and from that allow the players' actions tell a story. The complete control provided by a fighter may make the game more real to the player, but the larger scale of a sports game may provide more sense of story. Or, it may be that the direct control of the fighter makes for a more personal story, and the large scale of a sports game makes for a more epic story. In either case, neither the fighter approach nor the sports simulation approach to story and intention is right or wrong. Each elicits a different set of reactions from the player. As a designer, you must understand the ramifications of tool usage if you're going to create the experience you intend.

33

Ahhh, so what?

Tools as a vocabulary for analysis present a way to focus on what player experience the designer wishes to create. In this high-level introduction to FADT, I have focused on intention and perceived consequence, with less attention to story. (And what story is mentioned is slanted toward the player-driven.) This is not because these are the only tools or even the best tools. However, as we start to analyze our designs and the player experience provided by the tools we use, it's vital we try to understand what our medium is good at.

Games are not books; games are not movies. In those media, the tools used (camera placement, cuts, zooms, music cues, switching narrators, and so on) are used to manipulate viewers or readers, to make them feel or react exactly the way the director or author wants them to. I believe the challenge and promise of computer game design is that our most important tools are the ones that involve and empower players to make their own decisions. That is something that allows each player to explore him or herself, which is something our medium is uniquely equipped to do.

So I look to tools to help me understand that aspect of game design and to maximize the player's feeling of involvement and self. But that's because that's the kind of game I want to make. Each designer must choose the game he or she wants to create and use the tools available to craft that experience.

Hopefully, I have presented enough examples of the tools and tool-based analysis process to provide a useful overview. Of course, I only mentioned a few tools, but, as stated previously, this article was not intended to be exhaustive or complete. It's a justification for us to begin to put together a vocabulary. For this to become genuinely useful, we must engage in discussion and analysis to get a set of tools we like and then refine those tools until they are well understood. With that, we can start to do more careful analysis of the stuff we like and don't like in current games and work to improve future ones. And we can talk to each other more about design innovations, not just technical ones.

We will have to invest a lot of time if we're to generate a full list of tools we've used (or should use) in our work. There are resource economies, learning, player power-up curves, punishment/reward and many others to consider. And each tool could have an article written just about it—how it has been used over time, what games use it particularly well or poorly, and different aspects of it. Similarly, it would be great to take a game such as *Mario* or *Warcraft* and really deconstruct it, perform as complete an analysis as possible to see if that would be useful. This article is simply a primer to scratch the surface and give examples of this sort of process.

I make no assumption that tools are necessarily useful. Many people may find them overly pedantic. And there's clearly a danger of people starting to use words such as "intention" and "consequence" in the same way that terms and phrases such as "non-linear," "endless variety," or "hundreds of hours of game play" are used meaninglessly. Not surprisingly, that's not the intent.

FADT offers a potential framework for moving the design discussion forward—no more, no less. Although it's no magic bullet, the hope is for this framework to be broadly useful and allow collaborative analysis and refinement of the game design practice, leading to better designs, more interesting products, and satisfied players. If it's not the right framework, we should figure out why and determine what is the right framework. And then we'll work to evolve and develop it together.

TOOLS FOR CREATING DRAMATIC GAME DYNAMICS

Marc LeBlanc

Source: Game Developer's Conference (GDC), 1999, 438–459. Reprinted in Katie Salen and Eric Zimmerman (eds), *The Game Design Reader: A Rules of Play Anthology* (Cambridge, MA: The MIT Press, 2006), pp. 438–459.

Context

The topic for my essay comes from my first lecture at the Game Developer's Conference (GDC) in 1999, and owes some of its inspiration to my colleague Doug Church and his work on formal abstract design tools. At that time, it was becoming clear that our discourse on game design needed more of a conceptual framework, a way to place the individual topics of discussion in their proper aesthetic context. In the five years since, I have strived to develop such a framework, through my practical work as well as through my Game Tuning Workshop, held annually at the GDC. The essay represents those five years of refinement.

Introduction: stories and games

In the study of game design, comparisons to traditional narrative forms—prose, theater, film and TV—are inevitable. The advent of digital games has brought games and stories closer together than ever before. In the 1970s and 80s, text adventures like Zork gave us a new way to combine play with prose. Today, video games like Zelda and Grand Theft Auto possess the sights, sounds, characters, and plots that we might expect to see in a feature film. Given so many points of similarity between modern games and traditional stories, it's natural for game designers to look for ways to incorporate the tools and techniques of storytelling into their own craft.

But the power of games as a story vehicle is hardly a new idea. The ancient Egyptian game of *Senet*—which, along with Go, is one of the top contenders for the title of "oldest game known to humanity"—tells the story of the passage through the underworld to the land of the dead. During the height of its three millennia of popularity, players of Senet believed that the game was an oracle for mystical divination. The events of the game foretold what the player might one day experience in his own passage through the afterlife.

Since the ancient days of Senet, we have seen countless other games with a vast diversity of fictional meanings and metaphors: games about warfare and conquest, about courtly intrigue, about sleuthing detectives and robber barons, and about nothing at all. We have also seen how games can *become* stories, as when a sporting event is transformed into the news of the day—or the stuff of legend. We have seen works of fiction that incorporate games as narrative devices, like a movie that culminates in a climactic bike race, or a boxing match, or a game of Chess. In these examples of stories about games, the story no longer relies on the *metaphor* of the game, but on the events of the game itself: the plans and gambits, the bluffs and stratagems, the reversals of fortune. The play of the game becomes a climactic struggle that builds to a satisfying conclusion. In other words, the game is *dramatic*.

It should be safe to say that drama is a desirable quality of games. Players often seek out games that are dramatic, and sometimes a game's drama becomes the primary motivation for playing. Drama is part of a game's play content; it's a kind of fun. Thus, as game designers, we strive to imbue drama into our creations, to create games that are climactic struggles in their own right.

The challenge of creating drama within a game is compounded by our limited control over the games we create. We don't—and can't—know the precise details of how our game will play out, each and every time it is played. We are not the authors of the events of the game; we cannot craft the game's drama directly, the way a storyteller scripts a story. Our task is more indirect. We cannot *create* drama; we can only create the circumstances from which drama will *emerge*.

As game designers, how do we go about the task of creating dramatic games? What tools can we use to guarantee a climactic struggle? These are the central questions we will be exploring over the next few pages. We'll gain a better sense of what drama *is* and *how* it happens. We'll identify the necessary ingredients for drama, and we'll uncover a collection of tools and techniques for introducing those ingredients into our game.

Mechanics, dynamics, and aesthetics

Our exploration of drama will be guided by a core framework of three separate aspects of games: mechanics, dynamics, and aesthetics. We can think of these three aspects as parts of the game play experience, or as perspectives from which a game can be viewed.

When we talk about *mechanics*, we are referring to all the necessary pieces that we need to play the game. This primarily refers to the rules of the game, but can also refer to the equipment, the venue, or anything else necessary for playing the game. The mechanics of Chess include not only the rules for how the pieces move, but other facts like the dimensions of the board. The mechanics of Baseball include not only the explicit rules of Baseball, but the physical laws that govern the game: gravity, energy, the limits of the human mind and body. The peculiarities of the venue are also part of the mechanics; Fenway Park's "green monster" is part of the mechanics of any game played there. In a video game like

Super Mario Sunshine, the mechanics would include the program code (which is a complete description of the game's rules) and all of its equipment, including the physical layout of the controller. If we think of the game as a *system*, the mechanics are the complete description of that system.

Dynamics refers to what might be called the "behavior" of the game, the actual events and phenomena that occur as the game is played. In Baseball, the different kinds of batted balls (e.g., fly balls, line drives, grounders, bunts) are part of the dynamics of the game. In Chess, the dynamics include tactical concepts like the knight fork or the discovered check, as well as structural concepts like the opening and the endgame. When we view a game in terms of its dynamics, we are asking, "What happens when the game is played?" The dynamics of a game are not mandated by its rules, and are not always easy to intuit from the rules themselves. It would take a fairly clever person to deduce the concept of a discovered check from the rules of Chess without ever having played the game. The relationship between dynamics and mechanics is one of *emergence*. A game's dynamics *emerge* from its mechanics.

A game's *aesthetics* are its emotional content, the desirable emotional responses we have when we play—all the kinds of fun that result from playing the game. A game can challenge our intellect (or our physical prowess). It can foster social interaction. It can stimulate our imagination. It can provide us with a vehicle for self-expression. All of these properties are part of the aesthetics of the game. A game's aesthetics emerge from its dynamics; how the game *behaves* determines how it makes the player feel. Understanding how specific game dynamics evoke specific emotional responses is one of the greatest challenges of game design.

In a sense, the mechanics of the game always exist, even when the game is not being played. We can think of a board game (or a video game) that sits on our shelf as a box full of game mechanics, waiting for us to take it down and set the game into motion. The dynamics of the game, however, only manifest while the game is being played. Our ability to reap the game's aesthetic content depends on our actually playing the game and bringing those dynamics to life. Thus, when we play a game, our experience can be described as a kind of causal flow that starts with its mechanics, passes through dynamics, and ends with aesthetics.

For players, the purpose of playing is to enjoy the game's aesthetic content. As game designers, our objective is to *create* that content. Our relationship to the game is opposite that of the players. We begin our work with a set of aesthetic objectives—emotional responses we *hope* to evoke in the players. Our task is to work backward, determining what dynamics will accomplish our aesthetic objectives, and from there design game mechanics that will create those dynamics. So when we design a game, our experience begins with aesthetics, passes through dynamics, and ends with a set of mechanics.

This framework of three schemas for understanding games—mechanics, dynamics, and aesthetics—allows us to refine the motivating questions of our inquiry into drama in games:

- How does drama function as an aesthetic of play?
- What kinds of game dynamics can evoke drama?
- From what kinds of mechanics do those dynamics emerge?

In the pages that follow, we will explore each of these topics in turn.

The dramatic arc: an aesthetic model for drama

The goal of our exploration is to discover ways to make our games more dramatic. We want drama, as an aesthetic objective of our game design, to be part of the game's emotional content. The first step is to formulate a good definition of drama. How will we know drama when we see it? We need some kind of yardstick we can hold up to our game design to determine how well it succeeds or fails at being dramatic, a yardstick that encompasses our understanding of what drama is and how it happens. We call such a yardstick an "aesthetic model." As tools for formalizing our design objectives, *aesthetic models* can help us know when we have achieved them, and if we're headed in the right direction.

Before we proceed, we must acknowledge that drama is only one aesthetic among many. There are many reasons to play a game, many kinds of fun to get out of a game. Games can challenge us, realize our fantasies, bring us into social contact, and provide many more kinds of experiences. Each kind of experience is a separate aesthetic pleasure with its own aesthetic model. Different aesthetics can coexist within the discipline of game design, and even within the design of a single game. When we design a game, we hope its players will experience many kinds of fun, not merely a single kind. Because two different games might deliver the same aesthetics in different proportions, depending on the priorities of the designer—and the players—our aesthetic model of drama is not going to be a grand unified theory that encompasses all kinds of play or fun. We're looking for a specific model that explains drama, and nothing else. Other, broader models also exist, but they are beyond the scope of this essay.

Our quest for an aesthetic model of drama starts with a picture. Recognize it?

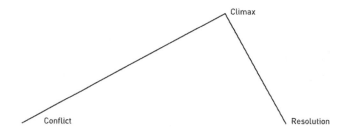

We've probably all seen this diagram at some point. The lines and proportions may be different, but the general shape is always the same. It visualizes the *dramatic arc*, the rising and falling action of a well-told story. The central conflict of a narrative creates *tension* that accumulates as the story builds to a climax, and dissipates as the conflict is resolved.

We can think of the diagram as a mathematical model. If we draw in the axes, it becomes a graph:

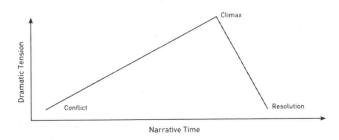

The mathematical model of drama imagines that dramatic tension is a kind of quantity that can accumulate and discharge, increase or decrease as time passes. That's not to say we could ever actually measure dramatic tension, of course. It's absurd to think that we could construct some kind of dramatic-tension-o-meter, a device that we could wave over the audience as a story is told, reading out the dramatic tension as a numerical value—no doubt measured in units called "millishakespeares." In that sense, it is not so much a quantity as a quality. Still, the idea that dramatic tension can increase and decrease is an important one for our diagram to have any meaning.

What is dramatic tension then? It's our level of *emotional* investment in the story's conflict: the sense of concern, apprehension, and urgency with which we await the story's outcome.

Drama as an aesthetic

The dramatic arc is an aesthetic model for stories; it's a statement about how stories convey their emotional content, and a yardstick that we can hold up to a story to see if it succeeds or fails at being dramatic. The dramatic arc is not a universal fact of all stories, but rather a desirable property of dramatic stories. The dramatic arc is a value statement. It says that well-told stories should possess dramatic tension, and that over time the tension should take on a particular shape, building toward the story's climax, and then dissipating.

What's so special about this particular shape? Why should the tension first rise and then fall, instead of first falling and then rising? Is this shape somehow intrinsically beautiful? Maybe, but most people don't leave a movie, thinking, "Wow, what a lovely dramatic arc!" The individual moments, and the emotions they evoked, are what stay with us.

Perhaps the dramatic arc is a part of the fundamental rhythm of human cognition. Something about it resonates with us, signaling to our subconscious: "This is a story. Pay attention!" It creates a context and a frame of mind where the individual moments become meaningful, powerful, and relevant. Perhaps it also serves to shape the story into an easily digestible cognitive morsel. It gives the story a sense of wholeness, that it is a complete work with a beginning, middle, and end.

In any case, the dramatic arc will serve as the cornerstone of our aesthetic model of drama. Let's spend some time exploring how dramatic tension emerges during game play, as well as techniques game designers can use to sculpt that tension into a well-formed dramatic arc.

Drama in games

In the context of a traditional narrative, it's natural to think of the dramatic arc as being handcrafted by the story's author. In the case of film or theater, the authors have complete control over every moment of the unfolding narrative. As game designers, we have a greater challenge. We must assure that our game will be dramatic, even when we don't have direct control over the narrative, a narrative that isn't scripted in advance, but rather *emerges* from the events of the game.

All drama originates from conflict. Indeed, without conflict, no dramatic tension will ever emerge. In a game, the conflict comes from the *contest* around which the game is built. Contests can take many different forms: some might challenge the player's intellect, others his stamina. Some might be competitions between multiple players; others might be solitaire challenges for a single player. Any of these contests provides the conflict necessary for drama.

How does tension emerge from a contest, and how does that tension change over time? Dramatic tension is the product of two different factors:

> **Uncertainty:** the sense that the outcome of the contest is still unknown. Any player could win or lose.
> **Inevitability**: the sense that the contest is moving forward toward resolution. The outcome is imminent.

Tension relies on these two factors in combination—neither is sufficient by itself. Without uncertainty, the outcome of the game becomes a foregone conclusion, and the players become spectators. Without inevitability, the outcome of the conflict seems distant. Players are given little incentive to invest their emotions in the contest.

To see these two factors at work, let's consider a typical game of Magic: The Gathering. The game begins as a blank slate: each player has a full deck of cards and nothing in play. In the first few turns, the players' ability to affect the outcome of the game is limited by their scant mana resources.[1] The outcome of the game is unknown, and seems miles away. As play progresses, certain game elements become ever more obvious signals that the game is moving toward a conclusion: the waning height of the players' decks, the scarcity of life points, and the increasing number of cards in play. Late in the game, the abundance of mana resources means that either player could change the game drastically in a

41

single move. The outcome of the game seems imminent, yet still hard to predict. Eventually, the stalemate is broken by a string of "power plays," from which one player will emerge with a clear advantage. That player will leverage the advantage into victory, or "die" trying. Either way, the game reaches its conclusion quickly. We can see how the dramatic tension of the game is regulated by the game dynamics: the escalation of resources and the "ticking clock" of the deck. These mechanisms sculpt the tension of the game into a proper dramatic arc.

Over the course of the game we expect the inevitability to increase and the uncertainty to diminish. The climax of the game happens at the moment of realization: the moment when the outcome of the contest is known, and the uncertainty has been dispelled. We can think of the time between the climax and the end of the game as dénouement, the process of resolving the tension created within the game.

Now that we understand the role of uncertainty and inevitability in creating dramatic tension, we can gain a better understanding of how these qualities can emerge from the dynamics of a game. Next, let's examine a handful of different game dynamics, and explore their roles in creating dramatic tension.

Game dynamics that produce dramatic tension

How exactly do uncertainty and inevitability emerge from game play? Quite often, they emerge independently of each other. That is, a game's uncertainty and its inevitability are evoked by different systems and dynamics. This is good news for game designers; it gives us finer control over the dramatic arc of the game, by allowing us to tune and adjust inevitability and uncertainty separately. It is also good news for our discussion because it allows our exploration to tackle inevitability and uncertainty as distinct topics.

In order to imbue our games with dramatic uncertainty, we need to create an ongoing sense that the game is *close*, that the contest is yet undecided. There are many techniques available to us, but all of them take one of two general approaches: force and illusion. *Force* is the approach of creating dramatic tension by manipulating the state of the contest itself. The game is close because we *make* it close, or at the very least we limit how much an advantage one player can have over another. *Illusion* is the approach of manipulating the players' perceptions so that the game *seems* closer than it is. Force and illusion are more of a spectrum than a dichotomy. In the pages that follow, we will explore techniques of pure force (e.g., cybernetic feedback systems) and techniques of pure illusion (e.g., fog of war) as well as techniques that combine the two (e.g. escalation).

Our discussion of dramatic inevitability will center on a single organizing concept: the ticking clock. The idea of the ticking clock is the sense of imminent resolution that gives a game its sense of momentum and forward progress. It stands as a constant reminder that the game will end, and soon. We will discuss how games create inevitability through ticking clocks that are both real and metaphorical.

We will begin our exploration with a very common source of dramatic uncertainty in games: cybernetic feedback systems.

Feedback systems as sources of uncertainty

Rules of Play provides a discussion of cybernetic feedback systems, and the ways in which they apply to games. A feedback system found in a game might be constructed like this:

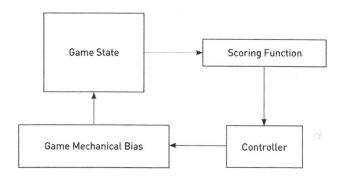

The *game state* is the complete status of the game at a particular moment. We can think of the game state as all the information you would need to put in a "save game" file for the game. In Checkers, the game state would include the positions of all the pieces, and indicate which player has the next move. In a first-person shooter, the state would include the name of the current level, the position of every object on the level, as well as the player's health and inventory. In a physical game like Basketball, the state includes not only the score and the time left on the clock, but the complete physical and mental state of all the athletes. Constructing a "save game" for a real physical sport (as opposed to a sports video game) would require a staggering amount of memory.

The *scoring function* is the *sensor* of the cybernetic feedback system. It is a rule of the game that gives us a numerical measurement of who is winning and by how much. Some games, like Basketball, have a score built into the rules. In this case, the scoring function might be the difference between the two scores (e.g., one team is ahead by six points). Other games, like racing games, have no explicit score. The scoring function would be some measurement based on the facts of the game. In a two-player car-racing game, the scoring function might be the distance between the two players' cars. The scoring function could even produce an aggregate number based on several different facts about the game, such as the distance between the cars and the amount of fuel in each car. A good scoring function produces a larger number the greater the winning player's lead, and produces the number zero when the game is tied.

The *game mechanical bias* is the *actuator* of the cybernetic feedback system. It is a rule of the game that gives one of the contestants an advantage over the other.

In Basketball, giving one team more players than the other would bias the game in favor of that team. In a death match game, giving one of the players twice as many points as the others would give that player an advantage.

The *controller* is the *comparator* of the cybernetic feedback system. It is a rule of the game that chooses which player receives the game mechanical bias; it makes its decision based on the scoring function.

As an example, let's consider the "handicap mode" found in many racing games. Handicap mode is a special game option designed to keep the race close: when one player falls behind, that player's maximum speed increases so that the player can catch up to the leader. We can think of this as a feedback system: the scoring function is the distance between the two racers, the speed boost is the game mechanical bias, and the controller is the rule that says the speed boost goes to the losing racer.

This kind of feedback system keeps the game close by driving the scoring function towards zero. Because it strives to make the difference in score as small as possible, it is called a "*negative* feedback system." We can imagine another feedback system—let's call it "spite mode"—that is the direct opposite of handicap mode. Using the same scoring function and game mechanical bias as handicap mode, spite mode would hand the speed boost to the *leading* racer. When one player gained an advantage over the other, spite mode would let that player keep the advantage for the rest of the game. This kind of feedback system strives to make the difference in score as *large* as possible, and so we call it a "*positive* feedback system."

Negative feedback as a source of uncertainty

Dramatic uncertainty depends on the player's perception that the outcome of the contest is unknown. Any game where the score is tied—or very close—is inherently uncertain. This means that negative feedback systems are a powerful tool for creating dramatic tension; by driving the scoring function toward zero, they create dramatic uncertainty.

In the example of the racing game in handicap mode, the negative feedback system helps sustain the dramatic tension of the game. It guards against the situation where one player takes an early lead and keeps it for the entire race. Thus the feedback system assures that the climax occurs late in the game, at a moment when one player's lead is large enough—and the time left in the game is short enough—that the feedback system cannot bring the players together before the end of the game.

Positive feedback as an aid to denouement

Toward the end of a game, positive feedback systems are sometimes useful for dispelling uncertainty, bringing about the climax, and creating a sense of finality and closure. Sometimes the negative feedback systems in the game can cause the game to stagnate. Positive feedback systems provide a mechanism for breaking the equilibrium and moving the game forward.

In Warcraft, the snowball effect of military conquest can be viewed as a positive feedback system. By attacking an opponent's infrastructure and capturing or destroying resources, one player can leverage a slight military advantage into a large one, and then leverage the large military advantage into victory. This process of routing the enemy dispels the dramatic uncertainty and creates a sense of closure. It is an end-of-game ritual that prepares the winner to win and the loser to lose.

Other sources of uncertainty

Feedback systems are one of the heaviest possible hammers available to game designers for sculpting the dramatic uncertainty of their game. Now let's explore some other kinds of game mechanics that create dramatic uncertainty. Many of the systems we are about to examine could be described as "illusory"; rather than altering the state of the game, they manipulate the player's *perceptions*.

Pseudo-feedback

The first two mechanisms we'll examine can be described as "pseudo-feedback." Quite frequently, these sorts of mechanisms create game dynamics that appear as if the game were being driven by a negative feedback system: when one player takes the lead, quite frequently the other player will catch up. When we inspect the inner workings of the game systems, however, we discover that there is no actual cybernetic feedback system present—just the perception of one.

Escalation

Escalation describes a game mechanic in which the score changes faster and faster over the course of game, so that there are more points at stake at the end of the game than at the beginning. The game show *Jeopardy* is a textbook example of escalation. The first round begins with questions worth $100 and ends with questions worth $500. More significantly, the value of all questions is doubled for the second round. This means that at the end of the first round, only one-third of the total available prize money has been given out, and roughly half of the game's total time has elapsed. The player perceives the game as being "half over," and measured in terms of *time*, it is. But measured in terms of *prize money awarded*, the game is only a third over. The player perceives that the game has progressed further than it really has. The escalation of prize money helps protect the dramatic uncertainty of the game; there is no first-round lead that can't be overcome in the second round. In the final round of the game, players can wager any amount of their prize money on a single question. We can think of this as yet another level of escalation, giving the trailing players one last all-or-nothing chance to overcome the leader.

Hidden energy

Imagine a racing game—one not driven by a feedback system—in which each player has a reservoir of "turbo fuel" to use during the race. The turbo fuel gives the player a speed bonus for as long as he holds down the "turbo" button on the controller. However, the reservoir only holds 30 total seconds of fuel in a race that will last a few minutes. The game is designed so that effective use of the turbo is the key to success.

In this game, one player might use turbo fuel to gain an early lead. That player would appear to be winning, with a score that was certainly higher, although achieved at a resource cost. If, however, we consider the whole state of the game—accounting for the players' resources in addition to their positions on the track—we see that the game is actually quite close. At some later time, the trailing player will choose to use his turbo fuel to close the gap, perhaps creating the illusion that handicap mode is in effect. This creates a sense of uncertainty as the true state of the game is revealed.

We can think of the turbo fuel as the "hidden energy" of the game. It is energy because it represents the potential to score, and it is hidden because it is not part of the player's own appraisal of the game scoring function. In sports like Basketball, the hidden energy is energy in the literal sense of the word; a team that takes the lead often does so at the expense of its own stamina, leaving itself vulnerable to a reprisal by the other team.

Another interesting example of hidden energy occurs in Pool. In Eight Ball, a player inches closer to victory each time the player sinks a ball. But the fewer balls the player has on the table, the fewer good shots there are to take, and the less likely the player's balls are to interfere with those of the other player. Each ball represents a liability (in that it must be sunk) but also an opportunity (to be an easy shot, and also to obstruct the opponent). Combined with the short-term positive feedback of the game (i.e., making a shot entitles you to another turn), the energy gives the trailing player a chance to catch up to the leader.

Hidden energy creates dramatic uncertainty by manipulating the player's incomplete understanding of the true score of the game. It creates artificial dramatic reversals of fortune by inflating and deflating the ostensible score of the game.

Fog of war

Strategy games like Warcraft and Civilization use a game mechanic called *fog of war*, which simulates limitations of game characters' ability to perceive and monitor the world around them. The "fog" covers all parts of the map that the players' units cannot see. As the players' resources develop, their units cover a greater area and push more of the fog back, giving the players progressively more information about the world. A player cannot see other players' resources unless the player commits units to scouting enemy terrain.

Fog of war represents a way of creating dramatic uncertainty by limiting the information available to the players. At the beginning of the game, players cannot predict the outcome of the contest, because they simply aren't given enough information. As the game progresses, more and more information becomes available, and the outcome of the game seems more and more certain.

Decelerator

The *decelerator* describes an obstacle that slows the players down late in the game. It makes the game seem closer by changing the scale and pace of the game.

A perfect example of a decelerator comes from that famous athletics-oriented game show of the 1990s, *American Gladiators*. At the end of each episode, the winner was determined by an obstacle course called "The Eliminator." One of the late obstacles of this course was a cargo net that the contestants had to climb. Climbing the net was slow work, so the trailing player would usually reach the net before the leading player had cleared it. The cargo net brought the players into physical proximity without necessarily changing the true score of the game. Measured in seconds, the distance between the players was the same as before they entered the cargo net, but measured in feet, the distance seemed much closer. The decelerator creates dramatic uncertainty by creating the illusion of a close game.

Interestingly enough, *American Gladiators* followed its decelerator with an *accelerator*. After the contestants climbed the cargo net, they would descend to ground level on a zip line. This acceleration would reveal the true difference in the players' positions (perhaps even exaggerate it), dispelling the uncertainty and resolving the tension created by the cargo net. It's no accident that the rising and falling action of the drama resembles the ascent and descent of the altitudes of the players.

Cashing out

Cashing out describes a game mechanic where the score of the game is reset to zero. The simplest example of cashing out occurs in the "best of 7" format used for the World Series and other tournaments, where the contest is actually several games played in succession. Although at the end of a single game of a series, the game is recorded as a win for one team, beyond that, the score no longer matters. The result is the same whether the game went into extra innings or was a blowout. Until one team wins its fourth game, both teams have a chance to win the series. Cashing out creates dramatic uncertainty by forgiving the trailing player's score deficit, and giving every player a chance to win, however unlikely.

Bomberman uses a similar form of cashing out. The game is played in rounds of a few minutes. Each round is a contest of serial elimination: players vie to blow each other up with bombs, and the last player standing wins a trophy. The first player to win three trophies from three separate rounds wins the game. During the round, players accumulate power-ups, becoming more and more powerful until elimination becomes inevitable, although nothing is carried over from one round to the next except for the trophy awarded to the winner. All the events of the round are cashed out and reduced to a single consequence: one player got the trophy and the others didn't. All power-ups are reset, and all mistakes are forgiven, giving each player a clean slate for the next round.

"The Eliminator" from the game show *American Gladiators* is another example of cashing out. Throughout a particular episode, contestants would

47

earn points for successes in each of the episode's events. The final event ("The Eliminator") was winner-take-all, but the player with the leading score was given a head start in the race, in proportion to the player's lead. In effect, points earned before the race were converted into seconds for the race. We can think of this conversion as a kind of cashing out. No matter how great the deficit, the trailing player has a chance to make it up, however slim that chance may be. We can also think of the moment where points are converted into seconds as an instantaneous moment of positive feedback, where an advantage in score is converted into a game mechanical bias.

Sources of inevitability

We've just explored five different ways that dramatic uncertainty can emerge from a game's dynamics. But uncertainty alone is not sufficient to create dramatic tension; we also need *dramatic inevitability*, the sense that the contest is moving forward toward a conclusion. If our contest appears as if it will never conclude— or not conclude any time soon—then it has no sense of urgency, and the dramatic tension is dispelled.

Uncertainty and inevitability are not opposites. Uncertainty concerns itself with the question, "Who will win?" whereas inevitability concerns itself with the question, "When will we know?" Our game is most tense at the moment both factors intersect: the outcome of the contest is unknown, but we feel that it will be determined imminently.

In games, dramatic inevitability emerges from any game mechanic that can function as a *ticking clock*, which gives the players a measurement of their progress through the game, as well as a sense of how far away the end might be. The clock also conveys a sense of forward motion: as time runs out, the players feel propelled toward the conclusion of the contest. Clearly then, a *literal* ticking clock—the time limit in sports like Basketball or in video games like Pikmin or Bomberman—is the simplest, most straightforward example of a game mechanic creating dramatic inevitability.

But literal time limits are not the only way the ticking clock manifests itself in game dynamics. We see it in the increasingly crowded game board in Go and Reversi, the waning deck sizes in Magic: The Gathering, the decreasing health bars in Virtua Fighter, the gradual filling-in of the word puzzle on Wheel of Fortune, and the depleting gold supplies in Warcraft. All of these "clocks" give us a measure of our progress through the game, warning us that the end is approaching; indeed, they can be characterized as *nonrenewable resources*, quantifiable assets within the game state that deplete over the course of play and are never replenished. When we consider *time* as a resource, we see that even the literal ticking clock falls within this category of nonrenewable resources. The notion of a nonrenewable resource is a powerful extension of the ticking clock concept—and a valuable nuts-and-bolts tool for game designers interested in assuring a sense of dramatic inevitability in their games.[2]

Other kinds of ticking clocks also exist. In the mystery board game Clue, the gradual accrual of information leads the game toward its inevitable conclusion. In a linear race game like SSX, the progress of play expresses itself in space rather than in time. The landmarks and checkpoints on the racecourse serve as reminders of the race's end. Many such games provide players with a "radar" overview of their linear progress through the level. These cues remind us of our place within the narrative, and of the constant forward motion toward an inevitable end. If hard-pressed, we could probably come up with a way to fit these concepts into our nonrenewable resource model of the ticking clock. (In Clue, can we think of ignorance as a resource?)

Rather than resort to such contrivances, we can identify an even more general model for the ticking clock: instead of nonrenewable resources, we can think of our ticking clocks as *nonreversible processes*. Nonreversible processes are exactly what they sound like: changes to the game state that can't be undone. Like a tightening ratchet, the process brings the game ever closer to completion, while at the same time prohibiting backward movement.

It should be clear that dramatic inevitability is all a matter of perception. In order for the ticking clock or nonreversible process to function as a dramatic device, the player must be able to perceive and understand its operation. A secret ticking clock does not convey the same sense of inevitability, nor does a nonreversible process whose workings are so complex that its nonreversible nature is not obvious.

Now let's take a look at an important historical example in which the lack of dramatic inevitability resulted in catastrophe. This example will give us a chance to flex our analytical muscles, as well as give us some perspective on the role and power of dramatic inevitability in games.

Twenty-one

The year 1956 saw the debut of the infamous game show *Twenty-One*, which became the centerpiece of the quiz show scandal. During the 1950s, the producers and sponsors of the show discovered that dramatic tension converted directly into big ratings and big business. They sought to sculpt their programs into ongoing narratives, with contestants cast as recurring characters. Many shows like *Twenty-One* resorted to rigging the results of the contest. The producers became authors, scripting not only the outcome of the game, but the dramatic details of its events.

Interestingly enough, it was only after the first episode that the producers of *Twenty-One* chose to rig the game:

> The show went on the air in 1956 and we felt that it had such great quality and content to it that we would not have to rig it. In fact, the first show of *Twenty-One* was not rigged and the first show of *Twenty-One* was a dismal failure. It was just plain dull.—*Dan Enright, Producer*

From then on, the producers decided to rig the game. Three years and one national scandal later, *Twenty-One* became an object lesson in the perils of "scripting" a game.

21/21 hindsight

Let's examine the dynamics of *Twenty-One* to see if we can find out why it was such a "dismal failure." We'll start with the rules.

Rules of Twenty-One (summary)

1   There are two players. Each player is in an isolation booth, and cannot see or hear the other player's play. Neither player knows the other's score.
2   Players score points by answering questions. The first player to 21 wins.
3   In the first round, each player is asked two questions. In subsequent rounds, each player is asked one question.
4   Before being asked the question, each player must choose how many points to wager on the question. Any number of points from 1 to 11 may be wagered. The player *must* wager at least one point, and *must* answer the question.
5   If a player answers the question correctly, the player gains the wagered points; if not, the player *loses* the wagered points. A player's score can't drop below zero this way.
6   At the end of a round, either player may choose to end the game and the player with the most points then wins.

Since each player is playing the game "in a vacuum," unaware and unaffected by the other player's choices, we can view a game of *Twenty-One* as two simultaneous solitaire games. Aside from the player's own score, an individual player has very little information to use when deciding whether or not to end the game. A player is free to play until one player drops from exhaustion, until his opponent chooses to end the game, or until he has earned an amount of points—let's say 19—that seems high enough to have a good chance of winning. So, we can say that each player is playing a solitaire game that only ends when one player reaches 19 points or more, and the winner is the player who reaches that value in fewer questions. This view will simplify our analysis of the game, at the very least by reducing the number of ending conditions from two to one.

Having made that simplification, it should be clear that the game lacks any kind of ticking clock. The only way that the game can end is for the score to increase, and points can be lost as easily as won—more easily, in fact. If scores were allowed to drop below zero, then the game might never end. Computer simulations bear our observations out (see below).

In the computer simulation, the score typically oscillates back and forth between 0 and 11. The game comes down to whether or not a player can answer two questions in a row. There is no sense of progress through the game; past

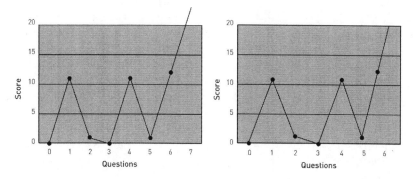

Two Simulated Games of Twenty-One

In the simulation, it was assumed that the player had a flat 40% chance of answering any question, wagered aggressively, and stopped at 19 points or more. In 1,000 simulated games, almost 42% of all questions resulted in a score of zero. The median game was 6 questions long, and the longest was 58.[3]

performance has essentially no meaning. We can see how the lack of a ticking clock dispels any hope of creating a dramatic arc.

How do our observations compare to history? We know that the first night of *Twenty-One* was plagued by zero-zero ties. Given that the score was zero 40% of the time in our simulations, this is hardly surprising.

Instead of fixing the game in the sense of rigging it, how might we fix the game in the sense of repairing the game design? There are many possible ticking clocks we could introduce: limit the total time to play, limit the number of questions or the number of wrong answers, and so forth. We could also try to salvage the notion that the score might function as the game's ticking clock by reducing or eliminating the penalty for a wrong answer. This might not be adequate if there were many rounds where neither player answered a question. We could handle that case explicitly: when neither player answered correctly, we would give each player one point, or perhaps reduce the number of points needed to win the game by one (from 21 to 20, then 19, etc.).

These are just a few examples among many; any game mechanic that causes the game to march forward to a guaranteed end has the potential to create the dramatic inevitability we need. Had the creators of *Twenty-One* realized the need to create dramatic inevitability within their game dynamics, they might have avoided a career-shortening scandal.

Resolving dramatic tension: denouement in games

So far we've examined several techniques for ratcheting up the dramatic tension in our games. But the dramatic arc shows us that tension shouldn't climb forever. Eventually the tension needs to reach a climax, change direction, and fade away.

When should the game's dramatic climax occur? How much time should pass between the climax and the end of the game? We've said that the climax occurs at the moment of realization, when uncertainty is dispelled and the outcome of the contest is known. Given that definition, it would seem that the climax of the game should occur as late as possible. After all, a contest whose outcome is known has ceased to be a game on some level: the players have become spectators. We could argue that such an interval should be as short as possible. On the other hand, there is also some value to providing the players with a denouement to resolve the tension and give them a sense of closure. We need to prepare the winner to win and the loser to lose. A game whose climax comes too late can seem to end too abruptly, catching the players off guard. In that case, the dramatic tension can linger, unresolved.

Sometimes, the resolution of the game's dramatic tension can occur after the end of play. In a social setting, this can happen informally as a kind of post mortem of the game by the players. Many computer games build "post-mortem" features into the product itself, such as the end-of-mission statistic screens in Warcraft or the game replay at the end of Civilization III. We can also see examples of this in movies whose story culminates in a climactic game. When the game ends, the movie goes on for a while afterward, in part to resolve tension created during play.

Summary

As game designers, we hope that our games will be climactic struggles; we strive to imbue our games with a sense of *drama*. In these pages, we explored the concept of drama in games.

We explored a framework of three schemas for analyzing games:

- **Mechanics:** the complete description of the game system; the rules and components we need to play the game.
- **Dynamics:** the way a game "behaves" when it is played. The strategies, events and behaviors that *emerge* from the mechanics of the game.
- **Aesthetics:** the emotional content of the game. The kinds of fun we have when we play. The emotional message we hope to impart as game designers.

We defined an *aesthetic model* for drama in terms of *dramatic tension*, the intensity of the struggle, and *dramatic structure*, the way that intensity changes over time. Good dramatic structure takes the shape of a *dramatic arc*, where the tension builds toward a climax and is resolved. We identified the two necessary ingredients for dramatic tension: *uncertainty*, the sense that the outcome of the game is still unknown, and *inevitability*, the sense that the end of the game is imminent.

At some length, we discussed a handful of different game dynamical tools for producing dramatic uncertainty: *cybernetic feedback, escalation, and hidden energy, fog of war, deceleration*, and *cashing out*. We examined how the dynamics of the "ticking clock" can create the inevitability we need for dramatic tension. We identified several different kinds of ticking clock: the *literal clock*, the *nonrenewable resource*, and the *nonreversible process*. We briefly explored the need for denouement in games.

The fruits of our exploration are a new set of conceptual tools for our game design toolbox. We can use these concepts to analyze the games we play, deconstruct their designs, and gain a greater understanding of how they succeed or fail at delivering their aesthetic content. We can also use them in designing games, to create and evaluate the game mechanics that will bring us closer to our aesthetic goals.

Beyond the study of drama, there is a larger inquiry to be made: other aesthetics to be examined, other mechanics and dynamics to be understood. The more of these game design elements that we explore, the larger our design toolbox will grow. The craft of game design will become a richer, more sophisticated, more powerful form of artistic expression.

Notes

1 In Magic: The Gathering, the fundamental game resource is called "mana." Almost all of the potent moves a players can make drain her mana resources. Each turn, a player has as much mana as the number of land cards she has in play. A player's land cards start in her deck, are drawn into her hand, and are put into play at a rate of one per turn. Thus an action's mana cost places a limit on how early in the game that action can be played; for example, an action costing five mana cannot (in general) be played before the fifth turn of the game.
2 Computer scientists will recognize the striking similarity between these nonrenewable resources and the "decrementing functions" used to prove whether a computer program terminates. Often, they are the same thing. On the other hand, a game's "ticking clock" does not always provide us with an ironclad proof that the game will halt; some ticking clocks depend on random events, or on the cooperation of the players. So we sometimes end up with a game that "probably" halts, or that halts if any player wants it to. Although forcing a proper decrementing function into a game can sometimes run counter to other design goals, sometimes it is exactly what is needed.
3 Random numbers for this simulation were generated using the MT19937 algorithm.

Bibliography

Salen Katie, and Eric Zimmerman. *Rules of Play: Game Design Fundamentals*. Cambridge, MA: MIT Press, 2004.

Piccione, Peter A. "In Search of the Meaning of Senet." *Archaeology*, July/August 1980: 55–58. Available online at www.cofc.edu/~piccione/piccione_senet.pdf.

Lucey, Paul. *Story Sense: Writing Story and Script for Feature Films and Television*. New York: McGraw-Hill, 1996.

"The Quiz Show Scandal," prod. Julian Krainin. *The American Experience*, PBS. Available online at www.pbs.org/wgbh/amex/quizshow/.

26

MDA

A formal approach to game design and game research

Robin Hunicke, Marc LeBlanc, and Robert Zubek

Source: *19th National Conference of Artificial Intelligence*, San Jose, California, 2004.

Abstract

In this paper we present the MDA framework (standing for Mechanics, Dynamics, and Aesthetics), developed and taught as part of the Game Design and Tuning Workshop at the Game Developers Conference, San Jose 2001–2004.

MDA is a formal approach to understanding games—one which attempts to bridge the gap between game design and development, game criticism, and technical game research. We believe this methodology will clarify and strengthen the iterative processes of developers, scholars and researchers alike, making it easier for all parties to decompose, study and design a broad class of game designs and game artifacts.

Introduction

All artifacts are created within some design methodology. Whether building a physical prototype, architecting a software interface, constructing an argument or implementing a series of controlled experiments—design methodologies guide the creative thought process and help ensure quality work.

Specifically, iterative, qualitative and quantitative analyses support the designer in two important ways. They help her analyze the *end result* to refine implementation, and analyze the *implementation* to refine the result. By approaching the task from both perspectives, she can consider a wide range of possibilities and interdependencies.

This is especially important when working with computer and video games, where the interaction between coded subsystems creates complex, dynamic (and often unpredictable) behavior. Designers and researchers must consider interdependencies carefully before implementing changes, and scholars must recognize them before drawing conclusions about the nature of the experience generated.

In this paper we present the MDA framework (standing for Mechanics, Dynamics, and Aesthetics), developed and taught as part of the Game Design and Tuning Workshop at the Game Developers Conference, San Jose 2001–2004 [LeBlanc, 2004a]. MDA is a formal approach to understanding games—one which attempts to bridge the gap between game design and development, game criticism, and technical game research. We believe this methodology will clarify and strengthen the iterative processes of developers, scholars and researchers alike, making it easier for all parties to decompose, study and design a broad class of game designs and game artifacts.

Towards a comprehensive framework

Game design and authorship happen at many levels, and the fields of games research and development involve people from diverse creative and scholarly backgrounds. While it's often necessary to focus on one area, everyone, regardless of discipline, will at some point need to consider issues outside that area: base mechanisms of game systems, the overarching design goals, or the desired experiential results of gameplay.

AI coders and researchers are no exception. Seemingly inconsequential decisions about data, representation, algorithms, tools, vocabulary and methodology will trickle upward, shaping the final gameplay. Similarly, all desired user experience must bottom out, somewhere, in code. As games continue to generate increasingly complex agent, object and system behavior, AI and game design merge.

Systematic coherence comes when conflicting constraints are satisfied, and each of the game's parts can relate to each other as a whole. Decomposing, understanding and creating this coherence requires travel between all levels of abstraction—fluent motion from systems and code, to content and play experience, and back.

We propose the MDA framework as a tool to help designers, researchers and scholars perform this translation.

MDA

Games are created by designers/teams of developers, and consumed by players. They are purchased, used and eventually cast away like most other consumable goods.

The production and consumption of game artifacts.

The difference between games and other entertainment products (such as books, music, movies and plays) is that their consumption is relatively *unpredictable*. The string of events that occur during gameplay and the outcome of those events are unknown at the time the product is finished.

The MDA framework formalizes the consumption of games by breaking them into their distinct components:

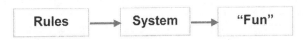

.... and establishing their design counterparts:

Mechanics describes the particular components of the game, at the level of data representation and algorithms.

Dynamics describes the run-time behaviour—of the mechanics acting on player inputs and each others' outputs over time.

Aesthetics describes the desirable emotional responses evoked in the player, when she interacts with the game system.

Fundamental to this framework is the idea that games are *more like artifacts* than media. By this we mean that the content of a game is its *behaviour*—not the media that streams out of it towards the player.

Thinking about games as designed artifacts helps frame them as systems that build behavior via interaction. It supports clearer design choices and analysis at all levels of study and development.

MDA in detail

MDA as lens

Each component of the MDA framework can be thought of as a "lens" or a "view" of the game—separate, but causally linked. [LeBlanc, 2004b].

From the designer's perspective, the mechanics give rise to dynamic system behavior, which in turn leads to particular aesthetic experiences. From the player's perspective, aesthetics set the tone, which is born out in observable dynamics and eventually, operable mechanics.

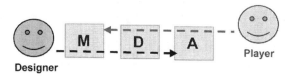

Designer   **Player**

The designer and player each have a different perspective.

When working with games, it is helpful to consider both the designer and player perspectives. It helps us observe how even small changes in one layer can cascade into others. In addition, thinking about the player encourages experience-driven (as opposed to feature-driven) design.

As such, we begin our investigation with a discussion of Aesthetics, and continue on to Dynamics, finishing with the underlying Mechanics.

Aesthetics

What makes a game "fun"? How do we know a specific type of fun when we see it? Talking about games and play is hard because the vocabulary we use is relatively limited.

In describing the aesthetics of a game, we want to move away from words like "fun" and "gameplay" towards a more directed vocabulary. This includes but is not limited to the taxonomy listed here:

1 **Sensation**
  Game as sense-pleasure
2 **Fantasy**
  Game as make-believe
3 **Narrative**
  Game as drama
4 **Challenge**
  Game as obstacle course
5 **Fellowship**
  Game as social framework
6 **Discovery**
  Game as uncharted territory
7 **Expression**
  Game as self-discovery
8 **Submission**
  Game as pastime

For example, consider the games Charades, Quake, The Sims and Final Fantasy. While each are "fun" in their own right, it is much more informative to consider the aesthetic components that create their respective player experiences:

Charades: Fellowship, Expression, Challenge.
Quake: Challenge, Sensation, Competition, Fantasy.
The Sims: Discovery, Fantasy, Expression, Narrative.
Final Fantasy: Fantasy, Narrative, Expression, Discovery, Challenge, Submission.

Here we see that each game pursues multiple aesthetic goals, in varying degrees. Charades emphasizes Fellowship over Challenge; Quake provides Challenge as a main element of gameplay. And while there is no Grand Unified Theory of games or formula that details the combination and proportion of elements that will result in "fun", this taxonomy helps us describe games, shedding light on how and why different games appeal to different players, or to the same players at different times.

Aesthetic models

Using out aesthetic vocabulary like a compass, we can define models for gameplay. These models help us describe gameplay dynamics and mechanics.

For example: Charades and Quake are both competitive. They succeed when the various teams or players in these games are *emotionally invested* in defeating each other. This requires that players have adversaries (in Charades, teams compete, in Quake, the player competes against computer opponents) and that all parties want to win.

It's easy to see that supporting adversarial play and clear feedback about who is winning are essential to competitive games. If the player doesn't see a clear winning condition, or feels like they can't possibly win, the game is suddenly a lot less interesting.

Dynamic models

Dynamics work to create aesthetic experiences. For example, *challenge* is created by things like time pressure and opponent play. *Fellowship* can be encouraged by sharing information across certain members of a session (a team) or supplying winning conditions that are more difficult to achieve alone (such as capturing an enemy base).

Expression comes from dynamics that encourage individual users to leave their mark: systems for purchasing, building or earning game items, for designing, constructing and changing levels or worlds, and for creating personalized, unique characters. *Dramatic tension* comes from dynamics that encourage a rising tension, a release, and a denouement.

As with aesthetics, we want our discussion of dynamics to remain as concrete as possible. By developing models that predict and describe gameplay dynamics, we can avoid some common design pitfalls.

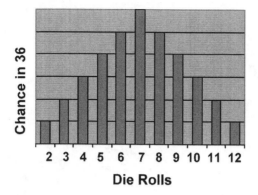

Probabilistic distribution of the random variable 2 D6.

For example, the model of 2 six-sided die will help us determine the average time it will take a player to progress around the board in Monopoly, given the probability of various rolls.

Similarly, we can identify feedback systems within gameplay to determine how particular states or changes affect the overall state of gameplay. In Monopoly, as the leader or leaders become increasingly wealthy, they can penalize players with increasing effectiveness. Poorer players become increasingly poor.

As the gap widens, only a few (and sometimes only one) of the players is really invested. Dramatic tension and agency are lost.

Using our understanding of aesthetics and dynamics, we can imagine ways to fix Monopoly—either rewarding players who are behind to keep them within a reasonable distance of the leaders, or making progress more difficult for rich players. Of course—this might impact the game s ability to recreate the reality of monopoly practices—but reality isn't always "fun".

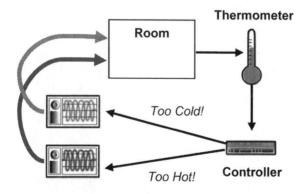

A thermostat, which acts as a feedback system.

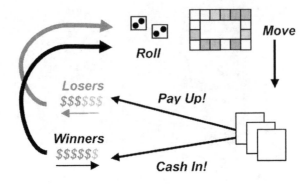

The feedback system in Monopoly.

Mechanics

Mechanics are the various actions, behaviors and control mechanisms afforded to the player within a game context. Together with the game's content (levels, assets and so on) the mechanics support overall gameplay dynamics.

For example, the mechanics of card games include shuffling, trick-taking and betting—from which dynamics like bluffing can emerge. The mechanics of shooters include weapons, ammunition and spawn points—which sometimes produce things like camping and sniping. The mechanics of golf include balls, clubs, sand traps and water hazards—which sometimes produce broken or drowned clubs.

Adjusting the mechanics of a game helps us fine-tune the game's overall dynamics. Consider our Monopoly example. Mechanics that would help lagging players could include bonuses or "subsidies" for poor players, and penalties or "taxes" for rich players—perhaps calculated when crossing the Go square, leaving jail, or exercising monopolies over a certain threshold in value. By applying such changes to the fundamental rules of play, we might be able to keep lagging players competitive and interested for longer periods of time.

Another solution to the lack of tension over long games of Monopoly would be to add mechanics that encourage time pressure and speed up the game. Perhaps by depleting resources over time with a constant rate tax (so people spend quickly), doubling all payouts on monopolies (so that players are quickly differentiated), or randomly distributing all properties under a certain value threshold.

Tuning

Clearly, the last step our Monopoly analysis involves play testing and tuning. By iteratively refining the value of penalties, rate of taxation or thresholds for rewards and punishments, we can refine the Monopoly gameplay until it is balanced.

When tuning, our aesthetic vocabulary and models help us articulate design goals, discuss game flaws, and measure our progress as we tune. If our Monopoly taxes require complex calculations, we may be defeating the player's sense of investment by making it harder for them to track cash values, and therefore, overall progress or competitive standings.

Similarly, our dynamic models help us pinpoint where problems may be coming from. Using the D6 model, we can evaluate proposed changes to the board size or layout, determining how alterations will extend or shorten the length of a game.

MDA at work

Now, let us consider developing or improving the AI component of a game. It is often tempting to idealize AI components as black-box mechanisms that, in theory, can be injected into a variety of different projects with relative ease. But as the framework suggests, game components cannot be evaluated in vacuo, aside from their effects on a system behavior and player experience.

First pass

Consider an example Babysitting game [Hunicke, 2004]. Your supervisor has decided that it would be beneficial to prototype a simple game-based AI for tag. Your player will be a babysitter, who must find and put a single baby to sleep. The demo will be designed to show off simple emotive characters (like a baby), for games targeted at 3–7 year-old children.

What are the aesthetic goals for this design? Exploration and discovery are probably more important than challenge. As such the dynamics are optimized here not for "winning" or "competition" but for having the baby express emotions like surprise, fear, and anticipation.

Hiding places could be tagged manually, paths between them hard-coded; the majority of game logic would be devoted to maneuvering the baby into view and creating baby-like reactions. Gameplay mechanics would include talking to the baby ("I see you!" or "boo!"), chasing the baby (with an avatar or with a mouse), sneaking about, tagging and so on.

Second pass

Now, consider a variant of this same design—built to work with a franchise like Nickelodeon's "Rugrats" and aimed at 7–12 year-old-girls. Aesthetically, the game should feel more challenging—perhaps there is some sort of narrative involved (requiring several "levels", each of which presents a new piece of the story and related tasks).

In terms of dynamics, the player can now track and interact with several characters at once. We can add time pressure mechanics (i.e. get them all to bed before 9 pm), include a "mess factor" or monitor character emotions (dirty diapers cause crying, crying loses you points) and so on.

For this design, static paths will no longer suffice—and it's probably a good idea to have them choose their own hiding places. Will each baby have individual characteristics, abilities or challenges? If so, how will they expose these differences to the player? How will they track internal state, reason about the world, other babies, and the player? What kinds of tasks and actions will the player be asked to perform?

Third pass

Finally, we can conceive of this same tag game as a full-blown, strategic military simulation—the likes of Splinter Cell or Thief. Our target audience is now 14–35 year old men.

Aesthetic goals now expand to include a fantasy element (role-playing the spy-hunting military elite or a loot-seeking rogue) and challenge can probably border on submission. In addition to an involved plot full of intrigue and suspense, the player will expect coordinated activity on the part of opponents—but probably a lot less emotional expression. If anything, agents should express fear and loathing at the very hint of his presence.

Dynamics might include the ability to earn or purchase powerful weapons and spy equipment, and to develop tactics and techniques for stealthy movement, deceptive behavior, evasion and escape. Mechanics include expansive tech and skill trees, a variety of enemy unit types, and levels or areas with variable ranges of mobility, visibility and field of view and so on.

Agents in this space, in addition to coordinating movement and attacks must operate over a wide range of sensory data. Reasoning about the player's position and intent should indicate challenge, but promote their overall success. Will enemies be able to pass over obstacles and navigate challenging terrain, or will you "cheat"? Will sound propagation be "realistic" or will simple metrics based on distance suffice?

Wrapping up

Here we see that simple changes in the aesthetic requirements of a game will introduce mechanical changes for its AI on many levels—sometimes requiring the development of entirely new systems for navigation, reasoning, and strategic problem solving.

Conversely, we see that there are no "AI mechanics" as such—intelligence or coherence comes from the interaction of AI logic with gameplay logic. Using the MDA framework, we can reason explicitly about aesthetic goals, draw out dynamics that support those goals, and then scope the range of our mechanics accordingly.

Conclusions

MDA supports a formal, iterative approach to design and tuning. It allows us to reason explicitly about particular design goals, and to anticipate how changes will impact each aspect of the framework and the resulting designs/implementations.

By moving between MDA's three levels of abstraction, we can conceptualize the dynamic behavior of game systems. Understanding games as dynamic systems helps us develop techniques for iterative design and improvement—allowing us to control for undesired outcomes, and tune for desired behavior.

In addition, by understanding how formal decisions about gameplay impact the end user experience, we are able to better decompose that experience, and use it to fuel new designs, research and criticism respectively.

References

Barwood, H. & Falstein, N. 2002. "More of the 400: Discovering Design Rules". Lecture at *Game Developers Conference*, 2002. Available online at: http://www.gdconf.com/archives/2002/hal_barwood.ppt

Church, D. 1999. "Formal Abstract Design Tools." *Game Developer*, August 1999. San Francisco, CA: CMP Media. Available online at: http://www.gamasutra.com/features/19990716/design_tool s_01.htm

Hunicke, R. 2004. "AI Babysitter Elective". Lecture at *Game Developers Conference Game Tuning Workshop*, 2004. In LeBlanc et al., 2004a. Available online at: http://algorithmancy.8kindsoffun.com/GDC2004/AITutorial5.ppt

LeBlanc, M., ed. 2004a. "Game Design and Tuning Workshop Materials", *Game Developers Conference 2004*. Available online at: http://algorithmancy.8kindsoffun.com/GDC2004/

LeBlanc, M. 2004b. "Mechanics, Dynamics, Aesthetics: A Formal Approach to Game Design." Lecture at Northwestern University, April 2004. Available online at: http://algorithmancy.8kindsoffun.com/MDAnwu.ppt

27

AN INTRODUCTION TO THE PARTICIPATORY AND NON-LINEAR ASPECTS OF VIDEO GAMES AUDIO[1]

Karen Collins

Source: Stan Hawkins and John Richardson (eds), *Essays on Sound and Vision* (Helsinki: Helsinki University Press, 2007), pp. 263–298.

It has been estimated that the average Westerner hears music for three and a half hours per day, most of which is in a linear form.[2] Like being locked onto a straight train track, it has been composed to start at one point and progress to another point.[3] A composer of music for linear media can predict how the music will sound from beginning to end for the listener, and compositions are constructed with this aspect taken for granted. The music of non-linear media like video games, however, works more like a major urban metro: At any time, we may want to be able to hop off at one station and hop onto another train going in a new direction. We may not get on at the end of this new train, but perhaps on one of the middle cars. The train may choose to speed up at night, or slow down through built-up urban areas. Every audio cue (train car) must be designed to stand alone, since there is no way to predict its hundreds of possible directions: There is no "correct" sequence of events for the train to follow. A unique relationship arises, then, between these cars and tracks, working with and connecting to one another.

The non-linear aspects of games audio, along with the different relationship the audio has with its audience, poses interesting theoretical problems and issues. Being an audio-visual form consumed on screen, it may seem at first logical in researching games audio to draw upon film and television theory; however, there are very distinct differences between these media for which new terminology and new theoretical approaches must be considered.[4] Although there has been significant academic research into related areas of multimedia and audio in terms of technology, communication, and development, work into the sonic aspects of audio-visual media has neglected games. Similarly, studies and theories of video games have, for the most part, disregarded the audio.[5] While there have been a scattering of articles published sporadically in the last few years, video games audio remains largely unexplored.[6] It is the aim of this paper, then, to begin to lay a few theoretical foundation stones upon which further research can be built, and to introduce to the reader some of the implications of the participatory nature of gaming in terms of both practical and theoretical perspectives.

To illustrate the discussion, I focus on two games, as they have both enjoyed considerable popularity and are easily obtainable to any researcher who may wish to examine them.[7] The first game, *Grim Fandango*, is an award-winning film-noir LucasArts PC adventure game released in 1998 and set in a Mardi Gras atmosphere in the land of the dead. The main character, Manny Calavera, is a travel agent for the Department of Death (D.O.D) who sets out on a journey to expose the corruption in the corporation, with the help of a rebel group known as the Lost Souls' Alliance. The game was designed by Tim Schafer, with music composed by Peter McConnell.[8] The second game is *The Legend of Zelda: Ocarina of Time* (hereafter discussed as *Zelda*), released by Nintendo in 1998 to much acclaim, selling almost nine million copies, and eventually achieving the number two spot on IGN Entertainment's 'Top 100 Games of All Time'.[9] It was later re-released with extended sequences as a bonus disk with *The Legend of Zelda: The Wind Waker* (Nintendo 2003). *Zelda* was so popular that instruments "inspired by" or "designed after" the sweet potato ocarina have since been sold, and one store even includes songs from the game in their marketing.[10] Created by Shigeru Miyamoto and composed by Koji Kondo, with sound design by Takuya Maekawa and Yoji Inagaki, the game follows the lead character, Link, through an adventure to save the land of Hyrule from Ganondorf, the king of evil who has invaded the Sacred Realm and stolen the Triforce of Power. Both of the games used to illustrate this paper are from the adventure genre, which requires puzzle solving skills and patience. These types of games have a tendency to be drawn out and complex, and the audio in the games is critical in helping the player to adapt to the many challenges that await them. Although audio in the adventure genre tends to be more elaborate than, for instance, simulators or sports games, the same functions and characteristics discussed below will generally apply. Nevertheless, it must be noted that audio can play a more limited role in certain genres of games, as I will discuss more fully below.

Video games sound is often referred to in a vague manner as "interactive", "adaptive" or "dynamic". An introductory text to Microsoft's audio development tool DirectX 9 suggests that these terms have different meanings, as it promises "software engineers and content creators the ability to create interactive, adaptive, *and* dynamic audio content" (Fay et al. 2004, back cover; my emphasis). A few attempts by those in the industry have been made to narrow down the meaning of the terms to refer to specific ways in which audio relates to a user in the context of gaming (see Bajakian et al 2003; Fay et al. 2004; Whitmore 2003). Although these more narrowly defined terms are not yet widely used, it is worth making the distinctions here.

Interactive audio refers to sound events occurring in reaction to gameplay, which can respond to the player directly. In other words, if for instance a player presses a button, the character on screen swings their sword and makes a "swooshing" noise. Pressing the button again will cause a recurrence of this sound. The "swoosh" is an interactive sound effect. *Adaptive* audio, on the other hand, "reacts appropriately to—and even anticipates—gameplay" rather than responding directly to the user (Whitmore 2003). As Todd Fay indicates, "in many ways, it is like interactive audio in that it responds to a particular event. The difference is that instead of responding to feedback from the listener/player, the audio changes according to changes occurring within the game or playback environment" (Fay et al. 2004, 6). An example is *Super Mario Brothers* (Nintendo 1985), where the music plays at a steady tempo until the time begins to run out, at which point the tempo doubles. I use the term *dynamic* audio to encompass both interactive and adaptive audio. Dynamic audio, then, is, audio which reacts to changes in the gameplay environment *or* in response to a user. There are several different ways in which dynamic audio interacts with a listener/player, and in which it acts within a game's diegesis, as outlined below.

Degrees of dynamic activity in games audio

Dynamic audio complicates the traditional diegetic/non-diegetic division of film sound.[11] The unique relationship in games posed by the fact that the audience is engaging directly in the sound-making process onscreen (discussed more below), requires a new type of categorisation of the image-sound relationship. Games sound can be categorised broadly as diegetic or non-diegetic,[12] but within these broad categories can be separated further into non-dynamic and dynamic sound, and then divided further still into the types of dynamic activity as they relate to the diegesis and to the player.

Apart from cut-scenes (movie sequences in which the player's input functions are impeded while a short clip to advance the plot is played), which are fixed in a linear fashion, the degrees of dynamic activity in a game are sometimes fluid, posing further difficulty in the classification of the sounds. For instance, in *Zelda's* Kokiri Forest, during the first portion of the game, we are continuously in daytime mode as we get trained in gameplay, and the Kokiri theme that plays throughout does not change except at those points where a player enters a building or encounters an enemy. While interactive, it is not adaptive at this point. After we complete our first major task and arrive at the next portion of the game (there are no distinct "levels" in this game), we then experience the passing of time, and can return to the forest. Now, if we return at night, the music has faded out to silence. At dawn, it will return to the main theme: the theme has become adaptive. In other words, a cue which is interactive or adaptive at one point in the game does not necessarily remain so throughout. Similarly, in *Asheron's Call 2: The Fallen Kings* (Turbine Software 2003), the non-diegetic music that plays in the background of scenes becomes diegetic when players decide to have their character play an instrument or sing along with the music. Not only has the music changed from non-dynamic to interactive, but it has also gone from non-diegetic to diegetic. As such, then, although I have distinguished levels of sound here, they must be viewed as fluid, rather than fixed, for many types of audio cues.

The most basic level of non-diegetic audio for games is the non-dynamic linear sounds and music found most frequently in the introductory movies or cut-scenes. In these cases, the player has no control over the possibility of interrupting the music (short of resetting or turning off the game). [13] In the introduction to *Zelda*, for instance, a short a dream sequence movie is played, explaining the plot. If the player does not start the game (leading to further cut-scenes), the entire introduction sequence loops. Similar plot advancement movies are spliced into *Grim Fandango*. At key points in the game, a pre-set cut-scene movie loads, leading us to the next stage in the plot. For instance, Manny meets with Salvador, the revolutionary, in his underground hideout to conspire to expose the inequities of the D.O.D. When Manny gives Salvador the moulded impression of his teeth (necessary for access to the building), a cut-scene ends that stage of the game (El Marrow) and leads us to the next location (the Petrified Forest). The music during this intermission cut-scene begins with the theme for the hideout, and then changes to that of the new location without the player's input: It is, in other words, linear, *non-dynamic, non-diegetic music.*

Non-diegetic audio can also contain various levels of dynamic activity. *Adaptive non-diegetic* sounds are sound events occurring in reaction to gameplay, but which are unaffected by the player's direct movements, and are outside the diegesis. As discussed above, the music in *Zelda* fades out at dusk and stops altogether during the night. At dawn, a quick "dawn theme" is played, followed by a return to the area's main theme music. The player cannot re-trigger these events (except by waiting for another day to pass). *Interactive* non-diegetic sounds, in contrast, are sound events occurring in reaction to gameplay, which can react to the player directly, but which are also outside of the diegesis. In *Zelda*, the music changes in reaction to the player approaching an enemy. If the player backs off, the music returns to the original cue. If the player manages to find the trigger point in the game, it is possible to hear both cues at the same time in the midst of a cross-fade. The player, then, controls the event cue, and can repeatedly trigger the cue, by, in this case, running back and forth over the trigger area.

There are also diegetic sounds ("source music" or "real sounds") in games, which can be non-dynamic, adaptive, or interactive. In *non-dynamic diegetic audio*, the sound event occurs in the character's space, but with which the character has no direct participation. These sounds of course occur in cut-scenes, but also take place in gameplay. For instance, in the underground hideout in *Grim Fandango*, Eva (a member of the resistance) is fiddling with a radio trying to tune in a particular station. Manny (the player's character) has no contact with the radio: Its sound is diegetic, but non-dynamic. Diegetic sounds can also be adaptive and interactive. To return to the night/day division of time in *Zelda*, at dawn we hear a rooster crow, and in the "day" sequences of Hyrule Field, we hear pleasant bird sounds. When the game's timer changes to night-time, we hear a wolf howl, crickets chirp, and various crows cawing. These sounds are diegetic and adaptive. On the other hand, *interactive diegetic sounds* occur in the character's space, with which the player's character can directly interact. The player instigates the audio cue, but does not necessarily affect the sound of the event once the cue is triggered. In *Grim Fandango*, there is a scene in the Calavera Café in which grease-monkey Glottis is playing a piano in the bar. If the player gives Glottis a VIP pass to the local racetracks, Glottis leaves the piano open. If the player then chooses, the main character Manny can sit down on the piano and play, triggering a pre-selected cue. More commonly, interactive diegetic sounds are sound effects, for instance, the sound Link's sword makes when cutting, or the footsteps of characters in games.

Finally, a level of even more direct audio interaction is that of *kinetic gestural interaction* in both diegetic and non-diegetic sound, in which the *player* (as well as the character, typically), bodily participates with the sound on screen. At its simplest level, a joystick or controller could be argued to be kinetically interactive in the sense that a player can, for instance, play an ocarina by selecting notes through pushing buttons on a controller; but more significantly, here I refer to when a player may physically, gesturally mimic the action of a character, dancer, musician, etc. in order to trigger the sound event. In other words, the player must physically play a drum in *Donkey Konga* (Namco 2003), or play a guitar in *Guitar Hero* (Red Octane 2005), for instance. These types of games have typically required the purchase of additional equipment to play outside the traditional joystick/controller that is included with the game's platform, although this will change with the release of Nintendo's Wii controller in 2006, which will make kinetic gestural interaction with sound much more common. With the Wii controller, in the latest Zelda game, *The Legend of Zelda: The Twilight Princess* (Nintendo 2006), the player must literally swing the controller to elicit a sword movement in the game, resulting in the sword swooshing sound.

There are, as shown, several different ways in which the player is connected to, participates in, or interacts with the sound of a game, and several ways in which this sound acts internally or externally to the game's diegesis. As the player is no longer a passive listener, but may be involved in invoking sound and music in the game, we must re-evaluate theories of reception. The notion that audiences might construct meaning from texts has come to be a subject of growing interest in cultural and media studies throughout the last few decades. The previous structuralist assumption that texts had a "preferred reading" to be decoded has given way to a post-structuralist theory of texts as having many meanings largely determined by the audience. This change in focus from the text to the audience has been referred to as the "return of the reader" or the "death of the author" and has been well documented elsewhere.[14] For example, if, in a film, the director wants an off-screen dog barking to inform the audience that there is a dog nearby, the sound designer records a dog bark and inserts it into the film's mix. The audience then hears the dog bark and recognizes that there is a dog nearby in the off-screen activity. Nevertheless, the audience brings their own meanings to that sound, which may be "my dog recently died and I am sad". In other words, the meaning is enriched by the *connotation* of the connotations. In terms of semiotic theory, I have elsewhere called this secondary level of signification "supplementary connotation" (Collins 2002). These are the unpredictable, individual and often personal connotations associated with a text.

However, even this approach does not account for media in which the audience plays an active role in the construction of the text. The traditional semiotic chain of communication from transmitter (the composer/sound designer) to channel (the sounds) to receiver (the audience) (Figure 1) is disturbed in games by the interplay between the player and the audio. In some cases, the player becomes a co-transmitter, and therefore, just as the audio in games is non-linear, it may be worth considering the communication chain as also non-linear, perhaps in a more circular fashion in which the receiver plays a more active role (Figure 2). Using the example of the dog barking, in this case, let us say that the player is in a driving game, and happens to take a curve too quickly just after the dog barks. The sound of the tires squealing is added to the transmission. In this case, the audience may interpret that supplementary connotation one level further, as "my dog recently died when he was hit by a car and I am sad and I hate cars", moving the train of thought away from the dog and to the car. The participatory nature of video games potentially leads to the creation of additional or entirely new meanings other than those originally intended by the creators by not only changing the reception, but also changing the transmission. We might refer to these meanings as "participatory supplementary connotations", as the original meaning (there is a dog somewhere) is maintained, but through our own experiences and through participation is supplemented by additional meanings.

Musical sound can, of course, also be affected by participation, as can be seen in *SingStar*, a PlayStation 2 game published by Sony in 2004, in which players can sing along with a selection of popular songs—rather similar to karaoke, although

Figure 1 Traditional semiotic approach to communication[15]

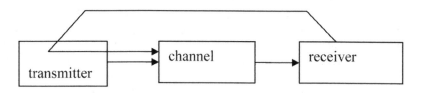

Figure 2 The impact of participation and non-linearity in gaming on communication: participatory supplementary connotations

the game component comes in to play when the game scores the player based on the accuracy of their vocals to the original recording. A player may choose to have fun by not attempting a high score, but by intentionally singing off-key or in an unusual way, changing the meaning of the original song. In fact, the competitive aspect and the rhetoric of superstardom is perhaps enough to change the meanings of the song for the audience. In less obvious ways, in most games the player has an active role in the overall sound of the game. Many player actions have sonic reactions, such as the firing of a gun, jumping, etc. and while the game may dictate where these sound events occur in some places, in other places the player may simply enjoy the sound and add a few jumps or gunshots into the mix. In some cases, a game's score is too closely synchronized to the action (a process known as "mickey-mousing" in film), [16] and the composer risks creating a musical "mini game" within the game. For instance, if the music's pitch ascends as a player climbs a flight of stairs, the player may choose to run up and down the stairs to play with the music, rather than with the game (Seflon 2006). Players, then, may choose to create new, unpredictable meanings from sounds in games, and thus are part of the creation of the whole resultant sonic landscape of a game. There are clearly many theoretical implications of games sound, and I will return to this idea later. First, however, it is necessary to understand some of the practical implications of games audio for sound designers and composers.

Dynamic audio: issues in non-linearity as it applies to games sound design and composition

Returning now to our metaphor of the urban metro as an illustration of non-linear music's structure, it is evident that this unpredictability may affect the audio in different ways. A player may at any time jump train cars, stop at stations, get on new trains, or change the direction of the car they are in. For composers, this unpredictable element can be very difficult to score. While scoring cues for specific gameplay events is fairly straight-forward, predicting how these cues may have to connect with other cues—what happens when two cars or tracks meet—can be very difficult. Moving smoothly from one music cue to another assists in the continuity of a game, and the illusions of gameplay, since a disjointed score generally leads to a disjointed playing experience, and the game may lose some of its immersive quality. There have been several approaches to the problems of transitioning between cues of music, and many scores use a variety of different transition types. Early games tended towards direct splicing and abrupt cutting between cues, though this can feel very jarring for the player (this was especially common in 8 and 16-bit games).[17] The most common transition is to fade out quickly, and then begin the new cue, or to cross-fade the two cues, which is to say, fade one out as the other cue fades in. Nevertheless, the transition can still feel abrupt, depending on the cues or the speed of the cross-fade. *Zelda* makes frequent use of this type of segue: In places where Link enters a building, the Kokiri theme music fades out completely, and then the "house" or "shop" music cue will begin. However, as mentioned above, when Link encounters a threatening enemy, a more subtle cross-fade will occur, and it is possible to situate the character half-way between both cues at the trigger point, in order to hear both cues simultaneously. To further assist in the smoothness of the cross-fades, the *Zelda* cues drop elements as the cue fades in or out, such as the disappearance of the snare-drum in advance of other instruments in the above situation. Another common type of transition is to use a quick stinger, also known as a stab (a quick shock chord). Particularly as one of the most abrupt transitions is to that of violent combat, the stinger—combined with the sound effects of violence (gunfire, sword clashes, etc.)—will obscure any disjointed musical effects that may occur. A stinger transition is used on the roof in *Grim Fandango*, for instance, when Manny scares away the last of the pigeons. We hear a squawking trumpet blast and then the music cue changes.

There are also a few more recent attempts at transitions that are more effective, but which are far more demanding on the composer, who must think of the music in non-linear and untraditional ways. For instance, some games use cue-to-cue transitions, so that when a new cue is requested, the current sequence plays until the next marker point (perhaps the next measure, or the next major downbeat), before triggering the new cue. This type of transition can be seen in *Grim Fandango*, which uses a LucasArts patented software engine called iMuse (Interactive Music Streaming Engine). The patent describes the cue-to-cue idea as follows:

> The decision points within the database comprise a composing decision tree, with the decision points marking places where branches in the performance of the musical sequences may occur . . . More specifically, each time a hook (allowing a jump to a new part of the sequence) or marker message is encountered in the musical sequence being played, it is compared with its corresponding value. If there is no match the message is ignored. If there is a match, a prespecified musical action occurs. (Land & McConnell 1994, 1, 14.)

The major difficulty with the cue-to-cue type of transition in most games, however, is the time lag: If the player's character is suddenly attacked by an adversary in a game, it may be a few seconds before the music triggers this event—far too much of a delay. Nevertheless, this approach is increasingly common, as composers write literally hundreds of cue fragments for a game, to reduce transition time and to enhance flexibility in their music.[18] Cue-to-cue transitioning is somewhat similar to the "transition matrix" method of scoring for a game. A transition matrix contains a series of small files which enable the game engine to analyse two cues and select an appropriate pre-composed transition. The cues must use markers to indicate possible places in the score where a transition may take place. This means that the composer must map out and anticipate all possible interactions between sequences at any marker point, and compose compatible transitions; an incredibly time consuming process (Fay et al. 2004, 406).

Further methods of transitions include layering approaches to song construction, in which music is composed in instrument layers with the understanding that at any time various instruments may be dropped and others may be added. This works well with some transitions, but again, it can be difficult to move quickly from cue to cue in a dramatic change. Instrument layers are also included as part of the iMuse patent, originally intended for MIDI, although it functions in *Grim Fandango* using pre-recorded sequences of WAV files. In one example, Manny stands on the docks and the underscore plays the 'Limbo' cue. If the player has Manny look at the moon, he will recite a poem, and high sustained strings are added to the original cue.

An example of a game using even more complex cue-to-cue and instrument layer transitions than those found in *Grim Fandango* or *Zelda* is *Russian Squares* (Microsoft 2002), in which the goal is to clear rows of blocks by matching colours. As each row is cleared, the music responds by adding or subtracting various layers of instrument sounds. The composer, Todd M. Fay, describes his approach as follows:

> *Russian Squares* uses instrument level variation to keep the individual cells from getting monotonous. Each music cell is anywhere from two to eight measures in length, and repeats as the player works on a given row . . . When combined with other instruments, these variations increase the amount of variation logarithmically. Most often, one to three instruments per cell use variation, and that gives the music an organic spontaneous feel, and prevents that all too familiar loopy feeling. Too much variation, however, can unglue the music's cohesion. (Fay et al. 2004, 373).[19]

I have transcribed ten cues (what Fay refers to as cells) to show how the layering approach functions in *Russian Squares*.[20] Each block represents one bar of music. The dotted lines indicate a change to a new cue sequence, which occurs with every row of blocks eliminated in the game. Cues have up to six instrument layers occurring at any time, although which layers occur in any cue is not necessarily relative to the one that comes before or after: the only constant is the steady synthesized electric bass line (instrument layer #1), though one percussion pattern is fairly consistent throughout (instrument layer #2). I have not included the addition of sound effects in the game, which occur with row clearances, time warnings, and unmoveable blocks.

Transitions are not the only difficulty facing a games composer: non-linearity in games has many consequences which affect how a game will sound. For instance, the relationship between the different types of audio occurring in a game leads to other complications for scoring. Stockburger (2005) identifies five different categories of sound events in games: speech (dialogue), zone (ambience), score (music), effects (diegetic game sounds) and "interface sound objects" (nearly exclusive to menu screens, sounds generally

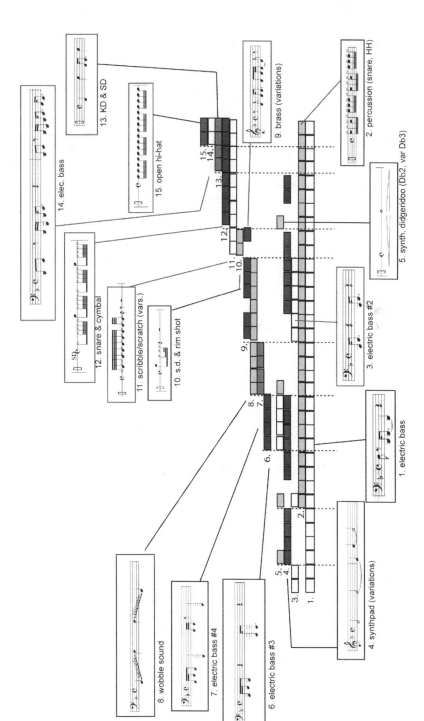

Figure 3 Russian Squares, 'Gravity Ride': Ten cues (ten minutes)

"not perceived as belonging to the diegetic part of the game environment"). Particularly since dialogue and the sound effects of, for instance, combat, are all mid-range, there is a constant risk of creating a "muddy" sound if the music also contains a lot of mid-range activity. For instance, if a player's character is in an open field, talking to a non-playing character, and is supposed to hear a gunshot in the distance, if the composer has chosen to include a lot of mid-range activity in that cue (such as, for instance, snare drums and guitar), the gunshot, the conversation and/or the music is going to be obscured. Whereas this has always been problematic in film sound and other linear media, in games, the added unpredictability of where these events may occur makes the mixing far more difficult a task. There is no real-time mixing of games audio (yet): There is nobody at the mixing desk to say when the effects should drop, or the music reduced, and so the result is sometimes a clash of sounds, dialogue, music and ambience. The consequence, therefore, is that some types of games—or some particular areas within a game—must be scored with potential mixing problems in mind, and action music cues may have high and low range frequencies, but with little in the middle range. Taken out of context, then, the music can at times sound awkward or unfinished. Another equally important issue relating to this mixing problem was raised by Anahid Kassabian in her discussion of the "evaporating segregation of sound, noise and music" (2003, 92). Kassabian suggests that the soundscape of games has impacted on recent film scores, such as *The Matrix* (1999), where the distinction between sound design and underscore is greatly reduced. Similar disintegration between sound effects and music are occurring in hip-hop and electronic music where sound effects (or "non-musical sound") regularly make appearances in songs (see Collins 2002). This raises the further possibility that games sound is influencing approaches to musical production in popular and cinematic music and that the consequences—or results—of non-linearity in music extend beyond non-linear media.[21]

Multi-player games (games played at home with other players, or games that can be played online with other users) pose another challenge to composers. If a game is designed to change cues when a player's health score reaches a certain critical level, what happens when there are two players, and one has full health while the other is critical (Seflon 2006)? Or, if a particular sonic trigger is supposed to occur at a specific point in the game, a decision must be made as to whether it occurs when both players have entered the target area, and triggered the sound event, or when just one player has entered. There are also some interesting musical opportunities opened up by multi-player games, such as spontaneous "jam sessions" between characters/players, in a game like *Asheron's Call 2*, mentioned above, in which different species of characters play different types of instruments, and the interaction between players causes changes to the music (see Fay et al. 2004, 473–499). In this way, players are encouraged to interact with each other, and to play music together.

The length of gameplay is another critical aspect that distinguishes games from linear media, and as such also introduces new difficulties for composers. The non-linear nature of games means that gameplay length is indeterminate. A player may get stuck and never complete a game, or start and stop a game repeatedly. Compounding this is LucasArts' new Euphoria technology, using artificial intelligence, in which what were previously pre-programmed game events are now unscripted and random. "You'll never be able to predict exactly what will happen, no matter how many times you've experienced a certain scenario", they promise.[22] The composer, of course, cannot compose an infinite number of cues for a game, although games do now have an increasing numbers of cues to reduce the amount of looping.[23] Well aware that games have a reputation for repetitive, looping music—but trapped by the many hours of music required in a game—composers now commonly re-use cues in other areas of a game, to reduce the amount of unique cues needed, but without creating a repetitive sounding score. This requires careful compositional planning, and often a reduction in dramatic melody lines so that the cue is less memorable.

Related to this temporal predicament is the concept of "listener fatigue": games are designed to be played multiple times, and repeated listening can be tiring, especially if a player spends a long time on one particular area of the game. Games have begun to incorporate timings into the cues, so that if the player does get stuck on a level, the music will not loop endlessly, but will instead fade out. McConnell (1999) uses this technique extensively in *Grim Fandango*. He explains, "Another compositional approach to writing state (non-diegetic) music is to start with a short flourish, or 'stinger', and then end or fade the music and let the ambient sound effects take over". Composer Marty O'Donnell elaborates in his discussion of the *Halo: Combat Evolved* score (Bungie Software 2001), "there is this 'bored now' switch, which is, 'If you haven't reached the part where you're supposed to go into the alternative piece, and five minutes have gone by, just have a nice fadeout.'" (Cited in Battino & Richards 2005, 195).

Implications of dynamic sound on the functions of games audio

The dynamic, non-linear aspects of gameplay also impact the role and functions that audio serves in games. While games audio typically maintains all of the functions found in film or television sound, (see Berg 1973; Cohen 1999; Chion 1994; Gorbman 1987; Kozloff 1988; Lissa 1965; Manvell & Huntley 1975; Smith 1998), there are also some distinct differences in the ways audio functions in games. Depending on genre, platform and on the player's familiarity with a game, some games can function without sound altogether, or with altered or substituted sound or music selected by the player. Games such as *Twisted Metal 4*, (989 Studios 1999) for instance, allow the player to remove the game's music and replace it with their own chosen CD. *Grand Theft Auto: San Andreas* (Rockstar Games 2004) has "radio stations" available so that a player can select the kinds of music that they want to hear. Games for portable players such as Play Station

Portable or Game Boy Advance are designed with the knowledge that these games are often played in the presence of other people and may require silence. As such, these devices often have much more limited capabilities for sound, and the audio is typically designed to serve a lesser role. Subsequently, the functions I describe below cannot be said to hold true for all games.

External to the games themselves is the economic impact that gaming has on various industries (and vice versa), including those of film and popular music. Increasingly, games are used as marketing tools and have become part of media franchises that may include film or television spin-offs. Games publisher Electronic Arts formed EA Trax as a marketing partner with labels "so as to not only find new music in all of our games, but hopefully create a music destination that gamers can rely on".[24] Electric Artists, a music marketing agency, recently published a white paper on video games and music after surveying "hard-core gamers", releasing such impressive statistics as: "40% of hard-core gamers bought the CD after hearing a song they liked in a video game"; "73% of gamers said soundtracks within games help sell more CDs"; and "40% of respondents said a game introduced them to a new band or song, then 27% of them went out and bought what they heard".[25] With such impressive statistics, it appears indicative of a new relationship to popular music in general. After all, it is unlikely that equal numbers of people purchase a CD after hearing a song on the radio.

The interplay between audience and audio has other impacts on the ways in which popular music is consumed. In the case of *Guitar Hero* or *SingStar* (Sony 2004), there is a direct participatory and performance aspect to listening to the songs. In many music games, the player is placed in the role of the star, the performer, even if these games are meant primarily for home play.[26] *SingStar* advertises other mini-games on its web site, declaring "Live the life of a rock star, kick back in your limo, create your own look and more".[27] A question arises, then, as to whether this fantasy changes the relationship between the audience and the music, or whether it has the same role as, for instance, playing "air guitar" and imagining being part of the band.

There are also aesthetic implications of the commercial aspects of games sound. A major repercussion of choosing licensed music is that there is limited adaptability or interactivity inherent in the music. Licensed songs are (primarily) designed as linear music, and therefore the placement of this music in games, (other than music games like *SingStar*), is generally limited to more linear aspects of gameplay (cut-scenes, title themes, credits, etc.), as is the *type* of game where such music may be appropriate. Certain types of games have become associated with specific genres of music, depending on who the target audience of the game is. Driving games, for instance, require "driving music" and are more likely to include popular songs with a repetitive "groove". Sergio Pimentel, who acquired the music for *Driver: Parallel Lines* (Reflective 2006), for instance, commented that he drove his car around listening to many types of music until he found the right "feel" for the game (2006), a combination of hip-hop and rock. To a certain degree, intertextual referencing and new semiotic connotations associated with the placement of linear music in games may occur.

The direct participation between a player and the audio takes on a new role in kinetic gestural games. These games are designed to have players directly physically participate and respond to the sound. Of course, such games are enjoyable—as is evidenced by their popularity—but the music is also sometimes intended as part of the edutainment role of some of these games (as in training basic motor skills in toddlers, for instance), or designed for aiding in physical fitness, such as *EyeToy Kinetic* (Sony 2005), which is clearly implicated in the marketing of these games. The sound in the case of kinetic games serves as a main motivating factor, arousing the player physically, and is also the part of the game on which the player must focus attention and with which the player must respond.

This changing role from passive to active listening is an important element of sound in games. A crucial semiotic role of sound in games is the preparatory functions that it serves, for instance, to alert the player to an upcoming event. Anticipating action is a critical part of being successful in many games, particularly adventure and action games. Notably, acousmatic sound—that is, sound with no clear origin visually—may inspire us to look to the direction of a sound, to "incite the look to go there and find out" (Chion 1994, 71, 85). This function, while present in films (even if we cannot force the camera to go in that direction, we mentally look there, argues Chion), is far more pronounced in games, as sound gives the player cues to head in a particular direction or to run the other way.[28] For instance, in *Zelda*, a giant rolling boulder is heard and grows in volume as it approaches—giving the player fair warning of an impending danger. The player is aware of the sound and will listen out for the boulder as they traverse that particular area in order to decide the appropriate time to move. As Marks explains, "Without [the audio], the player doesn't have any foreshadowing and won't know to take out their weapon or to get out of the room until it is too late. While this can lead to a learning experience for a player, repeatedly dying and having to start a level over can be frustrating enough to stop playing the game." (2003, 190.)

Particularly important to games is the use of sound symbols to help identify goals and focus the player's perception on certain objects. As Cohen describes, sound focuses our attention, as when a "soundtrack featuring a lullaby might direct attention to a cradle rather than to a fishbowl when both objects are simultaneously depicted in a scene" (2001, 258). In *Zelda*, the lesser enemies all have the same music, and beneficial items like gems or pieces of heart likewise all have the same or similar sounding cues. In other words, symbols and *leitmotifs* are often used to assist the player in identifying other characters, moods, environments and objects, to help the game become more comprehensible and to decrease the learning curve for new players. The use of recurrent musical themes can help to situate the player in the game matrix, in the sense that various locales or levels are usually given different themes. By listening to the music, the player is able to identify their whereabouts in the narrative and in the game. In the *Legend of Zelda*, for instance, musical themes play a key role, such as 'Saria's Song', the theme taught to the main character by his friend, Saria. The recurrence of the theme in several places helps otherwise seemingly disparate scenes hold together and provides a degree of continuity across a game that takes weeks to finish, while reminding the player of previous scenes. It also serves to reinforce the theme in the player's mind, so that when they learn to play the theme on the ocarina, it sounds familiar, and when they must recall the theme at specific points in the game, it will be likely remembered (Whalen 2004).

Music, then, can be used to enhance the overall structure of the game. These can include direct structural cues, such as links or bridges between two scenes, or which indicate the opening or ending of a particular part of gameplay. A drop to silence (the "boredom switch") can also tell the player that they should have completed that segment of the game, and that the game is waiting for a player to overcome a particular challenge or exit the area. A pause or break in music can indicate a change in narrative, or, continuous music across disparate scenes can help to signal the continuation of a particular theme (Cohen 1999, 41). For games like *Vib Ribbon* (SCEI 1999), the music can literally *create* the structure of the gameplay. Released in Japan for the Playstation, the game allows the user to input his or her own music CDs, which then influences the game's generation of level mapping. The game scans the user's CD and makes two obstacle courses for each song (one easy and one difficult), so that the game is as varied as the music the player chooses. Although this case is fairly unique, the potential certainly exists for using music to influence structures or to personalise games, as has been explored in audio games, specifically designed for the visually impaired.

Equally important in reinforcing elements of gameplay is the dialogue, which can, for instance, disclose clues, or assign goals (Kozloff 2000, 5). For example, there are often hints and goals given in the dialogue in *Grim Fandango*. When Eva tells us she needs our teeth, for instance, we have to go and find an object that will suffice before we can progress in the game. Listening to dialogue, then, becomes a key element in solving the game. Sound and dialogue can likewise reveal details about places or characters—whether they are a friend or a foe, for instance, either by their musical accompaniment or by the accent/language/timbre of their voice and voice-over narrations can let us access a character's thoughts and feelings (Kozloff 2000, 5). In *Grim Fandango*, the stereotyped accents play a key role in quickly understanding characters. South American Salvador is the revolutionary; the men criticizing capitalism in the jazz bar speak with a beat poet lingo, while the corporate boss, Don Copal, has a generic American accent. Changes in voice or accent are used to indicate other changes in gameplay: If the player chooses to have Manny take a drink of gold leaf liquor, his words slur for a while, providing a little added humour. While much of the verbal interplay between player and game has traditionally been text based, with lines selected or typed in by the player, future games will undoubtedly be more vocal, with players literally speaking to a game's characters.

Part of the role of dialogue—and audio in general—in a game is the suspension of disbelief, adding realism or creating illusion. The illusion of being immersed in a three-dimensional atmosphere is greatly enhanced by the audio, particularly for newer games which may be developed in 7.1 surround sound. Even more simple stereo effects still have a considerable impact. In *Grim Fandango*, for example, the sound changes in the Calavera Café based on the character's location, and follow the character's proximity to the piano using stereo location and occlusion effects. In addition to spatial acoustics helping to create an environment, the music, dialogue and sound effects help to represent and reinforce a sense of location in terms of cultural, physical, social, or historical environments. For instance, the song playing at the Day of the Dead Festival in *Grim Fandango*, 'Compañeros', uses a blending of rural folk and Mexican mariachi band music, with trumpet, violin, guitar, *vihuela* and *guitarrón*. This is contrasted by 'Swanky Maximino', which plays in the office of Maximino, the gambling kingpin. Explains composer Peter McConnell,

> I wanted to evoke the sounds of speakeasies of the Prohibition Era, those of the smaller "big" bands that played in clubs in such places as Harlem in the heyday of the Thompson gun-toting gangster . . . The music he would listen to, and the kinds of bands he would hire to play at the club, would reflect that sense of opulence as well. The main part of the music is inspired by recordings of the early Ellington band, when the Duke led the musical part of the Harlem Renaissance in the late twenties.[29]

While this function of game audio does not differ significantly from that of film, it must be recalled that a game may take thirty to forty hours to complete even when the "correct sequence" of events are known, and audio plays a crucial role in helping the player to recall places and characters, and to situate themselves in such a massive setting.

Another important immersive element Gorbman (1987) and Berg (1973) both discuss in relation to film is the historical function of covering distracting noises of the projector in the era of silent movies. A similar function may be attributed to games sounds created for an arcade environment. Arcade games have tended to have less polyphony and more sound effects and percussion, as part of the necessity of the environment, which meant that the games must be heard over the din to attract players. In consoles designed for home gameplay, music may mask the distractions of the computer fan, or sounds made by the surrounding environment (Cohen 1999, 41). I myself, for instance, crowded into a small apartment with a roommate, often turn the sound up on my headphones when working or gaming, to drown out telephone conversations, the snow plow outside, or other noises that serve to distract my attention. Although this has less of an effect on the audio than that of the arcade games, merely having a constant soundscape in a game can help the player to focus on the task at hand in a distracting environment.

Finally, adding to the immersive effects of gameplay is the communication of emotional meaning, which occurs in games audio in much the same way as in linear media. Here, a distinction must be made between communication of meaning through music, and mood induction: "Mood induction changes how one is feeling, while communication of meaning simply conveys information. One may receive information depicting sadness without him or herself feeling sad." (Rosar in Cohen 2001, 42.) Mood induction and physiological responses are typically experienced most obviously when the player's character is at significant risk of peril, as in the chaotic and fast boss music (the final major enemy of a level or series of levels in a game) in *Zelda*, for instance. In this way, sound works to control or manipulate the player's emotions, guiding responses to the game. As many studies of video games violence show, many players are considerably emotionally involved in games.[30] Where games differ from linear media in terms of this relationship is that the player is actively involved in their character—there are consequences for actions that the player takes. If the character dies, it is the player's "fault", as this is not necessarily a pre-scripted event out of the player's control. I would argue that this creates a different, (and in some cases perhaps more intense) relationship between the player and the character(s).[31]

The impacts of the dynamic aspects of game audio

The ways in which audio is used and functions in a game, as we have seen, are impacted by many factors. I have shown elsewhere how the technological limitations of historical games audio consoles are critical to the understanding of the construction of sound in games as well as its semiotic implications (see Collins 2006b). Although recent games systems have overcome many of the constraints of the past, the issues of participation and non-linearity bring forth many unique complications which have both practical and theoretical implications.

There are clearly many interesting problems which face games composers and sound designers, and the issue of non-linearity in sound is crucial to our understanding of games audio, as the factors which influence composition and sound design clearly influence the sound's aesthetics. In considering games audio, there are new consumption modes, new production modes and new listening modes which distinguish themselves from linear media. I have discussed the ways in which transitions impact a game, and how an inappropriate transition may result in a loss of the immersive characteristics of a game. Composers have begun to use cue fragments to adapt to this problem, but the issue calls forth aesthetic, as well as technological complications. To return to our metaphor of the metro station, not only may the passenger jump at any time to another car, but the emotional impact of that jump must also be considered in the transition. For example, if the first car was full of happy people laughing, even a cross-fade to an angry car may leave the passenger emotionally confused. The music, then, must be scored in subtle ways to build up to any dramatic emotion. Without a click-track to follow, the best the composer can hope for is to score general moods rather than direct timings to actions. Timbres are more limited, as abrupt changes from, say, trumpet jazz to heavy metal guitar are going to be awkward.

As discussed, popular music is playing an increasingly more significant role in games. Statistics suggested that gamers purchase a considerable proportion of music that they hear in a game. As such, this raises the possibility that repetition—or the associated enjoyment with play that occurs in a game—may influence the decision to purchase. More noteworthy, perhaps, is the fact that in many games it is unlikely that the player will hear the entire song, but instead may hear the first opening segment repeatedly, particularly as they try to learn a new level. The possible implication of this may be that, in the future, songs selected for games may be created with the idea that the player may not ever hear more than the first part of the song, thus changing the ways in which popular music is constructed.

Unlike in most film and television—in which music is usually designed to be absorbed on a purely subconscious level as "unheard melodies" (Gorbman 1987),[32] audio in games typically serves more of an active function, and at times must be carefully listened to in order to make the correct response. Depending on the type of game, turning off the sound, or failure to pay attention to the sonic cues, can lead to loss of points or even a character's demise. Ultimately, sound functions and is consumed in games in different ways than those of other media, and as such, our relationship to sound in games must be theorised differently from ways of the past.

I have shown that the issue of participation may require new semiotic models to understand how meaning is communicated in games, introducing the idea of "participatory supplementary connotations", since existing models rely on the notion that the receiver has no input on the transmission. There are further questions relating to reception that are raised by games, particularly the non-linear aspects which may indicate changing conceptions of time in our culture. Kramer, for instance, suggests that "just as discontinuous life-styles are becoming the norm and just as the continuity in modern time-arts is of a very different order than that in classical time-arts, so non-linear modes of experiencing pre-contemporary music are contrasting with, and even supplanting, our traditional and in a sense nostalgic well-ordered time-experiences" (1973, 124.) Kramer links the growth in non-linearity in Western music to both technological advances and social discontinuity. Perhaps the non-linear aspects of games audio are indicative of a wider cultural paradigm shift, as previous changes in music have also reflected their times (see Atalli 1985, Tagg 1996, etc.). Does the reception of non-linear games audio correspond with other contemporary non-linear audio, or does the experience of gaming change or influence the reception of non-linearity?

There are clearly issues of temporality in games music that require further exploration but are outside the scope of this paper. The length of gameplay, as discussed, is different from that of film—it could be one minute, or twelve hours, for instance, that a player chooses to engage in that mode. It may be that the same segments of music in the same order are only heard once in a game or it may be that one piece is looped for hours. The resultant implications for the composer are a reduction of dramatic melodies, but what impacts do cue fragments—and the mutability of the music—have on a player? With the adaptability of cue fragments, the player may hear what is essentially one long song for the length of their gameplay—how does the lack of a structured beginning, middle and end affect the listener's reception of the music? If all of our paradigms for thought are based on linearity, what are the wider implications of having the ability to conceive of ideas in a nonlinear framework?

It may be necessary to draw on theories of drones and the loss of time sometimes associated with their reception,[33] or on some of the theories of new temporality and non-linearity in music discussed by such authors as McClary (2000), Tagg (1996), Kramer (1973 and 1981), etc. Kramer's notion of "vertical time" may be useful in understanding games audio, as he suggests vertical time "consists of relationships between ever-present layers of the dense sound world, whereas form in linear music consists of relationships between successive events" (1981, 551). Kramer argues,

> The result is a single present stretched out into an enormous duration, a potentially infinite "now" that nonetheless feels like an instant . . . it does not begin but merely starts, does not build to a climax, does not purposefully set up internal expectations, does not seek to fulfill any expectations that might arise accidentally, does not build or release tension, and does not end but simply ceases. (1981, 549.)

Likewise, repetition, looping and its implications have been explored further by many authors (Garcia 2005; Katz 2004; Middleton 1996; Spicer 2004; Stillar 2005, etc.), although whether the loop in context with the visual image and dynamic nature of the gameplay is received differently than loops in linear popular music still remains an unanswered question. Garcia (2005) explains how the repetition of seemingly short musical units can generate pleasure over extended periods. Has games audio helped looping to become more acceptable in popular music, by changing the way it is received and listened to? These ideas and concepts are not limited to sound. In a game like *Zelda*, the player has the option to change perspectives and point of view in the game. While the default is a third-person point of view, the player can opt for first-person point of view, as well as change the angle of viewing, in a sense becoming the director and influencing the way visual imagery is produced and consumed in games. Just as MTV helped to influence new styles in film editing,[34] we need to now consider video games as a major cultural influence with implications on both practice and theory in popular music and cultural theory in general.

Notes

1 I would like to acknowledge the kind guidance and advice of the editors and other readers of preliminary drafts of this paper, particularly Paul Théberge and John Richardson. By "video" games I refer to all digital games, including those on computers, consoles, mobile phones, etc.
2 Tagg 2002, 1.
3 This is not to suggest that all music—or even all Western music—is linear. See for instance, Kramer 1981 for further discussion of non-linearity in music. I have borrowed the train metaphor from Griffin 1998.

4 Comparisons with film music have, unfortunately, fallen prey to implying games (at least, those of the past) are inferior to that of film. For example, David Bessell tells us that a particular game gives us "a rather one-dimensional impression in comparison to most film scores" 2002, 138. Bessell does acknowledge that there are difficulties in scoring dynamically, but the solutions he suggests—such as the approach taken by Boulez in using random sequences (2002, 142)—were ideas that had, in fact, been used in games going back to at least those of the Commodore 64 in the early 1980s (see Collins 2006a). It is quite common for games to introduce randomization, though perhaps in subtle ways. For instance, Marty O'Donnell and Jay Weinland of Bungie Studios inform us, "If you sit in one place in *Halo* listening to a piece of music, you will notice that it never plays back exactly the same way twice due to the randomization of the permutations. The music was edited so that the 'in' sound file plays seamlessly into any of the main loop permutations, and the main loop permutations can play seamlessly into the 'out' soundfile when the piece is stopped by the script. These main loop permutations contain unique elements, so as they are randomly played back, the piece takes on a new flavor each time you hear it" (in Fay et al. 2004, 421).

5 See for instance Wolf 2001 or Wolf & Perron 2003. A great majority of work into games has centered on their violence, but other approaches in the field of ludology have been increasing in the last decade.

6 Such as Bessell 2002, Stockburger 2005, and Whalen 2004. One issue facing game audio musicologists has been transcription and copyright. With many old games companies now defunct—and many old games simply not giving credit to composers—it has been difficult to publish in some areas.

7 Emulators, which can re-create the N64 platform on a home PC, are downloadable from the Internet, as are ROMs, the games themselves. Nintendo makes it clear on their website that these devices are illegal, and did not respond to my requests for special permission to use them for research purposes. Nevertheless, N64 consoles and games are available quite affordably on E-Bay and in used games stores.

8 Sound design and production by Michael Land, Clint Bajakian, Nick Peck, Andy Martin, Jeff Kliment, Michael McMahon, Julian Kwasneski, and Kristen Becht. It is worth noting that such a large audio group is rare, and is typically only seen at larger studios. In many smaller games companies, the composers also serve as sound (effects) designers. With larger companies, such as Nintendo or LucasArts, these roles are often divided and sometimes filled by several people.

9 According to IGN's Top 100 Games. IGN Entertainment is part of Fox Interactive Media, and is one of the largest reviewers of interactive media. Internet source, available http://top100.ign.com/2005/index.html (5.3.2006).

10 See for instance http://www.songbirdocarina.com/zelda_songs.html. See also Lark in the Morning, http://www.larkinthemorning.com (6.4.2006).

11 It may be useful to refer also to other approaches to sound theory. Scott Curtis, for instance, suggests a division of "isomorphic" and "iconic" uses of sound to replace the diegetic/non-diegetic dichotomy. Isomorphic "refers to the close matching of the image and sound—that is, a relationship based on rhythm in both the action and the music" (1992, 201), whereas iconic sounds have an analogous relationship between sound and image—"visual elements and the timbre, volume, pitch, and tone of the accompanying sound" (1992, 202). However, this distinction does not help us to understand the ways that the audience interprets the sounds in relation to the fictional on-screen world, and so is unhelpful to the present argument.

12 And could be sub-divided further, for instance, as Michel Chion has elaborated in his discussion of the diegetic/nondiegetic divide (1994), or Gorbman's "metadiegetic" subjective sound categories (1987, 450), Branigan's "intradiegetic" (1984, 68) and Bordwell & Thompson's "internal diegetic" (1990, 256), etc. Although the use of the

division of diegetic/nondiegetic is called into question in contemporary film studies because of its inability to deal with these other categories of sound, I do not wish to further complicate the issue here. My point is that the relationship of the audio to the player and to their character in games is different than in film because of the participatory nature of games.

13 Cut-scenes require "a dramatic score to grab a player's attention and motivate them to make it through the next level to see the next movie. These offerings often serve as a reward to the player, where they are able to watch the on-screen action and inwardly pride themselves for making it happen." See Marks 2001, 190.

14 See for instance, Moores 1993.

15 See also Tagg 1999, 11. Although the concept of supplementary connotation may be latent in Tagg's concept of codal interference, it is not clearly conceptualized: " when transmitter and receiver share the same basic store of musical symbols but totally different sociocultural norms and are basically 'understood' but that 'adequate response' is obstructed by other factors, such as receivers' general like or dislike of the music and what they think it represents, or by the music being recontextualised verbally or socially".

16 Although the term "score" is more commonly used to refer to printed musical compositions, it is the term commonly used by those in the games industry to refer to music composed for games. Increasingly, interactive audio compositions are being scored, orchestrated by professionals, and recorded by choirs or orchestras.

17 I rely on personal experience and the experience of some of my students for this observation.

18 Cue fragments are also referred to as "audio chunks" amongst games composers. Troels Folmann calls them "microscores". Folmann's score for *Tomb Raider: Legend* (Eidos 2006), for instance, contained over three hours of music in more than five hundred individual cues. Folmann 2006.

19 The book provides detail and examples from the composition. I use the 'Gravity Ride' track for this discussion. The game is part of the XP Plus package offered by Microsoft.

20 The layout of my transcription is borrowed from Garcia 2005. The blocks of bars are laid out in much the same fashion as sequencing software. The passage of time is followed from left to right, with each block representing one bar of music. Each vertical layer in the stack of blocks represents a new instrument sound.

21 There are of course other reasons for this sound/music disintegration. Recent technology has made this far easier than in the past, for instance. I would speculate that one of the most significant contributing factor to this idea is the changing role of the *sound effects editor* to *sound designer* in the last few decades and the subsequent more creative uses of non-musical sound in film. Blair Jackson, sound designer for television show *Twin Peaks*, for instance, described his approach to sound in one scene, "they went into the scene with music, then favored the effects, and then went out of it musically. It happened so seamlessly you didn't realize it wasn't one continuous flow of sound. It was all part of the 'musical score.'" See Forlenza & Stone 1993, 110.

22 From the LucasArts press release, Indy Game Features *Euphoria* Technology. April 27, 2006. Internet source, available: http://www.indianajones.com/videogames/news/news20060427.html (05.05.2006).

23 Algorithmic generation of cues is likely a major area to be reconsidered in the coming years.

24 EA Trax Interview, internet source, http://www.music4games.net/f_eatrax.html (22.1.2005).

25 See "Video Games of Note" on http://www.electricartists.com/videogamesofnote_whitepaper_0314.pdf (22.1.2005).

26 It is interesting to note that the original version of *Singstar* featured a single-player mode, but this function was dropped in later releases of the game, indicating a clear preference for group play.

27 See the *SingStar* website, http://www.singstargame.com/ (28.5.2006).

28 Stockburger 2005 provides a fairly extensive analysis of what he terms the "spatialising functions in the game environment", focusing on what he has called the "dynamic acousmatic function", which, he elaborates, is distinguished from film by the "kinaesthetic control over the acousmatisation and visualisation of sound objects in the game environment".

29 Internet source, available http://www.lucasarts.com/products/grim/grim_files.htm (5.6.2006).

30 See Gentile et al, 2004, Irwin & Gross 1995, or Calvert & Tan 1994, for instance. Of course, emotional involvement in games is not limited to violence. The *Guardian* had an article in which it discussed the emotional reaction to games, and reported later, "In response to the article, many gamers confess to having cried when Aeris died in *Final Fantasy VII*". See the games blog, http://blogs.guardian.co.uk/games/archives/2005/09/19/im_crying_here.html (05.05.2006). As a personal anecdote, I can recall a time when I first played *The Sims* (Maxis 2000). It surprised me that in a very short time I began to think of my life in *Sim*ean terms—adding friends, collecting objects, etc. I remarked on this somewhat disturbing realization to a friend, who commented that after playing *Roller Coaster Tycoon 2* (Infogrames 2002) she, too, had a similar experience looking at real-world buildings and trying to judge if they would fit into the game world she was constructing. Similarly, upon discussing a particularly stressful time recently with a games sound designer friend of mine, he remarked, "you just need to find some power-ups". Concepts introduced in gaming had entered and become useful in our lives. While we could differentiate between the "real" world and the world of the game, we had begun to think of our lives as if we were living out a video game experience.

31 However, the active involvement of the player with a game also has other repercussions that can lessen the immersive quality, such as the player's fumbling with the controller, for instance. Even after playing a game for several hours, for example, I find that I forget what function some of the buttons have, and this can cause the immersive effects of the game to lessen.

32 There are of course exceptions, such as in commercials, in which a track becomes part of a product's branding. See Cook 2000, 21.

33 See for instance Hainge 2004.

34 See Dancyger 2001.

References

Attali, Jacques 1985: *Noise: The Political Economy of Music*. University of Minnesota Press, Minnesota.

Bajakian, Clint; David Battino & Keith Charley 2003: Group Report: What is Interactive Audio? And What Should It Be? The Eighth Annual Interactive Music Conference Project Bar-B-Q. Internet Source, available http://www.projectbarbq.com/bbq03/bbq03r5.htm (12.3.2006).

Battino, David & Kelli Richards 2005: *The Art of Digital Music: 56 Visionary Artists and Insiders reveal their Creative Secrets*. Backbeat Books, San Francisco.

Berg, Charles Merrell 1973: *An Investigation of the Motives for and Realization of Music to Accompany the American Silent Film, 1896–1927*. PhD Thesis, Department of Speech and Dramatic Art, University of Iowa.

Bessell, David 2002: What's That Funny Noise? An Examination of the Role of Music in *Cool Boarders 2*, *Alien Trilogy* and *Medievil 2*. In King, George & Krzywinska, Tanya (eds.) *ScreenPlay: Cinema/videogames/interfaces*. Wallflower, London.

Bordwell, David & Thompson, Kristin 1990: *Film Art: An Introduction*. McGraw-Hill, New York.

Calvert, S.L., & Tan, S. 1994: Impact of virtual reality on young adults' physiological arousal and aggressive thoughts: Interaction versus observation. *Journal of Applied Developmental Psychology*, 15, 125–139.

Branigan, Edward 1984: *Point of View in the Cinema: A Theory of Narration and Subjectivity in Classical Film*. Moulton, Berlin.

Chion, Michel 1994: *Audio-Vision: Sound on Screen*. Columbia University Press, New York.

Cohen, Annabel J. 1998: The Functions of Music in Multimedia: A Cognitive Approach. In Yi, S.W. (ed.): *Music, Mind & Science*. Seoul University Press, Seoul, 40–68.

Cohen, Annabel J. 2001: Music as a Source of Emotion in Film. In Juslin, Patrick N. & Sloboda, John A. (eds.) *Music and Emotion: Theory and Research*. Oxford University Press, Oxford, 249–279.

Collins, Karen 2002. *The Future is Happening Already: Industrial Music, Dystopia, and the Aesthetic of the Machine*. PhD thesis, Institute of Popular Music, University of Liverpool, Liverpool.

Collins, Karen 2006a: Loops and Bloops: Music on the Commodore 64. *Soundscapes: Journal of Media Culture.* Volume 8: February. Internet source, available http://www.icce.rug.nl/~soundscapes (3.3.2006).

Collins, Karen 2006b: Flat Twos and the Musical Aesthetic of the Atari VCS. *Popular Musicology Online*, Issue 1. Internet source, available http://www.popular-musicology-online.com (11.06.2006).

Cook, Nicholas 2000: *Analysing Musical Multimedia*. Oxford University Press, Oxford.

Curtis, Scott 1992: The Sound of Early Warner Bros. Cartoons. In Altman, Rick (ed.): *Sound Theory Sound Practice*. Routledge, London, 191–203.

Dancyger, Ken 2001: *The Technique of Film and Video Editing: History, Theory, and Practice*. Focal Press, London.

Fay, Todd M.; Selfon, Scott & Fay, Todor J. 2004: *Directx 9 Audio Exposed: Interactive Audio Development*. Wordware Publishing, Texas.

Folmann, Troels 2006: *Tomb Raider Legend*: Scoring a Next-Generation Soundtrack. Conference presentation for the Game Developer's Conference 2006. San Jose, California.

Forlenza, Jeff & Stone, Terri 1993: *Sound For Picture: An Inside Look at Audio Production for Film and Television*. Hal Leonard Publishing Corporation, Emeryville, CA.

Garcia, Luis-Manuel 2005: On and On: Repetition as Process and Pleasure in Electronic Dance Music. *Music Theory Online* Volume 11, Number 4. Internet source, available http://mto.societymusictheory.org/issues/mto.05.11.4/mto.05.11.4.garcia.html (12.2.2006).

Gentile, D.A.; Lynch, P.L.; Linder, J.R.; & Walsh, D.A. 2004: The Effects of Violent Video Game Habits on Adolescent Hostility, Aggressive Behaviors, and School Performance. *Journal of Adolescence* Issue 27, 5–22.

Gorbman, Claudia 1987: *Unheard Melodies: Narrative Film Music*. Indiana University Press, Bloomington.

Griffin, Donald S. 1998: Musical Techniques for Interactivity. *Gamasutra*. May 1, 1998, Vol. 2: Issue 18. Internet source, available http://gamasutra.com/features/sound_and_music/19980501/interactivity_techniques_03.htm (12.3.2006).

Grim Fandango Files 1998: Internet source, available http://www.lucasarts.com/products/grim/grim_files.htm (12.4.2006).

Hainge, Greg 2004: The Sound of Time is not *tick tock*: The Loop as a Direct Image of Time in Noto's *Endless Loop Edition* and the Drone Music of Phill Niblock. *Invisible*

Culture: Electronic Journal for Visual Culture, Issue 8. Internet source, available http://www.rochester.edu/in_visible_culture/Issue_8/hainge.html (12.4.2006).

IGN's Top 100 Games. Internet source, available http://top100.ign.com/2005/index.html (5.3.2006).

Irwin, A.R. & Gross, A.M. 1995: Cognitive Tempo, Violent Video Games, and Aggressive Behavior in Young Boys. *Journal of Family Violence* Issue 10, 337–350.

Kassabian, Anahid 2003: The Sound of a New Film Form. In Inglis, Ian (ed.) *Popular Music and Film*. Wallflower, London, 91–101.

Katz, Mark. 2004: *Capturing Sound: How Technology has Changed Music*. University of California Press, Berkeley.

Kozloff, Sarah 1988: *Invisible Storytellers: Voice-over Narration in American Fiction Film*. University of California Press, Berkeley.

Kozloff, Sarah 2000: *Overhearing Film Dialogue*. University of California Press, Berkeley.

Kramer, Jonathan D. 1973: Multiple and Non-Linear Time in Beethoven's Opus 135. *Perspectives of New Music*, Vol. 11, No. 2, 122–145.

Kramer, Jonathan D. 1981: New Temporalities in Music. *Critical Inquiry*, Vol. 7, No. 3, 539–556.

Land, Michael Z. & Peter N. McConnell 1994: Method and Apparatus for Dynamically Composing Music and Sound Effects using a Computer Entertainment System. United States Patent Number 5,315,057.

Lissa, Zofia 1965: *Ästhetik der Filmmusik*. Henscherverlag, Berlin. Translated and summarised by Tagg, Philip. Internet source, available http://www.mediamusicstudies.net/tagg/udem/musimgmot/filmfunx.html (2.4.2006).

Manvell, Roger & Huntley, John 1975: *The Technique of Film Music*. Focal Press, New York.

Marks, Aaron 2001: *The Complete Guide to Game Audio: For Composers, Musicians, Sound Designers, and Game Developers*. CMP Books, California.

McClary, Susan 2000: Temporality and Ideology: Qualities of Motion in Seventeenth-Century French Music. *Echo: A Music-Centered Journal*. Volume 2 Issue 2, Fall 2000. Internet source, available http://www.humnet.ucla.edu/echo (3.3.2006).

McConnell, Peter 1999: The Adventures of a Composer Creating the Game Music for Grim Pandango (*sic*). *Electronic Musician*. Internet Source, available http://emusician.com/mag/emusic_adventures_composer_creating/index.html (20.5.2006).

Middleton, Richard 1996: Over and Over: Notes towards a Politics of Repetition. Surveying the Ground, Charting Some Routes. Conference paper presented at *Grounding Music for the Global Age*, Berlin. Internet source, available http://www2.hu-berlin.de/fpm/texte/middle.htm (2.4.2006).

Moores, Shaun 1993: Interpreting Audiences: The Ethnography of Media Consumption. Sage, London.

Pimentel, Sergio 2006: Music Acquisition for Games. Conference presentation for the Game Developer's Conference 2006. San Jose, California.

Seflon, Scott 2006: Audio Boot Camp: Music for Games. Conference presentation for the Game Developer's Conference 2006. San Jose, California.

Smith, Jeff 1998: *The Sounds of Commerce: Marketing Popular Film Music*. Columbia University Press, New York.

Spicer, Mark 2004: (Ac)cumulative Form in Pop-Rock Music. *Twentieth-Century Music* 1/1, 29–64.

Stillar, Glenn 2005: Loops as Genre Resources. *Folia Linguistica* XXXIX/1–2, 197–212.

Stockburger, Axel 2005: The Game Environment from an Auditive Perspective. Internet source, available http:/www.audiogames.net/ics/upload/gameenvironment.htm (4.6.2006).

Tagg, Philip 1996: Understanding 'Time Sense'. Internet source, available http://www. mediamusicstudies.net/tagg/articles/timesens.html (20.4.2006).

Tagg, Philip 1999: Introductory Notes to the Semiotics of Music. Postgraduate class handout, Institute of Popular Music, University of Liverpool, Liverpool.

Tagg, Philip 2002: Notes on how Classical Music Became 'Classical'. Internet source, available http://tagg.org/teaching/classclassical.pdf (20.4.2006).

Video Games of Note. Internet source, available http://www.electricartists.com/ videogamesofnote_whitepaper_0314.pdf (22.1.2005).

Whalen, Zach 2004: Play Along: An Approach to Videogame Music. *Game Studies: The International Journal of Computer Game Research*, 4/1. Internet source, available http://www.gamestudies.org/0401/whalen (3.3.2006).

Whitmore, Guy 2003: Design with Music in Mind: A Guide to Adaptive Audio for Game Designers. *Gamasutra*. Internet source, available http://www.gamasutra.com/resource_ guide/20030528/whitmore_01.shtml (2.4.2006).

Wolf, Mark J.P. (ed.) 2001: *The Medium of the Video Game*. University of Texas Press, Austin.

Wolf, Mark J.P. & N. Bernard Perron (eds.) 2003: *The Video Game Theory Reader*. Routledge, New York.

Audio-visual references

Asheron's Call 2: The Fallen Kings. Turbine Entertainment 2003

Donkey Konga. Namco 2003

Driver: Parallel Lines. Sony 2006

Eye Toy: Kinetic. Sony 2005

Grand Theft Auto: San Andreas. Rockstar 2004

Grim Fandango. LucasArts 1998

Guitar Hero. Red Octane 2005

Halo: Combat Evolved. Bungie Software 2001

Legend of Zelda: The Ocarina of Time. Nintendo 1998

Legend of Zelda: The Twilight Princess. Nintendo 2006

Legend of Zelda: The Wind Waker. Nintendo 2003

Russian Squares. Microsoft 2002

Sims. Maxis 2000

SingStar. Sony 2004

Super Mario Brothers. Nintendo 1985

Tomb Raider: Legend. Eidos 2006

Twisted Metal 4. 989 Studios 1999

Vib Ribbon. SCEI 1999

28

IN THE LOOP

Creativity and constraint in 8-bit video game audio

Karen Collins

Source: *Twentieth-Century Music*, 4(2), 2007, 209–227.

Abstract

This article explores the sound capabilities of video game consoles of the 8-bit era (*c*.1975–85) in order to discuss the impact that technological constraints had on shaping aesthetic decisions in the composition of music for the early generation of games. Comparing examples from the Commodore 64 (C64), the Nintendo Entertainment System (NES), the Atari VCS, and the arcade consoles, I examine various approaches and responses (in particular the use of looping) to similar technological problems, and illustrate how these responses are as much a decision made by the composer as a matter of technical necessity.

Another example would be when you're faced with a guitar that only has five strings. You don't say, 'Oh God, I can't play anything on this.' You say, 'I'll play something that only uses five strings, and I'll make a strength of that. That will become part of the skeleton of the composition.

Brian Eno[1]

Introduction

Technological constraints are not new to musical composition, although most explorations of the subject have focused on twentieth-century concerns. Mark Katz, for instance, discusses how the 78-rpm record led to a standard time limit for pop songs, and how Stravinsky famously tailor-made *Sérénade en LA* to the length of an LP, even though the composer, in doing this, may have been driven by 'his penchant for self-imposed limitations'.[2] Critiques of 'hard' technological determinism as it relates to musical technologies have dominated the literature.[3] In its place has arisen a softer approach, notes Paul Théberge, in which 'traditional instrument technologies can sometimes be little more than a field of possibility within which the innovative musician chooses to operate. The particular "sound" produced in such instances is as intimately tied to personal style and technique as it is to the characteristics of the instrument's sound-producing mechanism.'[4] However, video games audio has been strangely absent from nearly all accounts of popular music technology. By examining video games of the 8-bit[5] era (approximately 1975 to 1985), we can see how technological constraint has shaped aesthetic decisions, some of which have impacted upon other gaming platforms and even other genres of music. As a number of recent studies of music technology have argued, I maintain that the relationship between technology and aesthetics is one of symbiosis rather than dominance – what Barry Salt refers to as a 'loose pressure on what is done, rather than a rigid constraint'[6] I shall show how, while some choices may be predetermined by technology, creative composers have invented ways in which to overcome or even to aestheticize those limitations.

The influence of early games audio has been underestimated. The continuing prominence of one particular sound, *Pac-Man's* 'waca waca' (the sound the character makes when eating), is clear evidence of the significance of this influence. In the 1980s the sound was incorporated into popular songs such as 'Weird Al' Yankovic's 'Pacman' and Buckner and Garcia's 'Pac-Man Fever', but it has more recently been used by Aphex Twin, Bloodhound Gang, DMX, Lil' Flip, and many more,[7] There has also been an increase in the popularity of 'micromusic', sometimes known as 'chiptunes' – songs based on 8-bit games machine sound. Malcolm McLaren has begun promoting the scene, and Beck released an EP of 8-bit remixes of some of his songs in 2005.[8] A small but dedicated scene of micromusicians has developed, making music from otherwise obsolete computers and games consoles, with bands like 8bitpeoples, Teamtendo, and the Reverse Engineers. Some might suggest that this is Generation-X retro-gaming nostalgia, as Reverse Engineers' Edward Jones seems to imply: 'When I was a kid, I didn't listen to pop music on the radio. I listened to music on computer games. My friends and I, we would make tapes of the songs from computer games and we would listen to those. They were the tapes we'd copy and pass around.'[9] But many of the composers in the scene are too young to have spent childhoods with the machines. Rather, they like the challenge of the limitations ingrained in the technology, as Teamtendo intimates: 'Working with this limited harmonic vocabulary forces you to be creative, and there are some very pleasant discoveries along the way';[10] or, as Goto80 says, 'it's fun working with such hardcore limits, forcing you to realize your ideas in other ways'.[11] When the constraints are looked upon with the attitude of these artists, or, for instance, with that of Brian Eno in the quotation at the beginning of this article, the results become part of a new paradigm for creating music.

The concern of this paper, however, is original games music rather than contemporary micromusic, since numerous micromusicians have incorporated more modern technology into their work. Many 8-bit machines are worth studying, but I shall limit my discussion to the most successful consoles – the

Atari VCS and the Nintendo Entertainment System (NES) – and the first major home-computer game system – the Commodore 64 (C64) – as well as early coin-operated arcade machines. Many of the machines that I have excluded (such as the Intellivision, ColecoVision, the ZX Spectrum, and the BBC Micro) used the same or similar sound chips to those discussed here.[12] I focus on two groups of games. The first consists of games that crossed platforms and spanned genres: *Arkanoid, California Games, Donkey Kong, Frogger, Ghosts 'n Goblins, Karate Champ, Maniac Mansion, Pac-Man, Tetris,* and *Ultima 3: Exodus.*[13] For the systems that did not have a port[14] of these games, comparable games were chosen. The second group comprises games designed specifically for each system, and so includes the best-known games from each, chosen on fan and industry ratings.[15] In several cases, each of the games studied also had a particular influence on the development of games in general. For instance, *Metroid* was one of the first examples of non-linear gaming on a home console; and *Super Mario Bros.* was one of the most successful franchises in games history, selling over 180 million games and making popular many features that are now standard.

Unlike film audio, which is strictly linear and commonly operates as 'diegetic' or 'nondiegetic',[16] games audio exhibits varying degrees of gameplay response, from the fairly simplistic song that remains constant throughout a game level but changes on completion of that level, to more complex relations of sounds and music that continue to respond to a player throughout a game. It is worth distinguishing between these types of interactivity. *Interactive* audio refers to sound events that occur in reaction to gameplay, responding to the player directly. For instance, a player presses a button, and the character on the screen jumps and makes a 'bleep' noise; pressing the button again will cause a recurrence of this sound. The 'bleep' is an interactive sound effect. *Adaptive* audio, on the other hand, responds to the gameplay environment. For example, the music might change as a timer in a game increases to a certain point. I use the term *dynamic* audio to encompass both of these types of interactivity – audio that reacts to changes in the gameplay environment or to the activity of a user.[17] In 8-bit audio there are several distinct degrees of dynamic sound:[18]

1   *Adaptive non-diegetic sounds.* These occur in reaction to gameplay but are unaffected by users once the game has begun, until a major new event triggers a new linear track, such as when a timer triggers new music. For example, in *Frogger* a song plays until the player manoeuvres his/her character up to a 'home base', or the time runs out, at which point a new track is triggered.
2   *Non-dynamic diegetic sound.* This occurs when a sound event takes place in a character's space but the character does not interact with it. An example is the thunder and rain sounds in the background of *Ghosts 'n Goblins.*
3   *Interactive diegetic sound.* This, on the other hand, refers to sound in a character's space with which the player's character interacts. For example, in *Maniac Mansion* a character must record music on a cassette recorder and play it back during the game.

4   *Non-dynamic non-diegetic audio.* This refers to sound that is part of an underscore that is unaffected by a player's movements, such as the cut-scene[19] after the second level of *Pac-Man*, in which gameplay is stopped so a quick 'film' can play.

5   *Interactive non-diegetic sound.* This refers to sound events occurring in gameplay that can react or adapt to the user, such as jump sounds, or music events warning of approaching danger, which can be switched off by moving in a new direction. Examples of these would be *Super Mario*'s jumping sound, or the 'boss' tune in *Mayhem in Monsterland*, which plays when a character is in the vicinity of a boss character; if the player backs up, the music returns to the 'normal'-level gameplay music.

Levels 4 and 5 are the most common of these categories of musical interaction, and are the focus of this paper.

The concept of 'the loop' presents another issue. Here, I take loops to mean 'self-contained units that may or may not be combined with other loops or non-looping material in a larger structure [. . .] In music production and sound design circles, a "loop" is a bit of audio – usually, though not exclusively, of short length – that can be played back repeatedly and potentially endlessly without noticeable gaps or disruptions between one instance of the loop and the rest'.[20] Loops, however, occur in different shapes and sizes, as we shall see below. At this point it is perhaps useful to engage with Middleton's concept of 'musematic repetition' and 'discursive repetition' – the 'riff' versus the 'phrase' in the discourse about loops.[21] We see both forms of repetition occurring in games audio, often at the same time, along with a longer loop of the entire 'song' or a sequence of loops at a larger-than-phrase level. For the sake of brevity I have termed these 'microloops', 'mesoloops', and 'macroloops'. Thus a two-note bass line may provide a (musematic) microloop which repeats twice in a two-bar (discursive) mesoloop, which is part of a longer, eight-bar macroloop 'song', which is looped throughout a level of gameplay.

The technology of 8-bit audio

The majority of 8-bit machines (and early arcade and pinball machines) used what is known as programmable sound generators (PSGs), which were subtractive synthesis chips that offered little control over timbre and were usually restricted to square waveforms, with limited possibility for manipulation. Many of these PSGs were created by Texas Instruments or General Instruments, but some companies, such as Atari and Commodore, designed their own sound chips to improve sound quality.

Many coin-operated arcade games of the 8-bit era used the General Instruments AY-8910 chip, which contained three tone-generators and a white-noise generator. Each channel allowed for individual control of frequency, volume, and envelope. Pitch was controlled by the somewhat limited frequency-division method, but the AY chip used a larger bit register to set the divisor, allowing for 4096 possible tones instead of the 1024 pitches on the other popular arcade chip, the

Texas Instruments SN76489.[22] Another common chip, designed by Atari, was the Pokey. Each channel had only a square-waveform option, and had a three-octave frequency register and control register (setting the distortion and its volume). One of the more advanced chips, the Curtis CEM3394, was introduced in 1984, but was used in only a handful of games. It had a single voice per chip, but that voice had selectable pulse, triangle, and sawtooth waveforms, rather than just the square waves of other PSG chips. Most games that used the chip had several of them on board – up to six, as in *Chicken Shift*, for example.[23]

Early games also used sound samples created with digital-to-analog converters (DACs) or pulse code modulation (PCM).[24] The downside to PCM sampling was the amount of space required to store the samples: as a result, most PCM samples were limited to those sounds with a short envelope, such as percussion and sound effects, which were suitable, as mentioned, for arcades requiring lots of explosive sounds to attract players, but unsuitable at the time for musical purposes. This could be one reason why we see advanced sound effects at a time of limited musical capabilities.[25] Speech chips, which could be used for short vocal samples or for sound effects, also became more prominent in the mid-1980s.[26] With separate chips to handle sound effects and voice, the primary sound-chip's noise channel could be freed up, allowing for the use of more complex percussion in the music, such as in *Discs of Tron*.

The sound chip in the Atari VCS, which also controlled graphics, was manufactured specifically by Atari and was known as the TIA chip. The audio portion had just two channels, so that music and sound effects could only be heard on two simultaneous voices mixed into a mono output. Each channel had a 4-bit waveform-control selector, but, of the sixteen possible settings, several were the same as or similar to others. Typically, the voice options were two square waves (one high, one bass), one sine wave, one saw wave, and several noise-based sound options useful for effects or percussion. The trouble with the tonal sounds, however, was that each had a different tuning (although two of the square-wave sounds were almost the same tuning), so the pitch value of the bass and the lead voice would often be different. Tuning sets could be quite variable, then, as some sets would allow for more bass notes, while others would allow for more treble, and since many sets would have conflicting tunings between bass and treble, they were, for most tonal compositional purposes, quite useless. To compound the problem, there were variations between the sound on the NTSC and PAL versions of the machine.[27] At times, pitches were awry by as much as fifty cents (half a semitone) between the European and American models.

The Nintendo Entertainment System's (NES) sound chip, created by composer Yukio Kaneoka and more advanced than that of the Atari, used a built-in five-channel PSG delivering two pulse waves, a triangle wave, a noise channel, and a sample channel. The pulse channels had an 11-bit frequency control, capable of about eight octaves, and four duty-cycle options (altering the harmonics to create a sound that could be quite smooth, but also, with adjustments, 'fat', or thin and 'raspy'). In addition, the channels had a 4-bit amplitude-envelope function, and one of the pulse-wave channels had a frequency-sweep function that could create portamento-like effects. The triangle-wave channel was one octave lower than that of the pulse waves, had only a 4-bit frequency control, and had no volume or envelope control. The fifth channel was a sampler, also known as the Delta Modulation Channel (DMC). There were two basic methods of sampling using this channel: PCM, used for speech, such as in *Mike Tyson's Punchout*; and direct memory access (DMA), which was only 1-bit and was most frequently used for percussion and sound effects.

While Nintendo represented the peak of console audio in the 8-bit era, the Commodore 64 (C64) was far in advance of other home PCs, having been originally conceived as a games computer, with sophisticated (for the time) graphics and sound designed to entice consumers frightened off by the more business-like IBMs. The sound chip (called the Sound Interface Device, or SID) was a three-plus-one generator chip, created by Bob Yannes in 1981.[28] Each tone on the chip could be selected from a range of waveforms – sawtooth, triangle, variable pulse (square wave), and noise. An independent ADSR envelope generator for each channel enabled the SID to imitate traditional instruments more accurately than did previous chips.[29] Each tone could also be subjected to a variety of effects and programmable filters, including ring modulation, commonly for sound effects like bells, chimes, and gongs. The noise channel of the C64 could also operate as a simple pulse-width modulation (PWM) sampler. PWM was used for sampling and to simulate a low-frequency oscillator (LFO) and could simulate a tremolo effect. The ability to sample sounds led to the inclusion of more realistic sound effects in many C64 games tunes. *Turbo Outrun*, for instance, included a 'scratch' sound and voice samples, as well as samples of pitched percussion instruments.

Early sound programmers and musicians needed to understand assembly language to engage the chips, which meant that most of the early composers for games were, in fact, programmers working on other aspects of a game. It is unsurprising, then, that many early games tended to employ pre-existing popular or classical music rather than specially composed music.[30] The fact that the audio programmers were often not musicians could also explain why, even after some of the earliest constraints were lifted, music was thrust to the side in favour of more advanced sound effects. It was, therefore, a combination of the technological constraints of the time and the social constraints surrounding the specialized knowledge required to engage the chips that helped to create the unique aesthetic of early games audio.

The clearest evidence of these constraints was the lack of music in many of the earliest games. Typically, arcade games of the late 1970s had short title and game-over music. Otherwise the music would usually play only when there was no game action, and would be composed with simple DAC samples, as *Circus* and *Rip Cord* illustrate. Gameplay music was introduced as early as 1978, when continuous sound began to be added, as in *Space Invaders* and *Asteroids*. Arguably, these games represent the first examples of dynamic non-diegetic music in a game: the music of *Asteroids* was limited to an accelerating two-note melody, and *Space Invaders'* descending, looping four-tone marching of alien feet sped up as the game progressed.

By 1980 arcade manufacturers were including PSG chips in their machines more often, and more melodic music began to take off. The earliest examples of musical loops in games date from this time: for instance, *Rally X*, which had a six-bar loop, and *Carnival*, which used Juventino Rosas's 'Over the Waves' waltz (1889). Most arcade games now had co-processors specifically to control sound, allowing for the simultaneous playing of action and music, although the majority still had no background music. By 1982 it became increasingly common to use more than one sound chip in a coin-operated game. In this way the music could continue to play without being interrupted by the sound effects having to use the same chip. But the additional sound chips tended to be used for more advanced sound effects rather than for an increase in the textural complexity of the music, for reasons to do with the arcade environment (as mentioned previously, subtleties of polyphony are unlikely to be captured in such an atmosphere), or with the fact that most early programmers were not musicians and were therefore more comfortable with sound effects. The trouble with using multiple chips became evident in some of these games: in *Chicken Shift*, for example, which used diegetic as well as non-diegetic music, the various sound sources often conflicted with each other, as when one song continued under lose/win cues and sound effects, resulting in a hilariously chaotic cacophony of noise. Generally speaking, the inclusion of background music, however simple, was not well established until long after the capabilities existed.

As with the arcade machines, the music of the domestic games consoles reflects their technological constrictions. The most obvious consequence of the tuning problems of the Atari VCS (discussed above) was the avoidance of harmony. The fact that the tuning could differ between different voices (for instance, a G may be available in the bass, but only a G $^{\#}$ in the treble) complicated the programming of harmony, and it is little wonder that few games had songs with both bass and treble voices. Another effect was the inclusion of less common intervals, such as the prominence of minor seconds in the songs, which was due to the reduced number of notes available.[31] A comparison of the same games on the VCS console with those on the arcade machines shows these constraints in action. Most Atari songs would drop the bass line, as in *Qbert* and *Crazy Climber*. The tunes for *Up 'n Down* had a noticeably different flavour (see Example 1), suggesting that the Atari's tunings may have had a significant role to play in the prominence of minor seconds: the tune changes from a bluesy F #-minor groove to a very unsettling version based in C minor, with a D♭, in the upper register.

The Nintendo Entertainment System (NES), by comparison, had a much wider tonal range, although the use of the tone channels reflects the constraints of its chip: typically, the two pulse channels provided chords or a solo lead, with the triangle channel acting as a bass accompaniment. The most obvious rationale for using the triangle as the bass was the limitations of the channel: the lower pitch, the reduced frequencies, and the lack of volume control. These limitations

Example 1 Music for *Up 'n Down*: (a) Arcade version (Sega 1983: 2 × SN76496); (b) Atari VCS version (Sega 1983).

meant that many of the effects that could be simulated with the pulse waves were unavailable for the triangle wave, such as the vibrato (pitch modulation), tremolo (volume modulation), slides, portamento, and so on. Also, by altering the volume and adjusting the timing between the two pulse channels, echo effects could be simulated, as in *Metroid*, a science-fiction game with an unusually eerie soundtrack.

As was the case with the other 8-bit systems, most Commodore 64 games of the first few years had very little music, and almost no background music. In fact, in contrast with the NES, some of the popular games, even those launched in the late 1980s, had little or no music of any sort. Of the 'Top 100 C64 games',[32] about ten percent had no background music at all, and the earliest examples of games – those dating from about 1983 to 1985 – had the least amount of music. Typically, music was only used outside of gameplay. The clearest examples of this are in the *California Games* series, in which there were simple background-music introductions to events, but the music stopped as soon as the event (and therefore gameplay) began. By the late 1980s and early 1990s, when the 16-bit machines (Super NES, Sega Mega Drive/Genesis) began entering the market, a change occurred, and the games were increasingly likely to have more non-diegetic music. This suggests that the pressure of the games systems market led Commodore to attempt to emulate or adapt to the games audio aesthetic of the other available systems.

Two major factors played a part in the creation of audio for the C64: the music on the Commodore was coded in assembly language, which was harder to program than NES's BASIC-based language, and the availability of memory. The fact that systems such as the Nintendo had an (arguably) inferior sound chip to that of the Commodore, but had more gameplay music, suggests that there is some correlation between the provision of music and the storage capacity of the games cartridges. Whereas most C64 games averaged about 30 kB (on cassette), 10 kB (on cartridges), or 60 kB (to a maximum of 170 kB) on a floppy disk before having to go to a multi-disk game, Nintendo's cartridges held up to 512 kB; and with the use of memory management chips, some games (such as *Kirby's Adventure*) could be expanded to 768 kB. The issue of memory was clearly linked to the amount of looping in the games. As one Commodore programmer/composer explains of a cover version of the *Short Circuit* movie theme used in a game, 'the [song conversion] was a nightmare since it's the tune right from the beginning of the movie with all the robotic short notes and arpeggios. The tune just built up so massive [*sic*] that the poor C64 was short of notes by about 30 seconds into it, so I had to fudge the end a bit and make it repeat, basically.'[33]

Despite a few early exceptions, it was not until about 1984 that looping began to gain prominence in games. This is most obvious when examining the ColecoVision games: there is a clear division between the mostly non-looping games of 1982 and 1983[34] and the games of 1984, most of which have loops.[35] A similar effect is evident in Nintendo's early games: the very first games – *Donkey Kong*, *Donkey Kong Jr*, *Popeye*, and *Devil World* – had only very short one- or two-bar loops (*Popeye*'s loop was eight bars, but it was the same two-bar melody at different pitches), whereas later games have much more extensive loops.[36] It would appear, then, that rather than being the consequence of the limited memory available on the systems, loops were, at least *in part*, an aesthetic that grew as the games became more popular and more complex. It could be that they were also reflecting the popular music of the time, as techno and hip hop were beginning to see mainstream exposure.

Approaches to looping in 8-bit audio

There were some interesting responses to the technology's limits. Composer Rob Hubbard partially overcame the memory constraints of the C64 by arranging code for the music in a series of modules containing a set of songs.[37] Each module may contain title music, in-game music, and game-over music using the same source code to share instrument tables and thus save space (each different timbre used in the game was set out in a table in advance and called upon when needed). Typically, each song had three separate instrumental sounds (one for each channel), and each of these was made up of a list of patterns (sequences) in the order in which they were to be played. The code would then refer to specific sections of the module, which were called upon when necessary, reducing the need to repeat coding and thus save valuable space. This module format, emulated by other composers, lent itself well to looping. Despite the fact that looping was often a result of technological constraint, there were many different approaches to the loop in 8-bit games. These can be summarized into five categories, which I shall now explore in further detail: accumulative form, random loops, pattern repeats in different registers, a mesoloop-built song, and variations in the order and length of loops.

Accumulative form (the gradual building up of a groove by adding sequential units cumulatively)[38] was reliant on smaller formal units (micro- or mesoloops) within larger compositions. Each small unit could be called up once and then repeated, in terraced fashion, so that it would not tax the memory of the machine. Evidence of this approach is seen in Commodore 64's *Tetris*. Not having the selectable looping background music that was an option on the NES, Wally Beben composed original music – one very long track (about 26 minutes: 13 kB) of smaller loops (see Example 2). In order to save space, certain micro- and mesoloops repeat (the bass/percussion line that begins the song repeats just one bar for about half the song, for instance) while a number of melodies are superimposed on to various accompaniments.

A second approach to space constraints – random generation – was seen occasionally in the arcades and on the Commodore. The coin-operated game *Frogger*, for instance, in which the player guides a frog past cars and over moving logs into a series of four 'safe' houses, used at least eleven different songs. The game begins in what I shall term the 'home' song, and when the player successfully guides a frog into a safe house, the song will switch to another song quite abruptly and then continue until the frog has either moved successfully into another safe house, at which point there is a new song, or died, in which case the music returns to the 'home' song. Since the maximum time that gameplay could continue before arriving at a safe house or dying was 27 seconds (much less as the levels increased and gameplay sped up), the songs did not rely on loops. Similarly, Jetsoft's *Cavelon* used what appears to be a random looping of sequences. The player moves about the screen capturing pieces of a door. Each time the player stops moving, the music stops. When the player obtains a piece of door, a brief win-item cue is heard and the loop changes randomly into a new sequence.

Some Commodore 64 composers were also adventurous with their coding, including the use of random number generators into the code to select from a group of loop options. For instance, *Times of Lore* used a random selection of guitar solos for the eleven-minute duration of the song. In this way the game's ten songs (comprising over thirty minutes of music) could fit into just 923 bytes, and the music sound a lot more varied than it otherwise would.[39] Random generation was also used in *Rock Star Ate my Hamster*, a rock management game in which a band practises, accompanied by a tune that draws from a random combination of sixteen sequences. In *California Games* random generation is built into the half-pipe event. Here, an opening sequence plays for seven seconds, followed (as long as the player stays up) by a random sequence drawing on a collection of sixteen possible choices, each one twenty-three seconds long. If the player falls, the first segment repeats.

Example 2 Music for the first part of *Tetris* (Wally Beben, Mirrorsoft 1987), Commodore 64.

a.

b.

Example 3 Music for *Lazy Jones* (Terminal Software 1984), Commodore 64: (a) 8-bar
track 1 (main gameplay) (b) 4-bar track 21.

The Atari VCS's *Clown Down Town* also offers a very unusual example of an
approach to looping. Its nearly atonal effect results from a mesoloop that repeats in
other registers and keys. Although looping was far less common on the VCS than
on other systems of the time – most likely because of memory limitations – the
character of this track suggests, perhaps, that if the gameplay was uncomplicated
and therefore did not take too much memory, the capabilities for longer tracks did
exist but were not exploited.

Another approach to looping was to use mesoloops that built up into one longer
song, as in the C64 game *Lazy Jones*, which had twenty-one mesoloops that were
selected in turn when the character entered or left one of the 'room' levels of
gameplay. There were eighteen rooms in total, and each room had its own four-
bar 'song' or mesoloop, which actually played like a segment of one greater
macroloop song (the title music). Even if the character left the room at, say, bar 3,
the rest of the loop would play before it would transition seamlessly back into the
theme song. Most of the loops worked well together, in part owing to the ragtime-
like microlooped bass lines, the similarity of timbres employed, and the fact that
the game used only two channels (see Example 3).

Finally, the length and order of loops were significantly different among
games, platforms, and genres. As the NES was the 8-bit system with the most
standardized background looping (both interactive and non-interactive), I focus
on it in the following discussion. Loops on the NES were of varying lengths,
depending on the genre: role-playing games and platform adventure games had

the longest loops; fighting games and arcade-like games, short loops; and puzzle games, mid-length loops. Racing games had little non-diegetic music (most just had engine sounds during gameplay), and flight simulators tended to be silent. The loops on the NES ranged in length from very short (5–10 seconds), to medium length (10–30 seconds), to very long (the longest I found was about a minute and a half). Most loops averaged about thirty seconds and consisted of four or five different sections. The longest loops were present in the adventure-style games, probably because players would spend longer on them than on other games, since they were designed to last for many hours before ending: a short loop would rapidly become irritating to the player.

Some other games looped only the last section in the song, rather than the entire song, as in the title themes to *Metroid* and *Lagrange Point*. In these cases there is therefore a mesoloop but no macroloop (A B C ||: D:||). The most obvious explanation for this type of loop is that the title themes were not meant to be left on: once the introduction and credits were played, the player would probably begin the game rather than finish listening to the music – a clear case of function leading the form. Some songs also had brief intros that were not included in the loop. So, for instance, *Castlevania* level 2 has a brief intro and then a looped segment that skips the intro (A||: B C D E:||). The 'overworld' or game level loops (the longest sections of gameplay) were typically the longest loops (30–90 seconds), containing the most varied and the longest sections.[40] Battle music (or 'boss' music) usually had much shorter loops than other sections, with only one or two mesoloops, the likely reason being that the quick succession added to the tension, and the fact that this part of the game usually lasted only a few seconds. There were several variations at the point of looping: typically, either the loop was designed so that the last section would fit seamlessly with the return to the beginning, or a small transitional bridge was made in between loops. Transitions commonly used a glissando or a rising scale lasting one or two bars.

The loops were built in sections ranging from one to eight bars. These might repeat, but were usually found in the macroloop only once, one after the other, before progressing to a new section, and rarely returning to the original unless the entire loop was beginning anew. Looking in more detail, we can break down each section to see the looping aspect of several songs. For instance, the sixteen-bar level 1 music of *Castlevania* (see Figure 1a) has a one-bar intro (A) that loops itself once before moving to B, which has a two-bar mesoloop (B and B'); this two-bar pattern also loops once. The C and D sections also have two-bar mesoloops that repeat once, and then the E section has one bar that loops. This entire A–E element then repeats in a macroloop.

In contrast, the 'Ambrosia' level music of *Ultima 3* has an eight-bar mesoloop, A, which repeats, followed by a four-bar mesoloop, B, which repeats, and a four-bar C section, which we hear only once before the entire song loops (see Figure 1b). Because of this, the macrolooping segment (sixteen bars) feels a bit less repetitive than some of the other, more rigid and straightforward loops. *Metroid's* 'Brinstar' level, on the other hand, has taken a completely different approach to the looping of sections, with most sections being a two-bar mesoloop but repeating in odd rather than even segments (see Figure 1c). By alternating the length of the mesoloops and alternating mesoloops themselves, the looping becomes less obvious and monotonous. There are also games that use less conventional looping, such as *Super Mario Bros.*, which has four-bar sections of typically two-bar mesoloops *nearly* repeating (with minor variation; see Figure 1d). This is one of the few games to repeat alternate sections before the entire song loops at the macro level.

Generally speaking, loops on the Commodore 64 were much longer than those of the NES, but this could be due to the fact that fewer songs were included overall, whereas the NES was more likely to have consistent interactive background music. It could be, however, that because the C64 developed separately in the USA rather than in Nintendo's Japanese home, its aesthetic tended towards full songs rather than short loops. In games that did have regular looping, these loop lengths were comparable to those of the NES, although there is a distinct lack of the transitional bridges seen on the NES in favour of seamless loops. In some cases, such as *Forbidden Forest*, the loops were abrupt, changing mid-stream depending on the interaction with gameplay.

By the late 1980s and early 1990s there were several Commodore games, such as *Mayhem in Monsterland* or the *Great Giana Sisters*, that clearly tried to copy the Nintendo game style. The latter was so similar to *Super Mario Bros.* that Nintendo successfully sued to have it pulled from stores. What is interesting is the fact that these games not only adopted NES-like gameplay and visuals, but also a distinctly NES style of music, suggesting that an associated, well-defined aesthetic was involved, rather than merely a technological component. Each game contained interactive background loops for 'overworlds', 'underworlds', and 'boss' music, in Nintendo style.

a. *Castlevania*, 'level 1' music (Konami/Nintendo, 1986)

Bars	1	2	3	4	5	6	7	8	9	10	11	12	13	14	15	16
Section	A	A	B	B′	B	B′	C	C′	C	C′	D	D′	D	D	E	E

b. *Ultima III: Exodus*, 'Ambrosia' level music (Origin/Nintendo, 1983)

Bars	1–8	9–16	17–20	21–4	25–8
Section	A	A	B	B	C

c. *Metroid*, 'Brinstar' level music, composed by Hirokazu 'Hip' Tanaka (Nintendo, 1986)

Bars	1–12						13–20				21–8	29–30
Section	A	A	A′	A′	A′	A	B	B	B	B′	C	Bridge

d. *Super Mario Bros.*, 'level 1: overworld' music, composed by Koji Kondo (Nintendo, 1985)

Bars	1	2–5	6–9	10–13	14–17	18–21	22–5	26–9	30–3	34–7
Section	Intro	A	B	B	C	A	D	D	C	D

Figure 1 Analysis of looping sections in four different games songs

Conclusions

The year 1984 seems to be a key point in the culmination of an 8-bit aesthetic that saw the establishment of loops, dynamic music, and various forms of polyphony. As *Tetris* and *Clown Down Town*, among others, demonstrated, since alternatives to this aesthetic were available, the games audio aesthetic was *chosen* as much as determined by the limitations of the available technology, yet each machine had a slightly different aesthetic that grew, in part, from the technology available. The most notable difference, perhaps, was that between the Commodore 64 and the NES. The extended capabilities of the C64's SID chip helped create more of a traditional rock-song approach to music, while the NES relied more on a series of loops. As composer Rob Hubbard says:

> Well, you know, part of that [sound aesthetic] is dictated by the fact that you have such limited resources. The way that you have to write, in order to create rich textures, you have to write a lot of rhythmic kinds of stuff [...] it's easier to try to make it sound a lot fuller and like you're doing a lot more if you use much shorter, more rhythmic sounds.[41]

The persistent practice of looping nicely illustrates the tensions between technology and aesthetic. As we have seen, various approaches to looping were certainly available and, at times, used. But straight short-looping remained the most prominent response to limited memory. Looping, then, appears to be as much an aesthetic choice as a factor predetermined by technology. But, as also mentioned, constraints were not just limited to the technology. The social constraints of the specialized knowledge required to programme the machines – and to write music – also impacted on the developing aesthetic, with many composers lacking formal musical training. The impact of this could very well be one of the reasons why sound effects were so prominent, and why some of the music in the 8-bit era was unconventional in many ways. After all,

> When musicians are faced with new pieces of equipment, they often tend to transfer their knowledge from previous experiences with similar equipment [...] Students often program 'outer space noises' or 'bubbling volcanos' [*sic*] because there is no need to conform to any performance standards. Is someone going to criticize your rendition of 'A Lawnmower Travelling through the center of the earth'? Certainly not, unless they are jealous because it sounds better than their 'Phase Dishwasher'.[42]

Sound aesthetics are the result of a culmination of knowledge, creativity, and constraint. Perhaps one of the reasons why we saw innovations such as the use of accumulative form and random generation was that the composers were programmers rather than musicians. We also saw that the constraints were not limited to

103

these two factors, but also to genre and gameplay narrative. For instance, *Frogger* had a specific time constraint in each level, to which the music had to keep. Sports games had little music, and role-playing games had a lot of lengthy loops.

It could also be argued that the looping elements of games audio could have been influenced by the popular music of the time. By 1984 – as we see, the real 'beginning' of the loop as a common aesthetic in games – hip hop had become mainstream, disco had come and gone, and techno was in the ascendancy. Although looping goes back further in time than these genres, by the mid-1980s looping and repetition were a distinct and important part of the popular repertoire because of the development of sequencers and drum machines. Repetition, therefore, was an aspect of games music that was as much an aesthetic choice as it was a result of the technology. It would appear, then, that despite some quite rigid technological constraints, as indicated in the Introduction, these were a 'loose pressure' on the development of games audio, rather than the deciding factor in 8-bit aesthetics.

Discography

Aphex Twin. *Pac-Man*. CD single, Ffrreedom 110. 1992.
Beck. *Hell Yes Remix*. EP, Interscope INTR-11325–1. 2005.
The Bloodhound Gang. *Hooray for Boobies*. CD, Interscope 90455. 2000.
Buckner and Garcia. *Pac-Man Fever*. CD, Columbia 37941. 1982.
DMX. *Flesh of my Flesh, Blood of my Blood*. CD, Def Jam 538640. 1998.
Lil' Flip. *U Gotta Feel Me*. CD, Sony 92411. 1998.
'Weird Al' Yancovic. *Dr Demento's Basement Tapes No. 4*. Cassette (fanclub-only release). 1981.

Games

Recordings, remixes, and MIDI versions of games music can be heard on many websites, including the Video Games Music Archive <http://VGMusic.com>, and VORC <http://www.vorc.org/>. Soundtracks featuring collections of early games sound also exist.

Arkanoid (coin-op, Nintendo Entertainment System (NES), Commodore 64). Taito, 1986. Nintendo sound composed by Hisayoshi Ogura; sound effects by Tadashi Kimijima; game designed by Akira Fujita. Commodore music composed by Martin Galway.*Asteroids* (coin-op). Atari, 1979.
Burger Time (ColecoVision). Coleco, 1984.
California Games (Commodore 64). Epyx, 1987. Music composed by Chris Grigg.
Carnival (coin-op). Sega, 1980.
Castlevania (Commodore 64, NES). Konami, 1987.
Cavelon (coin-op). Jetsoft, 1983.
Chicken Shift (coin-op). Bally, 1984.

Choplifter (ColecoVision). Coleco, 1983.

Circus (coin-op). Exidy, 1977.

Clown Down Town (Atari VCS). Walker – Rainbow Vision, date unknown.

Crazy Climber (coin-op). Midway, 1982.

Dance Aerobics (NES). Nintendo, 1989.

Devil World (Nintendo Famicom). Nintendo, 1984.

Discs of Tron (coin-op). Bally, 1983.

Donkey Kong (Nintendo Famicom/NES). Nintendo, 1982.

Donkey Kong Jr (Nintendo Famicom/NES). Nintendo, 1982.

Duck Hunt (NES). Nintendo, 1986.

Forbidden Forest (Commodore 64). Kosmi, 1983.

Frogger (coin-op). Konami, 1981.

Ghosts 'n Goblins (NES, coin-op, Commodore 64). Capcom, 1985. Commodore music composed by Mark Cooksey.

Great Giana Sisters (Commodore 64). Rainbow Arts, 1987.

Gyruss (ColecoVision). Parker Bros, 1984.

Jungle Hunt (coin-op). Atari, 1983.

Karate Champ (NES, coin-op, Commodore 64, Atari VCS). Nihon Bussan, 1984.

Kirby's Adventure (NES). Nintendo, 1993.

Lagrange Point (Famicom). Nintendo, 1989.

Lazy Jones (Commodore 64). Terminal Software, 1984.

Maniac Mansion (Commodore 64, NES). LucasArts, 1987. Music composed by Chris Grigg and David Lawrence.

Mayhem in Monsterland (Commodore 64). Apex, 1993.

Metroid (NES). Nintendo, 1986. Directed by Yoshio Sakamoto; music composed by Hirokazu Tanaka.

Mike Tyson's Punchout (NES). Nintendo, 1987.

Pac-Man (coin-op). Namco, 1980.

Popeye (NES). Nintendo, 1983.

Qbert (coin-op, Atari VCS). Parker Bros, 1983.

Rally X (coin-op). Namco, 1980.

Rip Cord (coin-op). Exidy, 1979.

Rock Star Ate my Hamster (Commodore 64). CodeMasters, 1988.

Space Invaders (coin-op). Midway, 1978.

Super Mario Bros. (NES). Nintendo, 1985. Music composed by Koji Kondo.

Tetris (Commodore 64). Mirrorsoft, 1987. Music composed by Wally Beben.

Times of Lore (Commodore 64). Microprose, 1988. Music composed by Martin Galway.

Turbo Outrun (Commodore 64). Sega, 1989.

Tutankhamun (ColecoVision). Parker Bros, 1982.

Ultima 3: Exodus (NES, Commodore 64). Origin Systems, 1983. Commodore music composed by Kenneth Arnold.

Up 'n Down (coin-op, Atari VCS). Sega, 1983.

Notes

1 In Aikin, 'Brian Eno'.
2 Katz, *Capturing Sound*, 3–5; cf. McLuhan, *Understanding Media*, 283.
3 See, for example, Taylor, *Strange Sounds*, 27; Théberge, *Any Sound You Can Imagine*, 160; and Katz, *Capturing Sound*.
4 Théberge, *Any Sound You Can Imagine*, 187.
5 'Bit' refers to the smallest unit of digital data. An 8-bit machine could simultaneously process eight binary digits (bits) of data.
6 Salt, 'The Evolution of Sound Technology', 37.
7 For details of recordings see Discography below.
8 *Hell Yes Remix*; see Discography.
9 Jones, 'Thingo of the Week: Micromusic', *Mondo Thingo* (2005), <http://www.abc.net.au/thingo/txt/s1083340.htm> (accessed 10 November 2007).
10 Katigbak, 'Game on'.
11 Carr, 'An Interview with Anders Carlsson AKA GOTO80'.
12 The AY series of chips, for instance, was used in the Sinclair ZX Spectrum, Amstrad CPC, BBC Micro, Atari ST, Sega Master System, and many arcade machines.
13 For further details see Games list below. For a discussion of the video game genre see Wolf, 'Genre and the Video Game'.
14 That is, no copy for the new system was released.
15 'IGN's Top 100 Games', <http://top100.ign.com/2005/index.html>; 'Game Music Poll Results', <http://top100.ign.com/2005/>; 'Best Games on the NES', <http://www.amazon.com/gp/richpub/listmania/fullview/3CQFUX11P973Y/103-3964422-8647012?ie=UTF8&%2AVersion%2A=1&%2Aentries%2A=0>; 'Top 20 NES Games' <http://www.nintendo-land.com/home2.htm?charts/nes.htm> (all accessed 10 November 2007).
16 Though, of course, not without disagreement or further subdivisions (see, for example, Gorbman, *Unheard Melodies*).
17 For a more detailed discussion of interactivity and dynamic audio see Collins, 'An Introduction to the Participatory and Non-Linear Aspects of Video Games Audio'.
18 These are my own distinctions and are not commonly used by games composers, or in early programming languages such as BASIC, which typically distinguished only between 'foreground' and 'background' sound. There are also a few cases of what I have termed 'kinetically gestural interactive sound' in 8-bit games, although this is extremely rare and so is left out of the discussion here. This refers to sound or music that occurs when the player, along with the character, physically interacts with the sound, such as in *Duck Hunt*, in which the player fires a gun at ducks, making shooting noises, or in *Dance Aerobics*, which required a 'power pad' on which the player would stand, interacting with the music.
19 A cut-scene is a movie that plays in a game, in which the player does not control any actions.
20 Stillar, 'Loops as Genre Resources', 199.
21 See Middleton, '"Over and Over"'.
22 For a basic introduction to waveforms and bit depths see Adobe's 'A Digital Audio Primer' at <http://www.adobe.com/products/audition/pdfs/audaudioprimer.pdf> (accessed 10 November 2007).
23 The technical specs for sound chips and consoles have been published in many places on the Internet. Many of these specs were originally released to programmers or in manuals so that users could program the chip, and they have since been published by fans, chiptunes creators, or those designing emulators – software versions of the consoles or computers for today's PC users. The MAME arcade emulator allows users to see the technical data of what chips were originally used for each game, and it gives accurate information on the emulation.

24 DACs typically used 6- or 8-bit digital values, with up to 256 different voltage levels. The programmer chose a sequence of numbers between 1 and 256 to determine the speed (and therefore the resulting frequency) of the sound. With PCM, essentially, an analog sound is converted into digital sound by taking many small samples of an analog waveform. The data is stored in binary, which is then decoded and played back. The fidelity of the sound depends on the sample rate or quantization – the number of bits representing the amplitude. The method is still used, for instance for DVDs or CDs, where the sample rate is 44 kHz, or 16-bit, but most early games could sample at a maximum of 22 kHz only.

25 One solution to the size issue was what is known as adaptive difference PCM (ADPCM). With the ADPCM method, the difference between two adjacent sample values is quantified, reducing or increasing the pitch slightly so as to decrease the amount of data required; this is somewhat similar to the way in which JPEG compresses a visual image. The fidelity of the sound, however, is reduced as compression rates are increased.

26 A variety of different types of speech chips were used, including ADPCM, PCM, and linear predictive coding (LPC). In several games Atari included a Texas Instruments TMS5220 (LPC) chip, which had been used in 'Speak 'n' Spell', the popular family electronic game.

27 Eckhard Stolberg explains the difference as follows: 'The Atari 2600 VCS produces it's [sic] sound with some shift registers of various lengths. The speed at which it shifts the registers can be set to either the pixelclock/114 or to the CPUclock/114, which means two shifts per scanline or a third of this. Since a NTSC VCS produces 262 scanlines per frame and 60 frames per second this results in output rates of 31440 Hz and 10480 Hz. PAL TVs produce only 312 scanlines and 50 frames, so the output rates are only 31200 Hz and 10400 Hz' (Stolberg, 'Atari 2600 VCS Sound Frequency and Waveform Guide').

28 Yannes had helped engineer Commodore's VIC-20, and would later go on to create the DOC chip for the 16-bit Apple IIGS and to found Ensoniq keyboards.

29 The tone oscillators had a range of between 0 and 3995 Hz, approximately the same range as a piano. There were two 8-bit registers for each channel, controlling frequency (meaning 16 bits in total, or 65,536 frequency possibilities for each voice, so that composers could 'detune' notes if they wished).

30 See Collins, 'Loops and Bloops'.

31 See Collins, 'Flat Twos and the Musical Aesthetic of the Atari VCS'.

32 According to downloads from <http://www.c64.com/> (accessed 30 October 2007).

33 Martin Galway interview, <http://www.c64hq.com/> (accessed 30 October 2007).

34 For instance, *Tutankhamun* (Parker Bros), *Jungle Hunt* (Atari), or *Choplifter* (Coleco).

35 For instance, *Gyruss* (Parker Bros), *Burger Time* (Coleco), or *Up 'n Down* (Sega).

36 All were released by Nintendo. For the NES, *Donkey Kong*, *Donkey Kong Jr*, and *Popeye* were released in 1986, but on the Famicom (the Japanese version), *Donkey Kong* and *Jr* were released in 1982, *Popeye* in 1983, and *Devil World* in 1984.

37 By using the RanSID Analyzer, it is possible to disassemble the code of SID tunes to see the way in which songs were written.

38 For an examination of accumulative form in popular music see Spicer, '(Ac)cumulative Form in Pop-Rock Music'.

39 Martin Galway on *Times of Lore* in *SIDfind*, <http://www.c64.org/sidfind/> (accessed 30 October 2007).

40 Many adventure games have 'overworlds' and 'underworlds', a light-side, aboveground setting versus an underground, dark and more dangerous setting. Typically, in a game such as *Super Mario Bros.*, one level may contain three 'overworlds', where players increase basic skills before facing the fourth, 'underworld' section of the level.

41 Rob Hubbard interview, <http://www.freenetpages.co.uk/hp/tcworh/int_6581.htm> (accessed 23 November 2005).

42 Righter and Mercuri, 'The Yamaha DX-7 Synthesizer'.

Bibliography

Aikin, Jim. 'Brian Eno'. *Keyboard* 7 (July 1981). Extract at <http://www.specht-h.at/ interview.htm> (accessed 30 October 2007).

Carr, Neil. 'An Interview with Anders Carlsson AKA GOTO80'. <http://www.remix64. com/index.php?interview_ anders_carlsson_aka_goto80> (accessed 30 October 2007).

Collins, Karen. 'Loops and Bloops: Music on the Commodore 64'. *Soundscapes: Journal on Media Culture* 8 (February 2006). <http://www.icce.rug.nl/~soundscapes/> (accessed 30 October 2007).

——. 'Flat Twos and the Musical Aesthetic of the Atari VCS'. *Popular Musicology Online*, Issue 1: *Musicological Critique* (June 2006). <http://www.popular-musicology-online.com/> (accessed 30 October 2007).

——. 'An Introduction to the Participatory and Non-Linear Aspects of Video Games Audio', in *Essays on Sound and Vision*, ed. Stan Hawkins and John Richardson. Helsinki: Helsinki University Press, 2007. 263–98.

Gorbman, Claudia. *Unheard Melodies: Narrative Film Music*. Indiana: Indiana University Press, 1987.

Katigbak, Raf. 'Game on'. *Montreal Mirror*, 27 October 2004. <http://www.montrealmirror. com/2004/102104/ nightlife2.html> (accessed 30 October 2007).

Katz, Mark. *Capturing Sound: How Technology has Changed Music*. Berkeley: University of California Press, 2004.

McLuhan, Marshall. *Understanding Media: the Extensions of Man*. Toronto: McGraw-Hill, 1964.

Middleton, Richard. '"Over and Over": Notes towards a Politics of Repetition. Surveying the Ground, Charting Some Routes'. Paper presented at the conference *Grounding Music for the Global Age*, Berlin, May 1996. Available at http://www2.rz.hu-berlin.de/ fpm/texte/middle.htm> (accessed 30 October 2007).

Peters, Michael. 'The Birth of Loop' (1996, modified 2004, 2006). <http://www.loopers-delight.com/history/ Loophist.html> (accessed 30 October 2007).

Pouladi, Ali. 'An Interview with Ben Daglish'. *Lemon* 64 (June 2004). <http://www. lemon64.com/interviews/ ben_daglish.php> (accessed 30 October 2007).

Righter, Dennis, and Rebecca Mercuri. 'The Yamaha DX-7 Synthesizer: a New Tool for Teachers', in *Proceedings of the 5th Symposium on Small Computers in the Arts*. Philadelphia: IEEE Computer Society Press, 1985.

Salt, Barry. 'The Evolution of Sound Technology', in *Film Sound: Theory and Practice*, ed. Elisabeth Weis and John Belton. New York: Columbia University Press, 1985. 37–43.

Spicer, Mark. '(Ac)cumulative Form in Pop-Rock Music'. *Twentieth-Century Music* 1/1 (2004), 29–64.

Stillar, Glenn. 'Loops as Genre Resources'. *Folia Linguistica* 39/1–2 (2005), 197–212.

Stolberg, Eckhard. 'Atari 2600 VCS Sound Frequency and Waveform Guide' (2000). <http://home.arcor.de/estolberg/texts/freqform.txt> (accessed 30 October 2007).

Taylor, Timothy D. *Strange Sounds: Music, Technology and Culture*. New York: Routledge, 2001.

Théberge, Paul. *Any Sound You Can Imagine: Making Music/Consuming Technology*. Hanover, NH: Wesleyan University Press, 1997.

Wolf, Mark J. P. 'Genre and the Video Game', in *The Medium of the Video Game*, ed. Wolf, foreword by Ralph H. Baer. Austin: University of Texas Press, 2001. 113–34.

29

PAC-MAN

Nick Montfort and Ian Bogost

Source: *Racing the Beam: The Atari Video Computer System* (Cambridge, MA: The MIT Press, 2009), pp. 65–79.

The arcade-inspired *Combat* was not difficult to fit onto the Atari VCS. It was one of the games developed alongside the console's hardware, influencing the latter's design. *Adventure* was inspired by *Colossal Cave Adventure*, but Robinett thoroughly reimagined the text game for the VCS platform, creating something with very different appearance and different gameplay. When Atari acquired the home console rights to Namco's hit arcade game *Pac-Man*, the company faced a different problem: that of porting the massively popular and recognizable game from a platform with totally different technical affordances.

Chasing the blinking coin-ops

In the late 1970s, space shooters like *Asteroids*, *Space Invaders*, and *Galaxian* reigned in the arcades. Sports-themed games like *Pong*, war games like *Tank* and *Battlezone*, and driving games like *Night Driver* filled out the typical tavern and arcade fare. Toru Iwatani, a Japanese designer, wanted to create a different game, one that would appeal to a broader set of players. Classic *Pac-Man* lore holds that Iwatani was pondering this design problem as he was eating a pizza. Looking at the pie with one slice removed, he saw a head with its mouth agape and imagined it as an anthropomorphized character who would eat things.[1] Iwatani devised the maze as a way to structure the eating, and gave the game the title *Pakku-Man*, derived from the Japanese onomatopoeia "paku-paku"—the sound of an opening and closing mouth during eating.

Pac-Man did fairly well in Japan, but the game enjoyed wild success in the United States. *Pac-Man* was more than a video game; it was a cultural sensation, featured on the cover of *Time* and spawning dozens of licensed products including clothing, trading cards, cereal, board games, a record (*Pac-Man Fever*), television shows, and consumer goods. There are many reasons for the game's success. Novelty was undoubtedly a part of it. Journalist Chris Green has argued that *Pac-Man* filled a space in popular culture between the second and third *Star Wars* films, making it a cornerstone in 1980s popular culture. But beyond these feats of novelty and timing, *Pac-Man* was, and perhaps still is, a game that everyone will be happy to play. The game's colorful, friendly characters made everyone want to try it—boys and girls, men and women alike. Green explained:

> *Pac-Man* feels like a cartoon, from the bouncy theme music to the animated eyes on the ghosts to the forlorn sound effect as Pac-Man is apprehended and shrinks away to nothingness. Far more so than any other game before it (and many that came after), *Pac-Man* possessed elements of drama, giving names to its avatars and featuring them in brief comic interludes that played out after the player had achieved a certain level of success.[2]

It was into this cultural context that Atari released its VCS version of *Pac-Man* in 1982. The home videogame market operated alongside the arcade videogame marketplace, both enjoying significant popular and financial success. Arcade games continued to be built on ever more sophisticated technical infrastructures—ones that were increasingly distant from the Atari VCS, whose design was now more than half a decade old. Still, the massive popularity of arcade games motivated ports of these increasingly sophisticated popular coin-op games. After the VCS port of *Space Invaders* enjoyed considerable success, partly rescuing Atari from the losses of 1977–1978, the company became even more interested in arcade ports. *Pac-Man* seemed like a fruit ripe for the plucking, or perhaps even the key to Atari's continued success.

From a very high level, at a glance, a VCS *Pac-Man* conversion might seem like it would be straightforward. Although *Adventure* was a huge risk—a game totally different in form from those that preceded it—the PDP-10 *Adventure* was also entirely unknown to a popular audience, so VCS consumers had no basis for comparison. *Pac-Man* involved adapting an extremely prominent arcade title whose gameplay, graphics, sounds, and even iconography and packaging were universally understood and already based on graphical display and collisions. The reality of the project was quite challenging. The game was programmed by Tod Frye in an irrationally short time: six weeks. Worse, the game was to be manufactured as a 4K ROM rather than using the 8K bank-switched ROM that had become possible by this time. This approach was taken to save money on what would become an irresponsibly large production run of more than ten million cartridges.

Adaptation is a long-standing concern in cultural forms of all kinds. In 1972, the year of *Pong*, the film adaptation of the Mario Puzo book *The Godfather* won the Academy Award for Best Picture. In 1980, the year *Pac-Man* ruled the arcade, the Oscar went to another film developed from a book, Robert Redford's adaptation of Judith Guest's 1976 novel *Ordinary People*. Adapting novels to films is not always simple, but both media forms are good at telling stories with strong, deep, subtle characterization. Adapting films to video games poses a different set of challenges, as is discussed in chapter 7.

Pac-Man, of course, was already a video game before it was a VCS cartridge. Porting a graphical video game from one computer platform (the arcade board) to another (the Atari VCS) does not demand a change in fundamental representational or functional mode. Both versions are games, rule-based representations of an abstract challenge of hunter and hunted. Where the two versions diverge is in their technical foundations—in their platforms. And in the case of this title, those differences were significant enough to doom the VCS rendition of Pac-Man, by some accounts even causing a major crash in the videogame market during 1983.

Bitmaps and mazes

The Pac-Man coin-op cabinet ran on a custom-made arcade system board. (Later, Rally X and Ms. Pac-Man used the same board.) It featured a Zilog Z80 CPU, a cheap eight-bit microprocessor that, along with the 6502, dominated the microcontroller market of the 1970s and 1980s.[3] At this time, arcade hardware was still much more advanced than home console hardware, because the latter needed to be so much cheaper to make home machines affordable. The Z80 CPU runs three times as fast as the 6502, but more significant differences are seen in the amounts of RAM and ROM. Pac-Man's boards hold 16K of ROM, 2K of video RAM, and 2K of general RAM. The VCS Pac-Man cartridge is has only 4K, a quarter of the ROM in Pac-Man's arcade incarnation. The 2K of RAM on the coin-op's board is sixteen times the amount in the Atari VCS. The home system, of course, has no video memory.

More important than the sheer amount of memory afforded by the arcade cabinet is how it was allocated and organized. Pac-Man's video display supports a resolution of 224×228 pixels, split up into a 28×36 grid of "characters" of 8×8 pixels each. In Pac-Man's case, a character is not a letter or number, but a bitmap tile. The 2K of video RAM is logically spit into two 1K segments, with one kilobyte used for character definitions and one for character colors. 1K is not enough storage to hold 224 eight pixel-square bitmaps, and the same number of palette colors would need to be stored somewhere, too. The coin-op is set up so that this space is used to store references to bitmap and color data. The program draws the video display by taking the character and color references in VRAM and looking up a corresponding bitmap or color defined in another 4K ROM chip soldered to the board. It is this 4K ROM that holds graphical data such as the maze parts, letters, and numeric digits.

Even before we get to the game's hero and villains, Pac-Man's method of drawing the maze demonstrates one of the major challenges in porting the game to the Atari VCS: time. In the arcade game, the programmer would load character values into video RAM once per maze, using the character tiles to create its boundaries. On the VCS, the maze is constructed from playfield graphics, each line of which has to be loaded from ROM and drawn separately for each scan line of the television display.

To be sure, mazes had already been displayed and explored in VCS games like Combat, Slot Racers, and Adventure. But these games had to construct their mazes from whole cloth, building them out of symmetrical playfields. The arcade

111

incarnation of *Pac-Mac* demonstrates how the notion of the maze became more tightly coupled to the hardware affordances of tile-based video systems. In the arcade game, each thin wall, dot, or energizer is created by a single character from video memory. Though the method is somewhat arcane, the coin-op *Pac-Man* also allowed up to four colors per character in an eight-bit color space. (Each character defined six high bits as a "base" color—which is actually a reference to a color map of 256 unique colors stored in ROM—with two low bits added for each pixel of the bitmap.) This method allows the hollow, round-edged shapes that characterize the *Pac-Man* maze—a type of bitmap detail unavailable via VCS playfield graphics. The maze of the VCS game is simplified in structure as well as in appearance, consisting of rectangular paths and longer straight-line corridors and lacking the more intricate pathways of the arcade game (Figure 1).

The arcade *Pac-Man*'s hardware also makes keeping track of the state of the maze relatively simple. Each pellet has a unique location on the tile grid. When a pellet is eaten, the program clears the corresponding character in memory, resulting in a plain black background. Tracking and displaying the current state of the pellets on the VCS is much more challenging. The pellets of the VCS *Pac-Man* are far fewer than the dots in an arcade *Pac-Man* maze, and are drawn using the same playfield graphics that define the maze borders. Because playfield graphics are used, the pellets are the same color as the walls, and are thin rectangles instead of dots—each pellet is composed of the smallest block of playfield available. The manual that comes with the VCS game tries to apologize for this divergence from the arcade version by renaming the pellets "video wafers."

The playfield, as previously noted, is formed using 20 bits of data, which are either doubled or mirrored, depending on the way the CTRLPF register is set. The original *Pac-Man* maze is horizontally symmetrical, which is very convenient. The pellets, however, disappear as the player eats them, and it is obviously impossible for *Pac-Man* to eat pellets symmetrically.

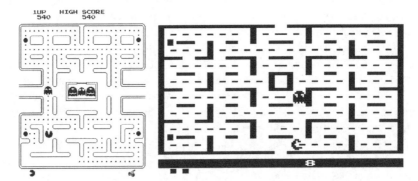

Figure 1 In the arcade *Pac-Man*, shown on the left, the screen is constructed of fairly high-resolution "characters," which are commonly called "tiles." What was possible on the Atari VCS using playfield graphics, as seen on the right, is not as impressive

To address this challenge, Frye employed a technique for drawing asymmetric playfields. To do this, the program must first set the playfield register graphics for the left half of the screen during horizontal blank. Then, as the electron beam passes across the screen, it must change those registers just before the second half of the screen starts. This technique requires careful processor timing as well as additional RAM storage for the state of each pellet. Worse yet, the positions for each remaining pellet need to be translated from data in RAM into the unique display requirements of the TIA playfield, which does not simply write its two and a half bytes in consecutive, high-to-low bit order. To get the dots on the screen, the program tracks their states separately from their positions on-screen, performing a series of computationally expensive bitwise operations to install the pellet data into the maze playfield locations, which in turn use up valuable RAM. Maze and pellet logic—relatively simple for the arcade cabinet, given its hardware affordances—were very challenging on the Atari VCS.

Sprites

In computer graphics, a *sprite* is a 2D image composited onto a 2D or 3D scene. The Atari VCS was designed to support two sprites, each a single byte in size, set via two memory-mapped registers (named GRP0 and GRP1) on the TIA. This design clearly shows the influence of *Pong* and *Tank*—games that feature two opponents, each controlled by a human player.

The coin-op *Pac-Man* also uses sprites, but once again, its platform design offers considerably greater flexibility than does the Atari VCS. *Pac-Man* has five moving objects on the screen at once: four monsters and Pac-Man himself. The Atari VCS provides graphics registers for two movable sprites, enough for two tanks (*Combat*) or a key and a dragon (*Adventure*). But the *Pac-Man* arcade cabinet hardware supports eight different moving sprites, each a bitmap of 16 × 16 pixels. Each of these shares the same graphical properties as tile "characters," but they can also be moved to a specific (x, y) coordinate on-screen. Bitmap data for up to sixty-four sprite graphics is stored separately, in yet another 4K ROM, like the one used for characters. This style of sprite—a movable bitmap—later became the standard for home console hardware and was used in many systems, including the Intellivision and the NES.[4]

The nature of VCS sprites is very different. When the programmer stores a value in the GRP0 or GRP1 register, the TIA displays that eight-bit pattern on-screen. A VCS sprite is thus always eight bits wide, although the TIA provided a few ways of modifying the appearance of sprites on-screen.

Though a sprite is a 2D image, it is drawn (like everything on the Atari VCS) one line at a time. Each sprite register can contain only the one byte of data that it needs for drawing a single scan line. To draw, for instance, a *Space Invaders* sprite, the program has to load the byte of graphics for the alien invader that corresponds to the current line on the television display and store that value in the proper sprite graphics register during the horizontal blank, in between the drawing of two lines. To position a sprite vertically, the program has to keep track of which lines of the display have sprites on them, and to compare the current line to that value in memory before drawing. The sprite is laid out in memory like so:

Bit	7 6 5 4 3 2 1 0	Sprite:
Line 0	0 0 1 1 1 1 0 0	XXXX
Line 1	0 1 1 1 1 1 1 0	XXXXXX
Line 2	0 1 0 1 1 0 1 0	X XX X
Line 3	1 1 1 1 1 1 1 1	XXXXXXXX
Line 4	1 0 1 0 0 1 0 1	X X X X
Line 5	1 0 0 1 1 0 0 1	X XX X
Line 6	0 1 0 1 1 0 1 0	X XX X
Line 7	0 1 0 1 1 0 1 0	X XX X
Line 8	0 1 0 0 0 0 1 0	X X

For both the Pac-Man character and the ghosts, the same sprite graphics can be used whether the character is facing left or right. The Atari VCS (like the arcade cabinet) provides a register switch that automatically flips the sprite graphics horizontally. The VCS Pac-Man character always faces to the side—never up or down. If VCS *Pac-Man* were able to look in those two directions, another two sets of three-frame animations would have been needed. Although the arcade board provides a facility for vertical sprite flipping in hardware, the very idea of such mirroring doesn't even make sense on the VCS, as the programmer must manually set up and draw sprites on an individual scan-line basis, not as a bitmap at a Cartesian coordinate.

Sprite graphics take up precious space in ROM. In the VCS *Pac-Man*, each sprite is eight blocks high, requiring eight total bytes to store. The game uses two sprite images for the ghosts—one for their normal state and one for their eaten state. Neither of these includes extra frames for animation. Pac-Man himself animates in three frames when he eats and in six frames when he is touched by a ghost and disappears. All together, that amounts to nine sprites, each one byte wide and eight bytes tall, for a total of 80 bytes used on ROM. This is a modest amount compared to the 192 bytes used for sprite data in *Combat*. By reducing the fidelity of the game's graphics and animation, Frye won back precious ROM space for the additional logic needed to set up the screen and move the ghosts. The need to save ROM points to a major difference between programming *Pac-Man* for an arcade board and programming it for the Atari VCS. The continuous 4K ROM provides greater flexibility than the arcade board, but far less total storage space.

The TIA also provides registers to set sprite colors: one named COLUP0 and the other COLUP1. In many early VCS games, including *Combat*, sprite colors were set once for the entire game. In later games, the program stored a different color value in one or both sprite color registers along with a different bitmap value. Multicolor sprites were implemented, too. These included Pitfall Harry in Activision's *Pitfall!* The careful observer can note color banding in most of these sprite graphics, though, which is not seen in the true bitmapped graphics of later platforms like the NES. This style of "stripe-colored" sprites is a particular trademark of VCS games. Mercifully for Tod Frye, the iconic Pac-Man of the arcade game is a single color, so no further ROM space or horizontal blank logic had to be expended to draw his yellow image convincingly.

Combat uses two sprites, each of which fires a corresponding missile—just what the TIA ordered, or what it was originally ordered to do. But games like Taito's *Space Invaders* were not designed with the peculiarities of the Atari VCS in mind. Sprites were different in many post-1977 arcade games. Most important, there were often more than two per screen! When faced with the rows of aliens in *Space Invaders* or the platoon of ghosts that chases *Pac-Man*, VCS programmers needed to discover and use methods of drawing more than two sprites, even though only two one-byte registers were available.

As discussed in the previous chapter, the TIA offers a set of horizontal motion registers for each of the sprites, the missiles, and the ball. The TIA also exposes another register called HMOVE to execute changes in horizontal motion. These registers were primarily intended to be set during a vertical blank—that is, between screen draws. For example, *Combat* repositions both player and missile horizontal positions each frame, then updates variables in RAM to ensure that the objects are drawn on the appropriate lines, and then updates the horizontal motion registers once at the start of the frame.

Larry Kaplan, one of the first developers to work on the Stella prototype, figured out that sprite data could be reset more frequently than once per frame. Because the VCS requires the program to control every line of the television screen, it is possible to change the sprite graphics' values and their horizontal positions more than once per frame. Kaplan first used this technique in *Air-Sea Battle*, one of the console's launch titles. In the game, multiple rows of enemies, one per row, pass back and forth across the screen. Each player controls a turret on the ground that can be aimed and fired at targets in the air. Multiple targets are presented by resetting the sprite graphics multiple times down the screen. Finally, when it is time to draw the ground, the sprite graphics and horizontal positions are reset for the player turrets.

Another variation of the horizontal movement technique helped bring *Space Invaders* to the system.[5] The trademark feature of the popular arcade game was the armada of slowly descending aliens, arrayed in rows and columns. The TIA, of course, didn't directly support a display of alien forces like this. Kaplan's *Air-Sea Battle* technique allowed multiple sprites to appear down the screen, but *Space Invaders* required multiple sprites in a horizontal line as well. Rick Maurer, the programmer for the VCS port of *Space Invaders*, discovered that strobing HMOVE while a line was being drawn would reposition objects immediately, even if they had already been drawn earlier in that line. The TIA, lacking any memory of what it has already done, begins drawing the data from its sprite graphics registers to the screen any time that HMOVE is reset. After one row of aliens had been drawn using this technique, Maurer had the program read and write new sprite graphics values from ROM to create a new row of aliens. On each row, the aliens could have a different appearance.

These two techniques, combined with the VCS's lack of a frame buffer and subsequent requirement that the programmer draw every scan line, allowed the VCS to overcome the apparent limitation of supporting only two sprites on-screen. Rather than changing both sprites and their positions every frame, one or both could be changed every line. Together, these approaches extended the originally imagined game design space on the Atari VCS, making the unit capable of playing games that were very different from the arcade hits of the mid-1970s. The importance of these exploits was not overlooked at the higher levels of the company. Discussing this technique in 1983, after he had become vice president of product development at Atari, Kaplan commented, "Without that single strobe, H-move, the VCS would have died a quick death five years ago."[6]

Despite the cleverness of these techniques, both vertical positioning and horizontal strobing required that sprites move together in vertical unison, if they were to move vertically at all. Some variations of *Air-Sea Battle* moved different enemy sprites at different rates of speed by writing new values to the horizontal motion registers, but the objects in that case only moved horizontally—never along both horizontal and vertical axes.

Unfortunately, the four *Pac-Man* monsters need to move horizontally and vertically, and to be independent of one another. Nothing like this had been done before on the Atari VCS. Yet, just as *Space Invaders* would have been unrecognizable without its characteristic rows of invaders, so *Pac-Man* would have been unrecognizable without its characteristic monster quadruplets.

To draw the four pursuers, programmer Tod Frye relied on a technique called *flicker*. Each of the four ghosts is moved and drawn in sequence on successive frames. Pac-Man himself is drawn every frame using the other sprite graphic register. The TIA synchronizes with an NTSC television picture sixty times per second, so the resulting display shows a solid Pac-Man, maze, and pellets, but ghosts that flicker on and off, remaining lit only one quarter of the time. The phosphorescent glow of a CRT television takes a little while to fade, and the human retina retains a perceived image for a short time, so the visible effect of the flicker is slightly less pronounced than this fraction of time suggests.[7] The fact that the monsters in *Pac-Man* were commonly referred to as "ghosts" apologized somewhat for the flicker and suggested the dimness of an apparition. The manual for the VCS rendition of *Pac-Man* included large illustrations of ghosts to drive the point home. The energizer dots are also comprised of sprite graphics, but they flash regularly, making their visual appearance less odd.

Later ports of games in the *Pac-Man* family, including the 1982 *Ms. Pac-Man* and the 1987 *Jr. Pac-Man*, used less visually intrusive techniques to draw the ghosts. Flicker was employed only when necessary, on one horizontal band of the screen rather than on every frame.

The flicker on the first VCS *Pac-Man* annoyed and disappointed many players. Part of the problem is the nature of human vision. The eyes can simply tire of the constantly flashing ghosts. Another part of the problem is the effect of flicker on gameplay. The flashing of the ghosts makes them harder to see, which is a major problem for a game that is all about pursuit.

Another problem with the visuals is even more subtle. In Iwatani's original game, each ghost has a different color, name, and behavior. This gives each of the opponents at least some sort of personality. The arcade game prominently introduces the monsters by name—Blinky, Inky, Pinky, and Clyde—during attract mode, when the machine is luring players to insert quarters, and Blinky is further fictionalized in the interstitial scenes between levels. No such transfer of characterization was possible on the Atari VCS, in part because the monsters cannot be distinguished from one another.

The flicker technique and the reuse of one sprite also made it necessary to abstract the bonus fruit in the game. Aesthetically, *Pac-Man* is already a very abstract game—even in the arcade. The player eats pellets and energizers, not burgers and cola. The addition of fruit fits the theme of eating and serves an additional purpose in the game design: considerable bonus points can be earned in return for steering Pac-Man in the right direction to get the fruit. The visual fidelity of these fruits, as well as the incongruity of their appearance, introduces an element of whimsy into the game. Because the maze is identical on each level, the fruit also marks achievement; players would talk about "reaching the apple stage" or "getting to the key" (the non fruit prize that is offered last) to note their progress and boast about their skill.

To avoid storing even more sprite data in ROM and drawing an additional flickering object that would result in even worse flicker, Frye represented each of the fruit bonuses with a single, even more abstract object: an orange box made of playfield graphics with a yellow player-one missile graphic filling its inside.

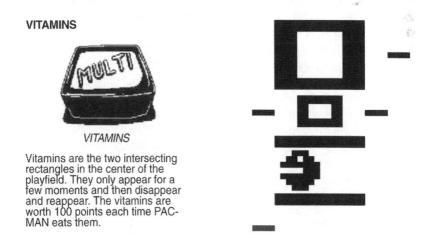

VITAMINS

VITAMINS

Vitamins are the two intersecting rectangles in the center of the playfield. They only appear for a few moments and then disappear and reappear. The vitamins are worth 100 points each time PAC-MAN eats them.

Figure 2 The manual for the VCS *Pac-Man* reimagines the bonus object, which is drawn using playfield graphics, as a "vitamin."

The object didn't change from level to level as it did in the arcade. In the printed manual for the game, Atari tried to fictionalize this technical decision by calling the bonus object a "vitamin," which was described as "two intersecting rectangles." In this case, the platform constrained the fiction of the game. The image of the vitamin in the manual even looks like a stylized version of the rectangular boxes shown on-screen, as shown in Figure 2.

Bank switching and *Ms. Pac-Man*

The VCS version was the first home console port of *Pac-Man*. Atari reportedly produced upwards of ten million cartridges in its first run. This was a very unusual production run, given that there was an active base of only ten million VCS consoles.[8] At the time, Atari executives reasoned that *Pac-Man*'s popularity in the arcade would drive purchases of VCS hardware, thus increasing demand for the game.

However, the cartridge's limitations and compromises led to less than anticipated interest in the game—much less. Atari did sell an impressive seven million copies of the game, but that still left millions to languish in the warehouse or to be returned unsold.[9] This was a massive financial disaster. In the wake of *Pac-Man*'s commercial reception, retailers began to mistrust the videogame industry. Their suspicions would be confirmed with even more licensed games of dubious quality that same year—most prominently, *E.T.: The Extra-Terrestrial*. *Pac-Man* contributed to a chain reaction of reduced retail commitment to home console video games, resulting in the so-called videogame crash of 1983, which is discussed in more detail in chapters 7 and 8. While larger companies like Atari and Activision survived in some form, the many smaller companies producing games for consoles quickly went out of business. It was not until Nintendo released its NES in 1985 that the U.S. videogame market recovered from this dark age.

In the videogame fan world, represented by posts from the Atari amateur community and fan-authored historical documents like Wikipedia's pages on the game, blame for the poor quality of the original VCS *Pac-Man* is leveled squarely at Frye and Atari. Indeed, both programmer and company may have overreached in their attempts to gobble dollars.

Frye developed the game from a prototype that he had been working on when Atari acquired the game rights. The company pressured him to use this incomplete version instead of starting over again so that the game could be released in time for the 1981 Christmas season. Despite the strong technical limitations under which he worked, Frye had an incentive to attempt the best work he could in the space and time he was given. Atari CEO Ray Kassar finally responded to the possibility of Frye and other senior programmers being hired away by offering them a royalty on sales of the cartridges they developed. Frye would get ten cents for every *Pac-Man* unit sold. Once the game shipped and money started rolling on, Frye made no secret of the wealth he was amassing. This didn't endear him to his coworkers, even though they were substantially better off because of the new royalty arrangement.[10] For Atari's part, the company rushed the game to market at the lowest possible cost in order to capitalize on the license alone rather than on a careful, well-crafted rendition of the game.

A year later, Atari released an adaptation of *Ms. Pac-Man* that responded to most of the gripes that players had about VCS *Pac-Man*. Part of this work was derivative of Frye's. Part of it benefited from the perfect hindsight of the original VCS *Pac-Man* debacle.

For one thing, the game used an 8K ROM instead of the 4K ROM that Frye was allotted for his project thanks to a technique called *bank-switching*. The 6507 microprocessor used in the Atari VCS featured only thirteen of the sixteen pins available in the 6502. This limitation reduced the total address space of the machine to 8K, of which 4K is devoted to RAM, the TIA, and the RIOT registers. This leaves 4K of address space for cartridge ROM. As *Pac-Man* demonstrates, limitations in ROM space are just as significant as limitations in computation time or RAM. A bank-switched cartridge partly relaxes this constraint, allowing the program to switch between multiple 4K ROM banks.[11]

The *Ms. Pac-Man* arcade game was itself a variation on *Pac-Man*, originally created by General Computing Company as a daughterboard that attached to the Namco *Pac-Man* board. The arcade game changed the appearance and layout of the maze, also adding three new mazes which appear on successive levels. It also revised the monster AI to make the behavior of the four opponents less evidently deterministic, changed the bonus fruit to move and bounce through the maze, and introduced new cut scenes to go with the fiction of Pac-Man's courtship.

The VCS *Ms. Pac-Man* made considerable use of the additional ROM space that bank-switching afforded. More ROM made it possible to have all four mazes in the game. Additional space for sprites allowed *Ms. Pac-Man* to face in all four directions, to feature better animation, and most important, to include game and character logos, bonus fruits, logos, interstitial screens, and an authentic arcade attract loop (Figure 3).

Fans and historians sometimes point to *Ms. Pac-Man* and later VCS *Pac-Man* hacks and rebuilds as evidence that *Pac-Man* could have been a much better game than it turned out to be. There is, for example, Nukey Shay's revision of Frye's cartridge, which adds credible arcade sounds, revised colors, better sprite graphics, and colored fruit.[12] Shay also tuned the speed and control interaction to better match the arcade. The game includes better renderings of the main eater and of the ghosts, including animated vertical orientations for Pac-Man. And it replaces the cloying VCS *Pac-Man* startup sound with a credible two-voice rendition of *Pac-Man*'s characteristic theme music—a remarkable feat, given the lack of similarity between Atari's sound registers and the *Pac-Man* board's custom three-channel waveform sound generator.

Despite all of this, it doesn't make sense to blame Frye for not accomplishing what Shay did, or to imagine that the VCS *Pac-Man* could have been a better game just because later versions of it were indeed more faithful adaptations. The situation of *Pac-Man*'s development and release was historically unique.

Figure 3 The VCS *Ms. Pac-Man* has bonus fruit, an attract screen, and other visual features that connect it to its arcade counterpart

The technical affordances of the Atari VCS itself are further bound, at any point in time, to the types of innovation that have already been accomplished on the platform, along with the player response to the previously released titles. Whether or not the videogame crash that hit in force in 1983 could have been averted, there is no question that a better version of *Pac-Man* could have been released in 1982, given the right circumstances. But those circumstances—a combination of intersecting issues in culture, business, and reception—did not arise. Part of that situation was the very intense demand for an adaptation of a hit arcade game in the first place, a possible signal of the cultural shift toward derivatives, licenses, and branded content as the first phase of cross-media consolidation took root.

If there is a general lesson that can be learned from *Pac-Man*'s fate on the Atari VCS, it is the importance of the framing and social context of a property—video game or otherwise—when adapting it for a particular computer platform. The VCS rendition of *Ms. Pac-Man* demonstrates that an artifact with a strong social and cultural context must carry some significant signs of that context into its adaptation. One videogame writer described the VCS game as "a pale imitation of the real thing," noting that "the cut-scenes were gone, the *paku-paku* sound effect was no more, and Iwatani's colorful, appealing graphic design was butchered."[13] Perhaps the most interesting feature of the VCS rendition of *Ms. Pac-Man* is that it includes an authentic arcade attract loop, dramatic interludes, and accurate *Ms. Pac-Man* logos on both the splash screen and the game screen. These features add nothing to the gameplay, but they provide an important frame for it. A home version of *Pac-Man*, it turned out, needed to simulate the arcade experience, with its sounds and video displays meant to draw players from afar, as much as it needed to allow players to pilot a yellow pizza-critter around an abstract maze.

Notes

1 In Kohler (*Power-Up*, 22), it is noted that the story of the missing pizza slice doesn't exactly describe a real event, but that Iwatani nevertheless likes the story and tells it as if it were true.
2 Green, "Pac-Man."
3 International Arcade Museum, "Pac-Man Videogame by Midway."
4 Even today, a movable object in a 2D or 3D world is often called a sprite. And handheld systems like the Game Boy Advance and Nintendo DS, both of which evolved from the Nintendo Entertainment System, offer even more complex hardware management for sprites.
5 Rick Maurer made an important innovation in *Space Invaders* in addition to this one. He introduced a cooperative two-player mode that was very suitable for a home system and not present in any form in the arcade game.
6 Quoted in Perry and Wallich.
7 The effect is different on an LCD display, which means that an emulated *Pac-Man* game will not look the same as one played on a CRT television.
8 Townsend, "The to Worst Games of All time."
9 Alexander, "Video Games Go Crunch."
10 Warshaw, *Once Upon Atari*, episode 2.
11 Control over memory banks is Memory-mapped, meaning that a VCS program writes to a specific location in memory to switch from one bank to another. This can be very helpful, but is net as useful as being able to address a large memory space directly. Often, some of the contents of one bank will have to be duplicated in another because it is impractical to switch back and forth at every point where it would be necessary.
12 Available to members of the AtariAge forums at http://www.atariage.com/forums/index.php?showtopic=54937.
13 Kohler, *Power-Up*, 24.

Bibliography

Texts

Alexander, Charles P. "Video Games Go Crunch." *Time* 122, no. 17, 17 October 1983. http://www.time.com/time/printout/0,8816,952210,00.html.

Davie, Andrew. "Atari Programming for Newbies." *AtariAge.com*, 2003. http://www.atariage.com/forums/index.php?showforum=31.

Green, Chris. "Pac-Man." *Salon.com*, 2002. http://dir.salon.com/story/ent/masterpiece/2002/06/17/pac_man/.

International Arcade Museum. "Pac-Man Videogame by Midway." *Killer List of Video Games*, 1995–2008. http://www.klov.com/game_detail.php?game_id=10816.

Kohler, Chris. *Power-Up: How Japanese Video Games Gave the World an Extra Life.* Indianapolis: Brady Games, 2004.

Perry, Tekla, and Paul Wallich. "Design Case History: The Atari Video Computer System." *IEEE Spectrum* 20, no. 3 (1983): 45–51.

Townsend, Emru. "The 10 Worst Games of All Time." *PC World*, 23 October 2006. http://www.pcworld.com/printable/article/id,127579/printable.html.

Video games

This section of the bibliography is organized by author. Whoever was originally credited as author of a video game when the game was originally released is considered to be the author for the purposes of this list. Since policies for attributing authorship vary, "Atari" is the author of all games published by that company, while individuals were considered the authors of Activision games. In all cases, including when games have a corporate author, we have indicated, to the best of our knowledge, the people who programmed, designed, and did other work on these games.

Atari. *Space Invaders*. Atari VCS. Programmed by Rick Maurer. 1980.
Nintendo. *Super Mario Bros.* Nintendo Entertainment System. Designed by Shigeru Miyamoto. 1985.
Nintendo. *The Legend of Zelda*. Nintendo Entertainment System. Designed by Shigeru Miyamoto. 1986.

Motion pictures

Warshaw, Howard Scott. *Once Upon Atari*. 2003.

30

GAME DESIGN AS NARRATIVE ARCHITECTURE

Henry Jenkins

Source: Noah Wardrip-Fruin and Pat Harrigan, (eds), *First Person: New Media as Story, Performance, and Game* (Cambridge, MA: The MIT Press, 2004), pp. 118–130.

The relationship between games and story remains a divisive question among game fans, designers, and scholars alike. At a recent academic Games Studies conference, for example, a blood feud threatened to erupt between the self-proclaimed ludologists, who wanted to see the focus shift onto the mechanics of game play, and the narratologists, who were interested in studying games alongside other storytelling media. The term "ludology" was coined by Espen Aarseth, who advocates the emergence of a new field of study, specifically focused on the study of games and game play, rather than framed through the concerns of pre-existing disciplines or other media. (Editors' note: Markku Eskelinen, in his response to this essay, points out that the term was introduced to computer game studies by Gonzalo Frasca. This introduction, according to Frasca, was in the Cybertext Yearbook–a publication coedited by Eskelinen and named for Aarseth's Cybertext [1997].) Consider some recent statements made on this issue:

> Interactivity is almost the opposite of narrative; narrative flows under the direction of the author, while interactivity depends on the player for motive power. (Adams 1999)

> There is a direct, immediate conflict between the demands of a story and the demands of a game. Divergence from a story's path is likely to make for a less satisfying story; restricting a player's freedom of action is likely to make for a less satisfying game. (Costikyan 2000, 44–53)

> Computer games are not narratives . . . . Rather the narrative tends to be isolated from or even work against the computer-game-ness of the game. (Juul 1998) For a more recent formulation of this same argument, see Jesper Juul (2001), "Games Telling Stories?"

> Outside academic theory people are usually excellent at making distinctions between narrative, drama and games. If I throw a ball at you I don't expect you to drop it and wait until it starts telling stories. (Eskelinen 2001)

I find myself responding to this perspective with mixed feelings. On the one hand, I understand what these writers are arguing against – various attempts to map traditional narrative structures ("hypertext," "Interactive Cinema," "nonlinear narrative") onto games at the expense of an attention to their specificity as an emerging mode of entertainment. You say "narrative" to the average gamer and what they are apt to imagine is something on the order of a choose-your-own adventure book, a form noted for its lifelessness and mechanical exposition rather than enthralling entertainment, thematic sophistication, or character complexity. And game industry executives are perhaps justly skeptical that they have much to learn from the resolutely unpopular (and often overtly antipopular) aesthetics promoted by hypertext theorists. The application of film theory to games can seem heavy-handed and literal-minded, often failing to recognize the profound differences between the two media. Yet, at the same time, there is a tremendous amount that game designers and critics could learn through making meaningful comparisons with other storytelling media. One gets rid of narrative as a framework for thinking about games only at one's own risk. In this short piece, I hope to offer a middle-ground position between the ludologists and the narratologists, one that respects the particularity of this emerging medium–examining games less as stories than as spaces ripe with narrative possibility.

Let's start at some points where we might all agree:

1   Not all games tell stories. Games may be an abstract, expressive, and experiential form, closer to music or modern dance than to cinema. Some ballets (The Nutcracker for example) tell stories, but storytelling isn't an intrinsic or defining feature of dance. Similarly, many of my own favorite games – Tetris, Blix, Snood – are simple graphic games that do not lend themselves very well to narrative exposition. Eskelinen (2001) takes Janet Murray to task for her narrative analysis of Tetris as "a perfect enactment of the overtasked lives of Americans in the 1990s – of the constant bombardment of tasks that demand our attention and that we must somehow fit into our overcrowded schedules and clear off our desks in order to make room for the next onslaught." Eskelinen is correct to note that the abstraction of Tetris would seem to defy narrative interpretation, but that is not the same thing as insisting that no meaningful analysis can be made of the game and its fit within contemporary culture. Tetris might well express something of the frenzied pace of modern life, just as modern dances might, without being a story. To understand such games, we need other terms and concepts beyond narrative, including interface design and expressive movement for starters. The last thing we want to do is to reign in the creative experimentation that needs to occur in the earlier years of a medium's development.

2   Many games do have narrative aspirations. Minimally, they want to tap the emotional residue of previous narrative experiences. Often, they depend on our familiarity with the roles and goals of genre entertainment to orient us to the action, and in many cases, game designers want to create a series of

narrative experiences for the player. Given those narrative aspirations, it seems reasonable to suggest that some understanding of how games relate to narrative is necessary before we understand the aesthetics of game design or the nature of contemporary game culture.

3   Narrative analysis need not be prescriptive, even if some narratologists – Janet Murray is the most oft-cited example – do seem to be advocating for games to pursue particular narrative forms. There is not one future of games. The goal should be to foster diversification of genres, aesthetics, and audiences, to open gamers to the broadest possible range of experiences. The past few years have been ones of enormous creative experimentation and innovation within the games industry, as might be represented by a list of some of the groundbreaking titles. The Sims, Black and White, Majestic, Shenmue; each represents profoundly different concepts of what makes for compelling game play. A discussion of the narrative potentials of games need not imply a privileging of storytelling over all the other possible things games can do, even if we might suggest that if game designers are going to tell stories, they should tell them well. In order to do that, game designers, who are most often schooled in computer science or graphic design, need to be retooled in the basic vocabulary of narrative theory.

4   The experience of playing games can never be simply reduced to the experience of a story. Many other factors that have little or nothing to do with storytelling per se contribute to the development of great games and we need to significantly broaden our critical vocabulary for talking about games to deal more fully with those other topics. Here, the ludologist's insistence that game scholars focus more attention on the mechanics of game play seems totally in order.

5   If some games tell stories, they are unlikely to tell them in the same ways that other media tell stories. Stories are not empty content that can be ported from one media pipeline to another. One would be hard-pressed, for example, to translate the internal dialogue of Proust's Remembrance of Things Past into a compelling cinematic experience, and the tight control over viewer experience that Hitchcock achieves in his suspense films would be directly antithetical to the aesthetics of good game design. We must, therefore, be attentive to the particularity of games as a medium, specifically what distinguishes them from other narrative traditions. Yet, in order to do so requires precise comparisons – not the mapping of old models onto games but a testing of those models against existing games to determine what features they share with other media and how they differ.

Much of the writing in the ludologist tradition is unduly polemical: they are so busy trying to pull game designers out of their "cinema envy" or define a field where no hypertext theorist dares to venture that they are prematurely dismissing the use value of narrative for understanding their desired object of study. For my money, a series of conceptual blind spots prevent them from developing a full understanding of the interplay between narrative and games.

First, the discussion operates with too narrow a model of narrative, one preoccupied with the rules and conventions of classical linear storytelling at the expense of consideration of other kinds of narratives, not only the modernist and postmodernist experimentation that inspired the hypertext theorists, but also popular traditions that emphasize spatial exploration over causal event chains or which seek to balance the competing demands of narrative and spectacle. "A story is a collection of facts in a time-sequenced order that suggest a cause and effect relationship" (Crawford 1982). "The story is the antithesis of game. The best way to tell a story is in linear form. The best way to create a game is to provide a structure within which the player has freedom of action" (Costikyan, 2000).

Second, the discussion operates with too limited an understanding of narration, focusing more on the activities and aspirations of the storyteller and too little on the process of narrative comprehension. "In its richest form, storytelling – narrative – means the reader's surrender to the author. The author takes the reader by the hand and leads him into the world of his imagination. The reader has a role to play, but it's a fairly passive role: to pay attention, to understand, perhaps to think . . . but not to act" (Adams 1999).

Third, the discussion deals only with the question of whether whole games tell stories and not whether narrative elements might enter games at a more localized level. Finally, the discussion assumes that narratives must be self-contained rather than understanding games as serving some specific functions within a new trans media storytelling environment. Rethinking each of these issues might lead us to a new understanding of the relationship between games and stories. Specifically, I want to introduce an important third term into this discussion – spatiality – and argue for an understanding of game designers less as storytellers and more as narrative architects.

Spatial stories and environmental storytelling

Game designers don't simply tell stories; they design worlds and sculpt spaces. It is no accident, for example, that game design documents have historically been more interested in issues of level design than on plotting or character motivation. A prehistory of video and computer games might take us through the evolution of paper mazes or board games, both preoccupied with the design of spaces, even where they also provided some narrative context. Monopoly, for example, may tell a narrative about how fortunes are won and lost; the individual Chance cards may provide some story pretext for our gaining or losing a certain number of places; but ultimately, what we remember is the experience of moving around the board and landing on someone's real estate. Performance theorists have described role-playing games (RPGs) as a mode of collaborative storytelling, but the Dungeon Master's activities start with designing the space – the dungeon – where the players' quest will take place. Even many of the early text-based games, such as Zork, which could have told a wide array of different kinds of stories, centered around enabling players to move through narratively compelling spaces: "You are facing the north side of a white house. There is no door here, and all of the windows are boarded up. To the north a narrow path winds through the trees." The early Nintendo games have simple narrative hooks – rescue Princess Toadstool – but what gamers found astonishing when they first played them were their complex and imaginative graphic realms, which were so much more sophisticated than the simple grids that Pong or Pac-Man had offered us a decade earlier.

When we refer to such influential early works as Shigeru Miyamoto's Super Mario Bros. as "scroll games," we situate them alongside a much older tradition of spatial storytelling: many Japanese scroll paintings map, for example, the passing of the seasons onto an unfolding space. When you adapt a film into a game, the process typically involves translating events in the film into environments within the game. When gamer magazines want to describe the experience of gameplay, they are more likely to reproduce maps of the game world than to recount their narratives. As I have noted elsewhere, these maps take a distinctive form – not objective or abstract top-down views but composites of screenshots that represent the game world as we will encounter it in our travels through its space. Game space never exists in abstract, but always experientially. Before we can talk about game narratives, then, we need to talk about game spaces. Across a series of essays, I have made the case that game consoles should be regarded as machines for generating compelling spaces, that their virtual playspaces have helped to compensate for the declining place of the traditional backyard in contemporary boy culture, and that the core narratives behind many games center around the struggle to explore, map, and master contested spaces (Fuller and Jenkins 1994; Jenkins 1998). Here, I want to broaden that discussion further to consider in what ways the structuring of game space facilitates different kinds of narrative experiences.

As such, games fit within a much older tradition of spatial stories, which have often taken the form of hero's odysseys, quest myths, or travel narratives. My concept of spatial stories is strongly influenced by Michel de Certeau (1988) The Practice of Everyday Life and Henri LeFebvre (1991), The Production of Space. The best works of J.R.R. Tolkien, Jules Verne, Homer, L. Frank Baum, or Jack London fall loosely within this tradition, as does, for example, the sequence in War and Peace that describes Pierre's aimless wanderings across the battlefield at Borodino. Often, such works exist on the outer borders of literature. They are much loved by readers, to be sure, and passed down from one generation to another, but they rarely figure in the canon of great literary works. How often, for example, has science fiction been criticized for being preoccupied with world-making at the expense of character psychology or plot development?

These writers seem constantly to be pushing against the limits of what can be accomplished in a printed text and thus their works fare badly against aesthetic standards defined around classically constructed novels. In many cases, the characters – our guides through these richly developed worlds – are stripped down to the bare bones, description displaces exposition, and plots fragment into a series of episodes and encounters. When game designers draw story elements from existing film or literary genres, they are most apt to tap those genres – fantasy, adventure, science fiction, horror, war – which are most invested in world-making and spatial storytelling. Games, in turn, may more fully realize the spatiality of these stories, giving a much more immersive and compelling representation of their narrative worlds. Anyone who doubts that Tolstoy might have achieved his true calling as a game designer should reread the final segment of War and Peace where he works through how a series of alternative choices might have reversed the outcome of Napoleon's Russian campaign. The passage is dead weight in the context of a novel, yet it outlines ideas that could be easily communicated in god-games such as those in the Civilization series.

Don Carson, who worked as a Senior Show Designer for Walt Disney Imagineering, has argued that game designers can learn a great deal by studying techniques of "environmental storytelling," which Disney employs in designing amusement park attractions. Carson explains,

> The story element is infused into the physical space a guest walks or rides through. It is the physical space that does much of the work of conveying the story the designers are trying to tell . . . Armed only with their own knowledge of the world, and those visions collected from movies and books, the audience is ripe to be dropped into your adventure. The trick is to play on those memories and expectations to heighten the thrill of venturing into your created universe. (Carson 2000)

The amusement park attraction doesn't so much reproduce the story of a literary work, such as The Wind in the Willows, as it evokes its atmosphere; the original story provides "a set of rules that will guide the design and project team to a common goal" and that will help give structure and meaning to the visitor's experience. If, for example, the attraction centers around pirates, Carson writes, "every texture you use, every sound you play, every turn in the road should reinforce the concept of pirates," while any contradictory element may shatter the sense of immersion into this narrative universe. The same might be said for a game such as Sea Dogs, which, no less than Pirates of the Caribbean, depends on its ability to map our preexisting pirate fantasies. The most significant difference is that amusement park designers count on visitors keeping their hands and arms in the car at all times and thus have a greater control in shaping our total experience, whereas game designers have to develop worlds where we can touch, grab, and fling things about at will.

Environmental storytelling creates the preconditions for an immersive narrative experience in at least one of four ways: spatial stories can evoke pre-existing narrative associations; they can provide a staging ground where narrative events are enacted; they may embed narrative information within their mise-en-scene; or they provide resources for emergent narratives.

Evocative spaces

The most compelling amusement park attractions build upon stories or genre traditions already well-known to visitors, allowing them to enter physically into spaces they have visited many times before in their fantasies. These attractions may either remediate a preexisting story (Back to the Future) or draw upon a broadly shared genre tradition (Disney's Haunted Mansion). Such works do not so much tell self-contained stories as draw upon our previously existing narrative competencies. They can paint their worlds in fairly broad outlines and count on the visitor/player to do the rest. Something similar might be said of many games. For example, American McGee's Alice™ is an original interpretation of Lewis Carroll's Alice in Wonderland.

Alice has been pushed into madness after years of living with uncertainty about whether her Wonderland experiences were real or hallucinations; now, she's come back into this world and is looking for blood. McGee's wonderland is not a whimsical dreamscape but a dark nightmare realm. McGee can safely assume that players start the game with a pretty well-developed mental map of the spaces, characters, and situations associated with Carroll's fictional universe and that they will read his distorted and often monstrous images against the background of mental images formed from previous encounters with storybook illustrations and Disney movies. McGee rewrites Alice's story in large part by redesigning Alice's spaces.

Arguing against games as stories, Jesper Juul suggests that, "you clearly can't deduct the story of Star Wars from Star Wars the game," whereas a film version of a novel will give you at least the broad outlines of the plot (Juul 1998). This is a pretty old-fashioned model of the process of adaptation. Increasingly, we inhabit a world of transmedia storytelling, one that depends less on each individual work being self-sufficient than on each work contributing to a larger narrative economy. The Star Wars game may not simply retell the story of Star Wars, but it doesn't have to in order to enrich or expand our experience of the Star Wars saga.

We already know the story before we even buy the game and would be frustrated if all it offered us was a regurgitation of the original film experience. Rather, the Star Wars game exists in dialogue with the films, conveying new narrative experiences through its creative manipulation of environmental details. One can imagine games taking their place within a larger narrative system with story information communicated through books, film, television, comics, and other media, each doing what it does best, each a relatively autonomous experience, but the richest understanding of the story world coming to those who follow the narrative across the various channels. In such a system, what games do best will almost certainly center around their ability to give concrete shape to our memories and imaginings of the storyworld, creating an immersive environment we can wander through and interact with.

Enacting stories

Most often, when we discuss games as stories, we are referring to games that either enable players to perform or witness narrative events – for example, to grab a light-saber and dispatch Darth Maul in a Star Wars game. Narrative enters such games on two levels – in terms of broadly defined goals or conflicts and on the level of localized incidents.

Many game critics assume that all stories must be classically constructed with each element tightly integrated into the overall plot trajectory. Costikyan (2000) writes, for example, that "a story is a controlled experience; the author consciously crafts it, choosing certain events precisely, in a certain order, to create a story with maximum impact." For a fuller discussion of the norms of classically constructed narrative, see Bordwell, Staiger, and Thompson (1985), The Classical Hollywood Cinema.

Adams (1999) claims, "a good story hangs together the way a good jigsaw puzzle hangs together. When you pick it up, every piece is locked tightly in place next to its neighbors." Spatial stories, on the other hand, are often dismissed as episodic – that is, each episode (or set piece) can become compelling on its own terms without contributing significantly to the plot development, and often the episodes could be reordered without significantly impacting our experience as a whole. There may be broad movements or series of stages within the story, as Troy Dunniway suggests when he draws parallels between the stages in the Hero's journey (as outlined by Joseph Campbell) and the levels of a classic adventure game, but within each stage, the sequencing of actions may be quite loose. Spatial stories are not badly constructed stories; rather, they are stories that respond to alternative aesthetic principles, privileging spatial exploration over plot development. Spatial stories are held together by broadly defined goals and conflicts and pushed forward by the character's movement across the map. Their resolution often hinges on the player reaching his or her final destination, though, as Mary Fuller notes, not all travel narratives end successfully or resolve the narrative enigmas that set them into motion. Once again, we are back to principles of "environmental storytelling." The organization of the plot becomes a matter of designing the geography of imaginary worlds, so that obstacles thwart and affordances facilitate the protagonist's forward movement towards resolution. Over the past several decades, game designers have become more and more adept at setting and varying the rhythm of game play through features of the game space.

Narrative can also enter games on the level of localized incident, or what I am calling micronarratives. We might understand how micronarratives work by thinking about the Odessa Steps sequence in Sergei Eisenstein's Battleship Potemkin. First, recognize that, whatever its serious moral tone, the scene basically deals with the same kind of material as most games – the steps are a contested space with one group (the peasants) trying to advance up and another (the Cossacks) moving down.

Eisenstein intensifies our emotional engagement with this large-scale conflict through a series of short narrative units. The woman with the baby carriage is perhaps the best known of those micronarratives. Each of these units builds upon stock characters or situations drawn from the repertoire of melodrama. None of them last more than a few seconds, though Eisenstein prolongs them (and intensifies their emotional impact) through cross-cutting between multiple incidents. Eisenstein used the term "attraction" to describe such emotionally packed elements in his work; contemporary game designers might call them "memorable moments." Just as some memorable moments in games depend on sensations (the sense of speed in a racing game) or perceptions (the sudden expanse of sky in a snowboarding game) as well as narrative hooks, Eisenstein used the word "attractions" broadly to describe any element within a work that produces a profound emotional impact, and theorized that the themes of the work could be communicated across and through these discrete elements. Even games that do not create large-scale plot trajectories may well depend on these micronarratives to shape the player's emotional experience. Micronarratives may be cut-scenes, but they don't have to be. One can imagine a simple sequence of preprogrammed actions through which an opposing player responds to your successful touchdown in a football game as a micronarrative.

Game critics often note that the player's participation poses a potential threat to the narrative construction, whereas the hard rails of the plotting can overly constrain the "freedom, power, and self-expression" associated with interactivity (Adams 1999). The tension between performance (or game play) and exposition (or story) is far from unique to games. The pleasures of popular culture often center on spectacular performance numbers and self-contained set pieces. It makes no sense to describe musical numbers or gag sequences or action scenes as disruptions of the film's plots: the reason we go to see a kung fu movie is to see Jackie Chan show his stuff. For useful discussion of this issue in film theory, see Donald Crafton (1995), "Pie and Chase: Gag, Spectacle and Narrative in Slapstick Comedy," in Kristine Brunovska Karnick and Henry Jenkins (eds.), Classical Hollywood Comedy; Henry Jenkins (1991), What Made Pistachio Nuts?: Early Sound Comedy and The Vaudeville Aesthetic; Rick Altman (1999), The American Film Musical; Tom Gunning (1990), "The Cinema of Attractions: Early Film, Its Spectator and the Avant Garde" in Thomas Elsaesser with Adam Barker (eds.), Early Cinema: Space, Frame, Narrative; Linda Williams (1999), Hard Core: Power, Pleasure and "The Frenzy of the Visible." Yet, few films consist simply of such moments, typically falling back on some broad narrative exposition to create a framework within which localized actions become meaningful. "Games that just have nonstop action are fun for a while but often get boring. This is because of the lack of intrigue, suspense, and drama. How many action movies have you seen where the hero of the story shoots his gun every few seconds and is always on the run? People lose interest watching this kind of movie. Playing a game is a bit different, but the fact is the brain becomes over stimulated after too much nonstop action" (Dunniway 2000).

We might describe musicals, action films, or slapstick comedies as having accordion-like structures. Certain plot points are fixed, whereas other moments can be expanded or contracted in response to audience feedback without serious consequences to the overall plot. The introduction needs to establish the character's goals or explain the basic conflict; the conclusion needs to show the successful completion of those goals or the final defeat of the antagonist. In *commedia dell'arte*, for example, the masks define the relationships between the characters and give us some sense of their goals and desires. See, for example, John Rudlin (1994), Commedia Dell'Arte: An Actor's Handbook for a detailed inventory of the masks and *lazzi* of this tradition.

The masks set limits on the action, even though the performance as a whole is created through improvisation. The actors have mastered the possible moves, or *lazzi*, associated with each character, much as a game player has mastered the combination of buttons that must be pushed to enable certain character actions. No author prescribes what the actors do once they get on the stage, but the shape of the story emerges from this basic vocabulary of possible actions and from the broad parameters set by this theatrical tradition. Some of the *lazzi* can contribute to the plot development, but many of them are simple restagings of the basic oppositions (the knave tricks the master or gets beaten).

These performance or spectacle-centered genres often display a pleasure in process – in the experiences along the road – that can overwhelm any strong sense of goal or resolution, while exposition can be experienced as an unwelcome interruption to the pleasure of performance. Game designers struggle with this same balancing act – trying to determine how much plot will create a compelling framework and how much freedom players can enjoy at a local level without totally derailing the larger narrative trajectory. As inexperienced storytellers, they often fall back on rather mechanical exposition through cut scenes, much as early filmmakers were sometimes overly reliant on intertitles rather than learning the skills of visual storytelling. Yet, as with any other aesthetic tradition, game designers are apt to develop craft through a process of experimentation and refinement of basic narrative devices, becoming better at shaping narrative experiences without unduly constraining the space for improvisation within the game.

Embedded narratives

Russian formalist critics make a useful distinction between plot (or syuzhet) that refers to, in Kristen Thompson's (1988) terms, "the structured set of all causal events as we see and hear them presented in the film itself," and story (or fabula), which refers to the viewer's mental construction of the chronology of those events (Thompson 1988, 39–40). Few films or novels are absolutely linear; most make use of some forms of backstory that is revealed gradually as we move through the narrative action. The detective story is the classic illustration of this principle, telling two stories – one more or less chronological (the story of the investigation itself) and the other told radically out of sequence (the events motivating and leading up to the murder).

According to this model, narrative comprehension is an active process by which viewers assemble and make hypotheses about likely narrative developments on the basis of information drawn from textual cues and clues. See, for example, David Bordwell (1989), Narration in the Fiction Film, and Edward Branigan (1992),

Narrative Comprehension and Film. As they move through the film, spectators test and reformulate their mental maps of the narrative action and the story space. In games, players are forced to act upon those mental maps, to literally test them against the game world itself. If you are wrong about whether the bad guys lurk behind the next door, you will find out soon enough – perhaps by being blown away and having to start the game over. The heavy-handed exposition that opens many games serves a useful function in orienting spectators to the core premises so that they are less likely to make stupid and costly errors as they first enter into the game world. Some games create a space for rehearsal, as well, so that we can make sure we understand our character's potential moves before we come up against the challenges of navigating narrational space.

Read in this light, a story is less a temporal structure than a body of information. The author of a film or a book has a high degree of control over when and if we receive specific bits of information, but a game designer can somewhat control the narrational process by distributing the information across the game space. Within an open-ended and exploratory narrative structure like a game, essential narrative information must be presented redundantly across a range of spaces and artifacts, because one cannot assume the player will necessarily locate or recognize the significance of any given element. Game designers have developed a variety of kludges that allow them to prompt players or steer them towards narratively salient spaces. Yet, this is no different from the ways that redundancy is built into a television soap opera, where the assumption is that a certain number of viewers are apt to miss any given episode, or even in classical Hollywood narrative, where the law of three suggests that any essential plot point needs to be communicated in at least three ways.

To continue with the detective example, then, one can imagine the game designer as developing two kinds of narratives – one relatively unstructured and controlled by the player as they explore the game space and unlock its secrets; the other prestructured but embedded within the mise-en-scene awaiting discovery. The game world becomes a kind of information space, a memory palace. Myst is a highly successful example of this kind of embedded narrative, but embedded narrative does not necessarily require an emptying of the space of contemporary narrative activities, as a game such as Half-Life might suggest. Embedded narrative can and often does occur within contested spaces. We may have to battle our way past antagonists, navigate through mazes, or figure out how to pick locks in order to move through the narratively impregnated mise-en-scene. Such a mixture of enacted and embedded narrative elements can allow for a balance between the flexibility of interactivity and the coherence of a pre-authored narrative.

Using Quake as an example, Jesper Juul argues that flashbacks are impossible within games, because the game play always occurs in real-time (Juul 1998). Yet, this is to confuse story and plot. Games are no more locked into an eternal present than films are always linear. Many games contain moments of revelation or artifacts that shed light on past actions. Carson (2000) suggests that part of the art of game design comes in finding artful ways of embedding narrative information into the environment without destroying its immersiveness and without giving the player a sensation of being drug around by the neck:

> Staged areas . . . [can] lead the game player to come to their own conclusions about a previous event or to suggest a potential danger just ahead. Some examples include . . . doors that have been broken open, traces of a recent explosion, a crashed vehicle, a piano dropped from a great height, charred remains of a fire.

Players, he argues, can return to a familiar space later in the game and discover it has been transformed by subsequent (off-screen) events. Clive Barker's Undying, for example, creates a powerful sense of backstory in precisely this manner. It is a story of sibling rivalry that has taken on supernatural dimensions. As we visit each character's space, we have a sense of the human they once were and the demon they have become. In Peter Molyneux's Black and White, the player's ethical choices within the game leave traces on the landscape or reconfigure the physical appearances of their characters. Here, we might read narrative consequences off mise-en-scene the same way we read Dorian Gray's debauchery off of his portrait. Carson describes such narrative devices as "following Saknussemm," referring to the ways that the protagonists of Jules Verne's Journey to The Center of the Earth keep stumbling across clues and artifacts left behind by the sixteenth-century Icelandic scientist/explorer Arne Saknussemm, and readers become fascinated to see what they can learn about his ultimate fate as the travelers come closer to reaching their intended destination.

Game designers might study melodrama for a better understanding of how artifacts or spaces can contain affective potential or communicate significant narrative information. Melodrama depends on the external projection of internal states, often through costume design, art direction, or lighting choices. As we enter spaces, we may become overwhelmed with powerful feelings of loss or nostalgia, especially in those instances where the space has been transformed by narrative events. Consider, for example, the moment in Doctor Zhivago when the characters return to the mansion, now completely deserted and encased in ice, or when Scarlett O'Hara travels across the scorched remains of her family estate in Gone With the Wind following the burning of Atlanta. In Alfred Hitchcock's Rebecca, the title character never appears, but she exerts a powerful influence over the other characters – especially the second Mrs. DeWinter, who must inhabit a space where every artifact recalls her predecessor. Hitchcock creates a number of scenes of his protagonist wandering through Rebecca's space, passing through locked doors, staring at her overwhelming portrait on the wall, touching her things in drawers, or feeling the texture of fabrics and curtains. No matter where she goes in the house, she cannot escape Rebecca's memory.

A game such as Neil Young's Majestic pushes this notion of embedded narrative to its logical extreme. Here, the embedded narrative is no longer contained within the console but rather flows across multiple information channels. The player's activity consists of sorting through documents, deciphering codes, making sense of garbled transmissions, moving step-by-step towards a fuller understanding of the conspiracy that is the game's primary narrative focus. We follow links between web sites; we get information through webcasts, faxes, e-mails, and phone calls. Such an embedded narrative doesn't require a branching story structure but rather depends on scrambling the pieces of a linear story and allowing us to reconstruct the plot through our acts of detection, speculation, exploration, and decryption. Not surprisingly, most embedded narratives, at present, take the form of detective or conspiracy stories, since these genres help to motivate the player's active examination of clues and exploration of spaces and provide a rationale for our efforts to reconstruct the narrative of past events. Yet, as the preceding examples suggest, melodrama provides another – and as yet largely unexplored – model for how an embedded story might work, as we read letters and diaries, snoop around in bedroom drawers and closets, in search of secrets that might shed light on the relationships between characters.

Emergent narratives

The Sims represents a fourth model of how narrative possibilities might get mapped onto game space. Emergent narratives are not prestructured or preprogrammed, taking shape through the game play, yet they are not as unstructured, chaotic, and frustrating as life itself. Game worlds, ultimately, are not real worlds, even those as densely developed as Shenmue or as geographically expansive as Everquest. Will Wright frequently describes The Sims as a sandbox or dollhouse game, suggesting that it should be understood as a kind of authoring environment within which players can define their own goals and write their own stories. Yet, unlike Microsoft Word, the game doesn't open on a blank screen. Most players come away from spending time with The Sims with some degree of narrative satisfaction. Wright has created a world ripe with narrative possibilities, where each design decision has been made with an eye towards increasing the prospects of interpersonal romance or conflict.

The ability to design our own "skins" encourages players to create characters who are emotionally significant to them, to rehearse their own relationships with friends, family, or coworkers or to map characters from other fictional universes onto The Sims. A glance at the various scrapbooks players have posted on the web suggests that they have been quick to take advantage of its relatively open-ended structure. Yet, let's not underestimate the designers' contributions. The characters have a will of their own, not always submitting easily to the player's control, as when a depressed protagonist refuses to seek employment, preferring to spend hour upon hour soaking in their bath or moping on the front porch.

Characters are given desires, urges, and needs, which can come into conflict with each other, and thus produce dramatically compelling encounters. Characters respond emotionally to events in their environment, as when characters mourn the loss of a loved one. Our choices have consequences, as when we spend all of our money and have nothing left to buy them food. The gibberish language and flashing symbols allow us to map our own meanings onto the conversations, yet the tone of voice and body language can powerfully express specific emotional states, which encourage us to understand those interactions within familiar plot situations. The designers have made choices about what kinds of actions are and are not possible in this world, such as allowing for same-sex kisses, but limiting the degree of explicit sexual activity that can occur. (Good programmers may be able to get around such restrictions, but most players probably work within the limitations of the system as given.)

Janet Murray's Hamlet on the Holodeck might describe some of what Wright accomplishes here as procedural authorship. Yet, I would argue that his choices go deeper than this, working not simply through the programming, but also through the design of the game space. For example, just as a dollhouse offers a streamlined representation that cuts out much of the clutter of an actual domestic space, the Sims' houses are stripped down to only a small number of artifacts, each of which perform specific kinds of narrative functions. Newspapers, for example, communicate job information. Characters sleep in beds. Bookcases can make you smarter. Bottles are for spinning and thus motivating lots of kissing. Such choices result in a highly legible narrative space. In his classic study The Image of The City, Kevin Lynch made the case that urban designers needed to be more sensitive to the narrative potentials of city spaces, describing city planning as "the deliberate manipulation of the world for sensuous ends" (Lynch 1960, 116).

Urban designers exert even less control than game designers over how people use the spaces they create or what kinds of scenes they stage there. Yet, some kinds of space lend themselves more readily to narratively memorable or emotionally meaningful experiences than others. Lynch suggested that urban planners should not attempt to totally predetermine the uses and meanings of the spaces they create: "a landscape whose every rock tells a story may make difficult the creation of fresh stories" (Lynch 1960, 6). Rather, he proposes an aesthetic of urban design that endows each space with "poetic and symbolic" potential: "Such a sense of place in itself enhances every human activity that occurs there, and encourages the deposit of a memory trace" (Lynch 1960, 119). Game designers would do well to study Lynch's book, especially as they move into the production of game platforms which support player-generated narratives.

In each of these cases, choices about the design and organization of game spaces have narratological consequences. In the case of evoked narratives, spatial design can either enhance our sense of immersion within a familiar world or communicate a fresh perspective on that story through the altering of established details. In the case of enacted narratives, the story itself may be structured around the character's movement through space and the features of the environment may retard or accelerate that plot trajectory. In the case of embedded narratives, the game space becomes a memory palace whose contents must be deciphered as the player tries to reconstruct the plot. And in the case of emergent narratives, game spaces are designed to be rich with narrative potential, enabling the story-constructing activity of players. In each case, it makes sense to think of game designers less as storytellers than as narrative architects.

References

Aarseth, Espen (1997). Cybertext: Perspectives on Ergodic Literature. Baltimore: Johns Hopkins University Press.

Adams, Ernest (1999). "Three Problems For Interactive Storytellers." Gamasutra, December 29, 1999.

Altman, Rick (1999). The American Film Musical. Bloomington: Indiana University Press.

Bordwell, David, Janet Staiger, and Kristen Thompson (1985). The Classical Hollywood Cinema. New York: Columbia University Press.

———. (1989). Narration in the Fiction Film. Madison: University of Wisconsin.

Branigan, Edward (1992). Narrative Comprehension and Film. New York: Routledge.

Carson, Don (2000). "Environmental Storytelling: Creating Immersive 3D Worlds Using Lessons Learned From the Theme Park Industry." Gamasutra, March 1, 2000.http://www.gamasutra.com/features/20000301/carson_pfv.htm.

Costikyan, Greg (2000). "Where Stories End and Games Begin." Game Developer, September 2000.

Crafton, Donald (1995). "Pie and Chase: Gag, Spectacle and Narrative in Slapstick Comedy." In Classical Hollywood Comedy, edited by Kristine Brunovska Karnick and Henry Jenkins. New York: Routledge/American Film Institute.

Crawford, Chris (1982). The Art of Computer Game Design. http://www.vancouver.wsu.edu/fac/peabody/game-book/Coverpage.html.

de Certeau, Michel (1988). The Practice of Everyday Life. Berkeley: University of California Press.

Dunniway, Troy (2000). "Using the Hero's Journey in Games." Gamasutra, November 27, 2000. http://www.gamasutra.com/features/20001127/dunniway_pfv.htm.

Eskelinen, Markku (2001). "The Gaming Situation." Game Studies 1, no.1 (July 2001). http://cmc.uib.no/gamestudies/0101/eskelinen.

Frasca, Gonzalo (1999). "Ludology Meets Narratology: Similitude and Differences between (Video) Games and Narrative." http://www.jacaranda.org/frasca/ludology.htm.

Fuller, Mary, and Henry Jenkins (1994). "Nintendo and New World Narrative." In Communications in Cyberspace, edited by Steve Jones. New York: Sage.

Gunning, Tom (1990). "The Cinema of Attractions: Early Film, Its Spectator and the Avant Garde." In Early Cinema: Space, Frame, Narrative, edited by Thomas Elsaesser with Adam Barker. London: British Film Institute.

Jenkins, Henry (1991). What Made Pistachio Nuts?: Early Sound Comedy and The Vaudeville Aesthetic. New York: Columbia University Press.

———. (1993). "x Logic: Placing Nintendo in Children's Lives." Quarterly Review of Film and Video, August 1993.

———. (1998). "Complete Freedom of Movement': Video Games as Gendered Playspace." In From Barbie to Mortal Kombat: Gender and Computer Games, edited by Justine Cassell and Henry Jenkins. Cambridge: The MIT Press.

Juul, Jesper (1998). "A Clash Between Games and Narrative." Paper presented at the Digital Arts and Culture Conference, Bergen, November 1998. http://www.jesperjuul.dk/text/DAC%20Paper%201998.html.

——. (2001). "Games Telling Stories?" Game Studies 1, no.1 (July 2001). http://cmc.uib. no/gamestudies/0101/juul-gts.

LeFebvre, Henri (1991). The Production of Space. London: Blackwell.

Lynch, Kevin (1960). The Image of the City. Cambridge: The MIT Press.

Murray, Janet (1997). Hamlet on the Holodeck: The Future of Narrative in Cyberspace. Cambridge: The MIT Press.

Ritvo, Harriet (1998). The Platypus and the Mermaid, and Other Figments of the Classifying Imagination. Cambridge: Harvard University Press.

Rudlin, John (1994). Commedia Dell'Arte: An Actor's Handbook. New York: Routledge.

Thompson, Kristen (1988). Breaking the Glass Armor: Neoformalist Film Analysis. Princeton: Princeton University Press.

Williams, Linda (1999). Hard Core: Power, Pleasure and "The Frenzy of the Visible." Berkeley: University of California Press.

31

THEORIZING NAVIGABLE SPACE IN VIDEO GAMES

Mark J. P. Wolf

Source: Stephan Günzel, Michael Liebe, and Dieter Mersch (eds), *DIGAREC Keynote-Lectures 2009/10* (Potsdam: Potsdam University Press, 2011), pp. 18–48.

Abstract

Space is understood best through movement, and complex spaces require not only movement but navigation. The theorization of navigable space requires a conceptual representation of space which is adaptable to the great malleability of video game spaces, a malleability which allows for designs which combine spaces with differing dimensionality and even involve non-Euclidean configurations with contingent connectivity. This essay attempts to describe the structural elements of video game space and to define them in such a way so as to make them applicable to all video game spaces, including potential ones still undiscovered, and to provide analytical tools for their comparison and examination. Along with the consideration of space, there will be a brief discussion of navigational logic, which arises from detectable regularities in a spatial structure that allow players to understand and form expectations regarding a game's spaces.

From simple single-screen games to elaborate adventure games requiring the exploration of convoluted networks of interconnections, space has always been an integral part of the video gaming experience; the graphical nature of video games seems to demand it. Decades of video game conventions and centuries of visual arts conventions help players to make sense of space, beginning with the division between a game's diegetic and non diegetic spaces, and ultimately to understand the way spaces construct a game's world. Yet although the ability to read and comprehend graphical representations is always the starting point of understanding space, interaction within and with a space is the means by which space is best understood. Interactivity is made up of choices, and choices are made up of options; and as spatial design often is an indication of movement options, it is also typically the basis for the indication of interactive possibilities. For example, most of the player's choices in even a simple game like SPACE INVADERS

(1978) involve four options: move left, move right, shoot, or do nothing; though the game features only one dimension of movement, three options are movement-related. Three-dimensional spaces suggest movement options along multiple axes, adding even more options to players' decision-making and dominating gameplay to an even greater extent.

Although players will mainly interact with tools, obstacles, and other characters within a game's spaces, navigation can be seen as interaction with space itself. Navigable space is space through which one must find one's way around, as opposed to a space in which one need not move, or a space in which one's movement is largely predetermined or so severely limited that one does not have the possibility of getting lost. Navigation is more than merely getting from one place to another; it is a cyclical process which involves exploration, the forming of a cognitive map of how spaces are connected, which in turn aids the decision-making processes employed by the player to move through those spaces for further exploration. Navigation, then, involves some degree of freedom of movement amidst connected spaces, the connections of which are explored and learned both by looking through and moving through them. After the first appearance of scrolling in Kee Games' SUPER BUG (1977) and the first screen-to screen cutting in Atari's ADVENTURE (1979), many games would show only a tiny fraction of their space onscreen at any given time, making spatial navigation and the building of a cognitive map an important part of gameplay. Any discussion of navigable space, then, should consider how a game's spaces are shaped, connected, represented, and manipulated, and how all of these affect navigation and navigational logic. To do so, we will need a generalized way of describing video game space and its configurations which can be applied in all cases and can be used as a means of comparing spatial constructions across games. And to do that we must first look, for a moment, at space itself.

Representations of space

The direct experience of physical space is understood though visual, sonic, haptic, and olfactic information which all aid in the mapping of space, but for most of us, visual information is the data most relied upon for the representation of space. For spaces represented in media forms, visual and sonic information are usually the only forms available for the representation of space. The human mind plays an active role as well; as Mark Wagner (2006:11) points out in his book on *The Geometries of Visual Space*, visual space is different than the physical space it seeks to represent and is often an affine transformation of it; he notes that "the geometry that best describes visual space changes as a function of experimental conditions, stimulus layout, observer attitude, and the passage of time". Wagner describes how visual space refers to physical space as we see it in lived experience; when we consider video game space, which is usually monocular, has reduced depth cues, and may not be fully three-dimensional in its construction, the potential variance from physical space is even greater.

A convenient way of categorizing spatial structures is dimensionality. As I have written elsewhere (Wolf 1997), many early games used planar, two-dimensional spaces, which can be described as being either a bounded single screen, a wraparound single screen, a space scrolling on one axis, a space scrolling on two axes, or a space divided into multiple screens depicting adjacent areas. In most of these games, two-dimensional space was used merely as a substitute for a three-dimensional space, such as those used for sports games or tank battles, rather than for an inherently two-dimensional scenario that required flatness. These games featured playing fields that were seen from above while the individual characters and objects on the fields were seen either in an overhead view or side view, giving the player a good sense of the spatial layout, and only those games which used off-screen space required navigation, and usually only a little of it at that.

Other games have a dimensionality that falls between two-dimensional spaces and ones that are computationally three-dimensional. These include games with independently-moving planes layered along the z-axis on which avatars may reside (as in SUPER MARIO BROS. (1985)), spaces with restricted z-axis movement (such as TEMPEST (1981), which only featured it in cut-scenes), spaces with oblique perspective that are largely only 2D-backdrops (such as ZAXXON (1982)), spaces that simulate 3D through the use of scaling sprites (such as POLE POSITION (1982)), and spaces with three-dimensional characters with limited movement and 2D-backdrops (such as TEKKEN (1994)). Such spaces, when they are large and complicated enough to require navigation, tend to still be only two-dimensional navigationally; player-character movement tends to be planar, even though there may be multiple planes of action, and the player's point-of-view tends to be more all-encompassing in games of such mixed dimensionality, as opposed to more immersive spaces that surround characters in three dimensions.

Three-dimensional spaces can also be non-navigable, like the live-action video sequences found in interactive movies, where the only navigation is narrative in nature. Even 3D-spaces involving true three-dimensional computation are often navigationally planar, though a first-person perspective makes navigation more challenging than an overhead view, and the malleability of video game spatial structures means that navigation has the potential to be far more difficult, and spaces far more confusing, than those of physical space.

Movement restrictions within spaces must also be considered, since avatars often cannot travel through all of a game's diegetic space. Games like PONG (1972), BREAKOUT (1976), SPACE INVADERS, and almost all paddle-based games, allow movement only back and forth along a line, one-dimensionally, though the player can affect things elsewhere; thus the rest of the space, which the player can see into but not move into, is still important in gameplay. While spatial navigation relies heavily on visual information, boundaries and barriers can exist without visual counterparts, and can only be discovered through the active exploration of a space; before spaces can be navigated they must be identified as navigable. Accounts of spatial navigation, then, must take all of these things into account.

Navigable space, as opposed to space in which no navigation is needed, is a space in which way-finding is necessary, a space made of interconnected spatial cells through which the player's avatar moves, a network often organized like a maze. All of the space may be present onscreen at once, as in certain maze games, but typically much of the space resides off-screen, and the accessibility, and even the discovery of off-screen areas, relies on a player's navigational ability. Additionally, obstacles may occlude spaces and their interconnections, while opponents and enemies may complicate navigational tasks and limit the time available for them. But before we consider all of these things, we should first define what we mean by spatial cells, the units with which navigable space is composed. Such a description should attempt to be useful in a general sense, not only for all existing video games, but also universal enough to include potential future designs.

Defining spatial cells

A video game spatial cell can be defined as a continuous 2D- or 3D-space which allows non-contingent two-way movement between all possible positions within that space, all of which is contained within some kind of boundary, such as a barrier or entrance regulating movement into and out of the space like a wall or doorway; a line of demarcation, like the line between two countries on a map or between squares on a chessboard; or a technical limitation, like a screen edge or a cut to another screen. Generally speaking, movement within a cell, since it does not cross a boundary, does not require navigation because the cell's space is available all around the player's avatar; it is when boundaries are crossed, and movement occurs from one cell to another, that navigation comes into play. This does not necessarily mean that all the space of an individual cell need be visible to the player all at once; in three-dimensional spaces seen with a first-person perspective, the cell's space will usually surround the player's avatar, who must turn around in order for all the space of the cell to be seen; but turning around and looking does not require the crossing of boundaries or movement from one cell to another, and thus does not require navigation. Navigation requires *movement*, either of the avatar along with its implied point of view, or even, in some cases, of the player's point of view itself, as in the solving of complex mazes presented on screen or on paper which the solver sees all at once. In such a situation, the solver's gaze must follow individual pathways through the maze in order to solve it, requiring navigation. For the solving of complex mazes on paper, a pencil or other pointer is often used, which becomes almost like a surrogate or avatar traveling through the maze along with the solver's gaze, making the process very similar to the playing of a third-person perspective video game.

The defining of spatial cells naturally depends on their boundaries, which may exist diegetically as walls, doorways, thresholds, or changes of terrain, or extradiegetically, such as screen edges or level changes which move a player to another space. Boundaries also serve multiple purposes, such as separating player positions, hallways, rooms, or territories, narrative locations or events, or areas of different levels of difficulty, and help the player to conceptualize the game in pieces, rather than as a large unwieldy whole. Practical reasons may exist for boundaries, such as programming limitations like memory allotment, load times, screen resolution, and render time, and other game design and gameplay concerns which address separate sections individually. Finally, boundaries can aid player motivation by giving players a sense of progress and accomplishment as each space is conquered, completed, or added, and they may also give a player a chance to rest between levels, view a cut-scene, save a game, and so on. Boundaries can range from very obvious barriers to subtle lines of demarcation awaiting a player's decision between a choice of passageways, and they may or may not be foregrounded by the game's action.

The boundary enclosing a spatial cell can further be divided into sections, each of which is either impassable or, when crossed, leads to a different location. These crossings or connections between spatial cells include such things as openings, pathways, tunnels, doorways, windows, variations in horizontal levels like stairs or platforms, transporters that send avatars to other locations, or simply screen edges which demarcate on-screen and off-screen space. Whether connections to adjoining spatial cells are hidden or obvious depends on such things as game design, player experience, and generic conventions.

Because boundaries can be broken into multiple connections between spatial cells, spatial cells can even be connected to themselves, making their own space navigable insofar as the player must learn how the spatial connections operate between different sections of the cell's boundary. An example would be the wraparound single screen found in ASTEROIDS (1979), in which the screen edges are connected to the edges directly opposite from them. While the operation of a space linked to itself in this manner seems fairly intuitive, especially if one is accustomed to cinematic conventions regarding the conservation of screen direction, other possibilities exist involving rotations and reflections; for example, a space which is linked to itself through a ninety-degree rotation, so that avatars leaving off the right side of the screen reappear moving up from the bottom of the screen, and so forth. Individual screen edges could be further subdivided into multiple boundary sections, and even neighboring sections on the same side of the screen could become connected.

The locating and using of the connections between spatial cells is a foundational part of navigation, and a cell's boundary can contain connections to many cells; so it is to these connections, and their variations, to which we must next turn.

Connections between spatial cells

Connections between spatial cells can be defined by their passability and visibility, and each of these traits can be further described regarding their reversibility and contingency, and whether they are open or closed. Each of these traits affects the player's ability to learn a game's spatial layout and navigate it successfully.

Passability refers to whether or not a connection between adjoining spatial cells is one that allows the player's avatar to move from one cell to the other. Such spaces need not be connected in the typical physical sense; for example, you could have pictures on the wall of a room which a player can click on and enter. The linking books in the MYST series operate in this way. Spaces could also be connected through the use of wormholes or transporters or other devices which allow transit between nonadjacent spaces. Connections which are initially closed but can later become opened or unlocked would still be considered passable. A connection is considered impassable only when no direct transit between connected cells is ever allowed. Passability is also in reference to the player's avatar in particular, since the player is the one doing the navigating; a connection that other characters are passing through but which never allows passage for the player's avatar would be considered impassable.

Visibility refers to whether a connection renders the space of an adjoining cell either visible, even partially, or completely obscured. In most cases, you can see into adjoining spaces before entering them. It is also possible for a connection to be impassable yet visible: for example, one can see adjoining spaces through windows, locked doors, or from high vantage points, even though in such cases the player cannot directly enter the spaces viewed from where they are. Impassible connections which still provide visibility aid in navigation since they give players information about how spaces are arranged, yet at the same time they can be frustrating since they do not allow movement into those spaces. Many games will often hint at spaces and spatial layouts in this way, giving players the navigational sub-goals of finding their way into the spaces seen. Numerous examples of this can be found in RIVEN (1997), where the grates of locked doors and high vistas tantalize players with glimpses of unexplored spaces. Spaces which are visible but cannot be traveled into are also usually used as vistas lining the borders of the game's diegetic world, to suggest a larger world beyond the spaces in which the game takes place, even though they are typically no more than simply 2-D backdrops draped around the game world's perimeter. Maps of spaces function in a similar manner, revealing spaces without showing them directly or allowing direct passage into them.

Connections that are passable, visible, or both can further be defined by their reversibility. *Reversibility* refers to whether a connection is two-way or one-way in nature. Whether players can cross over to another cell but still be able to return to the one from which they just came will determine the way they are able to explore a space, and sometimes the reversibility of a connection remains unknown until a player tries to pass through it both ways. An irreversible connection can also appear to be impassable, if one is on the receiving end of a one-way connection. A one-way connection can also result in the player's avatar being transported to another location, with nothing at that location to indicate that a one-way connection ends there. Therefore, a spatial cell may have one-way connections that end in the cell, yet do not pass through any specific boundary section; and there may be no prior indication that a cell is the endpoint of a one-way connection.

For example, in MYST (1993), the linking books of different ages return the player to the library on Myst Island, but there is nothing in the library to indicate that the ages link to it. Unless such connections follow some kind of rules, they can complicate a game's navigational logic. Likewise, while visibility is normally two-way between adjoining cells, connections similar to a one-way mirror are possible, wherein visibility is only available on one side of the connection. Views from surveillance cameras, for example, like those found in RIVEN, would be one example of one-way visibility.

Connections that are passable, visible, or both can also be defined by their contingency. *Contingency* refers to whether or not a connection always connects to the same place every time the avatar crosses it or looks through it. Most connections will always connect to the same spaces no matter what happens, while others, like certain doorways encountered by characters in the *Matrix* movies, change the destination cells of connections based on the state of different variables in the game. Those variables can include the state of the connection itself and how many times it has been used; for example, each use may take the avatar to a different place or narrative result. A contingent connection could also depend on the state of the player's avatar; for example, whether or not avatars have had a certain experience, or ability, or an object in their inventory. Contingencies can also be determined by the state of other parts of the game, like switches and levers, object positions, narrative branches, or other conditions. Some connections can randomly send the player to other spaces in the game (like the wormholes in EVE ONLINE (2003) or the 'Mass Relays' in MASS EFFECT (2007)), or even to other positions within the same spatial cell (like the hyperspace jump in ASTEROIDS). In the games NARBACULAR DROP (2005) and PORTAL (2007), players can use a special gun to create portals that connect to different areas and use them to move from one place to another.

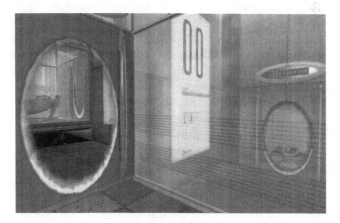

Figure 1 In portal (2007), players shoot holes that open into portals that connect disjoint spaces together (the three portals seen here are actually the same portal seen from different angles)

In the game PORTAL, the conservation of momentum that occurs when a player uses a portal is even used to solve certain puzzles and difficulties posed by the game's geography. Because of their dynamic nature, contingent connections can greatly complicate navigation, and can act as nexuses where spatial, temporal, and narrative structures intersect and determine each other.

Finally, the passability and visibility of a connection may each be either *open* or *closed*. Changing a connection from one to the other may be as simple as opening a door, or it may require a key or passcode to unlock and open it, or other actions or conditions. A connection that is closed and not easily opened may provide players with additional sub-goals that need to be pursued before navigation can continue, like the finding of a key. The fact that a connection can be open or closed should not be confused with the contingency of a connection; such connections are contingent only if they do not always connect to the same spaces and their connectivity changes. The issue of whether a connection is open or closed can be used to hide the impassable nature of a connection; for example, a player may encounter a locked door, and expect that it can be opened once the key is found. If it turns out that the game does not contain a key to open the door, then the connection is really an impassable one, if it can even be said to connect to anything at all; such a door could be no more than a detail in an uninteractive backdrop. Examples of locked doors that are never used and do not connect to anything appear in RETURN TO CASTLE WOLFENSTEIN (2001), as Espen Aarseth (2006) has pointed out.

Whether a connection is open or closed at any given time is often dependent on the player's actions, and as such it is really descriptive of the *state* of a connection, rather than its nature, which is described by such traits as passability, visibility, reversibility, and contingency. These four traits describe properties of connections; they may be initially misconstrued. A connection thought to be impassable may in fact turn out to only be closed once the means of opening the connection is found. Likewise, the visibility of a connection may be obscured or merely closed and able to be opened. Therefore, certain attributions are more difficult to confirm than others. Just as existence is more easily proven than nonexistence, connections can be proven to be passable, visible, reversible, and contingent, but they cannot be conclusively proven to be impassable, obscured, irreversible, or non-contingent without reference to the computer code that controls the game. Critical analysis, then, must be careful when describing connections in negative terms, since it is usually difficult to exhaustively experience all possible game states and conditions and be certain that one has discovered all the game's Easter eggs, although a game's structural logic may help to confirm or reject an analyst's assumptions regarding a game's overall spatial structure.

When passability, visibility, reversibility, and contingency are all taken into account, we find that there are 25 different types of connections possible between spatial cells, not including open and closed states which do not change the essential nature of the connection. The 25 types of connections are as follows:

1 impassable, obscured
2 impassable, visible (irreversible, contingent)
3 impassable, visible (irreversible, non-contingent)
4 impassable, visible (reversible, contingent)
5 impassable, visible (reversible, non-contingent)
6 passable (irreversible, contingent), obscured
7 passable (irreversible, contingent), visible (irreversible, contingent)
8 passable (irreversible, contingent), visible (irreversible, non-contingent)
9 passable (irreversible, contingent), visible (reversible, contingent)
10 passable (irreversible, contingent), visible (reversible, non-contingent)
11 passable (irreversible, non-contingent), obscured
12 passable (irreversible, non-contingent), visible (irreversible, contingent)
13 passable (irreversible, non-contingent), visible (irreversible, non-contingent)
14 passable (irreversible, non-contingent), visible (reversible, contingent)
15 passable (irreversible, non-contingent), visible (reversible, non-contingent)
16 passable (reversible, contingent), obscured
17 passable (reversible, contingent), visible (irreversible, contingent)
18 passable (reversible, contingent), visible (irreversible, non-contingent)
19 passable (reversible, contingent), visible (reversible, contingent)
20 passable (reversible, contingent), visible (reversible, non-contingent)
21 passable (reversible, non-contingent), obscured
22 passable (reversible, non-contingent), visible (irreversible, contingent)
23 passable (reversible, non-contingent), visible (irreversible, non-contingent)
24 passable (reversible, non-contingent), visible (reversible, contingent)
25 passable (reversible, non-contingent), visible (reversible, non-contingent)

While most of these connections are either passable or visible and can therefore provide the player with information useful to spatial navigation and the learning of the layout of a game's world, the first type of connection, which is both impassible and obscured, would seem to be a situation indistinguishable from the existence of no connection at all. Yet it is possible for connections that allow no movement or visibility between spaces to still provide navigational information and indicate an implied space. This can be as simple as the appearance of a locked door which implies an unseen adjoining space. Spaces can also be implied through the careful mapping of a game's space. For example, consider a three-by-three grid of adjoining screens that cut one to the next as the player moves through them.

As the player moves through the eight edge screens surrounding the middle screen, the mapping of the adjoining spaces reveals an implied space in between them in the center, which must exist, provided the overall space of the game's world is consistent, non-contingent, and Euclidean in nature. Another way to imply spaces is with a map showing spaces and their connections, without actually showing the spaces themselves or allowing access to them. Maps can even be used to imply space just by having blank spaces between other labeled spaces, showing that an area exists somewhere. Maps can provide a wealth of information

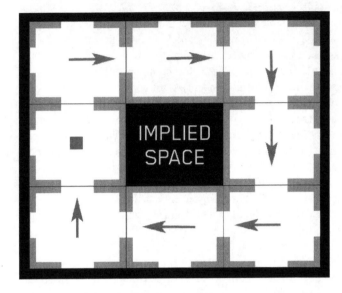

Figure 2 Spaces can be linked together in such a way as to imply other spaces in between them

about how spaces are connected, without allowing access to those spaces, or even allowing the player to look into them, since the map is only a representation of the space and not an image produced by a point of view looking into the space. While they can be one of the greatest aids to navigation, maps can be designed to provide as little information as possible about the actual spaces themselves, and even limit what can be implied regarding the status of their connections.

Of course, without a map, implied spaces can only be implied when the spatial structure in question is designed consistently around some kind of background logic upon which a player can rely. In the navigation of physical space, people rely on assumptions based on a Euclidean space in which Cartesian coordinates can be used, as is evident on most maps. Only for great distances do spherical distortions come into consideration. Just as 3D video games often rely on cinematic conventions to convey meaning, many also rely on assumptions about the Euclidean nature of space to aid players' navigation. But this not always need be the case, as the malleability of space in video games can easily allow for non-Euclidean configurations.

Non-Euclidean spatial structures

Although their use is relatively infrequent, non-Euclidean spaces appeared early in video game history and have continued to appear periodically since then, though their potential usage is still far from being realized. The Euclidean nature of video game space is due not only to its patterning after physical space to make it more comprehensible to players, but also because of the mathematical nature of the programming underlying the computational creation of space, which used to rely heavily on Euclidean Cartesian coordinate systems. Binary space partitioning 3D-engines, developed during the 1980s and early 1990s, would take a game-world space and recursively subdivide it into convex subsets, a hierarchical process resulting in a space-partitioning tree. Since binary space partitioning uses planes to divide spaces into subsets, there is an underlying assumption that the space is Euclidean. More recently developed portal-based systems, however, join spaces according to their connections, rather than where they are located in a larger grid of space, making non-Euclidean configurations easier to create (Laurila 2000). Like binary space partitioning systems, portal-based systems begin by drawing the sector the player is in, and then the other sectors visible from the player's sector, only they do not depend on an overall coordinate system, making non-Euclidean arrangements possible. Non-Euclidean geometry is even possible with a grid-based system, if a contingency system is used. For example, Ken Silverman's Build Engine for 3D Realms allows two rooms to occupy the same space on the grid, and decides which one will be rendered at any given time. Thus changes in the way spaces and their connections are conceptualized, and the programming methods that incarnate them in games, have opened up new spatial possibilities that have yet to be fully explored.

The space within individual spatial cells, then, is almost always Euclidean space when the cells are taken separately, and non-Euclidean spaces only arise through the way cells are connected to each other or to themselves. Thus the space within individual spatial cells is usually understood intuitively by players, even when the overall space of a game is designed counter to intuitive assumptions. So on the local level of the cell, space is almost always Euclidean, while on the global level it need not be at all.

There are several ways in which Euclidean cells can be connected so as to produce non-Euclidean structures. The first is to connect a single cell to itself in ways that violate Euclidean space. Single-screen games with wraparound space like ASTEROIDS are the most common example. The right and left sides of the screen are joined, as are the top and bottom, so that avatars leaving one side of the screen reappear on the opposite side. Mathematically, such a space is known as a 2-torus space, which is non-Euclidean because every line tracing the circumference of the torus is the same length, whether it lies on the inner or outer part of the ring. As mentioned earlier, another possible configuration for a single-screen space with four sides is one in which players leaving one side of the screen reenter through an adjacent side, rotated by ninety degrees.

Connections can also join together nested spaces of different sizes. For example in VENTURE (1981), some screens are enlarged areas of other screens, and cut to them when entered. And in ADVENTURE for the Atari 2600, castles are depicted onscreen with gates that are in the middle of the screen, yet the interiors of the black and white castles are each larger than a single screen. COSMIC OSMO (1989) subverts the assumption that a player's avatar remains a consistent size, and allows tiny spaces and openings to be entered, as the implied size of the avatar changes from one image of the game space to the next, even though the images are depicting different views of the same space.

Due to the way games depict three-dimensional spaces with two-dimensional images, the two can become interchangeable and open up possibilities for connections. An image might be used as a painting or photograph hanging on a wall, suggesting it is two-dimensional, but when a player clicks on it or moves into it, it can suddenly become three-dimensional. This effect can be used to create nested diegesis, for example, mini video games that can be played within the diegesis of other video games, like the 'Ship Chip Lander'-game found in COSMIC OSMO. The nesting of diegeses also has the potential to introduce interesting recursive loops into video games; COSMIC OSMO'S own title screen is seen on a Macintosh computer that appears within its own diegesis. Unfortunately, when the player clicks on the screen, the game does not become playable; though it could have easily been made to return the player to the title screen and begin the game again.

One-way spatial connections often violate Euclidean space. To cite an early example, SUPERMAN (1979) for the Atari 2600 had a subway depicted by a series of screens which had one-way connections by which the player exited into different parts of Metropolis. When the player makes the transition, the screen changes behind the avatar, leaving it in the same position, and there is no indication of the connection the avatar has just traversed. The linking books found in the ages of MYST return the player to the library on Myst Island in a similar fashion. More commonly, the moving up from one level of a game to a higher one is another instance of one-way movement, since the player usually cannot return to a lower level.

Another way to form a non-Euclidean structure is to join multiple cells together in ways that violate Euclidean space. For example, in the 'Lunatic Fringe'-level of DUKE NUKEM 3D (1996), there is a 720° circular hallway that the player must go around twice to return to the same position. Changing a few connections in a Euclidean arrangement of cells is usually enough to break the consistency and render the space non-Euclidean. It should be noted that connections in and of themselves are neither Euclidean nor non-Euclidean; it is the way they connect cells together that produces one kind of space or the other. It is only through movement and navigation, then, that the Euclidean or non-Euclidean nature of a space becomes apparent; most likely, a player will assume a Euclidean configuration until a structure's connectivity proves otherwise.

As mentioned earlier, in games like NARBACULAR DROP and PORTAL, players can create their own contingent non-Euclidean spatial connections. In ECHOCHROME (2008), players can even design their own non-Euclidean levels. Inspired by the work of M. C. Escher, ECHOCHROME features black-and-white line drawings of rotatable 3D structures, which obey different laws of perspective when rotated. The trailer (www.gametrailers.com/game/echochrome/5156) for the game describes and demonstrates the 5 perspective laws that the player must master:

- Perspective traveling: when two separate pathways appear to be touching, they are.
- Perspective landing: if one pathway appears to be above another, it is.
- Perspective existence: when the gap between two pathways is blocked from view and the pathways appear to be connected, they are.
- Perspective absence: when a hole is blocked from view, it does not exist.
- Perspective jump: when the mannequin jumps, it will land on whatever appears beneath it.

ECHOCHROME uses Jun Fujiki's Object Locative Environment Coordinate System, which translates the global three-dimensional space into a two-dimensional coordinate system locally around the avatar, and determines movement constraints based on the two-dimensional interpretation. Thus the game tests the player's ability to quickly shift back and forth between interpreting the game image as a two-dimensional space and as a three-dimensional space, since the manipulation of the space occurs in three dimensions, while the avatar's behavior requires a two-dimensional interpretation.

Finally, contingent connections can violate Euclidean space, unless there is some explanation for the way connections between spaces change; for example, an elevator that connects to different floors depending on the position to which it is moved. If the contingency of a connection renders a space non-Euclidean by changing a connection's destination cell, it may be the case that each of the resulting spatial structures is Euclidean and the only violation is a dynamic one, in which the space does not remain consistent over time; for example, if a particular room is replaced by another of the same size. Thus, spatial structures can become non-Euclidean in a spatial sense, through an unchanging network of connections that break Euclidean consistency, or become non-Euclidean in a temporal sense, through contingent connections that differ over time and break consistency in a dynamic way (in ECHOCHROME, for example, such contingent connections are based on the player's point of view).

Non-Euclidean spaces can be navigated once their constituent pieces and the connections between them are understood. But there are other difficulties that exist at a more local level. Some spaces can be more difficult to reconcile with the model of interconnected spatial cells I have been describing, and it is to these kinds of spaces that we must next turn.

Track-like spaces and other structures

Many games do not allow the kind of free exploration that necessitates the learning of the layout of a spatial structure, and an avatar's movements may be so restricted that navigational skills are not needed to play the game. For example, PONG, TEMPEST, and TETRIS (1985) all involve no navigation. But many racing games, driving games, and rail-based shooting games each have a space that is a gradually-revealed continuous strip of track-like space that the avatar or player's point-of-view moves along. Movement along such a track is typically one-way, and the speed of the movement may or may not be controlled by the player. Such games may require the player to steer around obstacles, shoot targets, or both, and often at a quick pace. Space in these games is experienced in largely a linear fashion, with little or no navigation occurring, because *steering* (which involves avoiding obstacles or staying within the bounds of a pathway) is different than *navigating* (which involves making choices and finding one's way around in a mazelike spatial structure). To consider these large, track-like spaces as single cells or even series of cells can be problematic, because free movement within them is usually not available, and because the player is unable to make choices that result in a change of destination. Both of these things are required for navigation, which requires not only a certain *type* of decision-making (which involves choosing which path to take out of several possibilities, based on the player's knowledge of the game's spatial structure), but a minimum *number* of such decisions as well, since the process of navigation is a cyclical one, involving exploration, the gathering of knowledge gained through exploration and the integration of new knowledge into existing knowledge, and finally the application of the integrated knowledge to further exploration.

Yet track-like spaces can be combined into navigable environments of spatial cells, and act like a cell within them. An example would be a vehicle that the player rides to a new location where exploration and navigation can resume. The same can be said for the mixing of two-dimensional, two-and-a-half dimensional, and three-dimensional spatial structures; they can be combined together in a game, like SUPER PAPER MARIO (2007), though most games typically limit their diegesis to a single type of dimensionality. If enough track-like spaces are joined together, with forking paths and decision points along the way, then navigation can gradually come into play again, as the network of track-like spaces becomes a maze.

Another kind of space is a large 3D space with obstacles or characters that obstruct the player's point of view, creating hidden spaces which are revealed and obscured as the obstructions move around. One such game space is organized around the surface of a sphere or other three-dimensional form, half of which faces the player and is visible and half of which faces away from the player and is hidden from view. For example, SUPER STARDUST HD (2007) and SUPER MARIO GALAXY (2007) feature small planets that the player's avatar traverses while avoiding enemies. Each of these spaces could be conceived as a single spatial cell, only half of which is seen at any given time, or as two cells whose boundaries change according to the player's movement; the visible area and the occluded area. In a similar fashion, the edges of the screen on scrolling landscapes change according to the avatar's positioning; such boundaries are conditional, as opposed to unchanging boundaries such as walls, mountains, or other fixed lines of demarcation.

The movement of the playing field relative to the avatar's position need not be the only exception. One could conceive of a video game in which the space of the game's world is dynamic. Instead of having fixed boundaries, spatial cells could have boundaries that are continually changing, expanding and shrinking, to the point where new spatial cells are coming into existence while others are going out of existence as they shrink down to nothing. SUPER MARIO GALAXY has a level in which spaces shrink and vanish after the player's avatar has passed over them, although even more complex expansion and contraction patterns could be designed. In such games, players would have to constantly keep on the move, to avoid getting caught in a cell that is disappearing, and they would also keep relearning the spaces and how they connect in order to navigate them. When the world and the player's mental map of it constantly changes, players can succeed only when they have a sense of the game's navigational logic.

Navigational logic

Navigational logic can be seen as being made up of four distinct kinds of things players must learn:

1   what spaces exist in the game's world (which includes those that can be accessed, those that are only seen but are inaccessible, and those that are neither accessible nor visible, but are only implied);
2   how those spaces are interconnected (which involves the learning of boundaries, obstacles, and geographical layout);
3   how interconnections between spaces work (in terms of their passability, visibility, reversibility, contingency, and how they are opened and closed); and
4   how spaces and their configurations change over time, if they do.

Of course, the learning process is simultaneous and cyclical, as each of these four things relies on the learning of the other three, and because spaces and their boundaries mutually define each other.

To investigate these questions we would next have to ask, how is each of these incorporated into gameplay? Are they foregrounded or backgrounded within the game's main objective, or are one or more of them involved in the game's main objective? What conventions are relied upon, and what kind of knowledge or experience is the player assumed to have? Different genres use them to differing degrees, with maze games, adventure games, and first-person shooting games the most likely to require more complex navigation. How much replaying of a game is necessary to learn its navigational logic, due to irreversible crossings or nonrepeatable events? The navigation of space may also involve the navigation of branching narrative possibilities, though at the same time these may also provide a player with clues to the navigation of space.

Spatial navigation can be made difficult either passively or actively. Elements that work passively against a player's ability to navigate include a game's design and the layout of its spaces: complex configurations can tax the player's memory, patience, and endurance. Non intuitive designs, especially non-Euclidean ones and ones involving contingency or irreversibility, can work against players usual assumptions and disorient them, requiring more exploration and trial-and-error in gameplay. Euclidean configurations tend to be the default in game design, especially for games in which navigation is not foregrounded or intended to be a challenge. If non-intuitive spatial structures are used, learning them will most likely be an important part of the game, if not its main objective. Finally, navigation can be passively thwarted by the lack of a consistent logic in the way game spaces and their connections operate. This differs from complex designs, since complex designs can be still be consistent and logical in the way they work, and it is usually more a result of poor design than deliberate design. Lack of a navigational logic is more likely to be seen as frustrating than as a challenge to be enjoyed.

Other things can actively work against the player's ability to navigate. Enemies who block connections, chase after players, and attack them, forcing them to respond, certainly make navigation more difficult. Even inanimate obstacles can block connections, making them impassable and obscuring visibility. Both enemies and obstacles demonstrate how other tasks can interfere or compete with navigational tasks, forcing players to prioritize and multitask, sometimes at the same time. Time constraints can act in a similar way, limiting the amount of time for exploration as well as for decisions regarding exploration. Narrative sequences can interrupt exploration, and possibly change a game's state in ways that affect navigation. Finally, if a game's spatial cells, the connections between them, and their contingencies continuously change during gameplay, navigation may become confoundingly complicated.

Spaces are created not only by software, but by hardware as well. To date, most games have been designed for a single, flat, rectangular screen. A few exceptions, like the Nintendo Virtual Boy and the Nintendo DS, have used multiple screens, although the Virtual Boy's screens were used together to produce a single stereo image. But new flat screen technologies, and developing technologies like flexible screens and electronic paper, will be able to help designers explore new screen configurations. Imagine playing even a simple game like PONG on a cylindrical screen which the player cannot see all at one time, and which must be physically turned as the game is played. Or PAC-MAN (1980) played on multiple screens on the sides of a cube, or even on a spherical screen in which Pac Man stays at the top of the sphere, which must be rotated to move him through the maze. Screens that the player cannot see in their entirety at any given time open up new design possibilities. Instead of having only on-screen and off-screen space, on-screen space would be further divided into on-screen space that the player can see and on-screen space the player can't see. Game events occurring simultaneously on multiple screens would act similar to games in which multiple actions are occurring on split screens, only they may be more difficult to monitor; six events occurring at once on the sides of a cube would not only place interesting demands on the mental aspects of gameplay, but on the physical ones as well, requiring dexterity and speed.

Likewise, interface devices (such as a joystick, controller, mouse, or keyboard) are usually used for moving a player's avatar through a two-dimensional plane of movement, which in turn determines what spaces are displayed. Some games turn these ideas around, so that the controllers manipulate the game's space directly, and this movement determines the avatar's movement, which is not directly under the player's control but instead is automated and responsive to changes in the spatial orientation of the surrounding environment, making spatial manipulation a prerequisite for spatial navigation. In some of these games, space is manipulated through the movement of the screen itself; position-sensing mercury switches have begun to make more of these games possible commercially, for example, on the iPhone. In other games, the screen itself stays stationary, while spaces are manipulated by conventional control devices. A brief analysis of one game in each category will help to examine the potential of spatial manipulation.

In ECHOCHROME, players manipulate space so as to change their viewpoint, which in turn changes the way the spatial structure behaves, opening and closing connections for the automated avatar. The main navigational challenge is the moving of the space combined with the constant perceptual shifting between the three-dimensional and two-dimensional interpretations of the game imagery, the first of which is needed for the manipulation of space while the second is needed to connect one space to another for the avatar's passage. Because the five rules of perspective are made explicit, players can adopt them more quickly, allowing them to concentrate on the puzzle aspects of the game. The automatic movement of the avatar can add a further time pressure, for example when it is heading for a hole or a gap that the player must hide by readjusting the perspective. The game could have been further complicated by the presence of monsters whose movements obey the same principles as the avatar, and who could be trapped and released in other areas of the structure as the perspective opens and closes connections. This would have required the player to focus on multiple areas of the game space simultaneously, and could create puzzles requiring the containment of monsters on geographically-isolated beams before certain moves could be safely completed. Perhaps we will see additional challenges like these in future iterations of the game.

A good example of the physical manipulation of space through analogous movements of the hardware on which the game space appears is Julian Oliver's game LEVELHEAD (2007), which uses a form of augmented reality. The player manipulates small cubes atop a pedestal, the movements of which are recorded by a small camera on the pedestal. The image from the camera appears on a large screen in front of the player, but this image has been processed by a computer so that the images of spaces within the cubes appear on the surfaces of the cubes facing the camera. When the player moves the cubes, the spaces shift perspective, and the avatar, a white silhouette of a walking man, moves as the cubes are tipped, passing from one space to another, and even from one cube to another.

Figure 3 Julian Oliver's LEVELHEAD (2007)—a game with an augmented reality interface

The cubes in LEVELHEAD each contain six different rooms, one on each face of the cube, and each room appears to occupy the entire interior of the cube. Through subtle clues like the position of the doorways and the color of the light spilling in through them, players must figure out how these rooms are connected, and also how the rooms in one cube are connected to rooms in the other cubes. The cube must be oriented properly so that the floor side of a room is on the bottom, something that can differ from one room to another. The game integrates game space and physical space in an interesting way, since players must watch their own hands interacting with the cubes on the big screen, in order to see the cube interiors composited into the image. The space in the large screen is that of the physical world of the player, being re-represented, and within it, the game's diegetic space is seen to reside, as though it were connected to the physical space of the player. Thus game space, physical space, and the interface itself are all combined in a unique way that makes the navigation of space, through spatial manipulation, the central challenge of the game.

As is the case with ECHOCHROME, the difficulty of LEVELHEAD could be increased with the addition of sub goals and enemies that chase the avatar through the space of the game. While the use of space in games like ECHOCHROME and LEVELHEAD is new, spatial navigation remains the games' central challenge. As more conventions regarding the use of non-Euclidean space and games with spatial manipulation become more common, spatial navigation may become only one of multiple tasks demanding a player's attention. As game screens, controllers, and other hardware devices evolve, and new software appears to integrate them into gameplay, new potential for spatial relationships will emerge, which in turn will affect the player's relationship to the game space and its navigational logic. Whatever the future of video games may hold in store, it is certain that questions regarding the design of video game spaces, how those spaces are connected, and how they are experienced, will remain essential to video game studies and the study of the human experience of spatial representations in general.

References

Aarseth, Espen (2007): "Doors and Perception. Fiction vs. Simulation in Games", in: *Intermédialités* 9, 35–44.

Laurila, Pietari (2000): "Geometry Culling in 3D Engines", posted October 9, 2000, on GameDev.net, http://www.gamedev.net/reference/articles/article1212.asp.

Wagner, Mark (2006): *The Geometries of Visual Space*, Mahwah, New Jersey and London, England: Lawrence Erlbaum Associates.

Wolf, Mark J. P. (1997): "Inventing Space. Towards a Taxonomy of On- and Off-Screen Space in Video Games", in: *Film Quarterly* 51, 11–23.

Wolf, Mark J. P. (2001): "Space in the Video Game", in: *The Medium of the Video Game*, ed. by M. J. P. Wolf, Austin: University of Texas Press, 52–75 [1997].

Wolf, Mark J. P. (2008): "Z-axis Development in the Video Game"in *The Video Game Theory Reader 2*, ed. by Bernard Perron and Mark J. P. Wolf, New York: Routledge, 151–168.

ADVENTURE (1979), Atari, Atari VCS 2600.
ASTEROIDS (1979), Atari, arcade (also ported to other systems).
BREAKOUT (1976), Atari, arcade (also ported to other systems).
COSMIC OSMO (1989), Cyan, Macintosh.
DUKE NUKEM 3D (1996), 3D Realms, Microsoft Windows (also ported to other systems).
ECHOCHROME (2008), PlayStation 3 (also ported to other systems).
EVE ONLINE (2003), online game.
LEVELHEAD (2007), downloadable game.
MASS EFFECT (2007), Bioware, Xbox 360, Microsoft Windows.
MYST (1993), Cyan, Macintosh (also ported to other systems).
NARBACULAR DROP (2005), downloadable game.
PAC-MAN (1980), Namco, arcade (also ported to other systems).
POLE POSITION (1982), Atari, arcade (also ported to other systems).
PONG (1972), Atari, arcade (also ported to other systems).
PORTAL (2007), Valve Corporation, downloadable (ported to various systems).
RETURN TO CASTLE WOLFENSTEIN (2001), Activision, Microsoft Windows (also ported to other systems).
RIVEN (1997), Cyan, Macistosh (also ported to other systems).
SPACE INVADERS (1978), Taito, arcade (also ported to other systems).
SUPER BUG (1977), Kee Games, arcade.
SUPER MARIO BROS. (1985), Nintendo, NES.
SUPER MARIO GALAXY (2007), Nintendo, Wii.
SUPER PAPER MARIO (2007), Nintendo, Wii.

SUPER STARDUST HD (2007), Housemarque, PlayStation 3.

SUPERMAN (1979), Atari, Atari 2600.

TEKKEN (1994), Namco, arcade.

TEMPEST (1981), Atari, arcade.

TETRIS (1984), Alexey Pajitnov, (ported to various systems).

VENTURE (1981), Exidy, arcade (also ported to other systems).

ZAXXON (1982), Atari, arcade (also ported to other systems).

The Matrix (1999), Andy Wachowski and Larry Wachowski, Australia/USA.

The Matrix Reloaded (2003), Andy Wachowski and Larry Wachowski, Australia/USA.

The Matrix Revolutions (2003), Andy Wachowski and Larry Wachowski, Australia/USA.

32

GAMIC ACTION, FOUR MOMENTS

Alexander R. Galloway

Source: *Gaming: Essays on Algorithmic Culture* (Minneapolis, MN: University of Minnesota Press, 2006), pp. 1–38.

A game is an activity defined by rules in which players try to reach some sort of goal. Games can be whimsical and playful, or highly serious. They can be played alone or in complex social scenarios. This book, however, is not about games in the abstract, nor is it about games of all varieties, electronic or not. There is little here on game design, or performance, or imaginary worlds, or nonlinear narrative. I avoid any extended reflection on the concept of play. Rather, this book starts and ends with a specific mass medium, the medium of the video game from the 1970s to the beginning of the new millennium. A few detours will be necessary along the way: to the cinema, and to the computer.

A video game is a cultural object, bound by history and materiality, consisting of an electronic computational device and a game simulated in software. The electronic computational device—the machine, for short—may come in a variety of forms. It may be a personal computer, an arcade machine, a home console, a portable device, or any number of other electronic machines.[1] The machine will typically have some sort of input device, such as a keyboard or controller, and also have some sort of intelligible surface for output such as a screen or other physical interface. Loaded into the machine's storage is the game software. Software is data; the data issue instructions to the hardware of the machine, which in turn executes those instructions on the physical level by moving bits of information from one place to another, performing logical operations on other data, triggering physical devices, and so on. The software instructs the machine to simulate the rules of the game through meaningful action. The player, or operator,[2] is an individual agent who communicates with the software and hardware of the machine, sending codified messages via input devices and receiving codified messages via output devices. Taking these elements in sum, I use the term "gaming" to refer to the entire apparatus of the video game. It is a massive cultural medium involving large numbers of organic machines and inorganic machines. Embedded as it is in the information systems of the millenary society, this medium will likely remain significant for some time to come.

Begin like this: If photographs are images, and films are moving images, then *video games are actions*. Let this be word one for video game theory. Without action, games remain only in the pages of an abstract rule book. Without the active participation of players and machines, video games exist only as static computer code. Video games come into being when the machine is powered up and the software is executed; they exist when enacted.

Video games are actions. Consider the formal differences between video games and other media: indeed, one *takes* a photograph, one *acts* in a film. But these actions transpire before or during the fabrication of the work, a work that ultimately assumes the form of a physical object (the print). With video games, the work itself is material action. One *plays* a game. And the software *runs*. The operator and the machine play the video game together, step by step, move by move. Here the "work" is not as solid or integral as in other media. Consider the difference between camera and joystick, or between image and action, or between watching and doing. In his work on the cinema, Gilles Deleuze used the term "action-image" to describe the expression of force or action in film. With video games, the action-image has survived but now exists not as a particular historical or formal instance of representation but as the base foundation of an entirely new medium. "Games are both object and process," writes Espen Aarseth, "they can't be read as texts or listened to as music, they must be played."[3] To understand video games, then, one needs to understand how action exists in gameplay, with special attention to its many variations and intensities.

One should resist equating gamic action with a theory of "interactivity" or the "active audience" theory of media. Active audience theory claims that audiences always bring their own interpretations and receptions of the work. Instead I embrace the claim, rooted in cybernetics and information technology, that an active medium is one whose very materiality moves and restructures itself—pixels turning on and off, bits shifting in hardware registers, disks spinning up and spinning down. Because of this potential confusion, I avoid the word "interactive" and prefer instead to call the video game, like the computer, an *action-based* medium.[4]

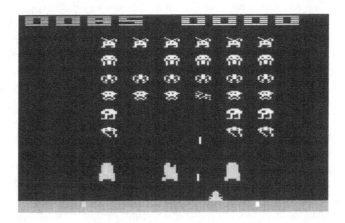

Space Invaders, Taito Corporation, 1978

Because of this, for the first time in a long time there comes an interesting upheaval in the area of mass culture. What used to be primarily the domain of eyes and looking is now more likely that of muscles and doing, *thumbs*, to be sure, and what used to be the act of reading is now the act of doing, or just "the act." In other words, while the mass media of film, literature, television, and so on continue to engage in various debates around representation, textuality, and subjectivity, there has emerged in recent years a whole new medium, computers and in particular video games, whose foundation is not in looking and reading but in the instigation of material change through action. And the most curious part of the upheaval is, to borrow what Critical Art Ensemble said once about hackers, that the most important cultural workers today are children.

People move their hands, bodies, eyes, and mouths when they play video games. But machines also act. They act in response to player actions as well as independently of them. Philip Agre uses the phrase "grammars of action" to describe how human activities are coded for machinic parsing using linguistic and structural metaphors.[5] Video games create their own grammars of action; the game controller provides the primary physical vocabularies for humans to pantomime these gestural grammars. But beyond the controller, games also have their own grammars of action that emerge through gameplay. These grammars are part of the code. They help pass messages from object to object inside the machine's software. But they also help to articulate higher-level actions, actions experienced in common game occurrences such as power-ups or network lag.

One may start by distinguishing two basic types of action in video games: machine actions and operator actions. The difference is this: machine actions are acts performed by the software and hardware of the game computer, while operator actions are acts performed by players. So, winning *Metroid Prime* is the operator's act, but losing it is the machine's. Locating a power-up in *Super Mario*

Berzerk, Stern Electronics, 1980

Bros. is an operator act, but the power-up actually boosting the player character's health is a machine act.

Of course, the division is completely artificial—both the machine and the operator work together in a cybernetic relationship to effect the various actions of the video game in its entirety. The two types of action are ontologically the same. In fact, in much of gameplay, the two actions exist as a *unified, single phenomenon*, even if they are distinguishable for the purposes of analysis. This book will not privilege one type of action over the other (as analyses of other media often do)—in video games the action of the machine is just as important as the action of the operator.

But, you may ask, where is the fun in a game played by an "operator" and a "machine"? Video games can be intensely fun. They immerse and enthrall. Time-wise, video games garner significant investment by players. This happens in gaming to an extent not seen in other mass media. Many games are rated at sixty or eighty hours of total gameplay; some, like *Sims Online* or *World of Warcraft*, far exceed that. But a video game is not simply a fun toy. It is also an algorithmic machine and like all machines functions through specific, codified rules of operation. The player—the "operator"—is the one who must engage with this machine. In our day and age, this is the site of fun. It is also the work site. I adopt the terms "operator" and "machine" not to diminish the value of fun, meaningful play but to stress that in the sphere of electronic media, games are fundamentally cybernetic software systems involving both organic and nonorganic actors.

As the great German media theorist Friedrich Kittler wrote, code is the only language that does what it says. Code is not only a syntactic and semantic language; it is also a machinic language. At runtime, code moves. Code effects physical change in a very literal sense. Logic gates open and close. Electrons flow. Display devices illuminate. Input devices and storage devices transubstantiate between the physical and the mathematical. Video games are games, yes, but more importantly they are software systems; this must always remain in the forefront of one's analysis. In blunt terms, the video game *Dope Wars* has more in common with the finance software *Quicken* than it does with traditional games like chess, roulette, or billiards. Thus it is from the perspective of informatic software, of *algorithmic cultural objects*, that this book unfolds.

Gamic action is customarily described as occurring within a separate, semiautonomous space that is removed from normal life. The French sociologist and anthropologist Roger Caillois writes that games are "make-believe," that they are "accompanied by a special awareness of a second reality or of a free unreality, as against real life."[6] The Dutch cultural historian Johan Huizinga agrees, writing that play transpires "quite consciously outside 'ordinary' life."[7]

Thus in addition to the previous split between machine and operator, a second analytical distinction is possible: in video games there are actions that occur in diegetic space and actions that occur in nondiegetic space. I adopt the terms "diegetic" and "nondiegetic" from literary and film theory. But in the migration from one medium to another, the meaning of the terms will no doubt change slightly.[8] The diegesis of a video game is the game's total world of narrative

Warcraft III, Blizzard Entertainment, 2002

action. As with cinema, video game diegesis includes both onscreen and offscreen elements. It includes characters and events that are shown, but also those that are merely made reference to or are presumed to exist within the game situation. While some games may not have elaborate narratives, there always exists some sort of elementary play scenario or play situation—Caillois's "second reality"— which functions as the diegesis of the game. In *PONG* it is a table, a ball, and two paddles; in *World of Warcraft* it is two large continents with a sea in between. By contrast, nondiegetic play elements are those elements of the gaming apparatus that are external to the world of narrative action. In film theory, "nondiegetic" refers to a whole series of formal techniques that are part of the apparatus of the film while still outside the narrative world of the film, such as a film's score or titles. With "nondiegetic" I wish to evoke this same terrain for video games: gamic elements that are inside the total gamic apparatus yet outside the portion of the apparatus that constitutes a pretend world of character and story. To be sure, nondiegetic elements are often centrally connected to the act of gameplay, so being nondiegetic does not necessarily mean being nongamic. Sometimes nondiegetic elements are firmly embedded in the game world. Sometimes they are entirely removed. The heads-up display (HUD) in *Deus Ex* is nondiegetic, while the various rooms and environments in the game are diegetic. Or in *Berzerk*, pressing Start is a nondiegetic act, whereas shooting robots is a diegetic act. Likewise, activating the Pause button in *Max Payne* is a nondiegetic act, but activating the slow-motion effect during a gunfight is a diegetic act. As will become evident, the nondiegetic is much more common in gaming than in film or literature, and likewise it will be much more central to my study. In fact, I find that the need to employ the concept of the diegetic at all stems not from a desire to reduce games

Deus Ex, Ion Storm, 2000

to narrative texts, but quite the opposite: since the nondiegetic is so important in video games, it is impossible not to employ the concept, even in a negative issuance. And indeed, in some instances it will be difficult to demarcate the difference between diegetic and nondiegetic acts in a video game, for the process of good game continuity is to fuse these acts together as seamlessly as possible.

The superimposition of these two orthogonal axes—machine and operator, diegetic and nondiegetic—is a deliberate attempt to embrace a broad theory of gamic action.[9] I wish to make room here for the entire medium of the video game. In this model, pressing Pause is as significant as shooting a weapon. Cheats are as significant as strategies. Other approaches might miss this. The four quadrants of these two axes will provide the structure for the rest of the chapter. Thus I offer here four moments of gamic action. Each will uncover a different perspective on the formal qualities of the video game.

Pure process

The first quadrant is about the machinic phylum and the vitality of pure matter. Consider Yu Suzuki's *Shenmue*. One plays *Shenmue* by participating in its *process*. Remove everything and there is still action, a gently stirring rhythm of life. There is a privileging of the quotidian, the simple. As in the films of Yasujiro Ozu, the experience of time is important. There is a repetition of movement and dialogue ("On that day the snow changed to rain," the characters repeat). One step leads slowly and deliberately to the next. There is a slow, purposeful accumulation of experiences.

Shenmue, Sega AM2, 2000

When games like *Shenmue* are left alone, they often settle into a moment of equilibrium. Not a tape loop, or a skipped groove, but a state of rest. The game is slowly walking in place, shifting from side to side and back again to the center. It is running, playing itself, perhaps. The game is in an ambient state, an *ambience act*. Not all games have this action, but when they do, they can exist in an ambience act indefinitely. No significant stimulus from the game environment will disturb the player character. *Grand Theft Auto III* defaults to the ambience act. Almost all moments of gameplay in *Final Fantasy X* can momentarily revert to an ambience act if the gamer simply stops playing and walks away. *Shenmue*, despite its clock, reverts to the ambience act. Things continue to change when caught in an ambience act, but nothing changes that is of any importance. No stopwatch runs down. No scores are lost. If the passage of time means anything at all, then the game is not in an ambient state. It rains. The sun goes down, then it comes up. Trees stir. These acts are a type of perpetual happening, a living tableau. Ambience acts are distinguishable from a game pause through the existence of micromovements—just like the small, visible movements described by Deleuze as the "affect-image." They signal that the game is still under way, but that no gameplay is actually happening at the moment. The game is still present, but play is absent. Micromovements often come in the form of pseudorandom repetitions of rote gamic action, or ordered collections of repetitions that cycle with different periodicities to add complexity to the ambience act. The machine is still *on* in an ambience act, but the operator is away. Gameplay recommences as soon as the operator returns with controller input. The ambience act is the machine's act. The user is on hold, but the machine keeps on working. In this sense, an ambience act is the inverse of pressing Pause. While the *machine* pauses in a pause act and the operator is free to take a break, it is the *operator* who is paused in an ambience act, leaving the machine to hover in a state of pure process.

The ambience act is an action executed by the machine and thus emanates outward to the operator (assuming that he or she has stuck around to witness it). In this sense, it follows the logic of the traditionally expressive or representational forms of art such as painting or film. The world of the game exists as a purely aesthetic object in the ambience act. It can be looked at; it is detached from the world, a self-contained expression. But there is always a kind of "charged expectation" in the ambience act.[10] It is about possibility, a subtle solicitation for the operator to return.

Likewise there is another category related to the ambience act that should be described in slightly inverted terms. These are the various interludes, segues, and other machinima that constitute the purely cinematic segments of a game. James Newman uses the term "off-line" to describe these moments of player passivity, as opposed to the "on-line" moments of actual gameplay.[11] Most video games incorporate time-based, linear animation at some point, be they the quick animations shown between levels in *Pac-Man*, or the high-budget sequences shot on film in *Enter the Matrix*. There is a certain amount of repurposing and remediation going on here, brought on by a nostalgia for previous media and a fear of the pure uniqueness of video gaming. (As McLuhan wrote in the opening pages of *Understanding Media*, the content of any new medium is always another medium.) In these segments, the operator is momentarily irrelevant—in the ambience act the operator was missed; here the operator is forgotten. But instead of being in a perpetual state of no action, the cinematic elements in a game are highly instrumental and deliberate, often carrying the burden of character development or moving the plot along in ways unattainable in normal gameplay. Cinematic interludes transpire within the world of the game and extend the space or narrative of the game in some way. They are outside gameplay, but they are not outside the narrative of gameplay. Formally speaking, cinematic interludes are a type of grotesque fetishization of the game itself as machine. The machine is put at the service of cinema. Scenes are staged and produced from the machine either as rendered video or as procedural, in-game action. Hollywood-style editing and postproduction audio may also be added. So, ironically, what one might consider to be the most purely machinic or "digital" moments in a video game, the discarding of operator and gameplay to create machinima from the raw machine, are at the end of the day the most nongamic. The necessity of the operator-machine relationship becomes all too apparent. These cinematic interludes are a window into the machine itself, oblivious and self-contained.

The actions outlined here are the first step toward a classification system of action in video games. Because they transpire within the imaginary world of the game and are actions instigated by the machine, I will call the first category *diegetic machine acts*. The material aspects of the game environment reside here, as do actions of non-player characters. This moment is the moment of pure process. The machine is up and running—no more, no less.

A subjective algorithm

But, of course, video games are not as impersonal and machinic as all this. The operator is as important to the cybernetic phenomenon of video games as the machine itself. So now let us look at an entirely different moment of gamic action. As will become apparent in chapter 4, this second moment is the allegorical stand-in for political intervention, for hacking, and for critique.

The second moment of gamic action refers to a process with spontaneous origins but deliberate ends. This is gamic action as a subjective algorithm. That is to say, in this second moment, video game action is a type of inductive, diachronic patterning of movements executed by individual actors or operators.[12] We are now ready to explore the second quadrant of gamic action: *nondiegetic operator acts*.

These are actions of configuration. They are always executed by the operator and received by the machine. They happen on the exterior of the *world* of the game but are still part of the game software and completely integral to the play of the game. An example: the simplest nondiegetic operator act is pushing Pause. Pausing a game is an action by the operator that sets the entire game into a state of suspended animation. The pause act comes from outside the machine, suspending the game inside a temporary bubble of inactivity. The game freezes in its entirety. It is not simply on hold, as with the ambience act, nor has the machine software crashed. Thus a pause act is undamaging to gameplay and is always reversible, yet the machine itself can never predict when a pause act will happen. It is nondiegetic precisely because nothing in the world of the game can explain or motivate it when it occurs. Pause acts are, in reality, the inverse of what machine actions (as opposed to operator actions) *are*, simply because they negate action, if only temporarily.

Another example of the nondiegetic operator act is the use of cheats or game hacks. Many games have cheats built into them. Often these are deliberately designed into the game for debugging or testing purposes and only later leaked to the public or accidentally discovered by enterprising gamers. Like a pause, the cheat act is executed from outside the world of the game by the operator. It affects the play of the game in some way. This action can be performed with hardware, as with the Game Genie or other physical add-ons, but is more often performed via the software of the actual game, using a special terminal console or simply pressing predetermined button sequences. Shortcuts and tricks can also appear as the result of additional scripts or software, as with the use of macros in *Everquest* or add-ons in *World of Warcraft*, or they can be outright cheats, as in the ability to see through walls in *Counter-Strike*. Cheats are mostly discouraged by the gaming community, for they essentially destroy traditional gameplay by deviating from the established rule set of the game. But macros and add-ons are often tolerated, even encouraged. Likewise the use of a hardware emulator to play a video game can introduce new nondiegetic operator acts (a pause act, for example) even if they did not exist in the original game.

Moving beyond these initial observations on the nondiegetic operator act, one can describe two basic variants. The first is confined to the area of setup. Setup actions exist in all games. They are the interstitial acts of preference setting, game configuration, meta-analysis of gameplay, loading or saving, selecting one player or two, and so on. The pause and cheat acts are both part of this category. It includes all preplay, postplay, and interplay activity.

Yet there exists a second variant of the nondiegetic operator act that is highly important and around which many of the most significant games have been designed. These are gamic actions in which the act of configuration itself *is the very site of gameplay*. These are games oriented around understanding and executing specific algorithms. All resource management simulations, as well as most real-time strategy (RTS) and turn-based games, are designed in this manner. In an RTS game like *Warcraft III*, actions of configuration can take on great importance inside gameplay, not simply before it, as with setup actions. In *Final Fantasy X* the process of configuring various weapons and armor, interacting with the sphere grid, or choosing how the combat will unfold are all executed using interfaces and menus that are not within the diegetic world of the game. These activities may be intimately connected to the narrative of the game, yet they exist in an informatic layer once removed from the pretend play scenario of representational character and story. These actions of configuration are often the very essence of the operator's experience of gameplay—simple proof that gaming may, even for limited moments, eschew the diegetic completely. (As I said in the beginning, the status of the diegetic will be put to the test here; this is one reason why.) Many simulators and turn-based strategy games like *Civilization III* are adept also at using nondiegetic operator acts for large portions of the gameplay.

But why should video games require the operator to become intimate with complex, multipart algorithms and enact them during gameplay? It makes sense to pause for a moment and preview the concept of interpretation that I take up more fully in chapter 4. For this I turn to Clifford Geertz and his gloss on the concept of "deep play." In the essay "Deep Play: Notes on the Balinese Cockfight," Geertz offers a fantastically evocative phrase: "culture, this acted document."[13] There are three interlocked ideas here: There is culture, but culture is a *document*, a text that follows the various logics of a semiotic system, and finally it is an *acted* document. This places culture on quite a different footing than other nonacted semiotic systems. (Certainly with literature or cinema there are important connections to the action of the author, or with the structure of discourse and its acted utterances, or with the action of reading, but *as texts* they are not action-based media in the same sense that culture is and, I suggest here, video games are. Geertz's observation, then, is not to say that culture is a text but to say that *action is a text*. In subsequent years this has resonated greatly in cultural studies, particularly in theories of performance.) In "Deep Play," Geertz describes play as a cultural phenomenon that has meaning. Because play is a cultural act and because action is textual, play is subject to interpretation just like any other text. The concept of "depth" refers to the way in which the more equally matched a cockfight becomes, the more unpredictable and volatile the outcome might be. The closer one is to an adversary, the more likely that entire reputations will be built or destroyed upon the outcome of the fight. So, in identifying deep play, Geertz demonstrates how something entirely outside play can be incorporated into it and expressed through it:

> What makes Balinese cockfighting deep is thus not money in itself, but what, the more of it that is involved the more so, money causes to happen: the migration of the Balinese status hierarchy into the body of the cockfight . . . . The cocks may be surrogates for their owners' personalities, animal mirrors of psychic form, but the cockfight is—or more exactly, deliberately is made to be—a simulation of the social matrix, the involved system of cross-cutting, overlapping, highly corporate groups—villages, kingroups, irrigation societies, temple congregations, "castes"—in which its devotees live. And as prestige, the necessity to affirm it, defend it, celebrate it, justify it, and just plain bask in it (but not, given the strongly ascriptive character of Balinese stratification, to seek it), is perhaps the central driving force in the society, so also— ambulant penises, blood sacrifices, and monetary exchanges aside—is it of the cockfight. This apparent amusement and seeming sport is, to take another phrase from Erving Goffman, "a status bloodbath."[14]

Play is a symbolic action for larger issues in culture. It is the expression of structure. "The cockfight is a means of expression," he writes.[15] It is an aesthetic, enacted vehicle for "a powerful rendering of life."[16]

I want to suggest that a very similar thing is happening in *Final Fantasy X* or *The Sims*. Acts of configuration in video games express processes in culture that are large, unknown, dangerous, and painful, but they do not express them directly. "The playful nip denotes the bite," wrote Gregory Bateson, "but it does not denote

Final Fantasy X, Squaresoft, 2001

what would be denoted by the bite."[17] Acts of configuration are a rendering of life: the transformation into an information economy in the United States since the birth of video games as a mass medium in the 1970s has precipitated massive upheavals in the lives of individuals submitted to a process of retraining and redeployment into a new economy mediated by machines and other informatic artifacts. This transformation has been the subject of much reflection, in the work of everyone from Fredric Jameson to Manuel Castells. The new "general equivalent" of information has changed the way culture is created and experienced. The same quantitative modulations and numerical valuations required by the new information worker are thus observed in a dazzling array of new cultural phenomena, from the cut-up sampling culture of hip-hop to the calculus curves of computer-aided architectural design. In short, to live today is to know how to use menus. Acts of configuration in video games are but a footnote to this general transformation. So the second classification of gamic actions I have proposed, nondiegetic operator acts, follows the same logic revealed in Geertz's analysis of the Balinese cockfight, or indeed Marx's understanding of social labor: just as the commodity form carries within it a map for understanding all the larger contradictions of life under capitalism, and just as the cockfight is a site for enacting various dramas of social relations, so these nondiegetic operator acts in video games are an allegory for the algorithmic structure of today's informatic culture. Video games render social realities into playable form. I will return to this theme in chapter 4.

With these first two moments of gamic action in mind, one can begin to see the first steps toward a classification system. The first moment of gamic action revealed diegetic machine acts, while the second moment revealed nondiegetic operator acts. I can now put together the first two axes in the classification scheme, pairing diegetic opposite nondiegetic and machine opposite operator (below).

The first two moments of gamic action therefore explore one of the diagonal relationships in this diagram. (Some of the other relationships in the diagram will be examined shortly.) The first diagonal relationship is between (1) the action experience of being at the mercy of abstract informatic rules (the atmosphere of the ambience act in *Shenmue*) and (2) the action experience of structuring subjective play, of working with rules and configurations (configuring and executing plans in *Final Fantasy X*). One motion emanates outward from the machine, while the other proceeds inward into the machine. One deals with the process of informatics, and the other deals with the informatics of process. Like *Shenmue*, the artfulness of games like *Myst* or *Ico* is their ability to arrest the desires of the operator in a sort of poetry of the algorithm. The experience of ambience, of nonplay, is always beckoning in *Ico.* Yet in nonplay, the operator is in fact moving his or her experience closer to the actual rhythms of the machine. In this way, the desires of the operator are put into a state of submission at the hands of the desires of the machine. This same masochistic fascination is evident in *Myst.* One doesn't play *Myst* so much as one submits to it. Its intricate puzzles and lush renderings achieve equivalent results in this sense. But with *Warcraft III* or *Civilization III* or any number of simulation games and RTSs, the contrapositive action experience occurs: instead of penetrating into the logic of the machine, the operator hovers

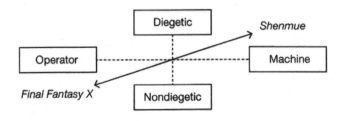

Ico, Sony Computer Entertainment, 2001

above the game, one step removed from its diegesis, tweaking knobs and adjusting menus. Instead of being submissive, one speaks of these as "God games." Instead of experiencing the algorithm as algorithm, one *enacts* the algorithm. In both cases, the operator has a distinct relationship to informatics, but it is a question of the composition of that relationship. *Shenmue* is an experience of informatics from within, whereas *Final Fantasy X* is an experience of informatics from above. Of course, the axes of my diagram still hold: *Shenmue* is primarily a game played by a machine, while *Final Fantasy X* is primarily a game played by an operator; and likewise *Shenmue* situates gameplay primarily in diegetic space, while *Final Fantasy X* situates gameplay primarily in nondiegetic space.

The dromenon

I have waited thus far to engage directly with the twin concepts of "play" and "game," perhaps at my peril, in order to convey the bounded utility of the two terms. As stated at the outset, a game is an activity defined by rules in which players try to reach some sort of goal. As for play, the concept is one of the least theorized, despite being so central to human activity.[18] Huizinga's work in the 1930s, culminating in his book *Homo Ludens*, and Caillois's 1958 book *Man, Play, and Games* both analyze play as a social and cultural phenomenon.

> Play is a voluntary activity or occupation executed within certain fixed limits of time and place, according to rules freely accepted but absolutely binding, having its aim in itself and accompanied by a feeling of tension, joy and the consciousness that it is "different" from "ordinary life."[19]

172

This definition, from Huizinga, is the distillation of his observations on the nature of play: that it is free, that it is not part of ordinary life, that it is secluded in time and place, that it creates order (in the form of rules), and that it promotes the formation of communities of players. Caillois, revealing an unlikely intellectual debt to the earlier book (Caillois was a leftist and friends with the likes of Georges Bataille; Huizinga was a cultural historian in the old school), agrees almost point for point with Huizinga on the definition of play: "It appears to be an activity that is (1) free, (2) separate, (3) uncertain, (4) unproductive, (5) regulated, and (6) fictive."[20]

Huizinga makes overtures for play being a part of human life in its many details. He argues for a direct connection to be made between play and culture, that play is not simply something that exists within culture, but on the contrary that culture arises in and through play. "We have to conclude," he writes, "that civilization is, in its earliest phases, played. It does not come *from* play like a babe detaching itself from the womb: it arises *in* and *as* play, and never leaves it"; or earlier in the text, "Culture arises in the form of play. . . . It is played from the very beginning."[21] But at the same time, Huizinga pays little attention to the material details of this or that individual moment of play. Instead he takes the concept of play as primary, stripping from it anything inessential. His rationale is that one must never start from the assumption that play is defined through something that is *not* play,[22] and hence play for Huizinga becomes unassigned and detached, articulated in its essential form but rarely in actual form as game or medium. In the end, it is the very irreducibility of play for Huizinga—the natural purity of it—that makes play less useful for an analysis of the specificity of video games as a medium. His book is so far removed from the medium that it can merely gesture a way forward, not provide a core approach.

While Huizinga and Caillois generally agree on the question of play, what distinguishes them is this: Caillois moves beyond the formal definition of play, which he claims is "opposed to reality," and moves further to describe the "unique, irreducible characteristics" of games in their "multitude and infinite variety."[23] This more materialist approach is where Caillois is most at home. He proceeds to map out four basic types of games (competitive, chance, mimicry, and panic or "vertigo" games), each of which may fluctuate along a continuum from whimsical improvisation to being rule bound. And unlike Huizinga, Caillois is not hesitant to mention actual games, as well as play activities, and group them together according to various traits. So in Caillois we have an attention to football and roulette, to kite flying and traveling carnivals.

But what Huizinga and Caillois have in common, and what confines their usefulness to the present single moment of gamic action, is that they both focus specifically on the individual's experience during play. As sociologists, they naturally privilege the human realm over the technological realm; play is an "occupation" or "activity" of humans (and also of some animals). As theorists of play, they naturally regard nonplay as beside the question. This is fine for understanding "play" or "game" in general, but it only partially suffices for understanding video games as a specific historical medium with definite tangible qualities. I have already described how in the ambience act, gameplay is essentially suspended, but does this mean that the ambience act is not part of what it means to play a video game? Or I have also described the use of hacks and cheats as nondiegetic operator acts, which both Huizinga and Caillois would argue by definition threaten play (cheaters are "spoil-sports," claims Huizinga), but does this mean that hacks and cheats are not part of what it means to play a video game? If the object of one's analysis is a medium in its entirety, must only those aspects of the medium that resemble play or a game be considered? Such an approach elevates an understanding of "play" or "game" pure and simple but, in doing so, ignores the vast detail of the medium in general. To arrive at a definition of video games, then, one must take Huizinga and Caillois's concept of play and view it as it is actually embedded inside algorithmic game machines.[24] This different approach, owing more to media studies than to cultural anthropology, tries to work backward from the material at hand, approaching the medium in its entirety rather than as an instantiation of a specific element of human activity. Only then may one start to sift through the various traces and artifacts of video gaming in order to arrive at a suitable framework for interpreting it. This is why I do not begin this book with Huizinga and Caillois, as any number of approaches would, but instead situate them here in this third moment, in the intersection of the playing agent and the diegetic space of gameplay.

This third moment illuminates action in the way that action is most conventionally defined, as the deliberate movements of an individual. Here Huizinga's understanding of the play element in sacred performances is revealing:

> The rite is a *dromenon*, which means "something acted," an act, action. That which is enacted, or the stuff of action, is a *drama*, which again means act, action represented on a stage. Such action may occur as a performance or a contest. The rite, or "ritual act" represents a cosmic happening, an event in the natural process. The word "represents," however, does not cover the exact meaning of the act, at least not in its looser, modern connotation; for here "representation" is really *identification*, the mystic repetition or *re-presentation* of the event. The rite produces the effect which is then not so much *shown figuratively* as *actually reproduced* in the action. The function of the rite, therefore, is far from being merely imitative; it causes the worshippers to participate in the sacred happening itself.[25]

Representation is a question of figuratively reshowing an action, Huizinga suggests, while play is an effect reproduced *in* the action. The dromenon, the ritual act, is thus helpful for understanding the third moment of gamic action: the *diegetic operator act*. This is the moment of direct operator action inside the imaginary world of gameplay, and it is the part of my schema that overlaps most with Huizinga and Caillois.

Diegetic operator acts are diegetic because they take place within the world of gameplay; they are operator acts because they are perpetrated by the game player rather than the game software or any outside force. Diegetic operator acts appear as either *move acts* or *expressive acts* (two categories that are more variations on a theme than mutually exclusive). Simply put, move acts change the physical position or orientation of the game environment. This may mean a translation of the player character's position in the game world, or it may mean the movement of the player character's gaze such that new areas of the game world are made visible. Move acts are commonly effected by using a joystick or analog stick, or any type of movement controller. In many video games, move acts appear in the form of player character motion: running, jumping, driving, strafing, crouching, and so on; but also in games like *Tetris* where the player does not have a strict player character avatar, move acts still come in the form of spatial translation, rotation, stacking, and interfacing of game tokens.

But parallel to this in operator gameplay is a kind of gamic act that, simply, concerns player *expression*. Even a single mouse click counts here. These are actions such as select, pick, get, rotate, unlock, open, talk, examine, use, fire, attack, cast, apply, type, emote. Expressive acts can be rather one-dimensional in certain game genres (the expressive act of firing in *Quake* or *Unreal*, for example), or highly complex, as in the case of object selection and combination in strategy or adventure games.

Some games merge these various expressive acts. In *Metroid Prime*, firing one's weapon is used interchangeably both to attack and to open doors. In fact, experientially these acts are equivalent: they both exert an expressive desire outward from the player character to objects in the world that are deemed actionable. That one expressive act opens a door and another kills a nonplayer character is insignificant from the perspective of gamic action. What is important is the coupling of acting agent (the player character) and actionable object.

Not everything in a game is available to the expressive act. There are actionable objects and nonactionable objects. Additionally, objects can change their actionable status. For example, an Alien Slave in *Half-Life* is actionable when alive but nonactionable when killed, or a gold mine in *Warcraft III* is actionable when producing but not when collapsed. Actionable objects may come in the form of buttons, blocks, keys, obstacles, doors, words, nonplayer characters, and so on. So in a text-based game like *Adventure*, actionable objects come in the form of specific object names that must be examined or used, whereas in *Metroid Prime* actionable objects are often revealed to the operator via the scan visor, or in *Deus Ex* actionable objects are highlighted by the HUD. Nonactionable objects are inert scenery. No amount of effort will garner results from nonactionable objects. The actionability of objects is determined when the game's levels are designed. Certain objects are created as inert masses, while others are connected to specific functions in the game that produce action responses. (During level design, some machine acts are also specified, such as spawn points, lights, shaders, and hazards.) Available expressive-act objects tend to have different levels of significance for

Tony Hawk's Pro Skater 4, Neversoft, 2002

different genres of games. Adventure games like *The Longest Journey* require keen attention to the action status of objects in the visual field. But in RTS games or first-person shooters, discovering the actionability of new objects is not a primary goal of gameplay; instead these genres hinge on interaction with known action objects, typically some combination of ammo, health packs, and monsters.

This discussion of diegetic operator acts, and the one before it on nondiegetic, may be documented through a sort of archaeological exploration of game controller design. Game controllers instantiate these two types of acts as buttons, sticks, triggers, and other input devices. So while there is an imaginative form of the expressive act within the diegesis of the game, there is also a physical form

176

of the same act. In a PC-based game like *Half-Life*, the operator acts are literally inscribed on various regions of the keyboard and mouse. The mouse ball movement is devoted to move acts, but the mouse buttons are for expressive acts. Likewise, certain clusters of keyboard keys (A, W, S, D, Space, and Ctrl) are for move acts, while others (R, E, F) are for expressive acts. But this physical inscription is also variable. While certain controller buttons, such as the PlayStation's Start and Select buttons, are used almost exclusively for nondiegetic operator acts, controller buttons often do double duty, serving in one capacity during certain gamic logics and in another capacity during others. For example, the Atari 2600 joystick, a relatively simple controller with button and directional stick, must facilitate all in-game operator acts.

The play of the structure

In "Structure, Sign and Play in the Discourse of the Human Sciences," Jacques Derrida focuses on the concept of play. He writes about how things "come into play," and refers to "the *play* of the structure," or the "play of signification," or even simply "the play of the world."[26] Or in *Dissemination*, he writes of the "play of a syntax," or the "play" of "a chain of significations."[27] So at a basic level, play is simply how things transpire linguistically for Derrida, how, in a general sense, they happen to happen. But the concept is more sophisticated than it might seem, for it gets at the very nature of language. After citing Claude Lévi-Strauss on the practical impossibility of arriving at a total understanding of language, that one can never accurately duplicate the speech of a people without exhaustively recounting every word said in the past, words in circulation today, as well as all words to come, Derrida seizes on this type of useless pursuit of totality to further explain his sense of the word "play":

> Totalization, therefore, is sometimes defined as *useless*, and sometimes as *impossible*. This is no doubt due to the fact that there are two ways of conceiving the limit of totalization. And I assert once more that these two determinations coexist in a non-expressed way in Lévi-Strauss's discourse. Totalization can be judged impossible in the classical style: one then refers to the empirical endeavor of either a subject or a finite discourse hopelessly panting after an infinite richness that it can never master. There is too much and more than one can say.

Then Derrida shifts to play.

> But nontotalization can also be determined in another way: no longer from the standpoint of a concept of finitude as relegation to the empirical, but from the standpoint of the concept of *play* [*jeu*]. If totalization no longer has any meaning, it is not because the infiniteness of a field cannot be covered by a finite glance or a finite discourse, but because the

nature of the field—that is, language and a finite language—excludes totalization: this field is in effect that of a *game* [*jeu*], that is to say, of a field of infinite substitutions in the closing of a finite group. This field only allows these infinite substitutions because it is finite, that is to say, because instead of being an incommensurable field, as in the classical hypothesis, instead of being too large, there is something missing from it: a center which arrests and grounds the play of substitutions. One could say—rigorously using that word whose scandalous signification is always obliterated in French—that this movement of play, permitted by the lack, the absence of center or origin, is the movement of *supplementarity*.[28]

The field of language is therefore not quantitatively but *qualitatively* inadequate. It is a question not of enlarging the field but of refashioning it internally. This process of remaking is what Derrida calls the movement of play.[29] Using the logic of supplementarity, play reconstitutes the field, not to create a new wholeness but to enforce a sort of permanent state of nonwholeness, or "nontotalization." Play is a sort of permanent agitation of the field, a generative motion filling in the structure itself, compensating for it, but also supplementing and sustaining it. "Transformative play," write Katie Salen and Eric Zimmerman, "is a special case of play that occurs when the free movement of play alters the more rigid structure in which it takes place."[30] Derrida describes this generative agitation as follows:

Play is the disruption of presence . . . . Turned towards the lost or impossible presence of the absent origin, [Lévi-Strauss's] structuralist thematic of broken immediacy is therefore the saddened, *negative*, nostalgic, guilty, Rousseauistic side of the thinking of play whose other side would be the Nietzschean *affirmation*, the joyous affirmation of the world in play and of the innocence in becoming, the affirmation of a world of signs without fault, without truth, and without origin which is offered to an active interpretation. *This affirmation then determines the* non-center *otherwise than as loss of the center.* And it plays without security. For there is a *sure* play: that which is limited to the *substitution* of *given and existing, present*, pieces. In absolute chance, affirmation also surrenders itself to *genetic* indetermination, to the *seminal* adventure of the trace.[31]

So although it is one of his most prized pieces of terminology, Derrida doesn't as much say what play is as use the concept of play to explain the nature of something else, namely, the structure of language. The word is lucky enough to be placed alongside other of Derrida's privileged oncepts; it is paired in this section with the supplement and the trace. And in *Dissemination*, the concept of play is described in such broad strokes and in such close proximity to writing itself that one might easily swap one term for the other. After describing the relationship between playfulness and seriousness in Plato, Derrida observes, "As soon as it comes into being and into language, play *erases itself as such*. Just as writing must erase itself as such before truth, etc. The point is that there *is* no *as such* where writing or play are concerned."[32] Play is, in this way, crucial to both language and signification, even if play erases itself in the act of bringing the latter concepts into existence.

So it comes full circle. With Huizinga, play was held aloft as a thoroughly axiomatic concept, irreducible to anything more phenomenologically primitive. But with Geertz, the pure concept is put to the rigors of a close reading, as any other textual form might be. And now with Derrida one is back to the concept of play as pure positivity. If Geertz's goal is the interpretation of play, then Derrida's goal is the play of interpretation. Play brings out for Derrida a certain sense of generative agitation or ambiguity, a way of joyfully moving forward without being restricted by the retrograde structures of loss or absence. And like Maurice Blondel's coupling of truth with action, Derrida sought to replace so-called textual truth with the generative tensions of active reading.

Now we are prepared to consider the fourth type of gamic action, that of *nondiegetic machine acts*. These are actions performed by the machine and integral to the entire experience of the game but not contained within a narrow conception of the world of gameplay. This is the most interesting category. Included here are internal forces like power-ups, goals, high-score stats, dynamic difficulty adjustment (DDA), the HUD, and health packs, but also external forces exerted (knowingly or unknowingly) by the machine such as software crashes, low polygon counts, temporary freezes, server downtime, and network lag. I say "narrow conception" because many nondiegetic machine acts such as power-ups or health packs are in fact incorporated directly into the narrative of necessities in the game such that the line between what is diegetic and what is nondiegetic becomes quite indistinct.

The most emblematic nondiegetic machine act is "game over," the moment of gamic death. While somewhat determined by the performance of the operator, or lack thereof, death acts are levied fundamentally by the game itself, in response to the input and over the contestation of the operator. A death act is the moment when the controller stops accepting the user's gameplay and essentially turns off (at least temporarily until the game can segue to a menu act or straight back to gameplay). This moment usually coincides with the death of the operator's player character inside the game environment (or otherwise with the violation of specific rules, as when missions are called off in *Splinter Cell*). The games created by Jodi are perfect experiments in nondiegetic machine acts in general and death acts in particular. The code of the machine itself is celebrated, with all its illegibility, disruptiveness, irrationality, and impersonalness. Jodi are what Huizinga calls spoilsports, meaning that their games intentionally deviate from the enchanting order created by the game:

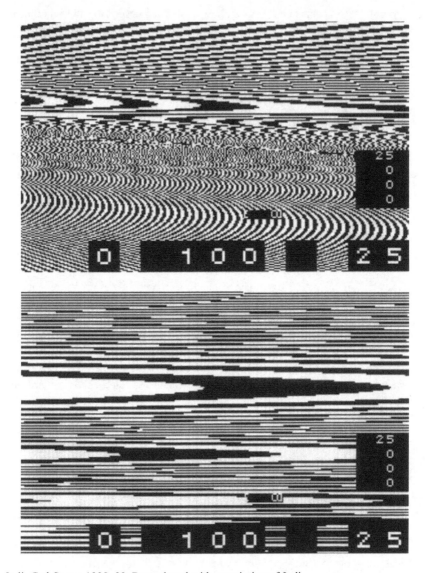

Jodi, *Ctrl-Space*, 1998–99. Reproduced with permission of Jodi

Inside the play-ground an absolute and peculiar order reigns. Here we come across another, very positive feature of play: it creates order, *is* order. Into an imperfect world and into the confusion of life it brings a temporary, a limited perfection. Play demands order absolute and supreme. The least deviation from it "spoils the game," robs it of its character and makes it worthless . . . . Play casts a spell over us; it is "enchanting," "captivating."[33]

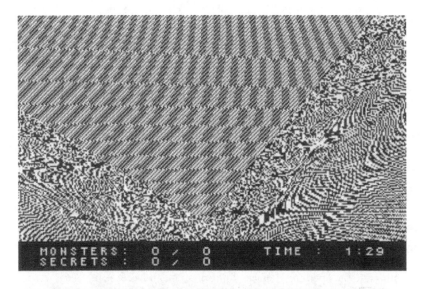

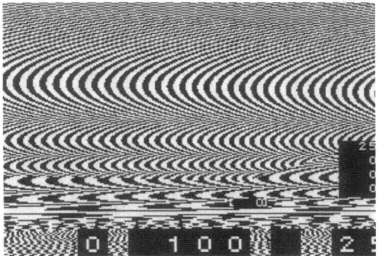

Jodi, *Ctrl-Space*. Reproduced with permission of Jodi

I cite this passage to highlight the dramatic disagreement between Huizinga's position and that of Derrida (or Jodi, if one was foolish enough to request they take a position on things). With Huizinga is the notion that play must in some sense create order, but with Derrida is the notion that play is precisely the deviation from order, or further the perpetual inability to achieve order, and hence never wanting it in the first place. Admittedly, the "game over" of a game is not *affirmative*, to use Derrida's Nietzschean terminology, but it is

181

certainly noncentering, putting the gamer into a temporary state of disability and submission.

The death act is, properly placed, part of the first type of nondiegetic machine acts that I will call the *disabling act*. These actions are any type of gamic aggression or gamic deficiency that arrives from outside the world of the game and infringes negatively on the game in some way. They can be fatal or temporary, necessary or unnecessary. So, as mentioned, all the following phenomena are included: crashes, low polygon counts, bugs, slowdowns, temporary freezes, and network lag. No action is more irritating to the gamer. Following Huizinga, these actions have the ability to destroy the game from without, to disable its logic. But at the same time, they are often the most constitutive category of game acts, for they have the ability to define the outer boundaries of aesthetics in gaming, the degree zero for an entire medium.

The second type of nondiegetic machine act comprises any number of actions offered by the machine that enrich the operator's gameplay rather than degrade it. These should be called *enabling acts*. They are the absolute essence of smooth runtime in gameplay. With an enabling act, the game machine grants something to the operator: a piece of information, an increase in speed, temporary invulnerability, an extra life, increased health, a teleportation portal, points, cash, or some other bonus. Thus receipt or use of the aforementioned items—power-ups, goals, the HUD (excluding any input elements), and health packs—all constitute enabling acts. The functionality of objects, or their *actionality*, must be taken into account when considering the status of enabling acts. Inert objects are not included here. This category is the most clear contrapositive to the diegetic operator acts discussed earlier.

It is perhaps important to stress that, while many of these enabling acts are the center of most games, they exist in an uneasy relationship to the diegetic world of the game. In fact, many enabling objects in games are integrated seamlessly into the world of the game using some sort of trick or disguise—what Eddo Stern calls "metaphorically patched artifacts"[34]—as with the voice recorders that are used as save stations in *The Thing* or the HEV suit charging stations that supplement health in *Half-Life* (or even erased from the object world of the game, as with the act of leaning against a wall to regain health in *The Getaway*). Thus the "xyzzy" command in *Adventure*, which teleports the player character to and from home base, is technically a nondiegetic machine act, but its nondiegetic status is covered over by the narrative of the game, which insists that the command is a magic spell, and thus, although it is nondiegetic, the command cooperates with the diegesis rather than threatening it. The same xyzzy logic is at work with the taxis in *Vice City* that, after the player character dies, transport him back to the previous mission. This wormhole through space and time reveals the tension often present in games whereby diegetic objects are used as a mask to obfuscate nondiegetic (but necessary) play functions.

Beyond the disabling and enabling acts, there is an additional category of nondiegetic machine acts worth mentioning. These are any number of *machinic embodiments* that emanate outward from a game to exert their own logic on the gamic form. For example, the graphic design of the aliens in the Atari 2600 version of *Space Invaders* is a direct embodiment of how a byte of data, equivalent to eight zero-or-one bits, may be represented as a strip of eight pixels turned on or off. The alien invaders are nothing more than a series of byte strips stacked together.[35] This is math made visible.

The shape and size of Mario in the NES version of *Super Mario Bros.* is determined not simply by artistic intention or narrative logic but by the design specifications of the 8-bit 6502 microchip driving the game software. Only a certain number of colors can be written to the NES screen at one time, and thus the design of Mario follows the logic of the machine by using only specific colors and specific palettes. But this is not a simple determinism on the macro scale of what exists on the micro scale. There are also other influences from the logic of informatics that affect the nature of certain gamic actions. One example is multithreading and object-oriented programming that creates the conditions of possibility for certain formal outcomes in the game. When one plays *State of Emergency*, the swarm effect of rioting is a formal action enacted by the game on the experience of gameplay and incorporated into the game's narrative. Yet the formal quality of swarming as such is still nondiegetic to the extent that it finds its genesis primarily in the current logic of informatics (emergence, social networks, artificial life, and so on) rather than in any necessary element in the narrative, itself enlisted to "explain" and incorporate this nondiegetic force into the story line (a riot) after the fact.

Other transformations in material culture may also reappear in games as nondiegetic emanations. Consider the difference between arcade games and home computer or console games. Arcade games are generally installed in public spaces and require payment to play. Computer and console games, on the other hand, exist primarily in the home and are typically free to play once purchased. This material difference has tended to structure the narrative flow of games in

Space Invaders alien as stack of ten bytes

two very different ways. Arcade games are often designed around the concept of lives, while console games are designed around health. For example, in arcade *Pac-Man*, a single quarter gives the player a fixed number of lives, whereas in *SOCOM* the player must maintain health above zero or else die. Arcade games are characterized by a more quantized set of penalties and limitations on play: one quarter equals a certain number of lives. Console and computer games, by contrast, offer a more fluid continuum of gameplay based on replenishment and exhaustion of a qualitative resource. Save stations extend this logic on the console and computer platforms, resulting in a more continuous, unrepeating sense of gameplay. And at the same moment in history, one may document the invention of the pause act as a standard feature of video games (the pause act is essentially absent from the arcade). *Super Mario Bros.*, which was released first for the arcade and then, famously, for the home console Nintendo Entertainment System, exists on the threshold between these two nondiegetic machine embodiments. On the one hand, the game retains the concept of lives familiar to the arcade format, but on the other hand, the game uses a variety of power-ups that strengthen the relative vitality of any single life. A single Mario life may be augmented and crippled several times before being killed outright, thereby exhibiting a primitive version of what would later be known as health. *Super Mario Bros.* was not the first game to do this, but it remains emblematic of this transformation in the early to mid-1980s. Games like *Gauntlet* accomplished the reverse: the game remained popular as an arcade game, yet it used an innovative technique whereby quarters bought health rather than lives.

It is in this sense that Derrida's conception of play becomes quite important, for nondiegetic machine acts can be defined as those elements that create a generative *agitation* or ambiguity—what Genette calls metalepsis—between the inside of the game and the outside of the game, between what constitutes the essential core of the game and what causes that illusion (literally, "in-play") to be undone. The lives-health distinction (or the graphic design of 8-bit sprites) did not impinge on the various narratives of arcade and early home games—they are well motivated in gameplay, but in many cases nondiegetic machine acts are consummate unplay, particularly when dealing with crashes and lags celebrated in the Jodi variant. Still, this does not exempt them from being absolutely intertwined with the notion of play. *Metal Gear Solid* celebrates this inside-outside agitation with the boss Psycho Mantis. The villain's supposed powers of mind control are so powerful that they break out of the game console entirely, at times pretending to interrupt the normal functioning of the television display. Mantis also uses his psychic powers to refer to other games that the player has played, a trick enabled by surreptitiously scanning files on the console's memory card. Then, in the most grievous violation of diegetic illusion, the player is required physically to move the game controller from port one to port two on the console in order to defeat Mantis. This brief moment of unplay does not destroy the game but in fact elevates it to a higher form of play. Even if the player does not believe that Mantis is a true psychic, the use of nondiegetic machine acts—requiring, in response, a nondiegetic operator act to continue playing—remains effective precisely because it follows the loop of supplementarity described in Derrida. The narrative follows faithfully enough to explain breaking the diegesis, and after the short diversion the player is safely returned to normal gameplay. Several other narrative games such as *Max Payne* contain similar "Mantis moments" where the game deliberately breaks the fourth wall. In a strange, drug-induced state, the Payne character breaks out of the diegetic space of the game to view himself as a sort of marionette within the world of gameplay:

MAX'S WIFE (voice-over): You are in a computer game, Max.

MAX (voice-over): The truth was a burning green crack through my brain. Weapon statistics hanging in the air, glimpsed out of the corner of my eye. Endless repetition of the act of shooting, time slowing down to show off my moves. The paranoid feel of someone controlling my every step. *I was in a computer game.* Funny as hell, it was the most horrible thing I could think of.[36]

This generative agitation may be explored further by looking at the interface of the first-person shooter. There are two layers at play here that would seem to contradict and disable each other. The first is the full volume of the world, extending in three dimensions, varied, spatial, and textured. The second is the HUD, which exists in a flat plane and is overlayed on top of the first world. This second layer benefits from none of the richness, dynamic motion, or narrative illusion of the first layer (a few notable counterexamples like *Metroid Prime* notwithstanding). The HUD has instead a sort of static, informatic permanence, offering information or giving various updates to the operator. In Derrida's vocabulary, the HUD exists as a supplement to the rendered world. It completes it, but only through a process of exteriority that is unable again to penetrate its core. The HUD is *uncomfortable in its two-dimensionality*, but forever there it will stay, in a relationship of incommensurability with the world of the game, and a metaphor for the very nature of play itself. The play of the nondiegetic machine act is therefore a play within the various semiotic layers of the video game. It is form playing with other form.

One should always speak of waning agitations or waxing agitations. In the diegetic machine act, the intensities of gameplay slow to near equilibrium, but at that same moment the game world is full of action and energy. The diegetic operator act is also defined through intensities, or *vectors* of agitation: the time-based unfolding of a game is never smooth or consistent but is instead marked by a wide variance in the agitation of movement, whereby one moment may be quite placid and unagitated, but another moment may be saturated with motion and violence. Often these differences in intensities are incorporated directly into gameplay—the shadows versus the light in *Manhunt*, for example, or the intensities of safe spaces versus hostile spaces in *Halo*. Nondiegetic operator acts, defined as they were in terms of configuration, are also about probabilistic customization and local calibrations of options and numbers (the depletion and augmentation of statistical parameters like hunger and energy in *The Sims*). And, as discussed, nondiegetic machine acts are about the various intensities of agitation between the various layers of the game itself, whether it be the agitation between two- and three-dimensionality, or between connectivity and disconnectivity, or between gameplay and the lack thereof. Games are always about getting from here to there. They require local differentials of space and action, not an abstract navigation through a set of anchored points of reference.

Taking all four moments together, one may revisit the earlier diagram. This is an incomplete diagram in many ways. To be thorough, one should supplement it with a consideration of the relationship between two or more operators in a multiplayer game, for the very concept of diegetic space becomes quite complicated with the addition of multiple players. Likewise the machine should most likely be rendered internally complex so that the game world could be considered in distinction to the game engine driving it. Nevertheless, the active experience of gaming is here displayed via four different moments of gamic action (below).

The interpretive framework presented in this chapter aims to be as inclusive as possible. I have deliberately avoided the assumption—incorrect, in my view—that video games are merely games that people play on computers. Such a position leads to a rather one-dimensional view of what video games are. I have also tried to avoid privileging either play or narrative, another tendency that is common in other approaches. There are many significant aspects of gaming that happen completely outside play proper (e.g., the setup act) or are not part of a traditional narrative (e.g., machinic embodiments). Thus I suggest that video games are complex, active media that may involve both humans and computers and may transpire both inside diegetic space and outside diegetic space.

In sum, because of my starting assumption—that video games are not just images or stories or play or games but *actions*—I have outlined a four-part system for understanding action in video games: gaming is a pure process made knowable in the machinic resonance of diegetic machine acts; gaming is a subjective algorithm, a code intervention exerted from both within gameplay and without gameplay in the form of the nondiegetic operator act; gaming is a ritualistic dromenon of players transported to the imaginary place of gameplay, and acted out in the form of diegetic operator acts; and gaming is the play of the

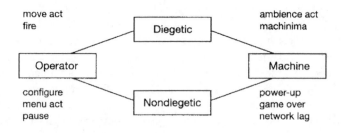

Gamic Action

Type of gamic action	Categories	Shape of action	Quality of action	Emblematic games
Diegetic machine act	Ambience act, machinima	Process	Informatic, atmospheric	Ico, Myst, Shenmue
Nondiegetic operator act	Acts of con-figuration, setup act	Algorithm	Simulation, material	Warcraft III, Flight Simulator, Final Fantasy X
Diegetic operator act	Movement act, expressive act	Play	Rule-based, singular	Tekken, Metroid Prime, Half-Life
Nondiegetic machine act	Disabling act, enabling act, machinic embodiments	Code	Swarms, patterning, relationality	Dance Dance Revolution, SOD, State of Emergency

structure, a generative agitation between inside and outside effected through the nondiegetic machine act. A theoretical analogue for the first moment would be the vitality of pure matter, the machinic phylum. For the second, it would be political intervention, hacking, critique, outside thought. The third would be desire, utopia, and the social. And a theoretical analogue for the fourth moment would be *écriture*, the supplement, the new. These are four moments, four suggestions. They should in no way be thought of as fixed "rules" for video games, but instead are tendencies seen to arise through the examination of the particular games listed here at this time. These are not ideal types; they are, rather, provisional observations that spring from an analysis of the material specificities of the medium.

Notes

1 I use the term "video game" with some inaccuracy. To be precise, a video game refers to a game played on a console using a video monitor. In such a specific definition, the term would exclude arcade games, games played on personal computers, those played on mobile devices, and so on. It is for simplicity's sake that I use "video game" in its colloquial sense as an umbrella term for all sorts of interactive electronic games.

2 Some suggest, and I partially agree, that "player" is a better overall term than "opera-tor." My goal in avoiding the term "player" is not to eliminate the importance of play, as will be evident later, but instead, by using "operator," to underscore the machinic, almost industrial, and certainly cybernetic aspect of much of human-computer interac-tion, of which gaming is a key part. Additionally, "operator" tames, if only slightly, the anthropomorphic myth of the distinctly and uniquely human gamer, and that can only be a good thing in my mind. Operators are, in a majority of instances, organic human players, but they may also be any type of intelligent play agent such as a bot or script. Hence the greater neutrality of the term "operator" appears fitting. Readers who are resistant should mentally cut and paste "player" for "operator" in the present chapter; the switch is entirely tolerable.

3 Espen Aarseth, "Computer Game Studies, Year One," *Game Studies* 1, no. 1 (July 2001). Aarseth uses the term "ergodic" to describe action in media. See Aarseth, *Cybertext: Perspectives on Ergodic Literature* (Baltimore: Johns Hopkins University Press, 1997).

4 I have never been happy with the word "interactivity." "I find the concept to be too broad to be truly useful," Lev Manovich writes. Because it is too broad, the concept is not included as a central principle of new media by Manovich. Most so-called old media are also interactive, he goes on to claim: "All classical, and even moreso modern, art is 'interactive' in a number of ways. Ellipses in literary narration, missing details of objects in visual art, and other representational 'shortcuts' require the user to fill in missing information." See Manovich, *The Language of New Media* (Cambridge: MIT Press, 2001), 55–56. This echoes what Umberto Eco calls the lazy machine: "Every text, after all, is a lazy machine asking the reader to do some of its work." See Eco, *Six Walks in the Fictional Woods* (Cambridge: Harvard University Press, 1995), 3. It is my contention, though, that traditional "texts" are not machines at all, at least not in the way that a computer is a machine. Thus I make a distinction between those art forms that require the physical action of both the user and the work for the work to exist, and those that do not. In the end, of course, such distinctions are largely strategic, aiming to elevate a new medium by laying claim to some space of aesthetic specificity, a pursuit repeated over and over in the various avant-gardes and artistic zig-zags of the modern era.

5 See Philip Agre, "Surveillance and Capture," in *The New Media Reader*, ed. Noah Wardrip-Fruin and Nick Montfort (Cambridge: MIT Press, 2003).

6 Roger Caillois, *Man, Play and Games*, trans. Meyer Barash (New York: Schocken Books, 1979), 10.

7 Johan Huizinga, *Homo Ludens: A Study of the Play-Element in Culture* (Boston: Beacon, 1950), 13.

8 Gérard Genette uses "extradiegetic" (instead of "nondiegetic") to designate the narrating instance itself, as opposed to the actual narration: "*Any event a narrative recounts is at a diegetic level immediately higher than the level at which the narrating act producing this narrative is placed.* M. de Renoncourt's writing of his fictive *Mémoires* is a (literary) act carried out at a first level, which we will call *extradiegetic*; the events told in those *Mémoires* (including Des Grieux's narrating act) are inside this first narrative, so we will describe them as *diegetic*, or *intradiegetic*." See Genette, *Narrative Discourse: An Essay in Method* (Ithaca, N.Y.: Cornell University Press, 1980), 228.

> The question of narrative is somewhat controversial in game studies: the narratologists claim that video games are simply interactive narratives, while the ludologists claim that games must be defined separately from the concept of narrative. At the end of the day, I side with the ludologists, but I find that the diegetic-nondiegetic split, despite being rooted in a theory of narrative, is still useful for understanding the different types of gamic action. For a good analysis of how narrative fits into gameplay, see Katie Salen and Eric Zimmerman, chapter 26 of *Rules of Play* (Cambridge: MIT Press, 2004), 377–419.

9 My distinction here is similar to the one made by Nick Montfort in his analysis of interactive fiction. His "commands" are my diegetic operator acts; "directives" are nondiegetic operator acts; "replies" are diegetic machine acts; and "reports" are nondiegetic machine acts. See Montfort, *Twisty Little Passages: An Approach to Interactive Fiction* (Cambridge: MIT Press, 2003), 25–28.

10 This phrase was suggested by Katie Salen.

11 James Newman, "The Myth of the Ergodic Videogame: Some Thoughts on Player-Character Relationships in Videogames," *Game Studies* 2, no. 1 (July 2002).

12 The purest form of this is probably found in Maurice Blondel, *Action (1893): Essay on a Critique of Life and a Science of Practice* (Notre Dame: University of Notre Dame

Press, 1984). James Somerville's *Total Commitment: Blondel's "L'Action"* (Washington, D.C.: Corpus, 1968) is a useful secondary source on Blondel's text. Blondel's interest is the irreducibility of action. Today the word "interactive" is often invoked to describe the coupling of user and machine, but Blondel's concept of action is more singular, more oriented around the individual life, or what he called the whole of man. "Yes or no, does human life make sense, and does man have a destiny?"—this query begins what is perhaps the most extensive and uncompromising consideration of action in the history of philosophy. "It is into action that we shall have to transport the center of philosophy" is his premise, "because there is also to be found the center of life" (3, 13). And so I take Blondel as inspiration, but not for the motivations of action, and not the consequences of action, nor the moral foundations of this or that action. Those related debates in the analytic philosophy tradition try to derail a study of pure action by reducing it to other topics, as if a study of causes and effects could shed any light on the actual phenomenon of doing. Blondel's book aims to answer, not unlike Descartes, a foundational question for human destiny. "In my acts," he wrote, "in the world, inside of me, outside of me, I know not where or what, *there is something*" (52). Indeed, the same theme has reoccurred often in philosophy, from Epicurus's "swerve" of atoms as they fall through space to Deleuze and Guattari's "refrain" abetting the forces of chaos.

13 Clifford Geertz, *The Interpretation of Cultures* (New York: Basic Books, 1973), 10.

14 Ibid., 436. The seeming irrationality of "deep play" in cockfighting goes against the source of the expression, which is found in Jeremy Bentham: "Take away from a man the fourth part of his fortune, and you take away the fourth part of his happiness, and so on . . . . It is to this head that the evils of deep play ought to be referred. Though the chances, so far as relates to money, are equal, in regard to pleasure, they are always unfavourable. I have a thousand pounds. The stake is five hundred. If I lose, my fortune is diminished one-half; if I gain, it is increased only by a third. Suppose the stake to be a thousand pounds. If I gain, my happiness is not doubled with my fortune; if I lose, my happiness is destroyed; I am reduced to indigence." See Bentham, *Theory of Legislation* (London: Trubner, 1871), 106.

15 Geertz, *The Interpretation of Cultures*, 444.

16 Ibid., 446.

17 Gregory Bateson, "A Theory of Play and Fantasy," in *Steps to an Ecology of Mind* (Chicago: University of Chicago Press, 1972), 180.

18 Indeed, for Schiller the play-drive is synonymous with man's moral freedom and his aesthetic experience. See, in particular, letters 14 and 15 of Friedrich Schiller, *On the Aesthetic Education of Man* (Oxford: Oxford University Press, 1967).

19 Huizinga, *Homo Ludens*, 28. A slightly more detailed summary of the concept appears earlier in the book: "Summing up the formal characteristics of play we might call it a free activity standing quite consciously outside 'ordinary' life as being 'not serious,' but at the same time absorbing the player intensely and utterly. It is an activity connected with no material interest, and no profit can be gained by it. It proceeds within its own proper boundaries of time and space according to fixed rules and in an orderly manner. It promotes the formation of social groupings which tend to surround themselves with secrecy and to stress their difference from the common world by disguise or other means" (13).

20 Caillois, *Man, Play and Games*, 43. A more verbose definition appears on pages 9–10.

21 Huizinga, *Homo Ludens*, 173, 46.

22 "All these [objectionable] hypotheses have one thing in common: they all start from the assumption that play must serve something which is *not* play." Huizinga, *Homo Ludens*, 2.

23 Caillois, *Man, Play and Games*, 10, 11.

24 Vilém Flusser, in a nod to Huizinga's own simple periodization from *Homo sapiens* to *Homo faber* to *Homo ludens*, underscores the eventual transformation of play into

algorithmic terms by using the word "program": "The new human being is not a man of action anymore but a player: *homo ludens* as opposed to *homo faber*. Life is no longer a drama for him but a performance. It is no longer a question of action but of sensation. The new human being does not wish to do or to have but to experience. He wishes to experience, to know and, above all, to enjoy. As he is no longer concerned with things, he has no problems. Instead, he has programs." Flusser, *The Shape of Things* (London: Reaktion, 1999), 89.

25 Huizinga, *Homo Ludens*, 14–15.

26 Jacques Derrida, *Writing and Difference* (Chicago: University of Chicago Press, 1978), 280, 278, 281, 292. The French *jeu* is translated as either "play" or "game," or, as one might say today, "gaming."

27 Jacques Derrida, *Dissemination* (Chicago: University of Chicago Press, 1981), 194, 95.

28 Derrida, *Writing and Difference*, 289 (translation modified by the author).

29 "If one takes the line of thought that runs from Heraclitus via Nietzsche to Deleuze and Derrida," McKenzie Wark writes, "one might rather say that play is a free movement that can engender more rigid structures. It is not the game that is the precondition of play, in other words, but play that is the condition of possibility of the game. Brian Massumi argues this most cogently in his book *Parables of the Virtual*." See Wark, "Designer Playtime," *Rhizome Digest*, January 5, 2004.

30 Salen and Zimmerman, *Rules of Play*, 305.

31 Derrida, *Writing and Difference*, 292 (translation modified by the author).

32 Derrida, *Dissemination*, 156–57.

33 Huizinga, *Homo Ludens*, 10.

34 Eddo Stern, "A Touch of Medieval: Narrative, Magic and Computer Technology in Massively Multiplayer Computer Role-Playing Games," http://www.eddostern.com/texts/Stern_TOME.html (accessed April 25, 2005).

35 This same machinic logic of image making is evoked in John Simon's 1997 Internet artwork *Every Icon*. The work draws every image that is combinatorially possible within a 32×32 pixel square by sequentially turning on and off pixels. In essence, the work is binary mathematics turned into image.

36 Remedy, "Part III, Prologue," *Max Payne* (New York: Rockstar Games, 2001) (italics mine).

33

IN DEFENSE OF CUTSCENES

Rune Klevjer

Source: Frans Mäyrä (ed.), *Proceedings of Computer Games and Digital Cultures Conference* (Tampere: Tampere University Press, 2002), pp. 191–202.

Abstract

The technique of cutscenes, as typically found in story-based action games, is placed within a wider discursive problematic, focusing on the role of pre-written narratives in general. Within a theoretical framework raised by Espen Aarseth, Markku Eskelinen and Marie-Laure Ryan, I discuss the relations between the ergodic and the representational, and between play and narration. I argue that any game event is also a representational event, a part of a typical and familiar symbolic action, in which cutscenes often play a crucial part. Through cutscenes, the ergodic effort acquires typical meanings from the generic worlds of popular culture.

Radical ludology

In his excellent article about configurative mechanisms in games, "The Gaming Situation" [5], Markku Eskelinen rightly points out, drawing on Espen Aarseths well-known typology of cybertexts, that playing a game is predominantly a configurative practice, not an interpretative one like film or literature. However, the deeply problematic claim following from this is that stories "are just uninteresting ornaments or gift-wrappings to games, and laying any emphasis on studying these kind of marketing tools is just waste of time and energy". This is a radical ludological argument: Everything other than the pure game mechanics of a computer game is essentially alien to its true aesthetic form.

The theoretical premise of this argument was introduced in Espen Aarseth's ground-breaking *Cybertext* [1], the first book to suggest a theory about play and narration as two distinct modes of discourse, not only located in literature, but as a dialectic fundamental to human activity in general. Through his concept of the *ergodic* Aarseth has provided an invaluable tool for investigating games as a unique form of expression, a distinct category of cultural activity not reducible to other and more established categories.

The ergodic signifies the general principle of having to work with the materiality of a text, the need to participate in the construction of its material structure. Some ergodic works lead us towards a fixed solution (a jigsaw-puzzle), others can be unpredictable and open-ended (an experimental hypertext novel). As a discursive mode, the ergodic can be contrasted to narrative discourse, where the user is invited only to engage in the semantics of the text and does not have to worry about its material configuration. Reading narrative is, as Eskelinen says, a purely interpretative practice. In narrative discourse the user is only a reader, not a co-constructor, not a player.

In any game, the ergodic is the defining discursive mode, not the narrative. This means that the user is basically involved as a player (doing ergodic work on the materiality of the text), not as a reader (interpreting on a semantic level). This may sound obvious (games are games), but it is an important theoretical premise if we are to avoid studying computer games as if they were just another narrative genre. Following the general perspective raised by Aarseth, both Jesper Juul [9] and Gonzalo Frasca [6] have developed more specifically game-oriented ideas about how to understand this basic distinction, centred around the Latin term *ludus*, both as a mode of textuality and as a mode of activity on a more general level. Correspondingly, all game research, including the study of computer games, would be labelled *ludology*.

There are good reasons why the ludic dimension of computer games deserves considerable theoretical attention. The field is still developing through an early stage, and it is important not to leave it open to affirmative appropriation by established disciplines and theories. Also, play and games as a cultural activity has received remarkably little attention, except as a subcategory within children's development studies. On the other hand – does it follow that other modes of discourse in a computer game are accidental to the gaming experience and hence less interesting to computer game theorists?

Should computer game studies be a sub-category of general game theory?

Radical ludology only takes us so far, mainly for two reasons:

a A computer game is a computing game. Play is transformed by the computer technology, producing distinctive new forms of challenge and attraction that can not be understood through concepts and theories developed to investigate non-computerized play. Although not the subject of this brief paper, both the procedural logic and the spectacular responsiveness of the computer as a media technology has indeed created unique, although not entirely new, textual attractions.

b A computer game (in the narrow, ludological sense of the term) frequently uses conventions of popular culture. In fact, game genres offering ergodic challenges within a fictional universe known from other media make up a large portion of the games that people actually buy and play today (sport and driving games being the other major commercial category). The marketing of these genres addresses the buyer primarily as a reader, packing their games with heavy intertextual references, most often based on expensive licences from the film industry. Already a standard convention, narration of events within this fictional universe is typically conveyed through cutscenes – cinematic sequences adressing the reader, putting the player on hold.

Within the radical perspective raised by Markku Eskelinen (inspired by Aarseth) this category of games can be nothing but a bastard discourse, an impure commercial practice that may well be appreciated by mainstream consumers, but cannot be taken seriously by computer game studies, other than as a discursive misunderstanding that probably will go away as games mature (or, admittedly, will live on due to the inherent corruption of mainstream entertainment). Expanding this logic, one could say that not only cutscenes, but any pre-written narrative, fixed path, scripted event or movie-based character is a sign of immaturity, a dependence on film parallel to the way much early film was dependent on the conventions of staged drama. A mature, involving gameplay would not need any "You are James Bond" or the like, especially not when forced upon the player through elaborate and game-spoiling cinematic narration.

Discursive modes

The problem with this line of argument is that the (necessary) theoretical project of articulating the principles of a specific discursive conflict seems to be confused with an ideology of 'pure' gaming. This ideology prescribes an ideal receptional mode of games, a strictly no-nonsense, gameplay-oriented attitude typical among the *real* (or 'hard-core') gamers – the 'cineastes' of the game world. This counter-establishment ideology of gaming, partly rooted in the dark arcades of the late 70's and early 80's, partly rooted in hacker culture, is instinctively sanctioned by a new breed of oppositional scholars, vaguely identifying mainstream players and mainstream commercial games with established theory.

There is a deliberate confusion of 'game' as a discursive mode and 'computer game' as an actual cultural product. This implies, rather conveniently, that the relevance of narration in any given computer game can be denounced simply by referring to the fact that 'games' and narratives are two different things. Originally suggested as tools for the study of computer game aesthetics, the concepts of ergodics and ludology turns into self-contained arguments for advocating the purity of games, targeting a broad category of games (story-based, single player action games) as unworthy of serious attention.

Alternatively, the purist can be less categorical, and argue like Espen Aarseth [2], seriously doubting the feasibility of games that try to integrate filmic narration:

> But there seems to be a limit to the usefulness of these kinds of modal crossovers, in that an audience will want the work to perform as either one or the other, and their own role to be either that of player or observer. [2]

Arguing like this, having no empirical evidence, or even indications, of what different kinds of audiences will actually want or not, is not as hazardous as it may seem. It is based on the assumption that two distinct discursive modes – of which the basic theoretical principles have been soundly established – cannot be mixed into new, stable, meaningful and enjoyable cultural practices. Consequently, a game (read: the cultural product) should stick to being a game (read: the discursive mode), in order to avoid being a confusing half-game. Therefore, we should not even bother to understand story-based action games as a phenomenon, as they are, and probably will always be, an artistic failure (even if consumers continue to enjoy 'modal crossovers' like *Metal Gear Solid*, for empirical reasons we do not know).

Contrary to the project of the die-hard ludologists, my general concern is how the 'alien' dimension of cultural conventions can work as an integrated part of the gaming experience. In this paper, this is not an empirical question about modes of reception in actual users (however interesting), but rather a call for a stronger interest in a typical textual practice, at once configurative and interpretative, both unique and intertextual. The most accentuated expression of such an impure duality is found in the oscillation between cutscenes and play in typical story-based action games. These games offer a highly structured, linear and progressive gameplay, framed by a pre-written story.

The gameplay of cutscenes

What can possibly be the reason for cutting up the players configurative activities with close-to-parodic, B-movie-type cinematic sequences? Let me first briefly look at some gameplay considerations, questioning the assumption that cutscenes are irrelevant or destructive to gameplay.

Framing gameplay in a single, linear story is convenient. A game within this genre needs a system of progression (with a clear goal), a reward structure, and the regular introduction of new elements (levels, enemies, weapons, skills). A simple, action-based story takes care of all this, offering a narrative project as a unifying logic. This narrative is *pragmatic*, as far as it serves as a plausible excuse for the construction of an interesting gameplay. The cutscene is an efficient tool for conveying this story, being more visually interesting than purely verbal narration, and more uncomplicated than distributing the necessary information through scripted events. But cutscenes also have strengths of their own, serving gameplay functions that cannot be taken care of through other means.

A cutscene does not cut off gameplay. It is an integral part of the configurative experience. Even if the player is denied any active input, this does not mean that the ergodic experience and effort is paused. A cutscene is never truly 'cinematic', no matter how poorly implemented it may be. In any case, it can not avoid affecting the rhythm of the gameplay. This need not be in the negative sense. For example, in the arcade-inspired *James Bond in Agent Under Fire* [12] (a fun game that makes up in spectacle and atmosphere for what it lacks in gameplay), the numerous but short cutscenes provide regular moments of release from intense action. They create a characteristic rhythm in which the regular interruption/ release is always expected. As a player you quickly learn the code, constantly being thrown rapidly in and out of bodily ergodic effort.

Still, a good cutscene has other qualities than just being 'rhythmically' well-implemented. Notably, it may work as a surveillance or planning tool, providing the player with helpful or crucial visual information. Another rather well-established convention is the 'gameplay catapult', building up suspense and creating a situation, only to drop the player directly into fast and demanding action-gameplay.

Both techniques are elegantly implemented in the gangster-themed *Grand Theft Auto III* [11], a game successfully combining story-based mission structure and a more open-ended gameplay. This unusual mix is enabled through the impressive simulation of a big, populated city for the player to play around in. The game also illustrates a significant gameplay-function of good cutscenes: reward by entertainment. The short, stylistic and humorous mission briefings in *GTA III* become a part of the gameplay's reward structure, independently of which new missions, items or weapons they may introduce. Some of them are good, some of them are not so good, but you will never know before you get there. This may not be a very sophisticated technique, but it adds extra motivation and satisfaction to the game. Chasing new cutscenes can be more fun than chasing bigger guns.

GTA III also features an interesting kind of in-game 'hybrid' carjump sequences, actually generated in real-time but looking much like a spectacular cutscene, a result of the triggered slow-motion effect and change of camera angle. Being both a simulation (run by the physics engine) and a sheer spectacle to sit back and watch, these jumps provide a striking illustration of the duality of computer games: At once representation and action, reading and configuration, communication and event, mediation and play.

Utterance

Doing away with the communicative dimension of computer games can only be a provisional, pragmatic tool, intended to highlight ergodic mechanisms. Neglecting reading and mediation altogether leads to an unnecessary pessimism towards the collaboration between narrative and the ludic as discursive modes. When Markku Eskelinen points to the fact that playing with a ball and telling stories are two different things [5], he is certainly making a relevant argument as far as discursive modes are concerned, but still his choice of example very conveniently hides the very contradiction (and sometimes dilemma) that makes computer games so fascinating as a peculiar textual practice: Unlike for example a game of football, they are *representational* events. A ball is not a sign, it is a ball. Football is not narrated, because it is not an utterance in the first place.

The easiest way to write off narration in a computer game, then, is to deny its relevance as an utterance. Being an act of signification, a computer game is what Kenneth Burke calls a *symbolic action* [4]. Much in line with Wayne C.

Booth's general argument in the classic *Rhetoric of Fiction* [3], Burke claims that all utterances (including literature) are rhetorical, in the sense that they testify to a motivation, a purpose of some kind. Because they are symbolic actions, holding pre-configured, rhetorical meanings, computer game events are not events like any events in the world. The actions I perform when I play, because they also have meanings within a pre-configured fictional world, are a part of a symbolic action of someone else. I may not pay any attention to it (being too busy playing), but my own actions speak to me in a voice which is not mine.

Espen Aarseth, although stressing that game events is a mode of textuality, nonetheless constructs a non-representational event-space within computer games. Given this premise, he can argue, as Eskelinen has done after him, that narration and play cannot co-exist on the same level in discourse. He claims that narration can only be *about* the events in a game, and that thinking otherwise would be to confuse the representation of an event with the event itself [2, page 35]. He is obviously unwilling to grant any significance to the fact that events in a non-abstract computer game are *already* representational, and therefore communicative, as they happen. Symbolic action is inscribed in all representational events. In story-based games, this symbolic act includes a narrative act. Narrative meaning does not depend on the user to perform a rhetorical reconstruction.

The paradox of make-believe

My interest in the pre-configured textuality of computer games is partly based on an empirical speculation: people buy and play computer games because they want the illusion of playing in fantastic, but familiar worlds. When they play, people do not generally want to be artists, expressing themselves in new ways. We do not want to make our own toys, even if our parents tell us so. Playing with a home-made (or imaginary) revolver is fine, but playing with an exact replica of a Colt 45 is much cooler.

Computer games presenting elaborate pre-written universes, containing typical narratives, are rhetorical-ludological bastards because we want them to be. We do not just want to play (as in football, chess or in *Tetris*), we also want to play make-believe. A 'story-game', as Aarseth calls it, offers a complete cultural configuration of a world – as much as it offers a specific ludic challenge. It is not just a set-up for play, but also an object of desire, a rhetorically structured illusion.

Any story-game is, of course, a contradiction. We want freedom of action, and we want to do the same as the hero from the movies does. The illusion of potent agency in a mythical world – as any representational event – is a paradox, creating conflict when we play. I remember playing "police and bank-robbers" when we were kids, and my younger brother caught me and my sister *before* we robbed the bank. He ruined the play. There is a prewritten narrative. Yes, we want to be free, to play, to master and to conquer, but we also want our actions to be meaningful within a mythical fictional universe. This is the paradox of make-believe, the contradiction between the given and the agency.

The inherent paradox of mimetic games is dramatically amplified by the computer as a toy, due to its strictly rule-based regime and immediate response, coupled with its ever-increasing representational powers. This is what creates the typical oscillation between cutscenes and play. Oscillation is a standard convention in story-based computer games, and my guess is that this form will not go away. On the contrary, it is becoming a new kind of artistic language, developing its own rules.

Not trying to understand this hybrid form (because games should not be like this) is to disregard computer gaming as an unified practice. If we (eventually) want to bring aesthetic analysis together with reception studies, we need speculative concepts and theories which make relevant hypotheses about what is actually going on when people play, theories addressing questions of understanding, identity and ideology. We must try to understand what happens when play meets mediation. The puristic ludological approach will leave us relatively helpless, forcing us to conclude that players are stupid, that they have been duped by the industry, or that they do not really like games.

The diegesis of dramatic events

Suggesting the classical concept of *mimesis* as a relevant tool for research on event-spaces, Marie-Laure Ryan [10] is more open to the question of narrative meanings in computer games than Eskelinen – and, possibly, Aarseth. However, she seems to agree about the crucial role of any eventual re-telling of computer game events. Using Plato's generic distinction between *mimesis* and *diegesis*, she searches for symbolic meaning in the *player's* diegetic act of narration. As a result, the relevance of narrative in computer games rather disappointingly hinges on the possibility of a diegetic re-telling that may never take place.

The concepts of representational event and symbolic action imply that we should focus less on *diegesis* as a method of narrative presentation (that is, presenting by telling instead of imitating), and instead take a clue from Gerard Genette's narratological adaptation of the term. To Genette, the *diegesis* is a fictional world, created by discourse [8]. The term comes in especially handy when there are fictional worlds within fictional worlds. This *diegesis* is not a method of presentation, but a level in discourse. Narration, as a mode of discourse, is the act of creating this *diegesis*. This narration may be a patchwork of dramatic and diegetic methods of presentation.

Narrative theory traditionally tries to explain a dramatic narrative from the spectator's point of view. As an actor in a play, *enacting* the events, your way of relating to the narrative would be very different. Also, a play may only be scripted on a general level, so that you would have to improvise the details. But still, as long as there is some kind of script limiting the range of events, the dramatic narrative would be a part of a narrative situation, establishing a *diegesis* in which certain events may take place. Actors do indeed act, do configure mimetic events, but they also interpret the symbolic action of an *implied author*.

The concept of implied author, according to Wayne C. Booth, is not about the physical and historical author, but signifies the author-in-the-text, the rhetorical voice implied by the text, a unifying focus of the reader's interpretation. In a computer game, there is also an implied author speaking, creating the diegetic world through general descriptions, through simulations, and through the pre-written events. The 'implied designer' may occasionally reveal signs of individuality, but as a general rule, he takes the form of a familiar, generic voice. The cutscene is a part of this typified symbolic action.

Narrated descriptions

The meaning of a representational event is partly established through the descriptive characteristics of the representation. Sniping a Colombian gangster in the head in *GTA III* is one thing. Doing the same to, say, a little girl would not be the same (consequently, there are no children in Liberty City). The difference between these two representations is partly rooted in their respective real-world references – a mean-looking adult male versus a pretty little girl – but also linked to a specific, typified universe constructed by the game. Within this familiar fictional ready-made, the mean-looking guy turns into (through a few, stylised hints) a very familiar gangster of the most ruthless, drug-dealing kind.

Also, the cartoonish, over-the-top style of this game-version of the gangster genre adds to the general feeling that aimless killing (for no ludic reason) is somehow permitted and cannot be taken very seriously. The cutscenes are highly stylised in terms of characters, dialogue, setting and cinematics, leaving the fictional world somewhere between the parody and the real thing.

In *GTA III*, it is very hard to define a representational level of 'description', independent of the narration that frames it. The gangster universe as a setting, and as a set-up for play, is partly founded on the formulaic stories told within it. The actions performed by the player, being representational events, become meaningful within the genre-based universe as a whole. 'Story' and 'fictional world' are two flips of the same coin – a pre-written, typified symbolic action, defining a typical identity of the playground. Even though we can imagine a similar fictional world without one, single, overarching story framing the gameplay, there would at least have to be recognisable narrative elements that could give some more genre-specific substance to an otherwise vague atmosphere of urban crime. In genre fiction, description evokes implied narratives, and narration evokes implied descriptions.

Constructing the representational event

The events taking place in a computer game are not just representational. As ergodic actions, they are also real events, establishing meanings which, by abstraction, can be imagined independently from the particular fictional universe in which they take place. Puzzle solving, exploring, confusion, dead ends, fragmentation, construction, destruction, search, loops, randomness, backtracking etc.

are formal categories, bearing cultural significances *irrespective* of different actualisations in specific game-worlds. Also, this concept of de-contextualized ergodic events is a very useful tool, enabling us to conceptualise the workings of a representational event.

A representational event is established through an *internal* relation between the pre-written and the ludic event. When there is only an external relation, there is no representational event. In the latter case, the ergodic effort is all about the configuration of the material discourse, revealing no other relation to the semantics of this discourse. A jigsaw puzzle is the classic example: The puzzle completes the picture, and that's all there is to it. There is no other relation between the puzzle-gameplay as such and the idea of building the Eiffel Tower.

Also, the gameplay-functions of the cutscene mentioned above, like the 'surveillance' or the 'catapult', are external relations. They do not contribute to the representational event as a symbolic action, but alter the structure of the ludic action. Similarly, the shapes of the Eiffel Tower provide recognisable patterns to the jigsaw-puzzle, making the ergodic challenge more accessible.

In any representational event, there is a *metaphoric* relation, an analogy, between the event and the representation. This internal relation between configuration and interpretation is not only found in games, but also in ergodic literature [1]. In Michael Joyce' classic *Afternoon: a story*, the ergodic effort of the reader is an actualisation of central ideas as they are (somewhat aphoristically) expressed in the lexia. An unstable cybernetic feedback loop is operating in a text celebrating the blessings of unstable textuality. This analogy makes the ergodic work-path a representational path. The representation is not an addition to the event, but absorbs it, enabling representational action jointly performed by the user and the machine.

Similarly, in a computer game, the cybernetic feedback loop between the player and the computer is also a representation of an action in a fictional world. The game event has a double function: it is both configurative and representational, operating on the material level as well as on the semantic level, referring to the machine (the toy) as well as to the fictional world.

In a computer game, a space of possible representational events is typically enabled through a simulation. The simulation is a *procedural* representation, representing rules, not events. In a strategy game like *Sim City*, the simulation establishes a characteristic analogy between the player-machine-relation and the player-world-relation: balancing parameters *is like* rational managment of a city. System A (the computer program) is analogous to system B (the city) – both systems being a specific interpretation of the other. When system B is interpreted in terms of system A, playing with the machine is the attraction [7]. When system A is interpreted in terms of system B, playing with a fictional world is the attraction.

In action games, because of real-time procedural representation of physical laws, the feedback loop of action-response-action is not operating only on the intellectual level. In *GTA III*, the ergodic involvement is crucially a matter of bodily (and partly automatized) interaction. When you play with the machine, it is *as if*, by analogy, you are a body in a world. A cutscene is a part of the more general strategy of providing a particularity to this body, and to this world. By inviting established fictional genres into the game, the cutscene places you as a typical subject in a typical world.

Fictional genre-worlds are not the only meaningful analogies enabling attractive representational events. A lot of computer games, from fishing-simulators to sport games, work wonderfully without them. Nevertheless, given that the typical stories of popular culture play a part in modern peoples lives, addressing our dreams and anxieties, they will also play a part in the favourite worlds we design for mimetic play.

A dream come true

The cutscene may indeed be a narrative of re-telling, as Ryan maybe would say, but more importantly: it is a narrative of *pre-telling*, paving the way for the mimetic event, making it a part of a narrative act, which does not take place after, but *before* the event. The cutscene casts its meanings forward, strengthening the diegetic, rhetorical dimension of the event to come.

In *GTA III*, narration always takes place as it is enacted – whether it is retold or not. When the boss of the Italian family tells me how important this next mission is, and how I am going to earn his trust on my way to mobster stardom if all goes well, the event-to-come is placed within the generic world of *Goodfellas* and *Miller's Crossing*. It is much like when you day-dream before a football match, imagining that the special girl you like is going to be in the audience and that you score the winning goal, saving the day and winning her heart, just like in the movies. And then, it turns out she is actually there, and everything actually happens that way. The match would not be the same without the previous narration of your day-dreaming. It would not have been a dramatic moment. Because of your day-dreams, this particular match turned out to be a dream come true.

Just like day-dreaming, the fictional genre gives vague expectations a form. Ergodic effort acquires new meaning through typical stories evoked by the pre-written. The cutscenes of *GTA III* play well on the genre. They do not tell elaborate back-stories, or try to explain complicated conspiracies. Style, setting, characters and simple stereotypical events bring the mobster stories to life. As a player-reader you are not just guided, you are spoken to. A recognisable rhetoric meets you; the voice of a genre. This voice is your dialogical partner, in a mythical world especially made for you. The distinct rhetoric of a fictional genre is perfectly suited to the single-player experience.

Playing story-games is an option. Many games do not cast any specific narrative expectations. Defending the importance of the pre-written is not based on epistemological claims about the all-encompassing narrative. It is based on an assumption about the role of stereotypes in our serious lives, about how the myths of popular culture play a part in our ergodic pleasures.

The conflict between narration and play is not a question of discursive levels – as if the first can only be *about* the other – but a conflict of agency. There is a balancing, and a struggle, between the agency of the story-game and the agency of the player. The mutual project of make-believe binds the two movements together. This project is a very persistent paradox, insisting on the combined pleasures of ergodic operation and symbolical seduction.

References

1   Aarseth, E. *Cybertext. Perspectives on Ergodic Literature*. John Hopkins University Press, Baltimore and London, 1997.

2   Aarseth, E. "Aporia and Epiphany in *Doom* and *The Speaking Clock*: The Temporality of Ergodic Art," in Ryan, M. (ed.). *Cyberspace Textuality. Computer Technology and Literary Theory*. Indiana University Press, Bloomington and Indianapolis, 1999.

3   Booth, W.C. *The Rhetoric of Fiction*. Harmondsworth, Penguin, 1987.

4   Burke, K. *The Philosophy of Literary Form: Studies in Symbolic Action*. New York, Vintage Books, 1957.

5   Eskelinen, M. "The Gaming Situation." *Games Studies 1* (July 2001), available at http://www.gamestudies.org/.

6   Frasca, G. "Ludology meets Narratology," available at http://www.ludology.com/, undated.

7   Friedman, T. "Making Sense of Software: Computer Games and Interactive Textuality," available at http://www.duke.edu/~tlove/simcity.htm/, undated.

8   Genette, G. *Narrative Discourse*. Translated by Jane E. Lewin. Oxford, Blackwell, 1980.

9   Juul, J. "Games Telling Stories? – A brief note on games and narratives." *Games Studies 1* (July 2001), available at http://www.gamestudies.org/.

10   Ryan, M. "Beyond Myth and Metaphor. – The Case of Narrative in Digital Media." *Games Studies 1* (July 2001), available at http://www.gamestudies.org/.

11   *Grand Theft Auto III*. Rockstar Games, 2001.

12   *James Bond 007 in Agent Under Fire*. Electronic Arts, 2001.

34

FEAR OF FAILING?

The many meanings of difficulty in video games

Jesper Juul

Source: Bernard Perron and Mark J. P. Wolf (eds), *The Video Game Theory Reader 2* (New York: Routledge, 2008), pp. 237–252.

Winning isn't everything

It is quite simple: When you play a game, you want to win. Winning makes you happy, losing makes you unhappy. If this seems self-evident, there is nonetheless a contradictory viewpoint, according to which games should be "neither too easy nor too hard," implying that players also want *not* to win, at least part of the time. This is a contradiction I will try to resolve in this essay.

- Question 1: What is the role of failure in video games?

The simplest theory of failure states that failing serves as a contrast to winning, that failure thereby makes winning all the more enjoyable. There is, however, much more to failure. The study of players discussed in this essay indicates that failure serves the deeper function of making players readjust their perception of a game. In effect, *failure adds content* by making the player see new nuances in the game. Correspondingly, the study shows that players have quite elaborate theories of failure as a source of enjoyment in games.

Even so, given the negative connotations of failing, would a game be better received if players did not feel responsible for failing, but rather blamed failures on the game or on bad luck?

- Question 2: Do players *prefer* games where they do *not* feel responsible for failing?

This study strongly indicates that this is *not* the case. Players clearly prefer feeling responsible for failing in a game; not feeling responsible is tied to a negative perception of a game.

In effect, this sharpens the contradiction between players wanting to win and players wanting games to be challenging: failing, and feeling responsible for failing, makes players enjoy a game *more*, not less. Closer examination reveals that the apparent contradiction originates from two separate perspectives on games: a goal-oriented perspective wherein the players want to win, and an aesthetic perspective wherein players prefer games with the right amount of challenge and variation. Nevertheless, these two perspectives still present opposing considerations—the goal oriented perspective suggests that games should be as easy as possible; the aesthetic perspective suggests that games should not be too easy.

To examine this, I will look at the role of failure and punishment. I am writing here about single-player games.[1]

Failure and punishment

Failure means being unsuccessful in some task or interdiction that the game has set up, and punishment is what happens to the player as a result. We can distinguish between different types of punishment for player failure[2]:

- *Energy punishment*: Loss of energy, bringing the player closer to life punishment
- *Life punishment*: Loss of a *life* (or "retry"), bringing the player closer to game termination
- *Game termination punishment*: Game over
- *Setback punishment*: Having to start a level over and losing abilities.

Losing energy brings the player closer to losing a life, and losing a life often leads to some type of setback. In this perspective, all failures eventually translate into setbacks, and the player's use of time and energy is the most fundamental currency of games.

Whereas early video games in the arcade, on the home console, or for personal computers, tended to force the player to replay the entire game after failing, many home games from the mid-1980s and later became much more lenient by dispersing save points, allowing the player to save the game, or letting the player restart at the latest level played even after game over. As a recent example of this design principle, after reaching game over in *Super Mario Galaxy* (Nintendo EAD Tokyo, 2007), the player loses of coins and collectables, but not overall progress in the game.

In the new area of downloadable casual games,[3] there is a movement from life punishment to energy punishment, with many games featuring energy bars, timers, or other types of soft evaluations of player performance as with the timer in *Big City Adventure: San Francisco* (Jolly Bear Games, 2007) (see Figure 1).

The psychological *attribution theory* provides a framework for examining different types of failure and punishment in games. According to attribution theory, for any event, people tend to attribute that event to certain causes. Harold K. Kelley distinguishes between three types of attributions that people can make in an event involving a person and an entity:

Figure 1 Big City Adventure: San Francisco—a timer gradually runs out. (Jolly Bear Games, 2007)

- *Person*: The event was caused by personal traits, such as skill or disposition
- *Entity*: The event was caused by characteristics of the entity
- *Circumstances*: The event was based on transient causes such as luck, chance, or an extraordinary effort from the person.[4]

In the case of receiving a low-grade for a school test, a person may decide that this was due to the (a) person—personal disposition such as lack of skill; (b) entity—an unfair test; or (c) circumstance—having slept badly, having not studied enough. This maps quite well to many common exclamations in video gaming: a player who loses a game can claim that "I am terrible at video games," "This is an unfair game," or "I will win next time."

During the research for this essay, I developed the hypothesis that energy punishment is being more widely used because it makes the cause of failure less obvious: If the game is over due to a single, identifiable mistake, it is straightforward for the player to attribute failure to his or her own performance or skill (circumstance or person), but if the game is over due to an accumulation of small mistakes, the player is less likely to feel responsible for failing, and the player should be less likely to experience failing as an emotionally negative event. This is the second question mentioned in the introduction: do players *prefer* feeling less responsible for failing?

Video game theory through game prototypes

To elaborate this discussion, a game prototype study was conducted. This is not without precedent. In a study made 25 years ago, Thomas W. Malone explored the question "Why are computer games so captivating?" by creating a number of game prototypes with the same core game, but with different features (music, scorekeeping, fantasy, types of feedback).[5] In order to explore the attraction of the variations of the game, he let some children play these prototypes and examined how long each prototype was able to keep the attention of young players. From this, he deduced a number of guidelines for developing games and interfaces.

Following Malone, the questions in this essay can be approached as empirical questions—*What do players prefer?* They can, however, also be approached as aesthetic questions—*What is a good game?* These are two historically separate approaches that I nevertheless believe can inform each other in the following.

In collaboration with the game company Gamelab, I developed a game prototype specifically designed to gather data on how players perceive failure. The custom game could be described as a combination of *Pac-Man* (Namco, 1980) and *Snake* (Gremlin, 1977): using the mouse, the player controls a snake that grows as the player collects pills; the player must avoid opponents; and a special power pill allows the player to attack opponents for a short while (see Figure 2).

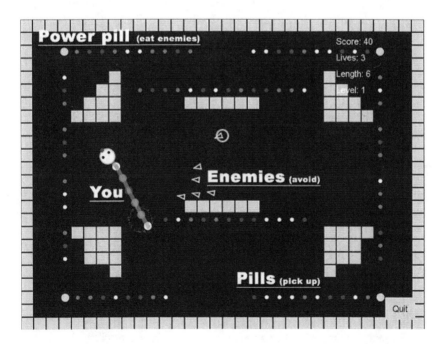

Figure 2 Game prototype for the test

205

The game was designed with two game modes, an *energy punishment* mode where the player would lose a tail part when hit by opponents, and a *life punishment* mode where the player could make only a single mistake before losing a life. In both games, the player has three lives, and the game consists of four levels. We attempted to balance the two games so that they were equally hard (as measured in the number of levels that players would complete). Another reason for developing a new game was that this would give insight to the players' initial experience of learning a new game, and be less a reflection of their previous experience with that game.

First test, offline

A preliminary test was conducted offline. Five males and four females from Gamelab's tester base participated. All participants had some experience with and interest in games, and came to the Gamelab offices (see Appendix 1 at the end of this essay for a description of the test procedure). Players were asked how they would rate the game had they found it on the Internet. The rating scale went from 1 to 10, with 10 being the best rating. Additionally, players were asked open questions about their views on failure in games.

Contrary to expectations, this small sample gave no indication that players preferred the energy punishment version of the game. On the other hand, there were indications that the players' ratings were closely tied to their performance in the game, such that a player performing badly would dislike the game, a player performing fairly well would like the game, but a player performing very well would *also dislike the game*. Given the interesting implications of this result, it was decided to focus on only one version of the game (energy punishment), and run a new test online with a bigger sample.

Second test, online

A total of 85 players were recruited online[6] and asked to play the game and answer a questionnaire (see Appendix 2 for a description of the test procedure). The players recruited were overwhelmingly male (73 out of 85), and the majority had a game console in their home (also 73 out of 85). Players were generally avid game players (see Figure 3).

Game rating vs. performance

Based on automated registration of player performances, player responses were placed into three categories, from a bad performance to a good performance:

1   Players that did not complete the game
2   Players that completed the game, losing some lives
3   Players that completed the game without losing any lives.

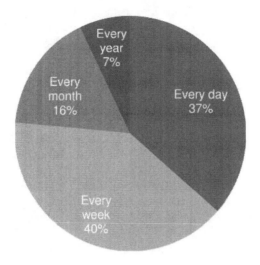

Figure 3 Game-playing frequency

By comparing the average game ratings with the performance of the players (Figure 4), we can see an indication that *winning isn't everything*: the most positive players were the ones that *failed* some, and then completed the game. Completing the game without failing was followed by a *lower* rating of the game (the statistical significance was the slightly weak $p<0.06$ for all three categories of player performance combined).

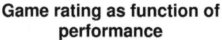

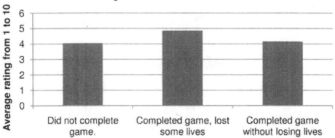

Figure 4 Player rating of game as function of performance

207

This runs counter to the simple idea that players enjoy a game more the better they do, but it vindicates the game design imperative that a game must be neither too hard nor too easy as argued by, for example, Fullerton et al.[7] This returns us to the second question, of whether feeling responsible for failing in a game will make players like the game less. In the test, players were asked why they failed or succeeded. Categories were based on attribution theory, but expanded into smaller subcategories:

- *Person* was split into "I am bad at this kind of game" and "I am bad at games in general" to capture difference between general player skills and player knowledge of specific genres
- *Entity* was asked via "The game was too hard"
- *Circumstance* was split into "I was unlucky" and "I made a mistake" in order to distinguish between the experience of losing due to chance and losing due to a strategic mistake.

As can be seen in Figures 5 and 6, players were slightly more likely to report being responsible for success ("figured out how to play right") than being responsible for failure ("made a mistake"). This is well-known phenomenon called *attribution asymmetry*, whereby individuals are more likely to attribute success to personal factors, and failure to external factors (Försterling 2001, 87–91).

Do players prefer games where they do not feel less responsible for failing? This seems not to be the case. On the contrary, even though players presumably on some level disliked being personally responsible for failing, the feeling of being responsible for failing was nevertheless tied to a *positive* rating of the game (see Figure 7).

Since players who never lost a life are not relevant, and too few players answered "I was unlucky" or "I am bad at this kind of game" for the results

Figure 5 Player attribution of success

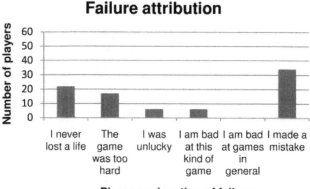

Figure 6 Player attribution of failure

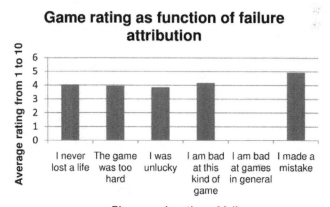

Figure 7 Rating as function of failure attribution

to be meaningful, we can see how players who answered "The game was too hard" rated the game compared with those who answered "I made a mistake." In this case, there is a clearer significance of $p<0.016$. In effect, this answers the second question of this essay—players *prefer feeling responsible* for their own failure. Or at least the negative emotions from failing are more than cancelled out by other factors. This result is parallel to a study of players playing the bowling mini-game in *Super Monkey Ball 2* (Amusement Vision, Ltd., 2002), in which players exhibited positive reactions when falling off the edge of the playing field, but negative reactions of watching the replay of the same event.[8] Although players do not want to fail, they may nevertheless enjoy it when feeling responsible for it.[9]

Players reactions when not failing

Do players have theories of the function of failure, and in that case, how do they frame them? To find out, players were asked if they had ever experienced a game that was too easy, and *"How do you know if a game is too easy?"* Answers were seen as falling into four categories based on their primary content. These are listed in Table 1 with example answers and percentages.

The first response type, "lack of challenge," is somewhat tautological.

Response (4) gives room for more interpretation: if a game being too easy is experienced as the game being shallow and uninteresting, it means that the role of failure is much more than a contrast to winning—failure pushes the player into reconsidering strategy, and failure thereby subjectively *adds content* to the game. The game appears deeper when the player fails; failure makes the game more strategic.

The next question is to what extent the results from this experiment map to players of published commercial games. In a discussion of the initial disappointing reception of the game *Shopmania* (Gamelab, 2006), Catherine Herdlick and Eric Zimmerman discuss how much of the criticism of the game came from the fact that it was perceived as too easy:

> In the original version of *Shopmania*, we approached the first several levels of the game as a gradual tutorial that introduced the player to the basic game elements and the core gameplay. This approach was based on

Table 1 Example answers and percentages

Answer type	Examples
1 Too easy, as lack of a challenge (36%)	"Not challenging enough." "Boring . . . doesn't provide further challenges." "I don't feel challenged. Of course that's a pretty predictable answer, but it's hard to put it any other way." "I get bored."
2 Too easy, as not failing (6%)	"When you never die. And beat it in a day." "It doesn't seem to challenge me—I never lose."
3 Too easy, as not being measured on performance (5%)	"I can do things I know are 'wrong' and don't get punished." "A game is too easy when you are progressing through the game automatically no matter how good you are playing."
4 Too easy, as not having to rethink strategy (27%)	"When I know exactly what to do and I can do it optimizing the result without (big) effort." "No challenge, going through the motions to complete it without any thought." "If the challenge and thought required to complete its objectives become second nature quickly or there is no need for such contemplation." "If the method for solving it is obvious and never fails."

210

the generally held casual game wisdom that downloadable games should be very easy to play, and that the frustration of losing a level should be minimized. However, the problem with going too far in this direction is that the game ends up feeling like interactive muzak: you can play forever and not really lose, and the essential tension and challenge of a good game are lost. From our analysis, players were telling us that the first seven or eight levels felt like a tutorial. By the third or fourth level, we had playtesters exclaiming out loud, "I get this game. Can I skip the tutorial?"[10]

One of the negative comments on *Shopmania* was about having seen the whole game too early:

"After 20 minutes, I felt like I saw the whole game . . . " (*Redesigning*)

The "saw" here probably does not refer directly to concrete graphics or level layouts, as much as it ties into some of the player comments in my experiment: The players complain about the game not pressuring them, not threatening with failure. Again, while players may dislike failure, *not* failing can be as bad as never succeeding.

Flow: the standard theory of failure and challenge

The standard psychological explanation for game failure and challenge is Mihaly Csikszentmihalyi's theory of *Flow* (see Figure 8), according to which the challenge of a given activity forms a narrow channel in which the player is in the attractive *flow* state.[11]

While flow theory does suggest that the player may oscillate between anxiety and boredom, it poses the banal problem that the standard *illustration* suggests a smooth increase in difficulty over time. Noah Falstein[12] has refined this to say that game difficulty should vary in waves—sometimes the game should be a

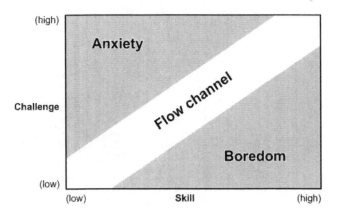

Figure 8 The flow channel. (Based on Csikszentmihalyi, 1990, 74)

little easy, sometimes a little hard, and that irregularity leads to enjoyment, as illustrated in Figure 9 An irregular increase in difficulty makes the player more likely to experience both failure and successes.

Conclusions: the contradictory desires of players

I initially discussed a contradiction between the observation that players want to win and the observation that players prefer games where they lose some, then win some. This leaves us with several opposing considerations indicating that games should be both easier and harder than they are:

1 The player does not want to fail (makes player sad, feel inadequate).
2 Failing makes the player reconsider his/her strategy (which makes the game more interesting).
3 Winning provides gratification.
4 Winning without failing leads to dissatisfaction.

Points (1) and (3) suggest that games should be very easy, whereas points (2) and (4) suggest that games should not be *too* easy. The actual relationship of game design and game playing is probably not as antagonistic as this seems. A more productive view is that games derive their interest from the interaction between these different considerations, and that the apparent contradiction comes from the fact that games can be viewed from two distinct frames of reference (see Figure 10). Playing a game entails (a) a goal-orientation as part of the activity, but a player also has (b) an outside view of the game that entails an aesthetic evaluation of

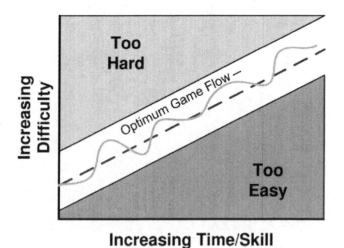

Figure 9 A better flow. (©2004 Noah Falstein)

game balance. This is the source of the contradiction discussed in the introduction, between players wanting to win, and players wanting not just to win.

The second question at the start of this essay is whether players would prefer *not* feeling responsible for failing, and whether the success of casual games consequently could be attributed to the fact that they tend to have energy punishment rather than life punishment, making failure seem less of a direct consequence of player actions. This idea seems to be largely disproved—player appreciation of the game was tied positively to feeling responsible for failure. This suggests that I had been focusing on the wrong part of the punishment system, and that the attraction of casual games is better explained as sparing use of *setback punishment*: failing in casual games is rarely tied to any substantial setback, and never to having to mechanically replay a game sequence.[13] Players still feel responsible for failing, but they are less likely to feel stuck in the game, being forced to replay a part of the game.

Finally, this research points to another layer of complexity in player behavior. That failure and difficulty is important to the enjoyment of games correlates well with Michael J. Apter's *reversal theory*, according to which people seek low arousal in normal goal-directed activities such as work, but high arousal, and hence challenge and danger, in activities performed for their intrinsic enjoyment, such as games.[14] This yields an extra complication in relation to the game *Shopmania* discussed previously: if the role of failure is to force players to discover new strategies in a game, why is this even necessary? Given that players enjoy a challenge, why do players not simply challenge themselves by finding new ways

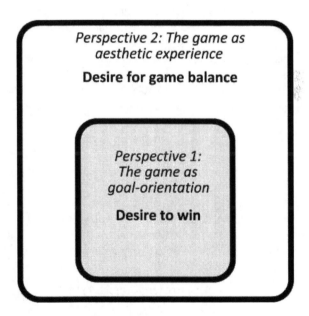

Perspective 2: The game as aesthetic experience

Desire for game balance

Perspective 1: The game as goal-orientation

Desire to win

Figure 10 Goal-oriented and aesthetic perspectives on a game

to play the game? Game designer David Jaffe goes as far as asserting that players are basically lazy and "WILL NOT use ANY mechanic they do not need to use. They will take the path of least resistance to get from A TO B."[15]

The conclusion must still be that players want to fail as well as win, but that players of the *single-player* games discussed here do *not* seek out additional challenge or depth if they do not have to. Perhaps single player games are perceived as designed experiences that players expect to be correctly balanced without having to seek additional challenges themselves?

Conversely, although the focus here has been on single player games, Jonas Heide Smith has documented how players of multiplayer games frequently handicap themselves to create an even playing field, effectively opening themselves to failure (Heide Smith 2006, 217–227). Multiplayer games and more open sandbox games seem to encourage players to undertake more challenge-seeking behavior.

The study raises a number of additional questions, but I believe the following are the most obvious ones to explore further:

- Is the relation between game rating and performance also consistent if the game is made easier or harder?
- How do players perceive difficulty in games without time pressure or failure states, such as "endless" mode in *Bejeweled 2* (PopCap Games, 2004) or *Sudoku*?
- In game development experience, it is certain that small changes to game designs *do* matter to players. To what extent can individual elements of a game design be isolated?
- To what extent can we extrapolate from one game to all games?
- Will the results of the test be different with a more "casual" audience?

I have argued that failure is central to player enjoyment of games. This is not that surprising, given conventional wisdom that a game should be balanced to match the skills of players. However, it is notable that failure is more than a contrast to winning—rather failure is central to the experience of *depth* in a game, to the experience of improving skills. The study supports the idea that that *growth*, the experience of learning, of adjusting strategies, of trying something new, is a core attraction of video games.[16] Hence the desire for game balance, losing some, winning some—the experience of variation in the challenge and difficulty of the game. *Failure adds content.*

If the classic tenet of storytelling is Aristotle's, that a story should have a beginning, a middle, and an end, the core tenet of games must be this: *a game should be neither too easy nor too hard.* This is more than the simple truism it sounds like. It reveals much deeper and more complicated facts about games, and players.

Acknowledgements

This research was done in collaboration with Gamelab in New York City, who provided facilities, discussion, feedback, and playtesting. Thanks to

T. L. Taylor, Jonas Heide Smith, Eric Zimmerman, Nick Fortugno, Chris Bateman, and Matthew Weise for comments. Thanks also to Svend Juul for statistical expertise.

Appendix 1: Offline test procedure

Participants were tested one at a time, and did not see or talk to other participants. Participants were informed that "We are working on a game, and we would like to hear your input. This is not a test of your skill; we would simply like to know what you think about the game."

Each player was asked to play the game until the game was over. It was noted on what levels players lost lives.

Each player was asked "Why did you fail?" and "Why did you complete the level?" The explanations were coded as being either due to *ability* (personal factor), *performance* (circumstance), or the *game* (entity).

After one game had been played, the player was interviewed.

Each player was asked to rate the game as follows: "If this was a game you found on the web, how would you rate it on a scale from 1 to 10, with 1 being the worst and 10 being the best?"[17]

Each player was asked to explain if he or she had ever played a game that was too easy.

Each player was asked how he or she could tell if a game is too easy.

Participants were not paid, but as game testing is often described as a way of entering the game industry, testers may have strong motivation for pleasing the company. This affects the confidence in the absolute judgments of the players, but since the testers' interest in pleasing the company will be statistically uniform, the data can be used relatively in correlation with other data from the test.

Appendix 2: Online test procedure

Players were recruited via the author's blog.

Players were told that "This is *not* a test of your skills, but a test of how you feel about playing a little game experiment"; players were not aware that the test concerned failure.

Players were directed to a page with instructions, as can be seen online at http://www.jesperjuul.net/test/rpt2/.

Players were directed to the game. The game consisted of four levels. The player had three lives.

When a player reached Game Over, either by completing all four levels or by losing all three lives, the player was directed to an online questionnaire. In the questionnaire, the player was asked to rate the game as follows: "Say you found this game on the Internet. On a scale from 1 to 10, with 1 being the worst game ever, and 10 being the best game ever, how would you rate this game?"

Only players who completed the entire questionnaire were included.

Notes

1 For studies of players in multiplayer settings, see Jonas Heide Smith, "Plans and Purposes: How Video Games Shape Player Behavior," PhD dissertation, IT University of Copenhagen, 2006, hereafter cited as Heide Smith; and Nicole Lazzaro,"Why We Play Games: Four Keys to More Emotion in Player Experiences," paper presented at the *Game Developers Conference*, San José, 2004. Abstract available online at <http://www.xeodesign.com/whyweplay games/xeodesign_whyweplaygames.pdf>.

2 Not all failure is punished in games—many smaller types of failure go unpunished, such as bumping into a wall.

3 Casual games are understood here as downloadable games that the player can play freely for typically 60 minutes, after which the game must be purchased to continue playing.

4 F. Försterling, *Attribution: An Introduction to Theories, Research and Applications* (London: Psychology Press, 2001), 46–47, hereafter cited as Försterling.

5 Thomas W. Malone, "Heuristics for designing enjoyable user interfaces: Lessons from computer games," in *Proceedings of the 1982 conference on Human factors in computing systems* (Gaithersburg, MD: ACM, 1982), 63–68.

6 Via the *Ludologist* blog. Available online at <http://www.jesperjuul.net/ludologist>.

7 Tracy Fullerton, Chris Swain, and Steven Hoffman, *Game Design Workshop: Designing, Prototyping, and Playtesting Games* (San Francisco: CMP Books, 2004), 249.

8 Niklas Ravaja, Timo Saari, Jari Laarni, Kari Kallinen, Mikko Salminen, Jussi Holopainen, and Aki Järvinen "The Psychophysiology of Video Gaming: Phasic Emotional Responses to Game Events," in *Changing Views: Worlds in Play. Proceedings of DiGRA 2005 Conference*, Vancouver, 2005. Available online at <http://www.digra.org/dl/db/06278.36196.pdf>.

9 The conclusions from the *Super Monkey Ball 2* study may not map to questions discussed in this essay, as *Super Monkey Ball 2* has a rewarding audiovisual feedback when the player fails compared to the more basic representation in the game prototype used here.

10 Catherine Herdlick and Eric Zimmerman, "Redesigning Shopmania: A Design Process Case Study," *IGDA Casual Games Quarterly* 2, no. 1 (2006), available online at <http://www.igda.org/casual/quarterly/2_1/index.php?id=6>; hereafter cited as *Redesigning*.

11 Mihaly Csikszentmihalyi, *Flow: The Psychology of Optimal Experience* (New York: Harper & Row, 1990).

12 Noah Falstein, "Understanding Fun—The Theory of Natural Funativity," in *Introduction to Game Development*, ed. Steve Rabin, 1 (Charles River Media, 2005), 71–98.

13 This is also due to the fact that casual games tend to contain much randomness, making every replay of a single level is a bit different from the previous.

14 J. H Kerr and Michael J. Apter, *Adult Play: A Reversal Theory Approach* (Amsterdam: Swets & Zeitlinger, 1991), 17.

15 David Jaffe, "Aaaaaaaaannnnnnnndddddd Scene!," *Jaffe's Game Design*, November 25, 2007, available online at <http://criminalcrackdown.blogspot.com/2007_11_25_archive.html>.

16 This is close to what Nicole Lazzaro calls "hard fun" (2004).

17 Since there is no universal scale for rating games, little can be deduced from the individual rating, but ratings can be used comparatively to examine player perceptions of game quality.

Part 5

VIDEO GAME THEORY, METHODOLOGY, AND ANALYSIS

35

CHANGING THE GAME

Bernard DeKoven

Source: *The Well-Played Game* (New York: Doubleday, 1978), pp. 39–59. Reprinted in Katie Salen and Eric Zimmerman (eds), *The Game Design Reader: A Rules of Play Anthology* (Cambridge, MA: The MIT Press, 2006), pp. 518–537.

Context

In 1968 the School District of Philadelphia hired me to write a curriculum for elementary school children. Although the original intention was a curriculum in theater, the curriculum I produced in 1971 was in children's games. In games, I found a form of theater that was native to childhood, universally—a theater of great social power and emotional depth, with an extensive repertoire. The curriculum was based on one single insight about games: it's a lot easier to change the game than it is to change the people who are playing it. It was this one observation that served as the basis for the training program I developed for the New Games Foundation, for the work I've done in game design and group facilitation, and most recently, my book *Junkyard Sports*. "Changing the Game" is a chapter from my book, *The Well-Played Game* (New York: Doubleday, 1978).

We've seen that a game can change. We've seen that the very game we're playing can become something we never intended it to be.

We made the change. It changed because of the way we were playing it.

It changed for the worse when we lost control. We didn't just lose control, we actually surrendered it to other people with whom we weren't even playing. As a result, though we were all involved in the game as much as we possibly could be, none of us was able to enjoy it. We couldn't even see that it was just a game, that it wasn't for real, that we were only playing.

It changed for the better when we discovered a different source of control. When that kid took his chair with him during the game of musical chairs, he established for us all a new way of seeing the game we were playing together.

But suppose what we really want to do is to play a game together, and every time we think we understand what game we are playing, somebody changes it. Suppose we are feeling so playful that we destroy the game together. If that's what we want to do—destroy the game—then everything's fine. But suppose we really want to play a *game*.

219

An example:

We start out with a game of dodgeball. We've been playing it for about five minutes. We're beginning to get the sense of what it means to play it well. At the same time, we're not quite committed to the game—we're not really into it yet. You're an ender and you throw the ball at me. I catch it. Now, according to what we understand to be the rules of the game, we're supposed to trade roles. Since I caught the ball, I get rewarded. Since you didn't hit me, you get punished.

In a moment of high cuteness, I decide to keep the ball. I just stand there, holding the ball against my stomach. And then, as soon as I notice that other people have noticed, I run.

So, people start running after me. I dribble teasingly. I dash madly. I run circles. The chase is on.

Then, just as it seems we've agreed that we're playing some kind of chasing game, I throw the ball to you.

You're shocked, so you throw the ball back to me. I'm tired, so I throw the ball back to you. Then you notice that others have noticed, so you take the ball and run. And then, as soon as you see someone getting too close, you throw the ball back to me.

Ah, keep away. All right. Good game. But then, when somebody gets the ball, instead of throwing it or running with it, she lies on top of it.

People try to get it away from her. Other people try to keep them from getting close to her.

Another game. What game is it? I don't know, do you?

Somebody steps on somebody else's hand. Somebody else steps on somebody else's hair. Some people really want to get the ball back. They're serious. They really want to start a game. Others don't know what's happening. Others are laughing hysterically.

It's all play and no game, all release and no control. No one can find the center. We have lost all responsibility—to the game, to the community, to ourselves.

We are not playing well at all.

Of play and games

There is a very fine balance between play and game, between control and release, lightness and heaviness, concentration and spontaneity. The function of our play community is to maintain that balance, to negotiate between the game-as-it-is-being-played and the game-as-we-intend-it-to-be. It is for that reason that we maintain the community.

On the one hand we have the playing mind—innovative, magical, boundless. On the other is the gaming mind—concentrated, determined, intelligent. And on the hand that holds them both together we have the notion of playing well.

The need for change

The balance between the playing mind and the gaming mind is never at an equilibrium. There is a dynamic tension between these two—a dialog. Playing well means playing within that dialog.

So the definition of playing well is the result of an ongoing process of negotiation and renegotiation. It changes as we do, sometimes drastically, sometimes subtly.

Suppose we're playing a game of volleyball. We're playing the regulation game: teams, rotation, points. It just so happens that I'm getting a little tired of playing that way. Something has changed. I don't like the way I'm playing anymore.

I could just walk away from the game. There are boundaries, and I could just step outside if I wanted to. But we are playing with small teams. I would be missed. I owe it to my team to stick it out until the game is over.

At the same time, I know I'm not playing well. The game isn't feeling right for me. My mind is wandering. I'm missing. I'm thinking about taking a nap. I'm wondering if the net is too high for me to put my toes through. I'm watching the shadows play. In fact, I'm not only missing the ball, I'm missing altogether.

So, there are times when playing the game as it is being played is a violation of the convention of the play community. I'm actually, in some way, interfering with the intention of the community. I'm not even trying to play well.

Though it is only fair, in terms of the game we're playing, that I continue playing, that I stick it out until the very end—though it is not only fair but also, in terms of my commitment to the team, obligatory that I remain in the game—I am cheating the community by the way I'm playing. The game is small enough for me to be felt. The balance between the playing mind and the gaming mind, between me and the other players is sensitive enough to perceive the shift. I am causing it to wobble. People are trying to play around me. There is a hole where I stand that is draining energy from the game.

It therefore becomes incumbent on me to do something about it. I could announce my problem to others in the community, but that would stop the game. I could quit, but that would be unfair to my team.

I can only see two other possibilities: I could try to focus myself in some way so that I could get back into the game, or I could try to somehow change the game itself.

If I select the first alternative, no one needs to know about it. I can withdraw within myself and argue myself back into the game. I can instruct myself to focus on the ball, to watch the seams, to notice how the light hits it.

But it isn't working. I'm focusing so intently on the ball that I forget to hit it. Somehow, the inner balance is getting shakier and shakier.

This leaves me with only one alternative.

I recognize that it is not always appropriate to change the game. It requires a sensitivity to the needs of the community as well as to my own needs. I am not sure that I am able to be sensitive enough to anything.

This leaves me with no alternatives at all.

Finding permission

I happen to notice that I did get more involved in the game when I was able to play close to the net. Perhaps my inner wanderings have something to do with the fact that I'm playing back.

During our next rotation, I go up to the net and ask if it's OK if I play there. Strangely enough, it is.

After all of this internal mishmosh, I discover that all I had to do was ask—that the permission was there all the time, and all I had to do was get it.

Here I was, trying to be so responsive to the needs of the community, and I totally forgot that the community we have created together was in response to the needs of each of us. My teammates knew that I was having trouble focusing on the game. It is in their own interest that I find the position that lets me play well.

Sure I can play front. Sure I can stay there as long as I need to. If it helps our game, why not?

The bent rule

We didn't really change a rule, we bent it. We made an exception, and it was clear to all of us that it was all right. If making an exception helps us have an exceptional game, anything is all right.

As the well-timed cheat helps restore the game to the players, the bent rule helps return the players to the game.

For example, suppose you're playing solitaire. Now you've gone through a modicum of effort to lay out the cards in their proper and officially authorized array. You have reached the point of play at which, though the game has been going for quite a while, you find you are about to lose. You almost won, but not quite.

Everyone knows that cheating at solitaire is an example of poor character. Even though there's no one around to call you on your cheating. Even though the only one you could possibly be cheating is yourself.

At this point in the game, either because of your highly evolved ability to rationalize, or because of your desire to see the game through, you decide to bend a rule. But, in order to maintain your sense of respectability, you decide to allow yourself only one small bend in one small rule. And then, if you still lose, you'll admit failure and pick up the cards and start all over again.

Now you're not doing a particularly admirable thing. You've admitted to yourself that, even if you win, you'll have won only because you cheated. Well, not cheated, exactly, but bent a rule. So in fact what you've done is to change the game. You're honest enough to admit to yourself that actually, in terms of the unchanging game, you have in fact lost. But, well, look at it this way: Now that you've lost, you can make up a new goal—how about seeing how long it takes to win? Maybe you'll have to bend a couple of rules. Maybe you'll even have to spindle, fold, and otherwise mutilate them, but, well, what does it matter now that you've lost?

So, you merely take the top card off the pile and place it underneath. Oh, joy! Behold what new possibilities have emerged!

The borrowed rule

If bending or breaking a rule is a bit too disturbing for the gaming mind to handle, we can employ a device which conforms a bit more at least to the letter of the law. We can borrow a rule from another game and attach it to ours.

After all, it's a real rule. It just wasn't part of the game when we started playing. But there's precedent.

Let's go back to your game of solitaire. As you know, there are many kinds of solitaire. In one kind, the rule is that you turn over every third card. In another, you turn over each card.

So, if turning over the third card, when you're playing a game like Canfield, is not yielding positive results, well then you can turn over every card, as in the game of Las Vegas solitaire, and see if that works.

Then, in some solitaires, you build up, in others, you build down. In some you play red on black, in others you play without regard to suit or color.

Thus, whenever another form of solitaire seems more advantageous to you, you simply switch to that form—announcing to yourself, of course, that you have in fact failed, and you're just employing this particular modification for the fun of it.

Sacredness

Rules are made for the convenience of those who are playing. What is fair at one time or in one game may be inhibiting later on. It's not the game that's sacred, it's the people who are playing.

It might have been true that, because of the way we were playing volleyball together, the rotation rule was superfluous. Suppose none of us cared what positions we were playing. Suppose the fact was that nobody wanted to stay in any particular position at all, that we were able to play together well enough no matter what position anyone held. Then, it's to no one's advantage to keep the rotation rule. Then, you might as well let me play where I want to play. Then we can all let each other play where we want to play.

Breaking or bending or borrowing a rule is only bad when we attempt to conceal it from each other or when it is done to the detriment of another player. When that happens, it's cheating for real. It violates not the sacredness of a rule but the spirit of the play community. Whenever we want to change the game, it's safest to make an open admission that that is what we're trying to do. Cheating for real is something that we try to conceal from each other. Telling each other helps keep the game in play.

It's just like Manny Kant used to say: "If I want to find out whether what I'm doing is OK, all I have to do is imagine what it would be like if everybody knew about it and did it too."

Bigger changes

There are many rules and, in fact, quite a few conventions which can be changed without drastically changing the game.

For example, we could play volleyball with a somewhat larger or smaller ball. We could increase or decrease the number of players on a side. We could raise or lower the net. None of these changes would keep us from playing volleyball. Any of them could help us play a better game.

I am not advocating changing the game for the sake of novelty. I am not saying that it is better to change the game than to keep it the same. I am merely pointing out that there are times—more times than one would think—when it is remarkably useful to the community as a whole and to the players in particular to have the power to change some of the rules.

The efficacy of change is, once again, a question of timing. If the change comes out of a realization that the game, as we are playing it, is no longer appropriate—if it is unquestionably clear that we are either playing too much or gaming too much—the change will be accepted because the change is necessary.

If it is the right time, we can change anything.

We can make up any kind of rule that we want to. We could make the court three feet wide. We could play volleyball with balloons. We could give everybody a ball. We could play with two nets. With four nets. With a moving net. Without a net. We could play silently, in the dark, with a luminescent ball. We could play on the ice. There could be three teams. Four. One.

As long as we make sure that it is the right time and that everyone understands and agrees to the rules, we can do anything we want to and still be playing well. OK, we might not be playing *the* game. But there is no "*the* game" for a play community. Any game whatever, as long as we are playing it well, is *the* game.

Too much change

Then there is the time when we become so fascinated by our power to change the game that we tend to get carried away by it all. We become so intent on celebrating our newly regained authority that all we want to do is change rules. We never keep the same rule for longer than five minutes. We change everything: sides, scores, balls, language, clothes. You name it, we change it.

At the beginning it's cute. It feels good to have this power back. It feels good to know that we have permitted each other to use it. However, after a while it tends to get a little disorienting. We are so excited about finding out all the wonderful ways we can change a game that we suddenly, crashingly, become aware of the fact that we no longer have a game to play.

If we are in a good humor at that particular moment, then everything is wonderful and we are restored. Maybe we will all go for a swim or something. Maybe we are actually able to settle on a particular variation and play it without changing anything.

If, on the other hand, one or several or all of us are not in such a state of willing hilarity, we could wind up without a community. It could happen. It has happened. A few of us feel, each, individually, that everybody else knows what's happening and we don't. We could feel that things have gotten out of hand, that people are being too silly. We could feel that we are somehow being attacked by all this wonderfulness.

We want to play, but we can find nothing solid to play with. There is no game for us to play. So we lose contact. We lose our sense of control. With loss of control goes loss of safety. With loss of safety goes loss of the willingness to play. Without the willingness to play, there is no play community.

Restoring balance

When we come back to the realization that the point of changing the game is so that we can play it well together, we discover that this is a more delicate task than keeping a game going, which, in turn, is a more delicate task than finding one to start with. The balance grows ever finer.

> Analogy: Think of a game as a sensitive instrument—a microscope, maybe. We can put anything at all, as long as it's small enough, under that microscope. Under low power we can see broad terrains. This is fascinating. We want to see them in greater detail. But as we increase the power of our microscope, we discover that it becomes more difficult to find the proper focus.

> Another analogy: One knob turns the TV on. Another knob selects the channel. A third one is for fine tuning. If you don't know how to work the knobs, you're not going to get the picture you're looking for.

The change thing can go too far. Eventually, we wind up totally unwilling to change the game any more. And then we go about trying to figure out how we can change the people who are playing it.

We have not only gone too far, we have gone completely off.

If anything needs change, it is much more logical to change the game than it is to change the people who are playing.

It is logical because the game isn't for real. It's something made up. It's something made up for the sake of those who are playing.

It's not only more logical, it's even wiser. If we all agree to change the game, the worst that can happen is that we'll wind up with a lousy game. But if our purpose becomes to change each other . . . . Frankly, I'd rather not even think about it.

So let us say that our play community has proclaimed a new morality, and inscribed in gold on our flag is the motto IF YOU CAN'T PLAY IT CHANGE IT, and woven into our banner are the words IF IT HELPS, CHEAT.

Now we find ourselves with an amazing, almost overwhelming freedom. We can change anything. Yes, there are regulations, but we are the ones who make them. There is no other authority than ours. We are the officials.

If we weren't so sure of our commonality—if we had any doubt about the objective, which we all share, of finding a game we can play well together—we simply couldn't handle all this freedom. We would get lost in it. We would take things personally.

Changing the game is the most delicate of all the things we're doing together. When we play a proven game—a game that has been played before—we are presented with a system of rules that has a balance of its own. Even if we ourselves have never played that game before, if the game is, officially, a game that works, we begin playing it with the knowledge that it is fair. We know that there are reasons for the rules.

Suppose we're playing tic-tac-toe. Maybe this is the first time we've played it. We don't really have to ask why we should be trying to get three instead of two or four in a row. We could try it that way, but ordinarily we wouldn't. We play the game according to its rules because we believe that the rules have been all thought out—that if we tried playing for two or four in a row the game wouldn't play well, we wouldn't be able to play it well together.

It just so happens that we are right. Tic-tac-toe doesn't work if we try for two in a row. Well, yes, we did try it. Curiosity, you know. But the first player always won. That wasn't very much fun—especially for the second player. But even for the first player as well: Who wants to play a game that you win before you start? Call that fun? Call that a well-played game?

So it seems to us that the game has been all figured out already—that every rule is what it should be. It's true. The game is as it should be. But it might also be the case that we aren't playing it well. That, in fact, we should change something about the game.

What would happen if we changed one of the rules?

We would definitely disturb the balance of the game. We would probably have to change other rules to restore it.

So we're on very shaky ground. Once we begin to change a rule, the only framework that is keeping us together is our intention to play well. Suppose it happens that you, playful person that you are, completely assured that you've no other goal than playing well and joyously—suppose it happens that you begin to wonder about my motivations. Maybe all I really want to do is beat you. Maybe that's why I'm so interested in changing the rules. I mean, what makes you so sure that I'm that community-minded?

All of which is to say that we cannot even begin to explore ways of changing the game until we are certain that we share the intention to play well together. This certainty is not found in the rules of any game. It lies in the nature of the relationship we are able to build with each other—in the establishment and the continual reaffirmation of our intention of playing well. It is found and maintained through the conventions of the play community.

But we have already played together enough to know that the game isn't really so very important.

Let's go back to tic-tac-toe. We now know how it's supposed to be played. We've played it many times. We know that we can play it well. We also know that the game isn't very interesting anymore. We've figured it out. When we play, the first player either wins or ties.

But we're interested in playing some tic-tac-toe-like game. We have pencils and plenty of paper. Rather than try to invent a new game, we decide that it would be easiest to start with one we already know.

Let's look at some of the things that we can change.

First of all, we know that the grid looks like this:

We also know that we could change how it looks. We could make it bigger or smaller or any way we wanted to:

Granted, if we get too creative with the grid designs, we'll wind up with something beautiful to behold but impossible to play with. Further granted, whatever way we change the grid, we're going to have to change other rules to restore the balance of the game. So maybe first we should take a look at the rules and get some sense of the range available to us.

One rule we know about is that the game is supposed to end when somebody gets three in a row. We could easily change that. We could make it four in a row, or five, or a hundred. Then we'd get to use the bigger grid. But how big should we make it? We'll have to play with it for a while to find out.

Or, maybe we'd like something other than a row. A circle maybe. How about three touching each other? Or four? Or how about four opposite each other?

There's a lot to explore. Maybe too much already. Maybe we should stop and just play with what we've already discovered. Let's see what the changes do. Let's see which changes we like best.

Well, we can always do that later. This is fun. Let's see what else we can change.

The rule is that whoever gets three in a row first is the winner. We could change the part about being first. We could say that whoever gets three in a row second is the winner. Why not? Maybe it'd be more fun that way. Maybe we could play better that way.

Then there's the rule about the tie game. Who says the tie game means that nobody wins? Maybe we both should win. Would that work? Would it still be fun?

Actually, I remember reading in one of my books on games about a version of tic-tac-toe called "Old Nick." This is the way it is played: Whenever a game is tied, the points go to Old Nick, and the next player to win also wins all of Old Nick's points. Sounds good. Sounds like it would add a tension that tic-tac-toe is lacking. Or maybe we could see if, at the end of twenty games, say, Old Nick has more points than either of us, and, if he does, then we would have both lost to him. Interesting, maybe.

Any other rules?

Well, how about the rule that you use X and O? Maybe we could use I and U. Of course, that wouldn't change the game any. We can really use any symbols that we want to as long as we can tell them apart. We could use colors instead of symbols. It wouldn't make a difference, really.

Maybe we like the way the game looks more when we use colors than when we use letters. That's reason enough to try it. Except that what we want to do is change the game so that we can play it better. And changing the symbols isn't enough of a change. It's interesting, though, that we can change some of the rules and not change the game at all.

So let's look for rules to change that really make a difference, that will really help us find the right game.

How about the rule that says you're supposed to draw a line through your three letters to prove that you've got three in a row? It helps us make sure that a win is really a win. But the strategies would be the same whether or not we use that rule.

So, to make the game different, to change it significantly, we have to find a rule to change that will result in a change of strategies.

I've got one that might prove drastic enough: the rule that you take turns.

Suppose I got two turns and then you got two turns. Would that foster the development of new strategies?

Do you have to take your turn? Could you pass? Would you ever find it strategically useful to pass?

What would happen if there were already some letters on the grid before the game started? The rule is that we start with an empty board. It is the rule, really, even if it's one we ordinarily take for granted. But suppose, even before the game began, there was an X in one corner and an O in the corner diagonally opposite? That'd be a real change, maybe.

Then there's the rule that we only use one kind of letter each. I mean, if I use X, I can't use Z too. Or maybe I could.

Maybe we could both use Z whenever we wanted to. Then we'd each have two letters to choose from. Sounds interesting, no? Maybe the Z could be a neutral letter, one that neither of us could use except to block someone? Or how about using the Z as a temporary block and saying that we could use that space for one of our letters only after a complete turn has passed?

What would happen if we could use each other's letters? That'd mean that either of us could win with an X or an O as long as that move completed a three in a row.

Actually, I've already tried that variation and it really makes for an interesting game. I play it just like tic-tac-toe, keeping all the other rules the same except for the one about whose marks are whose. I call this game "hypocrite." By giving it a name, I help officialize it. No, it's not tic-tac-toe we're playing, it's a much more sophisticated game called hypocrite.

How about the rule that you can't move a letter once it's been put down? Well, it's obvious that if we use paper and pencil to play the game and we allow each other to move letters around, we're going to wind up with a paper full of holes.

After all, there are only so many times you can erase before you discover you're beginning to erase the table instead of what's left of the paper.

So who says that we have to play with paper and pencil? We could make a grid out of wood if we wanted to. We could make pieces. Then we could really get things moving.

And then we could make a larger grid. How about a star-shaped grid? And then we could change the idea of getting three in a row to getting all your pieces on a star point. And then we could change the name of the game to something really official sounding, like Chinese checkers.

OK, before we get much further into this, let's extrapolate. It seems that there are rules which guide how we can change rules. Some of these are merely pragmatic. Others are a bit closer to conventional.

General definition of a changed game:
A variation which requires the development of a new strategy.

General purpose for changing a game:
The one you're playing is no longer giving you enough of a challenge for you to feel you want to play it well. You can play it well, but you're losing interest. Your gaming mind is bored. You're not playing the way you want to be playing. Or, vice versa, you can't play it well, the challenge is too big, your playing mind is overwhelmed, the game is too hard. The general purpose for changing a game, therefore, is to restore equilibrium.

Specific recommendation for technique:
Change one rule at a time. Change the rule and see what happens to the rest of the game. See what other changes you have to make in order to restore the balance. If you try to change too many rules, and the game doesn't work, you won't be able to tell why.

Universal definition of the working game:
What you are experiencing wellness in.

Another specific recommendation:
There are more rules than you realize. Many of them belong to a larger convention rather than a specific game. All of them can be changed. Some are subtle and take a long time to find. Cheat and see if anybody notices. Cheat openly so everyone can see it. If you think it's a rule but you're not sure, see what happens when you break it.

To bear in mind:
The reason you're changing the game. You're not changing the game for the sake of changing it. You're changing it for the sake of finding a game that works.

Once this freedom is established, once we have established why we want to change a game and how we go about it, a remarkable thing happens to us: We become the authorities.

No matter what game we create, no matter how well we are able to play it, it is our game, and we can change it when we need to. We don't need permission or approval from anyone outside our community. We play our games as we see fit.

Which means that now we have at our disposal the means whereby we can always fit the game to the way we want to play.

This is an incredible freedom, a freedom that does more than any game can, a freedom with which we nurture the play community. The search for the well-played game is what holds the community together. But the freedom to change the game is what gives the community its power.

This is a freedom which only works well as long as we don't *have* to use it. We need to know that we can change the game when we need to. We also need to know when we need to change the game.

So, like everything else we've looked at in the pursuit of the well-played game, changing a game only works sometimes. It can work against us as well as for us. It can confuse as well as clarify, destroy as well as empower. Only if the intention to play well is clearly, undeniably established and shared, only as long as that holds true does the play community hold true.

Handicapping

Another thing that might stand between us and the well-played game is our refusal to acknowledge our differences.

The game that I play well may not be the same that you play well. Your experience of wellness might be different from mine. We can acknowledge and validate the well-played game as it is experienced by each of us. But when we wish to play well together, we must discover the game that works for all of us.

Even though I'm playing as hard as I can, I'm not playing well. Even though I'm as focused as I can be, you're playing with an ease and a sense of mastery that is unavailable to me at this time in this game. I don't know the game as well as you do. I am not as familiar with its subtleties. You find yourself playing well, but the game we are playing together is not a well-played game.

We can look for another game—one with which we're both equally familiar. We could change the game we're playing. We could find other people to play with.

But suppose this particular game is the one we both want to play. I am as fascinated by the potential I am discovering in myself for playing this game well as you are fascinated by the excellence that you are able to manifest through this game. Can we find a way to play it well together? Can we make it even somehow—the challenge, the sense of play, the opportunity to play well?

Of course we can. We've already done it. When we were playing Ping-Pong together and we discovered, eventually, that in order for us to play this game well together you had to play with the wrong hand. That was the first step.

You gave yourself a handicap. You changed your criterion for playing the game well so that we could find a way of playing it well together. You found a way to make the game as new to you as it was to me.

As we play any one game, and play it repeatedly, with different people, we become more and more familiar with how we are when we are playing well. As we become more familiar with how we are, we become clearer about the sense of wellness that we are able to experience and manifest in the game. We are able to extend that experience with the game until we have reached such a stage of mastery that, assuming we have found someone who has reached a similar mastery, we can play well consistently, from the beginning to the end of the game. We may not be as "good" as a professional, but we do, in fact, delight in the way we are able to play.

Suppose I can play checkers well. We play together and discover that I am able to play well more often than you are. We play a game together and I win. You have momentary flashes of insight. I have a steady light of understanding. I see combinations that you don't. Just when you're sure something is about to happen and you've prepared yourself fully for it, I surprise you with something else. When the game ends, I have four pieces on the board and you have none.

What would happen if, next time we played together, I started the game with four fewer pieces?

I'd be a little less familiar with the game than I was before. I am less certain of the strategies that will work best under these conditions. I know that I won't be able to use the same opening. The game is newer to me. I won't be able to play it well the way I was able to play it well before. But it is now more likely that we will be able to play it well together.

Handicapping is used in order to equalize familiarity—to restore the balance between the different players' skills and understanding of the game. It is another evolution of the concept of fairness, stemming from a deeper understanding of the nature of the play community and its intention of playing well together.

Before we assumed a handicap, we were already playing fairly. We abided by the same set of rules. Neither of us cheated. But now the kind of fairness we are seeking is one that will assure both of us access to a well-played game.

Once we begin our exploration of handicapping, the possibilities for making the game work are again endless. If you play that well, and I don't, maybe you'd like to try it blindfolded? Maybe you can give me three free moves during the game? Or more if I need them? Maybe I can take a move back?

The convention of "no takebacks" has been helpful to us before. It has helped each of us become more familiar with the nature of the game. We have to deliberate more, to be more cautious. We have to be sure, before we make a move, that it is the move we really want to make. We have to plan ahead enough to see the implications of a move.

We have known, in our past experience of the game, too much sloppiness. Suppose, after you make your move, I deliberate for a while. It has opened up several possibilities, and I have to see which one is best. I enjoy this experience of deliberation. Then, just before I make my move, you want to take yours back. Now I have to deliberate all over again. I don't enjoy deliberation that much! At first, I find this effort, though slightly unsatisfying, not too much of a distraction. After a while, however, I find that my ability to sense the game is suffering. I have to plan also for the next event in which you decide to take your move back. So I'm slowed down. My opportunity to play well is slowed down. And finally I say, "Look, from now on, once you take your finger off the piece, your turn is over, OK?" I say that to you calmly, openly. If I have to say it again, I will be significantly less calm.

Thus the convention of no takebacks becomes part of the way in which we perceive the game. It becomes a convention to which we always adhere. On the other hand, it might just happen that, because of the differences between us, that convention would stand in the way of our having the opportunity to play well together. Suppose that we could play better if we both had the opportunity to take moves back?

Yes, it's not like life. In life, it doesn't seem that one can take a move back very easily. But we're only playing. We aren't ready to make the game that lifelike. Later, maybe, when we're both more familiar with how we play well together, we can up the stakes to make the game more interesting.

Absolute mastery over a game usually results in loss of interest. When we become too familiar with a game, we tend to drop it; like tic-tac-toe, it becomes too predictable.

In handicapping one or some of us so that we can all play well together, we are not, in fact, negatively affecting anyone's experience of the well-played game. Even though you, master that you are, have accepted a handicap, you are still playing well. You might not be as familiar with the game as you were, but that is as it should be, because we're playing together, and the game, whatever form it takes, is a result of how we are able to combine. It has nothing to do with trying to find out which one of us plays better. The focus is on how we play well, together.

The purpose of a handicap is not to limit anyone's access to playing well but rather to restore the challenge to all players. When you accept a handicap, you aren't holding back anything—you're increasing your-challenge, and addressing yourself to the challenge we have set before us as a play community.

When I'm playing with my children, I am aware how important it is to them that they have as much chance to win as I do. We all want the game to be fair. We all want to play as hard as we can so that we can experience playing well together.

Sometimes I wind up playing the game blindfolded, with my hands behind my back, while standing on one leg. Other times, I simply start off with a few checkers more.

We have found that it violates our mutual sense of fair play if I let them win. They know that I am playing poorly for their sake. Even though they enjoy winning, they get upset when they understand that I have held back. Even though it was for their sake that I wasn't playing as well as I could. Even though my intentions were parentally pure. The fact is that by letting them win I deprived us all of the opportunity to play well together.

232

Better that I handicap myself than handicap our opportunity to share a well-played game.

The score

Still another thing that we can change so that we can keep our game going well is what we give each other points for.

I don't think it will come as a shock to you to discover that you can play any game with or without score. Sometimes, as we've already found out, the best way for us to play Ping-Pong is just to volley. We could, if we wanted to, keep track of how many times we hit the ball. That could be our score, if we wanted one.

Obviously we could play tennis the same way we played Ping-Pong.

Usually, however, what happens after we volley with someone is that one of us sooner or later says, "OK, let's play the game." Which means: This volleying around was all well and good, but it was only a warm-up. Sure, the goal is to play well together. Sure, we can volley forever. But neither of us was playing very well. We were losing our focus—not really playing hard at all. So let's make it interesting again. Let's play for score.

Keeping track of the score doesn't make tennis into tennis. We can be playing without score. But part of tennis as we've come to understand it is in trying to make the other player miss. It increases the challenge because it makes us each try to be everywhere. You want to be as attentive, as present as I do. By trying to make each other miss we provide each other an invitation to awareness. We are saying, "Look, you want to be fully present, you want to be in a state of complete responsiveness and control, so see if you can get this one." Because that challenge is what we are asking from each other, because it helps each of us to experience playing well, it is right and good that I reward you with a point because you gave me a shot I couldn't return.

On the other hand, there are times when that kind of challenge is not what we need from each other in order to reach the well-played game together. There are times when the score becomes too important and we lose our focus on the game. There are times when we are giving each other points for things that are hurting our game.

Yes, when we're just volleying we're really playing a different game. It might be confusing to call it tennis. But, if what we intended to do was volley, if we found that well-played game by just volleying, then that's what we should be giving each other points for— keeping it going—even if we don't call the game tennis.

There's a tendency, as we begin to make things official, to think that only one particular form of a game is the real game. The fact is, any game we're playing is a real game. That's the fact. After all, the only thing that makes a game real is that there are people playing it.

But because we want to keep things clear, let's call tennis tennis and let's call our game something else. We can call it "volleytennis," "untennis," "cooperative tennis," "Chinese tennis"—we could even call it "flurtch" or "gronker" or "smunk." You don't change a game by giving it a different name. You give a game a different name because you're playing it a different way.

It's really amazing how much a game changes, how different it becomes, when you change what you are scoring for.

Let's score each other for bravery. Whenever either of us clearly risks limb, if not life, in the attempt to return a shot, that player, whether or not she actually succeeds in returning the ball, gets a point.

Let's score each other for grace, flow, harmony, endurance, agility. Let's score ourselves.

It all comes down to this: What do we want to get points for?

And then we discover that we can get points for anything. Anything. And each time we choose to score for something else, we change the game.

So, how about this: Maybe, since this is my first time playing, maybe I should get twice as many points for making the shot. Who says that everybody should get the same number of points for making it? Not me. I didn't say it.

The drastic change

And then, of course, there is the possibility that, though we can change the game infinitely, though we can constantly and continuously find ways we can make the game work, what we need to be doing is something else all together. That what we need to do, in fact, is forget the whole thing.

36

COMPUTER GAME SEMIOTICS

David Myers

Source: *Play & Culture*, 4(4), 1991, 334–345.

Abstract

I discuss symbols within the computer game and now those symbols are transformed during play. I develop a method of critically analyzing computer game structures utilizing a modified version of the semiotic square of Greimas. This analysis has goals somewhat similar to those of Propp (as applied to the study of folktales) and Levi-Strauss (as applied to the study of myth); however, this analysis also addresses recursive and deconstructive elements within computer game play elements that tend to undermine the more definitive conclusions of structuralism.

During study of computer game play, I have become increasingly concerned with relationships among the works of Vladimir Propp (1928/1968), Claude Levi-Strauss (1976), and Jacques Derrida (1967/1976, 1967/1978). In simplest terms, these concerns focus on the fundamental issues of formalism, structuralism, and deconstructionism that distinguish these critical approaches from one another and simultaneously—almost paradoxically—draw them together within the field of mass communications.

If we are to believe the results of bibliometrics (Beniger, 1988, 1990; Paisley, 1984; Reeves, & Borgman, 1983: Rice, Borgman, & Reeves, 1988), mass communications as an academic discipline has proliferated over the last few decades despite the "lack of a theoretical core" (Beniger, 1990, p. 698). The most fundamental and defining issues of communications as a discipline have been revealed, according to these analyses, only recently through the roundabout "convergence of several disciplines on the subject matter of communications" (Beniger, 1990, p. 713). What are these disciplines? They are those that I have come (in a much different, more roundabout way) to believe are more important to the analysis of computer game texts—"French structuralism or poststructuralism, hermeneutics or phenomenology, deconstruction or even semiotics" (Beniger, 1988, p. 213).

If this is true, then I feel justified in abandoning the variable analysis of mainstream mass communications research in favor of the participant-observation methods of cultural anthropology (Myers, 1987a), the controversial empiricism of Q-methodology (Myers, 1990c), and similar jaunts of play. Although the study of computer games seems at first glance trivial, it is significant that the serious consideration of topics and issues labeled frivolous and peripheral within the field of mass communications has led to many of the same conclusions as analyses of that field from much broader perspectives.

Goals and limits

During previous investigations of computer-game player behaviors and preferences (Myers, 1984, 1990a), I have observed the importance of computer game text (form and structure) in affecting and qualifying the computer-game playing experience. There are obvious patterns in computer game design and play that appear, at times, equally attributable to characteristics of the computer medium and characteristics of the human mind. The computer game is composed of Boolean operators combined into logical and finite, yet extremely complex, sequences. High-level sequences of this sort tend to evoke dramatic relationships during play and, therefore, to appeal patterned after interpretative processes within the human mind.

Realizing this, it is tempting to try to identify, as others have done (McLaughlin, 1990), physical structures within the brain that correspond to the creative experience of reading texts and playing games. The equally tempting alternative is to try to reproduce the functional equivalent of human interpretive processes outside the brain through artificial intelligence routines and other such mechanical procedures (Gardner, 1987; Posner, 1989). Yet, although both neurobiological and cognitive science approaches are enlightening, this analysis does not refer to them. The argument here is restricted to the symbolic (as opposed to the physical) structures of computer game play.[1]

Mine is ultimately a strategy of describing play with text by describing textual "playings." This strategy is most effective where the infinitive is given precedence over the noun. Unfortunately, such a strategy is difficult to follow in a largely noun-based language. For instance, I do not want to deal with isolated elements of the computer game text but rather with their relationships. Even then, my true topic is more properly these elements' "relationshipping" or, somewhat less exactly, their *relating*.[2]

Methodology

The task of identifying common elements within computer games appears relatively straightforward, but, even after begging the important question of proper units of analysis, there are numerous pitfalls. Propp's *Morphology of the Folktale* (1928/1968) was one of the first to demonstrate the methods and values of detailed structural analysis. In 1960. Levi-Strauss published a structuralist critique of Propp's formalism, which was followed in 1966 by Propp's rejoinder. Derrida was later to undermine both approaches in *Of Grammatology* (1967/1976) and *Writing and Difference* (1967/1978). It is useful here to summarize briefly the relevant positions of these three theorists.

Propp reduced the Russian wondertale to a sequence of abstract events, resulting in a formulaic sequence. As expressed in *Morphology of the Folktale*:

> A tale may be termed any development proceeding from villainy (A) or a lack (a), through intermediary functions to a marriage (W*), or to other functions employed as a denouement. Terminal functions are at times a reward (F), a gain or in general the liquidation of misfortune (K), an escape from pursuit (Rs), etc. (Propp, 1928/1968, p. 92)

This analysis eventually led Propp to the conclusion that . . .
To the variable scheme

$$ABC^*DEFG \frac{HJIK \downarrow Pr - Rs^uL}{LMJNK \downarrow Pr - Rs} QExTI \mid W^*$$

are subject all tales of our material. (Propp, 1928/1968, p. 105)

Levi-Strauss regretted that this analysis "lacks . . . context" (1976, p. 131). which, from his point of view, deprived Propp's abstract forms of their most crucial and informing characteristics. In his critique of *Morphology*, Levi-Strauss carefully distinguished form from structure: "Form is defined by opposition to content, an entity in its own right, but structure has no distinct content: it is content itself, and the logical organization in which it is arrested is conceived as property of the real" (Levi-Strauss, 1976, p, 115).

According to Propp (1984, p. 68), the argument between him and Levi-Strauss was that between an "empiricist and a philosopher." Yet, while Propp took refuge in his data—the folktale text—he did not necessarily seek to isolate interpretation from interpreter. Indeed, although Propp steadfastly supported the validity of examining the elements of the folktale out of their social and political contexts, he was also later to admit "morphology is sterile if it is not bound directly or indirectly to data from ethnology" (Propp, 1984, p. 71)

At the basis of the differences between Propp and Levi Strauss—and between formalism and structuralism—is the more synthetic perspective of the latter. Many of Propp's analytical elements of the folktale were combined and collapsed in subsequent structural analyses. These later analyses conceived variations in form or content as transformations of some more fundamental core structure. For instance, one result of Levi-Strauss' ethnological approach was to replace the rigid chronological sequences of Propp's folktale formulas with the more atemporal structures of myth.

Instead of Propp's chronological scheme . . . another scheme should be adopted, which would present a structural model defined as the group of transformations of a small number of elements. This scheme would appear as a matrix with two or three dimensions or more:

w	-x	1/y	1-z	...
-w	1/x	1-y	Z	...
1/w	1-x	y	-z	...
1-w	x	-y	1/z	...

and where the system of operation would be closer to Boolean algebra. (Levi-Strauss, 1976, p. 137)

Thus, in the Levi-Strauss analysis, the number of textual elements (w, x, y) is less significant and defining than the constant pattern of their transformations (w,—w, 1/w, 1—w). In opposition to Propp, Levi-Strauss defined textual elements without regard to their position in time (or syntagmatic aspects) and solely in terms of their relationships with each other. As a result, the Levi-Strauss matrix—wherein the omission of any single element (or element relationship) might have a ripple effect over the entire structure—is much more tightly integrated than Propp's formulas and requires a more holistic perspective (both inside and outside the text) during interpretation.

Matrix analysis of this sort is intriguing[3] but also, as others have commented (Schliefer & Veile, 1987), puzzling because Levi-Strauss offers no subsequent empirical elaborations concerning the application of this matrix to textual studies. Yet, upon learning of this model only after I had spent considerable time observing and cataloging computer game structures, I was immediately attracted to it by the similarities between it and computer game structures. These similarities are both logical/mechanical (mutual dependencies on Boolean algebra) and conceptual/symbolic (mutual dependencies on relationships as defining structural characteristics).

Subsequently. Greimas streamlined Levi-Strauss' and Propp's analyses in a series of works beginning with *Structural Semantics* (1966/1983). This volume attempted to establish a "descriptive metalanguage" for the "sciences of signification" (Greimas, 1960/1983, p. 161) through the study of patterns of binary relations among elements of meaning (or "semes"). Greimas later expressed his results inside a semiotic square—"the visual representation of the logical articulation of any semantic category" (Greimas & Courtes, 1979/1982, p. 308). (See Figure 1.)

The semiotic square is a logical mapping out of structural possibilities: for any content which can be understood as itself analyzable into binary opposition (S vs. non-S), the square, repealed and superposed, will exhaust the logical structural relations between its minimal elements. (Schliefer, 1983, pp. xxxii–xxxiii)[4]

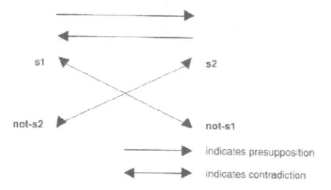

Figure 1 Greimas' (1987, p. 66) semiotic square: the elementary structure of signification.

Structural analysis of this sort, though appealing aesthetically, is frequently ambiguous in application and not entirely proof against deconstruction. One of Jacques Derrida's first widely publicized ventures into U.S. academia was at a 1966 lecture at Johns Hopkins University entitled "Structure, Sign, and Play." Both in that lecture and thereafter, Derrida (1967/1976, 1967/1978) attempted to undermine the structuralism of Levi-Strauss and others with reference to its logocentrism.

Logocentrism approaches are, in Derrida's terms, biased toward finding a center within a fundamentally noncentered text. Whereas structuralism, like formalism, ultimately seeks "a formula of algebraic power and simplicity" (Norris, 1982, p. 37), deconstructionism prefers to investigate those moments when a text "transgress[es] the laws it appears to set up for itself" (Selden, 1985, p. 87).

The conflict between deconstructionism and structuralism is similar to that between playing games and attempting to discuss that experience in a formulaic way. Though I have been overwhelmed by evidence of recurring patterns in computer game play and text (Myers, 1984, 1987a, 1990b), I have been often frustrated in my attempt to fully explicate those patterns within the context of the ephemeral relationship between player and plaything. In fact, it begins to seem as though that relationship—playing—requires a special sort of explication, one that somehow finds its most important meanings in its most inexplicable aspects (cf. the two interpretations of interpretation in Derrida. 1967/1978, p. 292ff).

In order to demonstrate further this conflict—and perhaps this frustration as well—1 would like to apply the Greimas logico-semantic (semiotic square) model to three representative computer games. It is this particular structural model, with the important addition of recursive relationships, that I have found most promising in explicating the symbolic structuring and restructuring of objects and events during computer game play.

Analysis

Chosen for analysis are three games that received the Overall Computer Game of the Year award during 1988, 1989, and 1990 from the popular publication *Computer Gaming World* (see Myers, 1990b, for a brief description of *CGW*). These games are best-sellers within the computer game marketplace, are innovative and complex in their designs, and represent the efforts of three entirely different designers or design teams (both British and American).

The games

Simcity, designed by Will Wright, was unable to find a willing publisher until almost 3 years after its completion. Ostensibly, the game puts the player in the role of city architect and manager. Successful game play results in a well run, cost-efficient city. This game was named Overall Game of the Year by *CGW* in 1988.

Populous was created by Bulldog, a British software company, and was introduced to the U.S. marketplace in 1989. *Populous* players—cast in the role of divine being—alter the environment of their game world to suit the needs of their population. They then use that population and their environment-altering powers (earthquakes, floods) to conquer a rival population. *Populous* won the *CGW* Overall Game of the Year award in 1989.

Railroad Tycoon requires the player to build a railroad empire through corporate financing, surveying and laying of track, and operating and dispatching trains. The designer of *Railroad Tycoon*, Sid Meier, has had previous commercial successes with the well-known computer games *F-19 Stealth Fighter* and *Pirates*. *Railroad Tycoon* was named Overall Game of the Year by *CGW* in 1990.

Game sequences

All three of these games are classified as strategy games by *CGW*—"games that emphasize strategic planning and problem-solving" (see Myers, 1990b)—and share many structural similarities. Propp reduced hundreds of Russian folktales to a relatively simple linear sequence of events. Is that possible here? Yes, each game proceeds in a linear fashion, of sorts, though *Populous* is different from the other two games in this respect.

The linear progression in *Populous* is bounded (that is, there is a definite end to the game). The sequence of player actions in *Populous* is roughly this:

1   Power (manna) transforms the player's game world. (Power → Transformation)
2   Transformations increase the player's population. (Transformation → Population)
3   Population increases the player's power. (Population → Power)

Thus, this sequence

Power → Transformation → Population → Power

might proceed indefinitely. But, in order to play the game successfully, the player must enact this sequence well and quickly enough to accomplish a singular goal: to destroy an enemy population controlled by the computer. Once either enemy or friendly population is destroyed, the game recycles and presents the player with another, slightly altered game environment in which play begins anew—with the same set of boundaries and goals.

The sequence of events is similar, but without such rigid designer-determined boundaries and goals, in *Simcity* and *Railroad Tycoon*. There are enemies (rival railroad builders) in *Railroad Tycoon*, but the destruction of these enemies (by buying their stock or driving their railroads into bankruptcy) does not end the game. *Simcity* has no obvious computer rival for the game player to compete against, yet both it and *Railroad Tycoon* move through time in a manner similar to *Populous*, with the accumulation of power replaced by the accumulation of money.

In *Railroad Tycoon*, the player uses money to transform the game world (cut down forests, lay railroad track). These actions have secondary effects (growth of cities, creation of industries) and enable the game player to charge for the transportation of passengers and cargo. These charges turn into profits, which provide funds for further transformations of the game world. Thus, there is this sequence:

Money → Transformation → Passengers → Money

In *Simcity*, the player uses money to transform the game world (cut down forests, create residential areas). These actions have secondary effects (growth of population, increased traffic) and enable the game player to tax city residents. These taxes turn into revenues, which provide for further transformations. Thus, there is again this sequence:

Money → Transformation → Population → Money

In all three instances, there is an important difference between these computer game sequences and the generic sequence Propp used to explain Russian folktales. The computer game sequences are *recursive*. That is, where Propp's sequence is linear, the computer game sequences are circular. And this circle does not always end where it begins; therefore, the computer game sequence is best visualized as a spiral of mounting complexity.

Where does this spiral end? *Populous* designers force an ending to this recursive sequence by imposing a single goal for the accumulation of power: the destruction of a rival power. There is no similar imposition on the game play of *Railroad Tycoon* and *Simcity*. The game sequences in these two games

241

end only in game defeat (loss of money or bankruptcy). If the player is not defeated, game play simply does not end. Larger and larger railroad empires are established: greater and more far-flung cities are created, bound only by the physical characteristics (disk space and memory size) of the machines on which the games are played.

What is the goal of play in these endlessly spiraling sequences? Propp's formalism fails us in this regard. Transformations take place, recursively, on several different levels during computer game play. Arranging events chronologically does not clearly indicate the degree to which previous events are reflected and affected by subsequent events. In order to understand the playfulness of recursive sequences, it is necessary to examine computer game play dimensionally as well as sequentially. And that requires the examination of structure as well as sequence. Therefore, advancing our analysis requires moving beyond Propp's formalism and considering the structural critiques of Levi-Strauss and Greimas.

Game structures

Within each of Propp's event categories (such as A, the category for villainy) there are many paradigmatic variations (i.e., A_{1-19}). And the structural relationships of these variations to each other are ultimately more significant to computer game analysis than the sequential (or syntagmatic) relationships Propp established among his broader categories of events.

Within the three computer games, there are obvious structural similarities of this atemporal (or paradigmatic) sort. For instance, in *Railroad Tycoon* and *Populous*, game opponents are computer-driven analogs of the game player. Though *Simcity* has no such game-player analog installed as enemy, the same obstacles facing the *Populous* player (earthquakes, floods) intervene during the building of *Simcity's* simulated cities. Thus, in all three cases, there are imbedded elements of conflict. These elements of conflict normally have the same power/money as the game player at the beginning of the game and are intended to be equal to the game player in every respect but one: the individual application of strategy.[5]

Recognizing these similarities, we can begin to express the conflict between player and game structurally and see along what dimensions it takes place. If we designate those elements of the game opposing the game player's actions as game opponents, there then exists a contrary relationship (Greimas, 1987, p. 49) between game players and game opponents, forming one half of Greimas' semiotic square. The latter half we may derive from the former—and from the Levi-Strauss matrix analysis. (See Figure 2.)

Left-side entries in Figure 2 are logically contrary to their right-side counter-parts, and all diagonally opposed entries are logically contradictory (Greimas, 1987, p. 49). Greimas called this diagram "an appropriate model by which to account for the first articulations of meaning within a *semantic microuniverse*" (1987, p. 66).[6] Difficulties in articulating the semantic microuniverse of the computer game immediately ensue.

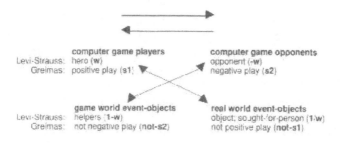

Figure 2 Greimas' semiotic square: adapted to explain computer game play

Contrariety is defined as "a relationship of reciprocal presupposition . . . where the presence of one [term] presupposes that of the other, and, conversely, where the absence of one presupposes that of the other" (Greimas & Courtes, 1979/1982, p. 61). We normally think of these relationships as between opposites, but opposites do not always exist in the clear-cut binary relationship that the semiotic square seemed to assume.[7] In *Railroad Tycoon*, for instance, there are *three* opponents to the game player, and each represents a slightly different sort of opposite to the game player—and to each other.

Contradiction is defined as "the cognitive act of negation" and also assumes a strictly binary relationship in which "the presence of one term presupposes the absence of the other, and vice versa" (Greimas & Courtes, 1979/1982, pp. 60–61). This relationship is very similar to that between figure and ground in which the ground provides the necessary contrast (background) for a figure to exist. Indeed, this particular interpretation of contradiction is supported by Greimas' indicating that contrary terms (s1 and s2) are subsets of their opposite, negated forms (not-s1 and not-s2).[8]

Negation, in this sense, establishes a particular context (figure and ground: s1 and not-s1); opposition creates an alternative context (s2 and not-s2). Relationships of opposition (contrariety: s1 and s2) are therefore of a more advanced level, necessarily leading to consideration of conversions (or equivalences) between different *contexts* (or, speaking geometrically, *dimensions*; or, speaking anthropologically, *cultures*) of meaning.

Basing the computer game, a "semantic microuniverse," on a process of moving from figure to ground and back again (context shifting) is particularly appealing because this process, like the chronological sequences observed earlier, is recursive. That is, context shifting is a process that constructs and deconstructs itself. Neither figure nor ground can be firmly fixed during play.

Thus, in *Railroad Tycoon*, the player is, at the beginning of the game, pitted against three computer-run opponents. However, at some point in the game, one or more of these opponents might be used as a helper (to block the invasion of a more formidable opponent) or as an extension of the player (by absorbing the opponent's railroad company into his or her own). Because of the interrelated characteristics of the semiotic square model, any such change in any one of the square's elements causes changes in all its other elements as well.

For instance, even when the player manages to seize control of *all* opponents in *Railroad Tycoon*—seemingly eliminating the game's source of conflict—the game does not end. By either transforming opponent to helper or by extending player structure into opponent structure, the contexts (game world and real world) are transformed and extended. And so the relationshipping, the playing, goes on.

Referring back to Figure 2, the game player who has seized control of all *Railroad Tycoon* opponents (s2)—a player who has previously been playing opposite individual game elements—now plays opposite the game as a whole. The original helper (not-s2) is transformed from game context to game *design* context, and so forth, in a spiral of increasing complexity wherein the original figures (s1 and s2) get increasingly closer to their ultimate grounds (not-s1 and not-s2).

Thus, we could create a more formal abstraction of Figure 2 (see Figure 3). At this point, as we begin to concentrate on the gradual movement (or transformation) of the self into the real world and the not-self into the play world that occurs during computer game play, we begin to lose touch with the atemporal permanence of structuralism and slide toward an increasingly deconstructionist interpretation of the play process.[9] For where is the center of the structure in Figure 3? The sought after object—the real-world ground that would encompass all possible figures– is in the lower right-hand quadrant: "objectiving." But this goal can never be achieved. It is a goal erected by the very process that negates its achievement: the process of "subjectiving," or playing.

> The concept of a centered structure is in fact the concept of a play based on a fundamental ground, a play constituted on the basis of a fundamental immobility and reassuring certitude, which itself is beyond the reach of play. (Derrida, 1967/1978, p. 279)

The spiral does not end because it cannot end not without destroying the playing. Play is, in fact, never a spiral, always a spiraling.

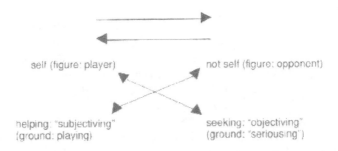

Figure 3 Greimas' semiotic square: adapted to explain play

Final comments

It is important to note that the three games examined here, whose sequences and structures are dominated by recursive context shifting, are very popular games. They are described in many reviews as particularly addictive games that completely absorb a player's interest. From personal experience and interviews with other players, I can say it is *very* common to play these games for 8 or more hours without pause, usually through the entire first night after purchase.

However, they are also real-time games; that is, things happen in these games regardless of whether the player is attentive to the game world or not. Only *Populous*, in fact, demands player action. Either *Railroad Tycoon* or *Simcity* may be allowed to run forward without player intervention. Railroads would extend, cities would grow, and players, we assume, would merely watch. But that never happens—at least not during those first sleepless nights.

The compelling structure of these games is as clearly real time (sequential) as dream time (nonsequential). It is difficult to say if either of these two aspects of game structure are dominant; they may not even be different. Certainly, however, it is the acting that is more defining than the action, the structuring that is more fundamental than the structure.

It can also be said that these computer games (and the compelling components of most others) are pervaded by structures of recursive context shifting. Indeed, play seems to function in this respect as a scaling mechanism, wherein microlevels of disbelief and its willing suspension somehow manage to bootstrap themselves into microlevels realities. It is this spiraling process that makes the computer game so addictive: replacing the physical context of reality with its symbolic representations ("objectiving") and then infinitely progressing those computer game symbols (including game player) toward an unachievable limit.

Notes

1 I would like to differentiate my approach from those that assign no particular intrinsic qualities of value or distinction to the text. The analogy here—based on logico-semantic models (Greimas, 1966/1983)—is that the computer game serves as a lens by and through which computer game play is focused and made manifest.
2 Difficulties of this sort seem to occur regularly in the analysis of play, which inevitably takes both high and low ground furthest from the point of attack. But then, this realization is a source of both frustration and energy because it seems to indicate that the essence of play is indeed somewhere round about.
3 Equally intriguing are parallels between the movement from structuralism to deconstructionism in literature and from S-matrix to quantum theory in physics: "Physicists have been seeking a unified field theory that . . . could integrate quantum physics and theories of astrophysics. The approach to language in structuralism and post-structuralism was likewise extended . . . to be a unified field theory . . . through a general theory to which the name semiotics has been attached" (Berman, 1988, p. 291). See also Bohm (1982).
4 Still another way of understanding the semiotic square is given in Schliefer (1983. p. xxxiii): "Nancy Armstrong has recently explained this scheme in this way: 'Once any unit of meaning (s1) is conceived, we automatically conceive of the absence of that

meaning (not-s1), as well as an opposing system of meaning (s2) that correspondingly implies its own absence (not-s2)."

5 Once again, for emphasis: These elements of conflict result from the paradigmatic transformation of game player to game opponent (and/or vice versa).

6 His use of the concept "semantic microuniverse" is intended to indicate the impact of culture and ethnolinguistic communities on the articulation and expression of meaning during syntagmatic discourse. Thus, though the semantic square seems to lie at the base of meaning-making, meaningful discourse (and its analysis) must also consider the cultural dimensions of discourse and what Greimas described as "privileged articulations, favor[ing] one microuniverse at the expense of another (wine culture in France, use of spring water in Turkey)" (Greimas, 1987, p. 66).

7 This questioning of the universal validity of binary relationships is indeed the basis of deconstructionist attacks against structuralism. "Any attempt to undo a particular concept is to become caught up in the terms which the concept depends on. For example, if we try to undo the centering concept of 'consciousness' by asserting the disruptive counterforce [opposite] of the 'unconscious,' we are in danger of introducing a new centre, because we cannot choose but enter the conceptual system (conscious/unconscious) we are trying to dislodge" (Selden, 1985. pp. 84–85). See also Berman, 1988, p 211ff; Derrida, 1967/1978, p. 283ff.

8 More specifically, Greimas used subset notation to explain the relationship between (the contraries (s1 and s2) and their subcontraries (not-s2 and not-s1) inside the semiotic square: "not-s1 ⊃ s2: not-s2 ⊃ s1" (1979, p. 308). However, his use of the term *figure* is quite different from my own (cf. Greimas & Courtes, 1979/1982. p. 120), which more nearly corresponds to the analysis in Seldon (1985, p. 106).

9 Though widely quoted recently, Derrida and deconstructionist approaches are not singular in their questioning of structures and structuralism. For other intriguing comments on the topic of recursive context shifting, see Koestler (1979) and his notion of holarchy.

References

Beniger, J.R. (1988). Information and communication: The new convergence. *Communication Research*, **15**, 198–218.

Beniger, J.R. (1990). Who are the most important theorists of communication? *Communication Research*, **17**, 698–715.

Berman, A. (1988). *From the new criticism to deconstructionism*. Chicago: University of Illinois Press.

Bohm, D. (1982). *Wholeness and the implicate order*. Boston: Routledge & Kegan Paul.

Brown, G.S. (1972). *Laws of form*. New York: Julian Press.

Derrida, J. (1976). *Of grammatology*. (G.C. Spivak, Trans.). Baltimore: Johns Hopkins University Press. (Original work published in 1967)

Derrida, J. (1978). *Writing and difference* (A. Bass, Trans.). Chicago: University of Chicago Press. (Original work published in 1967)

Gardner, H. (1987). *The mind's new science: A history of the cognitive revolution* (rev. ed.). New York: Basic Books.

Greimas, A.J (1983). *Structural semantics: An attempt at a method* (D. McDowell, R. Schleifer, & A. Veile, Trans.). Lincoln. NE: University of Nebraska Press. (Original work published in 1966)

Greimas, A.J. (1987). *On meaning selecting writings in semiotic theory* (P.J. Perron & F.H. Collins. Trans.). Minneapolis: University of Minnesota Press. (Original works published in 1970, 1973, (1983)

Greimas, A.J., & Courtes, J. (1982). *Semiotics and language: An analytical dictionary* (L. Crist, D. Patte, J. Lee. E. McMahon, II, G. Phillips, & M. Rengstorf, Trans.). Bloomington, IN: Indiana University Press. (Original work published in 1979)

Koestler, A. (1979). *Janus.* New York: Vintage Books.

Levi-Strauss, C (1976). *Structural anthropology.* Chicago: University of Chicago.

McLaughlin, C.D (1990). At play in the fields of the Lord: The role of metanoia in the development of consciousness. *Play & Culture*, **3**, 173–192.

Myers, D. (1984). The pattern of player-game relationships. *Simulation & Games.* **15**, 159–185.

Myers, D. (1987a). "Anonymity is part of the magic"; Individual manipulation of computer-mediated communication contexts. *Qualitative Sociology*, **10**, 251–266.

Myers, D. (1987b). A new environment for communication play: Online play, In G.A. Fine (Ed.), *Meaningful play, playful meaning* (pp. 231–245). Champaign. IL: Human Kinetics.

Myers, D. (1988). An argument for the study of play. *Issues in Integrative Studies*, **6**, 126–138.

Myers, D. (1990a). Chris Crawford and computer game aesthetics, *Journal of Popular Culture*, **24**(2), 17–28.

Myers. D. (1990b). Computer game genres. *Play & Culture*, **3**, 286–301.

Myers, D (1990c). A Q-study of computer game players. *Simulation & Gaming*, **21**, 375–296.

Norris, C. (1982). *Deconstruction: Theory and practice.* New York: Methuen.

Paisley, W (1984). Communication in the communication sciences. In B. Dervin & M.J. Voigt (Eds.), *Progress in communication sciences* (Vol. 5, pp. 1–43). Norwood, NJ: Ablex.

Posner, M.I. (Ed.) (1989). *Foundations of cognitive science.* Cambridge. MA: MIT Press.

Propp. V. (1968). *Morphology of the folktale* (rev. 2nd ed., L. Scott, Trans.). Austin, TX: University of Texas Press. (Original work published in 1928)

Propp. V. (1984), *Theory and history of the folklore* (rev. 2nd ed. A.Y. Martin & R.P. Martin. Trans.). Minneapolis: University of Minnesota Press.

Reeves, B, &. Borgman. C.L. (1983). A bibliometric evaluation of core journal in communication research. *Human Communication Research*, **10**, 119–136.

Rice, R. E, Borgman, C.L., & Reeves, B. (1988). Citation reworks of communication journals, 1977–1985: Cliques and positions, citations made and citations received. *Human Communication Research*, **15**, 256–283.

Seldon. R. (1985). *A reader's guide to contemporary literary theory.* Lexington, KY: University Press of Kentucky.

Schliefer, R. (1983). Introduction. In A.J. Greimas, *Structural semantics: An attempt at a method* (pp. xi–llvi). Lincoln. NF: University of Nebraska Press.

Schliefer. R., & Velie, A. (1987), Genre and structure: Toward an actantial typology of narrative genres and modes. *MLN*, **102**, 1122–1150.

37

COMPUTER GAME CRITICISM

A method for computer game analysis

Lars Konzack

Source: Frans Mäyrä (ed.), *Proceedings of Computer Games and Digital Cultures Conference* (Tampere: Tampere University Press, 2002), pp. 89–100.

Abstract

In this paper, we describe a method to analyse computer games. The analysis method is based on computer games in particular and not some kind of transfer from other field or studies—even though of course it is inspired from other kinds of analysis methods from varying fields of studies. The method is based on seven different layers of the computer game: hardware, program code, functionality, game play, meaning, referentiality, and socio-culture. Each of these layers may be analysed individually, but an entire analysis of any computer game must be analysed from every angle. Thereby we are analysing both technical, aesthetic and socio-cultural perspectives.

Introduction

Presented here is a method of analysis for computer game criticism. By focusing on different layers the aim is to analyse and thereby understand computer games better. The method of analysis is a bottom-up approach and like any method it has its flaws. As the main flaw one can see the losing of perspective by focusing only on fragments of the computer game. Thus, in order to minimise this flaw we should make a general description of the computer game in question before analysis. Thereby we shall be able to keep our perspective on the game as a whole, trying to be as thorough and objective as possible. This will turn out to be helpful in the later analysis. In order to show how the analysis method should be used, we analyse the computer game *Soul Calibur* by Hajime Nakatani (Namco, 1999) [1]. The method consists of seven layers: hardware, program code, functionality, gameplay, meaning, referentiality and socio-culture.

Describing the game

The description should be made from two different perspectives, because a computer game consists of two different levels: a) the virtual space, and b) the playground. These two levels may under special conditions combine, but normally they are kept apart. We find the same conditions in a game of chess. The board and the pieces represent the virtual space with its own intrinsic logic. The board, pieces and the two players situated in the surrounding space are all part of the playground. These two levels of course interact, but still they are in fact kept apart from one another. Like a puzzle picture we are only able to focus on one part at a time. If we focus on the virtual space we will be able to see the aesthetics and make-believe of the computer game, and if we focus on the playground we will be able to observe the culture around computer games. As already mentioned they of course influence each other since they are indeed both sides of the same coin.

Soul Calibur description

Soul Calibur is a 3D fighting game with lots of action and an adventure to tell.[1] The virtual space of *Soul Calibur* consists of characters combatting one another in arena fights using some kind of weapon. Each character has its own story and combat style, fighting in different arenas all over the world (except the Americas). The game is set for a fantasy adventure in the 16th century in which characters struggle against the evil sword Soul Edge. This setting is presented in a tale of sixteen chapters—one chapter for each character to be played. The tale being told is a sequel to the story in the game *Soul Blade*. The playground of the game consists of a television and a Dreamcast game console with two joypads. It is customary to play either alone against the characters in the game, or against one another using the joypad. A player needs a joypad in order to play, and one can interact with the game using the handle and buttons. On the screen each player

may see how well s/he is doing in the game. Players will be dealing with an arcade mode, time attack, survival mode and other combat modes including the mission battle mode in which the players travel the world. Here the player fights under special conditions against the computer, winning points to be used in the art gallery, the reward being lots of *Soul Calibur* artwork. The joypad control is as follows: A button is for a defensive guard stance; B button is for kick attack; while X and Y invoke horizontal and vertical attacks, respectively. These buttons and the handle may be combined into successive attacks, staggering attacks, throws, unblockable moves, soul charges, and lots of other techniques.

Layer 1: hardware

At this the lowest layer we find the hardware technology: wires, signals, hardware and components. This tells us about the physical nature of the playground and the computer as tool, medium, or toy. At this layer we have not even defined whether or not the computer is to be used as tool, medium, toy, or a combination of these possibilities. A computer may be used as both tool, medium, and toy since the computer is a very flexible electronic device. Of course if we use the computer using computer games, we are in fact dealing with the computer as a toy (or tool for fun) and as a medium. The computer in question may be very different depending on whether it is a mobile cell phone, home game console, or personal computer wired to the Internet or other network facilities. What can be done depend on the physical capabilities of the computer. This however does not tell much about what kind of games we have at hand.

Soul Calibur hardware

The hardware needed to play *Soul Calibur* is a Sega Dreamcast game console (1999) with two joypads, a CD-ROM with the game *Soul Calibur*, and of course the Dreamcast should be plugged to a television set. The Dreamcast console is able to handle more than 10 million polygons per second. I will not go further into the technical side of *Soul Calibur* and the Sega Dreamcast, since I am not an electronics expert. This aspect of the computer game should be analysed in its own right.

Layer 2: program code

Every computer game depends on code. Therefore program code is essential to the understanding of computer games. However this layer may be difficult to analyse since we may not have access to the source code and even if we had—we would not comprehend what is going on since we may not be able to translate the code into anything meaningful. These problems taken into account, the code still gives us a good clue to what the computer does. We are able to follow trails of action, and see what happens in different iterations. However, even without access to the code, we are still able to describe and analyse all the other layers of the computer game. Thus it is possible to indirectly understand the code according to other layers of the analysis—especially the functionality layer.

Soul Calibur program code

I must admit, I did not have access to the program code of *Soul Calibur*. This is partly because I did not know how to access the code, and partly because I would have very difficult time figuring out how the code worked. In a complete analysis of a computer game every layer of the computer game in question should be analysed, but it is still possible to make an analysis of a computer game without taking every layer into account. At least we recognize that we are not making a complete analysis of the game. Like for hardware program code may be analysed in its own right. Still much of the program code may be analysed indirectly from a functionality perspective.

Layer 3: functionality

The functionality depends on the code and the physical nature of the computer. Here we observe what the computer applications do. We are able to localise the computers' responses to user actions or integrated code signals. At this point of the analysis we focus on the behaviour of the computer and the computers interface reactions to user input. Espen J. Aarseth has defined a variety of the functionalities an application may have: dynamics, determinability, transiency, perspective, access, linking, and user function. Each of these functionalities has different variations, which have been thoroughly described by Espen J. Aarseth [2]. At this layer we are not even aware we are in fact dealing with a game—it might be any multimedia product or even other kinds of media program, here referred to as an application.

Dynamics: Text piece combinations are constant in a *static* application, while they may change in a *intratextonic dynamic* text. In a *textonic dynamic* application, text pieces may even change.

Determinability: An application is *determinate* if one text piece always follows another on command, if not, the application is *indeterminate*.

Transiency: If the mere passing causes text or actions to appear, the application is *transient*, otherwise it is *intransient*. A turn based game is *intransient*, while a real-time game is *transient*.

Perspective: The application is *personal*, if the user plays a strategic character, and *impersonal* if not.

Access: If all text pieces are readily available to the user at all time, the application has *random* access, if not the application access is *controlled*.

Linking: The application may have *explicit* hypertext links for the user to follow, or *conditional* links which may only be followed if certain conditions are met, or there may be no linking at all.

User function: Any application has an *interpretive* function, which we shall investigate further in the meaning layer. Additional functions may be *explorative*, in which the user chooses between different paths through the application. There may be a *configurative* user function, in which text piece combinations are in part chosen and created by the user. Finally, if text pieces and traversal functions may be permanently added, the user function is *textonic*.

Soul Calibur functionality

Soul Calibur has a textonic dynamics. During the game new characters will appear with new action sequences, giving new ways of playing the game. *Soul Calibur* is unpredictable to a certain degree. If the user pushes the same button or button-combination and if the character is same, it will produce the same result. At this point *Soul Calibur* is determinate and predictable. But when the user is up against a computer animated foe, foe's actions are unpredictable—even though the user acts in the same way. When the game has begun, *Soul Calibur* is intransient, meaning that time influences the game in such a way, that it alone changes what happens in the game. Since the user plays a strategic role as a character in *Soul Calibur*, the game has a personal perspective. Like most computer games the access is controlled. The user must carry out a task in order to get to a certain point in the game and this may only be done in a specific order when certain conditions are met (e.g. the user must win seven matches in order to type his or her tag). This makes linking conditional. The user functionality in *Soul Calibur* has a limited textonic feature, since the user is able to write tag at certain times. But mostly *Soul Calibur* has a configurative user function, where the player makes a choice, which influences the order of the game.

Layer 4: gameplay

At this layer we finally reach the game structure also known as gameplay. Here we recognise the computer software application as a game. Therefore we turn towards ludology; the study of games. Ludology acknowledges different game factors: positions, resources, space and time, goal (sub-goals), obstacles, knowledge, rewards or penalties [3]. These factors can be used to analyse any game not just computer games, but keep in mind that these distinctions are made to analyse games. In play (which of course is closely related to games) the goal, sub-goals and obstacles may be difficult to find. Any game or play is based on interaction between player(s) and the game itself.

Positions: These are the positions from which the game is perceived. They may be those of audience, players, or judges. The players are the most important, since they take active part in the game, but there might be other participants like team leaders, coaches or game masters. Positions will be further analysed in the socio-cultural layer.

Resources: These are the means by which the players are able to influence the game. This may be anything from a chess piece to a ball, or in the case of a computer game a computer controlled pixel images on the screen.

Space: The space is divided into the aforementioned space of the game, also known as *virtual space*, and the space of the real world from which the players influence the virtual space, which we shall refer to as the *playground*. As already mentioned, the two kinds of space may merge into one in some games.

Time: This is the time limit set for the game duration. Some games may have a definite time limit, others end when some sort of goal is reached, and again others just end when the players don't want to play anymore. In some games the main goal is to race against time.

Goal (sub-goals): The goal is what is needed to win the game. Sub-goals are what are needed to partially reach the main goal.

Obstacles: The challenge of the game comes from obstacles. These obstacles are set in order to prevent players from reaching their goal(s). Obstacles are, indeed, connected directly to the goal.

Knowledge: There exists different kinds of knowledge in a game: open knowledge (quite often the rules or statistics), hidden knowledge (e.g. strategy of other players), and random knowledge (e.g. rolling dice or other kinds of randomisation).

Rewards/penalties: Rewards or penalties can be anything from points, money, time, space or resources that may be won or lost during the game.

Soul Calibur gameplay

The player takes actively part in *Soul Calibur* by playing a character. There can be one player competing against computer controlled bot-characters, or two players can play against each other. The computer takes the position of the judge and the foe (in the case of bot-characters). The player controls the game with a joypad by which s/he controls a character in the game. The player chooses between different modes by moving the handle and pushing the A-button, and likewise s/he selects a character. When in some kind of combat mode, the player controls the character with the buttons and by moving the handle in different directions. The standard attacks are the same for each character, but they may be slower or faster in executing them, slower characters, however, tend to inflict more damage. Each character has lots of special attacks (e. g. Sophitia has a strike called *Heaven's Gate* which works when moving left twice, making a quick tap at the B-button, immediately followed by hitting the A-button).

The virtual spaces of *Soul Calibur* are different fighting arenas all over the world, while the playground is situated in front of a television screen. The arenas are always a limited space, and the player loses if s/he moves outside the arena. Most fights are played out with a time limit, depending on combat mode. Time is used as a measure of how good the player is, the quicker—the better. The goal is to win the game by knocking out the opponent, whether this is another player character or a computer controlled bot-character.

Sub-goals are to win, and thereby to get more characters to play with. The obstacles are of course the fighting opponent, but the limits of space and time are also important obstacles. In a mission battle mode there are lots of varied obstacles, from harsh time limits and difficult attacks to narrow ledge fights and poisonings of characters. Every game is fought one character against another, and when one party loses all its life or gets pushed off the arena, the other character wins. Remaining life is open to knowledge, and generally so are characters and weapons, too. In some mission battles, however, characters or weapons are hidden. The computer chooses strategy and bot-character at random. When fights are won, more and more information on characters becomes open knowledge. The player is rewarded with artwork, new characters and new outfits. The penalty for being wounded is loss of life. And when all life is lost, the player has to start all over again.

Layer 5: meaning

Here we find the semantic meaning of the computer game. This is best studied through the use of semiotics: the study of the meaning of signs. In some games we find lots of meaning, in others the meaning, if any is very abstract, and we may even find near meaningless games. Keep in mind though that there is no linkage between game quality (the significance of a game to particular gamers) and the semantic meaning of the game, since the game may indeed have it own intrinsic meaning, which cannot be measured from outside the game. But even though we may find narratives in games, they must primarily function as a game— otherwise it falls flat [4]. All the semantic meanings of the game are secondary to the gameplay's primary ludologic structure. The signs conveying meaning are indeed superficial, but still they help in putting the game into perspective. Two games may have exactly the same gameplay, but by having different ornamental signs and narratives (such as pictures, sounds and/or text) they convey different meanings of what is happening within the game.

Soul Calibur's meaning

The game makes sense, and does so by having a functioning gameplay and by creating meaning for the player. There are sixteen different characters—all of which have humanoid appearance. 'Taki' is a female ninja in a red ninja suit, using two knifes. 'Edge Master' on the other hand is an elderly man wearing a small chest armour and plus fours (knickers). He is able to use any weapon. The appearance of 'Lizard Man' corresponds to his name. This monster wears a cuirass (body armour), a short sword and a small shield. 'Mitsurugi' is a typical samurai with katana. 'Voldo' is an Italian pit fighter wearing a costume mainly made of leather straps, and he is using folding katars (scissor hands). This is just to name a few characters. Each of them has his or her own individual fighting style based on culture and personality. The designers have really worked hard on the choreography to create dramatic personalities. All of the characters play their own parts in the game's backstory. However, the player does not need to know these narratives in order to play the game, and the narratives have only superficial influence on the game. Therefore it is not fruitful to try to understand the game starting from these narratives. Still, they give some flavour to the experience. Likewise, the nineteen colourful 3D arenas of *Soul Calibur*, from Valentine Mansion in London to the Hokoji Temple in Kyoto have only a little impact on the gameplay, setting space limits for the arena fights, but they are visually impressive.

Layer 6: referentiality

Referentiality becomes apparent when comparing computer games with other games and other media. Here we target the characteristics of the game setting and genre. These characteristics are signs, ornaments or game structures that have originally been used in other media or other games, and which have been put into use in the game we are about to analyse. They give new meaning by transferring meaning from where it originally appeared (e.g. the game *Donkey Kong* refers to the movie *King Kong*). The setting is a sign system that helps us to relate to the virtual environment. These sign systems may have been taken from narrative genres or historical sources. We often find two types of genres present in computer games: 1) computer game genres, and 2) narrative genres. The computer game genres are genres like action/arcade, adventure, and strategy. The narrative genres may be based on literature, movies, or theatrical drama. However, it is not necessary for a narrative genre to be present. The computer game genres have lots in common with game genres in general. For example, Roger Caillois presents a ludological categorisation that introduces four game genres: agôn, alea, ilinx, and mimicry [5].

Agôn is a contest game, in which the player may win by being skilled; e.g., ball games, chess, or fencing.

Alea is a game of chance, in which the player wins by being lucky; e.g., dice play, lottery, or the roulette.

Ilinx is playing with vertigo; e.g., bungee jumping, parachuting, or the roller coaster.

Mimicry is role-playing; e.g., costume parties, playing doctor, and the theatre.

Agôn and alea are both mostly games, while ilinx and mimicry are mostly styles of play. Any of these game genres may be mixed and combined with each other. Most computer games depend on agôn, but often we find chance and role-playing elements in games, too. Ilinx is quite uncommon, but we find it to some degree in simulation games. Still this kind of vertigo does not normally appear directly in the game. Computer game genres like strategy, simulators, and arcade/action tend to be based primarily on contest of skill. But adventure games tend to be primarily based on role-playing—and narrative genres. While arcade/action, strategy and simulators use literary genres only as a setting, an adventure game profits from literary genres by using narrative structures. In classic adventure games the goal is to solve the puzzles in the story. The only chance the player has to do this is by knowing the genre and thereby knowing what to expect. This is how genres also work in general: they help us to understand the new by providing us with references to the old, and in that respect all genres are referential. Keep in mind that all genres may mix, but its easier to get a grip of what is going on if they are not mixed all together.

Soul Calibur referentiality

It is possible to play *Soul Calibur* with out knowing its references to others works. In this sense it is a work of art. However it does refer to other works. First of all it refers to *Soul Blade* (Namco, 1997), a fighting game with ten characters. Nine of these characters appear in *Soul Calibur,* too. *Soul Calibur* is an enhanced version of *Soul Blade* and a sequel to the chronicle of the blade Soul Edge. Second, it refers to the *Tekken* computer games from Namco. The Ninja Master Yoshimitsu appears as a rogue in *Soul Calibur*. But his first appearance was in *Tekken 1* (Namco, 1994) in which he fights for The King of the Iron Fist title. In the newest version *Tekken 4* Namco, 2001) Yoshimutsu is presented as follows: *As the leader of the Manji Party, Yoshimitsu dedicated himself to providing food, medical assistance, and shelter to the ever-increasing number of political refugees around the world. Unfortunately, with a constant lack of necessary funding and manpower, Yoshimitsu was unsure about the future of his organization.*[2] The difference between the *Soul Calibur* Yoshimitsu and the *Tekken 4* Yoshimitsu is that the *Tekken 4* Yoshimitsu has become a wraith. In *Soul Calibur* we are told an action-adventure tale that explains why: *However a spark from the demon sword struck Yoshimitsu's blade and it began to shed a strange aura. "Has my sword been possessed by evil? NEVER! IN MY NAME I WILL CONTROL THIS EVIL!"*[3]

In style both Tekken games, *Soul Blade*, and *Soul Calibur* is based on a combination of manga (japanese animation) and fantasy art (originating from the artist Frank Frazetta). But apart from this, we find that Tekken games *Soul Blade* and *Soul Calibur* follow the same line of computer games. They are of the same genre namely action/arcade fighting games, and what is more, there are fighting games going back to *Kung Fu Master* (Irem, 1984), *Double Dragon* (Technos— Mapefer, 1986), and *Mortal Kombat* (Acclaim, 1993) [6]. These games are all based on contests of skilled virtual fights and puppet master role-playing of dueling characters. It is no coincidence that we find many Japanese references in these games. In Japan we find a long tradition of philosophy and fighting techniques going hand-in-hand. Earlier we had the same tradition in Europe with knights representing honor and righteousness [7]. This of course opens up possibilities for further analysis of fighting styles, choreography and philosophies of martial arts and weapon mastery.

Layer 7: socio-culture

Finally we have the social layer in which we analyse the culture around computer games, thereby mostly observing the playground. We analyse the interaction not just between computer game and player but the interrelationship between all participants of the game. This means also addressing the relationship between the playground and the outside world. Focusing on the players, we observe the computer game target groups in terms of gender, age, and social status. These relations may again be analysed in comparison with the activities in the virtual world of the game. Lots of computer game studies have been done on socio-cultural matters from violence and marketing studies to gender and pedagogical studies. The problem is that they rarely actually research the games as cultural artefacts with aesthetic qualities. Still, the best of these studies may show how computer games are actually used in real life. To properly do so, it is important to understand the basic nature of game, play and culture. According to Johan Huizinga's theory, play and game are the origins of culture. Playing and games are culture in themselves, and culture will expand and prosper by freely exploring them [8].

Soul Calibur's socio-culture

To make an analysis on socio-cultural aspects of computer games demands a thorough focus on player's behaviours and the behaviour of other people involved. Another way is to present an analysis of socio-cultural behaviour based on personal experience. My personal experience with playing *Soul Calibur* is that it provides hours of entertainment among good friends. But more than that it is a game of power—more precisely, of symbolic power. Player's agony of losing to his or her friends and being taunted is indeed making the idea of symbolic power very concrete. But everyone knows this is only a game, so the player's failure only matters until his or her next victory and vice versa. What is even more important, the game can be played in lots of ways, and sometimes the player is up against the machine and all his or her friends are backing him or her up. In this way the game creates tension, but only to cope with tension—not to degrade, but to live through and experience the social structures associated with losing and winning.

Perspectives on computer game criticism

By using this method of analysis to study computer games, we may get a better understanding of how they work—and hopefully this may even help making better computer game designs. It is important to emphasise the ludic nature of computer games, because there have been many misguided computer game analyses based on narrative criticism. On the other hand there is computer game criticism, which has only focused on functionality thereby giving no clue to what is going on in general. Instead of pointing at narrativity as something that does not exist in computer games, or only focusing on functionality or ludology, we have tried to put these aspects into perspective by analysing them as different layers of the game. The reason for making a method of analysis or having computer games as the main subject of critical consideration, is that every aesthetic expression needs to be taken at its own premises, and not as be sub-categorised under another aesthetic discipline [9]. To comprehend computer games we must have an understanding of what game and play are, and to do so, we turn towards ludology. But more than that we turn towards a whole comprehension of the different layers from which computers game emanate. Each of these layers may be analysed individually, and we might only analyse one or a few of these layers. However, the other layers still exist and influence the true nature of the computer game.

Soul Calibur perspectives on criticism

In between the Dreamcast machine, the *Soul Calibur* program code, and the socio-cultural use of the game we have found different layers of aesthetic quality from functionality and gameplay to meaning and referentiality. We found a game of competition and puppet master style role-playing, a game of 16th century fantasy fighters in arenas all over the world. The game has an intrinsic gameplay based on martial arts and weapon mastery where players control the game through their actions. *Soul Calibur* functions as a game in itself, but also as a game pointing towards other games and the culture of martial philosophies.

Acknowledgments

I thank Espen J. Aarseth and Ian Dahl who have provided helpful comments on previous versions of this paper.

Notes

1 http://soulcalibur.com/
2 http://www.namcoarcade.com/tekken4/profile_yoshi.asp
3 http://www.soulcalibur.com/talessls/yose.html

References

1 Konzack, L. "Leg og lær med computerspil", in *Danskbogen: Danskfaget i de pædago-giske uddannelser.* (Petersen (ed.). Forlaget Klim, Aarhus, 2001), 25–48
2 Aarseth, E. J. *Cybertext: Perspectives on Ergodic Literature.* John Hopkins University Press, London, 1997.
3 Konzack, L. *Softwaregenrer,* Aarhus University Press, Aarhus, 1999.
4 Juul, J. "Games telling stories: a brief note on game and narratives", in *Game Studies 1,* (July 2001), http://www.gamestudies.org/0101/juul-gts/
5 Caillois, R. *Man, Play, and Games,* Free Press of Glencoe, New York, 1961.
6 Egenfeldt-Nielsen, S. & Smith, J. H. *Den digitale leg: om børn og computerspil,* Hans Reitzels Forlag, Copenhagen, 2000.
7 de Charny, G. *The Book of Chivalry,* University of Pennsylvania Press, Pennsylvania, 1996 (origin. 1352).
8 Huizinga, J. *Homo Ludens: A Study of the Play-Element in Culture,* Beacon Press, Boston, 1986.
9 Lewis, C. S. *An Experiment in Criticism,* Cambridge University Press, Cambridge, 1961.

38

PLAYING RESEARCH

Methodological approaches to game analysis

Espen Aarseth

Source: Digital Art and Culture conference, Melbourne, Australia, May 19–23, 2003, and also published in *Fine Art Forum*, 17(8), August 2003, and available at hypertext.rmit.edu.au/dac/papers/Aarseth.pdf.

Introduction

The study of game aesthetics is a very recent practice, spanning less than two decades. Unlike game studies in mathematics or the social sciences, which are much older, games became subject to humanistic study only after computer and video games became popular. This lack of persistent interest might seem odd, but only if we see traditional games and computer games as intrinsically similar, which they are not. We might try to explain this lack by noting that games are usually seen as trivial and low-brow by the aesthetic and theoretical elites who cultivate the analysis of artistic media objects: literature, the visual arts, theatre, music, etc. But this does not explain the fact that aesthetic studies of games are now possible, and even, in some academic environments, encouraged and supported with grants. What happened to cause this change?

A better explanation could be that these games, unlike traditional games or sports, consist of non-ephemeral, artistic content (stored words, sounds and images), which places the games much closer to the ideal object of the Humanities, the work of art. Thus, they become visible and textualizable for the aesthetic observer, in a way the previous phenomena were not.

However, this sudden visibility, probably also caused by the tremendous economic and cultural success of computer games, produces certain blind spots in the aesthetic observer, especially if he/she is trained in textual/visual analysis, as is usually the case. Instead of treating the new phenomena carefully, and as objects of a study for which no methodology yet exists, they are analyzed willy-nilly, with tools that happen to be at hand, such as film theory or narratology, from Aristotle onwards. The cautious search for a methodology, which we should have reason to expect of reflective practitioners in any new field, is suspiciously absent from most current aesthetic analyses of games.

This paper seeks to outline and promote a methodology for the aesthetic study of games, which, given the current nascent state of the field, will doubtless give way to more sophisticated approaches in the years to come.

It is a method rather than a theory, since the approach is empirical, and not limited to any particular theoretical result or model. It should also become clear that the method is not without problems, whose severity might be relative to the individual researcher and their resources.

Given the expressive richness of the genre, which is unprecedented in the history of media, the empirical approach chosen by the researcher becomes a critical issue. Any theoretical approach to game aesthetics implies a methodology of play, which, if not declared, becomes suspect.

Leveling the playing field

Given a newish empirical field, such as computer games, the obvious research question seems to be "How?" How do we investigate, and with what means? Although this question is crucial, and too often ignored by researchers, it is both too late and too early to ask it. Too late, because research using many different disciplines, from psychology to economics, is already well underway, and has been in some cases for decades; and too early, because there is another question that should be asked first, and never is. That question, of course, is "Why?"

Why do we want to make games and gameplay our object of study? Given a field which is interdisciplinary and empirically varied in the extreme, there are a great number of different reasons to do research, and a great number of types of research to pursue. A more or less complete list reads like the A-Z list of subjects from a major university. When faced with the rich and varied world of digital games, it is hard to think of a subject or discipline that *could not* in some way be used to study the field. The primary reason for this is that computer games are simulations, and simulations can, because of the principle of computer universality that Turing (1936) outlined, contain most other phenomena, such as machines or older media. This omni-potential for simulation means that computer games can portray, in principle, any phenomenon we would care to think about, and so, also in principle, no research area is excluded.

In the past, this has meant that games have been a relevant sub-theme in a large number of studies and approaches, and often used as a metaphor. All kinds of social interactions have been termed games, rightly or wrongly, and this superficial game-perspective has been applied to endless phenomena more or less pertinent to it. The concept or term "game" is always taken as a given, usually not worthy of separate investigation, or even of a cursory definition, but handy when we want to describe the *je-ne-sais-quoi* element of our primary, non-game object, whether it be a film, a novel, a play, a poem, a painting, a sculpture, a building, a relationship, or a piece of music. We often "play games" with the concept of game, but we don't take it seriously, since we are really talking about some other phenomenon.

So, what do we do when games become our most important cultural genre? Ideally, this situation should allow us to set up a scholarly field or discipline with the objective to study games. But in what way?

It seems clear that there cannot be *only one* field of computer game research. Already, approaches and studies from AI/computer science to sociology and education explode the field in almost a dozen directions. Like urban studies or epidemiology, a number of independent, different disciplines can be employed for a number of different reasons. The "Curriculum Framework" proposed by the International Game Developers' Association (IGDA) lists nine core topics that should be offered in game programs at universities:

- Game Criticism, Analysis & History,
- Games & Society,
- Game Systems & Game Design,
- Technical Skills, Programming & Algorithms,
- Visual Design,
- Audio Design,
- Interactive Storytelling, Writing & Scripting,
- Business of Gaming,
- People & Process Management

Each of these topics lists one or two pages of subtopics, with a total of over 200 subfields and disciplines. If we move out of the game developers' "practical" perspective, we might be able to add a hundred more.

With such variety, how can we even dream of creating a single field for the study of games? It should be obvious that the clinical psychologist with an interest in game-induced brain patterns has little or nothing in common with a 3D programmer seeking better algorithms for procedural shading. They certainly have no overlap in terms of methodologies.

Explicit discussions of methodology or of empirical selection (or, for that matter, reflections on the choice of theory) are very thin on the ground. A recent and notable exception to this, however, is Lars Konzack (2002) who sets out to construct a methodological framework for analyzing games. His attempt is probably the first, and the present paper is inspired by and indebted to his trailblazing. Konzack outlines

"seven different layers of the computer game: hardware, program code, functionality, game play, meaning, referentiality, and socio-culture. Each of these layers may be analysed individually, but an entire analysis of any computer game must be analysed from every angle. Thereby we are analysing both technical, aesthetic and sociocultural perspectives." (89)

Konzack then proceeds to analyze *Soul Calibur* (1999) according to his layers. His comprehensive approach seems very useful in at least three different respects:

261

Firstly, in the thorough analysis of a single, specific game, down to the last detail; secondly, as a general, descriptive, layered model of games; and finally, as a timely reminder of the many-sided, complex media machines that computer games are. However, while it is unfair to call his approach unpractical, its true strength lies probably in the theoretical model rather than as practical, step-by-step formula for game analysis. The strength of Konzack's model is also its weakness: the seven separated layers, which appear to be equally important. However, depending on one's perspective, it seems obvious that, say, gameplay is more important than hardware, and also, in most cases, than referentiality. Indeed, most games are not very interesting in all of these layers, and few present us with real innovations in more than one or two. An aesthetic analysis, just like a computer game, cannot afford to bore its audience, it must cut to the chase and zoom in on the elements that make the game interesting, whatever they are. Konzack's method is probably best used as an open framework, where the analyst can choose any 2–4 of the seven layers to work with, and ignore the rest. Furthermore, layers should not be seen in isolation, but probably analysed together for best effect.

A typology of game research

The elements we choose to examine are always predetermined by our motivation for the analysis. Why are we interested in this particular game? What is the point of our analysis? Given the large number of potential disciplinary perspectives discussed above, it seems that the list of motives and focal points could be equally large. For instance, it is unlikely that the same method would be fruitful in analysing both massively multiplayer games like *EverQuest* and puzzle/twitch games like *Tetris*. Also, the concept of "computer games" is quite weak, and notoriously hard to define in an interesting way. Do we include digitized versions of traditional board games? What about chess played by email? Programmed opponents for traditional games (artificial chess or checkers-players, say) dilute the concept even further. Could we identify a genre of "intrinsic computer games" that will help us exclude the games that are only trivially and "uninterestingly" digital, such as *Who wants to be a Millionaire* on CD-ROM? Perhaps it would be best to drop the term "computer game" altogether, and instead try to find a more suitable name for the phenomenon that interests us.

One such name would be "games in virtual environments."[1] This label fits games from *Tetris* via *Drug Wars* to *EverQuest*, while computerized toys like *Furby* and dice and card games like *Blackjack* are excluded. Non-computerized simulation games like *Monopoly* or *Dungeons and Dragons* would not be excluded, but perhaps that is a benefit rather than a problem. After all, the kinship between these and many computerized virtual-environment games is undeniable, so it makes good sense to actually include them.

Given this focus, what general elements do we find in "games in virtual environments"? I would like to point out three dimensions that characterize every game of this type:

262

- Gameplay (the players' actions, strategies and motives)
- Game-structure (the rules of the game, including the simulation rules)
- Game-world (fictional content, topology/level design, textures etc.)

Almost any game, from football to chess, can be described by this tripartite model. Since a game is a process rather than an object, there can be no game without players playing. Since these games are about controlling and exploring a spatial representation (see Aarseth 2000) the game must take place inside a clearly defined gameworld. And since all games have rules for advancing or losing, the game-structure of rules is perhaps the most fundamental of the three elements. Without rules to structure actions, but with a (virtual) world, we would have free play or other forms of interaction, but not *gameplay*.

These three levels could all be subdivided further, e.g. Gameplay: actions, strategies, social relations, players' knowledge, in-character communication, out-of-character communication, etc. They can be analysed separately, or combined: how does the combination of a certain game-structure and a certain game-world (arena) affect the gameplay? (E.g. how does changing the gravity from 1 to 3 affect the game?)

These interdependent levels have different weight in different games. In some games, typically multiuser roleplaying games, the first level dominates. In strategy and reaction-based games, such as *Command & Conquer* and *Tetris* or *Quake*, the rules dominate the game. And in world-exploration games, such as *Half-Life* or *Myst*, the Game-world is the dominant element. However, since all games are dominated by their rules, perhaps it is more accurate to say that in social games and world games, the rules dominate the experience *less* absolutely.

Perhaps more importantly in this context, by focusing on each of the three levels, we could identify three different types of games research perspectives:

- Gameplay: sociological, ethnological, psychological etc.
- Game-rules: Game Design, business, law, computer science/AI
- Game-world: Art, aesthetics, history, cultural/media studies, economics

In addition, combinations of the above could define more narrowly defined research areas, such as avatar-rights (rules&world), player-strategy or hacking (play&rules) or roleplaying (play&world).

My hypothesis is that there is a strong correlation between the dominant level of a game and the attraction it has as analytical object for certain disciplines and approaches. This is of course not surprising, but is should be acknowledged and perhaps guarded against when the purpose of the analysis is to produce general observations about games and playing.

But where is the method?

For any kind of game, there are three main ways of acquiring knowledge about it. Firstly, we can study the design, rules and mechanics of the game, insofar as these are available to us, e.g. by talking to the developers of the game. Secondly, we can observe others play, or read their reports and reviews, and hope that their knowledge is representative and their play competent. Thirdly, we can play the game ourselves. While all methods are valid, the third way is clearly the best, especially if combined or reinforced by the other two. If we have not experienced the game personally, we are liable to commit severe misunderstandings, even if we study the mechanics and try our best to guess at their workings. And unlike studies of films and literature, merely observing the action will not put us in the role of the audience. When others play, what takes place on the screen is only partly representative of what the player experiences. The other, perhaps more important part is the mental interpretation and exploration of the rules, which of course is invisible to the non-informed non-player. As non-players we don't know how to distinguish between functional and decorative sign elements in the game.

Once we have mastered the game ourselves, or other games in the same genre, non-involved observation and player interviews can be quite effective, and even provide insights that our own play could not produce. But informed game scholarship must involve play, just like scholars of film and literature experience the works first hand, as well as through secondary sources.

That said, how do we play? Is playing for analytical purposes different from playing for pleasure? That depends on our reason for the analysis. A journalist assigned a game to review for a mass audience will probably spend less time than a serious game scholar carefully dissecting a potential masterpiece. Another factor is of course the type of game. A multiplayer game requires the participation of others in our play, while a complex strategy game may require hundreds of hours in quiet contemplation.

As a player, we must assume one of a number of positions vis-à-vis the game. What type of player am I? Am I newbie, casual, hardcore? Do I know the genre? How much research should I do prior to playing? Do I take notes while playing? Keep a game-diary, perhaps? Or do I just go ahead and immerse myself, and worry about critical analysis later? Some games are fast, some are slow; should we approach them differently? Should we record ourselves while playing? How do we analyze a game we are not very good at?

As a non-player observer, the situation may seem easier, but is it? If I watch others play, how do I figure out their prior knowledge of the game? How do I choose my subjects? Every game involves a learning process, and this process is different for different players, depending on prior skills, motivation and context.

Styles of play

Richard Bartle (1996) offers perhaps the best analysis of players and playing we have seen so far. He presents a typology of four player types, and describes how the interactions between types influences the social atmosphere in the game. The four types are *socializers* (the players who play to enjoy the company of other players), *killers* (players who enjoy preying on and harassing other players), *achievers* (players who like to win and triumph) and *explorers* (players who enjoy discovering the game's secrets and hidden mechanics, including discovering and exploiting programming errors).

It seems Bartle has created a general model of human behaviour in virtual environments, and one which certainly could be used to classify game scholars as well. His typology is extracted from his active observations of the first MUDs, but his model works well with other types of games, and even beyond, with phenomena such as web portals. In almost any type of game, the drive to win, master and discover leads the players to socialize, trouble each other, impress, or find solutions that no one thought possible. A complex game, such as *Civilization*, *Deus Ex* or *GTA3* may be won in a matter of days or weeks, but due to the openness of the simulation and the collective ingenuity of players, the potential for new discoveries is endless.

After playing the multiplayer demo of *Return To Castle Wolfenstein* (the level called "beach invasion") for more than a year and a half, I am still occasionally amazed at what I see fellow players do. The game takes place on a Normandy beach, with one team defending a bunker as German soldiers, and the others playing as allies trying to invade it from the sea. At one point more than a year after the game was released, someone discovered that by exploiting the fact that players were invulnerable for the first seconds after they were revived by a medic, one could "fly" over the wall if one was revived next to a live grenade about to explode. Thus, by committing suicide, one could win the game in a novel way. This is clearly a Bartelian explorer at work, inventing a new strategy based on a weakness in the rule/simulation system. Far from an isolated case, the use of such exploits are typical in advanced gameplay. Some games, such as *GTA3*, even reward the player for certain innovative moves, such as spectacular car jumps (stunts). The dialectic between player inventiveness and game designers' need to balance realism and playability in the simulation can be regarded as a major source of creativity on both sides. Players find the discovery of exploitable bugs and loopholes in the games highly rewarding, while designers see the experiments of explorers as a challenge to their ability to predict the simulation's unwanted side effects. There is a fine line between a funny but harmless bug, and a game that is ruined by bug-exploiting players, especially in multiplayer games.

How should the game scholar approach exploitable games? Clearly, the explorers among us will enjoy this aspect, while the socialisers and killers (if there are any killers in our profession?) might ignore it. The achievers, on the other hand, will have a moral dilemma on their hands: should they play nice, or exploitatively?

This brings another style of play to our attention: the *cheater*. This lowly creature, for some reason not mentioned in Bartle's typology, can often be spotted far into the ranks of game scholars as well as among the average players. It is with great and increasing regret that one reads papers on game analysis where the author unashamedly admits that yes, I used a cheat code, or yes, I consulted a walk-through. In other fields this behaviour seems impossible, at least to admit openly. Imagine a professor of renaissance studies admitting to have used a Cliff or York Notes guide? While it is understandable that academics with not too much time on their hands find it difficult to spend the hundreds of hours necessary to master a game, and therefore give in to the temptation to zip through a game (typically a quest game) using the walkthrough, or (even worse) using the no-clipping or god-mode cheats, it is hard to imagine excellence of research arising from such practices. Where is the respect for the game? And, more importantly, how is the flavor of the game kept intact?

And yet, at times, most of us have done it.

Fear and loathing in Morrowind

After having played quest games for nearly twenty years, I am struck by the repetitiveness of the situation. Receive a task, find a solution, look for the next challenge. Or, in other words, explore, kill, explore some more, kill some more, etc. The two redeeming features of such games were improved graphics and, as a consequence, richer, better game worlds. From Crowther and Woods' original *Adventure* via *Myst* and *Duke Nukem* to *Half-Life, Serious Sam, No One Lives Forever, Max Payne* and beyond, the gameplay stays more or less the same, the rules likewise, but the game-world, as a corollary of Moore's Law, improves yearly (along with expanded development budgets). If not, the new games would never sell at all. Where is the new adventure game with retarded graphics that was successful? It does not exist. Take away the game-world, and what is left is literally the same game skeleton, give or take an algorithm. Bungie's quite successful first-person-shooter *Halo* was more or less a remake of their earlier hit *Marathon*, but with better graphics and an improved engine, of course. Science fiction futurism, medieval fantasy, or 20th century *noir*, the formula is the same: kill, explore, kill some more.

The linear structure of adventure games like these is unnoticed the first time you play one, and perhaps also the second or third game you play, but after a while the boredom hits, and even the most enjoyable game becomes un-re-playable. Another law than Moore's is probably at work here: the more linear, the less replayable. The corollary – the more nonlinear, the more replayable – also seems true.

One such nonlinear game is *Morrowind* (Bethesda Softworks, 2002), the third installment in *The Elder Scrolls* trilogy. *Morrowind* is set in a mysterious fantasy empire, with elves, orcs, various political and religious organizations, monster-infested waste lands, Imperial law enforcers, magical weapons, treasure dungeons, and more. *Morrowind* is a bildung-game in the tradition of *Rogue/Nethack, Ultima Underworld* and *Diablo*, where the player-character gathers strength and personal skills in a typical rags-to-riches scenario. Unlike these dungeon games, however, *Morrowind* is set in an open landscape, populated with small towns and occasional large cities, and plenty of underground crypts, caves and dungeons. The scale of the game-world is impressive, as is the variety of wildlife, people and vegetation, and even architectural styles.

The game starts with the player choosing/creating a character. This character is then let loose in the *Morrowind* world, freed from prison by the Emperor's order, and with some yet undefined task to perform in return. At first the world and your place in it is bewildering. The non-playing characters you meet are willing to talk to you, especially in the towns, where imperial guards keep order, but out in the open countryside monsters and villains will attack you on sight. Luckily, there are a few alternative means of transport, such as silt-riders (elephant-sized, strange-looking bugs) whose drivers will take you to the nearby towns for a few coins. Slowly you gather information and join guilds or factions to perform tasks that will make you rise in rank. As you perform these tasks and gather experience points you increase your skills. A quicker way to do this is to pay for private lessons from various eh.. personal trainers you meet here and there.

Little by little you learn to fight, to use magic and to navigate the world, and slowly the map of *Morrowind* expands to let you see more and more of the grand picture. The exact events as they happen, however, are completely unique from player to player. The first thing I did after having bought a suitable sword with my meager initial allowance, was to wander into a dungeon and get myself slaughtered by the despicable villain who lived there. Needless to say, much later when I happened by that region again, I sought a terrible revenge and afterwards looted his filthy abode, not finding anything of real value.

After my first unfortunate encounter, I learned my lesson and played much more carefully and cowardly, through numerous colorful adventures that space will not allow me to recount here. I learned that stealth and cunning get you much further than brawny behaviour. Money is very hard to come by at first, so I decided to leave my real-world morals behind, and steal whatever I could get away with. Most items in the game have owners, but you can still sell stolen goods to others. In particular, a dour book seller in Vivec, the largest city, became a favorite victim. I would visit his shop and stuff away a few dozen expensive volumes when he and the guard weren't looking. Then I would sell them to a merchant across the street. Eventually nearly half his three hundred books were gone, but since I was not actually caught in the act, the poor book seller never really noticed anything, regardless of his half-empty shelves. Later I discovered an even more profitable exploit, which wasn't even illegal. With all the selling, my merchant skill went through the roof. This meant that I could bargain well, and make much greater profits than a beginner would. So I would seek out the merchant with the most money, which happened to be an apothecary in the provincial town of Balmora, buy her most expensive item, a mortar, at a very reasonable price, and sell it back to her for a very nice profit. This I would repeat over and over, till she was out of money. I would then go upstairs and sleep in her bed for 24 hours (the time it takes for her money to regenerate) and start the process over.

With an unlimited supply of money, I could buy the training and weapons I wanted, and become a master fighter, the scourge of Morrowind. No monster too dangerous, no quest too hard. I could explore freely, and I could enter the most dangerous places I could find, such as the volcano at the center of the world. There, in a dungeon, lived a demon named Dagoth Ur, and this, finally, was an opponent worthy of my might and magic.

Until that moment, I had enjoyed a game with almost no linearity whatsoever. Any quest presented to me I could take or refuse, and little consequence would come of it. Sometimes a character would ask me to help him, and follow me around until I did, and I still remember with some shame a near-naked mercenary I promised to help find his gear, but had to abandon when he got stuck in a cave (the NPCs[2] have limited navigation skills, and get stuck easily). Occasionally I would do the wrong thing, as when I was on a mission to eliminate two Kwama mine robbers but killed two innocent miners instead (they were in the wrong place and fit the description . . .). But, all in all, these were happy times, exploring, fighting, and pearl-diving, in a vast landscape filled with countless wonders. I even learned to fly.

However, when I met Dagoth Ur, my world changed. Dagoth Ur was simply too powerful to kill, or, as he tauntingly pointed out, I did not have the right tools for the job. Hmm. Where to get those tools? I had a rough idea, but it would involve lots of tedious exploring, so curiosity got the better of me and I finally dropped out of the game and googled for a walkthrough.

That was a mistake. The walkthrough contained a wealth of information, about quests, characters and challenges I did not even know existed, and about a central quest that I had never heard of. So instead of simply finding the information I wanted, I was overloaded with information I had never asked for. This should have added depth to my impression of the game world, but it had the opposite, flattening effect: Instead of making me want to explore further, the walkthrough put me off playing the game! The magic was gone, and my personal investment in the world, after a week of playing, was totally devalued. I stopped playing. I still have fond memories of a great game, where my wish for an open, undirected game experience came true beautifully. However, the knowledge that there was a central quest, and that by following a recipe made by others I would be able to enact this quest, simply put me off further playing. I was no longer in love with the game.

The moral lesson here, for me at least, is that walkthroughs and other types of cheats can easily ruin the game. (They are not called "spoilers" for nothing.) But what about the methodology? My free, improvised play had not helped me to discover essential parts of the game. In failing to discover the main quest, I failed as a model player, in spite of my great enjoyment in the game. Perhaps there is a potential conflict between free enjoyment and game analysis, where cheats and walkthroughs that take away the game's challenges, must still be used to understand it. Of course, if I had had more patience and more time, then I might have discovered the main quest on my own.

The hermeneutic feed-back loops of play and non-play

How is determined by *why*. So what are the reasons for analysing games? And what, and how many, kinds of reasons are there? Game analysis is not just a critical/theoretical practice; gamers do it all the time. The primary objective/ meaning of most games, how to play well and win, demands an analytical approach. In order to progress through the learning stages of a game, the player must explore various strategies and experiment with different techniques. This kind of pragmatic analysis could be said to be present in the consumption of other genres also, but non-academic viewers or players do not regard their engagement with a new literary or cinematic work as a learning process, which every player of a new game must and does. While the interpretation of a literary or filmatic work will require certain analytical skills, the game requires analysis practiced as performance, with direct feedback from the system. This is a dynamic, real-time hermeneutics that lacks a corresponding structure in film or literature.

Reading a book or viewing a film does not provide direct feedback, in the sense that our performance is evaluated in real time. As Markku Eskelinen (2001) has pointed out, "in art we might have to configure in order to be able to interpret whereas in games we have to interpret in order to be able to configure." Our understanding of books or films, in the form of an essay or paper, might be evaluated externally by our peers or teachers. But to show that we understand a game, all we have to do is to play it well.

What will a typology of game analysis look like? There are at least to main types of analysis: playing and non-playing. Can these be subdivided further? It would be natural to assume that non-playing can only exist in one form, but this is not the case. Take, for instance, Eugene Provenzo's description (2001) of "U.A.C. Labs," the "mod" (modification) to *DoomII* made by one of the Columbine killers, Eric Harris. Provenzo claims that the characters in the modified game are unable to fight back, and that the *mod* clearly resembles the Columbine massacre. This remarkable claim is not confirmed by a walkthrough of Harris' mod, made by Ben Turner (1999). The Walkthrough shows commented screenshots from a typical Doom mod, consisting of two levels filled with the usual weapons and monsters, which Turner characterizes as "rather unimpressive". Judging by this walkthrough, it seems clear from Provenzo's description that he has not played, and probably not even seen the game he is describing. But then, neither have I. I also use a secondary source, but in this case, my source seems more trustworthy than the one used by Provenzo, who does not list any reference. Here we have two different kinds of non-playing analysis, one based on a walkthrough, and one most likely based on hearsay. While my use of a walkthrough puts me at a significant distance from the game itself, this is still better than Provenzo's position, which seems to allow for serious descriptive errors. I may not be sure that the walkthrough is the real thing, but nothing in Turner's report makes me suspect otherwise. Besides, I am quite familiar with the game that the mod is based on, having followed the *Doom* series from before the first release on the Internet in December 1993.

To generalize, we have several types of sources for our non-playing analysis:

- previous knowledge of genre
- previous knowledge of game-system
- other players' reports
- reviews
- walkthroughs
- discussions
- observing others play
- interviewing players
- game documentation
- playtesting reports
- interviews w/game developers

However, while some of these are better than others, it seems clear that it is in combination with hands-on playing experience that analysis has the best potential for success. But also, as the *Morrowind* example shows, non-play sources can significantly add to our play-based understanding. Like ergodic works in general, there are variations in the realization of the games which means that a collective pool of experience will always bring new aspects forward, as the Normandy Beach/*Wolfenstein* multiplayer example shows. Thus, it might be argued that for thorough game analysis, drawing on the experience generated by others is crucial, not merely useful. The hermeneutic circle of game analysis should include the game's player collective (the official company web site discussion board, fan web rings, and other user groups), and, if possible, direct observation of others playing, not merely reading of their reports and discussions. Since most aspects of play are non-verbal, observing player styles and techniques directly is invaluable, especially if we already know the game with some degree of intimacy.

Player strata in game analysis

When it comes to playing and player style, the playing analyst has a number of modes to choose from, depending on personal choice and game genre. Bartle's typology offer four distinct modes, with Cheating as a fifth. Combined with the experience axis of *newbie*, *casual* and *hardcore*, we get fifteen different player positions, although some, such as a "casual explorer," are less likely to occur than others. We could of course play the combinatorial game further and add game genre, theoretical foundation (Lacanian, player-response, feminist, semiotic etc.) and motivation (aesthetic, ethical, cultural etc.) and come up with a cornucopia of analytical combined modes and angles, but that will have to wait for future research. Instead, let us briefly examine the different strata of engagement that playing analysis allows.

First, we have superficial play, where the analyst plays around with the game for a few minutes, merely to make a quick classification and get a "feel" for the game, but without learning interface commands or structural features. Then there is light play, where the player/analyst learns enough to make meaningful progress in the game, but stops when progress is made. Then there is partial completion, when a sub goal or a series of sub goals has been reached. Total completion is of course only possible in games with defined endings, and not in games such as *Tetris* or *Space Invaders*. Repeated play and expert play are strata that usually come after total completion, unless the game genre is so familiar to the analyst that no substantial learning is necessary. The expert player is also, typically, a winner of multi-player games. The seventh stratum, innovative play, is seen when players invent totally new strategies and play the game not to win, but to achieve a goal by means that are not previously recognized as such by other players. The classic example of this is "rocket jumping" in *Quake*, where firing a rocket towards the floor while jumping will propel the player-avatar high in the air, but nearly every genre can provide examples. A famous example is the "peon rush" in *WarCraft II*, where a player wins by sending his builders to wipe out the opponent's builders, instead of progressing the normal way of first gathering resources, building barracks, training soldiers, etc.

Towards a methodology

How *do* we analyze games? It all depends on *who* we are, and *why* we do it. Scholars, gamers, critics and developers all have different needs and need for different methods. As scholars, we may also have different needs and motives, but it might still be possible to come up with common standards. Typically, we start out with a research question, such as "what is gameplay in adventure games?" or we might have encountered a new game which interests us in a puzzling way. If the empirical basis of our inquiry is not already given, we choose one or more games to give our question a target. Here we must be careful to choose games that not only will confirm our hypotheses, but also potentially refute them. Our choice should be well argued and thoroughly defensible.

Do we need theory? This might seem obvious, but as long as there are no really outstanding computer game theories (or, as it happens, hardly any at all), it would seem more important to present a well-argued analysis that commands previous scholarship and breaks new analytical ground. Importing and applying theories from outside fields such as literature or art history can be valuable, but not always and necessarily; and often non-theoretical, critical observations can contribute more to the field than a learned but theory-centered discussion. The question to ask here is, does the theory tell us something new about games, or is it discussed merely to be self-confirmed?

In gathering information about the game, we should use as many sources as possible. Playing is essential, but should be combined with other sources if at all possible. Games are performance-oriented, and our own performance might not be the best source, especially when we are analysing it ourselves. The analysis should also contain reflection on the sources used; where they come from, what could have been included, why did we select the ones we did, etc.

When concluding our analysis, we should match the results to the empirical basis. The cultural genre of games contains a rich variety of types and sub-genres, and too often generalizations are made on the basis of a few examples that are neither representative nor popular.

Naturally, methodological suggestions like the above has serious limitations. The game scholar may have a number of reasons for doing analysis, and most of them do not fit the prescriptive lens offered here. But critical self-awareness, in whatever form, should always be practiced.

Conclusion: playing for prestige?

For the playing analyst, the question of which position and stratum to attain is a question of skills, experience, ethics, motivation, and time. Although expert and innovative play are always hard and sometimes impossible to reach, they do imply that the (successful) analyst has understood the gameplay and the game rules better than others. A superficial cheater or a casual socialiser simply cannot be expected to reach a deep understanding of the games they examine. Then the question becomes, should we expect game scholars to excel in the games they analyze? This idea, while fairly militant, has some merit, especially if we look to other performing arts, where academic training is often combined with training for practical performance skills. As game scholars, we obviously have an obligation to understand gameplay, and this is best and sometimes only achieved through play. While our achievements as academics are measured by the quality of our publications rather than by our scores in *Tetris* and *Quake*, that quality is nonetheless also, at least for most of us, an indirect result of our playing skills. More crucial here than skills, however, is research ethics. If we comment on games or use games in our cultural and aesthetic analysis, we should play those games, to such an extent that the weight we put on our examples at least match the strata we reach in our play. Non-playing analysis, for whatever purpose, can only be strengthened by prior playing experience. But as my analytical misadventure in *Morrowind* showed, there must also be a balance between free play, analytical play, and non-play.

Acknowledgements

I wish to thank the anonymous DAC reviewers for their very valuable comments and criticisms.

Notes

1 For a longer discussion of "games in virtual environments," see Aarseth 2003.
2 Non-Playing Characters, computer-simulated persons in the game.

References

Aarseth, Espen (2000): "Allegories of Space: The Question of Spatiality in Computer Games" in Markku Eskelinen and Raine Koskimaa (eds.) *Cybertext Yearbook 2000*, University of Jyväskylä. (http://www.hf.uib.no/hi/espen/papers/space/)

Aarseth, Espen (2003): "Quest Games as Post-Narrative Discourse" in Marie-Laure Ryan (ed.) Narrative Across Media. University of Nebraska Press (in Press).

Bartle, Richard (1996): "HEARTS, CLUBS, DIAMONDS, SPADES: PLAYERS WHO SUIT MUDS." http://www.mud.co.uk/richard/hcds.htm

Eskelinen, Markku (2001): "The Gaming Situation" in Game Studies, Vol.1 Issue 1. http://www.gamestudies.org/0101/eskelinen/

Konzack, Lars (2002): "Computer Game Criticism: A Method for Computer Game Analysis", in CGDC Conference Proceedings, Frans Mayra (ed.), Tampere University Press 2002, pp 89–100. also available at http://imv.au.dk/~konzack/tampere2002.pdf

Provenzo, Eugene, Jr. (2001): "Children and Hyperreality The Loss of the Real in Contemporary Childhood and Adolescence" http://culturalpolicy.uchicago.edu/conf2001/papers/provenzo.html

Turing, Alan (1936): "On Computable Numbers, with an application to the Entscheidungsproblem," Proc. Lond. Math. Soc. (2) 42 pp 230–265 (1936–7); correction ibid. 43, pp 544–546 (1937). Also available at http://www.abelard.org/turpap2/tp2ie.asp.

Turner, Ben (1999): [untitled 'UAC Labs' walkthrough] http://www.worldlynx.net/bent/misc/uaclabs/

39

TOWARDS THE DEFINITION OF A FRAMEWORK AND GRAMMAR FOR GAME ANALYSIS AND DESIGN

Roberto Dillon

Source: *International Journal of Computer and Information Technology*, 3(2), March 2014, 188–193.

Abstract

The present paper defines an original approach to game analysis and design able to characterize a given game in a simple, yet efficient, way. Inspired by models widely used across the gaming industry, the proposed framework named A.G.E. is built by defining and layering different concepts: core player Actions, resulting Game-play and emotional Experience of players. These are all linked to each other by the game's own rules and goals to form a cohesive unit that can help in exposing the inner workings of any game. The model is then elaborated further into a regular grammar to provide a more formal and rigorous justification of the proposed framework and overall approach.

I. Introduction

Videogames, as a medium, have evolved considerably during their still young life: from basic monochrome squares on a CRT display to complex virtual worlds able to deliver highly spectacular and deeply emotional experiences.

As games become more and more pervasive in our modern society and are used not only to entertain but also to teach, convey complex messages and even as a medium for self-expression in the hands of talented indie developers, different analysis tools are needed for game designers to organize their ideas and creative processes. This is not only of paramount importance in a professional environment but even more so within the context of game development curricula where students need to be guided in the process of formalizing their ideas while also developing their analysis skills to understand different game genres for study purposes.

274

After a review of a few well known analysis models that served as a basis and inspiration for the proposed approach, an original framework will be presented and further elaborated into a regular grammar. By elaborating the same model under different forms that can be integrated together in the analysis process, we will be able to provide a comprehensive overview of the inner workings of a given game at different levels of abstraction to be used both in the classroom and in an actual working environment.

II. Related work

In this section, an overview of several different approaches related to game analysis, fun, and emotions experienced in games is presented as these build up the foundational knowledge upon which the present work is built. Most of the models here introduced have a strong background in psychology and focus on the study of subjective experiences inferred from the behaviour of participants so it is not surprising that different and complementary approaches have been proposed in the last few years to analyze games and explain why they are fun and engaging.

Lazzaro proposes a framework called "Four Fun Keys" [1] where the experience lived by the player is seen as different types of fun that are associated with a range of emotions. The first fun, called Hard Fun, is related to frustration and pride as the player can be proud when she overcomes a challenge and achieves its goal while she may feel frustrated by repeated failure. The second fun, named Easy Fun, is related to curiosity, with the player is willing to explore the possibilities offered by the game. The third fun is Serious Fun and is related to relaxation and excitement. Last we have the People Fun, which is related to the feeling of delight at being entertained and it is something best experienced in multiplayer games through interaction with other people.

In [2] Freeman proposed a vast collection of about 1500 rules and techniques grouped into 32 categories for evoking emotions in games. The whole collection was named Emotioneering™, which the author defined as "a vast body of techniques for evoking a breadth and depth of emotion in games, as well as for immersing a player in a role or in a game's world". Examples of techniques are "role induction" or "player chemistry towards NPC" to facilitate player's immersion into the virtual world.

Instead of proposing rules a-la Freeman, Jesse Schell's approach to game analysis and design involves a set of one hundred Lenses [3]. These "lenses" outline a set of questions, gathered from fields as diverse as psychology, architecture, music, visual design, film, software engineering, theme park design, mathematics, writing, puzzle design, and anthropology, that game designers should ask themselves to analyze their games and, ultimately, gain a better understanding of what makes games fun and interesting to play.

The MDA Framework (Mechanics, Dynamics, and Aesthetics) proposed in [4] is a well known approach among game designers that formalizes the consumption of games and their design counterparts by breaking them into three distinct components as shown in Figure 1.

As defined by its authors, "Mechanics describe the particular components of the game, at the level of data representation and algorithms. Dynamics describe the run-time behavior of the mechanics acting on player inputs and each others' outputs over time. Aesthetics describe the desirable emotional responses evoked in the player, when she interacts with the game system".

Aesthetics are clearly the most challenging part to analyze as they relate to the subjective experience of "fun" among players and, for this purpose, the MDA model proposes a specific taxonomy named "Eight Kinds of Fun". Specifically:

- Sensation: *Game as sense-pleasure*
- Fantasy: *Game as make-believe*
- Narrative : *Game as drama*
- Challenge: *Game as obstacle course*
- Fellowship: *Game as social framework*
- Discovery: *Game as uncharted territory*
- Expression: *Game as self-discovery*
- Submission: *Game as pastime*

So, for example, a game like "The Sims" [5] tends to elicit different types of fun including Fantasy, Narrative, Expression, Discovery, Challenge and Submission.

The 6–11 Framework [6] suggests that games can be so engaging at a subconscious level because they successfully rely on a subset of basic emotions and instincts which are common and deeply rooted in all of us. Specifically, the framework focuses on six emotions and eleven instincts shortlisted from those recurrent in psychology and analyzed in a number of well known treatises, like [7–9].

In particular, the six emotions are:

- Fear: one of the most common emotions in games nowadays. Thanks to the newest technologies, it is now possible to represent realistic environments and situations where fear can easily be triggered: think of all the recent survival horror games or dungeon explorations in RPG games for plenty of examples.

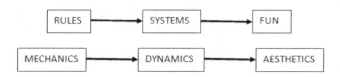

Figure 1 Consumption (top) and corresponding design structure of games (bottom) according to the MDA framework

276

- Anger: A powerful emotion that is often used as a motivational factor to play again or to advance in the story to correct any wrongs that some evil character did.
- Joy/Happiness: Arguably, one of the most relevant emotions for having a fun gaming experience. Usually this is a consequence of the player succeeding in some task and being rewarded by means of power ups, story advancements and so on.
- Pride: rewarding players and making them feel good for their achievements is an important motivational factor for pushing them to improve further and advance in the game to face even more difficult challenges.
- Sadness: Despite being an emotion that doesn't seem to match with the concept of "fun", game designers have always been attracted by it as a way to reach new artistic heights and touch more complex and mature themes.
- Excitement: most games worth playing should achieve this and it should happen naturally as a consequence of successfully triggering other emotions and/or instincts.

While the eleven core instincts taken into considerations are:

- Survival (Fight or Flight): the most fundamental and primordial of all instincts, triggered when we, like any other living being, are faced with a life threat. According to the situation, we will have to decide whether we should face the threat and fight for our life or try to avoid it by finding a possible way of escaping. This is widely used in many modern videogames, especially FPS and survival horror games.
- Self Identification: people tend to admire successful individuals or smart fictional characters and naturally start to imagine of being like their models.
- Collecting: a very strong instinct that motivates players to form patters of objects by completing sets with a common theme. It also relates to our hunting instinct and has been widely used in games since the early days of the medium.
- Greed: often we are prone to go beyond a simple "collection" and start amass much more than actually needed just for the sake of it. Whether we are talking about real valuable items or just multiple sets of goods and resources we need to build our virtual empire in a strategy game, a greedy instinct is likely to surface very early in many players' gaming habits.
- Protection/Care/Nurture: arguably the "best" instinct of all: the one that pushes every parent to love their children and every person to feel the impulse for caring and helping those in need.
- Aggressiveness: the other side of the coin, usually leading to violence when coupled with *greed* or *anger*. It is exploited in countless of games.
- Revenge: another powerful instinct that can act as a motivational force and is often used in games to advance the storyline or justify why we need to annihilate some alien or enemy.

- Competition: deeply linked with the social aspects of our psyche and one of most important instinct in relation to gaming, e.g. leaderboards. Without it, games would lose much of their appeal.
- Communication: the need for expressing ideas, thoughts, or just gossip, was one of the most influential for human evolution and it can be used to great effect in games too, while seeking information by talking to a non-playing character (NPC) or while sharing experiences with other players in chatrooms and forums.
- Exploration/Curiosity: all human discoveries, whether of a scientific or geographical nature, have been made thanks to these instincts that always pushed us towards the unknown.
- Color Appreciation: scenes and environments full of vibrant colors naturally attract us, whether it is an abstract or a photorealistic setting. Note, though, that this is not necessarily linked to technology prowess but it is more about the artistic use of colours to make graphics attractive regardless of the actual number of pixels.

Overall, the main idea behind the 6–11 Framework is that these emotions and instincts interact with each other to build a network or sequence that should, in general, end with "Joy" and/or "Excitement" to provide players with a meaningful and fun experience.

More formal and mathematical approaches to game analysis and design have also been proposed, for example in [10] where games are represented as abstract control systems in the form of a triple (F,S,M) where S is a set, M is a monoid and F is a (possibly partially defined) action of the monoid M on the set S, i.e., a map

$$F : S \times M \to S$$

In this model, M represents the input from the players, S represents the states of the different objects in the game and F all the possible ways player can manipulate and interact with those objects, in other words, the rules of the game.

III. The A.G.E. framework

Game design studies are still a very young field, often in between academia and the industry with academics and designers trying to analyze similar problems but from different perspectives and motivated by different needs. Unfortunately, this variety of approaches led to a complete lack of a common vocabulary and terminology, with commonly used terms like "mechanics", "rules", "dynamics" and "aesthetics" being interpreted and re-interpreted in slightly different, but significant, ways by different people.

For example, game designers like Brathwaite and Schreiber consider mechanics as synonyms of rules, spanning every phase of the game from the initial setup of game tokens onwards [11], while others, like Järvinen [12] or, more recently, Koster [13], tend to draw a clear distinction between the two. Similar disagreements can be found when trying to strictly differentiate between "mechanics" and "dynamics".

In the end, there is no common agreement on a definition for almost any term currently in use and different ones are being proposed and adopted in different contexts, as highlighted in [14].

Due to this very reason, instead of re-interpreting for the nth time the very same terms and risk further confusion, a new set of definitions will be used here to start anew and avoid any possible misunderstanding due to the lack of a common vocabulary.

Like the MDA model, the proposed approach breaks a game into three different layers of abstraction. Namely:

- **Actions**: the core, atomic actions that a player can perform in a game, usually described in terms of verbs. Examples are moving, jumping, kicking a ball, punching, shooting, taking cover etc.
- **Game-play**: the resulting play that players achieve by using and combining the available "actions". These can be either verbs or higher level concepts, for example: fighting, race-to-an-end, territorial acquisition etc.
- **Experience**: the emotional experience that engages players during the game. This will be described in terms of the 6–11 Framework.

As shown in Figure 2, each layer can be linked to the next by a set of "Rules", linking Actions to Game-play, and a set of "Goals", or challenges, linking Game-play to the Experience.

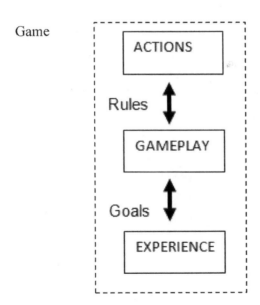

Figure 2 A schematic representation of the Actions, Gameplay, Experience (A.G.E.) model to describe a generic game

IV. Case studies

To understand how the A.G.E. theoretical framework can help us in practice to analyze and understand how successful games build up an engaging and enjoyable experience, we can apply it to a classic yet very simple arcade game named Frogger [15]. In Frogger the player controls a small frog that has to survive a set of different hazards across a trafficked road and river before finding a safe haven.

Our analysis starts from the Actions. To identify these, we should play the game and ask ourselves "what can we do in the game?". The answer here is very straightforward: the player can only move around the screen in four directions: left, right, forward and backward.

Once the Actions have been listed, the analysis can proceed to the Game-Play. Now we need to ask ourselves "What are the game rules allowing us to do? How do they allow us to interact with the game world?" or, in other words, "What are we actually doing in the game? What are we using the Actions for?"

In the case of Frogger, the game world is set to be a very hazardous environment with several dangers we need to avoid to reach the top of the screen. In game design terms, we can refer to these as originating a game-play about "avoidance" and "race-to-an-end". Indeed, reaching the end of the path is the game goal, which leads the analysis to the last stage: the Experience, where we have to make explicit how accomplishing the game goal make us feel.

Analyzing the Experience is clearly the most difficult part of the whole process since anything involving emotions can be very subjective. Anyway, by relying on the 6–11 Framework, it is possible to determine a most likely scenario. In this case, players would likely feel "excited" by the fast avoidance game-play, requiring high hand-eye coordination skills to avoid collision with the incoming vehicles and falling

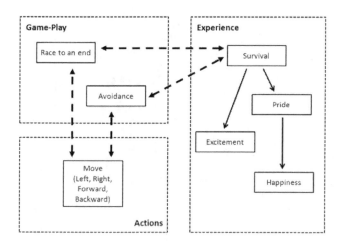

Figure 3 A.G.E. analysis for the classic arcade game Frogger (Konami, 1981)

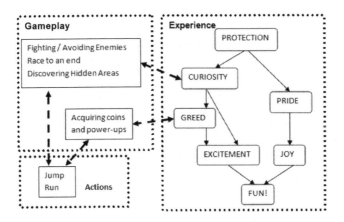

Figure 4 A.G.E. analysis for the original "Super Mario Bros" (Nintendo, 1985): Protecting Princess Peach is the first instinct to motivate the player. This, followed by Curiosity and Greed, can then effectively drive the platforming game-play to keep the exploration going

in the water. Players have to "survive" across the level. Once this is achieved, they would likely feel "proud" of having reached the end of the level safely and, henceforth, "happy" for their accomplishment. The analysis is exemplified in Figure 3.

As another example, in a platform game like "Super Mario Bros." [16], by repeating the previous analysis steps we can easily identify the core actions as "running" and "jumping" and realize how the rule "the player can kill enemies by landing on top of them" links the jumping or falling action to the "fighting enemies" game-play while the rule "player will progress to the next stage by reaching an end-level flagpole" links the core running and jumping actions to the race-to-an-end game-play.

Similarly, the ultimate goal of saving the princess serves as a motivation to link the fighting and race-to-an-end game-play to the emotional experience of players, namely "excitement" for the mission and "curiosity" for exploring new and secret areas while being the sole protector of the beautiful and elusive damsel in distress. Moreover, the analysis can also make us realize how, finding more and more coins while exploring the game worlds, can also trigger players' "greed" instinct, adding to the overall excitement for playing the game and, ultimately, lead to a fun and engaging experience.

A possible diagram for Super Mario Bros is shown in Figure 4.

V. Defining "games"

It is also worth noting that, through the proposed model, it is possible to outline a general definition of what a "game" actually is:

281

"a game is a system where one or more players perform different actions according to a set of predefined rules. These give a meaning, or purpose, to the former, leading to a gameplay aimed at reaching some goal or overcoming some challenge. In doing so, different instincts and emotions can potentially be evoked in the players, making them emotionally involved and engaged".

Where a 'system' is defined as a set of parts which are in relationship to each other to create a complex whole.

While many definitions of the word "game" exist, the one suggested above is in accordance to or, at least, does not contradict, many of the most popular ones like:

"A game is a system in which players engage in an artificial conflict, defined by rules, that results in a quantifiable outcome" [17]

Or

"A game is an activity among two or more independent decision-makers seeking to achieve their objectives in some limiting context" [18].

VI. Games described through a regular grammar

The A.G.E. model can also be formalized in terms of a simple regular grammar $G = \{N, \Sigma, P, S\}$, where N and Σ represent a set of non-terminal and terminal symbols respectively, P is a set of production rules and S is the start symbol. G would describe a language of gaming defined as follows:

$$L(G) = \left\{ a^n g^m e^q \mid n,m,q \geq 1 \right\} \tag{1}$$

where $N = \{A, G, E\}$ and $\Sigma = \{a, g, e\}$ with 'a', 'g' and 'e' being the individual actions, game-play and experience elements respectively. The starting symbol S and set of production rules P are defined as follows:

$$S \rightarrow aA \tag{2}$$
$$A \rightarrow aA \tag{3}$$
$$A \rightarrow gG \tag{4}$$
$$G \rightarrow gG \tag{5}$$
$$G \rightarrow eE \tag{6}$$
$$E \rightarrow eE \tag{7}$$
$$E \rightarrow \varepsilon \tag{8}$$

According to the actions, game-play and experience elements included in Figures 3 and 4, games like Frogger and Super Mario Bros would then be described respectively by strings like:

{move, avoidance, race to an end, survival, pride, happiness, excitement}
(9)

{run, jump, acquire coins and power-ups, fight/avoid enemies, discover hidden areas, race to an end, protection, curiosity, greed, pride, joy, excitement}
(10)

It is worth noting that, in this model, while the possible actions 'a' and game-play elements 'g' may possibly include hundreds of different items according to different game genres, the set of possible experiences 'e' can only include the 6 basic emotions and 11 instincts as originally identified by the 6–11 Framework. In the end, a game, to be properly formulated, should start with at least one action, followed by one or more game-play elements which are then used to elicit one or more specific emotions. All of which being related and linked to each other by the game's specific set of rules and goals.

VII. A.G.E. for game design and testing

By breaking a game into clearly separated levels of abstractions which can, nonetheless, be easily related to each other, it is not only easier to analyse games and understand how they manage to engage players but also to plan and conceptualize new ones. Game designers may start their creative processes by working on any specific level first and then expand on to the others. For example, we could start from a set of actions, like running and jumping, and then build some rules around them to draft the game-play, set challenges and goals and see if an emotional experience can actually develop into something coherent and engaging. Alternatively, other game designers may be more inclined to start by defining the type of game-play (eg. develop a platform game with plenty of hidden areas to explore) and then create goals, rules and actions accordingly or even start by drafting a desired experience first to motivate players and drive an interesting game-play, which will then be implemented by defining proper rules and actions. In the end, it is not really important in which specific conceptual level the game designer starts in but it is fundamental to be aware of the overall picture and know how to link the different layers by crafting appropriate rules and challenges to create a cohesive unit as shown previously in Figure 2.

Describing a game through the A.G.E. framework could also be beneficial during the testing phase: not only specific tests can be planned for verifying each action and see if they relate correctly to the game-play by abiding to the corresponding rules but, more interestingly, also valuable insights on the emotional experience can be gained. For example, testers could be asked to provide feedback on the emotional experience and point out specific emotions and instincts: would they emphasize the same ones as intended by the designers or something else? Indeed the 6–11 Framework has already been successfully used for game testing within the serious gaming field with encouraging results [19].

VIII. Conclusions

The proposed model allows for a schematic yet comprehensive view of a game and its inner workings in a rigorous and coherent approach that can be described both in an easily understandable graphical form and, more formally, as a regular grammar. Through the A.G.E. framework, games can effectively be referenced in terms of their core actions and game-play elements, leading to the arousal of a specific set of emotions and instincts that ultimately characterize their emotional appeal and engaging qualities.

Finally, the possibility of formalizing the analysis process into a grammar can also be useful for categorizing games in different ways, according to specific actions, game-play or emotions and see how these relate to different game genres. A classification and categorization of games following this approach is a possible area for further study and investigation.

References

1 N. Lazzaro, "Understand emotions," in "Beyond game design: nine steps toward creating better videogames," Chris Bateman, ed., Charles Rivers Media, 2009

2 D. Freeman, "Creating Emotions in Games: The Craft and Art of Emotioneering," New Riders Games, 2004

3 J. Schell, "The Art of Game Design: a book of lenses", Morgan Kaufmann, 2008

4 R. Hunicke, M. Leblanc and R. Zubek, "MDA: A Formal Approach to Game Design and Game Research", 19th National Conference of Artificial Intelligence, San Jose', CA., 2004

5 Maxis, The Sims, EA (PC), 2000

6 R. Dillon, "On the Way to Fun: an emotion-based approach to successful game design," AKPeters, Natick, MA, 2010

7 C.E. Izard, "Human Emotions," New York, Plenum Press, 1977

8 P. Ekman, "Basic Emotions," in T. Dalgleish and M. Power (Eds.) Handbook of Cognition and Emotion, John Wiley & Sons, Ltd., 1999

9 R. Plutchik, "A general psychoevolutionary theory of emotion," in "Emotion: Theory, research, and experience: Vol. 1. Theories of emotion", New York, Academic Press, 1980

10 S. M. Grünvogel, "Formal Models and Game Design", Game Studies, Vol.5(1), 2005

11 B Brathwaite and I. Schreiber, "Challenges for Game Designers," Boston, MA, Charles Rivers Media, 2008

12 A. Jarvinen, "Games without Frontiers: Theories and Methods for Game Studies and Design," Tampere, FIN, Tampere University Press, 2008 [13]

13 R. Koster, "Rules versus Mechanics," 2011. http://www.raphkoster.com/2011/12/13/rules-versus-mechanics/#more-3926

14 M. Sicart, "Defining Game Mechanics," Game Studies, Vol. 8(2), 2008

15 Konami, "Frogger", 1981

16 Nintendo, "Super Mario Bros", Nintendo (NES), 1985

17 K. Salen, E. Zimmerman, "Rules of Play: Game Design Fundamentals," MIT Press, p.80, 2003

18 C. Abt, "Serious Games," New York, Viking Press, p. 6, 1970

19 A. De Bakker, B. De Pacheco, C. D'Ipolitto, G. Xexeo, and J. De Souza, "Emotions in Business Game: Case Study in Desafio Sebrae," Proceedings SBGames 2011, Salvador, BA, Brasil, 2011

40

BOMBS, BARBARIANS, AND BACKSTORIES

Meaning-making within *Sid Meier's Civilization*

David Myers

Source: Matteo Bittanti (ed.), *Ludologica. Videogames d'Autore: Civilization and its Discontents. Virtual History. Real Fantasies* (Milan: Edizioni Unicopli, Costa and Nolan, 2005), original version available at http://www.loyno.edu/%7Edmyers/F99%20classes/Myers_BombsBarbarians_DRAFT.rft.

Introduction

I first found myself first writing about *Sid Meier s Civilization*—using it, along with Mark Baldwin's *Empire* (Interstel, 1987), as a prototypical example of computer strategy game's—shortly after the game's commercial release by Microprose just before Christmas, 1991 (Myers 1992).

In the succeeding decade, the game has seen two major revisions (*Civilization II*, Microprose, 1996; *Civilization III*, Infogrames, 2001), numerous supplements, mods, copy-cat designs, and, in the wake of widespread play and commercial success, a great variety of reviews, commentaries, and scholarly analyses—including those within the current volume. Over this period, my interest in the game—as a player and a critic—has seldom waned (though, admittedly, *Civilization III* tested that interest a bit). Most recently, in an extended study of computer games and play as semiosis (Myers *The Nature of Computer Games*), I devoted a chapter to the evolution of the *Civilization* game series, emphasizing components of *Civ* play that reflect recursive and transformative properties of cognitive play with computer games.

Now, in early 2004, *Sid Meier s Civilization* series remains one of the most interesting—and most fun—instances of a "builder," a computer strategy games in which player goals fall into the well-known (as coined by Alan Emrich[1]) "4X" categories: explore, expand, exploit, exterminate. But, perhaps even more intriguing is that *Civ* has become, in the brief history of computer gaming, a *mature* game—i. e., an illuminating example of how computer games are shaped and refined over time in response to the gathered experiences of their players. It is this maturity of *Civilization* play that I wish to emphasize in this essay: namely, the game's seemingly limitless *replayability* and the manner in which that replayability is critical to an understanding of cognitive play.

Saving, reloading, and replay

Replay is an integral component of the play process, and, as such, is not restricted to play with computer games. However, play with computer games displays informative manifestations of game replay—e. g., *save-and-reload* play.

All computer game players are familiar with save-and-reload strategies, which are applied within a great variety of games. In brief, saving-and-reloading involves initially playing some portion of a game (perhaps even its entirety), often less than satisfactorily; this portion of the game is then replayed, with some portion of that replay duplicative of the play preceding it. Common examples are found in first-person shooters in which the player-character dies in confrontation with a powerful opponent; the game player must then reload (or reboot) in order to face the same opponent again. This replay process gives computer game play a *spiral-like* (as opposed to a linear) trajectory (see Myers 1991).

Very similar replay occurs in action games, in role-playing games, and in computer strategy games such as *Civilization*. And, while there are subtle differences in the function of saving and reloading among computer game genres—at least partly justifying and verifying genre classification systems— the fundamental nature and basic characteristics of replay are common. Indeed, in many cases where the "saving" component of saving-and-reloading is either omitted or prohibited by game design, "reloading" and replay occur nevertheless. For instance, unlike home computer games, computer arcade games traditionally provide players no opportunity to save game positions and continue play at a later date. Yet arcade games derive their popularity—and their income—precisely from extensive replay.

Not only is replay common across computer game genres, but also across computer game histories—particularly within game histories as relatively long and detailed as that of *Civilization*. Replay in *Civilization* occurs both within the computer game proper (as I will describe hereafter) and also within the extended process of play which has resulted in *Civilization's* various versions, revisions, and alternate designs. Incorporating ubiquitous replay, the "spiral-like" trajectory of computer game play is more accurately *recursive*, wherein replay is both persistent, iterative and, most significantly, transformative.

The spiral-like history of *Civilization*

I have already detailed a history of *Civilization* design (Myers *The Nature of Computer Games*, 131–136); let me recount the pertinent aspects of that history here.

The first *Civilization* computer game—designed in tandem by Sid Meier and Bruce Shelley in 1991—originated as a redesign (or replay) of Frances Tresham's earlier board game (Hartland Trefoil, 1980). Ostensibly a simulation of the growth of ancient civilizations within the Mediterranean oval, the board game's most unique and compelling feature was its use of civilization "advances" which, at various points during game play, transformed that play. That is, these advances transformed the relative value of game units in such a way that game players were forced to revalue and redo their play (i.e., to replay). After a civilization advance had appeared, a pacifist player might be forced to adopt a more aggressive position; or an expansionist player might be forced to devote more time and attention to local city maintenance; or, more radically, a player with a previously unassailable position might realize that her newly transformed position was suddenly hopeless and be forced to start the game anew.

The Meier/Shelley design made much of these civilization "advances," turning them into the computer game's "World Wonders"—e. g., the Pyramids and the Sistine Chapel. World Wonders were such an important part of *Civilization* play that expert and winning play was determined almost solely by predicting and controlling when and under whose ownership the World Wonders appeared.

While other design elements and rules of the first *Civilization* computer game also involved contextual transformations—e. g., the tilling of virtual landscape by workers, and the celebratory benefits of an array of city improvements— the peculiar transformations wrought by the World Wonders were neither so localized nor so limited. Indeed, the World Wonder transformations were, in an important way, transformations of the game itself; as a result, it was practically impossible to learn the rules of the game until you had played—and replayed— those portions of the game in which those rules were transformed. For this reason, replay within *Civilization* was, over time, increasingly analytical and abstract, as the (re)player came to be guided by goals and strategies determined by *meta-rules* (e. g., rules for the transformation of rules) that, for novice players, were unavailable.

It is also interesting to note (see Myers *The Nature of Computer Games*, 132–134) that this repetitive, recursive aspect of *Civilization* game play was mirrored by (and perhaps even resulted from) the repetitive, recursive process of its design. During the design of the original *Civilization*, Shelley tended to be the game player, and Meier tended to be the game coder. Over the course of approximately a year prior to the release of *Sid Meier's Civilization*, Meier continuously varied the game code (transformed the rules governing game play), and Shelley continuously valued the game play (determined, according to meta-rules of play, which game rules should be further transformed in subsequent variations).

Through a similar but vastly extended process of play and replay, wherein the first release of the game was played, replayed, and valued within a growing community of players, *Civilization* spawned *Civilization II* and *III*. Both these games—most particularly *Civilization II*—were blatant redesigns of their predecessor(s). The redesigns attempted both to eliminate "bad" game elements and to expand and refine "good" game elements. What's most important is the degree to which "good" and "bad" were definitively determined only through the extended process of play and replay.

So we got our fun experts together and began the mammoth task of sorting through ideas . . . In the years since *Civilization* first appeared we have

> received literally thousands of letters, phone calls, and e-mail messages offering suggestion for improvements, additions, and sequels . . .
>
> Of course, the biggest potential pitfall in working on a game like this is that none of us wanted to go down in history as "they guys who broke *Civilization*"! . . . Every addition or change needed to be carefully weighted to make sure it wasn't doing more harm than good. (Reynolds, 179)

Game design elements common among (and thus proved by the test of replay within) all three games in the *Civilization* series included such crucial components as the transformation capabilities of the World Wonders, the basic goals of the 4X genre, and the game's (at least superficial) resemblance to the cultural history and characteristics of real-world civilizations. Game elements unique to the first *Civilization* (and thus at some point revised/removed during the redesign process) included the original game's visual appearance, its operating system, and the various rules which came to be associated with unsatisfactory—"broken"—play.

"Broken" rules in *Civilization* included—and, in fact, were characterized by—rules which allowed the game to be won by avoiding the transformations of replay. During broken play, the spiral-like progression of *Civilization* play—as envisioned by the game's designers and enjoyed by its players—was short-circuited. Commonly, this resulted from some imbalance within the rules which favored one portion of those rules (or rules-based strategies) over others; this imbalance drastically curtailed replay in that the game context then remained static—untransformed—from one game, or session of game play, to the next. That is, the game could be won—and won very quickly—in a manner that made the full range of World Wonder transformations largely irrelevant and, in some cases, entirely superfluous. If so, then over time and replay, the game became increasingly less fun.

> The Parallelia and Mongol strategies are game-beating strategies that exploit loopholes in versions 1.0 and 2.0 of *Civilization*. Both of them are fairly sure wins at any difficulty level, but they remove much of the enjoyment of playing *Civilization* . . . (Smedstad)

The challenge facing successive redesigns of any popular game such as *Civilization* is to add complexity and value without destroying the original games appeal. The redesign of *Civilization II* and *III* exemplifies the degree to which recursive replay was fundamental to the original *Civilization's* popularity. In all three games, learning the game rules remained a recursive process which, even once that process was well understood and widely practiced by the game's most dedicated players, preceded in a recursive fashion *without any certainty of a definitive outcome*.

> The spiral does not end because it cannot end—not without destroying the playing. Play is, in fact, never a spiral, always a spiraling. (Myers 1991, 343).

A theoretical interlude

Recursive replay, as observed within the behavior of computer game designers and players, is often referred to obliquely by game theorists and critics as either an inclusive process motivated by the peculiar characteristics of digital media (e. g., Bolter's and Grusin's *remediation*), or a more exclusive process narrowly focused on those stories, narratives, and other literary devices which are assumed to mediate computer game play (e. g., Aarseth's (1999) notion of a cyclical process alternating between *aporia* and *epiphany*). Here, however, recursive replay is more properly associated with basic human neurophysiology and universal cognitive practice, regardless of either the context in which that process operates (e. g., new media) or the objects upon which that process operates (e.g. "ergodic" texts). Assuming a natural-historical origin of play as a biological imperative, this process stands alone.[2]

Many analyses of computer games disagree. For instance, among technology-based theorists—including (with a broad brush) Lev Manovich and Friedrich Kittler—recursion and its manifestations as replay within computer games are shaped by and understood only with reference to some pre-existing social, cultural, and/or related technological context. Text-based theories—including those advanced by Aarseth (1997), Ryan, and much of the hypertext/IF group (e.g., Montfort)—most comfortably attach recursion and replay to a particular type of sign and symbol system, whether this system is as vague as language or as limited as narrative. Both these two theoretical positions—the tech-based and the text-based—seem to assume that the "meaning" of play and replay is largely predetermined by the unique constraints (or, sometimes, freedoms) that digital media and/or digital texts impose on computer game players and play.

In contrast, if recursive replay is indeed integral to play, and play is indeed integral to cognition, then computer game play need not be constrained (or explained) by external factors. The constraints of play—insofar as those constraints would be knowable through cognition—would be wholly determined by the boundaries of cognition. That is, play might well appear paradoxical (characterized by epistemic conflicts on the boundaries of the knowable); it might also appear instinctive (without any directly knowable cause). Play would, in such a scenario, appear to simply bootstrap itself into existence, either in ignorance or blatant disregard of game rules contrary to its most fundamental form.

Recursive replay within *Civilization*—and, in fact, replay within most computer games—displays many of these characteristics of paradox and self-determination. For instance, while computer games normally have clearly defined goals (the *Civilization* series has always had multiple winning conditions: military victory, cultural domination, winning the race to Alpha Centauri, etc.), the process necessary to achieve those goals involves transforming the game context in a manner that quite clearly moves those goals further away: the proverbial carrot on a stick. While players engage in such a paradoxical, recursive process instinctively during replay, often without full realization of its implications, game designers implement a cascading series of recursive goals more consciously and purposefully—most obviously as a series of difficulty levels which eventually recede beyond human capabilities.

> It was also clear that the forty bazillion or so hours of playing time which have occurred between 1991 and the present have served to vastly improve the world overall *Civ*-playing skills . . . Without making the game more difficult for beginners, we needed to crank up the challenge level significantly for all the jaded experts out there . . . Finally, we added the new Deity difficulty level for those who like their *Civ* really mean. (Reynolds, 181–182)

Certainly, over time, the *Civilization* redesigns have increased the number of player options—and related player challenges—far beyond the probability that any single player, during any single lifetime, will exhaustively complete them all. The appeal of such a multiplicity of game-related tasks (short of playing the game in its entirety) must then be found in the game's *perceived* completeability, regardless of how many goals or tasks are actually completed at the end of some interminable series of plays and replays. In such a context, the pleasures of play appear to result from two simultaneous and seemingly contradictory desires: first, the desire to conceive a clear end to play (e. g., in terms of designer-imposed goals); and second, a persistent unwillingness to reach that end. Only the first of these two might be significantly affected by game design; and, in fact, when confronted with designer-imposed goals which prove less than satisfactory—i. e., game goals too easily or too quickly achieved—recursive replay bootstraps itself: that is, players impose their own indeterminable goals—such as the herculean One-City Challenge (see van den Belt) in *Civilization II*.

The embedded "challenge" of a game is thus far less important than the player's perception of the challenging; and this perception is then less clearly motivated by any objective characteristic(s) of game design than by those phenomenological, self-determined process(es) embedded in an ongoing cognitive play. Successful game rules do not *construct* play; successful game rules *conform* to a pre-existing set of natural-historical rules governing cognitive play.

I pause to make this point clearly regarding play and replay within *Civilization* because implications and predictions are quite distinct among tech-based, text-based, and brain-based—as I have distinguished those three here—approaches to the study of computer game play. Most particularly, there are significant differences in the predictions these make concerning the *effects* of games and game play.

The *Civilization* series has the superficial trappings of a historical simulation. Indeed, some of the scenarios built into the game allow players to play on a realistically drawn (to some rough level of approximation) map of Earth; the names of the civilizations included in the game are the names of real-life nations and peoples; and the city improvements, unit types, and political systems referred to in the game are all represented at some basic, though often abstract, level of verisimilitude. In general, then, the signs and symbols of the *Civilization* series are similar to those signs and symbols found in more conventional accounts of human civilization and progress, e. g. history texts.

Further, many have found parallels between the "lessons" learned or the "stories" told during *Civilization* game play and various political ideologies and/or broad-based assumptions about the nature of Earth's peoples and their relationships. These lessons/stories have been, on different occasions, interpreted both positively (as opportunities for edification—e.g., Squire) and negatively (as advocating ideological perspectives peculiar to Western civilization—see the examples following). However, regardless of any normative issues involved, these lessons/stories are assumed to be embedded in the game design and, subsequently, within the play which that design motivates.

Based on how *Civilization* is actually played and replayed, I would like to use the remainder of this essay to debunk this notion.

Play and replay—with meaning this time

Cognitive play within the *Civilization* series is only marginally different from play within many other, similar computer games—most particularly those games within the 4X, builder genre. Cognitive play evokes a play and replay process which transforms signs and symbols just as often and just as radically as the World Wonders transform the game context within *Civilization*. This results in game signs and symbols having significantly different meanings than those meanings to which they are conventionally assigned outside the context of play.

Indiscriminate bombings

The initial release of *Civilization* generated a (sometimes quite heated) controversy concerning the game's implementation of nuclear power; let me give a brief background.

There are several victory conditions available within the *Civilization* games— some variable and chosen by the player before the game begins. Traditional and commonplace ways to win the game include (the typical war game fare of) destroying all your opponents and, a bit more imaginatively, winning a space race to Alpha Centauri. The space race victory condition can be chosen to guide play from the beginning of the game, or it can be selected as a fall-back position at any time a military victory proves unlikely. Computer-run civilizations, in fact, if sensing military defeat, devote their resources to the space race option— forcing the hand of opposing military commanders by changing the pace at which attacking forces must be mustered and deployed.

Such a sudden transformation of game context and goals—and related game rules—is a dedicated feature of the World Wonders, which, in the endgame, include the chief space-race determinant: The Apollo Project. Also included in

291

the *Civilization* endgame, for much the same reason—to move the game's goals a little further from the player's event horizon—is industrial pollution and, most particularly, pollution associated with nuclear power, plants, and bombs.

In the typical *Civilization* endgame, with over-large cities strewn across a modernist landscape, pollution and accompanying global warming become a major problem. In fact, the steadily increasing pollution rates—along with the late-game World Wonders—mark the final transformation of the game's early and mid-game goals to the endgame goals of either city destruction (the military version) or city exodus (the space race version).

Some have interpreted the implementation of nuclear power within the game and the resulting, inevitable decay of the *Civilization* landscape as carrying political connotations *beyond the context of the game*. The argument goes something like this:

> Players must . . . take care to preserve the environment. Too many large, polluting cities, for example, can lead to ecological disasters, ranging from the destruction of local environments to global warming. Pollution also affects the players' final score: players lose "civilization points" for every square of polluted terrain. Such features have led some to conclude that the game has an environmental message. Others have criticized the game for its cultural bias. Justin Hall, for example, remarks that the game reflects the "high technology late capitalist mindset of America." (Henthorne)

From the beginning, Sid Meier has consistently denied any intention of using the *Civilization* game designs as political statements, as indicated in this *CGOnline* interview:

> It's a gameplay factor. We very consciously avoid putting our political philosophy into the game. . . . Now, it did seem, and I think it turned out to be true, that building that element into Civilization, the pollution and things like that, gave you a new challenge as you got to the later parts of the game . . . So pollution became that kind of thing. (qtd. in Chick 2001)

And, given the common and characteristically incomplete nature of replay, it is problematic what portion of *Civilization* players (and critics) have gained full access to the later stages of the game and experienced the effects of pollution *in a recursive context of play*. Many obviously have and do, though it is also reasonable to assume that more players reach the final stages of the game (*any* game) on lower difficulty levels than they do on the highest possible difficulty level.

In any case, it is only during initial and novice play—which is most compatible with a linear reading of game as text—that *Civilization* game signs and symbols (i. e., game *signifiers*) might be reasonably associated with those pre-existing— often normative—values corresponding to the use (or misuse) of real-world factories, fossil fuels, and nuclear energies (i. e., real-world *signifieds*). During and after repeated play of *Civilization*, there are at least two factors which make this tentative association between game signifiers and real-world signifieds unlikely.

First, and most specifically as regards the *Civilization* series, the games are neither historical simulations nor historical texts, despite that fact that they are sometimes referred to as such—in both scholarly and popular publications (Squire; Caviness; Stephenson). There are technical reasons for this embedded in the game's semiotic structure (see Myers *The Nature of Computer Games*, 39–44), but let me simply note again that *Civilization* has been designed and redesigned, beginning with the original Meier and Shelley efforts, to quite clearly conform to an aesthetics of play rather than to construct a realistic model of human history. And, over the succeeding years, the games have retained the trappings of a historical simulation only in the most superficial and nominative sense.[3]

Second, and more importantly as regards computer game play in general, interactive game *play*—not game readings and not isolated game components and structures—most definitively map, measure, and give meaning to the signs and symbols within a game. The best test of this claim lies in the experiences of—and the choices made by—game players. Do these choices in any way reflect those cultural values commonly attributed to game components—e.g., the nuclear-power complex of signs—*outside the context of play*?

As an example of how and why *Civilization* players come to value game elements, consider again the alternative (and mistakenly included aberrant) strategies available to players of the original *Civilization*—the same version wherein the controversy concerning the use of nuclear power originated. One of the most aberrant of these strategies was the so-called "Mongol" strategy, a version of the well-known "rush" technique, which is often used as a first test of game balance and AI capabilities by players of turn-based and, in particular, real-time computer strategy games (e. g., the *Age of Empires* series).

The "value" of a Mongol strategy in *Civilization*—positive in terms of winning the game; negative in terms of curtailing replay (and fun)—was determined solely by its effect on the individual play experience. Certainly, the game rules allowing successful use of the Mongol strategy were not seen—by either players or critics of the game—as an editorial comment concerning the relative superiority of the Mongol civilization. These rules were simply ultimately, inevitably, not fun—and so these rules were ultimately, inevitably revised in subsequent game designs, *regardless of their value or meaning outside the context of play*. At the same time, complaints about the implementation of nuclear power within Civilization have seldom referenced any negative impact on the immediate play experience, and, subsequently, the function of nuclear power within the game has been changed very little in the game's successive revisions.

In general, socio-cultural critics of *Civilization's* ideological biases have not found it necessary to look at specific strategies employed by expert players prior to assuming widespread effects of those biases. Yet the most frequently discussed aspects of the game within dedicated player forums (e. g., Apolyton.net) are the relationships among in-game signifieds—without reference to or really any concern about their significance (or signification) outside the game context. As a result, these discussions of game rules and related strategies have greater relevance to other computer strategy games than they do to the real-world referents of the game's (from this point of view, arbitrarily chosen) signs and symbols. This is true both of the topics of player-based game analyses and of the methods employed by those analyses—both are quite different from the topics and methods employed by socio-cultural theorists.

Here, for instance, is a typical gamer's approach to valuing rush strategies as they (re-)appear within the single and multiplayer versions of *Civilization III*. (In this particular context, the aberrant Mongol strategy has evolved into a more efficient, virus-like form: the Infinite City Strategy or ICS.)

> Enter the first release of CivIII with its flog hack of pop-rushing, and for a while ICS was back with a vengence. Everything the Civ team had done to butt **** big city strategies, and there is no other term for it—such resource problems, worse corruption, harder unhappiness, more aggressive AI civs, less effective research for players than for AIs— made ICS ever more attractive . . .

> The recent patch is like a late Beta of a working game, the first release was like an Alpha. ICS is a good ma[r]ker of how well play tested a civ version was. It is an obvious, easy strategy, like "imp" from corewars, that crushes more elegant and complex strategies. If it works too well, then the version hasn't been well thought out. (Anonymous)

This particular player analysis—representative of many others—assigns value to new game elements (e. g. "pop-rushing") within the context of the entire *Civilization* game rules set (i. e., in relationship to rules determining "resource problems, worse corruption, harder unhappiness, more aggressive AI civ . . ." and so forth). This assignation occurs without reference to either the historical accuracy or the real-world value of game elements. And, importantly, this assignation occurs only as a result of knowledge gained through extensive replay.

If there is any most obvious bias in player analysis of this sort, it is the bias of the engineer in adopting a systems approach to determining game unit values. However, any such bias in methodology does not undermine the overwhelming tendency of game players to adjudicate game units, designs, rules, and related strategies according to their impact on *subjective* game experiences—or according to what I referred to earlier as an "aesthetic of play" (e.g., the reference to "elegant and complex" strategies above).

Barbarous treatments

The *Civilization* "barbarian" game element—appearing in the earliest portions of all games in the *Civilization* series—has received critical attention similar to that of pollution in the late game. Barbarian interpretations and values differ sharply in the analysis of game players and of socio-cultural critics.

In those analyses valuing *Civilization* game signs as at least some part of a colonialist/imperialist manifesto (Lemmes; Douglas; Poblocki), the treatment of barbarians as distinct from the more cultured, scientifically endowed, and eventually successful player civilizations forces game-world barbarians into a subordinate relationship with the player civilizations which reflects similar treatments imposed and assumptions held outside the game context.

> The equation that the player has to make between the Barbarian's level of nomadic activity and [the] threat they pose, points to a western mentality in which nomadic behavior is placed on the periphery of the culture as the 'other'. (Lemmes, 124)

> The Indians exist not as a civilization in their own right, but as an obstacle to be surmounted by civilization; in the [*Civilization*] game, as in Rowlandson's account, the enemy Indian Other is imagined as being the mechanism whereby the nascent American self is tested and found to be powerful. (Douglas, paragraph 17)

There is no doubt that recursive play as I have described it—reflecting basic patterns of human cognition—is universally involved in categorizing and, indeed, evoking oppositional relationships between self and other. However, there remains little evidence that the objects valued within such an opposition (i. e., signifiers of the "Other") carry the same meanings or significations inside the game as they do outside the game. There is even less evidence—and, in fact, there are contrary indications—that those objects carry the same meanings or significations inside play as outside play.

For instance, Douglas acknowledges that most players come to designate the barbarian villages as "goody huts," a label more clearly reflecting their role in the game than their ideological value to invading Western civilizations. From a gamer's point of view, in fact, the role of barbarians during play is more help than hindrance.

The most obvious function of the barbarians in the original *Civilization* design was to contribute to game's variable difficulty levels. However the impact of barbarians on game play is actually quite small, particularly when the game's difficulty level is set on anything other than its lowest levels. Barbarians indeed pose some threat to developing civilizations and neophyte game units, but this threat is minimal and can be, with little effort, avoided entirely by saving and reloading from a point prior to all barbarian-inspired disasters. Rather than treating (and valuing) the barbarians as an oppositional force, dedicated game players are much more likely to attempt to develop their early civilizations with the barbarians' aid.

This cooperative use of barbarians is vital to gaining a foothold in *Civilization* games played at the highest difficulty levels, where the computer-controlled civilizations inevitably attain very large and dangerous early leads in city production and development. Striking a lucky goody hut or two can mean the difference between surviving the game's early years or being quickly overrun by an aggressive adjacent civilization.

Realizing this, the computer-controlled civilizations seek out (and destroy) the goody huts very quickly, with races between civilizations often ensuing not to avoid confrontations with barbarians but to secure them for their own units.[4] There are also other subtle benefits of having barbarians on the map—e. g., improving the expertise of your units by sparring with barbarian units and allowing barbarians to fester in unexplored areas to serve as a temporary impedance to the growth of nearby civilizations. However, none of these functions of barbarians *during game play* appear to have any particular significance for critics of in-game barbarian representations. More commonly, text-based descriptions of barbarians—such as those found in game manuals (or game advertising)—are used as justification for assigning values and meanings to play within *Civilization*.

> Indeed, as an add informs, "we can match wits with greatest leaders of the world in an all-out quest to build the ultimate empire" (Civ3.com 2002), and we do become one of such nearly divine leaders with a capacity for altering the course of history (hence the popular classification of Civilization in the "you are the god" genre). The *telos*, however, is well known. If in the case of Hegel it was the Prussian state (Ferguson 1998: 30), the fetish-object of Meier's fantasies is the 'ultimate empire', the state that resembles most the end product of all human advancement, namely the United States of America. (Poblocki)

Text-based descriptions of game units, however, whether appearing in game-supported or supplementary publications—even when appearing as nominatives within the game itself—fail to reveal the manner in which those units are used during play and, as a result of that use, given value and meaning by players. It is well known, for instance, that game players commonly eschew written rules and instructions in favor of more direct and immediate play as a means of determining game goals. And, among dedicated game players, the more barbarian-like "Indians" (e. g., Iroquois) are usually considered more advantageously played than the (assumedly) less barbarian-like Americans.

In the back of the backstories

Civilization game elements—such as barbarians in early game play and nuclear power in late game play—are obviously interpreted and valued differently by game players than by those who find embedded in the *Civilization* games a set of values and meanings existing prior to and apart from game play. These embedded values and meanings can then be understood as a sort of ideological "backstory" to which gamer's need not—and most often do not—adhere.

I have made in the past (Myers "The attack of the backstories") the rather contentious claim that, in general, game backstories have no real relevance to computer game play and, in particular, inhibit rather than determine play within computer strategy games. This claim recognizes the degree to which (re)play deconstructs and revalues signs and symbols which are, in other contexts, more conventionally assigned value and meaning. As such, this claim is not intended to apply to *Civilization* alone but to the larger class of computer games which evoke repeated and recursive play. In his recent keynote presentation to the Austin Game Conference (2003), Raph Koster applies a similar argument to concerns that play within *Grand Theft: Auto* results in players learning that game's embedded "ethical implications."

> This is why gamers are dismissive of the ethical implications of games— They don't see *"get a blowjob* from a hooker, then *run her over."* They see *a power-up.* Koster)

However, there remains an important point unaddressed: What about those aspects of game play that might, with or without conscious intent, replicate pre-existing social and cultural values? Socio-cultural criticism, after all, may confuse the superficialities of game labels with the underlying mechanisms of game structures; but those game structures might nevertheless still be indicative of some ideological bias originating in some other context. Should all civilizations in the game, for instance, function according to the cultural identity of a single civilization (e.g., Poblocki's 'ultimate empire' above), then claims of ideological bias might well re-emerge.

> The [perfidy] of *Civilization's* cultural imperialism . . . sneaks into players' own activities, penetrating as deep as their own reconstructed body . . .
> The history of Western civilization is to a very high extent a history of the camouflage of power and the means of coercion . . . It is always difficult to spot power in the concept of culture (Wolf 2001, Said 1994) but in strategy computer games such as *Civilization* power is almost invisible because, at least at the level of rhetoric, it belongs to us. (Poblocki)

I have so far claimed that patterns and rules governing an "aesthetic of play" can be observed through the design and redesign of computer games; and I have given examples of this process at work in the evolution of the *Civilization* game series. Let us suppose now that this aesthetic of play is not merely at the root of game design and play, but also at the root of cultural bias, power, and "coercion."

For instance, while barbarians are not rightfully considered as a defining opposition to the human player in *Civilization*, other computer-controlled civilizations *are* placed in this sort of opposition. An undeniable theme in the game and its play is then a theme of opposition and conflict. Likewise, the most common manner in which the game is played, valued, and analyzed by its most dedicated players is through a systems-based approach which, through recursive play, exhibits an obvious debt to the methods and assumptions of positivist science.

Are there within the rules and nature of human play such seeds of opposition and contextualization, which, in their recursive application, create a "culturally biased" form of abstract thought? Or is some distorted aesthetic of play directly imposed on an otherwise culturally neutral cognitive template? There is even the possibility that the vagaries of play become irrevocably intertwined with the backstories of prevailing cultural contexts during the exercise of games as "configurative practices" (Eskelinen).

> [T]he hacker communities and digital game scenario sites suggest that the awareness of game rules—and the urge to rewrite them—often subverts the games' standing rules governing the way a game can be configured, but they also exceed the rules' ability to configure the operator's paths of thought. Such discourse includes discussion of the aesthetic qualities of the rules themselves . . . This is the two-way process of configuration—operator on game, game on operator—that digital game studies will have to address in the years ahead. (Douglas, paragraph 28)

Thus, regardless of how these might get into our play—through ourselves or through others—themes of power may yet seduce us.

Conclusion

I cannot here make any more detailed argument against assertions of critical theory[5]—other than to observe that while games (and "fun") exhibit important cultural differences, characteristics of play appear quite similar across cultures—and, in many respects, across species (see Beckoff and Byers). And therein I can draw a line in the sand of current computer game theory between those who would claim that the underlying mechanisms of games and game structures are determined by external factors and/or those texts which embody them and those who would claim that the fundamental mechanisms of play and play structures more accurately reflect their indelibly stamped and now internally fixed biological origins. This is, of course, not a new line[6] (sounding, as it does, suspiciously like the old nature-nurture saw). However, there are, in this case, some interesting and contrary predictions available to consider.

On one hand, if play serves as a deconstructive process—and replay serves even more so—then frequent and dedicated players of computer strategy games would be, over time, increasingly less likely to interpret or be affected by games as cultural statements, either consciously or unconsciously. Play and replay would be thus something of a natural de-culturalization process.

On the other hand, I suspect culturalists would maintain the opposite—that frequent and dedicated players of games are precisely the group mostly likely to be, over time, indoctrinated by the cultural values embedded in game texts and, therefore, mostly likely to exhibit cognitive and behavioral changes to that effect. We'll see.

Notes

1 Former writer/editor at *Computer Gaming World*, among other places and things.
2 Well, actually, I could say—in formal parallel with the tech-based theorists—that play is an inclusive process motivated by the peculiar characteristics of the brain. The key difference, then, between tech-based and brain-based theory is that, in the latter case, the brain must be considered an "external factor" constraining itself—resulting in, among other things, the common paradoxes of cognitive play (see Myers *The Nature of Computer Games*, 65–68). Subsequently, some might eliminate these paradoxes through a sleight-of-hand semantics, setting up a false dichotomy of brain and mind, or mind and consciousness, or consciousness and play. I rather think these paradoxes of cognition, as reproduced in cognitive play, should be acknowledged, accepted, and embraced.
3 Chick (2002) makes this point in what is possibly—well, probably—a more engaging way.
4 In fact, after assigning a positive in-game value to barbarians, many players of the earliest versions of *Civilization* used a saving-and-reloading strategy to invade the same goody hut over and over again until it produced its most valuable (otherwise randomly determined) goody—a strategy considered aberrant and curtailed in later game designs by determining the contents of all goody hut caches prior to a point where the game could be conveniently reloaded.
5 Well, actually (again), I could also say this: Unless we are willing to advocate theories of false consciousness and correspondingly dismiss both game designer intentions and game player systems of values as irrelevant in the face of a relatively superficial interpretation of games signs and symbols which, significantly, fails to acknowledge the function of replay in valuing and giving meaning to game elements, it is extremely difficult to validate the concerns of those who would claim that play and meaning-making within the *Civilization* game series are indicative of cultural biases peculiar to and caused by the ideological backstories of Western civilization.
6 See Clarke for a rehash of a debate over the effects of educational broadcasting services. The argument here is bit different from Clarke's, but the lines of demarcation are quite similar.

References

Aarseth, Espen. "Aporia and Epiphany in Doom and the Speaking Clock." *Cyberspace Textuality: Computer Technology and Literary Theory*. Ed. Marie-Laure Ryan. Bloomington: Indiana University Press, 1999. 31–41.

Aarseth, Espen. *Cybertext. Perspectives on Ergodic Literature*, Baltimore and London: Johns Hopkins University Press, 1997.

Anonymous [kilane royalist]. "ICS – Infinite City Strategy aka 'Chinese' Strategy." 25 Feb 2002. Online posting. Apolyton Civ3-Strategy Forum. 18 Jan 2004. <http://apolyton. net/forums/showthread.php?postid=773259#post773259>

Bekoff, Mark and John A. Byers. Eds. *Animal Play*. Cambridge, United Kingdom: Cambridge University Press, 1998.

Bolter, Jay David and Richard Grusin. *Remediation: Understanding New Media*. Cambridge, MA: MIT Press, 2000.

Caviness, Rochelle. History in Review: Civilization III. 2002. 14 Jan 2004. <http://www.largeprintreviews.com/civiii.html>

Chick, Tom. "The Teaching Game: All I Really Need to Know I Learned in Civilization." Jan 2002. CGOnline.com. 18 Jan 2004. <http://www.cgonline.com/features/020118-c2f1.html>

Chick, Tom. "The Fathers of Civilization: An Interview with Sid Meier and Bruce Shelley." Aug 2001. CGOnline.com. 18 Jan 2004. <http://www.cgonline.com/features/010829-i1-f1pg5.html>

Clarke, Richard E. "Media Will Never Influence Learning." 1994. 24 Jan 2004.<http://www.usq.edu.au/material/unit/resource/clark/media.htm>

Douglas, Christopher. "You Have Unleashed a Horde of Barbarians!": Fighting Indians, Playing Games, Forming Disciplines. Post Modern Culture 13.1 (Sep, 2002). 18 Jan 2004.<http://www.iath.virginia.edu/pmc/text-only/issue.902/13.1douglas.txt>

Eskelinen, Markku. The Gaming Situation. Game Studies 1.1 (Jul 2001). 24 Jan 2004.<http://www.gamestudies.org/0101/eskelinen/>

Henthorne, Tom. Cyber-Utopias: The Politics and Ideology of Computer Games. Studies in Popular Culture, 25.3 (Apr 2003). 20 Jan 2004. <http://pcasacas.org/SPC/spcissues/25.3/Henthorne.htm>

Kittler, Friedrich A. Gramophone, Film, Typewriter. Trans. Geoffrey Winthrop-Young and Michael Wurz. Stanford, CA: Stanford University Press, 1997

Koster, Raph. "A Theory of Fun." 2003 Austin Games Conference. Austin, Texas. 11–13 Sep 2003. 14 Jan 2004. http://www.gameconference.com/conference/raphkoster.pdf

Lemmes, Sybille. "On the Border: The Pleasure of Exploration and Colonial Mastery in Civilization III: Play the World." Level Up: Digital Games Research Conference Proceedings. Eds. Marinka Copier and Joost Raessens. Utrecht, the Netherlands: Faculty of the Arts, University of Utrecht, 2003. 120–129.

Manovich, Lev. Language of New Media. Cambridge, MA: MIT Press, 2002.

Montfort, Nick. Twisty Little Passages: An Approach to Interactive Fiction. Cambridge, MA: MIT Press, 2003.

Myers, David. "The Attack of the Backstories (and Why They Won't Win)." Level Up: Digital Games Research Conference Proceedings. Eds. Marinka Copier and Joost Raessens. Utrecht, the Netherlands: Faculty of the Arts, University of Utrecht, 2003. CD-ROM.

Myers, David. The Nature of Computer Games: Play as Semiosis. New York: Peter Lang, 2003.

Myers, David. "Time, Symbol Manipulation, and Computer Games." Play & Culture 5 (1992): 441–457.

Myers, David. "Computer Game Semiotics." Play & Culture 4 (1991): 334–345.

Poblocki, Kacper. "Becoming-State. The Bio-Cultural Imperialism of Sid Meier's Civilization." Focaal—European Journal of Anthropology 39 (2002): 163–177. <http://www.focaal.box.nl/previous/Forum%20focaal39.pdf >

Reynolds, Brian. "Designer's Notes." Sid Meier's Civilization II: Instruction Manual. Hunt Valley, MD: Micropose, 1996. 179–183.

Ryan, Marie-Laure. Narrative as Virtual Reality: Immersion and Interactivity in Literature and Electronic Media. Baltimore: Johns Hopkins University Press, 2001.

Smedstad, Gus. "Civilization dirty tricks." n.d. The Cheater's Guild. 18 Jan 2004.<http://www.cheaters-guild.com/cheat-display.asp?category=DirtyTricks&GameName=Civilization>

Squire, Kurt. Cultural Faming of Computer/Video Games. *Game Studies* 2.1 (2002). 14 Jan 2004. <http://www.gamestudies.org/0102/squire/>

Stephenson, William. The Microserfs are Revolting: Sid Meier's Civilization II. *Bad Subjects* 45(Oct 1999). 14 Jan 2004. <http://eserver.org/bs/45/stephenson.html>

van den Belt, Paul. "Civilization II: One City Challenge Strategy Guide." n.d. 18 Jan 2004. <http://www.paulvdb.cistron.nl/occ/occ.htm>

41

GENRE AND GAME STUDIES

Toward a critical approach to video game genres

Thomas H. Apperley

Source: *Simulation Gaming*, 37(1), 2006, 6–23.

Abstract

This article examines the notion of genre in video games. The main argument is that the market-based categories of genre that have been developed in the context of video games obscure the new medium's crucial defining feature, by dividing them into categories (loosely) organized by their similarities to prior forms of mediation. The article explores the inherent tension between the conception of video games as a unified new media form, and the current fragmented genre-based approach that explicitly or implicitly concatenates video games with prior media forms. This tension reflects the current debate, within the fledgling discipline of Game Studies, between those who advocate narrative as the primary tool for understanding videogames, "narratologists," and those that oppose this notion, "ludologists." In reference to this tension, the article argues that videogame genres be examined in order to assess what kind of assumptions stem from the uncritical acceptance of genre as a descriptive category. Through a critical examination of the key game genres, this article will demonstrate how the clearly defined genre boundaries collapse to reveal structural similarities between the genres that exist within the current genre system, defined within the context of visual aesthetic or narrative structure. The inability of the current genre descriptions to locate and highlight these particular features suggests that to privilege the categories of the visual and narrative is a failure to understand the medium. The article concludes by suggesting that the tension between "ludology" and "narratology" can be more constructively engaged by conceptualizing video games as operating in the interplay between these two taxonomies of genre.

In the introduction to "Theoretical frameworks for analyzing turn-based computer strategy games," Nick Caldwell (2004) muses over the notion of creating a "critical vocabulary" for computer games, concluding that different genres of game, even different subgenres of game, deployed such diverse *representational* strategies as to make general claims seem untenable . . . . Games might share some basic purpose—to entertain— but each new game that appeared on my screen could well have been in a different medium, or a different language, altogether [Emphasis added]. (p. 42)

I suggest that Caldwell's (2004) discussion marks a crucial problem in the study of video games: that they cannot be regarded as a consistent medium. Certainly, taken as a whole, the field of video games can hardly be considered to have a uniform—or consistent—*aesthetic*. Caldwell's statement indicates the crux of the problem: by focusing on the "diverse representational strategies" at the expense of other common features, the specific attribute of the video game medium is overlooked. *Interactivity*—the way in which the game is played, rather than watched—is a nonrepresentational feature common to all video games. By taking a critical approach to the understanding of genres of interactivity, useful observations can be made regarding the medium as a whole.

The claim of this article is that conventional video game genres rely overmuch on games representational characteristics. *Representational* in this case refers to the visual aesthetics of the games. Contra to conventional genres I argue that the nonrepresentational, specifically interactive, characteristics of video games should be deployed by game scholars to create a more nuanced, meaningful, and critical vocabulary for discussing videogames; one that can perceive the underlying common characteristics of games that might otherwise be regarded as entirely dissimilar if judged solely on representation.

This focus on interactivity as the dominant defining feature of video games requires careful consideration of that concept. Espen Aarseth (1997) criticizes the notion of interactivity in *Cybertext: Perspectives on Ergodic Literature*, arguing that: "it is a purely ideological term [that is] lacking any analytical substance" (p. 51). In reaction, Aarseth first introduces the concept of the "cybertext" to describe the intricate feedback system that exists in certain types of texts that are characterized by a "mechanical organisation" and an "integrated" reader (1997, p. 1).He then coins the term *ergodic* to describe the role of the human actor in the process of creating the cybertext; specifically, *ergodic* refers to the point that "non-trivial effort is required to allow the reader to traverse the text" (Aarseth, 1997, p. 1).Although Aarseth's formulation is not medium specific, in the context of this article, the notion of "interactivity" refers to the ergodic actions taken in order to play a video game. The concern of this article is to examine critically the various types of "non-trivial" efforts involved in the ergodic "traverse" of video games.

I suggest that the primary problem with conventional video games genres is that rather than being a general description of the style of ergodic interaction that takes place within the game, it is instead loose aesthetic clusters based around video games' aesthetic linkages to prior media forms. Conventional video game genres implicitly follow what Jay David Bolter and Richard Grusin (1999) in *Remediation:*

Understanding New Media describe as the "logic of remediation." Remediation being "the formal logic by which new media refashion prior media forms" (1999, p. 273). Bolter and Grusin (1999) describe two strategies of remediation: transparent immediacy and hypermediacy. Transparent immediacy seeks "to get to the real by bravely denying the fact of mediation" (p. 53). Hypermediacy— conversely—draws attention to the act of mediation, "by multiplying mediation to create a feeling of fullness, a satiety of experience, which can be taken as reality" (Bolter & Grusin, 1999, p. 53). By examining video games in the context of ergodic rather than representational genre, the "neatness" of Bolter and Grusin's (1999) notion of remediation as the recycling of representational aesthetics across mediums is challenged, as something more than the visual is operating, requiring the tracing of genealogical trajectories that looks beyond video games aesthetic borrowing from cinema and television.

The established genres of video games, while being substantially different from literary or filmic genres, still emphasize representation over any notion of interactivity. Bolter and Grusin (1999, p. 81), for example, argue that interactivity is supplementary to representation, that it merely makes the representation more realistic, as an object can be potentially manipulated and acted upon even though it is virtual. Aarseth (2004, p. 52) refutes the configuration of interactivity as secondary to either narrative structure or visual representation in "Genre Trouble: Narrativism and the Art of Simulation." In "Simulation Versus Narrative: Introduction to Ludology," Gonzalo Frasca (2003) delineates two approaches to the study of video games; the narratological; those approaches that rely on narrative paradigms, and the ludological; which rather than seeking to understand games through their narrative or representational strategies, "focus[es] on the understanding of [their] structure and elements—particularly [their] rules— as well as creating typologies and models for explaining the mechanics of the games" (p. 222).

To ludological scholars, the way in which video games differ from prior media forms is that as James Newman (2002) states in "The Myth of the Ergodic Videogame: Some Thoughts on Player-Character Relationships in Videogames": "the pleasures of video game *play* are not principally visual, but rather kinaesthetic"(p. 2). As *kinesthesis* is defined as being the muscular effort that accompanies the motion of the body, I suggest that Newman in this case refers to the interactive effort required to keep the flow of the game in motion, making the concept synonymous with Aarseth's (2004) notion of ergodicity. Furthermore, Newman's (2002) configuration underscores the importance of the ergodic work of the player rather than the mechanical rules of the game as the central determinant of the players' experience.

Although Caldwell (2004) is confounded by the diverse representational strategies of video games, other scholars have approached the question of genre with a will to capture its dynamism and variety. In "Genre and the Video Game," Mark J. P. Wolf (2001, pp. 116–117) sets out to classify video game genres along the lines developed by the Library of Congress Moving Imagery Genre-Form Guide.

The 42 categories listed in Wolf's adapted taxonomy of genre are a testament to the diversity of the medium. However, for the sake of brevity, this article will utilize case studies of four of the more popular video game genres: simulation, strategy, action, and role-playing games. Following these case studies, this article will discuss the implications of a shift from representational to ergodic understanding of genre in video games. However, first it is necessary to trace the development of genre as it pertains to video games in both its popular and critical contexts.

Video game genres

In response to the divergent characteristics of video games, useful scholarship has been done in an effort to establish a notion of genre. This helps to put a rough framework on the divergent field. Although Jesper Juul (2001, p. 3) in "Games Telling Stories: A Brief Note on Games and Narratives," is resistant to any notion of genre that questions the established industry categories, Mark J.P. Wolf (2001, p. 113) in "Genre and the Video Game" argues in favor of Thomas Schatz's (1981, p. 15) notion from *Hollywood Genres: Formulas, Filmmaking, and the Studio System*—that film-genre classification is a consensual agreement between the audience and the producers—be considered relevant to video games. This understanding of genre conceives it as flexible, dynamic, and integrated with the technology of video games.

However, it must be noted that players of games—that is, their audience—are not necessarily satisfied with the same generic conventions being endlessly repeated. The expectation is that the stability of genre will be tempered by innovation; this innovation may be technical, not necessarily stylistic. An example of the failure of the industry to meet the demands of the consumers is the suggestion made by Stephen Kline, Nick Dyer-Witheford, and Greg de Peuter (2003, pp. 104–105) in *Digital Play: The Interaction of Technology, Culture, and Marketing* that the widespread adoption of unimaginative, formulaic game design was a contributing factor in the collapse of the games industry in the United States between 1983 and 1984. Consumers had become so disgruntled with the rehashed and poorly designed generic fare being produced that the market for games halved within 2 years, and the industry, which is believed to have made as much as eight billion dollars in 1982, was suddenly struggling to survive. In *The Nature of Computer Games: Play as Semiosis*, David Myers (2003) emphasizes that game genres are the result of a particular dynamic of technological contexts and popularity and are therefore neither "fundamental or lasting" (p. 97). I suggest that the collapse of the games industry in 1983 to 1984 demonstrates that video game genres, however disparate, were not considered stable by their audience, genre was rather expected to evolve to exploit the ever-growing capacities of the hard ware on which the games were played.

This article marks a critical departure from Juul (2001), arguing that genre is a category that needs to be rethought with a critical perspective in mind, because the current established genres accepted by the audience and industry do not take into account the complex layering of genre that occurs within video games. The point of departure is based on the argument that Geoff King and Tanya Krzywinska (2002) make in the introduction to *ScreenPlay: Cinema/videogames/interfaces*, that games can be categorized on four levels: "according to platform, genre, mode and milieu" (p. 26). However, I suggest that King and Krzywinska's levels be understood as layers of ergodic interactivity, in particular, this requires a reconfiguration of their understanding of genre, which follows that typically used by the industry.

Genre

Of the four layers suggested by King and Kryzwinska (2002), "genre" has the most problematic designation. By using genre as a category—I maintain that—King and Krzywinksa (2002) are appealing to the type of categorization that is unique to video games: their ergodicity. However, in their discussion, they are satisfied with the demarcations of genres made by "the wider gaming community" (King and Krzywinksa, 2002, p. 26). In short, their approach to genre, while acknowledging that video games genres are necessarily different from those of film, is not critical. I suggest that this understanding of genre be replaced with Wolf's (2001, p. 114) alternative taxonomy of genre, which concentrates on the types of interactions that are available in the game, as distinct from the visual iconography. With the additional caveat that interactivity be focused on Aarseth's (1997) notion of the ergodic traversal.

Platform

The "platform" category of video game genre refers to the hardware systems on which the game is played. This includes personal computers, various consoles (Sony PlayStation 2, Nintendo GameCube, Microsoft Xbox, etc.), as well as handheld devices such as Game Boy Advanced, PDAs, and cellphones. Although this may seem unimportant, as it is common for popular games to shift across the various franchises, both Newman (2004, p. 44) in *Videogames*, and Will Brooker (2001) in "The Many Lives of the Jetman: A Case Study in Computer Game Analysis," point out that the specificity of design for a particular console may not be replicated when the software is adjusted to other hardware. Consequently, the experience of playing the game may be drastically different because of adjustments made to cope with a different style of controller or graphic interface. Furthermore, the platform used will often dictate the spaces, and social relations, in which the game takes place.

Mode

Of King and Krzywinska's (2002, p. 26) categories of genre, "mode" is the least clearly defined. This refers to the mode in which the "game world is experienced" by the players. I suggest that this appeal to environmental and experiential factors relates specifically to the spatial and temporal arrangements of the game. In the past, analysis of video games' space, and—more specifically—the ability of the player to move through space, has been a common focus. In *Hamlet on the Holodeck: The Future of Narrative in Cyberspace*, Janet H. Murray (1997, p. 132) uses the notions of the "maze" and the "rhizome" to contrast free movement with movement that is basically linear. In "The Art of Contested Spaces" Henry Jenkins and Kurt Squire (2003, p. 69) make a similar categorical observation using the terms, *hard rails* and *soft rails*, to distinguish between games in which the player's movements are tightly structured and those games which are multidirectional and multilinear.

A key aspect of "mode" noted by King and Krzywinska (2002, p. 26) is the way in which a particular game's mode may vary according to whether it is played multi- or single-player. This observation is supported by the ethnographic investigation of Sue Morris (2002, pp. 82–85) described in "First Person Shooters—A Game Apparatus," who points out the structural differences between the single- and multi-player versions of HALF-LIFE (1998). The single-player version of the game centers around following a linear narrative, whereas the multi-player version takes on a number of permutations in which the various players either stalk each other within the virtual environment or group together to compete against other groups in discreet episodes or "missions" (Morris, 2002, pp. 83–84). However, I suggest that the most significant—and potentially confusing—aspect of this genre is King and Kryzwinska's (2002, p. 26) claim that the "physical proximity" of other players is an aspect of mode. This infers that the environment encapsulated by "mode" is not solely virtual but extends into the physical also.

Milieu

Milieu is used to describe the visual genre of the video game. Several distinct established game genres of milieu exist: science fiction, fantasy, and horror being prominent. Aarseth (2004, p. 48)—and other ludologists—claim that this kind of "visual" aspect of the game is irrelevant to the mechanical rules of the simulation. Running counter to this, a growing body of work on horror-genre games argues that the effectiveness of the horror milieu is enhanced by using particular mechanical and structural rules (Carr, 2003, pp. 2, 7; Kryzwinska, 2002, p. 207). Thus, I suggest to construe this element of games as completely irrelevant is to ignore a key element of how games are structured.

Genre studies

Simulation

The simulation genre includes video games that simulate sports, flying and driving, and games that simulate the dynamics of towns, cities, and small communities. To use Bolter and Grusin's (1999) logic, most simulation games are located within

307

the notion of remediation, as their content and play is either repurposed from relatively common activities, and/or the depiction of those activities on media such as cinema and television. However, for ludologists the notion of simulation has much higher stakes. In "Genre Trouble: Narrativism and the Art of Simulation" Aarseth (2004, p. 52) argues that video games should be understood as a particular genre of simulation. This position is discussed more expansively by Frasca (2003, p. 222) in "Simulation Versus Narrative: An Introduction to Ludology," which argues that it is video games' roots in simulation that constitutes a break with prior media forms, as simulation has a different semiotic system from that of orthodox narrative media.

This genealogical connection between games and simulations is also identified by Myers in *The Nature of Computer Games: Play as Semiosis*. Myers (2003, p. 10) points out that both ADVENT (1976) and SPACEWAR! (1962) began as simulations: the former of a cave system, whereas the latter was of zero-gravity physics. However, Myers (2003) also notes a conflict between simulation and play, which differentiates his position from that of Aarseth (1997) and Frasca (2003). Regarding the design of SPACEWAR! he states: "although the game forced the two ships to accelerate and decelerate according to accepted laws of physics, the ships' rotation ultimately adhered only to laws of play" (Myers, 2003, p. 4). The strict adherence to "the real" demanded of the simulation gave way to the more pragmatic requirements of entertainment (Myers, 2003, p. 7). These contradictory demands that shape the simulation genre, highlight a broader conflict across the medium as a whole, between adherence to "the real" and pure entertainment.

To return to Bolter and Grusin's (1999) remediation argument, what these scholars are highlighting is that video games themselves are an example of the repurposing or remediation of the technology of the computer simulation. However, this places no imperative that video games be understood as simulations or even in the context of simulations. Cinema's technological origins in the scientific, "non-narrative" motion-capture technology of Eadwead Muybridge did not prevent the content of that medium from becoming dominated by narrative. However, to conceive cinema as a whole as primarily narrative, or in this case to conceive video games as simulations, places an undesirable conceptual homogeneity on the field.

Following Frasca's (2003) argument that all games are in some way simulations, what is particular about the conventional genre of simulation games is that they clearly remediate a "real" world activity. Within this is often the assumption—or the promise—that the game is "authentic" to the "real" activity, that the game will be a relatively accurate simulation, which does not subsume the authenticity of the simulation entirely within the demands of entertainment. For example in the subgenre of driving simulations, many games—like PROJECT GOTHAM RACING 2 and DAKAR 2 (2003)—clearly seek to simulate the activity of driving, through an accurate depiction of the physics involved in that process. Other games, such as CRASH NITRO KART and THE SIMPSONS: HIT AND RUN (2003) that also simulate driving, blatantly follow an entertainment paradigm. The latter of these games operates within its own internal logic, the physics that the game world obeys are remediated from the cartoon universe. As Bart explains to the neophyte player in the game's tutorial: "Press the A button to accelerate and use the left thumbstick or directional pad to steer. The B button is your break and reverse, the X button is your handbrake. You know, just like every driving game ever." Driving in THE SIMPSONS: HIT AND RUN (2003)—and as Bart infers— many other driving games, have been deliberately simplified in accordance with the demands of entertainment.

In contrast, PROJECT GOTHAM RACING 2 (2003) caters toward those players that demand a more authentic simulation; however, the complexities of gear shifting are optional and can be turned off by the player who does not desire such a degree of accuracy in the simulation. The real difference between the driving in the two games comes from the handling; for example, turning corners at high speed with the aid of the hand brake. In THE SIMPSONS: HIT AND RUN (2003), the technique was rather straightforward, and enabled the driver to turn rapidly without a dramatic loss of speed. This approach, when imported to PROJECT GOTHAM RACING 2 (2003) would invariably result in a temporary loss of control of the vehicle, as the game features a stricter adherence to the laws of physics. This divergence marks the way in which different games deal with the contradictory pressure noted by Myers (2003) between the "laws of physics" and the "laws of play."

Strategy

The examination of strategy games is crucial in offering an alternative to the argument that games remediate cinema. King and Krzywinska (2002, p. 14) point out that of all video games strategy games have the fewest cinematic associations. The strategy genre is usually divided into two subgenres: real time strategy (RTS) and turn-based strategy (TBS). Both RTS and TBS games have a similar aesthetic, a general god's eye-view of the actions taking place, with a tendency toward a more photorealistic depiction. However, both games, the TBS especially, cannot be considered remediated forms of any other orthodoxly conceived technological medium; rather they remediate the playing of the strategy table-top board game. Thus, this genre differs considerably from other genres in its visual aesthetic. Using Bolter and Grusin's (1999) logic of remediation to describe the strategy game also highlights a key aesthetic difference between this genre and others, in that it is hypermedia, deliberately drawing more attention to its interface as a same method of conveying information, due to the considerable amount of information that needs to be accessed and contextualized to play the game.

The integrity of the strategy genre is complicated by many games that although not of the genre, may still be played strategically. Myers (2002, p. 68) argues that strategic play is associated with expert play. Expert players contextualize relationships between certain values within the game-world in order to obtain the best possible outcomes (p. 44). The beginner player is engaged with the play of the game on the level of response. The expert player—in addition to that level of engagement—is organizing and valuing variables within that system (p.177). It is important to note that for Myers, this activity may take place outside of the game per se and involve contextualizing information gleaned from secondary sources—Internet sites, chat rooms, bulletin boards, conversations with other players, game magazines—as well as prior play of the particular game (p. 17).

The beginning player of an Action Game like BUFFY THE VAMPIRE SLAYER (2002), will proceed through the various challenges unable to make informed choices regarding the various options available to them. As play progresses, the beginning player will discover that various foes have different points of vulnerability, and furthermore, various weapons, styles of attack, and environmental factors in the game may be exploited in order to dispatch the enemy with greater efficiency. Each piece of information informs their future play; eventually all the variables that the player controls will be contextualized, consequently, they will have the information to be able to chose the best response to a given situation. For example, the beginner player when confronted with zombies would not necessarily know that of the various weapons available to them the shovel would be the most useful, while the expert player will switch between weapons often in order to exploit the weaknesses of their opponents. The strategic play of the expert player comes from a combination of knowing the various options available and being able to correctly value them within the game context. This process is ongoing, as the player learns more about the values of the variables. The strategy genre is made from games that emphasize the ongoing play of contextualization.

Lev Manovich's (1996, p. 184) description of postindustrial perceptual labor in "The Labour of Perception" captures the key distinction between the activity of playing a strategy game and a game of another genre. In that article, he distinguishes between two types of perceptual labor, one which implicitly describes the contemporary computer-mediated or cybernetic work-space, and a second that he argues represents the new kind of perceptual labor of the postindustrial society. He argues that the contemporary workspace is characterized as a constant engagement with overwhelming amounts of information, creating "a constant cascade of cognitive shocks that require immediate interventions," which he compares to the playing of a video game (1996, p. 185). The new situation, that of postindustrial labor, Manovich (1996, p. 185) describes as waiting for something to happen. Instead of a constant barrage of information, the worker will monitor a situation waiting for something that will require their intervention. It is to this latter situation that the strategy genre is closer, although the TBS game also shares many similarities with other genres.

To return to the simulation genre with this distinction in mind, I maintain that they operate along a pole of degrees of engagement in ergodic activity. By ergodic activity, I am referring to the kinds of attention that is paid to the interface, the way that the player watches the game screen and the kinds of movements involved by the player in operating the simulation. In this case, the activities involved in a driving simulation like PROJECT GOTHAM RACING 2 (2003) are characterized by detailed attention to the game-screen and constant interaction with the controller during the ergodic part of the play. In these games, the player has to constantly perform kinaesthetic actions, manipulate the controller, following the visual cues supplied by the screen. I suggest that games based on an ergodic performance are analogous to Manovich's (1996) description of the contemporary cybernetic workplace. The players' eventual success or failure at the game is determined by their skill at integrating and contextualizing the various activities involved within the physical rules of the simulation.

However, the activities involved in playing SIM CITY (1989) and THE SIMS (2000) are more strategic; in the SIM CITY (1989) series in particular the player must integrate information from, and make calibrations on, several screens in order to make effective interventions on a process of development that is already underway. The player has to manipulate the simulation as it progresses through time in order to get the result with the most utility. This may involve long periods of surveillance, where the player makes no direct interventions, as they accumulate funds, or anticipate the success or failure of a particular decision that can only be revealed in the process of time. This activity based around observation and intervention, resembles Manovich's (1996) description of the postindustrial workplace. I suggest that the difference in the ergodic engagement indicate two useful subgenres of interactivity. The first group are characterized by the players' crucial role in performing the ergodic process, whereas the second group are characterized by the interventions the player must make to bring the ergodic process to the desired end. The variety of activities involved in both intervention and performative computer games indicate disparate genres of nontrivial engagement.

This critical distinction provides a useful dichotomy for conceptualizing the mental process of the player. Ted Friedman (1999) in "Civilization and Its Discontents: Simulation, Subjectivity, and Space," argues that simulation games are characterized by process of the player learning gradually to think like the game:

> The constant interactivity in a simulation game—the perpetual feedback between a player's choice, the computer's almost instantaneous response, the player's response to that response, and so on—is a cybernetic loop, in which the line demarcating the end of the player's consciousness and the beginning of the computer's world blurs. (P. 137)

The performative games share this aspect to a degree, but they emphasize a physical response that requires the cybernetic integration of the games' challenges into the players' cognitive, kinaesthetic, and perceptual functions. Intervention games are outside of this constantly performative physical feedback loop. Newman (2002) argues that the notion of the "cybernetic feedback loop" can be applied to video games as a whole. Citing Friedman's (1999) work, Newman (2002) states that the linkage between player and game-world should be considered "as an experiential whole that synthesis, action, location, scenario, and not merely as a bond between subject and object within a world" (p. 8). The crucial point here is that the strategy genre of video games emphasize a particular mental process that is found in all video games; furthermore, this process indicates that in the ergodic process the boundary between play and player becomes blurred (see Myers, 2003, p. 144). This blurring is significant in the understanding of video games, and video game genres, as it indicates the inseparability of the player and the text.

Action

The action genre consists of two major subgenres: first-person shooters and third-person games. Although the first-person games are played as if the screen were the players' own vision, third person are played with avatars that are fully visible to the player. According to the categories suggested by King and Kryzwinksa (2002), this distinction is made along the lines of the "mode" genre, as it refers to the players' perceptual engagement with the game environment. These subgenres are demarcated through a remediation of terminology from cinematic perspective, which is based once again on the literary definitions of narration. Cinema that uses first person primarily or as a dominant form of narrative is almost unheard of, although is often used briefly with in a film dominated by third-person narrative as a technique to create identification. Third person is far more common, and is historically the dominant perspective in cinema. The third-person film is characterized by the viewer watching the action unfold through the camera narrator rather than through the eyes of a particular character.

This purely visual distinction collapses within the computer game medium for two reasons. First, Anne-Marie Schliener (2001, pp. 222–224) in "Does Lara Croft Wear Fake Polygons? Gender and Gender Role Subversion in Computer Adventure Games," Barry Atkins (2003, pp. 44–45) in *More Than a Game: The Computer Game as a Fictional Form*, and Mia Consalvo (2003, p. 331) in "Zelda 64 and Video Game Fans: A Walkthrough of Games, Intertextuality, and Narrative," all argue that the player identifies with their avatar, even through they are viewed in the third person. The avatar acts as a virtual prosthetic that acts as the connecting point between the player and the virtual environment. In "Nintendo and New World Travel Writing: A Dialogue," Henry Jenkins and Mary Fuller (1995, p. 61) argue that the avatar serves a function rather like that of a cursor in a more conventional computer-mediated environments (for example *Microsoft Word*), to link the perceptual to the cognitive and kinaesthetic aspects of the game. Second, all first-person games utilize some kind a visual technique that creates a static object that functions as an avatar to link the kinaesthetic, cognitive, and perceptual within the game-space, in the form of a gun or arm that extends out from the bottom of the screen into the virtual world or a gun-sight superimposed onto the center of the screen. This shows that, crucially, whether the perspective be first or third person in visual appearance, in order to experience the virtual world of the game, the player and game must be linked by a static physical locator that acts as an indexical axis that connects the players' gaze and kinaesthetic actions to the virtual game world.

Action games in particular are often intensively performative, in a manner distinctly different from other genres of performative games, in that it is action games that will often require the player to engage in extreme nontrivial actions in order to make the ergodic traversal. In many action games, the player must actually perform a desired action by selecting the correct inputs, while in other genres of video games, the player will merely select the desired action and the computer will determine the performance of that action. For example, in the action game THE LORD OF THE RINGS: RETURN OF THE KING (2003), in order to attack a foe the character must maneuver their avatar in range of the selected foe and then select an attack based on a combination of buttons. The effectiveness of the attack will vary according to the type of foe faced, as the more powerful the foe, the more difficult it is to perform the combination that is most useful against them. To slay an orc champion, in THE LORD OF THE RINGS: RETURN OF THE KING (2003), the player could use the combination Y, Y, B, Y, called the "Shield Cleaver," which will first smash the foes' shield, then knock them to the ground, and then strike them while they are vulnerable. However, failure to follow the sequence with the precise order and timing will result in a less effective, or even ineffective attack.

The performative element described is extremely different to the combat in the action and/or role-playing game STAR WARS: KNIGHTS OF THE OLD REPUBLIC (2003), where the player selects a target and then selects an attack, the computer then determines whether the attack fails of succeeds based on the skill and abilities of the character the avatar represents rather than the skill of the player. Games like this allow a strategic intervention in the performance, whereas action games—exemplified by THE LORD OF THE RINGS: RETURN OF THE KING (2003)—are performative to the extreme. The abilities possessed by the avatar of the player must be activated by a technical performance by the player. Atkins (2003) describes the process of discovering the correct technical performance as creating a "moment of gaming cinema [that] requires the continuing active participation of the player if it is to be successfully realised" (p. 39). This type of performance, of game-play virtuosity, represents a considerable nontrivial effort, and furthermore, this effort suggests a type of "textual" mastery that represents a significant break with prior media, that cannot be explain easily with the notion of remediation.

Role-playing

The genre of adventure or role-playing games (RPG) is closely tied to the literary genre of fantasy. Both King and Krzywinska (2002, p. 29), and Bolter and Grusin (1999, p. 94) describe the genre as remediated Tolkien. This assertion misses a key stage in the mediation and remediation process of the RPG: the pencil-and-paper role playing game, of which the most widely known is DUNGEONS AND DRAGONS (1974). To emphasize the importance of addressing this oversight it is necessary to briefly explain the difference between pencil-and-paper role-playing and "Tolkien" as a stand-in for the fantasy genre as a whole.

DUNGEONS AND DRAGONS (1974) differed considerably from fantasy literature, in that the game was primarily a set of rules for interaction between players and the fantasy environment. One of the players would take on responsibility for the environment and minor characters (the DM, or Dungeon Master), whereas the other players would create one or more characters to play within the world created by the DM. The story took place in the imagination of the players, as they each described their actions and the DM in turn described the results of their actions, perhaps referring to the rules, and to die rolls—should the rules demand a random factor. The key change in the role-playing game that came with the remediation into video game format is that— initially—they lost their primarily social aspect, as the original games were single player. In most computer RPGs, the computer replaces the role of the DM, not only in facilitating the players' actions within the fantasy world but in creating the fantastic environment in which those actions take place.

By acknowledging that remediation to computer significantly alters the RPG, in become possible to explore what exactly is lost in the process. In an interview with www.WomenGamers.Com, Gary Gygax, cocreator of DUNGEONS AND DRAGONS (1974) points out: "the player assumes a character model and takes action in that environment, without any real role-playing at all. Try suggesting something to a computer that isn't in the program, of course" (Gel214th, 2000). To expand this point, I maintain that the key difference between pencil-and-paper RPGs and computer RPGs is that the game is no longer a collectively produced fantasy, but one which takes place within an official fantasy world with strictly defined parameters. Furthermore, it shifts the focus of the games from role-playing, and character development, to a series of purely functional physical challenges where success is measured by the accumulation of rewards. As Newman (2002, p. 1) argues, the character in the computer RPG is not valued in terms of a character in a novel or another medium but only in terms of a set of characteristics.

I suggest that key to understanding this shift to valuing characters in video games in terms of characteristics is Myers' (2003, p. 19) notion of "character transformations." This notion is of particular importance in the role-playing genre as it is through character transformations that the character develops. In STAR WARS: KNIGHTS OF THE OLD REPUBLIC (2003) the player is given periodic opportunities to assign new skills to their characters, which transforms the role of that character within the game. As the game contains over one hundred assignable "feats" and "powers" the various combinations possible are myriad, and are contextualized within the game and assigned relative values through the game's play, in much the same way as the variables within the strategy game. The remediation of role-playing to computers changed the focus of the games from character development to the acquisition of characteristics that are contextualized and valued through play.

The contextualization of these transformative characteristics potentially involves quite complex understandings of the various characteristics and their transformative roles. Myers (2003, p. 12) describes this as a specific cultural knowledge. He implies that RPGs operate intertextually, as the context of the game is often larger than the individual game: "significations conducted during current game play more and more often referred to a single, all-encompassing context determined beyond the immediacy of current game play" (Myers, 2003, p. 117). The context comes not from the game itself, but by the contextualizing play of many individuals who collectively form a discourse that assigns value to the various transformations. Myers states, "Websites, fanzines, cheat sheets, walkthroughs, message boards, and a variety of supplemental publications provided further extensions to and reinforcements of the . . . game context" (2003, p. 178). RPG—rather than losing their social aspect through remediation— formed the beginnings of the notion of the game community. This genre of video games, although not remediating the communal aspect of pencil-and-paper role-playing tapped into an already formed community that was based partially about contextualizing character transformations. The development of the Internet has led to a proliferation of official, and unofficial, game-based or game-centered communities, which eventually included all genres of video games.

These communities primarily use bulletin boards or blogs to communicate, although some of the more popular sites may also have a chat room. Most games that are primarily played online, such as STARCRAFT (1998), HALF-LIFE: COUNTERSTRIKE (2000), and MEDAL OF HONOR ALLIED ASSAULT (2002) have incorporated chat functions into the game to allow players on the same team to communicate, or to abuse and taunt members of opposing teams. However, Massive Multi-player Online RPGs (MMORPGs) blur the boundary between game and community completely; in "Computer Game Studies: Year One" Aarseth (2001, p. 2) describes this shift as the social arena of the game becoming the game itself. Thus, I suggest that MMORPGs should be conceptualized as a convergent technology. In *New Media: An Introduction*, Terry Flew (2002, p. 18) defines convergence as "the bringing together of the computing, telecommunications, and media and information sectors." Convergence has allowed a complex and participatory practice to be remediated. The only factor lacking in the new MMORPGs that differentiates them from pencil-and-paper role-playing games is that they lack the DM, whose role is replaced by the programmed environment and augmented by company employees who monitor the interactions between players'. I suggest that adventure or RPGs are an example of the notion of remediation. However, the focus on the visual and on immediacy as a strategy of remediation, glosses over the complex, social and participatory nature of play which is apparent in convergent MMORPGs, and which also exists in other games— either within the game in the form of chat, or outside in the form of extra-textual Web-based chat and bulletin boards. In the case of MMORPGs, the remediation is not simply one of content, but also of a social practice.

Discussion

Returning to Caldwell's (2004) argument that the divergent representational aesthetics of video games make it impossible to conceive them as a cohesive field,

I suggest that what is lost in understanding genre in purely visual terms in relation to video games is a notion of the various other generic features that can serve to both recognize similarities between games and to mark key distinctions. What is crucially important to video game genres is to be able to think of each individual game as belonging to several genres at once. This point forms the basis of the critical understanding of genre across all mediums. Steve Neale (2000, p. 16) in *Genre and Hollywood* points out that while some film genres are indeed organized around the visual iconography of the film—for example the Western and Film Noir—other genres like melodrama and comedy have no consistent iconography and their generic classification refers to the films' narrative structure. I suggest that this points to the heterogenous and multifaceted use to which the notion of genre is put, as—in the case of cinema as Neale points out—genre is used in a way that both marks its distinct qualities and connects it back to prior media forms that it is remediating.

Video games may share many features with other media forms; however, I believe that it is crucial to acknowledge that running contra to the "neat" categories defined by the industry are emerging "messy" categories that cross the traditional boundaries of video game genres to place visually disparate games into new circuits of connectivity. It is by turning to the notion of "interactivity" in particular, that these new notions of video game genre are able to emerge from the domination of remediated genre categories. This shift away from the visual and narrative understanding of video game genres is the key point of departure for this article. Although it follows others who have demarcated this territory, it also follows as a strategic move the notion of ludology. Although I find the ludological position questionable, I agree with Patrick Crogan's (2004, p. 13) reflection upon it in "The Game Thing: Ludology and Other Theory Games" that the primary virtue of this "movement" has been the problematization of the smooth application of narrative theory to new media.

The general acceptance of this aspect of the ludologists' argument is follows a key development in the study of new media in general. The ludologists' concern that narrative is not entirely relevant for understanding games is accompanied by a more deep-seated ambivalence toward narratives from some scholars within the field of new media. In "Digital Filmmaking and Special Effects," Sean Cubitt (2002, pp. 26–27) argues that narrative is just one possible system of organizing new media and suggests that the structure and use of new media like Photoshop encourages a system of organization that he dubs "post narrative spatialization."

In particular, the removal of narrative as the key concept in understanding video games reflects a major strand of contemporary film studies. Following the work of Tom Gunning (1989) in "An Aesthetic of Astonishment: Early Film and the (In)Credulous Spectator," there has been a tendency toward connecting the emergent genre of special effects blockbuster with the non narrative and spectacular origins of early cinema. The move away from narrative has reinvigorated contemporary cinema studies as well as the study of video games. As King and Krywinska (2002, p. 3) point out, examining games in the light of cinema benefits the study of cinema as it encourages questioning of orthodox understanding of film inter-pretation. The end of narrative as the paramount defining feature of media is heralded in video games.

However, this turn away from narrative should be accompanied by an acknowledgement that video games, as well as being games are also, at least in part, textual, in that they make reference to what is outside of the game. Both Newman (2004, pp. 57–58) and Mia Consalvo (2003, p. 331) rally against the notion that all meaning in games is derived independently of context. Video games, they argue independently, are understood intertextually, through other media texts and through the shared experience of gaming. Certainly, to revisit the example of THE SIMPSONS: HIT AND RUN (2003), Bart's self-reflexive instructions to the player explicitly acknowledges an implied agreement between game designers and gamers that driving games—at least—will have rather similar sets of inputting controls. This agreed form of interaction suggests a consistent genre has been established. This contradicts Aarseth's (2004, p. 48) argument that games cannot be understood intertextually. Rather, they are played in negotiation with, and through understanding of, other video games. Consalvo (2003) widens the influences that shape the experience of play, arguing that game players bring to bear a wide range of medium-specific and general media in the production of meaning from a game: "They do not . . . discard knowledge of all other media while engaging with a primary text. Rather, they approach all of these media intertextually with knowledge of all informing all of their actions' (pp. 331–332). In support of this notion Newman (2004) states:

> Videogames do not exist within a vacuum. Rather, they reside, are produced, and are encountered within a web of intertextuality in which explicit and implicit references to other media forms proliferate in videogames, and in which videogames are referred to aesthetically and stylistically within other media. As such, advertising and marketing materials, not to mention the various and extensive tie-ins and spin-offs such as movies and cartoons, must be considered alongside the content of the game. (Pp. 57–58)

Conclusion

Through a critical examination of the current video game genres, a tension between an understanding of genre in terms of ergodicity or interactivity, and an understanding of video games purely in terms of the remediation of prior representational media emerges. Of the genres selected for examination, both the strategy and role-playing genres have their roots in pre-computer forms of play; whereas the simulation genre can be compared to nonentertainment computer simulations; finally the action genre is implicitly connected to cinema through its deployment of the terminology of that medium to mark key generic distinctions. Despite the clear connects to prior media forms, I maintain that a critical approach to video game genres in the light of ergodic interactivity suggests that a more useful generic layering exists. Both simulation and strategy provide general tropes for understanding video games as a whole. In addition, the genre of simulation also suggests that games can be organized according to how authentically they follow the rules of simulation as opposed to the demands of entertainment. The strategy genre highlights the distinction between games that require the constant attention and performance of the player, and those that require a more distant approach characterized by intervention. The action genre demonstrates a particular category of hyper-performative games, whereas the crucial element of the role-playing genre is understanding the way that generic conventions circulate between and within communities of players.

By shifting the focus of genre in video games from the imbroglio of visual, narrative, and interactive terminology to a specific focus on genres of interactivity, I suggest that a space is created that allows the scholar to examine games in a way that can classify them according to their underlying similarities rather than their superficial visual or narrative differences. This shift marks the unique function and role of video games within contemporary media.

Author's note

I would like to thank my wife Susana Mendéz Apperley, for her support and help during the process of producing this article, it is dedicated to her. Furthermore, I would like to thank Scott McQuire and Kate Hannah for their assistance and criticism during the writing process.

References

Aarseth, E. (1997). *Cybertext: Perspectives on ergodic literature.* Baltimore: The John Hopkins University Press.

Aarseth, E. (2001). Computer game studies, year one. *Game Studies, 1* (1). Retrieved 7 May 2005 from http://www.gamestudies.org/0101/

Aarseth, E. (2004).Genre trouble: Narrativism and the art of simulation. In N. Wardrip-Fruin & P. Harrigan (Eds.), *FirstPerson: New media as story, performance, and game.* Cambridge, MA: The MIT Press.

ADVENT. (1976). Will Crowther and Don Woods.

Atkins, B. (2003). *More than a game: The computer game as a fictional form.* Manchester, UK: Manchester University Press.

Bolter, J. D., & Grusin, R. (1999). *Remediation: Understanding new media.* Cambridge, MA: The MIT Press.

Brooker, W. (2001).The many lives of the Jetman: A case study in computer game analysis. *Intensities: The Journal of Cult Media, 2.* Retrieved 7 May 2005 from http://www.cult-media.com/issue2/Abrook.htm

BUFFY THE VAMPIRE SLAYER. (2002). The Collective, Electronic Arts.

Caldwell, N. (2004). Theoretical frameworks for analysing turn-based computer strategy games. *Media International Australia, 110,* 42–51.

Carr, D. (2003). Play dead—genre and affect in Silent Hill and Planescape Torment. *Game Studies, 3*(1). Retrieved 7 May 2005 from http://www.gamestudies.org/0301/carr/

Consalvo, M. (2003). Zelda 64 and video game fans: A walk through of games, intertextuality and narrative. *Television and New Media, 4* (3), 321–334.

CRASH NITRO KART. (2003). Vicarious Visions, VU Games.

Crogan, P. (2004). The game thing: Ludology and other theory games. *Media International Australia, 110,* 10–18.

Cubitt, S. (2002). Digital filmmaking and special effects. In D. Harries (Ed.), *The new media book* (pp. 2627). London: BFI.

DAKAR 2. (2003). Acclaim, Acclaim.

DUNGEONS AND DRAGONS. (1974). Gary Gygax and Dave Arneson, TSR.

Flew, T. (2002). *New media: An introduction.* Melbourne, Australia: Oxford University Press.

Frasca, G. (2003). Simulation versus narrative: Introduction to ludology. In M. J. P. Wolf & B. Perron (Eds.), *The video game theory reader.* New York: Routledge.

Friedman, T. (1999). Civilisation and its discontents: Simulation, subjectivity and space. In G. M. Smith (Ed.), *On a silver platter: CD-ROMs and the promises of a new technology* (p. 137). New York: New York University Press.

Gunning, T. (1989). An aesthetic of astonishment: Early film and the (in)credulous spectator. *Art &Text, 34,* 31–45.

HALF-LIFE. (1998). Valve Software, Sierra Entertainment.

HALF-LIFE: COUNTERSTRIKE. (2000). Counterstrike Team, Sierra Entertainment.

Gel214. (2000, October 10). *Interview with Gary Gygax RPG Legend.* Retrieved 20 March 2005 from http://www.womengamers.com/interviews/garygygax.php

Jenkins, H., & Fuller, M. (1995).Nintendo® and new world travel writing: A dialogue. In S. G. Jones (Ed.), *Cyber society: Computer-mediated communication and community* (p.61).Thousand Oaks, CA: Sage.

Jenkins, H., & Squire, K (2003).The art of contested spaces. In L. King (Ed.), *Game on: The history and culture of video games* (p. 69). London: Lawrence King.

Juul, Jesper. (2001). Games telling stories? A brief note on games and narratives. *Game Studies, 1,* 1. Retrieved 29 September 2005 from http://www.gamestudies.org/0101/juul-gts/

King, G., & Krzywinska, T. (Eds.). (2002). *ScreenPlay: Cinema/videogames/interfacings.* London: Wallflower Press.

Kline, S., Dyer-Witheford, N., & De Peuter, G. (2003). *Digital play: The interaction of technology, culture, and marketing.* Montreal, Canada: McGill-Queen's University Press.

Kryzwinska, T. (2002). Hands-on horror. In G. King & T. Kryzwinska (Eds.), *ScreenPlay: Cinema/videogame/interfaces* (pp. 207). London: Wallflower Press.

THE LORD OF THE RINGS: RETURN OF THE KING. (2003). EA Games, EA Games.

Manovich, L. (1996).The labour of perception. In L. Hershman Leeson (Ed.), *Clicking in: Hot links to a digital culture* (pp. 184–185). Seattle: Bay Press.

MEDAL OF HONOR ALLIED ASSAULT. (2002). 2015, EA Games.

Morris, S. (2002). First person shooters—a game apparatus. In G. King & T. Krzywinska (Eds.), *ScreenPlay: Cinema/videogames/interfacings* (pp. 82–85). London: Wallflower.

Murray, J.H. (1997). *Hamlet on the Holodeck: The future of narrative in cyberspace.* New York: Free Press.

Myers, D. (2003). *The nature of computer games: Play as semiosis.* New York: Peter Lang.

Neale, S. (2000). *Genre and Hollywood.* London: Routledge.

Newman, J.(2002).The myth of the ergodic videogame: Some thoughts on player-character relationships in videogames. *Game Studies, 2*(1), 1–8.

Newman, J. (2004). *Video games.* London: Routledge.

PROJECT GOTHAM RACING 2. (2003). Bizarre Creations, Microsoft.

Schatz, T. (1981). *Hollywood genres: Formulas, filmmaking, and the studio system.* Philadelphia: Temple University Press.

Schliener, A.-M. (2001). Does Lara Croft wear fake polygons? Gender and gender role subversion in computer adventure games. *Leonardo, 34* (3), 222–224.

SIM CITY. (1989). Maxis, Maxis.

THE SIMS. (2000). Maxis, Maxis.

THE SIMPSONS: HIT AND RUN. (2003). Radical Entertainment, VU Games.

SPACEWAR! (1962). Steve Russell, Peter Samson, Dan Edwards, and Martin Graetz.

STAR WARS: KNIGHTS OF THE OLD REPUBLIC. (2003). BioWare, LucasArts.

STARCRAFT. (1998). Blizzard Entertainment, Blizzard Entertainment.

Wolf, M.J.P. (Ed.). (2001). *The medium of the video game.* Austin: University of Texas Press.

42

CAMERA-EYE, CG-EYE

Videogames and the "cinematic"

Will Brooker

Source: *Cinema Journal*, 48(3), Spring 2009, 122–128.

I used to be good at games. I was good at the only *Space Invaders* machine in South London, in 1979. I was the first kid to have a ZX Spectrum in my school, in 1982. I published in the national games magazine *Crash* when I was seventeen. But since the age of eighteen and my first degree, I've concentrated on cinema. So this article comes from a film studies perspective; I've relied on game experts for many of my examples. Because I'm no longer good enough at games, I haven't been able to play through to witness most of these scenes first-hand. I've had to watch them at a secondary remove, as records of other people's achievement. That is, I've had to watch game scenes as *films*.

Of course, one of the reasons I focused on cinema is that you couldn't study games academically in 1988. You couldn't even take a degree solely in cinema: my degree was unusually progressive, offering fifty percent film and a token module in television. Since then, film studies has become higher status, moderately established, and respectable—on the middle-rung of the ladder between the academic study of television, games, and comics at one end, and literature at the other. By extension, complaints about the careless adaptation of *Doom* (Andrej Bartkowiak, 2005) and *Daredevil* (Mark Steven Johnson, 2003) may rage across discussion boards but rarely make it beyond fan communities, whereas issues about the adaptation of Austen or *Atonement* (Joe Wright, 2007) from their original literary texts are debated in broadsheet newspapers.

The "videogame" film

Because fidelity to the original is of low priority when porting from games to cinema, direct adaptations of videogames—with rare exceptions—have little in common with the aesthetics and conventions of the source material, and resemble the game primarily only in mise-en-scène and costume design. *Lara Croft: Tomb Raider* (Simon West, 2001), for instance, ignores the opportunity to re-create the player's experience by having Lara "seen to die, even if only on one occasion, and then to be able to restart a sequence, game-style, for another attempt." Its occasional references to the game-world constitute "insubstantial nods . . . rather than anything central to the structure or form of the film."[1]

However, a more general conception of the "videogame-style film" can be established from references to diverse movies that incorporate game conventions while not adapting a specific game. On a broad aesthetic level, the term "video game" is used to connote spectacular, showy displays of effects at the expense of subtext and character, as in: Tony Scott's bravura digital camerawork in *Déja Vu* (2006);[2] the spectacle that overwhelms ideas in *I, Robot* (Alex Proyas, 2004);[3] *The Matrix's* emotionless, uninvolving stunts (Andy and Larry Wachowski, 1999);[4] the exhibition bouts between CGI monsters in *King Kong* (Peter Jackson, 2005);[5] and the dense, detailed, but artificial action sequences of George Lucas's *Star Wars* prequels (1999, 2002, 2005).[6] More directly, critics and fans have identified specific videogame memes in films, such as the progression through levels, power-ups, and signature moves in *Ong-Bak* (Prachya Pinkaew, 2003),[7] the "get all weapons" cheat code in *The Matrix*,[8] and the platform-jumping in *Attack of the Clones* (George Lucas, 2002) droid factory. These are regarded as playful, knowing quotations and in-jokes along the lines of the Lara Croft "nods" or, in the latter case, as cynical cross-marketing through the placement of a scene that was immediately adapted to PlayStation and Xbox.

Finally, "videogame" style in films suggests a certain form of narrative, based on the cycles of character-death and reset. Charles Ramirez Berg traces the "Tarantino effect" in recent cinema to the influence of postmodern resistance to master narratives, of hypertext links, and of videogames, which "repeatedly take players back to the same situations."[9] Similarly, Jeff Gordinier identifies the "PlayStation Generation" of twenty-first-century-filmmakers, who "mess with narrative in new ways [. . .] mess with time, with space, with the laws of physics and the structure of story" and "bring to their movies the cut-and-paste sensibility of video games and the internet."[10] This is the reading of videogame conventions that leads Warren Buckland to identify "videogame logic" in Luc Besson's (1995) *The Fifth Element's* "serialised repetition," including a "feedback loop" and "space warp,"[11] and prompts Margit Grieb and Kate Stables to discuss *Run Lola Run* (Tom Twyker, 1999) and *Groundhog Day* (Harold Ramis, 1993) respectively as game-style cinema because of their looping mini-narratives and retelling of the same story with variations, like repeated attempts at the same level.[12] Like Berg and Gordinier, Grieb's discussion of *Run Lola Run* links the repetition and non-linearity that structure the film's narrative not just to games but to other forms of digital media—"websites, hypertext stories, interactive CD-ROMs."[13]

The implications of this overlap between cinema and games are mixed: on one hand, importing videogame conventions suggests a fast-and-loose, "cut-and-paste" resistance to traditional narrative rules, with overtones of rebellious youth (Berg describes "playing with narration" as "cool and fun," and refers to Tarantino's "wild" techniques). On the other hand, videogame aesthetics are associated with empty spectacle and cynical attempts at cross-platform marketing, both of which are presumed to take precedence over character and traditional storytelling. Common to both readings is a sense of digital novelty and technological innovation, whether in the bold slicing and reworking of story like a word-processed document, the web-style clicking through branching narratives, or the flashy showcasing of state-of-the-art effects.

The deliberate association with a lower-status form like videogames brings a movie down to a trashier, edgier, funkier level; it sacrifices any claims to serious art (unless it also carries the exotic kudos of "foreign" cinema, such as anime) but it gains a hip attitude. *Crank* (Mark Neveldine and Brian Taylor, 2006), reviewed in *Film Journal International* as "among the most mindless action films ever made, but . . . a helluva video game," is a prime example of this trade-off.[14] The movie refers explicitly to gaming conventions and history, both superficially (screens from the 1980 arcade game *Berzerk!* and a pastiche of the PC game-emulator MAME) and on the level of storytelling. Its plot is made up of fast-paced missions with a single goal; its visual perspective switches from ground-level chase to Google Earth map views. Its aesthetic is *Grand Theft Auto*, and it makes the debt clear with visual nods to *GTA's* producers, Rockstar Games. The film was written off by one reviewer as "the latest stab by Hollywood to cash in on the violent video game craze," and, tellingly, slated for its similarity to "any recent output by Tony Scott."[15] The movie's teen-punk response to criticism, in turn, is built into its opening credits, in the form of a high-score table: "FUC," "YOU," "ASS," "HOL."

The "cinematic" game

The connotations of the "cinematic" in videogaming are very different. King and Krzywinska identify an assumption within the industry that "more cinematic equals 'better' . . . a judgement accepted by many reviewers."[16] Cinema, as they recognize, has greater cultural prestige and a "standing higher in our dominant cultural hierarchies . . . a factor that adds to its potential appeal to the games industry."[17] Mark J. P. Wolf's taxonomy of on- and off-screen space in games is based on the same implicit approach of elevating the study of gaming through a comparison with film theory and cinematic form—just as theories of authorship, borrowed from literature, dignified popular cinema in the 1950s and 60s. Wolf finds a parallel between the scrolling of *Defender* (Williams Electronics, 1982) and the panning in Edwin S. Porter's *Life of an American Fireman* (1903) and Cecil Hepworth's *A Day with the Gypsies* (1906), while D. W. Griffith's cuts between adjacent spaces match the cuts between neighboring rooms in Atari's *Adventure* (1978).[18]

If these overlaps between the evolution of spatial storytelling in early (1900s) cinema and early (1970s) gaming were the result of technological limitations—in both cases, a static "camera"—by the mid-90s the process had become one of deliberate emulation. As Jo Bryce and Jason Rutter note, since the advent of the PC CD-Rom and the CD-driven PlayStation, both offering increased storage capacity, game designers of the late 1990s worked towards the holy grail of "interactive movies"—"movies," in this case, implying mainstream Hollywood.[19] Games from the mid-90s onwards attempted to incorporate this "cinematic" sense in a range of ways. Full-motion video, with real actors and sets (such as the casting of Mark Hamill and Malcolm McDowell in *Wing Commander III* [Origin, 1994]) proved to be a fad, phased out and replaced by pre-rendered, CGI sequences created on a more powerful computer than the games console itself. Ironically, this incorporation of high-quality, "filmic" visuals tended to disrupt the player's immersion in the diegesis, breaking the flow between cut-scene and gameplay.[20] Cut-scenes therefore improved, paradoxically, by becoming less smooth and polished; bridging scenes were increasingly generated "in-engine," created on the fly by the console, with no discrepancy in visual quality; and *Half-Life* (Valve, 2000) introduced a radical shift by keeping all exposition within the game-space, avoiding the shift between "playing" and "viewing."[21]

Capcom's *Resident Evil* games of 1997–1999 fit Wolf's theory of a parallel evolution between cinematic and game grammar by forcing the player to work within fixed camera angles, linked through the conventions of classical continuity editing. However, as King and Krzywinska note, "predetermined framing of this kind acts like that of a film . . . at the expense of player freedom," and this fixed camera positioning is, like full-motion video, rare in contemporary gaming.[22]

Twenty-first-century games continue to incorporate cinematic (and televisual) motifs—most obviously in their title sequences and credits and the use of "letterboxing" (appropriating TV's mediation of cinema) to signify a cut-scene[23] but also through in-game pastiche: the "bullet time" of *Max Payne*, inspired by John Woo through *The Matrix*, the *Saving Private Ryan* (Steven Spielberg, 1998) simulation in *Medal of Honor: Allied Assault* (EA, 2002), and the slow-motion stunt replays in *GTA: San Andreas* (Rockstar, 2004), which recall a range of sources from *Bullitt* (Peter Yates, 1968) to *Terminator 2* (James Cameron, 1991). The "realism" these games aspire to is a mediated truth—the experience not of being at war, but being in a war film. Similarly, King and Krzywinska recognize that within sports simulations, the "primary point of reference is television coverage of the sport, rather than the experience of the sport itself."[24] That games continue to simulate mediated experience is underscored by the way they digitally recreate the view through a camera lens, rather than the human eye: the golf game *Links 2004* (Microsoft, 2003), like the strategy war game *Ground Control* (Sierra, 2000) and the SF combat of *Halo: Combat Evoked* (Microsoft, 2001), incorporates the analogue oddity of lens flare; Max Payne experiences drug hallucination through a fish-eye lens, while *GTA: Vice City* (Rockstar, 2002) signifies rain through droplets on a glass surface, even when the player is outside a car.[25] Similarly, *American McGee's Alice* (EA, 2000) and *Silent Hill 4: The Room* (Konami, 2004) employ simulations of flickering, scratched celluloid as part of their horror repertoire.[26]

The videogame camera-eye and the cinematic avant-garde

Overall, however, the trajectory within games of the current decade has been away from a slavish emulation of the cinematic and towards the evolution of visual storytelling techniques that establish a unique mode, distinct from cinema— or more precisely, distinct from mainstream Hollywood. The experiments in "interactive movies" have demonstrated an unworkable tension between the cinematic (in terms of continuity editing and conventional film grammar) and the playable. Full-motion video cut-scenes break the player out of immersion in the diegesis, arguably like inter-titles in early films. Fixed camera angles restrict player movement and freedom, leading to an "on-rails" experience like a theme-park ride, rather than a convincing simulation. As Wee Liang Tong and Marcus Cheng Chye Tan conclude in their chapter on narrative space across the two forms, while many games "have intentionally mimicked and even attempted to out-do movies," what has emerged is "a distinctive mode of visualisation . . . [games are] unlike movies because they lack defining cinematic cues." Above all, it is "the employment of a free-ranging camera that breaks the rules of conventional cinema."[27] Again, the key term is *conventional* cinema.

Videogaming is currently dominated by two key camera positions, those of the Third-Person Shooter (TPS) and the First-Person Shooter (FPS). While, as noted, games are still dedicated to reproducing the visual effects of an analogue lens, these two key camera modes are very different from the camera-eye, and the associated editing, of mainstream cinema. The FPS point of view is generally assumed to have originated with *Wolfenstein 3D* (id, 1992), though it has precursors in the arcade game *Battlezone* (Atari, 1980) and the ZX81 *3D Monster Maze* (New Generation, 1982). *Wolfenstein* led to *Doom* (id, 1993), which led to *Quake* (id, 1996); these and further variants refined the details, texture, and lighting of the game environment, but retained the fundamental premise that the game "camera" represents the player's point of view. The TPS point of view can be traced to *Super Mario 64* (Nintendo, 1996), where it appears as a literal flying-eye camera, independent of the Mario avatar; the mode evolved through *Tomb Raider* (Eidos, 1996) and became the dominant POV in Rockstar's *Grand Theft Auto* when the series went 3D in 2001. In contrast to the FPS, this virtual camera "corresponds to no actual pair of eyes in the gameworld. The point of view from which we see Lara Croft is constantly moving, swooping, creeping up behind her and giddily soaring above, even diving below the putative floor level."[28]

Neither of these modes is conventionally "cinematic." We see a POV similar to the FPS in horror and science fiction, putting us in the position of the "Other"— the Terminator's digital scans of a barroom, or the Predator's infra-red vision. We witness Murphy's transformation to RoboCop through his helpless eyes (Paul Verhoeven, 1987) as we share Jean-Dominique Bauby's locked-down vision in *The Diving Bell and the Butterfly* (Julian Schnabel, 2007). Similarly, cinema invites us to share a character's enhanced vision through binoculars (see *Star Wars: A New Hope* [Lucas, 1977]) or a zoom lens (*Rear Window* [Alfred Hitchcock, 1954]).

Of course, the first-person POV shot is part of conventional film grammar—but it is a small part, a shot sparingly used. A sequence in an FPS game, from start until death, is a continuous point-of-view shot, and a technique so rare in cinema that its uses can be quickly listed: most obviously, the unsuccessful experiment of the first-person film noir, *The Lady in the Lake* (Robert Montgomery, 1947), and the scenes where we jack into a character's cerebral cortex in *Strange Days* (Kathryn Bigelow, 1995). *The Blair Witch Project* (Daniel Myrick and Eduardo Sanchez, 1999) and *Cloverfield* (Matt Reeves, 2008), which may seem to come closest to feature-length FPS, differ in that their point of view is explicitly a camera, which shakes, blurs, can be set down and passed from one character to another—quite distinct from the smooth, steady view of gaming, where the virtual "camera" is not held separate from the body, but embedded behind the eyes. (Tellingly, the television comedy *Peep Show* (Jesse Armstrong et al., 2003 onward) is shot from precisely this point of view, for its unnerving, uncanny effect.) The movie adaptation of *Doom* incorporated a first-person sequence as a novelty, another token nod to the source material, but switched back to conventional continuity editing for the majority of the film.

Where do we see the fluid, soaring, unbroken TPS camera in cinema? Again, the occasions stand out as remarkable. Orson Welles choreographed a swooping crane shot for the opening of *Touch of Evil* (1958); more recently, *Children of Men* (Alfonso Cuarón, 2006) and *Atonement* (Joe Wright, 2007) faked lengthy, mobile shots with a combination of camera rigs and CGI. As with the FPS, the most notable aspect of the third-person POV in games is (after its mobility) its *lack of cuts*: a technique that aligns it not with conventional Hollywood, but with Hitchcock's playful experiment in *Rope* (1948), with Greenaway's long tracking shots, with Tarkovsky's lengthy takes, with the unblinking stare at violence in *Irreversible* (Gaspar Noè, 2002) and *Hidden* (Michael Haneke, 2005); with rarities like *Timecode* (Mike Figgis, 2000) and *Russian Ark* (Alexander Sokurov, 2002).

The dominant camera of videogames, then, is far closer to that of *art cinema* than to mainstream Hollywood. The videogame's vision of "reality" is Bazinian, not Eisensteinian. Its virtual camera starts, records what happens without turning away, and cuts only at the end. While "videogame cinema," as discussed above, seems to imply an aesthetic of cut-and-paste and flashy, funky superficiality, the FPS and TPS modes actually look nothing like a Tony Scott movie. As cinema, the videogame would be not youthful rebellion, but the mature challenge of the avant-garde.

Notes

1 Geoff King and Tanya Krzywinska, "Introduction," in *ScreenPlay: Cinema/ Videogames/Interfaces*, ed. Geoff King and Tanya Krzywinska (London: Wallflower, 2002), 19.

2 Cammila Albertson, *All Movie Guide*, http://www.amazon.ca/Deja-Vu-Tony-Scott/dp/ B00005JPD0 (accessed March 17, 2008).

3 John Dale, *Autology*, August 9, 2004, http://blogs.warwick.ac.uk/johndale/tag/ culture/?num=20&start=20 (accessed March 17, 2008).

4 David Edelstein, cited in Henry Jenkins, *Convergence Culture: When Old and New Media Collide* (New York: New York University Press, 2006), 121.

5 C. Woodward, "King Kong Two Disc Special Edition," *DVD Active* (2002), http://www.dvdactive.com/reviews/dvd/king-kong-two-disc-special-edition2.html?post_id=64476&action=quote (accessed March 17, 2008).

6 Claudia Puig, "10 Movies That Sat Us Straight Up," *USA Today*, December 24, 2002, http://www.usatoday.com/life/movies/news/2002-12-23-top-ten-side_x.htm (accessed March 17, 2008).

7 Nathan Lee, "Traditional Storytelling, Video-Game Style," *New York Sun*, February 11, 2005, http://www.nysun.com/article/9068 (accessed March 17, 2008).

8 King and Krzywinska, "Introduction," 19.

9 Charles Ramirez Berg, "A Taxonomy of Alternative Plots in Recent Films: Classifying the 'Tarantino Effect,'" *Film Criticism* 31 (2006): 6.

10 Jeff Gordinier, cited in Kimberly A. Owczarski, "The Internet and Contemporary Entertainment: Rethinking the Role of the Film Text," *Journal of Film and Video* 59, no. 3 (Fall 2007): 3; see also Jenkins, *Convergence Culture*, 119.

11 Warren Buckland, "Video Pleasure and Narrative Cinema: Luc Besson's *The Fifth Element* and Video Game Logic," in *Moving Images: From Edison to the Webcam*, ed. John Fullerton and Astrid Soderberg Widding (London: John Libbey, 2000), 162.

12 Margit Grieb, "Run Lara Run," in King and Krzywinska, *ScreenPlay*, 161; Kate Stables, "Run Lara Run," *Sight and Sound* 11, no. 8 (August 2001): 19.

13 Grieb, "Run Lara Run," 165.

14 Bruce Feld "Crank," *Film Journal International* (2008), http://www.filmjournal.com/filmjournal/reviews/article_display.jsp?vnu_content_id=1003087415 (accessed March 17, 2008).

15 Brian Orndorf "Crank," *FilmJerk*, September 2, 2008, http://www.filmjerk.com/reviews/article.php?id_rev=916 (accessed March 17, 2008).

16 King and Krzywinska, "Introduction," 6.

17 Ibid., 7.

18 Mark J. P. Wolf, "Inventing Space: Toward a Taxonomy of On- and Off-Screen Space in Video Games," *Film Quarterly* 51, no. 1 (Autumn 1997): 15–16.

19 Jo Bryce and Jason Rutter, "Spectacle of the Deathmatch: Character and Narrative in First-Person Shooters," in King and Krzywinska, *ScreenPlay*, 161; Stables, "Run Lara Run," 66.

20 Geoff King and Tanya Krzywinska, *Tomb Raiders and Space Invaders: Videogame Forms & Contexts* (London: I.B. Tauris 2006), 135; Sacha A. Howells, "Watching a Game, Playing a Movie: When Media Collide," in *ScreenPlay*, 114–115.

21 Howells, "Watching a Game," 120.

22 King and Krzywinska, "Introduction," 13.

23 Howells, "Watching a Game," 118.

24 King and Krzywinska, *Tomb Raiders*, 136.

25 Ibid., 102–103.

26 See Ewan Kirkland, "The Self-Reflexive Funhouse of Silent Hill," *Convergence: The International Journal of Research into New Media Technologies* 13, no. 4 (2007): 410–411.

27 Wee Liang Tong and Marcus Cheng Chye Tan, "Vision and Virtuality: The Construction of Narrative Space in Film and Computer Games," in King and Krzywinska, *ScreenPlay*, 109.

28 Steven Poole, *Trigger Happy: The Inner Life of Videogames* (London: Fourth Estate, 1999), 145–146.

43

COLOR-CYCLED SPACE FUMES IN THE PIXEL PARTICLE SHOCKWAVE

The technical aesthetics of *Defender* and the
Williams arcade platform, 1980–82

Brett Camper

Source: Mark J. P. Wolf (ed.), *Before the Crash: Early Video Game History* (Detroit, MI: Wayne State University Press, 2012), pp. 168–188.

In today's gaming press, it's common enough to hear about pixel shaders, polygons per second, the Cell chip, and the network speed and latency of our current game hardware—the Xbox 360, the Playstation 3, the iPhone, or the latest PC graphics boards. This technical fetishization is not always helpful in assessing games as meaningful play experiences, but it does tell us something about the underlying materials that those games are made from. Computing platforms are about constraints, the techniques they do or don't allow a game designer or artist to use, qualitative and quantitative differences in visual style: the raster-based pixels that dominated the 8-bit and 16-bit PC and console eras, the sparse, brightly lit early arcade vector graphics of *Asteroids* (1979) or *Major Havoc* (1983), the 3-D filled-polygon graphics and lighting effects that have ruled the cutting edge since the 1990s. But in gaming history, we rarely hear this level of technical depth applied to earlier eras. Here I hope to redirect some of our current technical obsessions, going back to the pioneering arcade games released by Williams Electronics between 1980 and 1982, beginning with one of the best-selling and most challenging arcade games of all time: *Defender* (1980).

We often don't think of an arcade game as running on a *platform* in the way that we naturally do for home computers—the Commodore 64 or Apple II then, Windows 7 or OS X now—or dedicated gaming consoles (the Atari VCS or the PlayStation 3). But that's exactly how many arcade makers came to think of them: as stable, repeatable hardware designs that could be repurposed or incrementally tweaked across different games, providing a common set of capabilities that both simplified the game development process and drove down the costs of manufacturing, distribution, and other logistics. Usually, we assume that the platform comes first, and the games programmed for it are second. Yet, especially in video games' formative years, this progression was often flipped, with particular game designs shaping platform hardware directly. In *Racing the Beam*, their study of the Atari VCS, Montfort and Bogost describe the ways in which Atari's home console was built, from the circuit board level up, with the previous arcade successes *PONG* (1972) and *Tank!* (1974) in mind, and the latter was expanded into the VCS pack-in *Combat* (1977) (both games were released in the arcade by Kee Games, a wholly owned subsidiary of Atari intended to foster the illusion of industry competition). They also note that Steve Wozniak included key features, such as color graphics, in the Apple II home computer hardware based on his prior experience developing the *Breakout* (1976) arcade board.[1]

When Williams Electronics designed their 1980 arcade hit *Defender*, they established a foundational hardware platform that they would go on to use for six more titles, beginning with the sequel *Stargate* in 1981. They continued with further commercial and critical successes in 1982 with *Robotron: 2084, Joust,* and *Sinistar.* But that year the company also released two offbeat and less-known experiments: *Bubbles* (see Figure 1), in which a player-controlled soap bubble scrubs a sink clean while defending from approaching vermin, growing ever-larger in a mechanic that anticipates Namco's *Katamari Damacy* (2004) by 25 years; and *Splat!*, a one-on-one food fight with conveyor belts of food and a bizarre mechanic that triggers the detachment of the player character's head. While the core hardware remained constant across all seven machines, Williams expanded the platform incrementally to serve individual game designs: *Robotron* necessitated dedicated graphics-blitting chips to draw its overwhelming hoard of enemies on a single screen, while *Sinistar* was noted for the speech synthesis of its menacingly omniscient antagonist. This essay introduces this influential video game platform through a close analysis of *Defender*'s visual aesthetics, its technical underpinnings, and its relationship to other games of its day. In doing so, I aim to bring Montfort and Bogost's concept of *platform studies* to the realm of the early arcade.

From *Defender* onward, the computing hardware for all seven early Williams games is organized across five circuit boards: the main CPU and video board, responsible for running the game code, juggling the unfolding game state in 48KB of RAM (random-access memory), and assembling the screen graphics in real-time; the ROM (read-only memory) board, which holds all static data in the game (such as code and graphics that "make up" the game and persist when the machine is turned off), also totaling 48KB of memory; the sound board, with its own CPU and ROM for generating sound effects; the interface controller, handling player input from the cabinet in the form of joystick and button presses; and the power supply, providing electricity not only to the other boards, but also to the cabinet itself, powering elements like the lights above the monitor and behind the "marquee" advertising the game up top. For our graphical analysis of *Defender*, it is the CPU, video, and RAM elements that are most influential.

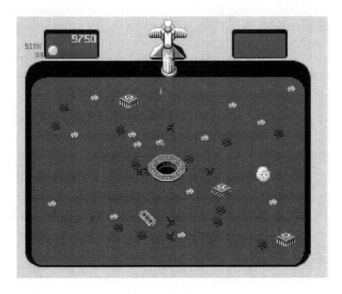

Figure 1 From 1980 to 1982, Williams released seven arcade games that shared the same basic hardware platform. Among classics such as *Defender* and *Joust* are lesser known titles with unusual premises: in *Bubbles*, the player cleans a sink

All early Williams arcade games use the 1MHz Motorola 6809E chip as their main CPU, driving the core game logic and coordinating with other elements of the platform, such as the dedicated sound and graphics hardware. The 6809 is an 8-bit processor first released in 1977, a follow-up of sorts to two other influential chips of the era: the Motorola 6800 (1974), and the MOS Technology 6502 (1975); the latter, the 6502, was the basis for many of the most well-known and successful computing platforms of the 8-bit era, including the Commodore 64, Atari VCS, and Nintendo Famicom (known as the Nintendo Entertainment System, NES, in the United States). The 6809 itself was also used in home-based computer and game consoles, including the short-lived, vector-based Vectrex game system, Radio Shack's TRS-80 Color Computer, and in Japan, Fujitsu's FM-7 personal computer.

As arcade emulation pioneer Aaron Giles notes, "the 6809 was hugely popular for arcade games, being used by Williams, Namco, Konami, Exidy, Atari, and a whole host of other game manufacturers."[2] According to the list of game ROMs supported by the popular (and de facto authority) Multiple Arcade Machine Emulator (MAME), an impressive 660 of the 8544 currently compatible ROM images are from games using a 6809 processor in some capacity (though not all of these games use a 6809 as the main CPU; in many cases, the chip could serve an auxiliary purpose, such as for specific sound or graphics tasks, or as a companion CPU).[3] In other words, 7.7 percent of all MAME ROMs, representing games from the 1970s through today, rely on 6809 emulation. Influential 6809-based arcade games beyond those from Williams include *Qix* (1981), *Mappy* (1983), *I, Robot* (1983), *Gyruss* (1983), and *Tower of Druaga* (1984), among others. However, according to MAME, Williams's *Defender* is the earliest 6809 game, and the series of successful Williams games from 1980–83 may certainly have contributed to the establishment of the chip as a standard arcade building block.[4]

Indeed, in a January 1979 *BYTE* magazine article chronicling the history of the 6809 processor, chip designers Joel Boney and Terry Ritter cite games and other consumer-oriented products as a core business driver not only of the 6809 but of the entire industry, the necessary motivator to move microprocessor development beyond the earlier, unwieldy mainframes that had dominated academic and early business computing: "Only when microprocessors entered high volume markets (hobby, games, etc.) did the manufacturers begin to make money and thus provide a credible reason (and funds) for designing future microprocessors."[5] Enter Williams Electronics, Namco Ltd., Taito Corporation, and the other companies that established the arcade format—a new hybrid between consumer electronics manufacturers and media entertainment publishers.

Like many companies seeking to understand and enter the very young arcade market of the 1970s, the first computer-driven arcade game that Williams created was a straight copy of Atari's *PONG* (1972): it was called *Paddle Ball* and was released in 1973. *Paddle Ball* was computationally simplistic, with one collector noting that the game "pre-dates the practical application of a processor chip. The computer board is 'one big processor,'" with a matrix of individual logic chips strung together in place of a single CPU.[6] Although *Paddle Ball* likely made Williams more comfortable in this new market, the true start of their creative and commercial success—and historical importance for gaming—was *Defender*, the first of the games to use the arcade platform described in this chapter, released in 1980.

Defender is known for its notorious difficulty and frantic pace, with *Edge Magazine* giving it the nod for #6 on its list of "The Best 50 Games of the 1980s": "With its daunting array of controllers (five buttons and a joystick), a range of bad guys sporting complex behaviours, plus a weird control system drenched in inertia . . . Eugene Jarvis's uniquely challenging creation for Williams remains one of the most difficult-to-master video games ever conceived."[7] *Defender* pioneered new gameplay concepts and technologies, such as the use of a "mini-map" or radar for tracking gamespace beyond the visible screen area, an inaugural distinction it shares with Atari's *BattleZone* (1980). Both games debuted at the Amusement and Music Operators Association (AMOA) trade show in 1980, and the idea appears to have been simultaneously developed independently. Although *Defender* was not the first game to provide continuous screen scrolling (a breakthrough first found in Kee Games/Atari's top-down racing game *Super Bug* in 1977), it is likely the first side-scrolling shooter, making it an influence on the entire genre of spaceship-centric, 2-D shoot-'em-ups popularized by titles such as Konami's *Gradius* (1985) (though not a true genre ancestor, as there are significant conceptual differences in gameplay style, spatial modeling, and goal structure between *Defender* and such titles). Another notable element is the mountainous terrain that comprises the planetary surface above which the player flies, providing a more naturalistic variation in the environment than the typical hard-edge, straight-line game graphics.

From a technological historical perspective, however, the most immediately striking aspect of *Defender* is its raw sense of speed, an ability to present the player with fluid, split-second-decision scenarios as immersive as those of any present-day gaming technology—despite its lowly 1MHz processor, which was responsible not only for all gameplay logic, but also for "pixel-pushing" its 60-frames-per-second graphics in tandem. How is *Defender* able to accomplish this with such relatively under-powered hardware? Its aesthetic style is closely matched to its particular technical architecture, and perhaps surprisingly, the game's most distinctive effects are arguably the result of a *lack* of the type of dedicated tile-and-sprite graphics hardware that became common on competing arcade platform designs.

What do I mean by a lack of hardware? When *Defender* was released in 1980, two key conceptual models for storing screen graphics were maturing in parallel. The first and most straightforward model is that used by *Defender*: the *framebuffer*, an area of (usually contiguous) memory that stores a value for each pixel on screen. One obvious advantage of the framebuffer is that it is easily graspable, with a logic that directly mirrors the way the video monitor is physically constructed: one pixel location on screen, one pixel location in memory. As the monitor's electron gun scans across the screen, the video hardware reads the corresponding pixel location in memory. For game aesthetics, the most important advantage of the framebuffer is flexibility—each pixel can be manipulated individually. But as Aaron Giles explains, this flexibility is also the model's downside: "Keep in mind that a typical arcade game is approximately 256 pixels by 256 pixels, so even just clearing the screen requires $256 \times 256 = 65,536$ operations. If each operation takes 4 clock cycles, then that is about 1/4 of a second on a 1 MHz CPU!"[8] There are simply too many pixels for the processor to keep up.

To solve this problem, hardware designers developed a second screen graphics model: the *tile-map*. In a tile-map, the screen is divided into a grid of smaller areas ("tiles"), typically 8x8 pixels each for this era of hardware. A limited number of 8×8-pixel tiles are stored for the common, repeatable elements in the game world. For example, arbitrarily shaped "walls" can be easily created by stringing together tiles for horizontal and vertical wall segments, with 90- or 45-degree corner pieces used to join them. At heart, the basic logic behind a tile-map is no different from that of LEGOs or other common toys that construct larger structures from a small set of individual pieces. Instead of needing to store one location in memory for each pixel, the programmer need only store one location in memory for *each tile*: the tiles are numbered, with each tile value mapping (hence, the name) to a unique type of 8x8-pixel tile. To draw the screen, the hardware first reads the tile number, and then looks up the pixel pattern for that tile. From a hardware performance standpoint, the primary advantage of the tile-map over the framebuffer is an exponential reduction in the amount of memory needed to store one screen's worth of information—and by extension, an equal reduction in the amount of processing power and time needed to make changes to that screen. Giles does the math: "a game with 256 by 256 pixels would need a 32 by 32 tilemap to cover that area with 8x8 graphics tiles . . . At 4 cycles per operation, clearing the screen happens in a brisk 1/250th of a second for a 1 MHz CPU."[9] In short, the tile-map requires *64 times less* memory and processing time.

The framebuffer and tile-map hardware models coexisted in the industry, and Giles points out that outwardly similar games of the same genre took different routes in their graphics implementations: Taito's *Space Invaders* (1978) used a classic framebuffer, while Namco's *Galaxian* (1979) introduced the tile-map model—most likely as a competitive response, enabling the more sophisticated enemy-swooping patterns for which the latter is known, not to mention freeing up memory to allow for color graphics (*Space Invaders* was a strictly 1-bit, monochrome experience). The framebuffer used by *Defender* and subsequent Williams games has a visible area of 292×240 pixels. This screen resolution is distinct from, yet similar in scale, to the other arcade games of its era: *Space Invaders* (1978) was 224×240 pixels, *Galaxian* (1979) was 224×256, and *Pac-Man* (1980) and *Mappy* (1983) were both 224×288. But whatever the reason, the exact 292×240 resolution was not a common one, and according to MAME's game list was used almost exclusively by Williams games.[10]

Each of these 70,080 pixels is one of 16 colors, chosen by the programmer from a total selection of 256 possible colors. A palette of 16 simultaneous colors is a widely shared feature of early 1980s graphics hardware: the Commodore 64, MSX, and PC EGA home computers all use 16-color palettes, as do fellow arcade games such as *Pac-Man* and *Mappy*.

However, in all of those preceding examples, the 16 colors are fixed; the specific set of colors is literally baked into the hardware, either in the graphics chip itself, such as in the Commodore 64's VIC-II, or on a dedicated chip called a "color PROM" in the case of an arcade board.[11] The Williams platform, by contrast, gives the designer considerably more control, allowing the particular 16 colors displayed at any one time to be manipulated by the programmer. In hardware, each color is defined as a single byte, or 8 bits, allocated as 3 bits of red, 3 bits of green, and 2 bits of blue. Forced to partition 8 bits across 3 colors, it is no accident that the blue is short-changed. When a human perceives brightness on an RGB video screen, the eye is 10 times more sensitive to green than to blue: the green contributes about 71 percent of the sensation of brightness, the red 21 percent, and the blue a mere 7 percent.[12] This blue perception imbalance has a long history of influence in the design of display hardware, right up to today—Google's Nexus One mobile phone, for instance, uses an AMOLED display with subpixels that intentionally provide more physical resolution for the green components, de-emphasizing the red and blue.[13] For the early 1980s Williams games, the practical consequence of the 3-3-2 RGB bit pattern is that for each color definition, the programmer can mix colors by choosing from eight levels of intensity for red and green each, but only four such levels for blue.

While the visible screen area is 292×240, the underlying video memory area is larger, with a full capacity of 304×256 pixels (see Figure 2). Why the discrepancy? As with almost all 1980s video hardware that output to a CRT-based, NTSC television, portions of the screen were often deliberately omitted. At the heart of the CRT television is an "electron gun" that is constantly scanning the screen from left to right, top to bottom, literally shooting onto the glass. TVs of the time (especially those from the 1970s or earlier) were often poorly calibrated, and there was no guarantee that the screen's edges would align from set to set. To alleviate the problem, hardware designers stuck to a "safe zone," with the discarded video areas known as "overscan." Even though Williams was designing arcade games with their own dedicated monitors, rather than games for home televisions, they still had to contend with individually calibrated monitors in arcades across the country. The need to avoid manual maintenance wherever possible influenced arcade hardware platform design.

There is also a hardware convenience to the particular 256 pixel height. Unlike most video framebuffers (especially on contemporary platforms), which are organized in a linear, horizontal fashion with bytes incrementing pixel locations from left to right, the Williams framebuffer is laid out vertically, two columns of pixels at a time: a zigzag pattern that traces two pixels right, then skips down one row and back two pixels before continuing (see Figure 3). The two-column layout is due to the platform's palette depth of 16 colors. Each pixel is stored in 4 bits

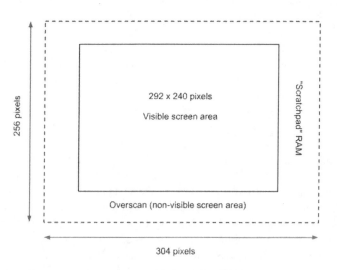

Figure 2 The Williams arcade platform had a total video framebuffer size of 304×256 pixels, but only 292×240 pixels were visible; the nonvisible areas were used to adjust for monitor differences and could be co-opted by the programmer as extra "scratchpad" RAM

(since 4 bits contain a number between 0 and 15), meaning that two pixels are stored in every byte (which consists of 8 bits). Thus each byte in the framebuffer corresponds to two pixels side by side. But a 256-pixel height is relevant because it allows framebuffer locations to be easily encoded in a single 16-bit number. Thanks to the properties of binary math, if the "lower" 8 bits represent the Y coordinate, and the "upper" 8 bits the X coordinate, then the Y coordinate will automatically "wrap" from 255 to 0 as it fills up, causing the X coordinate to increment as well.

So with a total framebuffer resolution of 304×256 (77,824 pixels), the current screen state is stored across 38,912 bytes, or exactly 38KB of RAM. Given that the Williams platform contains a total of 48KB of RAM, we can see that the screen graphics are by far the most dominant memory component, eating up almost 80 percent of all available memory. The remaining 10KB of RAM is used to keep track of all other "live" aspects of gameplay: player and enemy positions, orientations, speeds, the current level and scores, time limits, and anything else that the system would have to remember to keep the game running. Keep in mind that RAM is only used for transient, "per-play" information; persistent data that remains when the machine is turned off—such as the character graphics, level layouts, and actual game code—is stored in the nonvolatile ROM chips.

10KB may not sound like a lot compared to today's generous RAM allowances, when 2GB (or more) of RAM is common on typical desktop or laptop computers— over 43,000 times that of the Williams game board. But the constrained spatial areas of the games (a single-screen layout in *Joust, Robotron, Bubbles,* and *Splat!*, for instance, while *Defender, Stargate,* and *Sinistar* allow screen scrolling but within a limited area) keep this allocation reasonable and, indeed, comfortable.

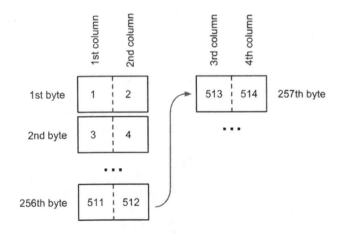

Figure 3 The framebuffer is organized in a zigzag pattern, with pairs of side-by-side pixels stacked vertically on top of each other: 256 bytes and 512 pixels per column. The numbers in each box indicate the pixels' sequential positions in memory

For example, the source code for the Atari 7800 port of *Robotron* (gameplay was certainly not identical to the arcade version, but presumably similar in scope) reveals that the game tracks up to 80 simultaneous enemies, with 16 bytes allocated for each enemy: 1 byte to indicate the type of creature; 2 bytes to hold X and Y screen locations; 7 bytes for values related to the direction, speed, and animation frame of the character's movement; and 6 bytes for other miscellaneous information.[14] The game state for these 80 enemies, easily the largest single group of game objects, consumes 1280 bytes of memory, or only 12.5 percent of the available 10KB RAM.

On the other hand, memory was not so plentiful that it was taken for granted or wasted by Williams programmers. Especially for arcade collectors, one graphical hallmark of these Williams games is a jittery, multicolored pattern of dots and lines sometimes visible on the right side of the screen: this video confetti is the slim, 12-pixel gutter between the 292-pixel edge of the screen that is intended to be visible, and the full 304-pixel area of memory that lies underneath. Given that some of this memory was nominally marked as "video RAM," yet was not intended to be actually *seen*, the programmers used it as an extra "scratchpad" area, storing other nongraphical data there instead. But when the monitor's horizontal positioning is not configured to precisely line up with its physical seating in the arcade cabinet, these hijacked scratchpad pixels find their way onto the screen: "Basically, some of the scratchpad RAM being used by the program is being scanned by and displayed by the video circuitry."[15] Quirks like these lay bare the relationship between hardware and game phenomenology; for a more contemporary equivalent, we can look to how the effect of "polygon seams" in some 3-D games—particularly the ability to see between them—alters the player's experience of game objects as supposedly "solid" geometry, and changes the nature of gameplay by revealing elements that were originally intended to be hidden.

So due to memory and speed limitations, the central graphics tenet of a 1980s-era, framebuffer-based game such as *Defender* is to change as *few pixels as possible* from frame to frame. *Defender* runs at a very smooth clip of 60 frames per second (fps). For comparison, film runs at 24fps and U.S. television stores one full frame per 30fps but interlaces alternating frames to simulate a higher rate of change. If we continue to use Giles's assumption of 4 CPU cycles per pixel operation, we can estimate that the 1MHz processor can alter the framebuffer values of 524,288 pixels per second (262,144 byte operations, with two 4-bit pixels drawn per byte): about 8,700 pixels per frame. In some respects, this does not seem to be much of a hindrance. There are 70,080 visible pixels on *Defender*'s 292×240-resolution screen, so the game is able to alter a theoretical maximum of 12.4 percent of the screen area per frame (1/60th of a second). On the other hand, this precludes certain graphic world models, most notably the smoothly scrolling background graphics that would become dominant on tile-map-based hardware like the Nintendo Entertainment System (NES), with *Super Mario Bros.* (1985) the quintessential example. Such games change more than 100 percent of their pixels per frame (a background layer covering the entire screen, plus the sprite characters and objects drawn atop it: some pixels will appear across multiple layers and will need to be drawn more than once, hence a per-frame pixel throughput that exceeds 100 percent). Tile-map-based platforms often included hardware-enabled scrolling features like X and Y offset registers that allowed them to accomplish this with relative ease: when drawing the screen, the video hardware would simply shift the entire tile-map over by a small pixel increment, obviating the need for the programmer to redraw the entire screen in software.

Yet even with its 12.4 percent pixel change ceiling—in actuality a highly optimistic limit that does not account for game or display logic necessary to decide which pixels to draw where—*Defender* does offer continuous side-scrolling and did so very early in the life of arcade platforms, before the effect was common. Two core graphical tactics are harnessed to enable the scrolling effect, and both depend on the game's sparse, sci-fi aesthetic of strong colors against a solid black background. The first is a multicolored field of stars drawn on that background. These "stars" are each a single pixel, and they quickly twinkle in and out, frequently changing color. The star field is a simple mechanism for creating a point of reference, an illusion of motion that the world is "scrolling" by, and it offers several advantages. Most obviously, because the field is sparse, there are very few pixels to redraw when the entire field must be "moved." And because the stars are constantly twinkling, there are even fewer of them visible at any one time than the eye perceives. Several screen captures (via MAME emulation) revealed no more than 14 stars simultaneously visible, dispersed across an area roughly half the size of the entire screen: that's a mere 0.04 percent of the total pixels in that screen area, an extremely efficient ratio of active to passive pixels.

Another more subtle advantage of the starfield is that because it changes so rapidly itself, it is not important to preserve the field's "integrity" when player or enemy characters travel across it. That is, unlike a "pictorial" background that must be carefully replaced pixel by pixel as a graphic moves "on top" of it, a star in *Defender*'s background will as likely as not have already conveniently disappeared by the time the player's spaceship uncovers it. The nature of the starfield makes any potentially "lost" pixels essentially undetectable by the player. In fact, all of the game's character graphics—the player's spaceship, the enemies, and so on—are drawn with a black background that covers up any graphical layer behind it: if you look closely as the player flies near the bottom of the screen, the terrain in the background will be blocked out. This is because the hardware lacks support for sprites, a feature that in later platforms would provide for transparency in character graphics. The starfield background helps to make this shortcut less noticeable. The game's liberal use of black spaces is well suited to its limitations.

The second tactic that provides *Defender*'s smoothly scrolling world is the mountainous terrain drawn across the bottom third of the screen. The surface is rendered in a fine-line style, a trail of brown pixels that wanders up and down, forming a vaguely planetary silhouette. As with the starfield, the terrain is arranged with economy, a single pixel drawn per X coordinate: a total of 292 pixels across the visible width of the screen. At first glance, the mountain terrain is purely decorative. It is, like the starfield, a non-interactive graphical element that has no direct impact on game state. The player does not crash into it, nor can it be used for cover from enemy fire or to avoid detection. Yet it is far from "useless." Like the starfield, its true role is as a perceptual indicator, a physical frame against which the player can correlate the position of his own ship and those of his enemies while the entire screen space is shifting. In fact, because it is a continuous line, is drawn in a stable, easier to see color, and is fixed in the world across time (unlike the twinkling stars), the terrain is the backbone that establishes the game's spatial model. A game with tile-based hardware would have taken this scrolling background for granted; *Defender*, predating the widespread use of such a model, relies on compact alternatives.

Defender's approach to motion and spatial navigation is notable for its divergence from both its contemporaries and its genre successors. The game creates a sense of depth and layer separation through parallax scrolling: the starfield, ground terrain, and player's ship all move at different speeds that adjust as the player accelerates (see Figure 4). It is unusual, by later-established genre conventions, that there is no stationary, visual "grounding" element in *Defender*. In most scrolling games, at least one of the player's avatar, foreground, and background graphics layers is moving at a constant speed (or not moving at all in the case that the player's avatar is stationary). Shoot'em-ups such as *Gradius* have a constantly scrolling, "forced" background progression, with the player able to perform constrained movements within that moving screen frame. In side-scrolling platformers like *Super Mario Bros.* (1985), either the world foreground scrolls in lock-step with the player (causing the player sprite itself to be fixed as the level moves forward), or the player navigates the level while the background stays in place (both modes are often seen in the same game, depending on level design, player backtracking vs. moving forward, etc.). But in *Defender*, these graphic layers are often all accelerating relative to one another. The player graphic does eventually become stationary once it has reached top speed—though in any case there is little practicality to playing the game at this velocity; the gamespace and enemy AI encourage strategic maneuvers rather than cowboy running-and-gunning. This relative layer parallax would likely not have been possible on a hardware platform with built-in scrolling. Although later "16-bit" platforms did often provide multiple scrolling layers that could move at different speeds, the cutting edge of *Defender's* era was the much simpler single layer with smooth, per-pixel scrolling control.

In the realm of world simulation, *Defender* (along with *BattleZone*, as previously mentioned) initiated the use of *off-screen action* as a significant focal point of player attention. As noted, it is not the first title in which off-screen space *exists*, but it does appear to be the initial introduction of player multitasking to core gameplay psychology, requiring the player to track both enemies and their human prey spread across the level, each of which can be both visible and invisible. It further complicates this mental tracking with the use of multistage gameplay. Although the primary player goal is to simply shoot all enemies before they are able to reach the human characters at the bottom of the screen, the game

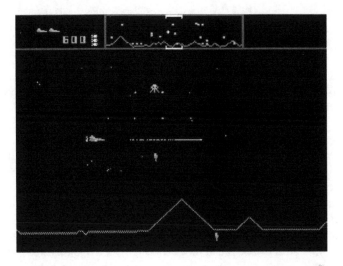

Figure 4 Defender's graphics are sparse and derive much of their impact from color and motion. Key elements are visible here, including the mini-map radar at the top of the screen, the player's laser beam streaking across the screen, and the single-pixel line that forms the mountain range along the lower third of the screen

also enables more sophisticated "recovery" operations. If an enemy does reach a human, that human is captured and carried upward by the enemy toward the top of the screen, rather than being killed on contact. The player can recover from this situation and avoid losing points by shooting the enemy, and then catching the suddenly falling human before it impacts the ground. The use of multiple-screen spaces, dependent-move sequences, and fallback goals reflects the game's desire to split the player's attention as widely as possible—the ungrounded, relative graphical velocities of player/foreground/background are part of this effort—but also to temper its own difficulty by adhering to a fair and logical system that reward mental orchestration.

Also peculiar is *Defender's* presentation of a side-scrolling gamespace that wraps. This has the effect of equalizing the direction of play: flying from right-to-left is just as effective as the left-to-right movement standard to the vast majority of other horizontal flying/shooting games (Namco's *Sky Kid*, 1985, is an unusual example of a right-to-left scrolling shooter). Several forms of wrapping space are common to games of *Defender's* era, yet they usually fall into other categories: single screens with objects that wrap at the edges (as in *Asteroids* and *Pac-Man*), or top-down four-directional scrolling (as in *Super Bug*). *Defender's* single-axis, wraparound space forms a conceptual cylinder and runs counter to the the genre of horizontal 2-D shooters that followed it starting with Konami's *Scramble* in 1981, in which there was a presumed progression along one direction and through a non-repeatable space. And from a technical perspective, the smaller wrapping space requires less data than would a longer linear level. From our historical vantage point of established side-scrolling genres, *Defender* is a fascinating case for its techniques that did *not* become genre precedents, more so than for those that *did*—though the impact of the mini-map/radar user interface pattern should not be forgotten and remains highly influential to this day.

The essence of *Defender*'s phenomenology is its feeling of speed and (what is best described as) "power," an unforgiving, lightning-fast, and always colorful response to in-game action. We have seen how *Defender* constructs a spatial environment by minimizing its pixel deltas. The same approach is behind two techniques that animate the action within that world. The first is a family of graphics algorithms broadly known as *particle systems*. Simply put, particle systems orchestrate the animation of a group of individual graphical entities (the "particles"), to form a perception of a larger, coherent object. Particle system effects can be used in a relatively humble, lo-fi manner as they are in *Defender*, as groups of individual pixels that form explosions, laser beams, and teleportation. But the style has also been used extensively in graphics and scientific research to model complex substances and motion such as fluid dynamics and gas clouds. Likewise, particle effects have played a prominent role in special effects for commercial films.

One does not have to wait long to observe *Defender*'s particle system effects: on the game's title screen, the *Defender* logo materializes from an array of pixel clumps (about 4 to 8 pixels each), yellow and red rectangles that converge from all directions, from screen edge to center, joining together to spell out the game's name. Particles are also the visual vehicle any time the player's ship materializes (at game start or when the "hyperspace" teleportation is activated) or is destroyed; likewise for enemy spawn and death animations. Particle effects are efficient because they can spread a relatively small number of pixels across a large area, moving and coloring those pixels in a way that presents a much larger object—and one more sophisticated and flexible than a typical game sprite, constrained by its invisible rectangular fence. They are also able to construct a feeling of action-at-a-distance. The most effective use of particles in *Defender* is the player's laser beam: when fired, the beam streams across the screen as a single, pixel-high line, solid at its leading edge, stuttering and re-forming in the trailing half. The player can strafe up and down the field, stacking these beams. It is a far more striking enabler of player power than the typical individual bullet of the shoot-'em-up genre. As with the star field, the laser beam requires minimal pixel redraw. It is drawn by adding pixels forward, with the back portion of the beam following a fixed toggle pattern—4 pixels on, 2 pixels skipped; 3 pixels on, 1 pixel skipped; and so forth—that acts as a mask as the pixels stream by. Only a few pixels need be removed while in transit, until the entire beam exhausts itself and disappears all at once.

A similarly powerful particle effect is used when the player's ship is destroyed, replaced by a cluster of 2×2-pixel rectangles that scatter in all directions, "erasing" the game's surroundings as they go: as the ship remnants pass over the star field, enemies, and even the world's ground terrain, they leave a black trail in their wake. This is technologically convenient, as the game simply back-fills the trail of the moving particles with solid black, rather than actually storing and redrawing the original pixel colors that were underneath. But this software shortcut also creates an emotionally effective feeling of decay and immediate obliteration: the simulation of the game world collapsing before the player's eyes, as if it no longer meaningfully existed without them.

Whereas the starfield and mountain terrain are examples of ways in which *Defender* has to work extra hard to create graphical layers of space that would have been easily accessible in arcade games with tile and sprite hardware, its particle effects are the opposite. Because particle effects operate by manipulating individual pixels across the framebuffer, the style simply would not have been possible on a system dependent on tiles and sprites, in which the lowest common denominator is a rectangular group of pixels more commonly sized at 8×8 or larger, and often constrained to particular patterns of location. Many hardware-native sprite implementations support a maximum number of sprites per scanline: 4 per line on the MSX, and 8 per line on the Commodore 64, for example. From a platform studies perspective, it is key that the particle effects of *Defender*, so central to its visual style and animation, would have been unavailable on later arcade hardware that from other points of view would be considered more "advanced."

Another technical feature that is key to the game's aesthetic is color-cycling, used extensively and cleverly by *Defender* (and later Williams games, especially *Robotron*) to create an impression of greater color variety and motion. Earlier, I described how the Williams platform allows the programmer to choose 16 colors for simultaneous display. Each of these colors is referenced by a number; for example, if color number 2 is defined as red, then all pixels in the framebuffer that are set to the value 2 display as red. Color-cycling is the ability, enabled by some graphics hardware, to change those color definitions "on the fly." For example, by changing color number 2 from red to green, we can instantaneously change *all* red pixels on screen to green, without changing any of the actual pixel values themselves in the framebuffer. This is because each time the video hardware redraws the screen (60 times per second), it is first reading the 16 color values set by the programmer, then correlating those to each pixel value in the frame, as it draws them one by one. The memory and computational benefits of color-cycling are obvious: anywhere from hundreds to tens of thousands of pixels can be changed in bulk, all by manipulating a single byte in the color lookup table.

Of course, the technique has limitations. Most animations require more than a simple mass-color change, instead requiring that individual pixels be manipulated to "move" across the screen, as when an entire character graphic must be repositioned. But color-cycling can be harnessed to construct motion effects such as wave or ripple patterns, by smoothly animating a band of colors with brightness levels along a single hue—commonly used for water, fire, or other "fluids." Alternatively, a block of palette values can all be set to the same actual color, with one contrasting color cycled through the band, a "shockwave" effect as the contrast color makes it way through the palette. For example, with 15 blacks and 1 red, the particular color number coded as red can be rapidly changed from

0 to 15, causing the appearance of a red line animating through space (to set this up, the framebuffer is stacked with pixel lines of increasing color numbers: a row of color 0 pixels, a row of color 1 pixels, etc.).

Color-cycling is a constant feature of *Defender*. There appears to be literally no point in the game's operation, from the title screen to the attract mode to the gameplay, during which color-cycling is not actively in use. Almost all of the core visual features of the game are enhanced by the technique: the twinkling star field, the laser beam, the explosion of the player's ship. But color-cycling is also used in more subtle and more ostentatious ways. The cockpit of the player's ship, a mere 3-pixel row, cycles to bring the ship to mechanical life, a noticeable contrast to typically static game sprites (and requiring no additional ROM to store animation frames). (The cockpit animation is even replicated in the mini-ships shown at the top of the screen, representing the number of lives the player has remaining.) A triangle behind the ship's tail end cycles through random colors, mixing to form a fiery exhaust that appears to propel the player forward. More generally, color-cycling pervades the non-diegetic game elements such as in-game scores, the high score board, the Williams logo on the title screen, and almost all text appearing anywhere. In short, like *Defender*'s stars, mountains, and particle effects, color-cycling is used to enable gameplay through minimal computational change. Yet it also sets the game's frenetic, loud, brightly lit ambiance, as identifiable a historical feature as its difficulty or game mechanics.

The next evolutionary step for the Williams arcade platform came in 1982, with *Robotron: 2084*, the quintessential single-screen "survival" game, the player surrounded by a claustrophobia-inducing mob of robots. *Robotron* is best known for its introduction of a dual-joystick control scheme: one eight-way joystick controls the player's movement, while another determines the direction of the player's shot. This allowed for the player to move and shoot in two directions at the same time, enabling more nuanced maneuvers such as strafing and backing away. The most significant technical difference between *Robotron* and *Defender*, however, is the addition of two "blitter" chips, dedicated graphics hardware that could quickly move rectangular blocks of pixels back and forth between video RAM and other general memory. The blitter chips were literally game-changing because they allowed the programmer to orchestrate the mass movement of pixels without having to expend more than a few cycles of primary CPU. Blitters were a hardware feature necessitated by designer Eugene Jarvis's vision for *Robotron* with up to 80 characters on screen simultaneously, it simply would have been impossible to "push" the required number of pixels in software (see Figure 5).

How fast were the Williams blitters? Aaron Giles notes that the theoretical maximum is about 1 megabyte per second (1MB/s), based on the chips' 4MHz clock and the underlying hardware's 8-bit data bus.[16] However, by instrumenting his original Williams hardware and capturing the output on a PC, collector Sean Riddle explicitly tested the blitters and pegged their real-world performance at about 910 KB/s (about 10 percent below the theoretical limit).[17] At 60 fps, this equates to roughly 31,000 pixels per frame—impressive considering that the

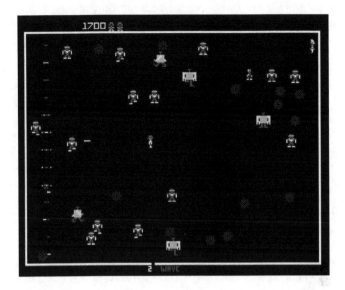

Figure 5 The overwhelming number of simultaneous on-screen characters in *Robotron: 2084* led to the addition of «blitters» to the Williams arcade platform: specialized chips that are dedicated to moving rectangular blocks of pixels at high speed

entire screen's framebuffer is only around 70,000 pixels. In actuality, the pixel throughput is lower: programmers must carefully time their character blits to stay in sync with the video beam drawing the screen, or to keep characters from erasing or overlapping one another, for example. The flexible nature of Williams's blitters parallels the hardware philosophy of their pixel framebuffer. Although many game hardware platforms provided hardware support for sprites, as noted previously these often carried limitations on sprite size, shape, and position (especially maximum number of sprites per scanline). The Williams games, by contrast, were limited only by the total throughput of the blitter chips themselves, with real impacts on gameplay. In their 1982 ostrich-battle game *Joust*, for example, the enemy flight and chase patterns are unencumbered by hardware limitations; characters can fluidly move between areas of the screen, allowing the programmers to focus more on the game's surprisingly sophisticated flight physics, with spatially freed enemies that appear more intelligent than typical lumbering arcade sentinels.

Williams's blitters also offer a nice example of hardware "limitations" proactively harnessed for game design. When the screen becomes filled with too many characters for the blitter to fill, it buckles under the weight, and the game literally slows down, allowing the player to pull off complex moves and daring escapes "in slow-motion." Game designers and players are familiar with this slowdown effect of the 8-bit era, providing a built-in trigger for managing difficulty that became an intentional design tactic of the 2-D shoot-'em-up genre. In fact, slowdown is not only artificially introduced into such games today, but has also found its metaphorical way into the periodic slow-motion scenes known as "bullet time" in many contemporary titles. The meaningful integration of hardware blitter speed into gameplay has also meant that programmers who seek to emulate arcade platforms must be keenly aware of low-level computing; again, Aaron Giles: "I'm currently working on an update to the early Williams games that will factor this [maximum blitting speed] in, in the hopes that Robotron might slow down enough to match the arcade (a number of folks have noticed that Robotron runs too fast in MAME at the higher levels)."[18]

With the foundation created by *Defender* and its sequel *Stargate*, and the addition of the blitter chips for *Robotron*, the Williams platform held steady through 1982, seeing the further release of *Joust, Sinistar, Bubbles,* and *Splat!* These seven arcade titles leave a remarkable legacy, running the gamut from familiar to strangely alien. While *Defender* and its siblings helped establish key user-interface (UI) components such as the mini-map and design approaches to off-screen space and multi-tasking, they also often applied control schemes and logic that can feel unorthodox by today's gameplay conventions: the "reverse" button in *Defender*, the frantic head-on collisions between player and asteroid in *Sinistar*, the soap bubble avatar of *Bubbles*. These games come from a period of rapid innovation, when the models of both hardware and game mechanics that we take for granted as "classic" today were still being established. Technical design plays a crucial role in the development of the gaming medium, but not in a technologically determinative fashion—instead often flowing in equal directions between hardware and game design. And this tension is especially relevant and illustrative in the early arcade era, when the designers creating the game rules and the physical machines were not from separate companies, with different professional, artistic, or economic goals, but instead were often the same or closely linked as a team.

Notes

1 Nick Montfort and Ian Bogost, *Racing the Beam* (Cambridge, MA: MIT Press, 2009), 13–15.
2 Aaron Giles, "Aaron's MAME Memories, Part 4: The Joy of Common Hardware," accessed April 9, 2010, http://aarongiles.com/mamemem/part4.html.
3 MAME ROM search by CPU, Motorola 6809, accessed April 9, 2010, http://maws.mameworld.info/maws/srch.php?page=1&cpu=134&by=year.
4 MAME ROM search by CPU, Motorola 6809.
5 Joel Boney and Terry Ritter, "The 6809," *BYTE Magazine*, January-February, 1979.
6 "Williams 1973 Paddle Ball," accessed April 9, 2010, http://www.vintagecomputer.net/paddle_ball.cfm.
7 "The 50 Best Games of the 1980s," EDGE Online, accessed April 9, 2010, http://www.edge-online.com/features/the-best-50-games-of-the-1980s?page =0%2C5
8 Aaron Giles, "The Universal Platform, Part 1," accessed April 9, 2010, http://aarongiles.com/?p=211.
9 Ibid.
10 MAME ROM search by screen resolution, 292x240, accessed April 9, 2010, http://maws.mameworld.info/maws/srch.php?resolution=292x240.

11 Aaron Giles, "Aaron's MAME Memories Part 3: Hunting for Color PROMs," accessed April 9, 2010, http://www.aarongiles.com/mamemem/part3.html.

12 "Luminance (relative)," *Wikipedia*, accessed April 9, 2010, http://en.wikipedia.org/wiki/Luminance_%28relative%29.

13 "Nexus One display and subpixel pattern," accessed April 9, 2010, http://blog.javia.org/nexus-one-display-and-subpixel-pattern/.

14 *Robotron: 2084* computer program source code, Atari 7800 platform, accessed April 9, 2010, http://www.atarimuseum.com/videogames/consoles/ 7800/games/.

15 "Robotron Tech: Lines at top of screen" [USENET forum discussion], accessed April 9, 2010, http://www.popularusenetgroups.com/showthread.php?p=2193088#post2193088.

16 Aaron Giles, "More about blitters," accessed April 9, 2010, http://aarongiles.com/?p=104.

17 Sean Riddle, "Blitter Test Files," accessed April 9, 2010, http://seanriddle.com/blittest.html.

18 Aaron Giles, "More about blitters."

44

PROCEDURAL RHETORIC

Ian Bogost

Source: *Persuasive Games: The Expressive Power of Video Games* (Cambridge, MA: The MIT Press, 2010), pp. 1–64.

In 1975, Owen Gaede created *Tenure*, a simulation of the first year of secondary school teaching, for the PLATO computer education system.[1] The program was intended to give new high school teachers an understanding of the impact of seemingly minor decisions on the teaching experience. The goal of the game is to complete the first year of teaching and earn a contract renewal for the next. During play, the player must make successive decisions, each of which affects different people in different ways. Some decisions may please the students but contradict the principal's educational philosophy. Others may provide a higher quality educational experience but put performance pressure on fellow teachers, causing workplace conflict. The player can monitor the state of affairs by listening to student reactions, requesting a conference with the principal, or overhearing gossip in the teacher's lounge.

The game is played primarily through responses to multiple-choice questions whose aggregate answers change principal, teacher, and student attitudes. For example, at the start of the game, the player must take a job interview with his prospective principal. The principal may ask about the player's educational philosophy or his willingness to advise student organizations. Later, the player must choose a grading methodology, classroom rules, student seating arrangements, and a curriculum plan. The simulation then presents the player with very specific quandaries, such as how to manage another teacher's students at a school assembly, whether or not to participate in the teacher's union, dealing with note-passing in class, contending with parents angry about their children's grades, and even managing students' difficult personal issues, such as home abuse.

No decision is straightforward, and the interaction of multiple successive decisions produces complex social, educational, and professional situations. Situations are further influenced by the gender of the teacher, the influence of the principal, student learning styles, and other subtle, social factors. In one run of a recent PC port of *Tenure*, Jack, one of my best students, had been arriving late to class.[2] I could choose to ignore his tardiness, talk to him privately, or give him detention. I chose to talk with Jack about the problem, which earned me praise from the principal, whose progressive philosophy encouraged direct contact and student empathy. However, after speaking with the student, I learned that his tardiness was caused by Mr. Green, the math teacher, who had been holding class after the bell to complete the last problem on the board. Now I was faced with a new decision: confront Mr. Green, make Jack resolve the issue and accept the necessary discipline, or complain to the principal. Asking the student to take responsibility would avoid conflict with my colleague and principal on the one hand, but would put Jack in an uncomfortable situation on the other, perhaps changing his opinion of me as a teacher. Confronting Mr. Green might strain our relationship and, thanks to lounge gossip, my rapport with other teachers as well. Complaining to the principal might cause the same reaction, and might also run the risk of exposing me as indecisive. All of these factors might change given the outcome of other decisions and the personalities of my fellow teachers and principal.

Tenure makes claims about how high school education operates. Most notably, it argues that educational practice is deeply intertwined with personal and professional politics. Novice teachers and idealistic parents would like to think that their children's educations are motivated primarily, if not exclusively by pedagogical goals. *Tenure* argues that this ideal is significantly undermined by the realities of school politics, personal conflicts, and social hearsay. The game does not offer solutions to these problems; rather, it suggests that education takes place not in the classroom alone, but in ongoing affinities and disparities in educational, social, and professional goals. *Tenure* outlines the *process* by which high schools really run, and it makes a convincing argument that personal politics indelibly mark the learning experience.

I suggest the name *procedural rhetoric* for the new type of persuasive and expressive practice at work in artifacts like *Tenure*. *Procedurality* refers to a way of creating, explaining, or understanding processes. And processes define the way things work: the methods, techniques, and logics that drive the operation of systems, from mechanical systems like engines to organizational systems like high schools to conceptual systems like religious faith. *Rhetoric* refers to effective and persuasive expression. Procedural rhetoric, then, is a practice of using processes persuasively. More specifically, procedural rhetoric is the practice of persuading through processes in general and computational processes in particular. Just as verbal rhetoric is useful for both the orator and the audience, and just as written rhetoric is useful for both the writer and the reader, so procedural rhetoric is useful for both the programmer and the user, the game designer and the player. Procedural rhetoric is a technique for making arguments with computational systems and for unpacking computational arguments others have created.

Procedural and *rhetoric* are both terms that can impose ambiguity and confusion. Before trying to use the two together in earnest, I want to discuss each in turn.

Procedurality

The word *procedure* does not usually give rise to positive sentiments. We typically understand *procedures* as established, entrenched ways of doing things. In common parlance, *procedure* invokes notions of officialdom, even bureaucracy: a procedure is a static course of action, perhaps an old, tired one in need of revision. We often talk about procedures only when they go wrong: *after several complaints, we decided to review our procedures for creating new accounts.* But in fact, procedures in this sense of the word structure behavior; we tend to "see" a process only when we challenge it.[3] Likewise, procedure and the law are often closely tied. Courts and law enforcement agencies abide by *procedures* that dictate how actions can and cannot be carried out. Thanks to these common senses of the term, we tend to think of procedures as fixed and unquestionable. They are tied to authority, crafted from the top down, and put in place to structure behavior and identify infringement. Procedures are sometimes related to ideology; they can cloud our ability to see other ways of thinking; consider the police officer or army private who carries out a clearly unethical action but later offers the defense, "I was following procedure." This very problem arose in the aftermath of American brutalization of Iraqi war prisoners at Abu Ghraib in 2004. Field soldiers claimed they followed orders, while officers insisted that the army did not endorse torture; rather individual soldiers acted alone. No matter the truth, the scenario raises questions about the *procedures* that drive military practice. In his report on prison practices, Major General Marshal Donald Ryder noted the possibility of altering "facility procedures to set the conditions for MI [military intelligence] interrogations."[4] In this case, the procedures in question dictate the methods used to interrogate prisoners. One might likewise think of interactions with line workers in retail establishments. When asked to perform some unusual task, such employees may be instructed to balk, offering excuses like "that's not our policy." Policy is a synonym for procedure in many cases: an approach, or a custom; a process for customer relations. In both these cases, procedures constrain the types of actions that can or should be performed in particular situations.

In her influential book *Hamlet on the Holodeck*, Janet Murray defines four essential properties of digital artifacts: procedurality, participation, spatiality, and encyclopedic scope.[5] Murray uses the term *procedural* to refer to the computer's "defining ability to execute a series of rules."[6] Procedurality in this sense refers to the core practice of software authorship. Software is composed of algorithms that model the way things behave. To write procedurally, one authors code that enforces rules to generate some kind of representation, rather than authoring the representation itself. Procedural systems generate behaviors based on rule-based models; they are machines capable of producing many outcomes, each conforming to the same overall guidelines. Procedurality is the principal value of the computer, which creates meaning through the interaction of algorithms. Although Murray places procedurality alongside three other properties, these properties are not equivalent. The computer, she writes, "was designed . . . to embody complex, contingent behaviors. To be a computer scientist is to think in terms of algorithms and heuristics, that is, to be constantly identifying the exact or general rules of behavior that describe any process, from running a payroll to flying an airplane."[7] This ability to execute a series of rules fundamentally separates computers from other media.

Procedurality in the computer-scientific sense preserves a relationship with the more familiar sense of *procedure* discussed above. Like courts and bureaucracies, computer software establishes rules of execution, tasks and actions that can and cannot be performed. I have argued elsewhere that procedurality can be read in both computational and noncomputational structures.[8] As cultural critics, we can interrogate literature, art, film, and daily life for the underlying processes they trace. But computational procedurality places a greater emphasis on the expressive capacity afforded by rules of execution. Computers run processes that invoke interpretations of processes in the material world.

For my purposes, procedural expression must entail symbol manipulation, the construction and interpretation of a symbolic system that governs human thought or action. As Steven Harnad argues, computation is "interpretable symbol manipulation" in which symbols "are manipulated on the basis of rules operating only on the symbols' shapes, which are arbitrary in relation to what they can be interpreted as meaning."[9] The interpretation of these systems, continues Harnad, "is not intrinsic to the system; it is projected onto it by the interpreter."[10] Computation is representation, and procedurality in the computational sense is a means to produce that expression. As Murray suggests, computer processes are representational, and thus procedurality is fundamental to computational expression. Because computers function procedurally, they are particularly adept at representing real or imagined systems that themselves function in some particular way—that is, that operate according to a set of processes. The computer magnifies the ability to create representations of processes.

The type of procedures that interest me here are those that present or comment on processes inherent to human experience. Not all procedures are expressive in the way that literature and art are expressive. But processes that might appear unexpressive, devoid of symbol manipulation, may actually found expression of a higher order. For example, bureaucracy constrains behavior in a way that invokes political, social, and cultural values. Consider the example of retail customer service as an invocation of processes. Imagine that you bought a new DVD player from a local retailer. Upon installing it, you discover that the device's mechanical tray opens and shuts properly, but no image displays on the television. You assume it is defective. Most stores offer a return policy in such cases, so you take the player back to the store and exchange it for a new one.

Now imagine that you buy the DVD player late one evening on the way home from work. You lead a busy life, and unpacking a DVD player isn't the first thing on your mind. You leave it in the box for a week, or two, and then finally take it out and connect it, discovering that it doesn't work properly. You are frustrated but still pressed for time, and you don't get back to the retailer for the return until the following week. The store would be happy to take your return, but they note that you purchased the item more than fourteen days ago. The store's stated policy is to accept consumer electronics returns only within two weeks of purchase. In this case, the retailer's employees may try to enforce their return policy, invoking the rules of a process. But you might reason with the clerk, or make a ruckus, or ask to see a supervisor, or cite your record of purchases at the store in question. Swayed by logic, empathy, or expediency, the store might agree to accept the return—to bend the rules or *to break procedure*, as we sometimes say.

Let's replace the human agents with computational ones. Now imagine that you purchased the DVD player from an online retailer. The return process is no less codified in procedure, but this time a computer, not a human, manages your interface with the procedure. You receive the package and, as before, you delay in opening and installing it. By the time you realize the item is defective, you have exceeded the stated return window. But this time, the return is managed by the retailer's website software. Instead of speaking with a person, you must visit a website and enter your order number on a return authorization page. A computer program on the server performs a simple test, checking the delivery date of the order automatically provided by the shipping provider's computer tracking system against the current date. If the dates differ by more than fourteen days' time, the computer rejects the return request.

Situations like this help explain why we often despise the role of computers in our lives. They are inflexible systems that cannot empathize, that attempt to treat everyone the same. This is partly true, but it is not a sufficient explanation of *computational* procedural expression. When the human clerks and supervisors in the retail store agree to forgo their written policy, they are not really "breaking procedure." Instead, they are mustering new processes—for example, a process for promoting repeat business, or for preventing a commotion—and seamlessly blending them with the procedure for product returns. This distinction underscores an important point about processes in general and computational processes in particular: often, we think of procedures as tests that maintain the edges of situations. Disallow returns after two weeks. Diffuse customer incidents as quickly as possible. This also explains why we think of procedures as constraints that limit behavior. Max Weber pessimistically characterized the rationalist bureaucratization of society as an "iron cage." When the asceticism of Puritanism was extended into daily life, argues Weber,

> it did its part in building the tremendous cosmos of the modern economic order. This order is now bound to the technical and economic conditions of machine production which today determine the lives of all the individuals who are born into this mechanism. In [Calvinist Richard] Baxter's view the care for external goods should only lie in on the shoulders of the "saint, like a light cloak, which can be thrown aside at any moment." But fate decreed that the cloak should become an iron cage.[11]

Weber's point is that mechanization overemphasizes rationalism. But in fact, procedures found the logics that structure behavior in *all* cases; the machines of industrialization simply act as a particularly tangible medium for expressing these logics. The metaphor of the cloak may suggest easy shedding of procedure, but the saint must immediately don a new cloak, symbolizing a new logic. Both cloak and cage brandish processes; one is simply nimbler than the other.

While we often think that rules always limit behavior, the imposition of constraints also creates expression. In our example, the very concept of returning a defective product is only made possible by the creation of rules that frame that very notion. Without a process, it would perhaps never even occur to us that defective or unwanted products can be returned. And yet, this state of affairs too implies a process, which we give the shorthand *caveat emptor*, let the buyer beware. When we do things, we do them according to some logic, and that logic constitutes a *process* in the general sense of the word.

This clarification in mind, there is no reason one could not model the more complex, human-centered product return interaction computationally. For example, the computer system might also recall the customer's previous purchases, forgoing the cutoff policy for frequent buyers. It might even reason about the customer's future purchases based on a predictive model of future buying habits of similar customers. We think of computers as frustrating, limiting, and simplistic not because they execute processes, but because they are frequently programmed to execute simplistic processes. And the choice to program only a simplistic process for customer relations exposes yet another set of processes, such as corporate information technology operations or the constraints of finances or expertise that impose buying off-the-shelf software solutions instead of building custom solutions.

Processes like military interrogation and customer relations are cultural. We tend to think of them as flexible and porous, but they are crafted from a multitude of protracted, intersecting cultural processes. I have given the name *unit operations* to processes of the most general kind, whether implemented in material, cultural, or representational form.[12] Unit operations are characterized by their increased compression of representation, a tendency common over the course of the twentieth century, from structuralist anthropology to computation. I use this term to refer to processes in the general sense, for example, the coupling of a cultural process and its computational representation. I also use *unit operation* to distinguish one process in interleaved or nested procedural systems, for example, the concept of customer loyalty as distinct from transaction age in the case of a process for managing product returns.

Since processes describe the way simple and complex things work, sometimes they are nonobvious. In some cases, we want to conceal procedure—for example, many people read the U.S. Army's ambiguous response to Abu Ghraib as a sign that high-ranking officials in the military, those with the authority to set the procedure, endorsed torture. In other cases, the process is too complex to apprehend immediately. We tend to ask the question *how does this work?* in relation to such processes. This sentiment probably conjures images of mechanical devices like wristwatches, where procedural understanding implies taking a set of gears apart to see how they mesh. But procedurality can also entail the operation of cultural, social, and historical systems. In these cases, asking *how does this work?* requires taking a set of cultural systems apart to see what logics motivate their human actors.

351

A notable example comes from microbiologist Jared Diamond's Pulitzer Prize-winning book *Guns, Germs, and Steel*, an alternative approach to understanding history (discussed further in chapter 9).[13] Instead of recording the events of human history, Diamond looks at configurations of material conditions like geography and natural resources and asks how they produce structural, political, and social outcomes. These outcomes in turn recombine with their underlying material conditions to produce new historical moments. For example, the lush agricultural conditions in the fertile crescent, along with the similar climates in the east-west axis of Eurasia, set the stage for rapid advances in agriculture across that continent, leading to adequate food surpluses that allowed societies to pursue activities like politics and technology. Such an approach to history goes far beyond the relation between contemporaneous events, asking us to consider the systems that produce those events.

Steven D. Levitt's work on microeconomies also exposes processes. Levitt and Stephen J. Dubner authored the *New York Times* bestseller *Freakonomics*, a populist account of Levitt's sometimes unusual microeconomic analysis. Levitt claims that human behavior is fundamentally motivated by incentives.[14] He uses this assertion to explain the seemingly incomprehensible function of numerous communities of practice, from real estate agents to sumo wrestlers to drug dealers. In one of his more controversial claims, Levitt argues that the massive drop in crime across the United States in the 1990s was caused by the legalization of abortion in 1973.[15] Levitt and Dubner explain:

> In the early 1990s, just as the first cohort of children born after *Roe v. Wade* was hitting its late teen years—the years during which young men enter their criminal prime—the rate of crime began to fall. What this cohort was missing, of course, were the children who stood the greatest chance of becoming criminals. And the crime rate continued to fall as an entire generation came of age minus the children whose mothers had not wanted to bring a child into the world. *Legalized abortion led to less unwantedness; unwantedness leads to high crime; legalized abortion, therefore, led to less crime.*[16]

Using written rhetoric, Levitt and Dubner walk us through an explanation of the causal relationship that leads, in their proposition, from legalized abortion to reduced crime. They are describing a social process, the operation of interrelated legal policy and social welfare. Notably, the two end this explanation with a formal logical syllogism (italicized above), a structure I will return to below in the context of rhetoric.

These abstract processes—be they material like watch gears or cultural like crime—can be recounted through representation. However, procedural representation takes a different form than written or spoken representation. Procedural representation explains processes *with other processes*. Procedural representation is a form of symbolic expression that uses process rather than language. Diamond and Levitt make claims about procedural systems like history and crime, but they do not inscribe those claims in procedure—they write them, just like I wrote the description of product returns above. In fact, each and every analysis of videogame-based procedural rhetoric I will perform in this book necessarily *describes* the function of processes. These written descriptions attempt to explain the procedural ones, which are made up of rules rather than letters.

Procedural representation itself requires inscription in a medium that actually enacts processes rather than merely describe them. Human behavior is one mode of procedural inscription. Human actors can enact processes; we do so all the time. The clerk, the supervisor, and the army private all enact procedures. Even very young children can consciously enact procedures with great success: crossing the street, tying one's shoes, and setting the table are all unit operations in cultural and social processes. Nondigital board and card games offer further examples of human-enacted processes; the people playing the game execute its rules. But human behavior is a challenging medium to muster for arbitrary expression. It is difficult to coerce even a small group of people to execute a particular process again and again, without rest and without incentive. Because procedurality is intrinsic and fundamental to computers, and because computers are much more flexible as an inscription medium than human agents, they are particularly suited to procedural expression.

In her call for meaningful interactive drama, Janet Murray advocates for procedural authorship. Such effort, says Murray, "means writing the rules by which the text appears as well as writing the texts themselves. It means writing the rules for the interactor's involvement, that is, the conditions under which things will happen in response to the participant's actions." Murray cites Joseph Weizenbaum's *Eliza* program as an early example of this kind of procedural expression.[17] *Eliza* modeled a therapist, responding to users' text-based input in much the same way one would expect from a real Rogerian psychologist. Here is a sample exchange from Weizenbaum's original *Eliza*, which ran on MIT's MAC time-sharing system in the mid-1960s (capitalized lines are computer responses):

Men are all alike.
IN WHAT WAY?
They're always bugging us about something or other.
CAN YOU THINK OF A SPECIFIC EXAMPLE?
Well, my boyfriend made me come here.
YOUR BOYFRIEND MADE YOU COME HERE
He says I'm depressed much of the time.
I AM SORRY TO HEAR YOU ARE DEPRESSED
It's true. I am unhappy
DO YOU THINK COMING HERE WILL HELP YOU NOT TO BE UNHAPPY
I need some help, that much seems certain.
WHAT WOULD IT MEAN TO YOU IF YOU GOT SOME HELP
Perhaps I could learn to get along with my mother.

TELL ME MORE ABOUT YOUR FAMILY
My mother takes care of me.[18]

As a technical experiment, *Eliza* is an example of natural language processing (NLP); the computer takes the user's input, parses it into units of meaning that the program can understand, and then assembles and presents a response, including the proper grammatical transformations to maintain the illusion of language fluency. *Eliza* seeks out keywords such as "I am" or "you" and manufactures transformations based on them. The computer program has no real understanding of the meaning of the user's input; rather, it is taking that input and spinning it into a possible conversation. *Eliza* is a machine for generating conversations according to procedures.

Of course, the Rogerian psychologist is not the most meaningful real-life interlocutor—such a therapist converses with the patient, encouraging him or her toward "self-actualization" through empathy, mostly in the form of repetition intended to encourage reflection. Since *Eliza*, considerable research in the field of artificial intelligence has centered on the creation of similar agents. Some agents are meant merely to process bits of data, like keyword searches or security tools. Other agents have more lofty goals, hoping to create believable characters whose behavior is authored procedurally with special-use computer languages.[19] These are expressive agents, meant to clarify, explore, or comment on human processes in the same vein as poetry, literature, and film. No matter their content, these computer programs use processes for expression rather than utility. As an inscriptive practice, procedurality is not limited to tool-making.

Procedurality versus the procedural programming paradigm

Speaking of computer languages, I would like to make a few notes to help reduce confusion for readers who come equipped with different (although not incompatible) notions of procedure, especially for those who come from a background in computer science. I am using *procedural* and *procedurality* in a much more general sense than it sometimes takes on in that field. In computer science, a *procedure* is sometimes used as a synonym for a subroutine—a function or method call. A procedure contains a series of computational instructions, encapsulated into a single command that can be called at any time during program execution. Some imperative computer languages, such as Pascal, even reserve the word *procedure* to declare a subroutine in code, as the following example illustrates.

```
procedure foo(var n: integer)
begin
    writeln('foo outputs ', n);
end;
begin
    i:= 1;
    while i <= 10 do foo(i);
end.
```

In other cases, *procedural* is used to describe a particular approach to computer programming, one typically called the *procedural programming* paradigm. Procedural programming is a paradigmatic extension of the notion of *procedure* as subroutine. As a programming method, procedural programming became privileged over unstructured programming, in which all code exists in a single continuous block. In Assembly and early versions of BASIC, programs were written as long lists of code with branches (Assembly's BNE, BEQ, and JMP) or execution flow statements (BASIC's GOTO).[20] Procedural programming allowed increased readability and management of complexity, at a slight cost in program performance. Procedural programming also offered the ability to reuse the same code throughout a program through procedure calls, functions, and multiple files. Strong proponents of the more recent paradigm of object-oriented programming may shudder at my liberal use of the term procedural, but I am not referring to the programming paradigm. Object-oriented programming extends the modularity introduced by procedural programming and therefore owes the latter a conceptual debt, but this relationship is not relevant to my purposes here. Rather, I understand procedurality as the fundamental notion of authoring processes.

Procedural figures, forms, and genres

Just as there are literary and filmic figures, so there are procedural figures. These are distinct from and prior to forms and genres. Procedural figures have much in common with literary figures like metaphor, metonymy, or synecdoche; they are strategies for authoring unit operations for particularly salient parts of many procedural systems. Noah Wardrip-Fruin has used the term *operational logics* to refer to the standardized or formalized unit operations that take on common roles in multiple procedural representations.[21] He identifies two operational logics that are particularly common, graphical logics and textual logics. Graphical logics are very frequently found in videogames; they include such procedural figures as movement, gravity, and collision detection. These fundamental figures ground innumerable videogames, from *Spacewar!* to *Pong* to *Pac-Man* to *Doom*. In many videogames, the player controls an object, agent, or vehicle that he must pilot in a particular manner—toward a goal or to avoid enemies or obstacles. Graphical logics frequently encapsulate procedural representations of material phenomena, such as moving, jumping, or firing projectiles. Object physics and lighting effects offer additional examples, meant to depict changing environments rather than character movement. In the videogame industry, sets of graphical logics are often packaged together as a *game engine*, a software toolkit used to create a variety of additional games.[22]

Wardrip-Fruin also cites textual logics as a common procedural trope. NLP, mentioned above, is an example of a textual logic, as are the text parsers inherent to Z-machine text adventure games and interactive fiction, such as *Zork*.[23] Additional logics include those procedural tropes used for text generation, such as n-grams, a probability distribution derived from Markov chains and first suggested by cyberneticist Claude Shannon. N-grams are sequences of a specified number (*n*) of elements from a given sequence, where probabilities determine which members of the sequence are most likely to be selected next. They are really sequential logics, but when applied to text generation they can be used to predict and construct textual phrases based on probability distributions of the subsequent word or phrase given a starting word or phrase. For example, in the sequence "where are" a likely subsequent word might be "you."[24]

Outside of videogames, procedural tropes often take the form of common models of user interaction. Elements of a graphical user interface could be understood as procedural tropes, for example, the scrollbar or push-button. These elements facilitate a wide range of user interactions in a variety of content domains. Operational logics for opening and saving files are also reasonable candidates; these tropes encapsulate lower-level logics for getting handles to filestreams and reading or writing byte data. We might call the former group of procedural tropes *interface logics*, and the latter *input/output (IO) logics*. Just as game engines accumulate multiple, common graphical logics, so software frameworks like Microsoft Foundation Classes (MFC) and Java Foundation Classes (JFC) accumulate multiple, common interface logics, IO logics, and myriad other logics required to drive the modern computer operating system.

Taken together, we can think of game engines, frameworks, and other common groupings of procedural tropes as commensurate with forms of literary or artistic expression, such as the sonnet, the short story, or the feature film. These collections of procedural tropes form the basis for a variety of subsequent expressive artifacts. On its own, the sonnet is no more useful than the physics engine, but both can be deployed in a range of expressive practices. A classical Newtonian mechanics simulation can easily facilitate both war (projectile fire) and naturalism (ballooning), just as a sonnet can facilitate both religious (John Donne) and amorous (Shakespeare) expression.

Procedural genres emerge from assemblages of procedural forms. These are akin to literary, filmic, or artistic genres like the film noir, the lyric poem, or the science fiction novel. In videogames, genres include the platformer, the first-person shooter, the turn-based strategy game, and so forth. When we recognize gameplay, we typically recognize the similarities between the constitutive procedural representations that produce the on-screen effects and controllable dynamics we experience as players.

Procedural representation is significantly different from textual, visual, and plastic representation. Even though other inscription techniques may be partly or wholly driven by a desire to represent human or material processes, only procedural systems like computer software actually represent process with process. This is where the particular power of procedural authorship lies, in its native ability to depict processes.

The inscription of procedural representations on the computer takes place in code. Just like *procedure*, the term *code* can take multiple meanings. Lawrence Lessig has taken advantage of the term's ambiguity to address the similarity between code in the legal sense and code in the programmatic sense: "In real space we recognize how laws regulate—through constitutions, statutes, and other legal codes. In cyberspace we must understand how code regulates—how the software and hardware that make cyberspace what it is *regulate* cyberspace as it is."[25] But in legal systems, code is regulated through complex social and political structures subject to many additional procedural influences, just like the soldiers in Abu Ghraib and the clerk at the retail return counter. In computational systems, code is regulated through software and hardware systems. These systems impose constraints, but they are not subject to the caprice of direct human action.

Rhetoric

Like procedurality, rhetoric is not an esteemed term. Despite its two and a half millennia-long history, *rhetoric* invokes largely negative connotations. We often speak of "empty rhetoric," elaborate and well-crafted speech that is nevertheless devoid of actual meaning. *Rhetoric* might conjure the impression of *hot air*, as in the case of a fast-talking con who crafts pretentious language to hide barren or deceitful intentions. Academics and politicians are particularly susceptible to this sort of criticism, perhaps because we (and they) tend to use flourish and lexis when coherence runs thin, as in this very sentence. Rhetoric is often equated with a type of smokescreen; it is language used to occlude, confuse, or manipulate the listener.

However, turgidity and extravagance are relatively recent inflections to this term, which originally referred only to persuasive speech, or oratory. The term *rhetoric* (ῥήτωρική) first appears in Plato's *Gorgias*, written some 2,500 years ago, in reference to the art of persuasion. The term itself derives from the rhetor (ῥήτωρ), or orator, and his practice, oratory (ῥήτωρεύω).[26] Rhetoric in ancient Greece—and by extension classical rhetoric in general—meant public speaking for civic purposes. Golden age Athenian democracy strongly influenced the early development of rhetoric, which dealt specifically with social and political practices. Rhetoric was oral and it was public. The rhetor used his art on specific occasions and in particular social contexts—the law court and the public forum. A well-known example of this type of rhetoric is Plato's *Apology*, in which Socrates defends himself against accusations that he has corrupted the youth of Athens— *apology* here refers to the Greek term ἀπολογία, a defense speech. In the context of public speech and especially legal and civic speech, rhetoric's direct relation to persuasion is much clearer. Spoken words attempt to convert listeners to a particular opinion, usually one that will influence direct and immediate action, such as the fateful vote of Socrates' jury.

In golden age Athens, there was good reason to become versed in rhetorical technique. Unlike our contemporary representative democracies, the Athenian system was much more direct. Citizens were required to participate in the courts, and anyone (i.e., any male) could speak in the assembly. Unlike our legal system, with its guarantees of professional representation, Athenians accused of a crime were expected to defend themselves (or to find a relative or friend to speak on their behalf). Furthermore, Athenian juries were huge—usually 201 members but often many hundreds more depending on the importance of the case. The average citizen untrained in oratory not only might find himself at a loss for words but also might experience significant intimidation speaking before such a large group.

Rhetorical training responded to this need, partly motivated by lucrative business opportunities. The title character in Plato's *Phaedrus* speaks of books on the subject of rhetoric (ἐν τοῖς περί λόγων τέχνης), and Socrates subsequently recounts the technical advice these books proffer:[27]

Socrates:	Thank you for reminding me. You mean that there must be an introduction [προοίμιον, *prooemion*] first, at the beginning of the discourse; these are the things you mean, are they not?—the niceties of the art.
Phaedrus:	Yes.
Socrates:	And the narrative [διήγησίν, *diegesis*] must come second with the testimony [τεχμήρια] after it, and third the proofs [πίστωσιν, *pistis*], and fourth the probabilities [ἐπιπίστωσιν, *epipistis*]; and confirmation and further confirmation are mentioned, I believe, by the man from Byzantium, that most excellent artist in words.
Phaedrus:	You mean the worthy Theodorus?
Socrates:	Of course. And he tells how refutation [ἐλεγχόν, *elenkhos*] and further refutation [ἐπεξέλεγχον, *epexelenkhos*] must be accomplished, both in accusation and in defense. Shall we not bring the illustrious Parian, Evenus, into our discussion, who invented covert allusion and indirect praises? And some say that he also wrote indirect censures, composing them in verse as an aid to memory; for he is a clever man.

. . .

But all seem to be in agreement concerning the conclusion of discourses, which some call recapitulation [ἐπάνοδον, *epanodos*], while others give it some other name.

Phaedrus:	You mean making a summary of the points of the speech at the end of it, so as to remind the hearers of what has been said?
Socrates:	These are the things I mean, these and anything else you can mention concerned with the art of rhetoric.[28]

Socrates' negative opinion of textbook rhetoric notwithstanding (see below), the *Phaedrus* offers evidence of the method by which fifth-century Greeks thought oratory could be best composed. Speakers should begin with an introduction *(prooemion)*, then continue with a description or narration of events *(diegesis)*, followed by proof and evidence *(pistis)* and the probabilities that such evidence is sound *(epipistis)*. The speaker should then refute the opposing claim *(elenkhos)*, and then refute it once more *(epexelenkhos)*. Finally, the speech should end with a conclusion, including a recapitulation *(epanodos)* of the argument.

These techniques form the basis for rhetorical speech; they describe how it works and they instruct the speaker on how best to use rhetoric in any situation. Technical rhetoric, as this type is sometimes called, is useful for the layperson but perhaps too simplistic for the professional orator. Numerous other techniques developed around imitating skilled orators. These experts usually charged for their services, and they were called *sophists*. Sophistic rhetoric was taught by demonstration and practice, not by principle like technical rhetoric. In some cases, a demonstration of sophistic rhetoric resembled the performance of epic poetry, where narrative fragments were memorized and reassembled during recitation.[29] Other techniques included parallelism in structure, syllabic meter, and tone.[30]

The popularity of books and sophistry bred critique. Such approaches motivated the work of Socrates, Plato, and Aristotle, who rejected the social and political contingency of the court and the assembly in favor of more lasting philosophical truths. Socrates and Plato privilege *dialectic*, or methods of reasoning about questions toward unknown conclusions, over rhetoric, which crafts discourse around known or desired conclusions. In Plato's *Georgias*, Socrates exposes rhetoric as a form of flattery, intended to produce pleasure, not knowledge or justice.[31]

Aristotle resuscitated rhetoric, joining it with his notion of causality. In the *Physics*, Aristotle articulates four causes, the material, formal, efficient, and final. The material cause is the material out of which a thing is made; the formal cause is the structure that makes it what it is; the efficient cause is that which produces the thing; and the final cause is the purpose for which it is produced.[32] A table, for example, is made of wood (material cause), crafted to have four legs and a flat surface (formal cause) by a carpenter (efficient cause) for the purpose of eating upon (final cause). For Aristotle, rhetoric has three possible ends, or final causes, and therefore he distinguishes three varieties of rhetoric: *forensic, deliberative*, and *epideictic*. Forensic (or judicial) rhetoric aims for justice, as in the purview of the law courts. Deliberative (or political) rhetoric strives for public benefit, as in the case of the assembly. Epideictic (or ceremonial) rhetoric aims for honor or shame, as in the case of a private communication.[33] Aristotle avoids Plato's dismissal of rhetoric, arguing that rhetorical practice as a whole has the final cause of persuasion to correct judgment.

In the *Rhetoric*, Aristotle accomplishes this corrective through an approach to rhetorical practice that aligns it with knowledge instead of sophistry. Responding to Plato, Aristotle attempts a systematic, philosophical approach to the art of persuasive oratory. This approach borrows much from the idea of oratory process from technical rhetoric, and a great deal of Aristotle's rhetorical theory addresses the style, arrangement, and organization of persuasive speech. For Aristotle, rhetoric is defined as "the faculty of observing in any given case the available means of persuasion."[34] The adept rhetorician does not merely follow a list of instructions for composing an oratory (technical rhetoric), nor does he merely parrot the style or words of an expert (sophistic rhetoric), but rather he musters reason to discover the available means of persuasion in any particular case (philosophical rhetoric). This variety of rhetoric implies an understanding of both the reasons to persuade (the final cause) and the tools available to achieve that end (the efficient cause), including propositions, evidence, styles, and devices. Most importantly, Aristotle offers a philosophical justification for rhetoric that moves it closer to dialectic, the philosophical practice of reason that Socrates and Plato deliberately opposed to rhetoric. In particular, Aristotle draws a correlation between two modes of human reason, induction (ἐπαγωγή) and deduction (συλλογισμός, *syllogism*). In rhetoric, the equivalent to induction is the example (παράδειγμα, *paradigm*), and the equivalent to deduction is the enthymeme (ἐνθύμημα). Examples advance the claim that a certain proposition is a part of a set of such (allegedly true) cases, and therefore equally true. Enthymemes advance the claim that a certain proposition is true in light of another's truth value. Unlike syllogisms, in which both propositions and conclusions are given explicitly, in enthymeme the orator omits one of the propositions in a syllogism.[35] For example, in the enthymeme "We cannot trust this man, as he is a politician," the major premise of a proper syllogism is omitted:

> Politicians are not trustworthy. (Omitted)
> This man is a politician.
> Therefore, we cannot trust this man.

The enthymeme and the example offer instances of a broad variety of rhetorical figures developed by and since Aristotle. Like procedural figures, rhetorical figures define the possibility space for rhetorical practice. These figures are many and a complete discussion of them would be impossible in the present context. However, many rhetorical figures will be familiar by virtue of our common experience with them: antithesis (the juxtaposition of contrasting ideas); paradox (a seemingly self-contradictory statement that produces insight or truth); oxymoron (a highly compressed paradox); aporia (feigning flummox about the best way to approach a proposition); irony (evoking contrary meaning to yield scorn). These and other rhetorical figures found the basis of rhetorical tactics. Combining these with the structural framework of introduction, statement, proof, and epilogue, Aristotle offers a complete process for constructing oratory.[36]

Rhetoric beyond oratory

Unlike his Roman counterparts Cicero and Quintilian, Aristotle does not explicitly define rhetoric as the art of *verbal* persuasion, although it is unlikely that any other rhetorical mode occurred to him. Classical rhetoric passed into the Middle Ages and modern times with considerable alteration. The use of rhetoric in civil contexts like the court never disappeared entirely, and indeed it remains a common form of rhetoric today; our modern politicians soapbox just as Plato's contemporaries did. But the concept of rhetoric was expanded beyond oratory and beyond direct persuasion. Effectively, rhetoric was extended to account for new modes of inscription—especially literary and artistic modes. Rhetoric in writing, painting, sculpture, and other media do not necessarily make the same direct appeals to persuasion as oratory. Rhetoric thus also came to refer to *effective expression*, that is, writing, speech, or art that both accomplishes the goals of the author and absorbs the reader or viewer.

Persuasion as a rhetorical goal persists, but it has changed in nature. In classical rhetoric, oral persuasion primarily served political purposes. It was enacted when needed and with particular ends in mind. The effectiveness of oratory related directly to its success or failure at accomplishing a particular, known goal. And because citizens often got only one shot at oratory—as is the case in Socrates' defense speech—one can point to the clear success or failure of rhetorical techniques. In discursive rhetoric, persuasion is not necessarily so teleological. Writers and artists have expressive goals, and they deploy techniques to accomplish those goals. The poststructuralist tendency to decouple authorship from readership, celebrating the free play of textual meanings, further undermines the status of persuasion. Here, persuasion shifts from the simple achievement of desired ends to the effective arrangement of a work so as to create a desirable possibility space for interpretation. In contemporary rhetoric, the goal of persuasion is largely underplayed or even omitted as a defining feature of the field, replaced by the more general notion of elegance, clarity, and creativity in communication. When understood in this sense, rhetoric "provides ways of emphasizing ideas or making them vivid."[37] Success means effective expression, not necessarily effective influence.

Despite the apparent dichotomy between classical and contemporary rhetorics, the two share one core property: that of technique. Rhetorics of all types assume a particular approach to effective expression, whether it be oral, written, artistic, or otherwise inscribed. Today, spoken and written expression remain deeply relevant to culture. The spoken and written word enjoys a long rhetorical tradition— Aristotle's techniques remain equally useful, and indeed equally put to use, by contemporary orators. Sonja Foss, Karen Foss, and Robert Trapp have attempted to reposition rhetoric outside of any particular mode of inscription. The three define rhetoric "broadly as the uniquely human ability to use symbols to communicate with one another."[38] However, as Kevin DeLuca points out, on the "very next page"[39] Foss, Foss, and Trapp also argue that "the paradigm case of rhetoric is the use of the spoken word to persuade an audience."[40] While rhetoric might include nonverbal transmission, these modes still maintain a tenuous relationship, and are at risk of appearing inferior to verbal discourse.

The influential twentieth-century rhetorician Kenneth Burke marks an important change in the understanding of rhetoric. Because people are inherently separate from one another, we seek ways to join our interests. Burke identifies this need as the ancestor of the practice of rhetoric. He extends rhetoric beyond persuasion, instead suggesting "identification" as a key term for the practice.[41] We use symbolic systems, such as language, as a way to achieve this identification. Burke defines rhetoric as a part of the practice of identification, as "the use of words by human agents to form attitudes or induce actions in other human agents."[42] While rhetoric still entails persuasion for Burke, he greatly expands its purview, arguing that it facilitates human action in general. Persuasion is subordinated to identification (or the more obscure term *consubstantiality*, which Burke uses to characterize identification), and using rhetoric to achieve an end is only one possible use of the craft for Burke.[43] Rhetoric becomes a means to facilitate identification and to "bridge the conditions of estrangement that are natural and inevitable."[44]

In addition to expanding the conception of rhetoric, Burke also expands its domain. Following the tradition of oral and written rhetoric, he maintains language as central, but Burke's understanding of humans as creators and consumers of symbolic systems expands rhetoric to include nonverbal domains. He does not explicitly delineate all the domains to which rhetoric could apply; instead, he embraces the broadness of human symbolic production in the abstract. "Wherever there is persuasion," writes Burke, "there is rhetoric. And wherever there is 'meaning,' there is 'persuasion.'"[45]

Visual rhetoric

The wide latitude Burke affords rhetoric won him both champions and critics, but his approach advances the rhetorical value of multiple forms of cultural expression, not just speech and writing.[46] Thanks to the influence of Burke, and amplified by the increasingly inescapable presence of non-oral, nonverbal media, increasing interest has mounted around efforts to understand the rhetorical figures and forms of these other, newer modes of inscription that also appear to serve rhetorical ends. In particular, the emergence of photographic and cinematic expression in the nineteenth and twentieth centuries suggests a need to understand how these new, nonverbal media mount arguments. This subfield is called *visual rhetoric*. Marguerite Helmers and Charles A. Hill explain:

> Rhetoricians working from a variety of disciplinary perspectives are beginning to pay a substantial amount of attention to issues of visual rhetoric. Through analysis of photographs and drawings, graphs and tables, and motion pictures, scholars are exploring the many ways in which visual elements are used to influence people's attitudes, opinions, and beliefs.[47]

Visual communication cannot simply adopt the figures and forms of oral and written expression, so a new form of rhetoric must be created to accommodate these media forms. Helmers and Hill argue that visual rhetoric is particularly essential in the face of globalization and mass media. Visual images on television, clothing, retail storefronts, and public spaces are nearly ubiquitous, offering a strong incentive to understand the rhetoric of such media. Moreover, the profusion of photographic, illustrative, and cinematic images increases with the rise in cheap, accessible digital photography and video techniques coupled with the instant, worldwide distribution on the Internet. Politicians and advertisers use visual images as much as, if not more than, they use spoken and written words. In reference to these and related uses of images, visual rhetoricians ask, "how, exactly, do images persuade?"[48]

Aristotle took great pains to reconnect rhetoric with philosophical discourse. A common thread in visual rhetoric addresses the relative merit of visual communication as emotional versus philosophical. As Hill explains,

> It is likely that verbal text, because of its analytic nature (being made up of discrete meaningful units) and because it is apprehended relatively slowly over time, is more likely to prompt systematic processing, while images, which are comprehend wholistically and almost instantaneously, tend to prompt heuristic processing.[49]

Images may lack the kind of deep analysis afforded by textual interpretation, a sentiment that resonates with concerns over the use of images in propaganda. According to Hill, images are more "vivid" than text or speech, and therefore they are more easily manipulated toward visceral responses.[50] This use of images has been especially popular in advertising, a subject to which I will return in chapter 5. Advertisers, notes Hill, "don't want to *persuade* people to buy their products, because persuasion implies that the audience has given the issue some thought and come to a conscious decision. Instead, advertisers want to . . . compel people to buy a product without even knowing why they're buying it—as a visceral response to a stimulus, not as a conscious decision. And this is best done through images."[51] Hill offers no final conclusions about the potential for images to serve more reflective rhetorical purposes, but he does point out that visual rhetoric should not strive "to banish emotional and aesthetic concerns."[52]

J. Anthony Blair argues that visual rhetoric needs a theory of visual argument to escape this trap. Blair argues that, like Hill's psychological vividness, "symbolic inducement" alone is inadequate for a theory of rhetoric.[53] Rather, visual rhetoric requires visual "arguments" which "supply us with *reasons* for accepting a point of view."[54] Blair advances the rather ambiguous view that visual images cannot make propositional claims—the very notion of a "visual argument" stands at the edge of paradox.[55] The acid test for a visual argument, according to Blair, is "whether it would be possible to construct from what is communicated visually a verbal argument that is consistent with the visual presentation."[56] Blair admits that such an argument could never be equivalent to the visual argument, but that the test is necessary to determine whether an image has propositional content. Verbal rhetoric remains privileged, with images mainly useful for "evocative power."[57]

The preferential treatment afforded to verbal rhetoric underscores the continued privilege of speech over writing, and writing over images. Philosopher Jacques Derrida argued against the hierarchy of forms of language, giving the name *logocentrism* to the view that speech is central to language because it is closer to thought.[58] In the Western tradition, speech is thought to derive from thought, and writing from speech. Detractors of visual rhetoric like Blair could be seen as logocentric in arguing that images derive from writing and are thus more distant from thought, less conducive to persuasive expression.

David S. Birdsell and Leo Groarke oppose this position. Visual argument does exist, but it takes a necessarily different form from that of verbal argument; images are, after all, a different mode of inscription from writing. Birdsell and Groarke call the "prevalent prejudice that visual images are in some way arbitrary vague and ambiguous" a "dogma that has outlived its usefulness."[59] Objections claiming that images are sometimes vague are unconvincing, for spoken and written language is also vague at times. Visual argument, argue Birdsell and Groarke, is simply constructed differently than verbal argument. The two also observe that the rapid changes in visual culture make visual cultural contexts crucial in considerations of visual argument.

Randall A. Lake and Barbara A. Pickering offer several tropes for visual argument and refutation, including substitution, in which an image is replaced in part of a frame with connotatively different ones, and transformation, in which an image is "recontextualized in a new visual frame, such that its polarity is modified or reversed through association with different images."[60] Examples of transformation include the "reframing" and "mobile framing" techniques used by filmmakers. Keith Kenney points out that documentarian Ken Burns liberally uses these gestures to reveal portions of an image in order to draw selective attention to its constituent parts, which then complete the visual argument.[61] Editorial cartoons, a favorite example of visual rhetoricians, use similar techniques, encouraging the viewer to break down the image into constituent parts, each of which advances a portion of the argument.

Kevin Michael DeLuca attempts to address visual argument through the concept of "image event," a kind of visual documentation of a rhetorical strategy.[62] He draws examples from large-scale environmental demonstrations, such as the (failed) 1975 Greenpeace attempt to disrupt the Soviet whaling vessel *Vlastny* by positioning activists in inflatable boats between the harpoon and the whale. DeLuca argues that despite the failed actions of Greenpeace's Save the Whales campaign, they succeed in their rhetorical purpose, namely drawing massive worldwide attention to the problem in question. DeLuca makes convincing claims that these situationist-style interventions actually influence future policy, but I would argue that they do not deploy visual rhetoric in the true sense of the word. To be sure, images of the Greenpeace actions appear to be partly, even largely responsible for subsequent protests and rejoinders toward environmental policy changes, but the actions themselves are designed to generate provocation, not to make arguments for policy changes.

The profusion of visual images recommends a subfield of rhetoric, but visual rhetoric remains an emerging discipline. The very notion of a visual rhetoric reinforces the idea that rhetoric is a general field of inquiry, applicable to multiple media and modes of inscription. To address the possibilities of a new medium as a type of rhetoric, we must identify how inscription works in that medium, and then how arguments can be constructed through those modes of inscription.

Digital rhetoric

Visual rhetoric offers a useful lesson in the creation of new forms of rhetoric in the general sense. One would be hard pressed to deny that advertisements, photographs, illustrations, and other optical phenomena have some effect on their viewers. To be sure, visual rhetoric is often at work in videogames, a medium that deploys both still and moving images. A study of visual rhetoric in games would need to address the disputes of the former field, especially the rift between psychological and cultural discourses about manipulation and phenomenal impact on the one hand and logical deliberation on the other. But despite its possible value to digital media, visual rhetoric cannot help us address the rhetorical function of procedural representation. To convincingly propose a new domain for rhetoric, one is obliged to address the properties of the persuasive medium in particular, and the general practice of persuasion on the other. Visual rhetoric simply does not account for procedural representation. This is not a flaw in the subfield of visual rhetoric; there is much value to be gained from the study of images in all media. But in procedural media like videogames, images are frequently constructed, selected, or sequenced in code, making the stock tools of visual rhetoric inadequate. Image is subordinate to process.

Unfortunately, many efforts to unite computers and rhetoric do not even make appeals to visual rhetoric, instead remaining firmly planted in the traditional frame of verbal and written rhetoric in support of vague notions of "the digital." *Digital rhetoric* typically abstracts the computer as a consideration, focusing on the text and image content a machine might host and the communities of practice in which that content is created and used. Email, websites, message boards, blogs, and wikis are examples of these targets. To be sure, all of these digital forms can function rhetorically, and they are worthy of study; like visual rhetoricians, digital rhetoricians hope to revise and reinvent rhetorical theory for a new medium. James P. Zappen begins his integrated theory of digital rhetoric on this very note: "Studies of digital rhetoric," he writes, "help to explain how traditional rhetorical strategies of persuasion function and are being reconfigured in digital spaces."[63] But for scholars of digital rhetoric, to "function in digital spaces" often means mistaking subordinate properties of the computer for primary ones. For example, Laura J. Gurak identifies several "basic characteristics"[64] of digital rhetoric, including speed, reach, anonymity, and interactivity.[65] Of these, the first three simply characterize the aggregate effects of networked microcomputers. On first blush the last characteristic, interactivity, appears to address the properties of the computer more directly. But Gurak does not intend *interactivity* to refer to the machine's ability to facilitate the manipulation of processes. Instead, she is thinking of the more vague notion of computer-mediated discussion and feedback, essentially a repetition and consolidation of the other three characteristics.[66]

Other digital rhetoricians likewise focus on the use of digital computers to carry out culturally modified versions of existing oral and written discourse; letters become emails, conversations become instant message sessions. Barbara Warnick has argued that the more populist, nonhierarchical structure of the web facilitated opposition to the standards of traditional media. For example, Warnick explores zines and personal websites as welcome alternatives to top-down commercial media like print magazines.[67] Others want educators, especially secondary and postsecondary instructors, to provide stylistic training in increasingly indispensable digital forms like email and the web. Richard Lanham has made a case for digital rhetoric's place in the broader "digital arts," encouraging higher education to address the changing composition practices brought on by so-called new media.[68] Both Warnick and Lanham's proposals are reasonable and valuable. But they focus on revisions of existing cultural and expressive practices; the computer is secondary. What is missing is a digital rhetoric that addresses the unique properties of computation, like procedurality, to found a new rhetorical practice.

This challenge is aggravated by the fact that rhetoric itself does not currently enjoy favor among critics of digital media. In one highly visible example, new media artist and theorist Lev Manovich has argued that digital media may sound a death knell for rhetoric. Writing about web interfaces, Manovich doubts that hypertext could serve a rhetorical function:

> While it is probably possible to invent a new rhetoric of hypermedia that will use hyperlinking not to distract the reader from the argument (as is often the case today), but rather to further convince her of an argument's validity, the sheer existence and popularity of hyperlinking exemplifies the continuing decline of the field of rhetoric in the modern era . . . . World Wide Web hyperlinking has privileged the single figure of metonymy at the expense of all others. The hypertext of the World Wide Web leads the reader from one text to another, ad infinitum . . . . Rather than seducing the user through a careful arrangement of arguments and examples, points and counterpoints, changing rhythms of presentation, . . . [hypertext] interfaces . . . bombard the user with all the data at once.[69]

One can raise numerous objections to Manovich's claims. For one, he has a rather curious view of hypertext that seems to equate hypermedia with media gluttony. Manovich seems to think that web pages present links in an attempt to substitute their linkage for their content, causing endless, haptic clicking on the part of the user. Meaning is tragically, "infinitely" deferred. This claim is especially curious given the prehistory of hypertext in Vannevar Bush's conceptual Memex and Ted Nelson's Xanadu.[70] These systems were conceived largely as tools to *increase* the correlation between documents, as material manifestations of manual cross-reference. Today, hypertext on "ordinary" websites is frequently used in this fashion; they provide additional information or resources to the user who wishes to confer them. Frequently, these resources take the form of supporting arguments, evidence, or citation, very old and very traditional tools in written rhetoric.

While Manovich considers the nature of the hyperlink, he ignores the computational system that facilitates hypermedia in the first place. Chris Crawford has used the term *process intensity* to refer to the "degree to which a program emphasizes processes instead of data."[71] Higher process intensity—or in Crawford's words a higher "crunch per bit ratio"—suggests that a program has greater potential for meaningful expression. While hypertexts themselves exhibit low process intensity, the systems that allow authorship and readership of web pages exhibit high process intensity. A web browser must construct a request for a page using the proper format for the Hypertext Transfer Protocol (HTTP) that carries requests between the computer and a server. The computer must then create a connection to the server via Transmission Control Protocol (TCP), which in turn communicates the request via Internet Protocol (IP), the communication convention that transports data across the packet-switched network that comprises the Internet. The server hosting the requested web page must then interpret the request, retrieve the requested document, and prepare it for transmission back to the user's computer via the same protocols, HTTP atop TCP/IP. IP guarantees delivery of all packets in a request, so the receiving computer's network layer must determine—all in code—whether all the packets have been received, which ones are out of order, and which need to be resent owing to corruption or loss. Once received, reordered, and reconstructed, the web browser must then take the textual data that the server has returned and render it in the browser. This too takes place in code. The web page is made up of Hypertext Markup Language (HTML), which the browser must parse, making decisions about which elements to place where and in what format on the user's screen. Then the web browser repeats the process for other resources referenced in the HTML document, such as other embedded HTML pages, images, script files, or stylesheets.

These technical details may appear to have little to do with Manovich's claims about the endless progression of hyperlinks on a web page. But the aggregate software systems that facilitate web-based hypertext are what make it possible to link and click in the first place. The principal innovation of the web is the merger of a computer-managed cross-referencing system with a networking system that supports heterogenous clients. More plainly put, Manovich ignores the software systems that make it possible for hyperlinks to work in the first place, instead making loose and technically inaccurate appeals to computer hardware as exotic metaphors rather than as material systems. Continuing the argument above, he compares hypertext to computer chipsets: "individual texts are placed in no particular order, like the Web page designed by [artist collective] antirom for HotWired. Expanding this comparison further, we can note that Random Access Memory, the concept behind the group's name, also implies a lack of hierarchy: Any RAM location can be accessed as quickly as any other."[72] Manovich compares the HotWired website to RAM not because computer memory facilitates the authorship of websites, but because the website was designed by a group that uses a pun on a computer chip term in their name—a different chip from RAM, as it happens, Read Only Memory, or ROM.

Manovich admits that a new rhetoric of hypermedia is "probably possible," but clearly he has no intention of pursuing one. Gurak and Warnick are not cynical about rhetoric and communication, but they focus on digital communities of practice, treating the computer primarily as a black-box network appliance, not as an executor of processes. In short, digital rhetoric tends to focus on the presentation of traditional materials—especially text and images—without accounting for the computational underpinnings of that presentation.

Rhetorician Elizabeth Losh neatly summarizes this inconsistency among digital rhetoricians. "In the standard model of digital rhetoric," she argues, "literary theory is applied to technological phenomena without considering how technological theories could conversely elucidate new media texts."[73] While I admit that there are useful interrogations of digital media that focus on reception over the technological structure (Losh's own work on the way digital artifacts take part in the public sphere is such a one), my contention here is that approaches to digital rhetoric must address the role of procedurality, the unique representational property of the computer.

Procedural rhetoric

With these lessons in mind, I would now like to put the concepts of *procedurality* and *rhetoric* back together. As I proposed at the start of this chapter, *procedural rhetoric* is the practice of using processes persuasively, just as verbal rhetoric is the practice of using oratory persuasively and visual rhetoric is the practice of using images persuasively. Procedural rhetoric is a general name for the practice of authoring arguments through processes. Following the classical model, procedural rhetoric entails persuasion—to change opinion or action. Following the contemporary model, procedural rhetoric entails expression—to convey ideas effectively. Procedural rhetoric is a subdomain of procedural authorship; its arguments are made not through the construction of words or images, but through the authorship of rules of behavior, the construction of dynamic models. In computation, those rules are authored in code, through the practice of programming.

My rationale for suggesting a new rhetorical domain is the same one that motivates visual rhetoricians. Just as photography, motion graphics, moving images, and illustrations have become pervasive in contemporary society, so have computer hardware, software, and videogames. Just as visual rhetoricians argue that verbal and written rhetorics inadequately account for the unique properties of visual expression, so I argue that verbal, written, and visual rhetorics inadequately account for the unique properties of procedural expression. A theory of procedural rhetoric is needed to make commensurate judgments about the software systems we encounter every day and to allow a more sophisticated procedural authorship with both persuasion and expression as its goal.

Procedural rhetorics afford a new and promising way to make claims about *how things work*. Consider a particularly sophisticated example of a procedural rhetoric at work in a game. *The McDonald's Videogame* is a critique of McDonald's business practices by Italian social critic collective Molleindustria. The game is an example of a genre I call the anti-advergame, a game created to censure or disparage a company rather than support it.[74] The player controls four separate aspects of the McDonald's production environment, each of which he has to manage simultaneously: the third-world pasture where cattle are raised as cheaply as possible; the slaughterhouse where cattle are fattened for slaughter; the restaurant where burgers are sold; and the corporate offices where lobbying, public relations, and marketing are managed. In each sector, the player must make difficult business choices, but more importantly he must make difficult moral choices. In the pasture, the player must create enough cattle-grazing land and soy crops to produce the meat required to run the business. But only a limited number of fields are available; to acquire more land, the player must bribe the local governor for rights to convert his people's crops into corporate ones. More extreme tactics are also available: the player can bulldoze rainforest or dismantle indigenous settlements to clear space for grazing (see figure 1). These tactics correspond with the questionable business practices the developers want to critique. To enforce the corrupt nature of these tactics, public interest groups can censure or sue the player for violations. For example, bulldozing indigenous rainforest settlements yields complaints from antiglobalization groups. Overusing fields reduces their effectiveness as soil or pasture; creating dead earth also angers environmentalists. However, those groups can be managed through PR and lobbying in the corporate sector. Corrupting a climatologist may dig into profits, but it ensures fewer complaints in the future. Regular subornation of this kind is required to maintain allegiance. Likewise, in the slaughterhouse players

Figure 1 In Molleindustria's *The McDonald's Game*, players must use questionable business practices to increase profits

can use growth hormones to fatten cows faster, and they can choose whether to kill diseased cows or let them go through the slaughter process. Removing cattle from the production process reduces material product, thereby reducing supply and thereby again reducing profit. Growth hormones offend health critics, but they also allow the rapid production necessary to meet demand in the restaurant sector. Feeding cattle animal by-products cheapens the fattening process, but is more likely to cause disease. Allowing diseased meat to be made into burgers may spawn complaints and fines from health officers, but those groups too can be bribed through lobbying. The restaurant sector demands similar trade-offs, including balancing a need to fire incorrigible employees with local politicians' complaints about labor practices.

The McDonald's Videogame mounts a procedural rhetoric about the necessity of corruption in the global fast food business, and the overwhelming temptation of greed, which leads to more corruption. In order to succeed in the long-term, the player must use growth hormones, he must coerce banana republics, and he must mount PR and lobbying campaigns. Furthermore, the temptation to destroy indigenous villages, launch bribery campaigns, recycle animal parts, and cover up health risks is tremendous, although the financial benefit from doing so is only marginal. As Patrick Dugan explains, the game imposes "constraints simulating necessary evils on one hand, and on the other hand . . . business practices that are self-defeating and, really just stupid."[75] The game makes a procedural argument about the inherent problems in the fast food industry, particularly the necessity of overstepping environmental and health-related boundaries.

Verbal rhetoric certainly supports this type of claim; one can explain the persuasive function of processes with language: consider my earlier explanation of the rhetoric of retail store return policies, or Eric Schlosser's popular book and film *Fast Food Nation*, which addresses many of the issues represented in *The McDonald's Videogame*.[76] But these written media do not express their arguments procedurally; instead, they describe the processes at work in such systems with speech, writing, or images. Likewise, it is possible to characterize processes with visual images. Consider a public service campaign called *G!rlpower Retouch*, commissioned by the Swedish Ministry of Health and Social Affairs. The goal of the campaign was to reduce the fixation on physical appearance caused partly by unrealistic body images in magazines and media. Forsman & Bodenfors, the agency hired to execute the campaign, created a click-through demo that explains how photo retouchers make significant changes to the bodies of their already striking models, hoping to render them even more perfect.[77] The demonstration depicts an attractive, young blonde on the cover of a fictional magazine. The user is then given the opportunity to undo all the photo retouches and individually reapply them. A textual explanation of the technique is also provided.

G!rlpower Retouch unpacks a process, the process of retouching photos for maximum beauty. It uses sequences of images combined with written text to explain each step. The artifact makes claims about images, so it makes reasonable use of images as propositions in the argument. *Retouch* even deploys the Aristotelian tactic of example, using a single model image to depict feature modifications common to all model images—eyes, teeth, lips, nose, jawline, hair, breasts, and so forth. The piece makes claims about the process of retouching, which is itself facilitated by the procedural affordances of image editing software like *Adobe Photoshop*. However, *Retouch* does not deploy a procedural rhetoric, since it does not use representational processes to explain the actual processes used in photo retouching. That said, one could imagine a procedural version of the same argument. Simply replicating a photo editor would supply the needed procedurality, but not the required rhetoric. The steps needed to accomplish the individual effects are complex and require professional-level command of the tools. Instead, a procedural implementation might abstract a set of editing tools particular to model editing, for example a "thinning" tool for waists, arms, and hips. Shadow and highlighting tools could be added for cheeks, hair, and breast augmentation. Instead of clicking through a sequence of images that explain the retouching process, the user would be put in charge of implementing it himself. A procedural implementation would accentuate and extend the use of paradigmatic evidence in the existing version of *Retouch*. In its current implementation, the piece depicts only one model. Her archetypical appearance makes her an effective example, and her three-quarter perspective pose allows the authors to address both face and body modifications. But a procedural version of the same argument would facilitate a variety of different images, full-body, head-and-shoulders, different body types, and so forth. Such a system might also allow the user to load his own photos, or photos from the Internet; these would serve as the data on which the retouching processes could run. Such a capacity would extend the rhetorical power of example.

Another, similar online consumer-awareness tool makes strides in the direction of procedural rhetoric while resting comfortably in the domain of visual rhetoric. PBS Kids maintains a website for young viewers, hosting show pages, games, and other interactive features.[78] Among the features is "Don't Buy It," a minisite that seeks to educate kids about the tricks advertisers use to turn kids into consumers.[79] The site features simple quizzes to help kids understand media manipulation (coincidentally, among them is a much simpler version of *G!rlpower Retouch* for food advertising).[80]

One of these features is *Freaky Flakes*, an interactive program that allows the user to design a cereal box. Unlike *Retouch*, *Freaky Flakes* asks the user to construct a box from the ground up, starting with its color. Textual information explains the benefits of each color, for example, "Orange stimulates the appetite and is one of the most popular cereal box colors." Next the user selects a character, again reading textual descriptions, for example, "The superhero is a great choice because little kids prefer fantasy characters to pictures of real people." Next the user enters a cereal name; the program advises him to "pick a name that is an attention grabber." Then the user selects one of four banners to add to the box to add marketing appeal, such as "Outrageous Crunch!" which "makes your cereal seem fun and exciting to eat." Finally, the user selects a prize to place inside, following advice about gender identification such as "Tattoos appeal to boys and girls." The user can view the completed box (see figure 2) or make a new one.

The argument *Freaky Flakes* mounts is more procedural than *Retouch*, but only incrementally so. The user recombines elements to configure a cereal box, but he chooses from a very small selection of individual configurations. *Freaky Flakes* is designed for younger users than *Retouch*, but the children who watch PBS Kids also likely play videogames much more complex than this simple program. Most importantly, *Freaky Flakes* fails to integrate the process of designing a cereal box with the supermarket where children might actually encounter it. The persuasion in *Retouch* reaches its apogee when the user sees the already attractive girl in the fake magazine ad turned into a spectacularly beautiful one. This gesture is a kind of visual enthymeme, in which the authors rely on the user's instinctual and culturally mediated idea of beauty to produce actual arousal, jealousy, or self-doubt. *Freaky Flakes* offers no similar conclusion. The user creates a cereal box, but every box yields the same result (even combining the superhero and the princess ring yields the congratulatory message, "Your box looks great!"). A more effective procedural argument would enforce a set of rules akin to the tactics advertisers use to manipulate kids, while providing a much larger possibility space for box authorship. Within this space, the user would have the opportunity both to succeed and to fail in his attempt to manipulate the simulated children buying the cereal. Through multiple designs, the user might home in on the logic that drives the advertisers, resulting in increased sales of his virtual cereal. This gesture represents a procedural enthymeme—the player *literally* fills in the missing portion of the syllogism by interacting with the application, but that action is constrained by the rules. That is to say, a set of procedural constraints would determine which combinations of design strategies influence kids more and less successfully.

Let's revisit verbal and visual rhetorics' stumbling blocks in light of these two examples of potential procedural rhetorics. Charles Hill pointed out that images offer greater "vividness" than verbal narration or written description. Vivid information, he argued, "seems to be more persuasive than non-vivid

Figure 2 PBS's *Freaky Flakes* offers a simple representation of practices of children's advertising
Courtesy of KCTS Television. © 2004 KCTS Television. All rights reserved.

information."[81] J. Anthony Blair countered that vivid images may increase presence, but they do not necessarily mount arguments. Even if images successfully cause viewers to take certain actions, those viewers are more likely manipulated than they are persuaded. Visual arguments, argues Blair, "lack [the] dialectical aspect [of] the process of interaction between the arguer and the interlocutors, who raise questions or objections."[82] Procedural rhetoric must address two issues that arise from these discussions: first, what is the relationship between procedural representation and vividness? Second, what is the relationship between procedural representation and dialectic?

To address the first question, I reproduce a table from Hill's essay, which he names "A comprehensive continuum of vividness."

Most Vivid Information	actual experience
	moving images with sound
	static photograph
	realistic painting
	line drawing
	narrative, descriptive account
	descriptive account
	abstract, impersonal analysis
Least Vivid Information	statistics

Immediately one can see that procedural representation is absent from this continuum. Simulation does not even make the list. Further yet, Hill accounts for no computational media whatsoever. I would be less inclined to quibble with the exclusion had Hill not called the continuum "comprehensive," indicating his intention to cover representational forms and their relationship to vividness fully.[83] Procedural representation is representation, and thus certainly not identical with actual experience. However, procedural representation can muster moving images and sound, and software and videogames are capable of generating moving images in accordance with complex rules that simulate real or imagined physical and cultural processes. Furthermore, procedural representations are often (but not always—see below) interactive; they rely on user interaction as a mediator, something static and moving images cannot claim to do. These capacities would suggest that procedurality is more vivid than moving images with sound, and thus earns the second spot on the continuum, directly under actual experience.[84] However, other factors might affect the relative vividness of procedural representations. For example, a simulation that accepts numerical input and generates numerical output might seem more akin to an abstract, impersonal analysis or even a set of statistics, falling to the bottom of Hill's continuum. Recalling Crawford's notion of process intensity, I would submit that procedural representations with high process intensity and with meaningful symbolic representations in their processes—specimens like interactive fiction, software, and especially videogames—certainly earn a spot above moving images on the continuum. Given this caveat, procedural representation seems equally prone to the increased persuasive properties Hill attributes to vividness.

What about procedural representations' relationship to dialectic? Hill argues that images are comprehended "wholistically and instantaneously," whereas verbal texts are apprehended "relatively slowly over time" as a result of their "analytic nature."[85] Interestingly, Hill characterizes the latter as "made up of discrete meaningful units," a property somewhat similar to my characterization of procedurality as the configuration of logical rules as unit operations. Blair's objection to visual arguments centers around images' reduced ability to advance propositions, a requirement of rhetorical argument. The visual argument Blair names most effective is the famous 1964 Lyndon Johnson television spot known as the "Daisy Ad."[86] Here is an account of the ad as accurately described by Wikipedia (www.wikipedia.org):

> The commercial begins with a small girl picking the petals of a daisy while counting slowly. An ominous-sounding male voice is then heard counting down as the girl turns toward the camera, which zooms in until her pupil fills the screen, blacking it out. Then the countdown reaches zero and the blackness is replaced by the flash and mushroom cloud from a nuclear test. A voiceover from Johnson follows: "These are the stakes! To make a world in which all of God's children can live, or to go into the dark. We must either love each other, or we must die." Another voiceover then says, "Vote for President Johnson on November 3. The stakes are too high for you to stay home."[87]

Blair argues that this visual image *does* make an argument "in the sense of adducing a few reasons in a forceful way."[88] In particular, the ad invokes a visual enthymeme that completes a syllogism:

> Increasing nuclear proliferation will likely lead to the destruction of humanity.
> Goldwater supports nuclear proliferation (omitted).
> Therefore, electing Goldwater may lead to the destruction of humanity.

Nevertheless, argues Blair, the ad "does not embody dialectic completely. In particular, it "does not permit the complexity of such dialectical moves as the raising of objections in order to refute or otherwise answer them."[89]

How does such an example compare with procedural representation? For one part, procedural rhetorics do mount propositions: each unit operation in a procedural representation is a claim about how part of the system it represents does, should, or could function. *The McDonald's Videogame* makes claims about the business practices required to run a successful global fast-food empire. My hypothetical revision of *Freaky Flakes* makes claims about the techniques advertisers use to design cereal boxes, as well as claims about children's culturally and psychologically influenced responses to specific box configurations. These propositions are every bit as logical as verbal arguments—in fact, internal consistency is often assured in computational arguments, since microprocessors and not human agents are in charge of their consistent execution.[90]

What about raising objections? One might argue that many computational systems do not allow the user to raise *procedural* objections—that is, the player of a videogame is usually not allowed to change the rules of play. Many critics have objected to this tendency, calling for games that allow players to alter core simulation dynamics to allow alternative perspectives. Most famously, Sherry Turkle has criticized[91] *Sim City*[92] for its failure to include alternative taxation-to-social services dynamics, a debate I have discussed in detail elsewhere.[93] Applying this objection to our current examples, one might point out that users of *Freaky Flakes* cannot make alterations to the designers' conception of advertising manipulation.

I have two responses to this objection. For one part, the type of user alteration Turkle and others call for is not the same as the dialectical objections Blair requires of arguments. One raises objections to propositions in the hopes of advancing conflicting or revisionist claims. Conversely, one allows user alteration in order to construct an artifact that accounts for multiple perspectives on a particular subject. One usually makes rhetorical claims precisely to *exclude* opposing positions on a subject, not to allow for the equal validity of all possible positions. For example, in the case of *Freaky Flakes*, one might object that the underlying model for advertising influence presumes the media ecology of consumer capitalism. This is a reasonable objection; but such a wholesale revision might imply a different simulation entirely, one that would be outside the expressive domain of the artifact. However, procedural representations often do allow the user to mount procedural objections through configurations of the system itself. In my hypothetical procedural revision of *Freaky Flakes*, the player might attempt to find inconsistencies in the creator's model by designing boxes that both produce socially responsible messages and appeal to children.

For another part, all artifacts subject to dissemination need not facilitate direct argument with the rhetorical author; in fact, even verbal arguments usually do not facilitate the open discourse of the Athenian assembly. Instead, they invite other, subsequent forms of discourse, in which interlocutors can engage, consider, and respond in turn, either via the same medium or a different one. Dialectics, in other words, function in a broader media ecology than Blair and Turkle allow. This objection applies equally to all rhetorical forms—verbal, written, visual, procedural, or otherwise.

Just as an objection in a debate would take place during the negation or rebuttal of the opponent rather than in the construction of the proponent, so an objection in a procedural artifact may take place in a responding claim of a verbal, written, visual, or procedural form. Such objections are not disallowed by the Daisy ad or by *Freaky Flakes*; they merely require the interlocutor to construct a new claim in another context—for example a responding TV spot or software program.

Consider an example of a procedural representation that addresses both of these concerns. *The Grocery Game* is a website that gives subscribers access to a special grocery list, sorted by grocery store and U.S. location.[94] The game's premise is this: supermarkets structure their pricing to maximize consumer spending on a short-term basis; they count on families buying enough groceries for about a week's time and then returning for more the following week. Buying in this fashion inevitably costs more, as consumers don't take advantage of the cost leverage afforded by bulk purchases of staples. *The Grocery Game* addresses this issue by automating the research necessary to produce lists of common products that maximize weekly coupon and in-store specials for a given week, while encouraging larger purchases of basics to last many weeks. Despite its name, "The List" is really a procedural system designed to maximize savings through strategic use of coupons and stockpiling. The game's method is clarified on the website:

> The Grocery Game is a fun, easy way to save hundreds of dollars on groceries each month. TERI'S LIST [the founder's name is Teri] reveals the "rock bottom" prices on hundreds of products each week and matches them up with manufacturers' coupons for the best possible savings at your local supermarket. The Grocery Game has exclusive databases that track manufacturers' coupons along with weekly sales and specials, both advertised and UN-advertised. With TERI'S LIST, the days of time consuming work required for effective couponing are over. The Grocery Game does all the hard work and research, presented in a quick reference format on the internet each week, as TERI'S LIST. Members log in, spend a few minutes with a pair of scissors, and they're off to win The Grocery Game!

The game has a goal (save as much money as possible) and a set of simple rules (stockpiling and couponing) that constitute its procedural rhetoric. A subsequent procedural system trolls grocery stock and advertising lists to produce a savings-maximized shopping plan tuned to a particular locality, based on the two tactics just mentioned.

The Grocery Game makes two major claims. For one part, it claims that the grocery business relies on weekly shopping for higher profits. Playing for a month and checking one's grocery budget against a previous month easily confirms this claim. For another part, the game claims that grocery shopping is fundamentally an exercise in spending as little money as possible. One might raise several objections to this claim: gastronomy is an experience central to human culture and should not be blindly replaced with frugality; buying the cheapest products for a given week sidesteps considerations like business ethics and the sustainability of growers and manufacturers; the cheapest products are sometimes, and perhaps often, at odds with ideal nutritional goals; a lowest-common-denominator grocery list assumes that all families are the same, while in fact every family has specific tastes and health considerations (such as food allergies); stockpiling requires storage space, which supports an undesirable obsession with material property. *The Grocery Game* has a hard time responding to these objections, although it is possible to pick and choose among the items the search algorithm generates.

While the game does not provide the user with direct access to the search algorithms that generate its lists, so that a user could wage these objections in code, it does provide a flourishing community of conversation. The message boards have entire threads devoted to savings for a particular week. This variation on the high-score list replaces hierarchical performance with discourse—an opportunity to share how well you did according to your own particular goals. It's not just about winning; it's also about telling people what you did and how you did it. Cash savings are winnings in a literal sense. To a lesser extent, so is fooling the grocery industry by refusing to play by their profit-maximizing rules. But the real winnings seem to come from what people do with what they save. Here's an example from the boards:

> i [*sic*, throughout] have been a lister for 1 year now. grocery shopping has changed 100% for me. i dreaded every single minute of being in a market. now, i find it to be fun. i average 100.00 a week in savings and spending 150.00. Today, i was able to purchase the dvd "Holes" for my children. It is because of the great savings weekly that i am able to purchase things like that "big ticket" item with ease.[95]

The community discourse at the game's message boards are not always related to objections to its underlying procedural rhetoric, but the availability of this forum facilitates active reconfiguration of the game's rules and goals, a topic to which I will return in chapter 11.

Interactivity

Procedural representations do not necessarily support user interaction. Many computational simulation methods make claims about processes in the material world, but limit user participation significantly. Take a simple computational model like the Monte Carlo method, a statistical sampling technique used to approximate the results of complex quantitative problems. The classic example of the Monte Carlo method in practice is the so-called Buffon's needle problem. George-Louis Leclerc, Comte de Buffon, posed the following question: If a needle of a particular length is dropped at random onto a horizontal surface ruled with parallel lines drawn at a greater than the length of the needle, what is the probability that the needle will cross one of the lines?[96] In a computational model of the Monte Carlo algorithm, the user might configure the length of the needle and the distance of the lines, then run the operation. Similarly, in a physical simulation, such as a demonstration of rigid body collision or mechanical dynamics, a human operator might configure the size and mass of objects or the relative force of gravity, elasticity, and other properties before observing the result.

A more complex and expressive example of a procedural system with limited user interaction can be found in Chris Crawford's 1990 game about global ecology, *Balance of the Planet*.[97] In the game, the player sets global environmental policies. The game challenges players to balance global ecological and economic forces through taxation and expenditure. However, each of the player's policies sets a complex set of interrelated relationships in motion. For example, forest clearing changes the carbon dioxide levels, which affect global warming. The player enacts policy by adjusting sliders to change underlying policies (see figure 3), executing the results, and again revising the policies.

The Monte Carlo simulation, physical simulations, and *Balance of the Planet* all accept simple user input and configuration, perhaps the most basic type of input to a computer program other than merely executing and automatically returning results based on hard-coded parameters. *Interactivity* is an entrenched notion in studies of digital media. Janet Murray rightly calls the term "vague" despite its "pervasive use."[98] Murray argues that the simple manipulation of a computational system, the "mere ability to move a joystick or click on a mouse" is not sufficient cause for "agency"—genuine embodied participation in an electronic environment.[99] Rather, such environments must be meaningfully responsive to user input. This state of affairs constitutes one of Murray's four properties of the computer, its *participatory* nature. "Procedural environments," she argues, "are appealing to us not just because they exhibit rule-generated behavior, but because we can induce the behavior . . . . the primary representational property of the computer is the codified rendering of responsive behaviors. This is what is most often meant when we say that computers are *interactive*. We mean they create an environment that is both procedural and participatory."[100]

As *Balance of the Planet* suggests, procedural rhetorics do not necessarily demand sophisticated interactivity. But we might ask if procedural rhetorics *benefit* from sophisticated interactivity. Following Murray, *sophistication* in this context does not refer to *more* or *more frequent* interaction, the kind that more buttons or faster hand-eye responses would entail. Rather, sophisticated interactivity means greater responsiveness, tighter symbolic coupling between user actions and procedural representations. *Balance of the Planet* offers a terrifically sophisticated procedural model of global ecology, but its coupling of user action to the game's causal model is weak, reducing both empathetic and dialectical engagement.

Another way to understand the role of interactivity in procedural rhetoric is through the concept of *play*. The weak coupling between model and experience in *Balance of the Planet* does not arise from a poverty of procedural representation. Rather, it arises from the awkward way that representation is exposed to the player. Play is a complex concept with a long and arduous intellectual history in numerous fields. Rather than understand play as child's activity, or as the means to consume games, or even as the shifting centers of meaning in poststructuralist thought, I suggest adopting Katie Salen and Eric Zimmerman's useful, abstract definition of the term: "play is the free space of movement within a more rigid structure."[101] Understood in this sense, play refers to the possibility space created by processes themselves. Salen and Zimmerman use the example of the play in a mechanism like a steering column, in which the meshing gears creates "play" in the wheel, before the turning gesture causes the gears to couple. In a procedural representation like a videogame, the possibility space refers to the myriad configurations the player might construct to see the ways the processes inscribed in the system work. This is really what we do when we *play* videogames: we explore the possibility space its rules afford by manipulating the game's controls.

Figure 3 Chris Crawford's 1990 title *Balance of the Planet* offers a sophisticated model of interrelated environmental issues

While *Balance of the Planet* sports a very large possibility space, the game's controls and feedback system make it difficult for players to keep track of the decisions they have already made and to see the aggregate effects of those decisions. The game is *hard to play*; that is, it is difficult to understand the processes at work inside and the nature of the possibility space those processes create.

In the context of procedural rhetoric, it is useful to consider interactivity in relation to the Aristotelian enthymeme. The enthymeme, we will remember, is the technique in which a proposition in a syllogism is omitted; the listener (in the case of oratory) is expected to fill in the missing proposition and complete the claim. Sophisticated interactivity can produce an effective procedural enthymeme, resulting in more sophisticated procedural rhetoric. Sometimes we think of interactivity as producing user empowerment: the more interactive the system, the more the user can do, and the better the experience. For example, many players and critics have celebrated *Grand Theft Auto III (GTAIII)*[102] as a game that allows the player to "go anywhere, do anything."[103] This sentiment is flawed for several reasons. First, the game does not actually allow the player to "do anything"; rather, in the words of one reviewer, *"GTAIII* let you do anything you wish, within the parameters of the game."[104] The "parameters of the game" are made up of the processes it supports and excludes. For example, entering and exiting vehicles is afforded in *GTAIII*, but conversing with passersby is not (see chapter 3 for more on this subject). This is not a limitation of the game, but rather the very way it becomes procedurally expressive. Second, the interactivity afforded by the game's coupling of player manipulations and gameplay effects is much narrower than the expressive space the game and the player subsequently create. The player performs a great deal of mental synthesis, filling the gap between subjectivity and game processes.

Previously, I have argued that the ontological position of a videogame (or simulation, or procedural system) resides in the gap between rule-based representation and player subjectivity; I called this space the "simulation gap."[105] Another way to think about the simulation gap is in relation to rhetoric. A procedural model like a videogame could be seen as a system of nested enthymemes, individual procedural claims that the player literally completes through interaction. If *Balance of the Planet* increased player interaction by adding more sliders to move, it would not necessarily become more expressive or more persuasive. On Hill's vividness continuum, *Balance of the Planet* might land closer to the realm of abstract analysis, despite its rich procedural policy model. However, if it increased the coupling between the computer's procedural rhetoric and the exposition of that rhetoric, its persuasive value would likely increase as well. Ironically, Chris Crawford himself has offered a definition of interactivity that addresses this very problem: "I choose to define it [interactivity] in terms of a conversation: a cyclic process in which two actors alternately listen, think, and speak. The quality of the interaction depends on the quality of each of the subtasks (listening, thinking, and speaking)."[106] In the case of *Balance of the Planet*, the player does a lot of meaningful listening and thinking, but not much meaningful speaking. The computer does a lot of meaningful thinking, but not much meaningful listening or speaking. Maximizing all three does not necessarily optimize expression—*GTAIII* does limited computational listening and thinking, for example—but understanding the relationship between the three can offer clues into the rhetorical structure of a procedural argument.

Videogames

I have chosen to explain and exemplify the function of procedural rhetoric in a subcategory of procedural expression, namely, videogames. There are several reasons I privilege this medium over other procedural media, and over other computational media in particular.

For one part, videogames are among the most procedural of computational artifacts. All software runs code, but videogames tend to run more code, and also to do more with code. Recalling Crawford's term, videogames tend to offer more process intensity than other computational media. Videogames tend to demand a significant share of a computer's central processing unit (CPU) resources while running; they are more procedural than other computational artifacts. As I write this paragraph, my computer is running twelve major applications, including the active one, resource hog *Microsoft Word*, and some seventy total processes to run the machine's underlying systems—window management, networking, graphics, audio, and so forth. Despite this immodest quantity of activity, my CPU remains 75–85 percent idle. The quantity of processes and the amount of random access memory (RAM) they consume does not necessarily correlate with their process intensity. Modern videogames often require another processor devoted to processing graphics instructions, a graphics processing unit (GPU). Videogames regularly drive computer hardware upgrades; physics processing units are slowly emerging as another tool to extend the power of the CPU. Process-intensive programs like videogames are not guaranteed to mount more interesting or sophisticated procedural rhetorics, but they are predisposed to do so.

For another part, videogames are generally a more expressive subgenre of computational media than other types, for example, productivity software.[107] By expressive, I mean that videogames service representational goals akin to literature, art, and film, as opposed to instrumental goals akin to utilities and tools. All software structures experience, including productivity software, and much has been written about the ways word processors, spreadsheets, and web applications influence our conception of the world (to cite just one example, Friedrich Kittler has written about the ways WordPerfect, coupled to the MS-DOS operating system, structures writing practice).[108] But videogames are uniquely, consciously, and principally crafted as expressions. As such, they represent excellent candidates for rhetorical speech—persuasion and expression are inexorably linked.

For yet another part, videogames are often interactive in the particular way I described above; they require user action to complete their procedural representations. As such, they provide particularly promising opportunities for the procedural translation of rhetorical devices like enthymeme. Interactivity guarantees neither meaningful expression nor meaningful persuasion, but it sets the stage for both. Sid Meier, designer of *Civilization*, has argued that gameplay is "a series of interesting choices."[109] Interesting choices do not necessarily entail *all* possible choices in a given situation; rather, choices are selectively included and excluded in a procedural representation to produce a desired expressive end. For example, *The McDonald's Videogame* includes control of cattle slaughtering but abstracts control of restaurant line-workers for a rhetorical end: to force the player to make decisions with social and political implications.

Greater interactivity is often considered especially engaging, or "immersive." The interactivity of (good) videogames might locate those games higher on the "vividness spectrum" discussed earlier, producing more vivid experience thanks to the player's active involvement. But I want to suggest that vividness comes not from immersion, but from abstraction. The values common to virtual reality and computer graphics assume that the closer we get to real experience, the better. This sentiment corresponds directly to the vividness spectrum, with the best interactivity coming closest to real experience. But meaning in videogames is constructed not through a re-creation of the world, but through selectively modeling appropriate elements of that world. Procedural representation models only some subset of a source system, in order to draw attention to that portion as the subject of the representation. Interactivity follows suit: the total number and credibility of user actions is not necessarily important; rather, the relevance of the interaction in the context of the representational goals of the system is paramount. Videogames offer a particularly good context for this selective interactivity.

Finally, I will admit that I have a particular fondness for videogames. I am a videogame critic and a videogame designer, and I am devoted to the process of connecting videogames with the history of human expression. In my previous book, *Unit Operations*, I argued for a comparative understanding of procedural expression, using the concept of unit operations to define the elements of procedural representation common across media. In this book, I argue for a similar understanding with respect to rhetoric. As I have already suggested, rhetoric in its contemporary sense refers to both persuasion and expression, and so a study of procedural rhetoric shares much in common with a study of procedural expression. Despite my preference for videogames, I should stress that I intend the reader to see *procedural rhetoric* as a domain much broader than that of videogames, encompassing any medium—computational or not—that accomplishes its inscription via processes. I hope my choice of videogames as examples of procedural rhetoric inspires both an increased appreciation of that medium and inspiration to study procedural rhetorics in other media.

Persuasive games

I give the name *persuasive games* to videogames that mount procedural rhetorics effectively. Before addressing persuasive games in this sense, it is worth diffusing some of the other ways videogames and persuasion have intersected, so as to distinguish my approach from others'.

Starting with Bushnell's *Computer Space*, arcade games have shared much in common with pinball and slot machines.[110] They accepted coins as payment, and one of their main design goals entailed persuading players to insert (more) coins. In the arcade industry, this is called "coin drop." Andrew Rollings and Ernest Adams have discussed the effect of coin drop on the design of such games: "Arcade operators care little for richness, depth, and the aesthetic qualities of a game as long as it makes a lot of money for them. This requires some fine balancing. If a game is too hard, people will abandon it in disgust, but if it is too easy, they will be able to play for a long time without putting any more money in."[111] Procedural rhetoric might be deployed in such games, but more often persuasion is accomplished through more basic appeals to addiction and reinforcement. Shuen-shing Lee explains such persuasion via Geoffrey R. Loftus and Elizabeth F. Loftus's 1983 study *Mind at Play*:[112]

[*Mind at Play*] sorts out two types of psychological configurations embedded in game design that aim to get players addicted to gaming. The first type, "partial reinforcement," is that utilized by slot machines which spit out coins intermittently to reward a gambler. The experience of being occasionally rewarded often drives the gambler to continue inserting coins, in hopes of another win or even a jackpot. Arcade game designers have cloned the same reinforcement strategy in their games. Surprises such as score doubling, weapon upgrading, expedient level advancing may pop up randomly during the gaming process to heighten the player's intrigue, stimulating continued playing.[113]

Partial reinforcement is certainly a type of persuasion, but the persuasion is entirely self-referential: its goal is to cause the player to continue playing, and in so doing to increase coin drop. Despite its relationship to gambling and other addictive activities, partial reinforcement is an interesting and worthwhile area of inquiry that can help game designers understand how to produce experiences that players feel compelled to continue or complete. However, this kind of persuasion is not my concern here. Instead, I am interested in videogames that make arguments about the way systems work in the material world. These games strive to alter or affect player opinion outside of the game, not merely to cause him to continue playing. In fact, many of the examples I will discuss strive to do just the opposite from arcade games: move the player from the game world into the material world.

As arcade games suggest, there are reasons to leverage videogames for goals orthogonal to those of procedural expression. The increasing popularity of and media attention paid to videogames means that merely producing and distributing a videogame may have its own persuasive effect. When Gonzalo Frasca and I co-designed *The Howard Dean for Iowa Game* in 2003, it became the first official videogame of a U.S. presidential candidate. While the game did deploy procedural rhetorics (see chapters 4 and 11 for more), the very existence of an official Howard Dean game served its own rhetorical purpose, further aligning the candidate with technology culture.[114] In another, similar example, Elizabeth Losh has reflected on the government's creation of *Tactical Iraqi*, a learning game designed to teach U.S. soldiers Arabic language and customs in order to help them accomplish military missions in the Middle East.[115] Losh, who studied the game as a field researcher and has written lucidly about her moral and rhetorical conflicts in doing so, later mused about its true rhetorical function in an online discussion forum:[116]

> In the wake of all the publicity that *Tactical Iraqi* has received in the last few months, I find myself with an even more serious reservation about the game, which crystallized after reading Max Boot's article, "Navigating the 'human terrain,'" in which Boot, a senior fellow at the Council on Foreign Relations, enthuses about visiting "the Expeditionary Warfare School, where captains study Arabic by playing a sophisticated computer game complete with animated characters." It was then that I realized that the purpose of the game might be rhetorical not pedagogical. Despite what the researchers thought they were doing, perhaps it was primarily intended to SHOW the teaching of Arabic to policy makers and the general public not actually TEACH Arabic more effectively. Traditional classroom teaching doesn't make for a good media spectacle, but a video game might.[117]

Tactical Iraqi cannot be accused of sporting low process intensity. As an engineering effort, it deploys sophisticated procedural models of language understanding, simulated gestures, and cross-cultural communication. But, Losh suggests, as an expressive artifact, the project might serve an agenda different from its primary one, namely drawing attention to a videogame training system to distract critics from America's military occupation of Iraq. Again, such a gesture is undeniably rhetorical, but its rhetoric is accomplished through media speech, not through processes. I will return to the substitution of procedural rhetoric for audience correlation in the context of advertising in chapter 5.

Videogames created with a more genuine interest in expression and persuasion may still underplay procedurality in favor of visual images. The commercial game industry dazzles buyers with high-fidelity images of increasingly greater verisimilitude, but these images do not necessarily couple with advances in procedural representation. In 2004, the American Legacy Foundation commissioned *Crazy World*, a game in service of their ongoing antismoking campaign, best known for its rhetorically powerful "the truth"-themed television ads. Built around a satirical carnival world that coincided with the foundation's advertising campaign at the time, the game sports very high production values, visuals, and sound—the very factors that contribute to vividness, according to Charles Hill. But the procedural rhetoric in the game is weak. In a press release, one of the creators describes a mechanic in the game:

The game, which is aimed at a wide audience, ages 18–50, was created to show both smokers and non-smokers the dangers of cigarettes using humor and irony. Players score points by avoiding moving green puffs of radioactive smoke. If they get caught in the smoke, they mutate into an alien-like form. "The idea is to attract people to entertain themselves and keep the message within context—to play for fun," [Templar Studios president Peter] Mack said.

A game like *Crazy World* may speak through visual rhetoric alone, or at least principally. The use of highly polished visual and sound design builds an expectation of authority. Images hypnotize many consumers, and even the largest videogame companies often repackage the same games with improved (or simply different) graphics. Considerable attention and investment has gone into improving the visual fidelity of commercial games, including the move to high definition and higher polygon models on the now-current Xbox 360 and PlayStation 3 consoles. Visual fidelity implies authority. Likewise, simplistic or unrefined graphics are often taken as an indication of gameplay quality. Just as a poor or "generic" package design can turn consumers away from a quality product, so the skin of a procedural rhetoric might influence player enticement. The 2004 Republican National Committee game *Tax Invaders*, which barely succeeds in replicating the rudimentary graphics of the classic arcade game *Space Invaders*, is an example of the latter (for more on this game, see chapter 3).[118]

The tenuous coupling between visual appearance and procedural rhetoric also hinders videogames that seek to make persuasive statements about issues in the material world, but fail to adopt effective procedural representations for those issues. One common pitfall is borrowing a procedural form from an existing game or game genre and skinning it with new graphics. Such a one is *Congo Jones and the Raiders of the Lost Bark*, a game about deforestation sponsored by the nonprofit Rainforest Foundation.[119] The game borrows its game-play from 2D platform games of the *Super Mario Bros.* variety.[120] The player controls a monkey who must find and defeat the president of the World Bank. The player must jump from platform to platform to avoid flying chainsaws, while attempting to reach and defeat the bank president.

Congo Jones adopts no procedural representation—and therefore no procedural rhetoric—of its own. Instead, it borrows the notion of progress through abstract obstacles as an object lesson for deforestation's struggle against the World Bank (who had supported logging in the Congolese rainforests). The game makes no claims about possible reasons to oppose the World Bank, nor how to do so, although it does succeed in positing the World Bank as an archetypal opponent, the "boss monster" of the game. The game might or might not be effective in building "awareness" about the issue, but it certainly does not mount a procedural argument about the topic. Or more precisely, it does not mount its *own* procedural rhetoric; it adopts processes of obstacle avoidance and goal pursuit from platform games and reinscribes them onto deforestation.

385

Congo Jones borrows gameplay and applies a graphical skin—a visual rhetoric—atop it. Another common technique is to borrow gameplay and apply a textual skin—a verbal rhetoric—atop it. An example of such a game is *P.o.N.G.*, created by the Global Arcade art collective.[121] The game's website explains that the game features "a few different variations of the classic Pong, each with just a little different play on the language of globalization."[122] The result is a direct copy of *Pong* in which the ball is replaced by words that might arise in discussions of globalization *(neoliberalism*, $$, etc.). The player must bat these back and forth with the paddle, as one might "exchange words" in a conversation on the topic. While the Global Arcade's mission statement announces their commitment "to make information about globalization interesting, engaging and interactive," *P.o.N.G.* serves as little more than a sight gag, perhaps not even articulating expression adequate to warrant the moniker of *digital art*.

The notion of adopting *Pong*'s back-and-forth procedural mechanic or *Super Mario Bros.'* platform mechanic as rhetorics for discourse might have promise, but *P.o.N.G.* and *Congo Jones* do not make meaningful use of those processes in their arguments. *Tax Invaders*, which I mentioned above and discuss in detail in chapter 3, is an example of a game that borrows a videogame form and successfully mounts its own procedural rhetoric atop it.

A more successful procedural rhetoric can be found in the 1982 title *Tax Avoiders*, an unusual game for the Atari Video Computer System (popularly known as the Atari VCS or Atari 2600).[123] Conceived by Darrell Wagner, a "Licensed Tax Consultant and former IRS Revenue Agent," the goal of the game is to become a millionaire by amassing income and avoiding red tape and audits.[124] The player controls a human character, John Q, who must collect income (represented by dollar-sign icons) and avoid red tape (represented by an abstract tape icon). After each fiscal quarter the player has the opportunity to shelter income in investments, which are represented as sprites on screen, or to store income in a portfolio, represented as a briefcase sprite (see figure 4). A second sprite oscillates between an IRS agent, a CPA, and an investment advisor. The player always loses an audit, and 50 percent of his income is lost to taxes. A CPA charges a small fee but always makes new tax-sheltered investments available. The investment advisor can maximize returns on sheltered investments. At the end of this interstitial phase, the player's remaining income is taxed and he returns to work.[125]

Tax Avoiders mounts an interesting and relatively complex procedural rhetoric about tax avoidance strategies. The fact that these techniques are mapped onto movement, a graphical logic, is perhaps not ideal, but it is also not detrimental to the argument. The player must run around to collect income, literally *avoiding* red tape. Likewise, he must avoid the IRS agent while racing to *catch* investment opportunities before their window of opportunity closes. These metaphors of locomotion correspond quite well to the abstract processes of work, investment, and taxation.

Finally, I would like to make a distinction between persuasive games, procedural rhetoric, and the rhetoric of play. In contemporary game studies, considerable attention has been paid to the relationship between games and play—and this is a worthwhile pursuit. However, my interest here is not in the function of play, nor in videogames as a subdomain of play activities. Rather, my interest is in the function of procedural representation as it is used for persuasion, and in videogames as a subdomain of procedural media. In particular, I should draw a distinction between procedural rhetoric and what Brian Sutton-Smith has called "rhetorics of play," or ways "play is placed in context within broader value systems."[126] While we both use the term *rhetoric*, we use it in different contexts, although not in entirely different ways. Sutton-Smith discusses the rhetorical modes of play itself: the ways theorists present play as a human cultural activity. As Katie Salen and Eric Zimmerman explain, Sutton-Smith's rhetorics of play "identify how games and play embody ideological values and how specific forms and uses of play perpetuate and justify these values."[127] Sutton-Smith's project is a general one, focused on the cultural role of play, not the culturally embodied practice of playing specific games. He identifies seven rhetorics of play, including play as progress, fate, power, identity, the imaginary, the self, and frivolity, each of which orchestrates play in different ways and for different ends under the same ostensible name (hence the ambiguity).[128] Sutton-Smith musters these rhetorics to attempt to explain the reasons people play, and the cultural function of that play.[129] His approach is broad and macroscopic, investigating play itself as a cultural activity that serves multiple purposes, purposes which often complicate one another.

I am discussing the rhetorical function of procedural expression in the tradition of representation rather than the tradition of play. This said, Sutton-Smith's rhetorics may prove useful in contextualizing procedural rhetorics

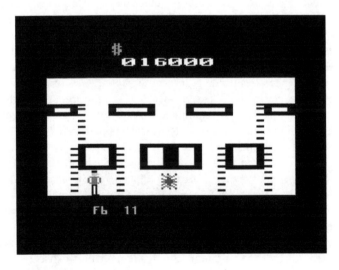

Figure 4 Although the Atari VCS title *Tax Invaders* may look simplistic, it constructs a sophisticated procedural rhetoric about tax strategy

among the values of play. This is not an effort I will attempt here, but which Salen and Zimmerman attempt in their text on game design, *Rules of Play*. The two suggest *The Landlord's Game* (the conceptual precursor to the popular board game *Monopoly*) as an embodiment of Sutton-Smith's rhetorics of power and progress. Unlike *Monopoly*, *The Landlord's Game* opposes land monopoly, instead advocating the single tax proposed by economist Henry George. As Salen and Zimmerman explain:

> Despite the strong similarity between The Landlord's Game and Monopoly, there are distinct (and wonderfully incongruous) differences in the rhetorics each evokes. While the play rhetorics of progress and power apply to both games, The Landlord's Game was distinctly anti-capitalist in its conception. The game's conflict was not premised on property acquisition and the accumulation of monopolies, but instead on an unraveling of the prevailing land system. Because properties in the game could only be rented, there was no opportunity for domination by a greedy land baron or developer.[130]

Without realizing it, Salen and Zimmerman helpfully clarify the difference between Sutton-Smith's *rhetorics of play*—the global, cultural roles for exploring themes like ownership and property—and the *procedural rhetoric of a game*—the local argument *The Landlord's Game* makes about taxation and property owner-ship. Salen and Zimmerman do not actually apply Sutton-Smith's rhetorics of play, a gesture that shows how macroscopic the latter's approach really is. On the one hand, they admit that progress and power "apply" abstractly to both *The Landlord's Game* and *Monopoly*. On the other hand, their analysis relies not on these higher-level categories, but on the specific function of the rules of each game, for example rental as collective equity versus ownership as individual lev-erage. When Salen and Zimmerman say that there are "distinct . . . differences in the rhetorics each evokes," they refer not to Sutton-Smith's cultural rhetorics, but to the procedural rhetorics of the two specific games, *The Landlord's Game* and *Monopoly*. In fact, Salen and Zimmerman's analysis of the procedural rhetorics of these games is quite mature, revealing the way the rules of the games make fun-damentally different arguments about land ownership, despite having apparently similar boards and gameplay dynamics.

The difference between rhetorics of play and procedural rhetoric should now be clear. Sutton-Smith's rhetorics of play characterize broad cultural contexts, while procedural rhetorics express specific patterns of cultural value. Despite their invocation of Sutton-Smith as a figure at the intersection of rhetoric and games, Salen and Zimmerman are actually invoking the more ordinary notion of rhetoric as persuasive and expressive discourse.[131] Although they claim to "take the word 'rhetoric' from Brian Sutton-Smith's remarkable treatise *The Ambiguity of Play*," really they take the word from its more general classical and modern roots, applying it to the analysis of games.[132] There may be value in applying

Sutton-Smith's rhetorics of play to specific procedural rhetorics, perhaps for comparative anthropological purposes. But as Salen and Zimmerman unwittingly demonstrate, the more useful intersection between rhetoric and play is one that unpacks the particular rules of a particular game in a particular context, not the more general intersection between modes of play in general. This distinction mirrors the one that separates representational discourse from sociological discourse. Clearly cultural context influences the creation of and interaction with games. But the games we create can also support, interrogate, or oppose those cultural contexts.

Persuasive games versus serious games

Topics like taxation, deforestation, and globalization are not the usual subject matter of videogames; furthermore, the games about these topics discussed above are very arcane, so much so that I doubt many readers would have chanced upon all three before. Procedural rhetoric is not limited to such anomalous specimens; in the following pages I discuss numerous commercial games that have enjoyed great market success. But one often uses persuasion in the context of domains like economics, business, and politics. As it happens, an entire subdomain of videogame development has erupted around such topics, known as *serious games*. What, if anything, differentiates persuasive games from serious games?

Interrogating the relationship between seriousness and play is nothing new. Dutch anthropologist Johan Huizinga struggled with the ambiguous link between seriousness and play in his classic study *Homo ludens*. On the one hand, Huizinga notes that play "is the direct opposite of seriousness."[133] But on further investigation, he argues that "the contrast between play and seriousness proves to be neither conclusive nor fixed."[134] Huizinga notes that one can "play seriously," that is, with great devotion and resolve,[135] but seriousness does not seem to include the possibility of play, making the latter of a "higher order" than seriousness.[136] Despite this status, play helps constitute social and cultural functions of great gravity, according to Huizinga, including religion, politics, and warfare. Huizinga remains conflicted to the end on the interrelation between play and seriousness. As such, it is not surprising that scholars, business people, and developers thought they had fallen upon something new in "reuniting" seriousness and play.

An early example of the new collusion of seriousness and gameplay comes in Clark C. Abt's 1970 book *Serious Games*, which addresses the use of analog games (board games, role-play, etc.) in education, science, government, and industry. In his first chapter, titled "The Reunion of Action and Thought," Abt offers a definition of serious games: "We are concerned with *serious games* in the sense that these games have an explicit and carefully thought-out educational purpose and are not intended to be played primarily for amusement."[137] Abt quickly admits that this does not mean that serious games "are not, or should not be entertaining," but the message is clear: serious games are created under the direct influence and guidance of external institutional goals.

When the Woodrow Wilson International Center for Scholars unearthed the moniker "serious games" as the name for their new videogame initiative, they did so without direct reference to Abt's proposal thirty years earlier. Rather, the name arose fairly spontaneously. Wilson Center Director of Foresight & Governance David Rejeski and consultant Ben Sawyer were trying to title a white paper Sawyer had written for the center. The two had a subtitle—"Improving Public Policy through Game-Based Learning and Simulation"—but they wanted a snappy title to entice readers. Rejeski had been reading Michael Schrage's 1999 book *Serious Play: How the World's Best Companies Simulate to Innovate*, a call for businesses to foster play as an agent for innovation.[138] Schrage cites Abt in his book, and Rejeski, perhaps influenced by conscious or unconscious memory of that reference, suggested "Serious Games" as a title.[139] Since then, Woodrow has founded and funded the Serious Games Initiative, an ad hoc networking and knowledge-sharing group with a thriving membership.[140] Its primary activities include collecting resources, facilitating contacts between government/industry and developers, and running meetings and conferences on its core topics, including the Serious Games Summit, a large biannual conference (on whose advisory board I happen to serve). Interestingly, the Initiative's goals read very similarly to Abt's 1970 definition: "the goal of the initiative is to help usher in a new series of policy education, exploration, and management tools utilizing state of the art computer game designs, technologies, and development skills."[141] Mirroring Abt's goals with nondigital games, the Initiative seeks to couple videogames to the needs of modern institutions. Their mission statement asks, "How can we quickly expand the application of computer-based games to a much wider range of key challenges facing our government and other public or private organizations?" Abt's "carefully thought out educational purpose" and the Serious Games Initiative's focus on "government and other public or private organizations" both suggest that serious games are crafted in the service of officials, especially officials of governments or corporations. The language used to advertise the Serious Games Summit confirms this sentiment; under a header reading "Gaming for your Industry" follows a list of institutional interests: education, government, health, military, corporate, first responders, science.[142]

If the notion of "seriousness" is what distinguishes this group's efforts from other types of videogaming, it is worth briefly interrogating the term and its relationship to their endeavor. *Serious* is a word with many meanings, and it should no longer be sufficient merely to oppose it to *entertainment*, the major mover-and-shaker in the videogame marketplace.

Serious can mean *solemn*, implying emotionlessness and sobriety. One might think of the drill sergeant, the librarian, or perhaps even the IRS agent as an agent of this type of seriousness: *she shot me a serious look and I reconsidered my itemizations.*

Serious can mean *weighty*, implying consequence and demanding consideration. One might think of authority figures like teachers, parents, or religious leaders using this meaning of the term when addressing the particularly foolish (not serious) plans of pupils, offspring, or followers: *Don't tell me to calm down, son! Marriage is a serious commitment.*

Serious can mean *grave*, implying severity and foreboding. One might think of officials making statements about unthinkable acts of war, disease, or suffering: *Two of the five miners remain hospitalized in serious condition.*

Serious can mean *highbrow*, implying intellectualism and profundity. One might think of academics, artists, curators, and more generally snobs insistent on segregating weighty matters from light ones: *James is a serious artist, he doesn't make that pop-culture drivel.*

All of these ways of understanding *serious* have something in common: they rely on a point of reference that affirms the seriousness of a subject in relation to some nonserious alternative. Solemnity responds to behavior outside a known, desired code of conduct; weightiness responds to behavior thought to lead to crucial and perhaps irreversible decision; gravity suggests an opposite and always undesirable condition; and snobbery isolates worthwhile pursuits from insignificant ones. Furthermore, these meanings suggest that seriousness is often deployed in the service of institutions: governments, corporations, healthcare systems, religious beliefs, cultural communities, and so forth. Seriousness implies actions that support the goals and progress of these institutions.

Such a conception of seriousness is coincident with Abt's use of the term in relation to board games and the Serious Games Initiative's use of the term in relation to videogames. Serious games are videogames created to support the existing and established interests of political, corporate, and social institutions. To apply this principle to the industry domains of the Serious Games Summit proves a simple task. Educational games translate existing pedagogical goals into videogame form; government games translate existing political goals in videogame form; health games provide doctors and medical institutions with videogame-based tools to accomplish their existing needs; military games help armies and soldiers address existing global conflicts with new, cheaper, and more scalable simulations; corporate games provide executives with videogame-based tools to accomplish their existing business goals; first responder games offer simulated views of already known methods of response to natural disaster or terrorist incident; and science games provide appealing videogame-based tools to clarify known principles and practices.

Such goals do not represent the full potential of persuasive games. If persuasive games are videogames that mount meaningful procedural rhetorics, and if procedural rhetorics facilitate dialectical interrogation of process-based claims about how real-world processes do, could, or should work, then persuasive games can also make claims that speak past or against the fixed worldviews of institutions like governments or corporations. This objection—which bears some resemblance to Socrates' opposition to sophistic and technical rhetoric in the fifth century BCE—suggests that persuasive games might also interrogate those institutions *themselves*, recommending correctives and alternatives.

If we wanted to retain the term *serious games*—a questionable goal—then two other meanings stand out as potential ways of understanding the phrase. First, *serious* can imply care and attention to detail, especially as such care leads to reflection: *I will give your ideas serious thought.* This meaning is related to weightiness, but carries the sense of open discourse, of the possibility of finding new structures of thought not immediately given by a current worldview. Second, and more esoteric, *serious* can imply substance, a window onto the underlying structure of a thing. This use may be limited to informal discourse; a sentiment like *dude, that is a serious cheesecake* implies that the specimen presented offers a fundamental insight into the nature, even the apotheosis of the thing in general.[143] "Serious games" in this sense—a sense commensurate with what I intend persuasive games to mean—would deal with the exposition of the fundamental structure of existing situations intended to invoke support, doubt, or debate about their validity or desirability, or universality. These are not games in the service of governments, corporations, educational institutions, and their kindred but games that challenge such institutions, creating opportunities to question, change, or eliminate them.

The notion of the serious as the underlying structure of a system is particularly compatible with the concept of procedurality. Procedural representation depicts how something does, could, or should work: the way we understand a social or material practice to function. I connect this idea to contemporary philosopher Alain Badiou's notion of the *situation*, a "structured presentation" of a *multiplicity*, a particular ontological arrangement.[144] Badiou applies transfinite set theory to philosophy, understanding being to mean *being a member of.* The gesture of including a concept in a situation is akin to the set-theoretical notion of belonging, which Badiou names the *count-as-one*.[145] I have previously correlated the count-as-one with the unit operation, the gesture of conceiving of a particular process as an encapsulated concept.[146] Badiou further understands situations to have a *state*, the logic by which the elements in a situation are counted as one—or the reasons why the structure is organized in the way it is.[147] It is the state that is commensurate with "seriousness" as the nature of a thing, the reasons that make it what it is. Badiou further articulates a concept called the *event*, which offers a chance to disrupt the state of a situation and reinvent it, wholly anew, under a different organizing logic, a topic I will return to in chapter 11.[148]

Despite the possibility of rescuing serious games under the definition I have just offered, I do not want to preserve the name. Instead, I would like to advance persuasive games as an alternative whose promise lies in the possibility of using procedural rhetoric to support *or* challenge our understanding of the way things in the world do or should work. Such games can be produced for a variety of purposes, be they entertainment, education, activism, or a combination of these and others. The concept of serious games as a counter movement apart from and against the commercial videogame industry eliminates a wide variety of games from persuasive speech. It is a foolish gesture that wrongly undermines the expressive power of videogames in general, and highly crafted, widely appealing commercial games in particular. As I will show in the following chapters, many games carry messages, make arguments, and attempt meaningful expression. This should not surprise us; indeed, all media resonate on a variety of registers. I want to encourage developers and critics to pay more mind to the way such messages, arguments, and expressions are constructed through procedural rhetorics, in videogames of all kinds.

Persuasive games versus persuasive technology

Since the late 1990s, Stanford University experimental psychologist B. J. Fogg has been advancing a concept he calls *captology*. The simple definition Fogg gives on his research group's website is this: "Captology is the study of computers as persuasive technologies. This includes the design, research, and analysis of interactive computing products created for the purpose of changing people's attitudes or behaviors."[149] Fogg's research has produced a book entitled *Persuasive Technology: Using Computers to Change What We Think and Do*.[150] Given the strong similarity between the phrases *persuasive technology* and *persuasive games*, I would like to address the differences between my approach and that of Fogg.

The most important distinction mirrors the difference between persuasive games and serious games. Just as the Serious Games Initiative implicates videogames in the service of existing goals, so captology does for computer technology in general. Captology, says Fogg, "does not include . . . unintended outcomes; it focuses on the attitude and behavior changes *intended* by the designers of interactive technology products."[151] Admittedly, this understanding is far closer to my goals than that of the Serious Games Initiative; Fogg does not appear to explicitly correlate captological persuasion with institutional ideologies. However, further interrogation shows that captology is not fundamentally concerned with altering the user's fundamental conception of how real-world processes work. Rather, it is primarily intended to craft new technological constraints that impose conceptual or behavioral change in users.

To this end, Fogg suggests seven types of persuasive technology tools, which I list, define, and exemplify below.

> **Reduction**—"using computing technology to reduce complex behavior to simple tasks," exemplified by the capitoladvantage.com website, which simplifies political participation by presenting a user with contact information for all of his elected officials based on zip code input.[152]
>
> **Tunneling**—"leading users through a predetermined set of actions, step by step," illustrated by the registration or electronic payment systems on many websites.[153]
>
> **Tailoring**—"provid[ing] information relevant to individuals to change their attitudes or behaviors or both," as by scorecard.org, which provides information about polluting institutions local to a user based, again, on zip code input.[154]

Suggestion—"an interactive computing product that suggests a behavior at the most opportune moment," such as roadside speed-monitoring radar systems, which display a driver's speed as he passes.[155]

Self-Monitoring—"[a] type of tool that allows people to monitor their attitudes or behaviors to achieve a predetermined goal or outcome," for example, digital heart-rate monitors.[156]

Surveillance—"computing technology that allows one party to monitor the behavior of another to modify behavior in a specific way," such as Hygiene Guard, a system that monitors hand washing in the retail service industry.[157]

Conditioning—"a computerized system that uses principles of operant conditioning to change behaviors," such as Telecycle, an exercise bike which, when pedaled to a target speed, clarifies the image on a television screen in front of the cycle.[158]

Perhaps these tools offer valid ways of using technology to alter behavior. But not one of them deploys rhetoric; instead, all of Fogg's techniques use technology to alter actions or beliefs without engaging users in a discourse about the behavior itself or the logics that would recommend such actions or beliefs. Some techniques are more obviously guileful than others, such as the hand washing surveillance system or the website registration system. The approaches that do admit user awareness assume that the user has already understood and accepted the larger reason that the technology inscribes. For example, a self-monitoring technology like a heart-rate monitor assumes an understanding and acceptance of the relationship between cardiovascular exercise and long-term health. Thus, while captology does not explicitly align itself with the service of existing social, political, or corporate institutions, its formal structure—as tactics given a particular, established situation—only allows persuasive technology to work in the service of existing material ends, rather than the reasons one would want to pursue those ends.

More strongly, captology appears to rely only on psychological, not dialectical user responses. This is not surprising given Fogg's background as an experimental psychologist, but he seems generally dismissive of the tradition of philosophical rhetoric, which aligns persuasion with logical argument and discourse. In the nearly three hundred pages of *Persuasive Technology*, Fogg devotes only a half-page sidebar to the subject of rhetoric, dismissively labeled "A Brief History of Persuasion Studies."[159] In this sidebar, Fogg exposes his opinion that psychological methods are inherently more desirable than philosophical ones:

> Today the formal study of persuasion continues to be advanced, primarily through research in social psychology, which began during the early part of the 1900s. Inspired largely by the U.S. government's need to persuade citizens to support war efforts, social psychologists established ambitious research programs to determine what caused people to change their attitudes and behaviors. Later, marketers and advertisers

built on the insights gleaned from social psychology, systematically investigating how influence works and often applying their findings to help corporations prosper.[160]

The lack of irony and scrutiny in the discussion of government-funded social science studies for covert manipulation suggests that Fogg is perhaps unaware of the ideology he himself inhabits: one in which existing power structures always devise ethical and desirable goals. Fogg himself is caught in a worldview that limits his understanding of computational persuasion, one driven partly by corporate and government grant funding for his own research. Despite Fogg's suggestion that *captology* acronymizes "computers as persuasive technologies," the phrase itself conjures the sense of *capture*, of arrest and incarceration by an authority. A better name for Fogg's work would perhaps be *manipulative technology*.

On a less critical note, persuasive technology differs from persuasive games because the former does not deal fundamentally with procedurality. Fogg does discuss the use of simulations in persuasion, including nods to videogames (principally as examples of conditioning, "keeping the player playing," the broader context of which coin-drop is an example), but the majority of his examples rely on presenting data to the user (turning zip codes into lists of data) or mirroring the result of sensor input back to the user (the speed check or the heart-rate monitor).[161] Reduction and tunneling might provide useful frames for procedural rhetorics, but Fogg does not explicitly align them with procedural representation; as is, his examples all exhibit low process intensity.

Black and white boxes

As a final note of clarification, I would like to say a few things about the function of computer code in my analysis of procedural rhetoric. If computational expression is fundamentally procedural, and if computational procedural expression is crafted through code, then what is the role of code in the practice and analysis of procedural rhetoric?

Since each figure and form of a procedural rhetoric in software and videogames must be constructed with code, it might seem impossible to analyze or discuss them without digging into the code itself. Verbal rhetoric, after all, has identified dozens of figures for the authorship of spoken and written arguments with an eye toward persuasion. Is the same not possible for procedural rhetoric? I believe that it is, but nevertheless none of the analyses you will read herein cites or extrapolates code.

Code is not usually available in compiled software like videogames. Software subsystems are closely held trade secrets, and one simply cannot "open up" *The Sims* or *Grand Theft Auto III* to look at the code running beneath. In software development and testing, there is a name for this distinction. To watch a program's effects and extrapolate potential approaches or problems (in the case of testing) in its code is called *black-box* analysis. Such analysis makes assumptions about the actual operation of the software system, assumptions that may or may not be true. To watch a program's effects and identify actual approaches or problems in its code is called *white-box* analysis (or sometimes, *glass-box* analysis). Such analysis observes the effects of the system with a partial or complete knowledge of the underlying code that produces those effects. Some white-box analysis can be performed without direct access to code. Examples include architectural descriptions from conference presentations about development techniques, as have been made about *The Sims*, or commonalities in documented subcomponents, as could be done for the Renderware engine at the heart of *Grand Theft Auto*. I have previously discussed the way early arcade console games use of common hardware components, and first-person shooters' use of common game engines, each influenced the design of multiple games built on the same platform.[162] Publicly documented hardware and software specifications, software development kits, and decompiled videogame ROMs all offer possible ways of studying the software itself. Such study can shed important light on the material basis for videogame experiences. An understanding of code supplements procedural interpretation. In particular, a procedural rhetorician should strive to understand the affordances of the materials from which a procedural argument is formed. For attorneys, this means understanding the legal code and judicial process. For computational critics, it means understanding the affordances of hardware, software frameworks, and programming languages.[163] This type of expertise is a subset of both procedural criticism and procedural rhetoric, and it is a worthwhile course of study in both fields. But such resources are hardly guaranteed for every computational artifact.

This lack of visibility concerns some critics. Part of Sherry Turkle's criticism of *Sim City* had to do with the simulation's black-box nature, which she saw occluding its position on such matters as tax policy. "Opening the box," in Turkle's opinion, would allow players to see how the simulation runs, providing better ability to critique. The problem with this objection is that the player *can* see how the simulation runs: this is, in no trivial way, what it means to play the game. Turkle's real beef is not with *Sim City*, but with the players: they do not know how to play the game critically. Understanding the simulation at the level of code does not necessarily solve this problem. Even understanding the simulation via some intermediary system poised between the code and the existing interface—some have proposed "policy knobs" that could alter the simulation rules of a game like *Sim City*—does not guarantee an understanding of making and interacting with arguments as processes rather than words. Rather than addressing this problem from the bottom up through code literacy, we need to address it from the top down through procedural literacy, a topic I will return to in chapter 9. Part of that practice is learning to read processes as a critic. This means playing a videogame or using procedural system with an eye toward identifying and interpreting the rules that drive that system. Such activity is analogous to that of the literary critic interpreting a novel or the film critic reviewing a film—demanding access to a computer program's code might be akin to asking for direct access to an author's or filmmaker's expressive intentions. Despite the flaws of twentieth-century critical theory, one notion worth keeping is that of dissemination, the irreversible movement of the text away from the act of authorship.[164] "Simulation authors," says Gonzalo Frasca, "do not represent a particular event, but a set of potential events. Because of this, they have to think about their objects as systems and consider which are the laws that rule their behaviors. In a similar way, people who interpret simulations create a mental model of it by inferring the rules that govern it."[165] In such simulations, says Frasca, "the goal of the player would be to analyze, contest and revise the model's rules according to his personal ideas and beliefs."

Persuasive games and procedural rhetoric

As examples like *Tax Avoiders, P.o.N.G.*, and *Congo Jones and the Raiders of the Lost Bark* suggest, procedural rhetoric is not automatically a part of computational expression, and a great deal of attention is required to construct coherent—let alone effective—procedural rhetorics. In the three sections that follow, I will consider approaches to and examples of procedural rhetorics in three domains, namely, politics, advertising, and education. I have chosen these fields for several reasons. For one part, they are areas I know something about—I have worked professionally in all these areas, I have done academic research and writing in all these areas, and I have created videogames in all these areas. For another part, these represent typical domains for discussions of rhetoric and persuasion in general, and thus are low-hanging fruit for procedural rhetoric and persuasive games. For yet another part, they offer clear goals and referents in the material world. Exposure to procedural rhetorics in politics, advertising, and education should plant the seeds for the interrogation of other, perhaps more subtle expressive domains. And finally, together these three areas cover a broad swath of human social experience, areas that have become largely broken in contemporary culture, and areas I believe videogames can help restore, and not just in small part.

Notes

1 Owen Gaede, *Tenure* (Minneapolis: Control Data Corporation, 1975). PLATO was a computer instruction system first developed at the University of Illinois in 1960, The name is an acronym for Programmed Logic for Automatic Teaching Operations. The system was commercially produced by Control Data Corporation (CDC) until the 1990s, and despite its eventual failure PLATO is acknowledged to have pioneered now-familiar tools like online forums, instant messaging, and multiplayer games. I am indebted to Noah Falstein for introducing me to this particular PLATO title.
2 Owen Gaede has also written a Windows version of *Tenure*, available at http://home. earthlink.net/~tenure/abourtenure.html/.
3 This is similar to Marshall McLuhan's suggestion that we see a medium only when we are moving beyond it.
4 Seymour M. Hersh, "Torture at Abu Ghraib," *New Yorker*, May 10, 2004.
5 Janet Murray, *Hamlet on the Holodeck* (New York: Free Press, 1997), 71.
6 Ibid.

7 Ibid., 72.
8 Bogost, *Unit Operations*.
9 Stevan Harnad, "Computation Is Just Interpretable Symbol Manipulation; Cognition Isn't," *Minds and Machines* 4, no. 4 (2004): 379.
10 Ibid.
11 Max Weber, *The Protestant Ethic and the Spirit of Capitalism*, trans. Talcott Parsons (London: Unwin Hyman, 1930), 181.
12 Bogost, *Unit Operations*, 3.
13 Jared Diamond, *Guns, Germs, and Steel* (New York: W. W. Norton, 1999).
14 Steven J. Levitt and Stephen J. Dubner, *Freakonomics: A Rogue Economist Explores the Hidden Side of Everything* (New York: William Morrow, 2005), 7.
15 Ibid., 137–141.
16 Ibid., 139. My emphasis.
17 Joseph Weizenbaum, "ELIZA—A Computer Program for the Study of Natural Language Communication between Man and Machine," *Communications of the ACM* 9, no. 1 (1966).
18 Ibid., 36–37.
19 For example, see Michael Mateas and Andrew Stern, "A Behavior Language for Story-Based Believable Agents," *IEEE Intelligent Systems* 7, no. 4 (2002).
20 The assembly instructions given here apply to the 6502 processor. The 6502 is an 8-bit processor widely used, in microcomputers of the 1980s, including the AppleII, the Commodore 64, the Atari 400 and 800, and, with modifications, as the 6507 in the Atari VCS (2600) and the Nintendo Entertainment System (NES). Assembly instructions may vary from processor to processor.
21 Noah Wardrip-Fruin, "Expressive Processing: On Process-Intensive Literature and Digital Media," Doctoral dissertation (Brown University, 2006).
22 For more on game engines and unit operations, see Bogost, *Unit Operations*, 56–66.
23 Infocom, *Zork* (Cambridge, Mass.: Infocom, 1980).
24 For more on the use of n-grams to construct computational, textual artifacts, see Noah Wardrip-Fruin, "Playable Media and Textual Instruments," *Dichtung Digital. Journal für Digitale Ästhetik* 5, no. 34 (2005).
25 Lawrence Lessig, *Code and Other Laws of Cyberspace* (New York: Basic Books, 1999), 6.
26 *Plato: Complete Works* (New York: Hackett, 1997), 453a.
27 Ibid., 266d.
28 Ibid., 266d–267d.
29 George A. Kennedy, *Classical Rhetoric and Its Christian and Secular Tradition* (Chapel Hill: University of North Carolina Press, 1999), 33.
30 Ibid., 34.
31 *Plato: Complete Works*, 464c.
32 Aristotle, *Physics*, trans. Robin Waterfield (Oxford and New York: Oxford University Press, 1999), 39 (II 33, 194b132).
33 Aristotle, *The Rhetoric and Poetics of Aristotle* (New York: McGraw Hill, 1984), 32 (I.33, 1358b–1355).
34 Ibid., 24 (I.22, 1355b–1326).
35 Ibid., 30–31 (I.32, 1358a–1358b).
36 Ibid., 199 (III 112, 1414a–1414b).
37 Kennedy, *Classical Rhetoric and Its Christian and Secular Tradition*, 3.
38 Sonja K. Foss, Karen A. Foss, and Robert Trapp, *Contemporary Perspectives on Rhetoric* (Prospect Heights, Ill.: Waveland Press, 1985), 11.
39 Kevin Michael DeLuca, *Image Politics: The New Rhetoric of environmental Activism* (New York: Guilford Press, 1999), 14.

40 Foss, Foss, and Trapp, *Contemporary Perspectives on Rhetoric*, 12.
41 Kennerh Burke, *A Rhetoric of Motives* (Berkeley and Los Angeles: University of California Press, 1969), 19.
42 Ibid., 41.
43 Ibid., 20.
44 Foss, Foss, and Trapp, *Contemporary Perspectives on Rhetoric*, 193.
45 Burke, *A Rhetoric of Motives*, 172.
46 See Foss, Foss, and Trapp, *Contemporary Perspectives on Rhetoric*, 214.
47 Marguerite Helmers and Charles A. Hill, "Introduction" in *Defining Visual Rhetorics*, ed. Charles A. Hill and Marguerite Helmers (Mahwah, N.J.: Lawrence Erlbaum Associates, 2004), 2.
48 Charles A. Hill, "The Psychology of Rhetorical Images," in *Defining Visual Rhetorics*, 25.
49 Ibid., 33.
50 Ibid., 37.
51 Ibid.
52 Ibid, 38.
53 J. Anthony Blair, "The Rhetoric of Visual Arguments," in *Defining Visual Rhetorics*, 44.
54 Ibid.
55 Ibid., 47.
56 Ibid., 49.
57 Ibid., 51.
58 Jacques Derrida, *Of Grammatology*, trans. Grayatri Chakravorty Spivak (Baltimore: The Johns Hopkins Press, 1974), 3, 11–23.
59 David S. Birdsell and Leo Groarke, "Toward a Theory of Visual Argument," *Argumentation and Advocacy* 33 (1996): 2.
60 Randall A. Lake and Barbara A Pickering, "Argumentation, the Visual, and the Possibility of Refutation: An exploration," *Argumentation and Advocacy* 12 (1988): 82.
61 Keith Kenney, "Building Visual Communication Theory by Borrowing from Rhetoric," in *Visual Rhetoric in a Digital World*, ed. Carolyn Handa (New York: Bedford St, Martins, 2004).
62 DeLuca, *Image Politics*, 1.
63 James P. Zappen, "Digital Rhetoric: Toward an Integrated Theory," *Technical Communication Quarterly* 14, no. 3 (2005): 319.
64 Ibid., 321.
65 Laura J Gurak, *Cyberliteracy: Navigating the Internet with Awareness* (New Haven: Yale University Press, 2001), 29.
66 Ibid., 44.
67 Barbara Warnick, *Critical Literacy in a Digital Era: Technology. Rhetoric, and the Public Interest* (Mahwah, N.J.: Lawrence Erlbaum Associates, 2002), 82.
68 Richard A. Lanham, *The Electronic Word: Democracy. Technology, and the Arts* (Chicago: University of Chicago Press, 1995), 17, 39, 76, 152.
69 Lev Manovich, *The Language of New Media* (Cambridge, Mass.: MIT Press, 2001), 77–78.
70 For concise coverage of these two important works, see their respective chaprers in Nick Montfort and Noah Wardrip-Fruin, eds., *The New Media Reader* (Cambridge, Mass.: MIT Press, 2003), 35–48, 301–338.
71 Chris Crawford, "Process Intensity," *Journal of Computer Game Development* 1, no. 5 (1987).
72 Manovich, *The Language of New Media*, 77.
73 Elizabeth Losh, Virtualpolitik: Digital Rhetoric and the Subversive Potential of Information Culture, manuscript in progress.
74 See chapter 7 for more on anti-advergames.

75 Patrick Dugan, "Hot off the Grill: la Molleindustria's Paolo Pedercini on The McDonald's Video Game," *Gamasutra*, February 27, 2006.
76 Richard Linklater, *Fast Food Nation* (Participant Productions, 2006); Eric Schlosser, *Fast Food Nation: The Dark Side of the All -American Meal* (New York: Harper, 2001).
77 See http://demo.fb.se/e/girlpower/retouch/.
78 See http://www.pbskids.com/, PBS is the American Public Broadcasting System, a public television network.
79 See http://pbskids.org/dontbuyit/.
80 See http://pbskids.org/dontbuyit/advertisingtricks/foodadtricks_burger2.html/.
81 Hill, "The Psychology of Rhetorical Images," 31.
82 Blair, "The Rhetoric of Visual Arguments," 51–52.
83 One might wonder if this omission suggests rhetoricians' general blindness toward computational media.
84 One could make additional claims about the relative vividness of different types of procedural interaction, for example screen-based applications as compared with augmented reality (AR), virtual reality (VR) or other forms. This is a valid question which I do not intend to address in the present context. That said, I do discuss physical interfaces in chapter 10, and the reader is referred there for more on this topic.
85 Hill, "The Psychology of Rhetorical Images," 33.
86 The spot is available online at http://www.pbs.org/30secondcandidate/timeline/years/1964b.html/.
87 See http://en.wikipedia.org/wiki/Daisy_(television_commereial)/.
88 Blair, "The Rhetoric of Visual Arguments," 52.
89 Ibid.
90 This does not imply that all procedural arguments are logically consistent, but merely that computationally implemented procedural arguments are assured to execute according to the particular logic a human author has imposed upon them.
91 Sherry Turkle, "Seeing through Computers," *American Prospect* 8, no. 31 (March 1997).
92 Maxis, *Sim City* (Alameda, Calif.: Brøderbund, 1989).
93 Bogost, *Unit Operations*, 100–109.
94 http://www.thegrocerygame.com/.
95 This sample was collected in October 2003 from the game's old messageboard system at http://pub28.ezboard.com/bterisshoppinglist/. The site has since created a new board and purged these previous messages.
96 The mathematician Laplace devised a solution to Buffon's needle problem that provided an efficient means of estimating the value of π.
97 Chris Crawford, *Balance of the Planet* (Self-published, 1990).
98 Murray, *Hamlet on the Holodeck*, 128.
99 Ibid.
100 Ibid., 74.
101 Katie Salen and Eric Zimmerman, *Rules of Play: Game Design Fundamentals* (Cambridge, Mass.: MIT Press, 2004), 28.
102 Rockstar Games, *Grand Theft Auto III* (New York: Take Two Interactive, 2001).
103 Eric Qualls, "*Grand Theft Auto: San Andreas* (Review)" (GamesFirst, 2004 [cited March 2, 2006]); available from http://gamesfirst.com/index.php?id=188/.
104 Adam Woolcott, "Grand Theft Auto Retrospective" (Gaming Target, 2005 [cited March 1, 2006]); available from http://www.gamingtarget.com/article.php?artid=4739/.
105 Bogost, *Unit Operations*, 107.
106 Chris Crawford. *The Art of Interactive Design: A Euphonious and Illuminating Guide to Building Successful Software* (San Francisco: No Starch Press, 2002).
107 When I say "videogames," I mean to include non- or low-graphical procedural works like interactive fiction and text adventures.

108 Friedrich Kittler, "There Is No Software," in *Literature. Media, Information Systems*, ed. John Johnston (Amsterdam: Overseas Publishers Association, 1997).

109 Andrew Rollings and Ernest Adams, *Andrew Rollings and Ernest Adams on Game Design* (New York: New Riders, 2003), 200.

110 Bushnell, *Computer Space.*

111 Rollings and Adams, *Andrew Rollings and Ernest Adams on Game Design*, 46.

112 Geoffrey R. Loftus and Elizabeth F. Loftus, *Mind at Play: The Psychology of Video Games* (New York: Basic Books, 1983).

113 Shuen-shing Lee, "I Lose, Therefore I Think: A Search for Contemplation amid Wars of Push-Button Glare," *Game Studies* 3, no. 2 (2003).

114 We discuss this matter further in Ian Bogost and Gonzalo Frasca, "Videogames Go to Washington: the Story Behind Howard Dean's Videogame Propaganda," in *Second Person: Roleplaying and Story in Games and Playable Media*, ed. Pat Harrigan and Noah Wardrip-Fruin (Cambridge, Mass.: MIT Press, 2007), 233–246.

115 Alelo Inc. and USC Information Sciences Institute, *Tactical Iraqi* (Los Angeles: Tactical Language Training LLC, 2005).

116 Elizabeth Losh, "In Country with Tactical Iraqi: Trust, Identity, and Language Learning in a Military Video Game" (paper presented at the Digital Arts and Cultures Conference, IT University, Copenhagen, Denmark, December 1–4, 2005).

117 See http://www.watercoolergames.org/archives/000526.shtml#c7429/.

118 Republican National Committee, *Tax Invaders* (Washington, D.C.: RNC/gop.com, 2004); Taito, *Space Invaders* (Tokyo: Taito, 1978).

119 Ben Woodhouse and Martyn Williams, *Congo Jones and the Raiders of the Lost Bark* (London: The Rainforest Foundation, 2004).

120 Nintendo, *Super Mario Bros* (Kyoto, Japan Nintendo, 1985).

121 Banff Centre and Global Arcade, *P.o.N.G* (San Francisco: Global Arcade, 1999).

122 See http:// www.globalarcade.org/pong/index.html/.

123 Dunhill Electronics, *Tax Avoiders* (American Videogame, 1982).

124 So reads the game's packaging and the cartridge label.

125 Some have observed that the mechanics of *Tax Avoiders* bear very close resemblance to those of the Atari 2600 title *Porky's*, based on the 1982 film of the same name. Dunhill Electronics created both games, although *Porky's* enjoyed much greater success, and perhaps understandably so. *Tax Avoiders* was the sole title released by American Videogame, which went bankrupt soon after its release, a victim of the so-called videogame crash of 1983. Bob Clark, *Porky's* (20th Century Fox, 1982); Dunhill Electronics, *Porky's* (Santa Clara, Calif: Fox Video Games, 1983).

126 Brian Surton-Smith, *The Ambiguity of Play* (Cambridge, Mass.: Harvard University Press, 1997), 8.

127 Katie Salen and Eric Zimmerman, *Rules of Play: Game Design Fundamentals* (Cambridge, Mass.: MIT Press, 2004).

128 Sutton-Smith, *The Ambiguity of Play*, 9–12.

129 Ibid.

130 Salen and Zimmerman, *Rules of Play*, 520.

131 I discuss ideology in more detail in the next section.

132 Salen and Zimmerman, *Rules of Play.*

133 Johan Huizinga, *Homo ludens* (New York: Beacon, 1955), 5.

134 Ibid.

135 Ibid., 8.

136 Ibid., 45.

137 Clark C, Abt, *Serious Games* (New York: Viking, 1970), 9.

138 Michael Schrage, *Serious Play: How the World's Best Companies Simulate to Innovate* (Cambridge, Mass,: Harvard Business School Press, 1999), 12–15.

139 The report in question is Ben Sawyer, "Serious Games: Improving Public Policy through Game-Based Learning and Simulation" (Washington, D.C.: Woodrow Wilson International Center for Scholars, 2002). The origin of the title was related to me in a personal communication with Ben Sawyer, March 31 2006.

140 See http://www.seriousgames.org/.

141 See http: // www.seriousgames.org/about2.html/.

142 See http://www.seriousgamessummit.com/home.html/. This messaging may change in the future, but it has been used lor the last three Serious Games Summits, one each per year held in Washington, D.C., in the fall and at the Game Developers Conference in the spring.

143 I have jokingly suggested that this particular use of *serious* must always be preceded by the informal vocative *dude*, as if to signal that the alternative, slang use of the term *serious* will follow. Cf. Stuart Moulthrop, "Taking Cyberculture Seriously" (paper presented at the Digital Arts and Culture Conference; ITU, Copenhagen, Denmark, December 1–4, 2005).

144 Alain Badiou, *Being and Event*, trans. Oliver Feltham (London and New York: Continuum, 2005), 25.

145 Ibid., 26.

146 Bogost, *Unit Operations*, 11–14.

147 Badiou, *Being and Event*, 95.

148 Ibid., 179.

149 See http://captology.stanford.edu/index.html#captologyOverview/.

150 B. J. Fogg., *Persuasive Technology; Using Computers to Change What We Think and Do* (San Francisco, Morgan Kauffman. 2003).

151 Ibid., 17.

152 Ibid., 33.

153 Ibid., 34.

154 Ibid., 37.

155 Ibid., 41

156 Ibid., 44.

157 Ibid., 46.

158 Ibid., 49.

159 Ibid., 24

160 Ibid.

161 Ibid., 51,

162 Bogost, *Unit Operations*, 55–64.

163 Jacques Derrida uses the term dissemination in his critique of Plato's preference of spoken to written discourse, arguing that centrality and authority elude meaning in all forms, whether textual, verbal, or otherwise. See "Plato's Pharmacy," in Jacques Derrida, *Dissemination*, trans. Barbara Johnson (Chicago: University of Chicago Press, 1981), 61–84.

164 Gonzalo Frasca, "Videogames of the Oppressed" (master's thesis, The Georgia Institute of Technology, 2001).

165 One form of this type of critical activity has been called "Software Studies," although much of this work still does not interrogate the cultural implications of computational systems through close readings of the software or hardware architectures that underlie them. For two good examples of the latter, see Brett Camper, "Reveling in Restrictions: Technical Mastery and Game Boy Advance Homebrew Software" (paper presented at the Digital Arts and Cultures 2005, IT University, Copenhagen, Denmark, December 1–3, 2005); Michael Mareas and Nick Montfort, "A Box, Darkly: Obfuscation, Weird Languages, and Code Aesthetics" (paper presented at the Digital Arts and Cultures 2005, IT University, Copenhagen, Denmark, December 1–3, 2005).

Bibliography

Abt, Clark C., *Serious Games*. New York: Viking, 1970.

Alelo, Inc., and USC Information Sciences Institute. *Tactical Iraqi* (videogame). Los Angeles, Calif.: Tactical Language Training LLC, 2005.

Aristotle. *Physics*. Translated by Robin Waterfield. Oxford and New York: Oxford University Press, 1999.

——. *The Rhetoric and Poetics of Aristotle*. New York: McGraw Hill, 1984.

Badiou, Alain. *Being and Event*. Translated by Oliver Feltham. London and New York: Continuum, 2005.

Banff Centre, and Global Arcade. *P.o.N.G.* (videogame). San Francisco, Calif.: Global Arcade, 1999.

Birdsell, David S., and Leo Groarke. "Toward a Theory of Visual Argument. "*Argumentation and Advocacy* 33(1996): 1–10.

Blair, J. Anthony. "The Rhetoric of Visual Arguments." In *Defining Visual Rhetorics*, edited by Marguerite Helmers and Charles A. Hill, 41–61. Mahwah, N.J.: Lawrence Erlhaum Associates, 2004.

Bogost, Tan. *Unit Operations: An Approach to Videogame Criticism*. Cambridge, Mass.: MIT Press, 2006.

Bogost, Ian, and Gonzalo Frasca. "Videogames Go to Washington: The Story Behind Howard Dean's Videogame Propaganda." In *Second Person: Roleplaying and Story in Games and Playable Media*, 233–246, edited by Pat Harrigan and Noah Wardrip-Fruin, Cambridge, Mass.: MIT Press, 2006.

Burke, Kenneth. *A Rhetoric of Motives*. Berkeley and Los Angeles: University of California Press, 1969.

Bushnell, Nolan. *Computer Space* (videogame). Mountain View, Calif.: Nutting Associates, 1971.

Camper, Brett. "Reveling in Restrictions: Technical Mastery and Game Boy Advance Homebrew Software." Paper presented at the Digital Arts and Cultures 2005, IT University, Copenhagen, Denmark, December 1–3, 2005.

Clark, Bob (dir.). *Porky's*. 20th Century Fox, 1982.

Crawford, Chris. *Balance o f the Planet* (videogame). Self-published, 1990.

Crawford, Chris. "Process Intensity."*Journal of Computer Game Development* 1, no. 5 (1987).

Crawford, Chris. *The Art of Interactive Design: A Euphonious and Illuminating Guide to Building Successful Software*. San Francisco, Calif.: No Starch Press, 2002.

DeLuca, Kevin Michael. *Image Politics: The New Rhetoric of Environmental Activism*. New York: Guilford Press, 1999.

Derrida, Jacques. *Dissemination*. Translated by Barbara Johnson. Chicago: University of Chicago Press, 1981.

Derrida, Jacques. *Of Grammatology*. Translated by Gayatri Chakravorty Spivak. Baltimore: The Johns Hopkins Press, 1974.

Diamond, Jared. *Guns, Germs, and Steel*. New York: W. W. Norton, 1999.

Dugan, Patrick. "Hot Off the Grill: la Molleindustria's Paolo Pedercini on The McDonald's Video Game." *Gamasutra*, February 27, 2006.

Dunhill Electronics. *Tax Avoiders* (videogame). American Videogame, 1982.

Fogg, B. J. *Persuasive Technology: Using Computers to Change What We Think and Do*. San Francisco, Calif.: Morgan Kauffman, 2003.

Foss, Sonja K., Karen A. Foss., and Robert Trapp. *Contemporary Perspectives on Rhetoric*. Prospect Heights, Ill.: Waveland Press, 1985.

Frasca, Gonzalo. "Videogames of the Oppressed." Master's thesis, The Georgia Institute of Technology, 2001.

Gaede, Owen. *Tenure* (videogame). Minneapolis: Control Data Corporation, 1975.

Gurak, Laura J. *Cyberliteracy: Navigating the Internet with Awareness*. New Haven: Yale University Press, 2001.

Harnad, Stevan. "Computation is Just Interpretable Symbol Manipulation; Cognition Isn't." *Minds and Machines* 4, no. 4 (2004): 379–390.

Hersh, Seymour M. "Torture at Abu Ghraib." *New Yorker*, May 10, 2004.

Hill, Charles A. "The Psychology of Rhetorical Images." In *Defining Visual Rhetorics*, edited by Marguerite Helmers and Charles A. Hill, 25–40. Mahwah, N.J.: Lawrence Erlbaum Associates, 2004.

Huizinga, Johan. *Homo ludens*. New York: Beacon, 1955.

Infocom. *Zork* (videogame). Cambridge, Mass.: Infocom, 1980.

Kay, Alan, and Adele Goldberg. "Dynamic Personal Media" (1977). In *The New Media Reader*, edited by Noah Wardrip-Fruin and Nick Montfort, 391–404. Cambridge, Mass.: MIT Press, 2003.

Kennedy, George A. *Classical Rhetoric and Its Christian and Secular Tradition*. Chapel Hill: University of North Carolina Press, 1999.

Kenney, Keith. "Building Visual Communication Theory by Borrowing from Rhetoric." In *Visual Rhetoric in a Digital World*, edited by Carolyn Handa, 321–343. New York: Bedford St. Martins, 2004.

Kittler, Friedrich. "There Is No Software." In *Literature, Media, Information Systems*, edited by John Johnston, 147–155. Amsterdam: Overseas Publishers Association, 1997.

Lake, Randall A., and Barbara A. Pickering. "Argumentation, the Visual, and the Possibility of Refutation: An Exploration." *Argumentation and Advocacy* 12 (1988): 79–93.

Lanham, Richard A. *The Electronic Word: Democracy, Technology, and the Arts*. Chicago: University of Chicago Press, 1995.

Lee, Shuen-shing. "I Lose, Therefore I Think: A Search for Contemplation amid Wars of Push-Button Glare." *Game Studies* 3, no 2 (2003).

Lessig, Lawrence. *Code and Other Laws of Cyberspace*. New York: Basic Books, 1999.

Levitt, Steven J., and Stephen J. Dubner. *Freakonomics: A Rogue Economist Explores the Hidden Side of Everything*. New York: William Morrow, 2005.

Linklater, Richard. "Fast Food Nation." Participant Productions, 2006.

Loftus, Geoffrey R., and Elizabeth F. Loftus. *Mind at Play: The Psychology of Video Games*. New York: Basic Books, 1983.

Losh, Elizabeth. "In Country with Tactical Iraqi: Trust, Identity, and Language Learning in a Military Video Game." Paper presented at the Digital Arts and Cultures Conference, IT University, Copenhagen, Denmark, December 1–4, 2005.

Manovich, Lev. *The Language of New Media*. Cambridge, Mass.: MIT Press, 2001.

Mateas, Michael, and Nick Montfort. "A Box, Darkly: Obfuscation, Weird Languages, and Code Aesthetics." Paper presented at the Digital Arts and Cultures 2005, IT University, Copenhagen, Denmark, December 1–3, 2005.

Mateas, Michael, and Andrew Stern. "A Behavior Language for Story-Based Believable Agents." *IEEE Intelligent Systems* 7, no. 4 (2002): 39–47.

Maxis. *Sim City* (videogame). Alameda, Calif.: Brøderbund, 1989.

Moulthrop, Stuart. "Taking Cyberculture Seriously (Dude)." Paper presented at the Digital Arts and Culture Conference, ITU, Copenhagen, Denmark, December 1–4, 2005.

Murray, Janet. *Hamlet on the Holodeck*. New York: Free Press, 1997.

Nintendo. *Super Mario Bros.* (videogame). Kyoto, Japan: Nintendo, 1985.

Plato. *Plato: Complete Works.* New York: Hackett, 1997.

Qualls, Eric. 2004. "Grand Theft Auto: San Andreas (Review)." GamesFirst, http://www. gamesfirst.com/index.php?id=188/ (accessed March 2, 2006).

Republican National Committee. *Tax Invaders* (videogame). Washington, D.C.: RNC/gop. com, 2004.

Rockstar Games. *Grand Theft Auto III* (videogame). New York: Take Two Interactive, 2001.

Rollings, Andrew, and Ernest Adams. *Andrew Rollings and Ernest Adams on Game Design.* New York: New Riders, 2003.

Salen, Katie, and Eric Zimmerman. *Rules of Play: Game Design Fundamentals.* Cambridge, Mass.: MIT Press, 2004.

Sawyer, Ben. *Serious Games: Improving Public Policy through Game-Based Learning and Simulation.* Washington, D.C.: Woodrow Wilson International Center for Scholars, 2002.

Schlosser, Eric. *Fast Food Nation: The Dark Side of the All-American Meal.* New York: Harper, 2001.

Schrage, Michael. *Serious Play: How the World's Best Companies Simulate to Innovate.* Cambridge, Mass.: Harvard Business School Press, 1999.

Sutton-Smith, Brian. *The Ambiguity of Play.* Cambridge, Mass.: Harvard University Press, 1997.

Turkle, Sherry. "Seeing through Computers." *American Prospect* 8, no. 31 (March 1997).

Wardrip-Fruin, Noah. *Expressive Processing: On Process-Intensive Literature and Digital Media.* Doctoral dissertation, Brown University, 2006.

———. "Playable Media and Textual Instruments." *Dichtung Digital, Journal für Digitale Ästhetik* 5, no. 34 (2005).

Warnick, Barbara. *Critical Literacy in a Digital Era: Technology. Rhetoric, and the Public Interest.* Mahwah, N.J.: Lawrence Erlbaum Associates, 2002.

Weber, Max. *The Protestant Ethic and the Spirit of Capitalism.* Translated by Talcott Parsons. London: Unwin Hyman, 1930.

Weizenbaum, Joseph. "ELIZA—A Computer Program for the Study of Natural Language Communication between Man and Machine." *Communications of the ACM,* 9, no. 1 (1966): 36–45.

Woodhouse, Ben, and Martyn Williams. *Congo Jones and the Raiders of the Lost Bark (videogame).* London: The Rainforest Foundation, 2004.

Woolcott, Adam. 2005. "Grand Theft Auto Retrospective." Gaming Target, http://www. gamingtarget.com/article.php?artid=4739/ (accessed March 1, 2006).

Zappen, James P. "Digital Rhetoric: Toward an Integrated Theory." *Technical Communication Quarterly* 14, no. 3 (2005): 319–325.